The Palgrave Handbook of South–South Migration and Inequality

Heaven Crawley · Joseph Kofi Teye
Editors

The Palgrave Handbook of South–South Migration and Inequality

palgrave
macmillan

Editors
Heaven Crawley
United Nations University Centre for Policy
Research (UNU-CPR)
New York, USA

Joseph Kofi Teye
Centre for Migration Studies
University of Ghana
Accra, Ghana

ISBN 978-3-031-39813-1   ISBN 978-3-031-39814-8 (eBook)
https://doi.org/10.1007/978-3-031-39814-8

© The Editor(s) (if applicable) and The Author(s), under exclusive licence to Springer Nature Switzerland AG 2024. This book is an open access publication.

Open Access This book is licensed under the terms of the Creative Commons Attribution 4.0 International License (http://creativecommons.org/licenses/by/4.0/), which permits use, sharing, adaptation, distribution and reproduction in any medium or format, as long as you give appropriate credit to the original author(s) and the source, provide a link to the Creative Commons license and indicate if changes were made.
The images or other third party material in this book are included in the book's Creative Commons license, unless indicated otherwise in a credit line to the material. If material is not included in the book's Creative Commons license and your intended use is not permitted by statutory regulation or exceeds the permitted use, you will need to obtain permission directly from the copyright holder.
The use of general descriptive names, registered names, trademarks, service marks, etc. in this publication does not imply, even in the absence of a specific statement, that such names are exempt from the relevant protective laws and regulations and therefore free for general use.
The publisher, the authors, and the editors are safe to assume that the advice and information in this book are believed to be true and accurate at the date of publication. Neither the publisher nor the authors or the editors give a warranty, expressed or implied, with respect to the material contained herein or for any errors or omissions that may have been made. The publisher remains neutral with regard to jurisdictional claims in published maps and institutional affiliations.

Cover illustration: © Klaus Vedfelt/Getty Images

This Palgrave Macmillan imprint is published by the registered company Springer Nature Switzerland AG
The registered company address is: Gewerbestrasse 11, 6330 Cham, Switzerland

The paper in the product is recyclable.

Acknowledgments

The editors are grateful to the authors for their contributions to this Handbook and to Karl Landström for his editorial support.

Many of the contributors to this Handbook are part of the Migration for Development and Equality Hub—otherwise known as MIDEQ. Funded by the UKRI Global Challenges Research Fund (GCRF) (Grant Reference: ES/S007415/1), MIDEQ unpacks the complex and multi-dimensional relationships between migration and inequality in the context of the Global South. MIDEQ's work directly addresses knowledge gaps, decentring or decolonising the production of knowledge about migration and its consequences away from the Global North with the aim of ensuring that policy makers, programme specialists and donors have the understanding and evidence they need to harness the development potential of migration for individuals, households, communities and the countries of the Global South. More at www.mideq.org.

Contents

1 South–South Migration and Inequality: An Introduction   1
   Heaven Crawley and Joseph Kofi Teye

Part I Conceptualising South–South Migration

2 The Enduring Impacts of Slavery: A Historical Perspective on South–South Migration   25
   Veronica Fynn Bruey and Heaven Crawley

3 Recentring the South in Studies of Migration   47
   Elena Fiddian-Qasmiyeh

4 Writing the Refugee Camp: A Southern–Southern Correspondence   75
   Yousif M. Qasmiyeh and Elena Fiddian-Qasmiyeh

5 Migration Research, Coloniality and Epistemic Injustice   83
   Karl Landström and Heaven Crawley

6 Rethinking Power and Reciprocity in the "Field"   105
   Kudakwashe Vanyoro

7 What Does it Mean to Move? Joy and Resistance Through Cultural Work in South–South Migration   125
   Hyab Teklehaimanot Yohannes and Alison Phipps

Part II Unpacking "the South" in South–South Migration

8   Global Trends in South–South Migration 153
    Kerilyn Schewel and Alix Debray

9   The Dynamics of South–South Migration in Africa 183
    Joseph Awetori Yaro and Mary Boatemaa Setrana

10 Migration as a Collective Project in the Global South: A Case Study from the Ethiopia–South Africa Corridor 201
    Dereje Feyissa, Meron Zeleke, and Fana Gebresenbet

11 Migration and Inequality in the Burkina Faso–Côte d'Ivoire corridor 223
    Bonayi Hubert Dabiré and Kando Amédée Soumahoro

12 Unequal Origins to Unequal Destinations: Trends and Characteristics of Migrants' Social and Economic Inclusion in South America 247
    Victoria Prieto Rosas and Gisela P. Zapata

13 The Making of Migration Trails in the Americas: Ethnographic Network Tracing of Haitians on the Move 271
    Louis Herns Marcelin and Toni Cela

14 Migrant Labour and Inequalities in the Nepal–Malaysia Corridor (and Beyond) 295
    Seng-Guan Yeoh and Anita Ghimire

15 Inter-regional Migration in the Global South: Chinese Migrants in Ghana 319
    Joseph Kofi Teye, Jixia Lu, and Gordon Crawford

16 Inter-regional Migration in the Global South: African Migration to Latin America 343
    Luisa Feline Freier, Leon Lucar Oba, and María Angélica Fernández Bautista

Part III Inequalities and South–South Migration

17 Poverty, Income Inequalities and Migration in the Global South 371
    Giulia Casentini, Laura Hammond, and Oliver Bakewell

18	Gendered Migration in the Global South: An Intersectional Perspective on Inequality *Tanja Bastia and Nicola Piper*	393
19	Haitian Migration and Structural Racism in Brazil *Jailson de Souza e Silva, Fernando Lannes Fernandes, and Jorge Luiz Barbosa*	413
20	Climate Change and Human Mobility in the Global South *Ingrid Boas, Animesh Gautam, and Ademola Olayiwola*	435
21	Why, When and How? The Role of Inequality in Migration Decision-making *Caterina Mazzilli, Jessica Hagen-Zanker, and Carmen Leon-Himmelstine*	455
22	Overcoming and Reproducing Inequalities: Mediated Migration in the "Global South" *Katharine Jones, Heila Sha, and Mohammad Rashed Alam Bhuiyan*	477
23	The Design and Use of Digital Technologies in the Context of South–South Migration *G. Harindranath, Tim Unwin, and Maria Rosa Lorini*	499
24	Migrant Resource Flows and Development in the Global South *Edward Asiedu, Tebkieta Alexandra Tapsoba, and Stephen Gelb*	519
25	South–South Migration and Children's Education: Expanded Challenges and Increased Opportunities *Henrietta Nyamnjoh, Mackenzie Seaman, and Meron Zeleke*	543
26	Mapping the Linkages Between Food Security, Inequality, Migration, and Development in the Global South *Jonathan Crush and Sujata Ramachandran*	567

Part IV Responses to South–South Migration

27	The Governance of South–South Migration: Same or Different? *Francesco Carella*	587
28	Policies towards Migration in Africa *Joseph Kofi Teye and Linda Oucho*	609

29 Migration Governance in South America: Change and Continuity in Times of "Crisis" 631
Marcia Vera Espinoza

30 Perú and Migration from Venezuela: From Early Adjustment to Policy Misalignment 653
Jacqueline Mazza and Nicolás Forero Villarreal

31 The "ASEAN Way" in Migration Governance 679
Rey P. Asis and Carlos L. Maningat

32 Unfair and Unjust: Temporary Labour Migration Programmes in and from Asia and the Pacific as Barriers to Migrant Justice 699
Pia Oberoi and Kate Sheill

33 Migrant Political Mobilisation and Solidarity Building in the Global South 719
Mariama Awumbila, Faisal Garba, Akosua K. Darkwah, and Mariama Zaami

Index 741

Editors and Contributors

About the Editors

Heaven Crawley is Head of Equitable Development and Migration at United Nations University Centre for Policy Research (UNU-CPR) in New York, and holds a Chair in International Migration at Coventry University's Centre for Trust, Peace and Social Relations (CTPSR). Heaven has been Director of the Migration for Development and Equality (MIDEQ) Hub since 2019. The MIDEQ Hub is a global consortium of 18 research institutions, six international organisations, and numerous local and regional partners that aims to transform knowledge and understanding of the relationships between migration, inequality, and development in the context of the Global South. Heaven was previously head of asylum and migration research at the UK Home Office, Associate Director at the Institute for Public Policy Research, and managed an international research consultancy before returning to academia to establish the Centre for Migration Policy Research at Swansea University. She has served as a specialist adviser to the UK Parliament's Home Affairs Committee and Joint Committee on Human Rights on three separate occasions and as a patron/trustee to the Baobab Centre for Young Survivors in Exile, Asylum Justice and Migrant Voice.

Joseph Kofi Teye is the Director of Research at the Office of Research Innovation and Development at the University of Ghana and a Co-Director of the Migration for Development and Equality (MIDEQ) Hub. He is also an Associate Professor of Migration and Development in the Department of Geography and Resource Development of the University of Ghana. He holds a PhD in Geography from the University of Leeds. Joseph's current research interests include migration and development, migration policy development, environmental change and migration, and natural resource governance. He has written several journal articles and contributed chapters to a number of books. Joseph has participated (either as a PI or Co-I) in large research projects funded by international organisations, including UKRI, DFID, EU, ESRC, ACP Observatory on Migration, and IOM. He has also consulted widely for a number of international organisations and governments, and was the lead consultant for the development of national labour migration policies for Sierra Leone, Ghana, and Malawi.

Contributors

Edward Asiedu is a development economist and a Senior Lecturer at the University of Ghana Business School. He is also a JPAL MIT invited researcher, former post-doctoral research and teaching fellow at the Chair of Development Economics at the University of Passau, Germany, and currently a visiting Associate Professor at the Institute of Development Policy (IOB) University of Antwerp, Belgium as well as a researcher on the Migration, Development and Equality (MIDEQ) Hub. Edwards' research is centred around topics in development economics and finance, migration and development, behavioural economics, and the design and impact evaluation of development projects. His current research is taking place Ghana, Nigeria, Togo, and Liberia. Edwards holds a Ph.D. in Economics from the University of Gottingen in Germany and an M.A. in Economics from the University of Guelph, Ontario Canada, and a bachelor's degree (First Class Honors) from the University of Ghana.

Rey P. Asis is an activist and a migrants' rights advocate. Moving to Hong Kong to work as a regional secretariat member for the Asian Students Association in 2003, Rey became involved with the migrant workers' community there, learned about their struggles and contributed through teaching theatre arts, body movement, and public speaking. He is currently the Asia Pacific Mission for Migrants' programme coordinator for advocacy and campaigns.

Mariama Awumbila teaches at the Department of Geography and Resource Development, and also at the Centre for Migration Studies, both at the University of Ghana. Her research interests and publications are in the areas of migration, livelihoods and development, Migration Policy Development, and gendered dimensions of Africa's development. Mariama was the Ghana Director of the DFID funded Migrating Out of Poverty (MOOP) Research Consortium from 2010 to 2019 and Lead Consultant for the development of a national migration policy for Ghana among others. She is currently Co-Investigator for the Migration for Development and Equality (MIDEQ) Hub's work on Political Mobilisation and Transnational Solidarity. Mariama has served on several migration management Technical and Advisory Boards including the IUSSP Scientific Panel on International Migration. She currently Chairs the Ghana Inter Ministerial Technical Working Group for the establishment of a Ghana National Commission on Migration.

Oliver Bakewell is a Reader in Migration Studies at the Global Development Institute, University of Manchester. His work focuses on the intersections between migration and mobility and processes of development and change, with an empirical focus on migration within Africa. He is the Research Coordinator on Migration and Development for the Research and Evidence Facility of the EU Trust Fund for Africa and Co-Investigator for the Migration for Development and Equality (MIDEQ) Hub. Prior to joining GDI, Oliver spent over a decade at the Department of International Development at the University of Oxford where he was one of the founder members of the International Migration Institute and became Co-Director and then Director. Before taking up this role at Oxford, Oliver spent many years working with migrants and refugees both as a researcher and as a practitioner with a range of development and humanitarian NGOs. He holds a Ph.D. and M.Sc. in Development Studies from the University of Bath and a BA in Mathematics from the University of Cambridge.

Jorge Luiz Barbosa is a geographer with Ph.D. in Human Geography. He is currently a Professor in Human Geography at Fluminense Federal University (Brazil). Jorge is co-founder of Observatory of Favelas and is also a researcher and member of the board of directors for the Maria and João Aleixo Institute/UNIperiferias in Rio, Brazil. Jorge has published on urban development and peripheral communities

Tanja Bastia is a Professor of Migration and Development at the Global Development Institute at the University of Manchester. Tanja's research focuses on transnational migration for work, particularly on the relationship between power relations, mobility, and space. She has conducted multi-sited ethnographic research with Bolivian migrants in Bolivia, Argentina, and Spain. She is co-editor (with Ronald Skeldon) of the *Routledge Handbook of Migration and Development*; sole editor of *Migration and Inequality*

(2013, Routledge) and author of *Gender, Migration and Social Transformation: Intersectionality in Bolivian Itinerant Migrations* (Routledge, 2019). She is a Co-Investigator on the Migration for Development and Equality (MIDEQ) Hub, where she co-leads the Work Package on Gender Inequalities with Nicola Piper and Kavita Datta.

María Angélica Fernández Bautista is a research assistant at Universidad del Pacífico (UP) in Lima, Peru. She is a B.A. student in International Relations at the Pontificia Universidad Católica del Perú. María Angélica has participated in various academic projects and consultancies on migration and human mobility in Latin America, as well as leading various organisations that promote university students' research. Her research interests include refugee policies, human rights, feminism, soft power studies such as e-diplomacy and cultural diplomacy, and user experience (UX).

Mohammad Rashed Alam Bhuiyan is an Assistant Professor at the Department of Political Science, University of Dhaka (on study leave). Currently he is pursuing his Ph.D. in the Centre for Trust, Peace and Social Relations at Coventry University (CU) on the topic of migration intermediaries in the context of labour migration from Bangladesh to Malaysia. Prior to joining CU, Rashed completed an M.Sc. in Sustainable Development at the University of Exeter with a Commonwealth-Shared Scholarship. His expertise lies in studying migration and climate change, urban development, migrants' rights and wellbeing, and international political economy. Before embarking on his UK-based studies, Rashed worked at Dhaka University Refugee and Migratory Movements Research Unit (RRMRU) as a Research Associate. He has contributed to several research projects in collaboration with the University of Exeter, University of Sussex and University of Southampton.

Ingrid Boas is an Associate Professor and research coordinator at the Environmental Policy Group of Wageningen University (Faculty of Social Sciences). Since 2007 she conducts research on the subject of environmental change and human mobility, focusing on the everyday, trans-local, and geopolitical realities characterising this relation. Her latest Veni project was on environmental mobility in the digital age, for which she conducted research in Bangladesh and Kenya. Her Vidi project on climate change-related mobility in borderland contexts, involves research in the Bengal, West African, and Pacific borderlands. She is also a supervisor of numerous master and Ph.D. researchers, and serves as an expert for the UN and several NGOs.

Francesco Carella is a Senior Specialist on Labour Migration and Mobility at the International Labour Organisation. Since 2006 he has held positions with several UN entities (including UNHCR, IOM, UNDP and the UN Secretariat) in multiple locations—mostly in North Africa and Latin America—developing an expertise in migration governance, labour migration, migration and refugee law, forced labour, and human trafficking. Francesco holds a B.A. with Honours in European Social and Political Studies and an LL.B. Bachelor of Laws from University College London/University of London, and an M.A. in Politics and Public Administration from the College of Europe in Bruges, Belgium. His Master's thesis examined the migration–development nexus through the case study of EU–Morocco relations. Francesco is currently a part-time Ph.D. researcher at UCL exploring the impact of multi-level migration governance on the local socio-economic integration of migrants and refugees in cities.

Toni Cela is a Senior Research Associate in the Migration for Development and Equality (MIDEQ) Hub and Coordinator of the Interuniversity Institute for Research and Development (INURED) in Haiti. She received her terminal degree from Columbia University. Her research interests include anthropology of disaster and recovery; disaster health; anthropology of education; migration and education, Haitian youth identity formation, and diaspora and development. She has undertaken research with populations of Haitian origin in the US, Haiti, the Dominican Republic, Brazil, and Senegal. She has received numerous fellowships including the Council on Anthropology and Education Presidential Fellowship, the Phelps Stokes Fund for African Development Fellowship, the National Institutes of Health Diversity Fellowship, and the U.S. Fulbright Scholar award in Haiti.

Giulia Casentini is a research associate at SOAS University of London, where she works on poverty, inequality, and gender thematic work packages as part of the Migration for Development and Equality (MIDEQ) Hub. Giulia holds a Ph.D. in Anthropology at the University of Siena on border crossing, border construction, and political institutions in Ghana and in Togo. She was post-doc research fellow at the University of Pavia on migration networks in West Africa, with a focus on the historical dimension of mobility, inclusion/exclusion dynamics and current challenged represented by return migration. Her research interests often combine with experiences as consultant in international development: she worked with IOM and INTERPOL on child trafficking and labour migration in the cocoa sector in Ghana and Cote d'Ivoire, and with ICMPD on mixed migration flows, trafficking in persons, and smuggling on the Mediterranean route.

Gordon Crawford is Research Professor in Global Development at the Centre for Trust, Peace and Social Relations, Coventry University. He is also Honorary Professor, University of Freiburg, and was Director (Germany) of the Merian Institute for Advanced Studies in Africa (MIASA) at the University of Ghana from March 2018 until December 2020. He holds a Ph.D. in Political Studies, M.A. in Development Studies and B.A. (Hons) in Sociology. Gordon's work focuses on issues of democracy and human rights and on the struggles by social movements to secure and extend such rights. He is currently undertaking research on Cameroon's "Anglophone conflict". He has published widely in international journals. He is co-author of *Understanding Global Development Research: Fieldwork Issues, Experiences and Reflections* (2017, Sage) and co-editor of *Research Handbook on Democracy and Development* (2021, Elgar).

Jonathan Crush is Professor in the School of International Policy and Governance, and the Department of Political Science at Wilfrid Laurier University and the Balsillie School of International Affairs. He holds degrees from Cambridge, Laurier and Queen's Universities. His recent awards include the CIGI Chair in Global Migration and Development, the Laurier University Research Professorship, and an Honorary Professorship at the University of Cape Town. Jonathan is currently an Extraordinary Professor at the University of the Western Cape in Cape Town. He founded and directs three research networks: the Southern African Migration Program (SAMP at www.samponline.net), the African Food Security Urban Network (AFSUN at www.afsun.org) and the Hungry Cities Partnership (HCP at www.hunbgrycities.net). He is the Principal Investigator in the HCP's South–South Migration and Food Security Network (MiFOOD at www.hungrycities.net/mifood-project). He has published extensively on the migration and food security nexus, most recently in two edited collections: *Handbook on Urban Food Security in the Global South* (Edward Elgar, 2021) (with Bruce Frayne and Gareth Haysom) and *Transforming Urban Food Systems in Secondary Cities in Africa* (Palgrave Macmillan, 2023) (with Liam Riley).

Bonayi Hubert Dabiré has Ph.D. in demography and is a Lecturer-researcher with the Institut Supérieur des Sciences de la Population (ISSP) at the Université Joseph Ki-Zerboin Burkina Faso. Dabiré is Director of Research, Head of Training in Social Statistics, and Deputy Director of the ISSP. He is also a member of the Burkinabè Association of Demographers (ABDEM), the Union for the Study of African Populations (UAPS), and the International Association of French-speaking Demographers (AIDELF). The main areas of Dabire's research are migration and urban integration; migration and access to rural land; intra-urban mobility; the impact of public policies on migration; and programme evaluation and policy development. He is also currently a Co-Investigator leading the work of the Migration for Development and Equality (MIDEQ) Hub in Burkina Faso, and team leader of the project MiTraWA (Migration and translocalité in West Africa). Dabiré teaches courses on migration in the sociology department of the Université of Joseph Ki-Zerbo and has published widely.

Akosua K. Darkwah holds a Ph.D. in Sociology from the University of Wisconsin-Madison. She is currently an Associate Professor of Sociology at the University of Ghana where she has taught for two decades. Her research interests in the area of migration focuses primarily on intra-household dynamics in migrant families. Prior to her participation in the Migration for Development and Equality (MIDEQ) Hub, Akosua worked as part of the Migration out of Poverty (MOOP) Research Consortium. She has over sixty articles, book chapters, and working papers to her credit. In addition to her work as a researcher, Akosua K. Darkwah works actively in the publishing world. She has served as co-editor of *Ghana Studies* (2013–2016) and currently serves as one of the editors of *African Studies Review and Feminist Africa*. She has also held various administrative roles at the University of Ghana.

Jailson de Souza e Silva is a geographer with a Ph.D. in the Sociology of Education. Jailson is founder of the Observatory of Favelas and Maria and João Aleixo Institute/UNIperiferias in Rio, Brazil. He has extensive experience of work in academia, NGO, and public sector with contributions in the fields of urban policy, human dignity, and community development. Jailson has published on urban peripheries and peripheral groups. The key focus of his work and research has been around the contribution of a peripheral epistemology for policy and practice change. Jailson is Co-Investigator on the Migration for Equality and Development (MIDEQ) Hub, leading the project's work in Brazil.

Alix Debray is a doctoral researcher at the United Nations University institute on Comparative Regional Integration Studies (UNU-CRIS, Belgium). Affiliated to the Faculty of Economics and the Faculty of Primary Care and Public Health of Ghent University, she explores determinants and consequences of water-related migration in the African continent. Her current work investigates voluntary and involuntary immobility through mixed-method (quantitative and qualitative) interdisciplinary approaches. Specifically, her studies of (non-)migration aspirations dive into the role of place attachment and its impact on subjective wellbeing, life aspirations as well as broader agricultural development outcomes. Alix holds an engineering degree and has worked in the water sector for five years, covering water quality assessment, flood management, river restoration, and sustainable development. Her work also touched upon global water security and peace processes, influencing her interests for science-policy interfacing and cooperation, change management, and societal implications.

Fernando Lannes Fernandes is a geographer with PhD in Human Geography. He is currently a Reader in Youth and Community Work at University of Dundee (UK). Fernando has extensive experience in the NGO sector and has worked in direct collaboration with NGOs and government agencies. Fernando is a founder member of the Observatory of Favelas. He is also a member of the board of directors for the Maria and João Aleixo Institute/UNIperiferias in Rio, Brazil, and Co-Director for the Just Transition Hub (University of Dundee). Fernando has published in the fields of urban development, peripheral communities and youth with focus on peripheral epistemologies and the Global South. He is an associate senior researcher for the Migration for Development and Equality (MIDEQ) Hub in Brazil.

Dereje Feyissa is a Co-Investigator for the Migration for Development and Equality (MIDEQ) Hub focusing on the Ethiopia-South Africa corridor and also an Associate Professor at the College of Law and Governance, Addis Ababa University. Dereje is the author of two books, *The Oyda of Southern Ethiopia: A Study on Local economy and Society* (2011) and *Playing different Games: The Paradox of the Identification Strategies of Anywaa and Nuer in the Gambella region of Western Ethiopia* (Berghahn, 2011) and co-edited two further books, *Borders and Borderlands as Resources in the Horn of Africa* (James Currey, 2010) and *Ethiopia in the Wake of Political Reform* (Tsehay publishers, 2021). He has also published numerous articles in peer-reviewed journals and book chapters for edited volumes. Dereje's research interests cover migration, ethnicity and conflict and religion and politics. He is a board member of the Social Science research Council and editorial board member of the Journal of East African Studies.

Elena Fiddian-Qasmiyeh is Professor of Migration and Refugee Studies at University College London, where she is also the Co-Director of the UCL-Migration Research Unit, and Principal Investigator of a number of research projects, including *Southern Responses to Displacement* and *Refugee Hosts*. Elena's research focuses on experiences of and responses to conflict-induced displacement, with a particular regional focus on the Middle East. Drawing on a critical theoretical perspective, her work contributes to key debates surrounding refugees' and local host community members' experiences of conflict-induced displacement, the nature of refugee–host–donor relations, and both North–South and South–South humanitarian responses to forced migration. She is the author and editor of many books, including *The Handbook of South-South Relations* (2018), *Refuge in a Moving World* (2020), *South-South Educational Migration, Humanitarianism and Development: Views from Cuba, North Africa and the Middle East* (2015) and *The Ideal Refugees: Islam, Gender and the Sahrawi Politics of Survival* (2014).

Luisa Feline Freier is an Associate Professor of Political Science and International Development Research Centre (IDRC) Research Chair on Forced Displacement in Latin America and the Caribbean at the Universidad del Pacífico (Lima, Peru). Her research focuses on migration and refugee policies and laws in Latin America, south–south migration and the Venezuelan displacement crisis. Feline has published widely in both academic and media outlets, and has been interviewed on the Venezuelan displacement crisis in international media, including BBC, El País, La Presse and The Economist. She also has provided advice to various international institutions and organisations such as Amnesty International, ICRC, IDB, IOM, UNHCR, the World Bank, and the EU, and is Migration Research and Publishing High-Level Adviser of the IOM.

Veronica Fynn Bruey is a multi-award winner academic-advocate. Holding six academic degrees, Veronica has researched, taught, consulted, and presented at conferences in over 30 countries. She is author of five books as well as several book chapters and journal articles. She is the found/editor-in-chief of the Journal of Internal Displacement; co-editor of the Migration, Displacement, and Development Book Series with Rowman and Littlefield; co-lead of the Displaced Peoples Collaborative Research Network; lead of the Disrupting Patriarchy and Masculinity in Africa International Research Collaborative; president of the International Association for the Study of Forced Migration, and Co-Chair, Africa Interest Group, American Society of International Law. Veronica is the CAFA Distinguished Academic Early Career Award recipient (2023), the Australian National University International Alumna of the Year, 2021 and currently, the Director of Flowers School of Global Health Sciences. She is an aAssistant pProfessor of Legal Studies at Athabasca University. Veronica is a born and bred Indigenous Liberian war survivor.

Faisal Garba is a Senior Lecturer of Sociology at the University of Cape Town (UCT) where he convenes the Global Studies Programme (GSP) and directs the Migration and Mobility research cluster. He is Co-Investigator leading the Migration for Development and Equality (MIDEQ) Hub's work in South Africa and co-leads the work package on Migrant Transnational Mobilisation and Political Solidarity. In addition to migration and mobility, Faisal works on social movements and labour studies, social theory, and historical sociology. His most recent publication is a special issue of *Zanj: The Journal of Critical Global South Studies* on migrant migration and (in)equality in the Global South co-edited with Heaven Crawley and Francis Nyamnjoh.

Animesh Gautam (Mesh) is a junior researcher based out of the Environmental Policy chairgroup at Wageningen University and Research. They received their interdisciplinary M.Sc. degree in Tourism, Society and Environment from Wageningen University. Mesh's research interests lie in understanding the nexus between borders, mobilities and environmental change and focuses on the politics of competing environmental mobility regimes that shape (im)mobilities. Mesh's current work examines environment-driven tourism in the ecologically sensitive Eastern Himalayan Borderland state of Sikkim, India with a particular focus on the relations between environmental mobilities and governance of India's borders with Nepal and China. As a queer Nepali individual born and raised in the Eastern Himalayan Borderlands (Sikkim, India), Mesh's lived experiences, observations, and the questions posed by the social and environmental complexities in geographical borderlands have motivated their research interests.

Fana Gebresenbet is a researcher with the Migration for Development and Equality (MIDEQ) Hub and an Associate Professor of peacebuilding and development at the Institute for Peace and Security Studies of Addis Ababa University. He has co-edited two books, *Lands of the Future* (Berghahn, 2021) and *Youth on the Move* (Hurst, 2021), and published numerous journal articles and book chapters. Fana's research interests cover migration, the politics of development, political economy, and peacebuilding in Ethiopia and the Horn of Africa.

Stephen Gelb is a Senior Research Associate at ODI, London, and was previously Principal Research Fellow at ODI, leading on Private Sector Development. He has a PhD in economics and undertook research and policy analysis in South Africa for over thirty years, advising President Mbeki and the cabinet on inclusive growth, macroeconomic policy, and foreign direct investment after 1994. He has taught economics, political science, and development studies in South Africa, Canada, the US, and Switzerland. He has written on macroeconomics, foreign direct investment, inequality, and political economy in South Africa; on foreign direct investment and global value chains in Africa and Asia; and on migration and diaspora finance. His current research focuses on corporate corruption; on urban economics and enterprise development; value chains and FDI; and on diaspora finance and migrant-linked businesses. Stephen is a Co-Investigator on the Migration for Development and Equality (MIDEQ) Hub, focusing on resource transfers associated with migration in the Global South.

Anita Ghimire is a research director at the Nepal Institute for Social and Environmental Research in Kathmandu. She has a 4-year post-doctoral degree from University of Zurich, Switzerland and more than 14 years research experiences working on adolescent and young people, social norms and gender, migration and mobility, health, and DRRM. She has worked for a range of donors including FCDO, World Bank, IOM, UNICEF, and other UN agencies and with British, Swiss, Swedish, and Indian Universities. She is currently the country lead for two long-term research programmes—gender and adolescence (https://www.gage.odi.org/) and the Migration for Development and Equality (MIDEQ) Hub. Her work includes reports and policy briefs as well as visual materials for policy engagement and research uptake.

Jessica Hagen-Zanker is a Senior Research Fellow leading ODI's migration research and Co-Investigator on the Migration for Development and Equality (MIDEQ) Hub. Her research focuses on migration decision-making, particularly understanding how migration, economic, and social policies affect migrant decision-making; impacts of migration on migrants and their families; the interlinkages between migration and social protection, including access to social protection for migrant workers and refugees, portability, and the integration of humanitarian assistance into national systems. Jessica is an economist, and while she has extensive experience in the design, implementation, and analysis of household surveys, much of her research draws on mixed methods. Her work has covered a diverse range of countries in Europe, Sub-Saharan Africa, the Middle East, and South Asia. Alongside her research work, Jessica also engages in advisory work with policy stakeholders. Jessica holds a Ph.D. in Public Policy from Maastricht University.

Laura Hammond is Pro-Director of Research Knowledge and Exchange and Professor of Development Studies at SOAS University of London. She has been conducting research on conflict, food security, refugees, migration and diaspora in and from the Horn of Africa since the early 1990s. Among her research activities, she is PI of the Impact Acceleration Account on Migration, Displacement, Minorities and Marginalisation and Co-Investigator of the Work Package on Poverty and Inequalities for the Migration, Inequality and Development (MIDEQ) Hub. She is also Team Leader of the EU Trust Fund's Research and Evidence Facility on migration and conflict in the

Horn of Africa, and Team Leader of the London International Development Centre's Migration Leadership Team. She has undertaken consultancy for a wide range of development and humanitarian organisations. Laura is the author of *This Place Will Become Home: Refugee Repatriation to Ethiopia* (Cornell University Press, 2004), editor (with Christopher Cramer and Johan Pottier) of *Researching Violence in Africa: Ethical and Methodological Challenges* (Brill, 2011) and several books and journal articles.

G. Harindranath is Professor of Information Systems in the School of Business and Management at Royal Holloway, University of London. His work focuses on the social and organisational implications of digital technologies including ICT4D. He is an editorial board member of the *Journal of Information Technology*, Senior Editor of *Information Technology and People*, and Associate Editor of *Information and Management*. Hari is a Co-Investigator Migration for Development and Equality (MIDEQ) Hub in which his intervention work package seeks to understand the extent and ways through which digital technologies alleviate or exacerbate existing inequalities in the context of South–South migration, as well as successes and challenges facing the use of digital technologies for migrant-related development outcomes. Hari is a co-founder of the Association for Information Systems-affiliate conference, International Conference on Information Resources Management (ConfIRM).

Carmen Leon-Himmelstine has a Ph.D. in International Development from the University of Sussex. Currently she works as Research Fellow at ODI in the Gender Equality and Social Inclusion programme as part of the Migration for Development and Equality (MIDEQ) Hub and also as a Research Associate at SOAS University of London. Her research expertise is on the linkages and mutual impacts between social protection and migration. She has conducted primary research on social protection in Haiti (CLM programme), Burundi (Terintambwe programme) and Mexico (Oportunidades programme). Carmen also works on gender, education, economic empowerment, health and child poverty. She has a strong publication record ranging from academic articles, reports and literature reviews to policy briefs and conference papers on such topics.

Katharine Jones is Associate Professor at the Centre for Trust, Peace & Social Relations (CTPSR) at Coventry University (CU) and leads the Migration, Displacement & Belonging theme. She is also Co-Director of the Migration for Development and Equality (MIDEQ) Hub. Katharine has 25 years of experience in leading research related to migration, from within academia, civil society, for grant-making foundations and for international organisations. After completing her Ph.D. at the University of Manchester in 2012 and before joining academia in 2015, Katharine acted as a consultant to two UN agencies, the International Labour Organisation and International Organisation for Migration, leading large-scale multi-country programmes of work on rights, employment and migration. Her research and international policy advocacy primarily address migration intermediaries, especially the role of labour recruiters in neoliberal transnational labour markets. Katharine retains close civil society links and is on the Board of JustRight Scotland (JRS), a leading law centre on human rights and the Scottish Refugee Council.

Karl Landström is a Research Fellow in applied philosophy at the Responsible and Sustainable Business Lab (RSB), Nottingham Business School and a Research Associate with the African Centre for Epistemology and Philosophy of Science at University of Johannesburg. Karl holds Master's degrees in Education and Applied Ethics from Linköping University, and completed his Ph.D. in Philosophy of Social Science at Coventry University, during which he worked closely with the Migration for Development and Equality (MIDEQ) Hub. Karl's research is situated at the intersection of ethics and epistemology and contributes to debates about this intersection, particularly as they pertain to academic research practice and governance, by drawing upon a combination of feminist social epistemology, hermeneutics, and post- and decolonial theory.

Maria Rosa Lorini is a researcher and project management practitioner. She is working primarily on digital technologies and migration as part of the research team contributing to the Migration for Development and Equality (MIDEQ) Hub. The team works with migrants and digital tech experts to develop solutions that can be used to reduce inequalities. Prior to joining Royal Holloway, University of London and MIDEQ, she was a postdoctoral researcher at the University of Cape Town, working on co-design projects in the underserved communities of South Africa and collaborating with Oldenburg University on a Hub for Education on ICT for Sustainability. She has a background in civil society organisations as well. Between 2008 and 2012 she directed an HIV/AIDS and gender-based violence project in South Africa, and before that she worked for the United Nations Operation in Côte d'Ivoire on human rights and the rule of law.

Jixia Lu is a Professor at the College of Humanities and Development Studies, China Agricultural University, Beijing, China and Co-Investigator for the Migration for Development and Equality (MIDEQ) Hub. She was previously at the Institute of Development Studies (IDS) in the UK as a postdoctoral visiting scholar from 2012 to 2013, and at the South and Southeast Asia Research Center in Lund University, Sweden as visiting scholar in 2018. In recent years, Jixia's research has focused on China and international development, South–South Migration and development, and agrarian change in rural China. She has published over 50 journal articles in English and Chinese, including in *World Development*, *Journal of Peasant Studies*, *International Migration* and *Foreign Affairs Review (in Chinese)*.

Carlos L. Maningat is a Filipino researcher, activist and writer who focuses on topics ranging from labour flexibilisation, labour laws, migration, to gender and development. As legislative researcher at the House of Representatives, he has been working closely with migrants and migrant organisations in drafting pro-migrant legislation. Prior to his current work as legislative staff, Carlos served as head researcher of the Ecumenical Institute for Labor Education and Research, Inc. (EILER), a nongovernment organisation based in Quezon City, Philippines.

Louis Herns Marcelin is Co-Director of the Migration for Development and Equality (MIDEQ) and Professor at the University of Miami in Coral Gables, Florida. His research examines questions related to health, human security, migration and the roles of power, violence and marginalisation across the Americas. In 2007, he founded the Interuniversity Institute for Research and Development (INURED), a transnational and transdisciplinary institute that conducts high-level research and provides scientific training to early career and professional researchers in Haiti. He has been funded by the National Institutes of Health in the US, the Organisation for Economic Co-operation and Development (OECD) in Paris, the International Development Research Centre in Canada, and the World Bank, among others. He has received numerous awards and fellowships from the Woodrow Wilson Institute, the Rockefeller Foundation's Bellagio Center; the American Council of Learned Societies (ACLS), the Museu Nacional Universidade Federal Rio de Janeiro, and the Stellenbosch Institute for Advanced Study in South Africa, among others.

Jacqueline Mazza is a Senior Adjunct Professor of International Development and Latin American Studies at the Johns Hopkins University, School of Advanced International Studies (SAIS) at both SAIS-Europe in Bologna, Italy and SAIS-Washington in Washington, DC. She is the former Principal Labor Markets at the Inter-American Development Bank in Washington, DC and consultant to the World Bank and the International Labour Organization. Jacqueline is a recognised expert in the fields of migration, labour markets and

US foreign policy towards Latin America. She is the author of *Labor Intermediation Services in Developing Economies* (Palgrave Macmillan Press, 2017), *Venezuelan Migrants under COVID-19: Managing South America's Pandemic Amid a Migration Crisis* with Nicolás Forero Villarreal (Wilson Center for International Scholars, December 2020), and *Don't Disturb the Neighbors: the US and Democracy in Mexico* (Routledge Press). She holds her Ph.D. and M.A. in International Relations from Johns Hopkins University, SAIS.

Caterina Mazzilli is a Research Officer in the Humanitarian Policy Group at ODI. Her research focuses on migration policies, the links between migration and development, migration decision-making, and social protection for migrants. She holds a Ph.D. in Migration Studies from the University of Sussex, UK. Prior to working for ODI, Caterina worked as a post-doctoral researcher at Queen Mary University of London, as a doctoral tutor at the University of Sussex, and as an independent consultant for NGOs and IOs. She has long-standing experience in qualitative research and has published extensively in the fields of geography, sociology, and migration studies.

Henrietta Nyamnjoh is a researcher at the University of Cape Town and on the Migration for Development and Equality (MIDEQ) Hub. Henrietta has researched extensively on female migrants and recently completed a study titled "Migrant Margins: City-Making Across Durable Borders" which explores the everyday lives of Congolese women. Henrietta's research also focuses on childhood, exploring on the left-behind children of Cameroonian economic migrants in Cape Town. Her research interests include migration and mobility, transnational studies, childhood studies, and migration and food. Henrietta has published widely on these topics. Additionally, she is also interested in understanding religion in the context of migration. Henrietta has researched and published widely on religious healing among migrants in South Africa, drawing attention to migrants' appropriation of Information and Communication Technologies, Hometown Associations and migrant economy and everyday life.

Leon Lucar Oba is a teaching assistant at the department of Political Science at Pontificia Universidad Católica del Perú (PUCP) in Lima, Peru. He holds a BA in Political Science and Government from the Pontificia Universidad Católica del Perú. He has worked as a research assistant in academic projects and consultancies on migration and human mobility in Latin America, as well as decentralisation and civil society in Peru. His research interests include migration policies, religion and politics, social movements, and civil society in Peru and Latin America.

Pia Oberoi is Senior Advisor on Migration and Human Rights (Asia Pacific) for the United Nations Human Rights Office where she is responsible for developing and implementing research and institutional policy on migration and human rights in the region. Previously, she was the head of the migration unit at UN Human Rights headquarters in Geneva, where she led the Office's global work on policy and legal issues related to the human rights of migrants and people on the move and the intersections between migration and human rights. Before that, she headed the migrants' rights work of Amnesty International's International Secretariat, and has been an expert consultant on migration, refugee, and human rights issues for NGOs and policy think tanks in many regions. Pia is the author of *Exile and Belonging: Refugees and State Policy in South Asia* (2006) and has published and lectured extensively. She holds a D.Phil. in International Relations from St Antony's College, Oxford University.

Ademola Olayiwola is a Ph.D. researcher at the Environmental Policy Group at Wageningen University & Research, Netherlands. He received his M.Sc. degree in Governance and Regional Integration from the Pan African University, Cameroon. Ademola's research concerns with the conceptual and contextual relation between climate change, mobility, and governance, and focuses on the dynamics of intertwined geographies produced by such relation. His Ph.D. project focuses specifically on the Fulani pastoralists to explore how climate change impacts and discourse are shaping their movements within and around the border region, and the role that border politics as well as social and cultural histories of mobility play in these dynamics. Ademola's research interest draws from internship period at the Department of Peace and Security at African Union Commission in Addis Ababa, Ethiopia.

Linda Oucho is an established migration expert with over 10 years of experience leading the African Migration and Development Policy Centre (AMADPOC)—a research think tank based in Nairobi, Kenya. Linda's research focuses on labour migration, social protection of migrant workers, diaspora contribution to national development, forced displacements, poverty, climate change, and more recently youth, employment, and migration, among others. She has undertaken consultancies with IOM Kenya, Ethiopia and South Africa, ICMPD, AUC, UNDP, GIZ, IDRC, and FES and works closely with a number of national African governments including Kenya where she is an active member of the National Coordination Mechanism for Migration (NCM) advocating for the use of research to inform policy design and implementation. Linda also supports research and dialogue activities with Regional Economic Communities (RECs) such as the EAC, IGAD, ECOWAS, and SADC and interacts closely with the African Union as a technical expert.

Alison Phipps is UNESCO Chair in Refugee Integration through Languages and the Arts at the University of Glasgow and Professor of Languages and Intercultural Studies. She was De Carle Distinguished Visiting Professor at Otago University, Aotearoa New Zealand 2019-2020, Thinker in Residence at the EU Hawke Centre, University of South Australia in 2016, Visiting Professor at Auckland University of Technology, and Principal Investigator for AHRC Large Grant "Researching Multilingually at the Borders of Language, the body, law and the state"; for Cultures of Sustainable Peace, and Co-Director of the Migration for Development and Equality (MIDEQ) Hub. She is Ambassador for the Scottish Refugee Council. She is an academic, activist, educator, and published poet and a member of the Iona Community.

Nicola Piper a political sociologist, is Professor of International Migration and currently British Academy Global Professor Fellow at Queen Mary University of London, UK. Her research interests and extensive publications focus on international labour migration, the relationship between global and regional governance of migration, advocacy politics and gender dynamics, mostly applied to Asia. Nicola is co-editor of the international, peer-reviewed journal *Global Social Policy* and co-editor of two book series (Routledge's *Asian Migration* and Palgrave's *Mobility and Politics*).

Yousif M. Qasmiyeh is a scholar, poet and translator who completed his D.Phil. research at Oxford University on containment, the archive, and time in refugee writing in Arabic and English. He is the Joint-Lead of the Baddawi Camp Lab, as part of the Imagining Futures GCRF-Network+ project, and was Writer-in-Residence for the AHRC-funded Refugee Hosts project. His essays, poetry and translations have appeared in *Modern Poetry in Translation, Critical Quarterly, GeoHumanities, Cambridge Literary Review, PN Review, Stand, New England Review* and *Poetry London*. His collection, *Writing the Camp* (Broken Sleep Books, 2021), was a 2021 Poetry Book Society Recommendation and was selected as one of the Best Poetry Books of 2021 by the *Telegraph* and the *Irish Times*; was highly commended by the 2021 Forward Prizes for Poetry; and was shortlisted for the 2022 Royal Society of Literature Ondaatje Prize. His latest book is *Eating the Archive* (Broken Sleep Books, 2023).

Victoria Prieto Rosas is an Associate Professor at the Population Programme at the University of the Republic (Uruguay). She holds a Ph.D. in Demography from the Autonomous University of Barcelona. She leads the project "Using Internet-based data to quantify and sample international migrants: applications to examine recent immigration to Uruguay", funded by the Max Planck Society (Germany) and the National Agency for Research and Innovation (Uruguay). Victoria is also part of the coordinating committee of the Latin American Migration Project (LAMP) to expand ethno-surveys as a tool to research immigration in Latin America and is a member of the research group "Comparative Analysis of Migration and Displacement in the Americas" (CAMINAR). Her publications have focused on drivers of international migration, the social inclusion of immigrants and returnees in South American countries, and the assessment of traditional and non-traditional data to study human mobility.

Sujata Ramachandran is a Postdoctoral Fellow with the Hungry Cities Partnership (HCP) at the Balsillie School of International Affairs and in the Department of Political Science at Wilfrid Laurier University, Waterloo, Canada. Sujata received her Ph.D. in Human Geography from Wilfrid Laurier University and holds M.A. degrees from the University of Toronto and Jawaharlal Nehru University. She has extensive experience studying various aspects of migration in Canada, Southern Africa, and South Asia. Her research interests include migration and development, migrant integration, and migration governance. Sujata has been involved in the SSHRC-funded MiFOOD Project, which examines the neglected ties between migration and food security within the Global South. She is beginning work on the new NFRF-IDRC funded Women Feeding Cities Project on the pandemic's gendered impacts on the informal food retail sector in selected cities of Jamaica, Mexico, Mozambique, and Namibia. Sujata co-edits the MiFOOD Working Paper series.

Kerilyn Schewel is Co-Director of the Duke Program on Climate-Related Migration and a Lecturing Fellow at the Duke Center for International Development. Her research examines the root causes of human migration and immobility, with an emphasis on the themes of gender, youth, rural development, and climate change. Her work has been published in Social Forces, Population and Development Review, and International Migration Review, among others. Her book, *Moved by Modernity: How Development Shapes Migration in Rural Ethiopia*, is forthcoming with Oxford University Press. Kerilyn has additionally worked with the United States Agency for

International Development, International Labour Organization, and International Organization for Migration on policy-oriented publications addressing migration and development. She holds a Ph.D. in Sociology from the University of Amsterdam and an M.Sc. in Migration Studies from Oxford University. She previously held visiting researcher positions at Addis Ababa University and Princeton University.

Mackenzie Seaman is a mixed-methods migration researcher working with the Migration for Development and Equality (MIDEQ) Hub with expertise in gender and children. Her specific interest is in child and youth refugee movements both within the Levant and onwards to the Global North and she has experience working with child and youth migrants in/from Afghanistan, Central Europe, East and West Africa, the Levant and South Asia. Mackenzie has authored a variety of reports and publications centred on child and youth migrants and is a strong advocate for gender sensitive research methods, analysis, and reporting in the field. She holds a Master of Arts in Law and Diplomacy from the Fletcher School at Tufts University and a Bachelor of Arts in Political Science from the University of Michigan.

Mary Boatemaa Setrana is the Director of the Centre for Migration Studies, University of Ghana, Accra. She is the West Africa Chair on Forced Displacement funded by IDRC and a member of the 12 Chairs on forced displacement globally. Mary is a member of a number of migration governance advisory groups and networks. She is also an Advisory Board member of the African Research Universities Alliance (ARUA) Centre of Excellence on Migration and Mobility and the Centre for Forced Displacement in Boston University. Her research interests focus on migration and gender, migration governance and policy development, forced displacement, and return migration and reintegration. Mary is either the lead or co-researcher on a number of ongoing research projects including: Migration Decisions and the COVID-19 Pandemic; Migration for Development and Equality (MIDEQ) Hub; Migration and Social Transformation; Culture for Sustainable and Inclusive Peace; and Crises as Opportunities.

Heila Sha (Saheira Haliel) is a Research Fellow at the Centre for Research in Ethnic Minority Entrepreneurship (CREME) at Aston University. Her research expertise includes migration, cross-border trade, entrepreneurship, kinship, gender, marriage, family business, and socio-economic transformations in China. Saheira completed her Ph.D. at Max Planck Institute for Social Anthropology in Germany in July 2015. Her Ph.D. research focused on inter-generational transformations of family life, care, and gender relations in response to socio-economic transformations in Northwest China.

In April 2016, she joined the University of Sussex (UK) as a post-doctoral Research Fellow, where her research explored transnational lives, mobilities, and networks by applying multi-sited methodologies that bridge scales to connect globally diverse localities within transnational trading networks and commodity markets in the context of global trade liberalisation. After Sussex, Saheira was a Research Fellow at Coventry University, where she worked with Migration for Development and Equality (MIDEQ) Hub, with a particular focus on migration intermediaries and inequalities.

Kate Sheill has worked as an independent research and policy consultant since 2015, following many years working at human rights and feminist NGOs, and she is an expert in human rights, gender, sexuality, migration, and their intersections. She has consulted for a range of organisations including the United Nations Human Rights Office (OHCHR), International Labour Organization (ILO), Amnesty International, Asia Pacific Forum on Women, Law and Development (APWLD), and the Global Alliance on Traffic in Women (GAATW). She was the principal drafter of the Principles and Guidelines on the human rights protection of migrants in vulnerable situations for OHCHR, and her more recent work includes research on migrant worker housing in ASEAN, and policy reports on rights-based migration pathways in the Asia Pacific region, temporary labour migration programmes, and trafficking into online scam operations.

Kando Amédée Soumahoro has a Ph.D. in sociology and is a Lecturer-researcher in the Department of Sociology of the University Felix Houphouet-Boigny in Ivory Coast. He is also a permanent researcher at the Laboratory of Economic Sociology and Anthropology of Symbolic Belongings (LAASSE) and Associate Researcher at the Institute for Good Governance, Development and Foresight (IGDP and Co-Investigator leading the work of the Migration for Development and Equality (MIDEQ) Hub in Côte d'Ivoire. Kando is a member of the Mande Studies Association (MANSA), Ivoirian Education Research Association (AIRE) and APAD. Kando's centres of interest are towards questions of identity reconstructions related to health, inequalities, migration, the environment, conflicts, resilience, etc. In this respect, he has collaborated with centres and Research Center (CIRES/CAPEC, ORS), United Nations system agencies (WHO, UNFPA, UNICEF, WFP, OECD, UNAIDS, development agencies (GIZ, ENGENDER HEALTH and Institute of Development Studies (IDS) in UK-Brighton). Kando has published in both French and English at national and international level.

Tebkieta Alexandra Tapsoba is a Lecturer and researcher at the Higher Institute of Population Sciences, University Joseph Ki-Zerbo in Ouagadougou, Burkina Faso, and with the Migration for Development and Equality (MIDEQ) Hub. She has a PhD in development economics, and her research focuses on migration, remittances, and climate change, trying to understand how households use remittances as a hedge against the negative effect of climate change on living standards. Before coming to ISSP, Alexandra worked as a consultant for the International Organization for Migration and the Economic Community of West African States where she helped identify better ways of including migration questions in national censuses. Although the focus of Alexandra's research is on voluntary migration, it has expanded to include research on forced migration caused by conflicts and terrorism in the Sahelian region.

Tim Unwin CMG is an Emeritus Professor of Geography at Royal Holloway, University of London. He was Secretary General of the Commonwealth Telecommunications Organisation from 2011 to 2015, was Chair of the Commonwealth Scholarship Commission from 2009 to 2014, and over the last decade has worked closely with UN agencies, and particularly the ITU, UNESCO, and UNICEF. He has written or edited 16 books and more than 250 other publications, with his influential edited book *Information and Communication Technologies for Development*, being published by CUP in 2009, and his latest single authored book *Reclaiming ICT4D* being published by OUP in 2017. His research focuses on the inequalities caused by the use of digital technologies, and he has worked especially with people with disabilities, out of school youth, migrants, and women in patriarchal societies, seeking to help them overcome exploitation and the increasing inequalities caused by the design and propagation of digital tech.

Kudakwashe Vanyoro is a Lecturer in the Department of Anthropology in the School of Social Sciences at the University of the Witwatersrand, in Johannesburg, South Africa. Over the last decade, his research has focused on migration, temporality, borders, humanitarianism, knowledge politics, decolonisation, and governance in Africa. He is the author of a book titled *Migration, Crisis and Temporality at the Zimbabwe-South Africa Border: Governing Immobilities* (Bristol University Press, 2023). Alongside this forthcoming monograph, he has published in a number of academic journals in *Gender & Development, Refugee Survey Quarterly, Globalizations, Journal of Southern African Studies, Anthropology Southern Africa, The Lancet and Incarceration*. Kudakwashe has received accolades for his writing including the Mixed Migration Centre (MMC) Alternative Voices Competition Prize for writers under 30 and the International Association for the Study of Forced Migration (IASFM) 2022 Lisa Gilad Prize.

Marcia Vera Espinoza is a Reader at the Institute for Global Health and Development (IGHD) at Queen Margaret University, in Edinburgh, where she leads the Psychosocial Wellbeing, Integration and Protection Research Cluster. Marcia is a co-founding member of the research group Comparative Analysis in International Migration and Displacement in the Americas (CAMINAR). She is PI of the EU-AMIF project "New Scots Integration: A Pathway to Social and Economic Inclusion", and Co-I of an RSE Research Grant to explore long-term refugee integration in Scotland. Marcia has recently published in *Comparative Migration Studies, Migration Letters, Forced Migration Review, Frontiers in Human Dynamics, Migration and Society, Geopolitics,* and *Global Policy,* among others. Her co-edited books include *The Dynamics of Regional Migration Governance* (Edward Elgar, 2019), *Latin America and Refugee Protection: Regimes, Logics and Challenges* (Berghahn Books, 2021), and *Movilidades y Covid-19 en América Latina: Inclusiones y Exclusiones en Tiempos de "Crisis"* (UNAM, 2022).

Nicolás Forero Villarreal is currently a SPILS fellow at Stanford Law School. He is a former adjunct professor at Universidad de los Andes and an international consultant on human security and international law. Nicolás is a recipient of the Bob Hepple Equality Law Fellow, Open Society Internship for Human Rights and Governance Grant (OSIRG) and a former Global Established Multidisciplinary Sites Fellow at the Johns Hopkins Bloomberg School of Public Health. He has participated in research projects on migrant's rights and the intersection of gender and disarmament in Latin America and Europe, and has collaborated with Control Risks, UNICEF, UNHCR, Equal Rights Trust and DCAF in different projects. Nicolás holds an M.A. in International Affairs from the School of Advanced International Studies at Johns Hopkins University, an LL.M. in international law, and an LL.B. from Universidad de los Andes in Bogotá, Colombia.

Joseph Awetori Yaro is a Professor of Human Geography at the University of Ghana. He combines a rich background in development studies and rural geography with extensive rural research experience in Ghana. He is currently the Principal of the University of Ghana Accra City, and the West Africa Regional Hub Coordinator for the Futures Agricultural Consortium. His specific research interests are in sustainable development in rural areas; migration; livelihoods and food security; climate change adaptation; land tenure and transnational land deals/grabs. Joseph is actively researching transnational land deals, South–South migration, trans-local livelihoods, and building local adaptive capacity to climate change and climate variability. He has authored several publications in these broad developmental themes and contributed to a range of policy strategies for agriculture, migration, and climate change.

Seng-Guan Yeoh is an Associate Professor in Social Anthropology in the School of Arts and Social Sciences, Monash University Malaysia. He is an urban anthropologist who researches primarily on the intersections between cities, religion, migration, and civil society in Southeast Asia. He also makes ethnographic documentaries. His current fieldwork sites are Malaysia, the Philippines, and Indonesia. Seng-Guan is Co-Investigator for the Migration for Development and Equality (MIDEQ) Hub co-leading the project's work in the Nepal–Malaysia Corridor. Seng-Guan holds a Ph.D. from the University of Edinburgh, Scotland.

Hyab Teklehaimanot Yohannes is a former refugee and an academic with a Ph.D. in *The Realities of Eritrean Refugees in a Carceral Age* from the University of Glasgow, where he currently works as a research associate. He is also a member of the RSE Young Academy of Scotland and has been appointed as a member of the International Survivors of Trafficking Advisory Council, where he assists the work of the Office for Democratic Institutions and Human Rights in combatting human trafficking. Additionally, Hyab is involved in several management and leadership roles, providing organisational oversight.

Mariama Zaami is a Senior Lecturer at the Department of Geography and Resource Development and an Interfaculty member of the Centre for Migration Studies (CMS), University of Ghana and a researcher on the Migration for Development and Equality (MIDEQ) Hub. Her research areas include gender and poverty, migration, immigration, race and ethnicity, globalisation and development, and livelihood change. Currently, she is working on migration within the ECOWAS subregion, focusing on the political mobilisation and solidarity building among migrants, gendered patterns of migration, and the implications on livelihoods, family welfare and access to community resources. She has published in national and international journals, including the *International Journal of Intercultural Relations*, *Journal of Family Issues*, *Canadian Ethnic Studies*, and *Ghana Journal of Geography*.

Gisela P. Zapata is an Assistant Professor in the Department of Demography and researcher at the Centre for Regional Development and Planning (CEDEPLAR) of the Federal University of Minas Gerais (UFMG), Brazil. She holds a Ph.D. in Human Geography from Newcastle University (UK). She is a fellow of the Brazilian Council for Scientific and Technological

Development (PQ2/CNPq) and member of the research group "Comparative Analysis on International Migration and Displacement in the Americas" (CAMINAR). Gisela leads the project "The interiorization strategy for refugees and migrants from Venezuela in Brazil: building evidence to inform gender-responsive policymaking" funded by UN Women (Brazil). Her research and publications have focused on international migration and displacement, migration policies, remittances, and the migration–development nexus in Latin America.

Meron Zeleke is an Associate Professor at the Center for Human Rights, Addis Ababa University and a researcher with the Migration for Development and Equality (MIDEQ) Hub. Meron has years of teaching and research experience at renowned academic institutions in Africa, North America, Europe, and Asia, and is a member of several international academic associations. She has rich research experience on numerous international and national academic research projects. Meron's core research expertise includes in areas of migration, gendered labour markets, violence against women, religion, and customary conflict resolution. She has extensively published in internationally renowned peer-reviewed journals on a wide range of topics such as religion, local institutions of dispute settlement, gender, and migration. She has also authored two books, edited books and journals, and contributed chapters to several edited volumes and entries in encyclopaedias including the Oxford Research Encyclopedia of African History. Meron is an international editorial board member of Islamic Africa (Brill) and the Editor in Chief of the *Ethiopian Journal of Human Rights*.

List of Figures

Fig. 7.1	Refugee-organised mass at St. Joseph's Roman Catholic Church, Cairo, Egypt	137
Fig. 7.2	Eritrean coffee celebration with Alison Phipps, Glasgow, Scotland	138
Fig. 8.1	Global South and Global North country categorisation from the Organisation for Women in Science for the Developing World (OWSD)	155
Fig. 8.2	Evolution of international migrant stocks, in millions of people	157
Fig. 8.3	Evolution of international migrant stock by gender, in millions of people	158
Fig. 8.4	Geographic groupings used for regional analyses	159
Fig. 8.5	Evolution of intra- and extra-regional migration per sub-region, in millions of people	161
Fig. 9.1	International migrant stock as a percentage of the total population in Africa	186
Fig. 9.2	Destination of African migrants globally	187
Fig. 9.3	Distribution of migrants on the continent	187
Fig. 9.4	International migrant stock in Africa	188
Fig. 9.5	Annual rate of change of the migrant stock in Africa	189
Fig. 9.6	Female migrants as a percentage of the international migrant stock in Africa	190
Fig. 9.7	International migrant stock as a percentage of the total population 1990–2020	191

Fig. 11.1	Evolution of international migration from Upper Volta, 1919–1960	226
Fig. 12.1	Estimated stock of the foreign-born population in South America by origin, 1990–2020	253
Fig. 12.2	Number of asylum applications received in South American countries by claimant's nationality, 2000–2019	254
Fig. 13.1	Haitian migration to the Latin American and Caribbean (LAC) region	278
Fig. 14.1	Total number of foreign migrant workers holding valid temporary work permits (PLKS) in Malaysia	297
Fig. 14.2	Total number of foreign migrant workers according to nationalities	298
Fig. 14.3	Number of Nepali migrant workers (with PLKS) by gender	299
Fig. 14.4	Total number of migrant workers by sectors and nationalities (with PLKS)	299
Fig. 16.1	African asylum seeker population in Latin American countries (2000–2022)	350
Fig. 16.2	African asylum seeker population in Latin American countries (2022)	351
Fig. 16.3	Total African refugee population in Latin American countries (1993–2022)	353
Fig. 16.4	Number of African migrants detained by Mexican immigration authorities (2007–2022)	353
Fig. 16.5	Top-10 irregular African migrant nationalities presented before Mexican immigration authorities	354
Fig. 19.1	Haitian migration to Brazil	422
Fig. 23.1	Word Art derived from the abstracts of the 74 papers reviewed	501
Fig. 24.1	Chinese FDI vs. US FDI to Africa, flow	526
Fig. 30.1	Perú: Net migration rates, 1960–2022	656
Fig. 30.2	Venezuelan migrants to Perú vs. all other migrants, 2014–2022	657
Fig. 30.3	International funding received by Perú for the Venezuelan migrant crisis	668

List of Tables

Table 1.1	Features of colonial South–South and globalised South–South migration (after Adil Khan & Hossain, 2017)	4
Table 2.1	Ten enslavers journey of African human cargo	30
Table 8.1	Top 20 regional corridors in the Global South	160
Table 8.2	Top 10 countries of origin and destination to/from the middle east	163
Table 8.3	Top 10 countries of origin and destination to/from Central Asia	164
Table 8.4	Top 10 countries of origin and destination to/from South Asia and South-East Asia	166
Table 8.5	Top 10 countries of origin and destination to/from China	168
Table 8.6	Top 10 countries of origin and destination to/from Africa	171
Table 8.7	Top 10 countries of origin and destination to/from Latin America	173
Table 9.1	Annual rate of change in the migrant stock from 1990 to 2020	191
Table 9.2	Annual rate of change in the migrant stock in Africa 1990–2020, by regions and sex	194
Table 12.1	Activity, unemployment, and informal employment rates by sex in urban areas for selected countries, circa 2018	251
Table 12.2	Main sociodemographic characteristics of recent immigrants in selected South American countries, circa 2018	255
Table 12.3	Main characteristics of migration and refugee legal frameworks in selected countries, 2022	257

Table 15.1	Reasons for migration to Ghana by gender (multiple response)	324
Table 15.2	Sector of main work of Chinese migrants in Ghana by gender	327
Table 16.1	Major African countries of origin of asylum seekers and refugees in Latin America, 2022	352
Table 16.2	Main host countries for African asylum seekers and refugees in Latin America	352
Table 31.1	Licensing requirements for recruitment agencies in ASEAN's main sending countries	684

1

South–South Migration and Inequality: An Introduction

Heaven Crawley and Joseph Kofi Teye

The Scale and Importance of South–South Migration

Although scholarly work on international migration overwhelmingly focuses on movements from the Global South to the Global North, South–South migration has been—and remains—a significant share of global population movements (Campillo-Batisai, 2022; Carrete, 2013; De Lombaerde et al., 2014; Gagnon, 2018; Leal & Harder, 2021; Melde et al., 2014; UNDESA, 2020). North–North and South–South migration showed surprisingly comparable volumes of international migration in 1990 and 2005, before a significant rise in South–South migration in 2020. As noted by Schewel and Debray (this volume), South–South migration was the predominant form of international migration in 1990, surpassed by South–North migration in 2005 and was slightly greater than South–North migration in 2020. International migration within the Global South appears to be on the rise, at least

---

H. Crawley (✉)
United Nations University Centre for Policy Research (UNU-CPR), New York, NY, USA
e-mail: crawley@unu.edu

J. K. Teye
Centre for Migration Studies (CMS),
University of Ghana, Accra, Ghana
e-mail: jteye@ug.edu.gh

in terms of absolute numbers and now constitutes over one-third of international migration in 2020 (UNDESA, 2020). In other words, there are more people migrating from one country to another within the Global South than there are people moving from the Global South to the Global North. In some places, almost all migration is to a neighbouring country in the Global South. Take for example, migration from Burkina Faso to Cote d'Ivoire, one of the largest migration flows in the world and one that is rarely talked about or analysed by migration scholars outside the region (Cross, 2020; Dabiré & Soumahoro, this volume).

Reflecting this, South–South migration is also increasing in absolute terms (Nawyn, 2016). For example, African countries hosted 24.7 million migrants in 2017, up from 19.3 million in 1990, a 28% increase (Gagnon, 2018). Almost all these migrants were born somewhere else in Africa: despite perceptions to the contrary, more than 80% of African migrants do not leave the continent (IOM, 2020). As noted by Gagnon (2018), conditions are ripe for this trend to continue with a significant increase in the number of children and youth alongside an increase in women's participation in the labour market and rapid urbanisation. When combined with increasing border controls in Global North, it seems almost certain that intra-regional migration within Africa will continue to rise. Within the Global South, Asia-to-Asia migration, especially that related to migration from slower-growing developing Asia to faster-growing developing Asia, is most significant. It is estimated that 87% of the 21 million migrants who entered the Asian region between 1990 and 2013 originated from other countries in Asia (Adil Khan & Hossain, 2017).

South–South Migration has a long history, albeit under differing economic and political conditions. Although South–South migration has always involved large numbers of people, the nature of these flows has changed over time. Historically, large scale migration South–South migration flows were mostly enforced and involuntary, involving both inter- and intra-regional destinations to various colonies of the Global North (Adil Khan & Hossain, 2017).[1] The transatlantic slave trade was one of the largest historical migrations between the countries of the Global South, taking place mainly between the countries of western, central and southern Africa and what is now known as Brazil (Bruey and Crawley, this volume). The forced migration of up to 14 million people as a result of the partition of India also represented a

---

[1] It is important to acknowledge that South–South migration has been a feature of societies across the Global South since the beginning of human history, however much of the documented history of migration is more recent and coincides with the creation of borders demarcating geographical territories from one another, e.g., the partition of Africa with The Berlin Conference of 1884–5.

very significant intra-regional flow (Leaning & Bhadada, 2022). Contemporary South–South migration is characterised by features that reflect this history but are driven by the neoliberal modes of production that have come to dominate national, regional and global economies (Table 1.1). According to Adil Khan and Hossain (2017), contemporary South–South migration is more likely to be through choice—albeit that these choices are often made in contexts of poverty and limited economic opportunities—as well as being predominantly intra-regional, temporary and cyclical in nature due to relatively high transaction costs and low net returns.

This raises the important question of whether South–South migration is different from South–North migration or migration between the countries of the Global North? While some question the distinctiveness of South–South migration (see, for example, Bakewell, 2009), others argue that South–South migrations have a number of features that are particular, and reflect the very different social, as well as economic and political, contexts within which migration takes place. These differences relate to: the distance of journeys; the nature of borders; the composition of migration flows; the migration–conflict nexus; regional migration governance; and the particularities of certain migration-related concepts and variables (De Lombaerde et al., 2014).

Firstly, contemporary South–South migration tends to take place over shorter geographical distances—often within countries or across immediate borders. This is mainly because the costs of migration are lower but also because of bilateral agreements between countries of the Global South. One example is the open border between Nepal and India, through which thousands of Nepalis migrate each year for work. Because of the open border agreement, Nepalis and Indians can move freely over the border, making it difficult to know how many Nepali migrants live and work in India at any time (Sharma & Thapa, 2013). Secondly, South–South migration is often irregular and those who move become undocumented, although this term can be misleading given that migration between countries, particularly neighbouring countries, has effectively become regularised over time even if it remains informal. The absence of documentation and formal regulation of flows means that estimations of South–South migration are likely far lower than the reality. This leads us to the third specificity of South–South migration: the nature of borders. Borders in the Global South have historically been less restrictive in terms of migration, not least because of weaker border enforcement capacities. This is particularly the case for Africa (Jonsson, 2009).

Fourthly, it has been observed that there are differences in the average composition of South–South compared with South–North migration flows,

Table 1.1 Features of colonial South–South and globalised South–South migration (after Adil Khan & Hossain, 2017)

Colonial South–South Migration
• Transatlantic slave trade to colonised South to meet colonial economic and production arrangements primarily in the plantation/mining sectors;
• Forced migration over shorter distances, often as indentured labour;
• Mainly intra- and inter-regional;
• Largely involuntary and enforced with no provision for return and/or "backward linkage'" (financial and social remittances) to the country/place of origin;
• Exploitation based with no migrant rights;
• Migrants socially excluded in receiving countries
Globalised South–South Migration
• With decolonisation most migrant workers were absorbed in their receiving countries where they continue to face social, political and economic barriers;
• Mixed drivers of migration between sending and the receiving countries including opportunities for migration as a voluntary option;
• Mostly intra-regional although some inter-regional movements have emerged more recently;
• Temporary and rotational ("cyclic") in nature and includes mainly low to semiskilled workers;
• Predominantly male but with a large proportion of female migrants in some geographical contexts;
• Modalities of migration include but not limited to: kinship networks; official formal means; a range of intermediaries;
• War and human rights abuse in some sending South countries contributes to involuntary/irregular migration;
• Migration represents a major source of foreign exchange earnings for the developing sending countries that accrue through remittances, and for receiving countries a major and also a cheap source of labour for infrastructure development and services sector;
• Governance deficits in both sending and receiving countries increase migrant vulnerabilities in terms of safety, security and welfare at both ends, and reduce net benefits;
• Low income and relatively high transaction costs prompt repeat or cyclical migration contributing to prolonged migrant absence that increase social costs at the individual and migrant household levels;
• Most national and international level research and policy discussions on migration prioritise issues concerning remittance and development financing rather than economic and social changes/costs incurred at the individual migrant and household levels

with the former being characterised by lower skills and educational levels (Hujo & Piper, 2007) and generally of a younger age. A fifth feature is related to conflict–migration nexus, which is likely to be more present in contexts of South–South migration (Jonsson, 2009). This is reflected in the fact that low- and middle-income countries in the Global South hosted 76% of the world's refugees and other people in need of international protection in 2022, a figure which was for a long time more than 85% (UNHCR, 2023).[2] Finally, migration takes place in the context of family and community structures which are often more important to decision-making than in the Global North where these processes are often more individualistic. Religion and spirituality (in varying forms) are also likely to play a more significant role.

Focusing on South–South migration therefore allows for the testing and either affirmation or modification of theories developed by migration scholars in an effort to understand why people migrate, who migrates, where they choose to migrate to and why and how well or poorly they integrate into the destination country. Studying South–South migration dynamics also allows us to re-consider and/or question the meaning and relevance of other social concepts and variables, and their relationship to other variables that have often emerged in a Northern context and were then uncritically transported into other contexts, for example, the nature of family/social networks, the role of religion and spirituality and the idea that migration might be a collective rather than individualised project (see De Lombaerde et al., 2014; Feyissa et al., this volume). Like Batisai (2022), many of the contributions to this Handbook examine the extent and ways in which emerging South–South theorisations resonate with migration realities in the broader Global South context, exposing, where necessary, gaps in existing theorisations which have originated in the Global North.

None of which is to say that South–South migration, or the countries in the Global South between which people move, are monolithic. As several of the authors in this Handbook note, the term "Global South" is contested (Fiddian-Qasmiyeh; Casentini, Hammond and Bakewell; Carella). It can be criticised for "flattening out" the vastly different histories of the countries of the Global South, implying that there is something inherently different about these countries from those of the Global North. For the purpose of this Handbook, we use the term "Global South" as "a territorial, relational, structural and political construct [which] is fundamentally about the distribution of power in the global system" (Sud & Sánchez-Ancochea, 2022, 1123). Like Sud and Sánchez-Ancochea (2022), we have chosen to approach the term Global South and, in turn, South–South migration, critically and with a recognition of the sometimes-contradictory meanings and uses of the term. We consider critical engagement with the term to be more important than discursive attempts to replace it. When not simplistically used to represent geographical space, we believe that this term has significant potential to

---

[2] The proportion of refugees and others in need of international protection has fallen because of the Russian invasion of Ukraine in 2012 which led to the forced displacement of millions of Ukrainians to neighbouring European countries.

consolidate and empower the various social actors that consider themselves to be in subalternised positionalities within global networks of power (Kloß, 2017). As Kloß (2017, 1) suggests, the Global South is not an entity that exists per se but has to be understood as something that is created, imagined, invented, maintained and recreated by the ever-changing and never fixed status positions of social actors and institutions. Reflecting this, we recognise the territorial South as dynamic, produced through the workings of history, geography and time, and as a place in which there are both centres and peripheries when it comes to political and economic power, for example South Africa in the context of the African continent and Brazil in the context of South America. In Asia, where the bulk of South–South migration occurs, two sets of countries provided the demand nodes of migration in the region—namely, the slow-growing Bangladesh, India, Pakistan, Sri Lanka and Nepal on the one hand, and faster-growing countries such as the oil-producing Middle East, fast-growing Malaysia, the Republic of Korea, Singapore and Thailand on the other (Adil Khan & Hossain, 2017). One of the most significant reasons for these patterns is that the countries of the Global South have experienced different growth trajectories, creating inequalities between and within the countries of the Global South as well as between South and North.

The Relationships Between Migration and Inequality

There is growing interest in the extent and ways in which migration can contribute to positive development outcomes and delivery of the Sustainable Development Goals (SDGs) (Ratha et al., 2013). This is reflected in the fact that development agencies and policy makers in the Global North are devoting significant resources to understanding migration's potential and implementing policies to reduce the associated costs. There has been rather less focus on the relationships between South–South migration and inequality.

As noted by Black et al. (2006) international migration is a powerful symbol of global inequality, whether in terms of wages, labour market opportunities, or lifestyles. But the potential for migration to reduce inequality and contribute to development is neither straightforward nor inevitable. Firstly, and perhaps most importantly, not everyone has access to the benefits of migration. The ability to migrate, and the conditions under which migration takes place, often reflects and reinforces existing spatial, structural and social inequalities including those related to gender, nationality, race, age and income. As many of the chapters in this Handbook show, these inequalities are often intersectional. They determine who is and is not able to migrate and under what conditions, as well as where people move to and the rights and the resources that they are able to access. Importantly, migration can increase as well as reduce inequality. For example, income inequalities in countries of origin can be expected to increase with international migration, particularly for the most marginalised groups in society, for example, women. This is because the poorest of the poor seldom have the means to migrate (McKenzie, 2017).

Secondly, increased barriers to migration, irregular and precarious journeys, poor labour conditions, and a lack of rights for migrants and their families can create new inequalities. In other words, vulnerability and violence is not inherent to migration but is also created (or allowed) by States, for example, by refusing or failing to provide access to a legal status and documentation, by failing to provide access to safe and legal migration routes or by choosing not to effectively regulate employers and businesses who exploit migrant workers. Disjointed and top-down policy and legal frameworks can also serve to dehumanise migrants by focusing on economic outcomes to the neglect of human experiences and well-being.

Thirdly, the countries of the Global South are locked into unequal relations with the Global North because of colonialism and their incorporation into systems of unequal exchange (Hickel et al., 2022). Recent research by Hickel et al. (2022) confirms that the "advanced economies" of the Global North rely on a large net appropriation of resources and labour from the Global South, extracted through induced price differentials in international trade. When measured in Northern prices, the drain amounted to $10.8 trillion in 2015, and $242 trillion over the period from 1990 to 2015—a significant windfall for the North, equivalent to a quarter of Northern GDP and similar to the windfall that was derived from colonial forms of appropriation. Unequal exchange is a major driver of underdevelopment and global inequality which limits the potential contribution of migration to development.

The depth and extent of the inequalities facing migrants globally was revealed by the COVID-19 pandemic. As reflected in some of the contributions to this Handbook, COVID-19 was not the "great equaliser" some claimed, but rather served as an amplifier of existing inequalities, including those associated with migration (Crawley, 2020). The pandemic severely disrupted access to the opportunities associated with migration, undermining the potential developmental benefits and creating new challenges for policy efforts aimed at securing improved outcomes for migrants and their families.

Refugees and displaced populations living in crowded and unhygienic conditions were often unable to protect themselves from the virus, faced increasing economic precarity and found themselves excluded from measures to alleviate poverty and hunger. The threat to refugees came not only from material (in)security, but from increasing exclusion and exceptionalism associated with the politics of protection with governments in Europe, the US and some countries in the Global South who used the pandemic as an excuse to double-down on border closures and/or dip into their migration policy toolboxes to demonstrate the robustness of their response to it (Crawley, 2021).

Although the relationships between migration and inequality are profound, they remain largely under-analysed in the context of the Global South, and indeed more generally. While the migration and inequality have been studied extensively as separate theoretical and conceptual domains, few have theorised the direct links between them (Bastia, 2013; Muyonga et al., 2020). Moreover, where inequality is considered there is a tendency to focus on income inequalities to the exclusion of all others (Palmary, 2020). Indeed, the majority of studies on inequality are based on analysis at the individual level, often focusing on remittances and generally using income as the measurement parameter. There is a neglect of broader structural inequalities that limit possibilities and opportunities and place some population groups in precarious conditions while maintaining others in areas of privilege that provide them with greater access to social services and, therefore, greater social mobility. There is clearly a need for more in-depth investigation of the nexus between non-income inequalities and migration as well as the unpacking of the contextual factors behind inequality and migration using both qualitative and quantitative approaches (Muyonga et al., 2020). Additionally, Muyongo et al. (2020) strongly encourage the use of specialist migration surveys to improve the body of knowledge on this subject. This Handbook addresses these gaps, and it does so primarily by drawing on the knowledge of scholars and practitioners living and working in the countries of the Global South.

The Importance of Global South Perspectives

Migration scholarship is heavily skewed towards the Global North where research is largely designed and led, and where governments and international organisations increasingly fund research to inform policy development (Nawyn, 2016). As a result, the Global North's interests shape dominant research themes, producing a disproportionate focus on South–North migration and categories of migrant defined in law and policy to make sense of—and increasingly contain—migration flows. This picture is inevitably partial. In the case of Africa, for example, numerous works produced across disciplines—from history (e.g., Ibadan School of Historiography) to African Studies (e.g., Institute of African Studies, University of Ghana Law, Makerere University)—do not form part of the literature or archive of migration studies (Crawley et al., 2022). The result is that important and path-breaking conceptual and theoretical works on the making of political communities that span North Africa and parts of the Arab world seldom inform thinking in the field of African migration and the contemporary making of societies. As noted previously by Teye (2021):

> [s]cholars in the Global North tend to misunderstand or misinterpret mobility patterns. For instance, because they are in Europe, they just see an influx of people coming to Europe, especially since 2015…So, when the story is led by people that only see the people coming and they don't see the other people that are circulating within the region, they will not be able to tell our story better than we can. That is why we think the knowledge production has to shift towards the Global South, so that we decolonise that knowledge.

Moreover, much migration scholarship has been dominated by a "paradigm of absence" (de Souza e Silva, 2021), which focuses on what the Global South (and its people) lack in relation to an idealised (but deeply flawed) colonial cultural and educational model. This approach can serve to stigmatise migration and those that move in ways that simply reinforce rather than challenge dominant (anti-) migration narratives.

This Handbook, by contrast, is dominated by the views and perspectives of those living in, or originating from the Global South with more than two-thirds of the chapters being written by Global South scholars. These contributions provide new insights into migration processes in the Global South and some of them directly challenge dominant migration theories developed by scholars in the Global North which ignore context specific economic, political and social processes. By assembling a set of empirically informed works that grapple conceptually with the relationship between migration and inequality from diverse Southern locations, this Handbook ensures both local relevance and trans-local comparative work that takes the South (in its varied specificities) as a serious analytical category (see also Crawley et al., 2022). Many of the contributors are part of the Migration for Development and Equality Hub—otherwise known as MIDEQ[3]—which

---

[3] The Migration for Development and Equality (MIDEQ) Hub is funded by the UKRI Global Challenges Research Fund (GCRF) (Grant Reference ES/S007415/1). More at www.mideq.org.

unpacks the complex and multi-dimensional relationships between migration and inequality in the context of the Global South. MIDEQ's work directly addresses knowledge gaps, decentring or decolonising the production of knowledge about migration and its consequences away from the Global North with the aim of ensuring that policy makers, programme specialists and donors have the understanding and evidence they need to harness the development potential of migration for individuals, households, communities and the countries of the Global South. The Hub's overarching vision is thus to disrupt dominant assumptions about the reasons why people move and the consequences of migration, deepening knowledge and understanding of the relationships between South–South migration, inequality and development. It does this by building interdisciplinary migration research capacity in the Global South that can challenge dominant narratives on migration and improve the lives of migrants, their families and the communities of which they are a part.

The Contributions to this Handbook

The Handbook is divided into four parts, each highlighting often overlooked mobility patterns within and between regions of the Global South as well as the intersectional inequalities faced by those who move. While most books on South–South migration focus on only one country or region, the Handbook takes a regional approach which allows for the comparison of findings from different geographical areas. A number of chapters employ the idea of "corridors" to describe the movement of people, goods, money, knowledge and skills between two places with socio-cultural, economic, political and historical dynamics that transcend national borders. This focus on corridors enables the contributors to the Handbook to examine the relationships within and between countries, countering the focus of much migration research on processes and outcomes in individual countries. Several chapters also analyse migration flows *between* different regions of the Global South (Teye et al., Freier et al., this volume).

Part I focuses on conceptualisations of South–South migration and begins with a historical perspective on migration between the countries of the Global South. Examining the lasting impacts of the transatlantic enslavement of Black African peoples as a precursor of contemporary forms of South–South migration, Bruey and Crawley argue that is impossible to understand contemporary forms and experiences of South–South migration without first understanding the history of migration between countries generally classified as the Global South and the enduring effects of slavery. The authors also highlight the impacts of slavery on contemporary inequality within Africa, including Liberia, where the return of captured and emancipated slaves led directly to the civil wars that devastated the country between 1989 and 2003, and significant displacement into other parts of West Africa.

Having situated South–South migration firmly in its historical antecedents of slavery and colonisation, the Handbook then turns to inequalities in the production of migration knowledge. As noted by Fiddian-Qasmiyeh, it has become increasingly mainstream to argue that redressing the Eurocentrism of migration studies requires a commitment to decentring Global North knowledge, however it is not clear what this means in practice for Global South scholarship. Her chapter highlights the diverse ways in which scholars have sought to redress Eurocentrism in migration studies, by challenging the relevance and applicability of classical concepts and frameworks in the South, addressing knowledge "blind spots" by studying migration in the South and South–South migration, and engaging critically with the geopolitics of knowledge production. The geopolitics of knowledge production are also explored by Landström and Crawley, who take stock of existing critiques of contemporary migration research and bring these debates into contact with ongoing debates among decolonial scholars and in feminist social epistemology. Drawing on the framework of epistemic injustice and oppression, the authors highlight issues of undue epistemic marginalisation, suggesting that these issues should be centred as a core concern as migration scholars who need to critically reflect upon the knowledge production and dissemination practices of their field. Understanding the processes through which epistemic injustices happen, rather than just the epistemic outcomes, can help us to identify ways to address the structural inequalities with which the production of migration knowledge is often associated. Structural inequalities in the production of knowledge are picked up in the chapter by Vanyaro, who explores how the distinction(s) implied by the term "fieldwork'", gives rise to false and misleading dichotomies that are problematic for any decolonial migration research praxis that tries to undo the bureaucratic damage of hegemonic ideas about research ethics. Exploring how "fieldwork" is undertaken in practice, Vanyaro argues that the dichotomies of "home" and the "field" conjured by this term negate an intermediate space between these two extremes in which social relationships, kinship ties and social value define the possible extent of the risk of migration research to further marginalise or protect migrants. What is needed, he suggests, is a paradigm shift in the kinds of ethics procedures as well as considerations in partnerships on migration studies which presume that power relationships between the researcher and the researched are somehow evened out when research is undertaken by African researchers working in African academic institutions.

Two of the contributions in Part I challenge migration scholars to find alternative ways of looking at South–South migration from non-economic perspectives and from the perspectives of those who move, including those who are forced to move due to conflict and human rights abuses. The contribution by Qasmiyeh and Fiddian-Qasmiyeh, combining critical reflections with poetry, is framed around the correspondence between the refugee camp and the process of writing—here, writing from the South—positing that writing the refugee camp into literature is both witnessing and archiving, and that refugees are not only wait-*ers* but makers of time. The chapter by Phipps and Yohannes questions what it means to move and critiques the Global North's measurement-heavy and largely economistic perceptions of migration which, the authors argue, obscure the humanity of forced migration. The chapter considers how art and cultural works serve as methods practised daily by migrants in contexts of violent (b)ordering, (dis)counting and survival, to maintain their identities and humanity, and to resist. The chapter concludes by stressing the need for cultural work mediated by arts-based research to unmask not only the humanity within the South–South migration but also the potent forces of comfort and discomfort.

The contributors in Part II unpack "the South" in South–South migration by providing both an overview of migration patterns and trends across the regions of the Global South—Africa, Asia and South America—and exploring the differences between them. Collectively these chapters highlight the existence of centres and peripheries *within* the Global South and the ways in which inequalities shape migration patterns and outcomes. In their contribution to global trends in South–South migration, Schewel and Debray review global, regional and county-level trends between 1990 and 2020 using the most geographically comprehensive database available on international migrant stocks (UN DESA, 2020). The author notes that over one-third of all international migration is between countries of the Global South, a greater share than South–North migration in 2020. This chapter shows most migrants from the Global South move to countries within their home region, particularly in areas like Sub-Saharan Africa, the Middle East and South America. However, extra-regional migration is on the rise as more international migrants travel further distances. Migration from South Asia to the Middle East is now the largest South–South intra-regional migration corridor in the world.

These trends are then unpacked at the country and regional levels. The first three chapters examine the relationships between migration and inequality in the context of the context of Africa. We begin with a chapter from Yaro and Setrana on the dynamics of South–South migration in Africa. Historically, colonialism has shaped movements within the African continent through inequalities in development processes and outcomes as well as infrastructural imbalances and forced movements. More recently, efforts by African states to enhance regional integration have played an important role in facilitating intra-African movements. The authors point out that while Africa is commonly represented as a continent of exodus, the vast majority of African migration occurs within the continent. This point is picked up by Feyissa, Zeleke and Gebresenbet who explore the idea that migration is a collective rather than an individual project, as typically assumed by migration scholars in the Global North. Their chapter, which draws on the case study of Hadiya migration to South Africa, critiques the individualist thrust in migration studies and the assumed "autonomous agency" of prospective migrants, especially in the context of the Global South. Finally, Dabiré and Soumahoro examine the sometimes-contradictory impacts of migration on inequalities in Burkina Faso and Côte d'Ivoire which represents one of the largest migration flows in the world with the cross-border movement of migrant workers to the cocoa plantations established by the colonisers in the northern areas of Côte d'Ivoire. The authors suggest that while this migration helps poor households through the transfer of resources, it also creates inequalities: inequalities between children whose parents migrate and those who do not, inequalities between households that do and don't receive remittances, and gender inequalities. In addition, once they arrive in Côte d'Ivoire, Burkina Faso migrants (Burkinabè) often face difficulties in securing good working conditions and rights.

The focus then turns to South America, starting with a chapter from Rosas and Zapata outlining trends and characteristics of migrants' social and economic inclusion in six countries: Argentina, Colombia, Chile, Ecuador, Peru and Uruguay. These countries have recently witnessed rising levels of intra-regional migration, diversification in the origins and motivations of flows, and/or have suddenly become immigration and transit countries. The authors argue that these transformations have added a layer of complexity to our understanding of the historic—and persistent—socio-economic inequalities that characterise the region, posing additional challenges to migrants' social and economic inclusion. These inequalities are reflected in the chapter by Marcelin and Cela which explores the making of migrant trails in the Americas through ethnographic tracing of Haitians on the move. The authors argue that migrant vulnerability often begins at home, signalling to governments and communities in transit and destination countries that they are people who are unprotected and easy to exploit. Haiti, they are, epitomises this continuum of intersectional inequities which create a path dependency for vulnerability. The authors use the concept of "circulation" to frame the fluid patterns of migration by Haitians who are caught on different migrant trails across the Americas, arguing that Haitians on the move—already unprotected and deprived of basic rights at home—carry their path dependency to complex vulnerability across the Americas where they experience unequal access to rights and social protection.

The final three chapters in Part II take us first to Southeast Asia for a chapter by Yeoh and Ghimire on migrant labour and inequalities in the Nepal–Malaysia corridor and beyond. Malaysia is an upper middle-income country heavily reliant on migrant labour from 15 different countries to work in the manufacturing, construction, plantation and service sectors. For Nepali citizens, Malaysia is a popular destination country in addition to the Gulf Co-operation Council (GOC) states, Nepalis constitute the third largest migrant labour force in Malaysia after Indonesians and Bangladeshis. Drawing on the concept of "migration infrastructure" (Xiang & Lindquist, 2014) as a point of departure, this chapter examines the range of pre-existing everyday and structurally imposed migration inequalities faced by Nepalis. It also elaborates on how these inequalities, which were relatively ignored or underplayed in the past, became accentuated and brought into public view during the COVID-19 global pandemic, and in its wake set in motion long overdue policy reforms.

The Handbook then turns to the topic of inter-regional migration in the Global South with two chapters that highlight the growing but under researched topic of those for whom South–South migration means moving between continents rather than just countries. In their chapter on the growing phenomenon of Chinese migration to Ghana, Teye, Lu and Crawford suggest, as earlier authors do, that migration has both positive and negative impacts on equality. Positively, the incomes and livelihoods of some Chinese migrants and Ghanaians who work for Chinese investors have improved, however, financial rewards have benefited some more than others, with increased income inequalities along gender and social class lines. Negative impacts also include environmental degradation, violation of Ghana's trade and mining laws, and exploitation of some Ghanaians by Chinese migrants. While Chinese migrants and their families left behind benefit through improved incomes and remittances, migration and associated financial flows contribute to a deepening of inequalities in migrants' sending areas. The drivers of African migration to South America are explored by Freier, Oba and Bautista who note that despite the media focus on African migration to Europe, African migrants are also undertaking longer and riskier journeys in search of better opportunities in destinations such as Brazil, Argentina and Mexico. The authors explain why African migrants are choosing South American host or transit countries, offering a refutation of classical "push–pull" models and instead, proposing that Africans migrate for a variety of reasons including personal aspirations. In so doing, the chapter aims to contribute to a better understanding of the dynamics of African migration to non-traditional destinations, and highlight avenues for further research in the field of African migration studies. It also emphasises the need to move away from simplistic explanations based on push–pull models and to recognise the agency and diversity of African migrants.

Having explored South–South migration patterns and trends, Part III of the Handbook turns to the inequalities associated with migration, drawing on data from the MIDEQ Hub and other research in the Global South, starting with three chapters that examine inequalities associated with poverty, gender and race from an intersectional perspective. In their overview of the relationships between poverty, income inequalities and migration in the Global South, Casentini, Hammond and Bakewell assess the ways in which income inequalities contribute to patterns of migration, the mechanisms by which resources are transferred back to places of origin and their impacts on poverty and income inequalities, and the impacts of migration on patterns of inequalities in places where people move. Reflecting the contributions in Part I, the authors take a critical approach which highlights the need to consider the historical dimensions involved in the political construction of the Global South as a category. In their contribution, Bastia and Piper explore the comparative dynamics of gendered processes and outcomes in the context of South–South migration with the aim of redressing an existing bias towards destination countries by placing greater emphasis on countries of origin and transnational social fields. By focusing on migrant precarity as workers, the analysis in this chapter also moves beyond the overwhelming focus on domestic work to highlight other overlooked sectors in which there are highly gendered patterns of migrant employment, such as manufacturing, agriculture and tourism. This theme is continued in the chapter on Haitian migration and structural racism in Brazil by Souza e Silva, Barbosa and Fernandes. Highlighting the socio-historical foundations of Brazilian structural racism, and in particular its articulation with sexism and institutional patrimonialism—the authors argue for the need to better understand how experiences in diverse socio-cultural and political contexts may influence perceptions, and even a supposedly "naïve" views on race and inequalities.

They also emphasise the need to acknowledge the distinct strategies adopted by Black migrants in contexts of structural racism.

The chapters that follow explore the inequalities that shape decisions to migrate and the role of specific drivers including climate change, food insecurities, as well as the role of intermediaries in the migration process. Boas, Olayiwola and Gautam provide a socio-political account of the ways in which the relations between climate change and human mobility manifest themselves in different regions of the Global South. Moving away from Global North assumptions that the relationships between climate change and mobility are straightforward, even obvious, the chapter demonstrates how climate mobility patterns are embedded within often uneven social and political dynamics which shape whether, how and to where people move. This involves socio-economic dynamics such as gender inequality, or policy developments such as donor agendas impacting local manifestations of climate mobility in the Global South, as well as the political role of state borders and how these influence the ways people can move in the context of climate risk. Crush and Ramachandran continue this theme by drawing attention to the underexplored linkages between food security, inequality, migration and development with respect to South–South migration. Building on core arguments reflecting on these ties and empirical studies from diverse sending and receiving contexts, they outline five distinctive ways in which these multi-dimensional relationships and interactions operate. Their analysis problematises the often-positive framing of the migration–development nexus.

The theme of inequalities in decisions to migrate is picked up in Mazzilli, Hagen-Zanker and Himmelstine's exploration of the ways in which migration decision-making intersects with both tangible and intangible inequalities. The emerging literature from the Global South shows that perceptions of inequality are multi-dimensional, intersectional and overlapping, and that they are shaped and experienced by migrants at different stages of the migration cycle. The authors argue that focusing on these perceptions can dramatically increase our understanding of migration decision-making. Building on this analysis, Jones, Sha and Bhuiyan argue that intermediaries play a critical role in understanding migration processes and outcomes, not least because increasing border controls and restrictions on movement mean that intermediaries make mobility possible in a world in which *im*mobility is often the norm.

The final set of chapters in Part III examines the impacts on South–South migration including the ways in which digital technology is harnessed to overcome inequalities (but can also create them), the relationships between migrant resource flows and development in the Global South and the extent and ways in which South–South migration both expands the challenges and increases the opportunities for children to access education. According to Harindranath, Unwin and Lorini, the use and design of digital technologies plays an important role in South–South migration, from migrant decision-making, orientation and route planning, to integration into host communities and connecting with those left behind. Digital technologies can be leveraged to increase access to opportunities and rights for migrants, thereby boosting migration's developmental benefits at the interface between migrants and host communities. However, the authors argue that structural inequalities in migration contexts mean that access and use of digital technologies are almost always socially contingent, often leading to further inequalities. In their chapter on migrant resource flows and development in the Global South, Asiedu, Tapsoba and Gelb examine three types of resource flows in South–South migration—financial flows of remittances and diaspora investment, trade flows of goods and services, and knowledge flows relating to skills development and production and organisational technology for enterprises. The authors point out that the South–South component of resource flows has barely been addressed in the existing literature, focusing overwhelmingly on North–South flows with greater aggregate value and ignoring the migrant and diaspora population from the Global South. They also argue that many resource flows are informal and that trying to "formalise" these will leave many—both migrants and citizens—in jeopardy because they will not have access to flows of finance, trade and knowledge. Taking account of South–South flows will be critical to harness the developmental benefits of migration and manage the potentially unequalising impacts of these flows. Nyamnjoh, Seaman and Zeleke examine the impacts of South–South migration on children's education, arguing that migration produces, mitigates and transforms educational inequalities, with such shifts generating impacts across generations and geographies. Through two case studies on South–South migration which focus on first-generation children born to Ethiopian parents and Ethiopian children who reunited with their parents in South Africa, and children in Ethiopia whose parents are migrants in South Africa, the authors explore migration's nuanced impacts on educational opportunities, aspirations and attainment, and how this in turn effects social mobility and inequalities.

Finally, Part IV explores responses to South–South migration, returning to a regional perspective in order to highlight the very significant differences that exist in migration policy approaches in Africa, Asia and South America where histories of migration, relationships to the Global North and governance structures vary significantly. The chapters also draw attention to the experiences and responses of migrants, including their ability (or otherwise) to access justice and rights and efforts to mobilise politically and build new forms of transnational solidarity that bridge both geographical and sectoral boundaries. Carella begins by asking the important question of whether the governance of South–South migration is, or should be, different from that taking place both to and within the Global North. The author approaches South–South migration as a complex and diverse phenomenon, the governance of which is rendered particularly challenging by inequalities at the global level, as well as between southern countries and within them. He argues that since South–South migration often occurs in challenging contexts characterised, among others, by the prevalence of labour market informality, irregular status and/or temporariness, it requires southern responses adapted to specific needs.

The specificities of migration governance in the Global South are reflected in the chapters that follow. In their analysis of policies towards migration in Africa, Teye and Oucho provide an overview of the measures taken by the African Union Commission and Member States to promote free movement of persons but note the slow and uneven process of implementation due to a lack of political will and resource constraints. Espinoza takes us to South America, providing us with an overview of recent South American migration governance in the context of significant shifts in migration patterns and dynamics associated, in particular, with the exodus of more than seven million Venezuelans. The author suggests that the changes in migration governance in South America over the last decade have been framed and justified through the lens of "multiple crises" and is characterised by fragmented and reactive measures, with practices that evidence both continuity and change. The development of this approach is leading to more control, the criminalisation of migration, increased migrant irregularity and less protection for people on the move. The focus on Venezuelan migration continues with the chapter by Mazza and Villarreal, who examine the arrival of large numbers of Venezuelans in Perú, where migration policies have changed dramatically over the course of the crisis. The authors find that Perú's restrictive policies have been both ineffective in reducing forced migration flows and counterproductive by inducing the increased marginalisation of Venezuelan migrants, inequalities which were further deepened by the COVID-19 pandemic.

We then move to southeast Asia, where Asis and Maningat provide an overview of what they describe as "the ASEAN way" in migration governance, which reflects both the refusal of Asian states to be part of international migration conventions while at the same time making efforts towards cooperation at a regional or sub-regional level. The authors explore the complex migration governance mechanisms in southeast Asia, highlighting the particular roles of national governments, civil society organisations, migrant workers and private recruitment agencies as well as the nuances that exist in between these actors. The limits and potential of "contestations from below" are also discussed. This theme continues with an analysis of temporary labour migration programmes in and from Asia and the Pacific by Oberoi and Sheill. The authors argue that while temporary labour migration programmes are a wide option for regular migration available to low-wage migrant workers from Asia and the Pacific, these programmes bring considerable risks to the well-being of the migrants and for their families including in their access to justice. Many, they argue, are consistently excluded by policy or practice from access to justice and remedies for human rights abuses whether in the workplace or outside. The authors argue that it is necessary to build an understanding of social justice as a societal organising principle that centres fairness in relations between individuals within society. This approach is emphasised in the final chapter of the Handbook in which Awumbila, Garba, Darkwah and Zaami examine the ways in which migrants within the Global South organise at the meso-level to defend and access their rights, and the solidarity that they build among themselves as migrants and with social movements, working class organisations and other civil society actors. Using the example of trade unions, the authors urge the need for political mobilisation actions to move away from conceptualisations of migrants as victims but rather as *actors*, capable of various initiatives and with whom they can build solidarity movements.

Taken as a whole, this Handbook represents an important contribution to our understanding of the nature of South–South migration in general, and its relationship to inequalities in particular. It moves us away from the frequently examined South–North and North–North movements to look instead at human mobility within the Global South, challenging dominant conceptualisations of migration and offering new perspectives and insights that can inform theoretical and policy understandings. As noted above, two-thirds of the chapters have been written by scholars living or, or originating from, the Global South, centring this knowledge and understanding in a way never previously seen. Moreover, because the Handbook takes a corridor and regional approach, it allows for a comparison of findings from different geographical areas, enabling us to consider whether South–South migration, in its forms and processes, outcomes and governance, different from those seen in the Global North.

One of the clearest conclusions we can draw from the Handbook is that the relationships between migration and inequality are varying and sometimes contradictory. As noted by others (see, for example, Palmary, 2020), there is little clear agreement about whether migration indeed reduces poverty or inequality. Rather what emerges from this Handbook, and from the wider literature, is an understanding that whether migration increases or decreases inequality is shaped by a large number of contextual and political factors as well as the historical contexts within which migration has developed and the responses of politicians and policy makers to this phenomenon. Understanding the relationships between South–South migration and inequalities in these contexts is a critical first step in harnessing the benefits of migration for development, and for the well-being of migrants and their families.

References

Adil Khan, M., & Hossain, M. I. (2017). The emerging phenomenon of post-globalized south-south migration: In search of a theoretical framework. In P. Short, M. Hossain, & M. Adil Khan (Eds.), *South-south migration*. Routledge.

Bakewell, O. (2009). South-south migration and human development. Reflections on African experiences. *IMI Working Papers* 15.

Bastia, T. (Ed). (2013). *Migration and inequality*. Routledge.

Batisai, K. (2022). Retheorising migration: A south-south perspective. In P. Rugunanan & N. Xulu-Gama (Eds.), *Migration in Southern Africa*, IMISCOE Research Series (pp. 11–26).

Black, R., Natali, C., & Skinner, J. (2006). Migration and inequality, World Development Report 2006 Background Papers.

Campillo-Carrete, B. (2013). South-south migration a review of the literature. ISS Working Paper No. 570, https://www.iss.nl/sites/corporate/files/Campillo_WP_South-South_migration_Lit-reviewannotated-bibly_22July_2013.pdf

Crawley, H. (2020). The great amplifier: COVID-19, migration and inequality. MIDEQ Blog 18 April 2020, https://www.mideq.org/en/blog/great-amplifier-covid-19-migration-and-inequality/

Crawley, H. (2021). The politics of refugee protection in a (post)COVID-19 world. *Social Science, 10*(81). https://doi.org/10.3390/socsci10030081

Crawley, H., Garba, F., & Nyamnjoh, F. (2022). Migration and (in) equality in the Global South: Intersections, contestations and possibilities. *Zanj: The Journal of Critical Global South Studies, 5*(1/2), 1–13. https://www.scienceopen.com/hosted-document?doi=10.13169/zanjglobsoutstud.5.1.0001

Cross, H. (2020). The Burkina Faso–Côte d'Ivoire migration corridor. In T. Bastia & R. Skelton (Eds.), *Routledge handbook of migration and development* (pp. 469–473). Routledge.

Gagnon, J. (2018). Understanding south-south migration. *OECD Development Matters*, https://oecd-development-matters.org/2018/12/17/understanding-south-south-migration/

Hickel, J., Dorninger, C., Wieland, H., & Suwandi, I. (2022). Imperialist appropriation in the world economy: Drain from the global South through unequal exchange, 1990–2015. *Global Environmental Change*. https://doi.org/10.1016/j.gloenvcha.2022.102467

Hujo, K., & Piper, N. (2007). South-South migration: Challenges for development and social policy. *Development, 50*, 19–25.

IOM. (2020). Africa migration report: Challenging the narrative, Ethiopia: International organisation for migration, https://publications.iom.int/books/africa-migration-report-challenging-narrative

Jonsson, G. (2009). *Comparative report: African migration trends*. International Migration Institute.

Kloß, S. T. (2017). The global south as subversive practice: Challenges and potentials of a heuristic concept. *The Global South, 11*(2), 1–17. https://doi.org/10.2979/globalsouth.11.2.01

Leal, D. F., & Harder, N. L. (2021). Global dynamics of international migration systems across South–South, North–North, and North–South flows, 1990–2015. *Applied Network Science, 6*(8). https://doi.org/10.1007/s41109-020-00322-x

Leaning, J., & Bhadada, S. (Eds.). (2022). *The 1947 partition of British India: Forced migration and its reverberations*. Sage.

De Lombaerde, P., Guo, F., & Neto, H. P. (2014). Introduction to the special collection: South–South migrations: what is (still) on the research agenda? *The International Migration Review, 48*(1), 103–112. http://www.jstor.org/stable/24542838

McKenzie, D. (2017). Poverty, inequality, and international migration: Insights from 10 years of migration and development conferences. *Revue D'économie Du Développement, 25*, 13–28.

Melde, S., Anich, R., Crush, J., & Oucho, J. (2014). Introduction: The south-south migration and development nexus. In R. Anich, J. Crush, S. Melde, & J. Oucho (Eds.), A new perspective on human mobility in the south, global migration issues (Vol. 3). Springer.

Muyonga, M., Odipo, G., & Agwanda, A. O. (2020). Interlinkages between migration and inequality in Africa: Review of contemporary studies. *AHMR African Human Mobility Review, 6*(1), 6–26.

Nawyn, S. (2016). Migration in the global south: Exploring new theoretical territory. *International Journal of Sociology, 46*, 81–84.

Palmary, I. (2020) Migration and inequality: an interdisciplinary overview. In T. Bastia & R. Skelton (Eds.), *Routledge handbook of migration and development* (pp.95–102). Routledge.

Ratha, D., Mohapatra, S., & Scheja, E. (2013). Impact of migration on economic and social development: A review of evidence and emerging issues. *World Bank Policy Research Working Papers*, https://elibrary.worldbank.org/doi/abs/10.1596/1813-9450-5558

Sharma, S., & Thapa, S. (2013). Taken for granted: Nepali Migraruin to India. *CESLAM Working Paper*, Kathmandu, https://www.ceslam.org/our-publications/taken-for-granted

De Souza e Silva, J. (2021). The peripheries as territories of potencies. *MIDEQ Blog*, https://www.mideq.org/en/blog/peripheries-territories-potencies/

Sud, N., & Sánchez-Ancochea, D. (2022). Southern discomfort: Interrogating the category of the Global South. *Development and Change, 53*(6). https://doi.org/10.1111/dech.12742

Teye, J. (2021). South-south migration has long been overlooked. Why? *New Humanitarian*, https://www.thenewhumanitarian.org/interview/2021/7/8/why-south-south-migration-has-long-been-overlooked

UNDESA. (2020). *International migrant stock 2020*. United Nations database, POP/DB/MIG/Stock/Rev.2020

UNHCR. (2023). *Global trends: Forced displacement in 2022*. Geneva: UNHCR, https://www.unhcr.org/sites/default/files/2023-06/global-trends-report-2022.pdf

Xiang, B., & Lindquist, J. (2014). Migration infrastructure. *International Migration Review, 14*(s.1), S122–S148.

Open Access This chapter is licensed under the terms of the Creative Commons Attribution 4.0 International License (http://creativecommons.org/licenses/by/4.0/), which permits use, sharing, adaptation, distribution and reproduction in any medium or format, as long as you give appropriate credit to the original author(s) and the source, provide a link to the Creative Commons license and indicate if changes were made.

The images or other third party material in this chapter are included in the chapter's Creative Commons license, unless indicated otherwise in a credit line to the material. If material is not included in the chapter's Creative Commons license and your intended use is not permitted by statutory regulation or exceeds the permitted use, you will need to obtain permission directly from the copyright holder.

Part I

Conceptualising South–South Migration

2

The Enduring Impacts of Slavery: A Historical Perspective on South–South Migration

Veronica Fynn Bruey and Heaven Crawley

Introduction: A Critical View of the Minority World and South–South Migration

South–South migration is not a new phenomenon. While the bulk of European's "discovery mission" to explore, colonise, and imperialise the world was based on North–South migration, the colonial project was also executed by The Netherlands, Portugal, France, Spain, and, especially, Great Britain "using export of population [Black African human cargo] to establish its imperial hegemony" (Cohen, 1995, 10). Africans carried to Brazil came overwhelmingly from Angola. Africans carried to North America, including the Caribbean, left mainly from West Africa. These South–North (Europe to the West African coastlines) and South–South (Western African coastlines to the Caribbean and South America) migration routes categorically dehumanised mass movement for nearly 400 years during what came to be known as the transatlantic slave trade. Fuelled by the incessant drive for consumerism, wealth, and greed, trafficking of Africans as human property became entrenched (Harley, 2015; Inikori, 2020). Over the period of the

---

V. Fynn Bruey (✉)
Legal Studies, Athabasca University, Athabasca, AB, Canada
e-mail: vfynnbruey@athabascau.ca

H. Crawley
United Nations University Centre for Policy Research (UNU-CPR), New York, NY, USA
e-mail: crawley@unu.edu

transatlantic slave trade, from approximately 1526 to 1867, between 11.8 and 12.5 million men, women, and children were captured and put on ships in Africa, and somewhere between 9.6 and 10.8 million arrived in the Americas.[1] These figures do not include those who were killed during the enslavement raids or those who died on their journey to the coast (Nunn, 2008). The transatlantic slave trade was likely the costliest in human life of all long-distance global migrations. Enslaved Africans were taken from African slaving coasts that stretched thousands of miles, from Senegal to Angola, and even around the Cape and on to Mozambique. Approximately half of the slaves embarked on ships in ports along the region of West Central Africa and St. Helena. Today, these regions are in the countries of Angola, Democratic Republic of the Congo, Gabon, and the Republic of the Congo. The majority of the rest were taken from West Africa, embarking in ports between the present-day countries of Senegal and Gabon, while a smaller number of slaves were captured in the southeast of Africa.[2] Of the estimated 12.5 million human cargo plucked out of Africa between 1501 and 1866, approximately 5.8 million (46.79%) disembarked in Brazil, 5.3 million (42.45%) in the Dutch, English, and French colonies of the Caribbean Islands; one million (8.49%) in Uruguay, and 305,326 (2.44%), a relatively small percentage, in what was to become the US (SlaveVoyages Operational Committee, 2021).

These bi-directional South–South currents are haunted by grave injustices sustained by war, violence, trauma, and, in the contemporary period, the omnipresence of deadly voyages arrested by drastic border securitisation and externalisation strategies intended to curb unprecedented migration from the Majority World. Understanding the largest inter-continental South–South migration phenomenon goes well beyond the mechanics of the actual journey: it is critical for making sense of the ongoing trauma, violence, and injustices that continue to plague migrants of colour and their descendants. By contrast, the movement of (predominantly) white men from the Northern to the Southern hemispheres still thrives on post-colonial control, neoliberal ideologies and doctrines (most notably the furtherance of capitalism), the extraction industry, land dispossession and genocide of Native Peoples, Big

---

[1] It is very difficult to know exactly how many people were enslaved and how many died on the long journey across the Atlantic. Lovejoy (1989) calculates a figure of 11,863,000 based on a review of the literature. Others put the figure between 12 and 12.5 million, see https://www.slavevoyages.org/ and https://www.gilderlehrman.org/history-resources/teacher-resources/historical-context-facts-about-slave-trade-and-slaveryThe UN puts the figure at more than 15 million https://www.un.org/en/observances/decade-people-african-descent/slave-trade#:~:text=For%20o ver%20400%20years%2C%20more,darkest%20chapters%20in%20human%20history. All acknowledge that some slaves went unrecorded, and that the available data contain errors that are difficult, if not impossible, to detect.

[2] https://www.statista.com/statistics/1150475/number-slaves-taken-from-africa-by-region-century/.

Tech expansion, illicit small arms trade, and globalisation across economic, social, geo-political, cultural, and military spectra (Williams, 2022). Today, South–South migration, a necessary but constant flow of "neighbours" in the Majority World (Alam, 2008) is encumbered with incredulous complexities, nuances, and relevance inextricably tied to slavery and indentured labour between fourteenth and nineteenth centuries (Melde et al., 2014).

The focus of this chapter is on the history of the transatlantic slave trade and, in particular, the role of the British Empire, as well as the continuing legacy of contemporary South–South migration (Adjisse, 2022; Carpi & Owusu, 2022). The chapter begins with a historical overview and reflection on present-day legacies of the transatlantic slave trade between countries in West Africa, the Caribbean, Latin America, and Oceania before turning to the lasting impacts of the trans-Atlantic enslavement of Black African peoples as a precursor of contemporary forms of South–South migration and associated responses, representation, challenges, and opportunities. The chapter also highlights the contemporary consequences of slavery for Liberia, where the return of captured and emancipated slaves led directly to the civil wars that devastated the country between 1989 and 2003, displacing an estimated 800,000 people internally with more than a million people travelling to neighbouring countries in West Africa in search of protection and the opportunity to rebuild their lives.

A note on terminology. In this chapter, instead of developing countries or the "Global South", we use the term Majority World interchangeably with the South to reflect the significant proportion of the world's population living in the Southern hemisphere, and also the fact that a significant proportion of all international migration takes place between these countries. According to the United Nations, there were 258,000 international migrants in 2017 (McAuliffe & Triandafyllidou, 2021; United Nations, 2018). In that same year, migration between the countries of the Majority World was approximately 37% of the total, and therefore higher than migration between South and North (35%) (International Organisation for Migration, 2022; see also Schewel and Debray, this volume). More migrants born in the South live elsewhere in the South (than in the North): 53% Dig down deeper and the rate increases even more: up to 79% in Middle Africa (Gagnon, 2018). Of migrants born in the Majority World, 53%, 71%, and 79% live in Africa below the Sahara (Mashanda, 2017). Similarly, rather than referring to advanced countries or the developed world, we use the term Minority World instead of North or Global North to represent countries, including Australia and New Zealand, which are economically and politically powerful but geographically located in the South.

An Overview of the Transatlantic Slave Trade

The Portuguese began the sale and trade in human beings in 1444, when 235 Black Africans were snatched from the west coast to be sold in Lagos, Portugal (Ames, 2018; de Zurara, 2010; Hatton, 2018). The erection of St George's Castle (or Sao Jorge de Mina) in Cape Coast, Ghana in 1482 gave the Portuguese a monopoly over the human cargo industry in what was then Gold Coast region. Now a tourist beach resort, Lagos has nothing to commemorate the Portuguese slavers' inhumane act, except for the Mercado de Escravos.[3]

While the Portuguese initiated the sale of Africans, others including the Dutch, French, Spanish, and, especially, the British, were also actively involved. Although Britain's involvement in the transatlantic slave trade officially began with royal approval in 1663, it started 100 years earlier in 1562, when John Hawkins traded enslaved Africans for ginger and sugar in a voyage approved by Queen Elizabeth I.[4] There was also a precursor to the British Empire's enslavement of human beings in 1624 when 50 white settlers were transported to Barbados and the Leeward Island (Antigua, Montserrat, St. Christopher, and Nervis) as indentured labourers. The goal was to turn the islands into a profitable agrarian enterprise by growing tobacco, cotton, and a new luxury plant, sugar cane (Beckles & Downes, 1985). Although they were poor people who were treated terribly, indentured servants were not slaves. They were bonded for five years of labour and, in return, received 10 acres of land. By the 1660s, the predominantly white indentured plant servants were displaced by the relatively few Native Peoples and imported African slaves. Unlike their forerunners the white indentured labourers, Black African slaves, and their children were chattel slaves owned by their masters and never allowed to return home ever again.

The large-scale involvement of the English in the slave trade started after 1660, when King Charles II and his brother James, Duke of York (later to become King James II), helped establish a company that would control all English business in African slave trading. By 1672, it had become the Royal African Company (RAC) and its symbol was an elephant with a castle on its back. The RAC had an absolute monopoly over the "triangular route"[5] by trading sugar from the Caribbean to England, extracting commodities

---

[3] The museum was first installed in 2009 and reopened in 2016 but was indefinitely closed in July 2022 during a visit by one of the authors to the Faro district of the Algarve Region.

[4] See https://heritagecollections.parliament.uk/stories/the-transatlantic-slave-trade/.

[5] The "triangular trade" was not a specific trade route, but a model for economic exchange among three markets. The triangular trade between Europe, West Africa and the New World is probably the best known.

from the Gold Coast, and transporting human cargo from Africa to English colonies in the Caribbean, South America, and the US (Pettigrew, 2013; Platt, 1975).

The RAC was prolific, shipping more enslaved African women, men, and children to the Americas than any other single institution during the entire period of the transatlantic slave trade. The RAC played a central role in establishing England's transatlantic slave trade, stealing market share from the Dutch and French slave trades, and in Africanising the populations of England's Caribbean plantations. In 1673, soon after the company's foundation, the English had a 33% share in the transatlantic slave trade. By 1683, that share had increased to 74% (Pettigrew, 2013, 11). Aided by the British government's own chartered entity, the RAC's triangular routes flourished, with the Company mounting 12,103 slaving voyages with 3,351 departing from London (Royal Museum Greenwich, 2023).

Between British ports, Africa, and the Americas, the largest cross-continental forced migration was a defining moment in history (Pettigrew, 2013; Scott, 1903). Between 1690 and 1807, an estimated 6 million enslaved Africans were transported from West Africa to the Americas on British or Anglo-American ships, with the RAC alone transporting 187,000 enslaved Africans, mostly from West Africa to its colonies in the Caribbean, South America, and the what became the US (see Table 2.1).[6] Many of the enslaved Africans transported by the RAC were branded DY, standing for Duke of York.[7] Notwithstanding the involvement of other European countries in the transatlantic slave trade, it is reasonable to say that the RAC perfected the act of selling Africans as disposable people in the largest South–South forced migration system.

On the first leg, ships leaving Britain and other countries were filled with goods, which were exchanged for enslaved Africans on the west African coast. These people were then transported across the Atlantic to be sold as slaves to work on plantations. The same ships then returned to Europe carrying "slave grown" produce, notably sugar, tobacco, and cotton which were consumed in high volumes and fuelled the Industrial Revolution benefitting businessmen, financiers, and landowners who ran and profited from the trade, as well as businesses, workers, and consumers (Harley, 2015; UK Parliament, n.d.). The ships of the Company enjoyed the protection of the Royal Navy, and

---

[6] The SlaveVoyages website is a digital initiative that compiles and makes publicly accessible records of the largest slave trades in history. The website provides details of the journeys made, the horrific loss of life during these voyages, the identities and nationalities of the perpetrators and the numerous rebellions that occurred. See https://www.slavevoyages.org/.

[7] See https://www.bl.uk/restoration-18th-century-literature/articles/britains-involvement-with-new-world-slavery-and-the-transatlantic-slave-trade.

Table 2.1 Ten enslavers journey of African human cargo

#	Enslaver	Year	# of captives	Embarkation port	Disembarkation ports
1	Royal African Company	1693–1715	186,592	Ghana, Nigeria, Benin, Central Africa, Guinea, Gambia, Niger, Sierra Leone, Angola, Guinea Bissau, Senegambia, Congo, Gabon	Jamaica, Barbados, the US (Virginia, Maryland and South Carolina), Nervis, Cuba, Antigua, Montserrat, St. Kitts, French Caribbean Colony, Martinique, Colombia, Cuba, Guadeloupe, British Caribbean, US Virgin Island, Mexico, Trinidad
2	Nieuw West Indische Compagnie	1713–1748	186,167	Benin, Congo, Ghana, Nigeria, Angola, Senegambia, Equatorial Guinea, Gabon, Ivory Coast, St. Eustatius	Dutch Caribbean Island, Surinam, St. Eustatius, St. Dominique, Haiti, Western Sahara, Guyana, Mexico, Colombia, Martinique
3	Boats, William	1763–1795	55,361	Nigeria, Ghana, Benin, Guinea, Congo, Central Africa, Sierra Leone, Angola	Barbados, Dominica, Jamaica, St. Vincent, British Virgin Island, St. Kitts, Bahamas, the US, French Caribbean, Colombia, Antigua, Grenada

(continued)

Table 2.1 (continued)

#	Enslaver	Year	# of captives	Embarkation port	Disembarkation ports
4	Apsinall James	1791–1807	52,279	Nigeria, Guinea, St. Helena, Cameroon, Congo, Angola, Ghana, Benin, Gabon, Sierra Leone, Benin	Jamaica, Dominica, British Caribbean Island, St. Vincent, Antigua, Virgin Island, Trinidad, Suriname, Haiti, Grenada, the US, Guyana, St Kitts, French Caribbean, Bahamas
5	South Sea Company / Asiento	1715–1739	50,130	Colombia, Jamaica, British Caribbean, Barbados, St Kitts, Dutch Islands	Spanish colony, Cuba, Colombia, Mexico, Curaçao, Puerto Rico, Guatemala, Haiti, Venezuela, British Virgin Island, Brazil
6	Gregson, William	1745–1793	4,717	Nigeria, Cameroon, Ghana, Benin, Central Africa, St. Helena, Angola	Jamaica, Dominica, Barbados, the US, St Vincent, Grenada, Antigua, Colombia, Guadeloupe, French Caribbean, St. Kitts, Guyana, Brazil, Haiti, British Caribbean, Guyana, Bahamas, Virgin Island, Cuba, Martinique, Suriname, St. Lucia

(continued)

Table 2.1 (continued)

#	Enslaver	Year	# of captives	Embarkation port	Disembarkation ports
7	Dawson, John	1760–1797	46,873	Nigeria, Benin, Sierra Leone, Ghana, Cameroon	Cuba, Jamaica, Guyana, Grenada, Trinidad and Tobago, Caracas, St. Kitts, Barbados, Spanish Caribbean, Dominica, Sierra Leone,
8	Case, George	1771–1808	45,585	Guinea, Benin, Angola, Congo, Ghana, Cameroon, Nigeria, Sierra Leone, Angola, Gabon	Guyana, Bahamas, the US, St., Kitts, St. Vincent, Trinidad and Tobago, Jamaica, British, Virgin Island, Grenada
9	James, William	1759–1779	44,102	Angola, Sierra Leone, Gambia, Liberia, Ghana, Benin, Nigeria, Brazil	St. Kitts, Jamaica, Tobago, Grenada, British Caribbean, Martinique, the US, Dominica, Antigua
10	Hodgson, Thomas	1753–1805	43,941	Sierra Leone, Ghana, Gambia, Liberia, Cameroon, Benin, Nigeria, Angola, Congo, Portugal	Jamaica, the US, Dominica, Barbados, St. Vincent, Grenada, St. Kitts,

Source SlaveVoyages Operational Committee, 'People of the Atlantic Slave Trade - Database', Enslavers Database the traders made good profits. However, slavery and the triangular trade with which it was associated, did more than just create a source of free labour for Britain: it built a network of systemic exploitation that became the backbone of the Industrial Revolution in Britain (Heblich et al., 2022), and ultimately gave rise to a capitalist global economy centred on the employment of enslaved Africans in large-scale commodity production in what was come to be known as the US (Inikori, 2020; Williams, 1994).

The transatlantic slave trade was a crime against humanity and arguably represented a genocide (Cooper, 2012). Unable to continue the enslavement of Indigenous Peoples in their new colonies owing to disease, famine, and conflict, European settler-colonists turned to Black African slaves to feed their compulsion for economic wealth. This wealth and power would never be shared with the source, enslaved Africans. In fact, after the transportation of human cargo was abolished in England with the enactment of the Abolition of the Slave Trade Act in 1807, an audacious compensation scheme was lavished on slave owners for losing their property. Some 46,000 slave owners, including relatives of John Gladstone, father of Victorian prime minister William Ewart Gladstone and Charles Blair, the great-grand father of Eric Blair (George Orwell), who was paid £4,442 (equivalent to about £3 m today), all walked away with the biggest bailout in British history (Olusoga, 2015).[8] While British slavers received a significant amount of money for losing their human chattel property, not a single penny was paid to those who had been enslaved (Olusoga, 2015). It should also be noted that while the abolition of slavery in 1807 eventually ended the human cargo business and the act of slavery itself in 1834 (Equiano, 1789; Turner, 1982), what immediately ensued was an institution of indenture or bonded labour migration (Anderson, 2009). Between 1834 and 1917, another long-term contractual South–South migration resulted in an estimated 2.0–2.2 million Africans, Chinese, Indians, Japanese, Javanese, and Melanesians being transported to British, Dutch, French, and Spanish colonies including Fiji, Hawa'ii, Samoa, Tahiti, Vanuatu, Ceylon (Sri Lanka), Burma (Myanmar), Malaysia, Uganda, Kenya, South Africa, Mauritius, Mayotte, Reunion, Suriname, Trinidad, Guyana, Cuba, Guadeloupe, Jamaica, Martinique, Peru, and Mexico (Allen, 2017; Ramsarran, 2008; Tinker, 1993).

---

[8] See also BBC, *Britain's Forgotten Slave Owners* https://www.bbc.co.uk/programmes/b063db18.

The Legacy of Slavery

The legacy of the slave trade pervades almost every aspect of contemporary life and is central to understanding contemporary South–South migration flows, and the experiences of those who move between the countries of the Majority World.

First, there was the impact on the countries to which slaves were shipped, especially Brazil, which remain deeply racialised even today (de Souza e Silva et al., this volume). Alongside Great Britain, the Portuguese empire shipped the highest number of slaves from Africa, and Brazil was the main destination. Once in Brazil, many slaves were forced to work on sugar *fazendas* (plantations) geared towards export-based markets and their work was difficult, demanding, and coercive. They were utterly dehumanised and treated as a community to be bought and sold. When slavery was eventually abolished in Brazil in 1888, far later than any other country in the Americas, the lives of Afro-Brazilians did not change drastically. Many freed slaves entered into informal agreements with their former owners, exchanging free labour in return for food and shelter. Meanwhile, white Brazilian elites, concerned they could become a minority, also implemented a policy of *branqueamento*, or "whitening", through European immigration which aimed to *limpar o sangue* (cleanse the blood) (dos Santos & Hallewell, 2002). This was justified on the grounds that Brazil could not flourish with a largely black population, a legacy that continues today through deeply racialised institutional structures and attitudes prevalent throughout contemporary Brazilian society.[9]

The ongoing impacts of the slave trade on countries in the Americas are highlighted by Engerman and Sokoloff (1997), who argue that differences in factor endowments implied differences in the reliance on slave labour, with dramatic consequences for the degree of inequality. Bertocchi (2016) also notes the work of Soares et al. (2012) who found a significant correlation between past slavery and current levels of inequality across a world-wide sample of 46 countries which included North-African and Southern-European recipients of African slaves. Bertocchi (2016) argues that the extreme historical inequalities—in wealth, human capital, and political power—associated with the slave trade exerted a permanent influence on economic development, since they favoured the endogenous formation of institutional structures that, rather than promoting growth, maintained the privileges of the elites against the interests of the masses. In Brazil, there

---

[9] See https://www.un.org/en/chronicle/article/racial-discrimination-and-miscegenation-experience-brazil.

continue to be widespread human rights abuses towards Afro-Brazilians and Black migrants, with poverty rates twice those of white Brazilians.[10]

The ongoing impacts of the slave trade are nowhere more apparent than in Haiti. First claimed by Spain in 1492 when Christopher Columbus landed on the island in search of spices, the country was ceded to France in 1665. The colonial economy of Saint-Domingue was based almost entirely on the production of plantation crops for export. Enslaved African slaves grew sugar in the northern plains around Cap Français, for example, and coffee in the mountainous interior. The slave system in Saint-Domingue was regarded as one of the harshest in the Americas, with high levels of both mortality and violence. To supply the plantation system, French owners imported an estimated 800,000 Africans to the colony (which, by comparison, is almost double the number of Africans carried to North America). Under French rule, Saint-Domingue grew to be the wealthiest colony in the French empire and, perhaps, the richest colony in the world, producing around 40% of the sugar and 60% of the coffee imported into Europe.

One of the most notable aspects of Haitian history is that the nation is the only one to have emerged as the result of a successful slave rebellion. From 1791 through 1804, enslaved people and their allies in Saint-Domingue fought a protracted revolution to win their independence from France. However, after securing independence and abolishing slavery, Haiti was severely punished by the international community and forced to make huge debt repayments to France, pushing the country into a cycle of debt that hobbled its development for more than 100 years. Reparations for slavery is the application of the concept of reparations to victims of slavery and/or their descendants. In Haiti the opposite has occurred, i.e., Haiti, a nation of slaves and the ancestors of slaves, has had to pay the enslavers. Once the wealthiest colony in the Americas, Haiti is now the Western Hemisphere's poorest country, with more than half of its population living below the World Bank's poverty line.[11]

Secondly, the slave trade had devastating—and enduring—impacts on the places in Africa from where slaves were taken, with implications for contemporary forms of South–South migration associated with both poverty and conflict. Slavery led to the transformation of entire economic, political, and legal systems in the areas of West Africa now known as Ghana,[12] Senegal

---

[10] See https://www.usw.org/blog/2017/in-grim-times-brazils-young-workers-take-charge-of-future.
[11] See https://www.worldbank.org/en/country/haiti/overview.
[12] See https://www.youtube.com/watch?v=s-To3HWs9l8.

(Fofana, 2020), and Nigeria.[13] Some states, such as Asante and Dahomey, grew powerful and wealthy as a result. Other states were completely destroyed, and their populations decimated as they were absorbed by rivals. Millions of Africans were forcibly removed from their homes, and towns and villages were depopulated. Generally, the consequence of internal conflict was increased political instability and in many cases the collapse of pre-existing forms of government (Lovejoy, 2000). According to Nunn (2008), the Portuguese slave trade was a key factor leading to the eventual disintegration of the Joloff Confederation in Northern Senegambia and also led to the weakening and eventual fall of the once powerful Kongo kingdom of West-Central Africa. Pre-existing governance structures were generally replaced by small bands of slave raiders, controlled by an established ruler or warlord. However, these bands were generally unable to develop into large, stable states (Nunn, 2008).

Evidence from research on the relationship between a country's history of slavery and subsequent economic performance suggests that these effects of the slave trades may be important for current economic development (Chanda & Putterman, 2005; Nunn, 2008). As noted by Whatley (2022), recent econometric research has found recurring evidence that the international slave trades underdeveloped Africa over the long term, an idea most closely associated with Walter Rodney and his book *How Europe Underdeveloped Africa* (Rodney, 1972). Whatley (2022) finds that the international slave trades encouraged decentralised African societies in catchment zones to adopt slavery as a defence against further enslavement. Moreover, fears of being captured and being enslaved led to significant migration due to insecurity, which in turn weakened agricultural production, the mainstay of many African economies at that time. Robbing African countries of their much-needed labour force by taking men and women at their prime and productive age not only affected the economic activities at that time but has been held responsible for the poverty experienced in the continent subsequently. Historical accounts suggest that the pervasive insecurity, violence, and warfare had detrimental impacts on the institutional, social, and economic development of societies (Nunn, 2008). In addition, it has been suggested that the slave trades may have generated a culture of mistrust, because of the way slaves were captured by other Africans through raids involving neighbouring communities, thus breaking the social bonds upon which trust is built (Bertocchi, 2016; Nunn, 2008). Because the slave trades weakened ties between villages, they also discouraged the formation of larger communities and broader ethnic

---

[13] See https://www.npr.org/sections/goatsandsoda/2020/10/01/917054760/a-nigerian-finds-hard-truths-and-hope-in-netflix-series-on-nigeria.

identities. Therefore, the slave trades may be an important factor explaining Africa's high level of ethnic fractionalisation today (Nunn, 2008), and the conflicts and associated migration flows with which this has been associated.

It is clear then that the transatlantic slave trade has contributed both directly and indirectly to contemporary forms of migration in Africa associated with poverty and conflict. Slavery radically impaired Africa's potential to develop economically and maintain its social and political stability (M'baye, 2006). Indeed, "the coerced population movement set into place by the trans-Atlantic slave trade was only the beginning of a very long mobilization process that has not yet stopped" (Bertocchi, 2016).

Slavery and the Protracted Displacement of Liberians in West Africa

We contextualise this chapter by focusing on a much-neglected and little understood nexus between the transatlantic slave trade and South–South migration: that of the protracted displacement of literally millions of people both inside and outside the small West African country of Liberia.

The conflict that led Liberians to flee to Ghana and other West African countries began in December 1989 but had its roots in the transatlantic slave trade and the formation of Liberia itself (Crawley & Fynn Bruey, 2022; Dick, 2002; Hampshire et al., 2008; Omata, 2012). Liberia was birthed out of the need to address the perceived "problem" of freed slaves being placed on the same legal equality with White people in the US following the abolition of slavery in 1819. Between 1820 and 1904 nearly 15,000 former slaves were returned from the US to the Colony of Liberia, marking a period of forced migration back to West Africa from the Americas. In 1847, the settlers signed a declaration of independence marking Liberia as the oldest republic in Africa. However, this did not mean that all people in the republic enjoyed the same rights and privileges. On the contrary, the former slave returnees—the so-called Americo-Liberians—who comprised less than 1% of Liberia's population ruled the nation as quasi-imperial masters until 1980, selectively manipulating the customs and traditions of the Indigenous Peoples to gain and reinforce their own control of Liberia's land, resources, and people. While in England ancestors of slavers are members of the House of Lords (Lashmar and Smith, 2020; Syal, 2020), in Liberia they are warlords turned into Supreme Court Justices and legislators (Fynn Bruey, 2018).

The consequences of this legacy of slavery ripple through into Liberia's more recent history of conflict and displacement. The two civil wars that devastated Liberia between 1989 and 2003 were rooted in a power struggle between former slave returnees from the US and various Indigenous groups, most of which had been excluded from participating in the state-building and development after the country was founded. In 1980, Samuel Doe, a junior level Indigenous military officer, led a successful military coup and overthrew the Americo-Liberian regime. During his presidency, Doe gave virtually all positions of power to people from his own Krahn language group and maltreated most other Indigenous groups (Frontani et al., 2009) and several further *coup d'état* attempts in the 1980s led to widespread civil conflict throughout the country. In 1989 Charles Taylor, an Americo-Liberian, formerly in Doe's government, overthrew Doe from his base in Côte d'Ivoire. At the beginning of the civil war, Taylor's regime targeted the Krahn and Mandingo Peoples who were viewed as Doe-supporters resulting in a civil war which lasted until 1996 when there was temporary peace that allowed for the 1997 elections. The elections resulted in Taylor's victory but fighting continued until 2003 (Dick, 2002; Hampshire et al., 2008).

A peace agreement, Taylor's resignation and exile to Nigeria in 2003 led to the United Nations declaring Liberia safe in 2004 and the onset of repatriation initiatives. However, the consequences of the conflict, as well as the longer history of forced migration, the violence, and the widespread inequalities with which the civil war was associated, linger on. By the official end of Liberia's war in 2003, an estimated 250,000 people had been killed and around half of the country's population of 2.8 million had been displaced. Approximately 800,000–1 million people were displaced within the country (Dick, 2002; UNHCR, 2006; Wyndham, 2006) and over a million people became refugees (Nmona, 1996; UNHCR, 2006). The scale of displacement in Liberia reflects its use as a deliberate tactic during the conflict (Dabo, 2012). But the Liberian conflict is not only notable for the scale of the violence and the fact that the casualties were often civilians: there were also particular impacts for specific groups of civilians. While its scale is contested (Cohen & Green, 2012), there is evidence that rates of rape and sexual violence against women and girls were very high (Jones et al., 2014; Swiss et al., 1998).[14]

Liberians began entering Ghana as refugees in mid- to late-1990, shortly after the outbreak of the civil war, choosing Ghana for its general stability, reasonable economy, and the widespread use of English. Others fled to different countries in the region including neighbouring Sierra Leone, Guinea, and Côte d'Ivoire, all of which experienced significant internal and

---

[14] See also http://www.unwomen.org/en/news/stories/2017/11/feature-reversing-the-tide-of-rising-violence-against-women-in-liberia.

external displacement due to conflict occurring between 1991–2002, 2002–2004, and 2010–2011. Liberians were initially brought to Ghana by air and sea, with navy ships and merchant vessels cooperating with the military branch of the Economic Community of West African States (ECOWAS) to bring refugees en masse (Dick, 2002). As noted by Dick (2002), the majority of refugees represented the average Liberian, but a substantial number of the initial arrivals were younger, well-educated, urban-based professionals from Liberia's capital of Monrovia or surrounding communities. By August 1990 the Ghanaian government set up an ad hoc Committee on Refugees in response to the arrival of an increasing number of Liberian refugees and agreed to use the abandoned church premises of Gomoa Buduburam in the Central Region of Ghana. Located in an agricultural settlement about an hour's drive east of Accra, the Buduburam Refugee Camp served as a reception centre for accommodating the influx of Liberian refugees. In September 1990, there were around 7,000 Liberians at Buduburam with a further 2,000 leaving the facility and self-settling in and around the Greater Accra region or communities nearby the Central Region (Dick, 2002). A decade later the number of Liberians living in Ghana had increased to around 42,000 living in three major refugee camps, the biggest of which was at Buduburam (Agblorti, 2011; Dako-Gyeke & Adu, 2017; Dick, 2002). Today, Liberians continue to live in Ghana and other parts of West Africa in a state of protracted displacement.

Conclusions

The transatlantic enslavement was a devastating cross-continental trade in human beings between the countries of the Majority World. Its impact continues to haunt descendants, traumatise families, racialise Black Africans, and destabilise communities across the globe. It has also led directly to violent conflicts such as that in Liberia which have driven intra-regional South–South migration. Moreover, putting an end to transatlantic enslavement was not the end of African oppression from European slavers. In fact, the Abolition of Slavery Act of 1807 gave rise to the dawn of the "Scramble for Africa" (Carmody, 2011; Chamberlain, 1974). Barely eight decades later, on 15 November 1884, 14 European countries and the US gathered in Germany for the Berlin Conference, the aim of which was to manage the continuous destruction of the fabric of Indigenous Africa (Craven, 2015; Stone, 1988). The continuity of oppressive European colonial stronghold on Africa which is strongly tied to violent conflict and poor governance as the impetus for (intra-regional) South–South forced migration is evident on a daily basis. The implications of colonialism for migration are well documented, not only in terms of the movement of people within and between the countries of the Majority World (see Bonayi and Soumahoro, this volume), but also in terms of migration law and policy (Mayblin and Turner, 2021) and the ways in which knowledge about migration is produced (Fiddian-Qasmiyeh, Landström and Crawley, Vanyaro, Phipps and Yohannes, this volume).

Finally, it is important to acknowledge the slave trade's "legacy of racism" which continues to haunt the world to this day and can be seen in contemporary forms of racism in both the Majority and Minority Worlds. Racial difference was invoked to justify the slave trade. As the trade grew, and Europe became wealthy, so too did theories about racialised hierarchies, Eugenics, and the equation between intellectual abilities and the subjugation of Africans (Jones, 2015; Otele, 2017).[15] As noted by Jones (2015), for example, "the colonial past is always present in Caribbean societies. It resonates in popular images of gender, race, class and sexuality, and discrimination on all of these grounds persists". Whiteness continues to signal social and cultural capital to this day, as evidenced by the concentration of white and lighter skinned people within the elite. According to UN chief Antonio Guterres, "[w]e can draw a straight line from the centuries of colonial exploitation to the social and economic inequalities of today…and we can recognize the racist tropes popularised to rationalise the inhumanity of the slave trade in the white supremacist hate that is resurgent today".[16] This, as much as anything else, confirms the need for a historical perspective on South–South migration, one which acknowledges the enduring legacy of slavery.

Acknowledgements Our thanks to Robert Fantauzzi for assisting with the literature review for this chapter. Part of this chapter was originally published as Heaven Crawley and Veronica Fynn Bruey, V. (2022). 'Hanging in the air': the experiences of Liberian refugees in Ghana. In J. K. Teye (Ed.), *Migration in West Africa* (pp. 107–127). Cham, Switzerland: Springer International Publishing.

---

[15] According to David Olusoga (2015), the book that arguably did most to disseminate racial ideas about Africans was written by a man who had never set foot on African soil. Edward Long was a slave owner and son of a slave owner, whose family was in Jamaica from the middle of the seventeenth century. Long's ideas about Black people and Africa were widely accepted as being rigorous and scientific, even though he had no scientific training, His book *The History of Jamaica* (1774) includes vitriolic denouncements of Africans as irredeemably inferior and perhaps not even human. See https://www.theguardian.com/commentisfree/2015/sep/08/european-racism-africa-slavery.

[16] See https://www.aa.com.tr/en/politics/slave-trades-legacy-of-racism-still-haunts-world-un-chief/2855473.

Bibliography

Adjisse, S. S. (2022). The legacy of the transatlantic and Indian ocean slave trades on contemporary intent to migrate in Africa. Presented at the 2022 Agricultural and Applied Economics Association Annual Meeting, Anaheim, CA: AgEcon Search. https://ageconsearch.umn.edu/record/322512?ln=en

Agblorti, S. K. M. (2011). Refugee integration in Ghana: The host community's perspective. New Issues in Refugee Research. http://www.unhcr.org/4d6f5f3f9.html

Alam, S. (2008). Majority world: Challenging the West's rhetoric of democracy. *Amerasia Journal, 34*(1), 88–98. https://doi.org/10.17953/amer.34.1.l3176027k4q614v5

Allen, R. B. (2017). Asian indentured labor in the 19th and early 20th century colonial plantation world. In *Oxford Research Encyclopedia of Asian History* (pp. 1–16). Oxford University Press. https://doi.org/10.1093/acrefore/9780190277727.013.33

Ames, P. (2018). Portugal confronts its slave trade past. *Politico*. https://www.politico.eu/article/portugal-slave-trade-confronts-its-past/

Anderson, C. (2009). Convicts and coolies: Rethinking indentured labour in the nineteenth century. *Slavery and Abolition, 30*(1), 93–109. https://doi.org/10.1080/01440390802673856

Beckles, H. (2016). *The first black slave society: Britain's "barbarity time" in Barbados, 1636–1876*. The University of the West Indies Press.

Beckles, H., & Downes, A. (1985). An economic formalization of the origins of black slavery in the British West Indies, 1624–1645. *Social and Economic Studies, 34*(2), 1–25.

Bertocchi, G. (2016). The legacies of slavery in and out of Africa. *IZA Jourrnal of Migration, 5*(24). https://doi.org/10.1186/s40176-016-0072-0

Carmody, P. R. (2011). *The new scramble for Africa*. Polity Press.

Carpi, E., & Owusu, P. (2022). Slavery, lived realities, and the decolonisation of forced migration histories: An interview with Dr Portia Owusu. *Migration Studies, 10*(1), 87–93. https://doi.org/10.1093/migration/mnac009

Chamberlain, M. E. (1974). *The Scramble for Africa* (0 ed.). Routledge. https://doi.org/10.4324/9781315833668

Chanda, A., & Putterman, L. (2005). State effectiveness, economic growth, and the age of states. In M. Lange & D. Rueschemeyer (Eds.), *States and development: Historical antecedents of stagnation and advance*. Palgrave MacMillan.

Cohen, D. K., & Green, A. H. (2012). Dueling incentives: Sexual violence in Liberia and the politics of human rights advocacy. *Journal of Peace Research, 49*(3), 445–458.

Cohen, R. (1995). Prologue. In R. Cohen (Ed.), *The Cambridge survey of world migration* (1st ed., pp. 1–10). Cambridge University Press. https://doi.org/10.1017/CBO9780511598289.001

Cooper, A. D. (2012). From slavery to genocide: The fallacy of febt in reparations discourse. *Journal of Black Studies, 43*(2), 107–126. https://doi.org/10.1177/0021934711410879

Craven, M. (2015). Between law and history: The Berlin conference of 1884–1885 and the logic of free trade. *London Review of International Law, 3*(1), 31–59. https://doi.org/10.1093/lril/lrv002

Crawley, H., & Fynn Bruey, V. (2022). 'Hanging in the air': The experiences of Liberian Refugees in Ghana. In J. K. Teye (Ed.), *Migration in West Africa* (pp. 107–127). Springer International Publishing. https://doi.org/10.1007/978-3-030-97322-3_6

Dabo, A. (2012) *In the presence of absence: Truth-telling and displacement in Liberia*. ICTJ/Brookings. https://www.ictj.org/publication/presence-absence-truth-telling-and-displacement-liberia

Dako-Gyeke, M., & Adu, E. (2017). Challenges and coping strategies of refugees: Exploring residual Liberian refugees' experiences in Ghana. *Qualitative Social Work, 16*(1), 96–112.

Dick, S. (2002). Liberians in Ghana: Living without humanitarian assistance. UNHCR New Issues in Refugee Research Working Paper No.57. http://www.unhcr.org/3c8398f24.html

Engerman, S. L., & Sokoloff, K. L. (1997). Factor endowments, institutions, and differential growth paths among new world economies: A view from economic historians of the United States. In S. Haber (Ed.), *How Latin America Fell behind: Essays on the economic histories of Brazil and Mexico, 1800–1914* (pp. 260–304). Stanford University Press.

Equiano, O. (1789). *The interesting narrative of the life of Olaudah Equiano: Or Gustavus Vassa, the African.* (2nd ed., Vol. 1). G. Vassa. https://anthologydev.lib.virginia.edu/work/Equiano/equiano-interestingnarrative.pdf. Accessed 19 December 2022.

Frontani, H. G., Silvestri, K., & Brown, A. (2009). Media image and social integration of Liberian and Togolese refugees in Ghana. *Africa Media Review, 17*(1/2), 51–75.

Fynn Bruey, V. (2018). *Warlords on trial: Prosecuting Libera's ex-combatans in foreign jurisdictions*. Conference Presentation, West Georgia, GA.

Fofana, D. M. (2020). Senegal, the African slave trade, and the door of no return: Giving witness to Gorée Island. *Humanities, 9*(3), 57. https://doi.org/10.3390/h9030057

Gagnon, J. (2018). Understanding South-South migration. *Development Matters*. https://oecd-development-matters.org/2018/12/17/understanding-south-south-migration/

Hampshire, K., Porter, G., Kilpatrick, K., Kyei, P., Adjaloo, M., & Oppong, G. (2008). Liminal spaces: Changing inter-generational relations among long-term Liberian refugees in Ghana. *Human Organisation, 67*(1), 25–36.

Harley, K. (2015). Slavery, the British Atlantic economy, and the industrial revolution. In A. B. Leonard & D. Pretel (Eds.), *The Caribbean and the Atlantic world economy*. Cambridge imperial and post-colonial studies series. Palgrave Macmillan. https://doi.org/10.1057/9781137432728_8

Hatton, B. (2018). *Queen of the Sea: A history of Lisbon*. C. Hurst & Co. (Publishers) Ltd.

Heblic, S. J., Redding, S. J., & Voth, H-J. (2022). Slavery and the British industrial revolution. *NBER Working Paper* 30451, Cambridge, Massachusetts. http://www.nber.org/papers/w30451

Henley, J. (2010). Haiti: A long descent to hell, *The Guardian*, 14 January 2010. https://www.theguardian.com/world/2010/jan/14/haiti-history-earthquake-disaster

International Organisation for Migration. (2022). *IOM and South-South and Triangular Cooperation* (p. 2). https://migration4development.org/sites/default/files/2022-09/SSC_IOM_factsheet_EXTERNAL_JULY%202022.pdf

Inikori, J. E. (2020). Atlantic slavery and the rise of the capitalist global economy. *Current Anthropology, 61*(S22), S159–S171.

Jones, C. (2015). Shades of white: Gender, race, and slavery in the Caribbean, *Open Democracy*. https://www.opendemocracy.net/en/beyond-trafficking-and-slavery/women-and-slavery-in-caribbean-whiteness-and-gilded-cage/

Jones, N., Cooper, J., Presler-Marshall, E., & Walker, D. (2014). The fallout of rape as a weapon of war: the life-long and intergenerational impacts of sexual violence in conflict. *ODI Research Report*. Overseas Development Institute. https://odi.org/en/publications/the-fallout-of-rape-as-a-weapon-of-war/

Lashmar, P., & Smith, J. (2020, December 12). *He's the MP with the Downton Abbey lifestyle. But the shadow of slavery hangs over the gilded life of Richard Drax*. The Observer. https://www.theguardian.com/world/2020/dec/12/hes-the-mp-with-the-downton-abbey-lifestyle-but-the-shadow-ofslavery-hangs-over-the-gilded-life-of-richard-drax. Accessed 29 January 2023.

Lovejoy, P. E. (1989). The impact of the Atlantic slave trade on Africa: A review of the literature. *Journal of African History, 30*, 365–394.

Lovejoy, P. E. (2000). *Transformations in slavery: A history of slavery in Africa* (2nd Ed.). Cambridge University Press.

Mashanda, T. (2017). Rethinking the term Sub-Saharan Africa. *The Herald*. Harare, Zimbabwe. https://www.herald.co.zw/rethinking-the-term-sub-saharan-africa/

Marcelin, L. H., Cela, T., & Shultz, J. (2016). Haiti and the politics of governance and community responses to Hurricane Matthew. *Disaster Health, 3*(4), 1–11.

M'baye, B. (2006). The economic, political, and social impact of the Atlantic slave trade on Africa. *The European Legacy, 11*(6), 607–622.

McAuliffe, M., & Triandafyllidou, A. (2021). *World Migration Report 2022*. International Organization for Migration (IOM). https://publications.iom.int/books/world-migration-report-2022

Melde, S., Anich, R., Crush, J., & Oucho, J. O. (2014). Introduction: the South–South migration and development nexus. In R. Anich, J. Crush, S. Melde, & J. O. Oucho (Eds.), *A new perspective on human mobility in the South* (Vol. 3, pp. 1–20). Springer Netherlands. https://doi.org/10.1007/978-94-017-9023-9_1

Nmoma, N. (1997). The civil war and the refugee crisis in Liberia. *XVII, 1997*, 4–5.

Nunn, N. (2008). The long-term effects of Africa's slave trade. *The Quarterly Journal of Economics, 123*(1), 139–176.

Nunn, N. (2017). Understanding the long-run effects of Africa's slave trades. *Vox EU/CEPR Column*. https://cepr.org/voxeu/columns/understanding-long-run-effects-africas-slave-trades

Olusoga, D. (2015). The history of British slave ownership has been buried: now its scale can be revealed. *The Observer*. 11 July, Online. https://www.theguardian.com/world/2015/jul/12/british-history-slavery-buried-scale-revealed

Omata, N. (2012). Struggling to find solutions: Liberian refugees in Ghana. *New Issues in Refugee Research, UNHCR Research Paper* No. 234. UNHCR.

Otele, O. (2017). Migratory flows, colonial encounters and the histories of transatlantic slavery. *International Migration Institute (IMI) Blog*. https://www.migrationinstitute.org/blog/migratory-flows-colonial-encounters-and-the-histories-of-transatlantic-slavery

Pettigrew, W. A. (2013). *Freedom's Debt: The Royal African Company and the Politics of the Atlantic Slave Trade, 1672–1752*. The University of North Carolina Press.

Platt, V. B. (1975). "And don't forget the Guinea voyage": The slave trade of Aaron Lopez of Newport. *The William and Mary Quarterly, 32*(4), 601. https://doi.org/10.2307/1919556

Ramsarran, P. (2008). The indentured contract and its impact on labor relationship and community reconstruction in British Guiana. *International Journal of Criminology and Sociological Theory, 1*(2), 177–188. file:///Users/veronicafynn/Desktop/admin,+Prabattie.pdf

Rodney, W. (1972). *How Europe underdeveloped Africa*. Bogle-L'Ouverture Publications.

Royal Museum Greenwich. (2023). *How did the slave trade end in Britain? Key facts about the trans-Atlantic slave trade*. https://www.rmg.co.uk/stories/topics/how-did-slave-trade-end-britain

dos Santos, S. A., & Hallewell, L. (2002). Historical roots of the "whitening" of Brazil. *Latin American Perspectives, 29*(1), 61–82.

Scott, W. R. (1903). The constitution and finance of the Royal African Company of England from it's foundation till 1720. *The American Histiorical Review, 8*(2), 241–259. https://www.jstor.org/stable/pdf/1832924.pdf

SlaveVoyages Operational Committee. (2021). *People of the Atlantic Slave Trade—Database. Enslavers Database*. https://www.slavevoyages.org/past/enslavers

Soares, R. R., Assunção, J. J., & Goulart, T. F. (2012). A note on slavery and the roots of inequality. *Journal of Comparative Economics, 40*, 565–580.

Stone, J. C. (1988). Imperialism, colonialism and cartography. *Transactions of the Institute of British Geographers, 13*(1), 57–64. https://doi.org/10.2307/622775

Syal, R. (2020, September 30). *Westminster's links to Britain's slave trade revealed in art survey.* The Guardian. https://www.theguardian.com/politics/2020/sep/30/westminsters-links-to-britains-slave-trade-revealedin-art-survey. Accessed 1 February 2023.

Swiss, S., Jennings, P. J., Aryee, G. V., Brown, G. H., Jappah-Samukai, R. M., Kamara, M. S., Schaack, R. D., & Turay-Kanneh, R. S. (1998). Violence against women during the Liberian civil conflict. *JAMA, 279*(8), 625–629.

Teye, J. K. (Ed.). (2022). *Migration in West Africa.* Springer International Publishing. https://link.springer.com/book/10.1007/978-3-030-97322-3

Tinker, H. (1993). *A new system of slavery: The export of Indian labour overseas 1830–1920* (2nd ed.). Hansib Publishing.

Turner, M. (1982). The baptist war and abolition. *Jamaican Historical Review, 13*, 31–41.

UNHCR. (2006). *Liberia: Strategies and program.* Government of Liberia Report. https://www.unhcr.org/home/PROTECTION/43eb16254.pdf

UK Parliament. (n.d.). *The transatlantic slave trade.* https://heritagecollections.parliament.uk/stories/the-transatlantic-slave-trade/

United Nations. (2018). *International migration report 2017.* UN. https://doi.org/10.18356/54684d14-en

Whatley, W. (2022). How the international slave trades underdeveloped Africa. *The Journal of Economic History, 82*(2), 403–441. https://doi.org/10.1017/S0022050722000110

White, E. C. (2018, June 16). The last ship to transport Africans to slavery was helmed by a Nova Scotian. The Coast Halifax. Nova Scotia. https://www.thecoast.ca/halifax/the-last-ship-to-transport-africans-to-slavery-was-helmed-by-a-nova-scotian/Content?oid=15402761

Williams, E. E. (1994). *Capitalism and slavery.* University of North Carolina Press.

Williams, E. E. (2022). *Capitalism and Slavery (This edition first published in Great Britain in Penguin Classics 2022).* Penguin Books.

Wyndham, J. (2006). The challenges of internal displacement in West Africa. *Forced Migration Review, 26*, 69.

Zhang, Y., Xu, Z. P., & Kibriya, S. (2021). The long-term effects of the slave trade on political violence in Sub-Saharan Africa. *Journal of Comparative Economics, 49*(3), 776–800.

de Zurara, G. E. (2010). *The chronicle of the discovery and conquest of Guinea.* Cambridge University Press.

Open Access This chapter is licensed under the terms of the Creative Commons Attribution 4.0 International License (http://creativecommons.org/licenses/by/4.0/), which permits use, sharing, adaptation, distribution and reproduction in any medium or format, as long as you give appropriate credit to the original author(s) and the source, provide a link to the Creative Commons license and indicate if changes were made.

The images or other third party material in this chapter are included in the chapter's Creative Commons license, unless indicated otherwise in a credit line to the material. If material is not included in the chapter's Creative Commons license and your intended use is not permitted by statutory regulation or exceeds the permitted use, you will need to obtain permission directly from the copyright holder.

3

Recentring the South in Studies of Migration

Elena Fiddian-Qasmiyeh

Introduction

In line with long-standing debates in diverse disciplines, over the past few years scholars have increasingly argued that redressing the Eurocentrism of migration studies requires a commitment to a "decentering of Global North knowledge" of and about migration (Fiddian-Qasmiyeh & Daley, 2018, 22; see Achiume, 2019; Grosfoguel et al., 2015, 2016; Pailey, 2019; Vanyoro, 2019).[1] However, it is less clear whether the "epistemic decolonization of migration theory" (Grosfoguel et al., 2015, 646, drawing on Quijano, 1991) necessarily means "recentering the South" in such studies. It is against this backdrop that this chapter explores a set of intersecting questions: What do

---

[1] An earlier version of this chapter was published as the introduction to a special issue of the *Migration and Society* journal of the same title. This chapter and the journal special issue more broadly, are informed by my ongoing project "Southern Responses to Displacement from Syria" (www.southernresponses.org), which has received funding from the European Research Council under European Union's Horizon 2020 Research and Innovation Programme (Grant Agreement No. 715582). The project combines attention to a particular *directionality* of both forced migration—from Syria to the neighbouring states of Lebanon, Jordan, and Turkey—and of *responses* to this displacement—by organisations, states, groups, and individuals from "the South"—while simultaneously critically examining the diverse ways that "the South" is understood, mobilised, and indeed resisted by differently positioned people, and tracing the power relations underpinning and emerging through and from these processes of migration, response, and conceptualisation/interpellation.

E. Fiddian-Qasmiyeh (✉)
Department of Geography, University College London, London, UK
e-mail: e.fiddian-qasmiyeh@ucl.ac.uk

© The Author(s) 2024
H. Crawley and J. K. Teye (eds.), *The Palgrave Handbook of South–South Migration and Inequality*, https://doi.org/10.1007/978-3-031-39814-8_3

decentring and recentring mean and what might these processes entail? What or who does the South refer to in contested academic, political, and policy domains? And whose knowledge is and should be involved in re-viewing the nature, and plural futures, of migration studies?

This chapter starts by delineating three ways that researchers have aimed to redress Eurocentrism in migration studies: (1) examining the applicability of classical concepts and frameworks in the South; (2) filling blind spots by studying migration in the South and South–South migration; and (3) engaging critically with the geopolitics of knowledge production. Building on this overview, the remainder of the chapter draws upon debates in migration studies and cognate fields to examine the preceding questions on decentring and recentring, different ways of conceptualising the South, and—as a pressing concern with regard to knowledge production—the politics of citation. In so doing, this introduction highlights a number of issues for further exploration and implementation as scholarly priorities.

Redressing Eurocentrism in Migration Studies

It has become increasingly mainstream to acknowledge that academic and policy studies of and responses to migration have been dominated by scholarship produced in the northern Hemisphere (e.g., Bommes & Morawska, 2005; Gardner & Osella, 2003; Piguet et al., 2018; Pisarevskaya et al., 2019). Indeed, migration studies, as an Anglophone institutional field of study, was first born in and dominated by scholarship from North America and, since the 1970s and 1980s, Europe.[2] In turn, the alignment of migration studies with the political and policy priorities of North American and European states has been widely documented and critiqued (e.g., Geddes, 2005; Scholten, 2018). For instance, it has been widely argued that studies of migration have often closely paralleled the interests of states that are the main funding sources for many academics in North America and Europe, and that often both explicitly and implicitly direct research agendas (Bakewell, 2008; Fiddian-Qasmiyeh, 2018; Geddes, 2005; Schinkel, 2018). As a means of highlighting connections with state priorities, researchers have traced both the predominance of particular themes and research questions in this field (e.g., Pisarevskaya et al., 2019) and particular directionalities and forms of migration. With reference to the former, for example, scholars have noted

---

[2] On the dominance of North American scholarship in migration studies' first decades as a field of study, and the more recent (post-1970s) "Europeanization" of migration research, see Bommes and Morawska (2005) and Piguet et al. (2018).

a long-standing focus on "classical" questions in migration studies. These include tracing the challenges of the integration of migrants in Europe and North America and developing analyses that provide insight into how to better manage and govern migration in and to such countries (ibid.; Adamson & Tsourapas, 2019). Concurrently, it has been recognised that the field has historically been dominated by studies of migration from the Global South *to* North America and Western Europe (i.e., processes of South–North migration), in spite of the greater numerical significance of internal and cross-border migration within and across the countries of the Global South (i.e., South–South migration) (Crush & Chikanda, 2018).

Indeed, given the long histories of migration in and across different parts of what is now often referred to as the Global South, Crush and Chikanda (2018, 394) remind us that "this blind spot is indicative of the hegemony of the Northern discourse on South–North migration, which has traditionally attracted widespread attention from scholars based in the North and has been assumed to have greater developmental value relative to other migration flows." Following the diagnosis of this "blind spot" and the "hegemony" of particular discursive frames of reference, one of the questions that emerges is how to redress this Eurocentric bias. Diverse responses have arisen accordingly, including the following three key approaches.

Examining the applicability of classical concepts and frameworks in the South

First, taking as their starting point the acknowledgement that many concepts in the field are far from universal, scholars have examined the applicability of a range of classical concepts and frameworks in countries that are not readily classified by scholars or politicians as "Western liberal democracies" (e.g., Adamson & Tsourapas, 2019; Natter, 2018).[3] In this vein, recent research has critically drawn on research in countries of the Global South to explore concepts, policies, and programmes originally developed from the vantage point of European states and "international" (read: northern-led) intergovernmental organisations.

For instance, the introduction and the subsequent five articles in a special themed section of the *Migration and Society* journal interrogate the concept of the transit state, a concept that, as guest editors Antje Missbach and Melissa Phillips note (2020), was originally developed to describe the nature

---

[3] On "African rearticulations of Western concepts" in the context of international relations, see K. Smith (2013).

and roles of countries on the European borderlands, such as Turkey or Ukraine (Düvell & Vollmer, 2009; Içduygu & Yükseker, 2012). In contrast, the special section explores the ways that state-level and local actors in six countries—Ecuador (Álvarez Velasco, 2020), Mexico (Vogt, 2020), Malaysia and Indonesia (Missbach & Hoffstaedter, 2020), Libya (Phillips, 2020), and Niger (Morreti, 2020)—negotiate being interpellated and mobilised "as" transit states and as (presumably compliant) gatekeepers. It also, "more importantly," examines how stakeholders within these "Southern positionalities" themselves perceive, conceptualise, and negotiate discourses of transit (Missbach & Phillips, 2020, 19).

Concurrently, Wurtz and Wilkinson (2020) explore how local faith actors in Mexico and Honduras conceptualise, interpret, and define two concepts—"innovation" and "self-sufficiency"—that have been heralded by policy makers and humanitarian practitioners from the Global North. In so doing, they challenge the secular framework that "reflects a predominantly Western, neoliberal ideology," providing important insights into how concepts and frameworks that are at the core of "international" humanitarian debates are conceived of, negotiated, and enacted in southern contexts (ibid., 146).

Studying Migration in the South and South–South Migration

A second approach that scholars, and indeed politicians, policy makers, and UN agencies, have pointed to in order to redress the above-mentioned "blind spot" is promoting, and funding, further studies of migration *in* the South (e.g., Nawyn, 2016a, 2016b) and *of* South–South migration (see Crush & Chikanda, 2018). In this light, research has documented and explored migration "in" and across countries of the Global South. For instance, Turner et al. (2020) examine the complex histories and experiences of internal migration in relation to the territorialisation of Vietnam's upland frontier regions, with a particular focus on Lào Cai Province on the country's border with China. In turn, Brankamp and Daley (2020) trace the ongoing legacies of colonial migration regimes between African societies, highlighting the ways that "African bodies as labour" have been racialised and subjected to different forms of discrimination and exclusion in postcolonial states like Kenya and Tanzania. In so doing, they stress that "considering long-term socio-historical trajectories is essential to understand contemporary hegemonic approaches to migration in Africa" (ibid., 125). In turn, Neil Carrier and Gordon Mathews explore connections between Eastleigh (Nairobi) and Xiaobei (Guangzhou)—two sites "that have become emblematic of much South–South migration and mobility"—arguing that South–South migration "offer opportunities for literal and social mobility—opportunities that the global North attempts to restrict for citizens of the South" (2020, 99).

Indeed, researching processes of South–South migration can be seen as redressing the above-mentioned historical imbalance, and as offering "an important corrective to Northern state and non-state discourses which depict the North as a 'magnet' for migrants from across the global South" (Fiddian-Qasmiyeh & Daley, 2018, 19). At the same time, however, the extent to which policy makers and politicians in Europe and North America have expressed an interest in better understanding and promoting South–South migration (e.g., IOM, 2013; Richter, 2018) raises concerns that "Northern actors might precisely be instrumentalising and co-opting Southern people and dynamics (in this case, migrants and migration flows) to achieve the aims established and promoted by Northern states and institutions" (Fiddian-Qasmiyeh & Daley, 2018, 19).

The Geopolitics of Knowledge Production

Such concerns resonate with a third approach: engaging critically with the geopolitics of knowledge production in this field. On the one hand, as Juliano Fiori (interviewed by Fiddian-Qasmiyeh, 2020) and Nasser-Eddin and Abu-Assab (2020) argue, researching migration in the South or about South–South migration per se can be seen as a continuation of normative and hegemonic research, policy, and political practices, rather than necessarily being part of a commitment to either "decentering" the North or "recentering" the South. On the other hand, Francesco Carella highlights "a recent trend … in both academia and practice whereby the 'Global South' has been developing its own understanding (or rather, multiple understandings) and critical analysis of migration, rather than having South-South migration concepts and models imposed from the 'Global North'" (interviewed by Fiddian-Qasmiyeh, 2020, 208). Indeed, as many researchers argue, there are multiple ways of knowing, including epistemological perspectives and methodological approaches that have been marginalised through the coloniality of knowledge (Quijano, 1991).

In effect, while many migration scholars are committed to testing the applicability of classical concepts and frameworks and filling empirical gaps by focusing on the particularities of migration in the Global South and South–South migration, a parallel constellation of debates has taken a different route to challenge the Eurocentric bias of migration studies. Among other things, such scholars aim to resist Eurocentrism by building on a range of long-standing theoretical and methodological interventions that can variously be posited as postcolonial, decolonial, and/or southern in nature[4] (e.g., Anzaldúa, 2002; Asad, 1975; Connell, 2007; Grosfoguel, 2011; Minh-ha, 1989; Ndlovu-Gatsheni, 2013; Quijano, 1991, 2007; Said, 1978; Santos, 2014; Smith, 1999; Spivak, 1988; Thiong'o, 1986). While internally heterogenous, such approaches have "traced and advocated for diverse ways of knowing and being in a pluriversal world characterised (and constituted) by complex relationalities and unequal power relations, and equally diverse ways of resisting these inequalities" (Fiddian-Qasmiyeh & Daley, 2018, 2). To illustrate, Aníbal Quijano has centralised the coloniality of power and knowledge (1991, 2007), while Amin (1972a, 1972b, 1985) and Chakrabarty (2000) have "provincialized" European and Eurocentric systems of knowledge that have been artificially constructed as "universal" by denying or marginalising the existence of "non-European" or "non-Western" forms of knowledge. Building on such works, scholars such as Raewyn Connell and Boaventura de Sousa Santos have proposed the urgency of recentring "Southern theories" (Connell, 2007) and "epistemologies of the South" (Santos, 2014). A range of disciplinary, epistemological, and methodological traditions have thus guided the deconstruction of hegemonic conceptual models used in mainstream North American and European migration studies to examine, explain, and "diagnose" the challenges faced by migrants throughout their journeys. As explored further below, doing so, for instance, requires interrogating and contesting, rather than taking for granted or reproducing, the "coloniality of the ways that terms like 'indigenous,' 'southern' [and, I would add here, 'the South'] … fix and contain those subjects and spatialities" (Jazeel, 2019, 10). Beyond testing the applicability of classical concepts in countries of the South, it involves resisting what Connell refers to as "methodological projection," through which "data from the periphery are framed by concepts, debates and research strategies from the metropole" (Connell, 2007, 64, cited in Jazeel, 2019, 11).

Such approaches may lead scholars to engage in what Robtel N. Pailey denominates "subversive acts of scholarship" (2019, 8), insofar as they are ways of acting against the grain. As I discuss further in the following section, this can include considering what it means to engage critically with "local" or "southern" perspectives not merely as data but as forms of knowledge,

---

[4] On the particularities of and differences between decolonial, postcolonial, and southern theories, see Dastile and Ndlovu-Gatsheni (2013) and Patel (2018).

and to acknowledge artistic production *as* forms of knowledge (i.e., see Qasmiyeh, 2020). It may involve "studying up" structures of inequality such as the humanitarian industry rather than "researching down" the lived experiences of refugees (see Farah, 2020); challenging traditional modes of research or humanitarian programming through implementing critical, participatory approaches to working with people affected by displacement (see Vera-Espinoza, 2020; Conti et al., 2020); or applying a "southern ethnography" lens to migration-related systems in the Global North (see Boano & Astolfo, drawing on AbdouMaliq Simone, 2020).

Indeed, importantly, where Koh (2020) and Jubilut (2020) centralise the roles of academics and universities from Southeast Asia and South America, respectively, in promoting nuanced studies of migration, decolonial and postcolonial scholars have also been attentive to the potential of provincialising European ways of being and knowing by shifting the geographical focus of the critical academic gaze—this includes the potential of seeing Europe through "Caribbean eyes" (Boatcă, 2018; see also Grosfoguel et al., 2015). As such, far from assuming that "recentering the South" must entail conducting more research in and about particular geographies associated with the Global South, challenging Eurocentric approaches to migration studies can also be grounded on critical writing vis-à-vis migration to the North. As evidenced in Tayeb Saleh's pivotal novel *Season of Migration to the North* (1969), there is of course a long history of critical reflections highlighting the very question of directionality as a decolonial stance, with more recent reflections building on such a tradition to argue that migration to the North is itself a form of "decolonial migration," going as far as to view "migration as decolonization" (Achiume, 2019, 1510, 1523).

Throughout, decolonial and postcolonial scholars have thus been critiquing the ways that particular directionalities and modalities of migration, and specific groups of migrants, have been constituted as "problems to be solved," including through processes that are deeply inflected by gender, class, and race. In so doing, many of these scholars are part of a broader collective that argues that there is a need to challenge the very foundations and nature of knowledge production—to "decolonise migration research" (Vanyoro, 2019)—and to acknowledge and resist the way that migration research is embedded within and reproduces neoliberal and neocolonial systems of exploitation.

In essence, what this brief summary of three key approaches to redressing Eurocentrism in migration studies highlights is that although these (and other) approaches often overlap in a given article or book, one can be a scholar who acknowledges the hegemony of northern and Eurocentric migration studies—with its tendency to prioritise researching migration from the South to the North through concepts and frameworks that are often aligned to European and North American state interests—without necessarily being interested in decolonial thinking or challenging neocolonial knowledge production or migration control. Equally, while decolonial scholars may prioritise studying migration through southern theories or epistemologies from the South, one can also be a postcolonial or decolonial scholar who (while critiquing these very constructs) conducts research in and in relation to the North rather than empirically exploring processes of migration taking place in and across the South.

Recognising a multiplicity of ways of redressing Eurocentrism in migration studies in turn leads us, in the following section, to the three questions outlined in the opening of this introduction: (1) what decentring and recentring might entail; (2) the meanings of "the South"; and (3) the broader politics of knowledge production in this field. While the following reflections are far from exhaustive, they raise questions for further exploration in terms of topics and thematics, but also in terms of broader approaches to conducting research, writing, and publishing in this field.

Decentring the North Qua Recentring the South?

I start this section by reasserting that although a focus on studying migration in the South may be a means of "recentering the South" in empirical terms—by filling a gap *in* knowledge—this does not necessarily "decenter" or challenge the dominance of and inequalities perpetuated by the original system, nor does it contest what is constituted *as* knowledge itself.

Indeed, gap-filling studies are open to similar critiques as those developed in response to studies of women in development that merely adopted an "add women and stir" approach (Fiddian-Qasmiyeh, 2014), thereby failing to challenge the systems that excluded women in the first place, and that sought to instrumentalise the "added" women to meet preexisting, externally established goals. In part, I introduce this reference to feminist critiques of the "add women and stir" method as a means of echoing Scarlett Hester and Catherine Squires's call—in their reflections on "*recentering* black feminism"—that we must be "willing to search for knowledge and theory outside of our discipline" (Hester & Squires, 2018, 344, emphasis added). Echoing these authors—who are writing from within the context of feminist critical race studies—highlights that debates on centring and recentring have been pivotal to diverse fields of study. Critical inquiry vis-à-vis those people, places, and processes that have historically been marginalised and erased extend from feminist theory (Hooks, 1984) to "recentering" or "adding and stirring" Africa into international relations (respectively, de Heredia & Wai, 2018; Smith, 2013). In the pages that follow, I draw on these cognate debates to reflect on the challenges and possibilities of engaging with the proposed processes of "decentering" and "recentering" in relation to migration studies.

The Politics of Recentring

In their 2018 edited collection, Marta Iñiguez de Heredia and Zubairu Wai advocate "taking Africa out of a place of exception and marginality, and *placing it at the center* of international relations and world politics" (n.p., emphasis added). While many scholars and activists advocate such a process, others contest the notion of recentring for different reasons. On the one hand, for instance, Achille Mbembe draws on the work of Ngugi wa Thiong'o to argue that "in Ngugi's terms, 'Africanization' is *a project of 're-centering.'* It is about rejecting the assumption that the modern West is the central root of Africa's consciousness and cultural heritage … Decolonizing (a la Ngugi) is not about closing the door to European or other traditions. It is about defining clearly what the centre is. And for Ngugi, Africa has to be placed at the centre" (2016, 35, emphasis added). Far from proposing an isolationist modus operandi characterised by rejecting European traditions, reifying a static geography, or solely conducting research "in" Africa, Mbembe reminds us that for Ngugi wa Thiong'o "Africa expands well beyond the geographical limits of the Continent. He wanted 'to pursue the African connection to the four corners of the Earth'—the West Indies, to Afro-America" (Mbembe, 2016, 35). In this sense, centring must intrinsically be viewed as a particular relational project, extending beyond a specific spatial referent: "After we have examined ourselves, we radiate outwards and discover peoples and worlds around us. With Africa at the centre of things, not existing as an appendix or a satellite of other countries and literatures, things must be seen from the African perspective" (Mbembe, 2016, 35).

On the other hand, however, Mbembe draws on the work of Frantz Fanon to stress that Africanisation itself is not "decolonization": placing "Africa" and "Africans" at the core can still, as Fanon critiqued, be characterised by xenophobia and the drive to expel "the foreigner," which, as Mbembe reminds us, "was almost always a fellow African from another nation" (ibid., 34; see Brankamp & Daley, 2020). In this sense, centring—whether "Africa,"

"Africans," or, in the context of this chapter, "the South"—can still be characterised by inequalities, and may, in fact, risk perpetuating systems of exclusion.

Indeed, in contrast to calling for recentring "as" decolonisation of knowledge, Sabelo Ndlovu-Gatsheni powerfully rejects calls to "bring Africa *back in*" (2018a, 283, emphasis added; also see 2018b). First, he argues that there is a need to shift from Vumbi Yoka Mudimbe's (1994) "idea of Africa" to the "African idea" proposed by Ngugi wa Thiong'o (2009, 74), and already hinted at in the quotes above. We could posit that this parallels arguments that while "the idea of the South" is a construct that artificially fixes and contains (to draw on Jazeel's words, quoted above), it may nonetheless be the case that "south*ern* ideas," theories, and epistemologies enable us to productively engage with the complexity of intersecting and mutually constitutive processes.

Second, Ndlovu-Gatsheni urges for a "shift from the simplistic discourses of negativity, alterity, peripherality, and marginality to the complex alternative decolonial ones of Africa that was both *'inside' and 'outside' simultaneously* and that continued to be a site of 'critical resistance' thought and self-assertion" (2018a, 284, emphasis added). Ndlovu-Gatsheni argues that "both the 'inside-ness' and 'outside-ness' of Africa are determined by coloniality giving it the character of an insider who is pushed outside and an outsider who is kept inside forcibly" (ibid.). In effect, beyond the diagnosis that "Africa" has been absent(ed) or marginal(ised), Ndlovu-Gatsheni "challenges the very premise of *the politics of bringing Africa back-in* as misguided and missing the complexity of Africa's position within the modern world system, world capitalist economy, and global imperial/colonial orders" (ibid., emphasis added).

Twenty years before Ndlovu-Gatsheni powerfully argued in this chapter that "Africa cannot be brought 'back in' to the bowels of Euro-North American-centric beast. It is already inside as a *swallowed* victim" (ibid., emphasis added),[5] the Chicana feminist theorist Gloria Anzaldúa spoke of, and against, "this kind of United Statesian-culture-*swallowing*-up-the-rest-of-the-world" (quoted in Lunsford, 1998, 16, emphasis added).

Anzaldúa also simultaneously confronted the inside-outside binary through her conceptualisation of *nosotras* (feminine "we" in Spanish):

---

[5] In turn, one of José Martí's most famous phrases, as an early critic of American imperialism (b. Havana, 1853), is "*Viví en el monstruo y le conozco las entrañas*" (I lived in the monster, and I know its entrails). With many thanks to Mette L. Berg for drawing my attention to this echo.

It used to be that there was a "them" and an "us." We were over here, we were the "other" with other lives, and the "nos" was the subject, the White man. And there was a very clear distinction. But as the decades have gone by, we, the colonized, the Chicano, the Blacks, the Natives in this country, have been reared in this frame of reference, in this field. So all of our education, all of our ideas come from this frame of reference. We are complicitous for being in such close proximity and in such intimacy with the other. Now I think that "us" and "them" are interchangeable. Now there is no such thing as an "other." *The other is in you, the other is in me.* This White culture has been internalized in my head. *I have a White man in here, I have a White woman in here. And they have me in their heads, even if it is just a guilty little nudge sometime ...* (Anzaldúa, quoted in Lunsford, 1998, 8, emphasis added)

By rejecting the false binary between the insider *nos* (the white "us," qua the "I," the subject) and the outsider *otras* (the colonised "them," the Other, the inferior object), Anzaldúa proposed the concept of (*nos* + *otras* =) *nosotras* ("we"). In this conceptualisation, each is constitutive of the other, albeit on terms and through processes that are not only unequal but embedded in different forms of colonial violence—or, as I discuss below, also with reference to her work (Anzaldúa, 2002, 25), "colonial *wounds.*"

Such a theoretical move posits that it is not only the case that there are multiple "we's," but also that the "we" itself is internally plural and is created relationally within, through, and against structures of inequality (Fiddian-Qasmiyeh, 2019a). While with somewhat different roots, this echoes analyses that argue that there are multiple Souths in the world, including "Souths" (and southern voices) within powerful metropoles, as well as multiple Souths within multiple peripheries (Connell, 2007; Sheppard & Nagar, 2004).[6] It resonates with assertions, such as those made by Urvashi Aneja, that historical and contemporary processes mean that "the South and the North alike 'can thus be said to exist and evolve in a mutually constitutive relationship,' rather than in isolation from one another" (Aneja, quoted in Fiddian-Qasmiyeh & Daley, 2018, 3). In turn, this parallels Ndlovu-Gatsheni and Kenneth Tafira's assertion that "the global South was not only invented from outside by

---

[6] As noted by Horner (2019), it is not only critical scholars who acknowledge the existence of multiple Souths, including Souths in the North, and vice versa (Sheppard and Nagar, 2014), but also representatives of quintessentially neoliberal institutions such as the World Bank. Among the examples shared by Horner to demonstrate the "blurring boundary" of traditional neoliberal "maps of development" (Sidaway, 2012) are the then World Bank President Robert Zoellick arguing in 2010 "that the term Third World was no longer relevant in the context of a more multipolar world economy" (Horner, 2019, 8), and the official 2016 announcement that the World Bank would be removing "the classification of 'developed' and 'developing' countries in the World Development Indicators" (Horner, 2019, 8).

European imperial forces but it also invented itself through resistance and solidarity-building" (2018, 131).

If we extend the challenges presented by Anzaldúa, Ndlovu-Gatsheni, and many others to the study of migration, this leads us simultaneously to critique the processes through which certain people, spaces, and structures constitute themselves as the centre/inside, and the processes that can reinscribe the power of that "centre" by aiming to "add and stir" that which has been (kept) outside. It is also, perhaps, to challenge the very binaries that underpin the project of decentring/recentring, since, in this framework, the North–South/core–periphery/centre–margin are always already mutually constitutive and mutually implicated in one another's being in (or exclusion from) the world.

Diagnosing bias and exclusionary processes can thus run the risk of recentring that which scholars ostensibly aim to challenge (see Horner, 2019; Madlingozi, 2018). In this regard, rather than "recentering," perhaps what is required is a process of "decentering" the hegemonic.

In the following section, I briefly turn to the implications of a number of the arguments outlined above—of simultaneity, relationality, and mutual constitutiveness, and the politics of decentring rather than recentring—for conceptualisations of "the South."

The "South" or "Southern Theories"?

If recentring is a contested proposition, so too is "the South." On the one hand, when used in the context of examining "migration in the Global South" or "South-South migration," it is often taken for granted that a geographical complex known as "the South" objectively exists, typically encompassing and equated with countries in or the entire regions of "Asia," "Africa," "Latin America," "the Middle East," and "the Pacific." In other contexts, authors such as Peace Medie and Alice Kang define "countries of the global South" as "countries that have been marginalised in the international political and economic system" (2018, 37–38). In this sense, "the South" is often adopted as an equivalent or substitution for the formerly popular and now widely disavowed terms of "the Third World" and "the developing world."[7]

---

[7] While "the South" is used in different ways by different authors, it is notable that contributors such as Francesco Carella highlight that the term "Third World" is no longer an "acceptable" frame of reference in the field of international migration policy, while policy makers are increasingly "doing" South–South in the field of migration (interviewed by Fiddian-Qasmiyeh, 2020). Indeed, the unacceptability of the term is widely acknowledged, not only by the World Bank (see Horner, 2019, 8), but also by proponents of the intellectual tradition of Third World Approaches to International Law (known by its acronym TWAIL; see Achiume, 2019). TWAIL advocates nonetheless continue to

While such classifications may be externally applied and/or imposed, it is equally the case that states have often *defined themselves* with reference to the Global "South." For instance, over 130 states *define themselves* as belonging to the Group of 77—a quintessential platform for "South-South" cooperation—in spite of the diversity of their ideological and geopolitical positions in the contemporary world order, their vastly divergent gross domestic product (GDP) and per capita income, and their rankings in the Human Development Index.[8] Indeed, a number of official, institutional taxonomies exist, including those that classify (and in turn interpellate) different political entities as being from and of "the South" or "the North" (see Fiddian-Qasmiyeh, 2015). Such emic and etic classifications have variously been developed on the basis of particular readings of a state's geographical location, of its relative position as a (formerly) colonised territory or colonising power, and/or of a state's current economic capacity on national and global scales (ibid.).

On the other hand, as already suggested above, the South and both the North–South and West–East binaries are just some of many constructs that have been interrogated for over four decades, including by scholars like Said (1978), Mohanty (1988), Escobar (1995), Kothari (2005), Connell (2007), and Ndlovu-Gatsheni and Tafira (2018). Among other things, these scholars have argued that far from being "either static or purely defined through reference to physical territories and demarcations" (Fiddian-Qasmiyeh & Daley, 2018, 3), geographical imaginaries of the South (and the Orient) have been invented, after Said (1978), through the active deployment of "imperial reason and scientific racism" (Ndlovu-Gatsheni & Tafira, 2018, 127). This "imperial reason and scientific racism" has constituted certain places, peoples, ways of knowing, and ways of being as inferior to or void of hegemonic (read Western/northern) systems of meaning.

Indeed, if such scholars have demonstrated the urgency of interrogating "the South" as a means of defining and containing geographical locations, it has nonetheless been widely used by theorists engaged in postcolonial and decolonial debates and politics in ways that are pertinent to the topic of this chapter and the Handbook of which it is part. For instance, Sujata Patel (2018, 32) follows both Connell (2007) and Santos (2014) in conceptualising "the South" as "a metaphor" that "represents the embeddedness of knowledge

---

argue that the usage of the term "Third World" is expedient precisely because "it provides the conceptual framing for counter-hegemonic discourse that unveils the close relationship between capitalism, imperialism and international law, and explains why international law has always disadvantaged Third World peoples" (Peel & Lin, 2019).

[8] For more detailed discussions and applications of the notion of "the South," and of diverse modes of definition and typologies vis-à-vis the "Global South," see Fiddian-Qasmiyeh (2015) and Fiddian-Qasmiyeh and Daley (2018).

in relations of power." Stressing its constitutive *relationality*, it is defined by Siba Grovogui as "an idea and a set of practices, attitudes, and relations" that are mobilised as "a *disavowal* of institutional and cultural practices associated with colonialism and imperialism" (2011, 177, emphasis added). Furthermore, as noted in the preceding section, Connell (2007) and Santos (2014) shift from using "the South" (as a noun) and instead respectively develop their focus on south*ern* theories (the adjectival) and epistemologies *of the South* (a fixed referent in the genitive construction).

From this standpoint, redressing Eurocentrism is not merely a matter of recentring "the South" by conducting research in and about countries in "the South" (as a fixed geographical descriptor), but instead requires a more radical and deeper shift. Returning to the question of recentring and decentring, Mignolo (2009, 3) proposes that this shift can only be achieved through "de-Westernisation," which, in his words, "means, within a capitalist economy, that the rules of the games and the shots are no longer called by Western players and institutions." It is, in his view, only through de-Westernisation that we can go beyond the insufficient step of aiming "to change the *content* of the conversation," and instead take up the essential challenge of "chang[ing] the *terms* of the conversation" (ibid., 4, emphasis added).

However, Mbembe disagrees with the diagnosis of "de-Westernization" as the solution. While he agrees that "decolonization is not about design tinkering with the margins," and, drawing on Fanon, holds that Europe must not be taken as a model or paradigm to be imitated or mimicked, he powerfully argues that "decolonizing knowledge is … not simply about de-Westernization" (2015, 24). As noted above with reference to simultaneity, relationality, and mutual constitutiveness, de-Westernisation is insufficient precisely because "the Western archive is singularly complex," and because this archive "contains within itself the resources of its own refutation" (ibid.). Indeed, the Western archive is "neither monolithic, nor the exclusive property of the West," and Mbembe maintains that "Africa and its diaspora decisively contributed to its making and should legitimately make foundational claims on it" (ibid.).

Pulling together the diverse strands of this chapter thus far suggests that changing the *terms* of the conversation, and changing the very "rules of the game" in this sense, arguably therefore requires transcending the model of "recentering" the South or of "decentering" the North/West. Instead, as suggested above, and as explored in more detail in the next section, it requires attention to the relational and situated nature of knowledge production (as has long been argued by feminist and decolonial thinkers alike[9]) and the broader geopolitics of knowledge.

The Politics of Citation: Beyond Diversity and Inclusion

Hester and Squires (2018, 344) remind us that although "recentering and historicizing race scholarship around black feminism is one approach to the issue of citational politics," inclusive citation is insufficient when it becomes little more than an exercise in "diversity management." Inter alia, Hester and Squires argue that, just as insisting that scholars cite white, European, or North American "experts" in the field is part of an exclusionary and hegemonic process, so too "the insistence that scholars cite particular, well-known, 'authorized' theorists of color, serves to police the boundaries: which fields and which scholars are permitted, and which scholars are unrecognized because their ideas haven't made their way into the authorized shortlist?" (ibid., 345). Going beyond "inclusion" as "diversity" thus requires careful consideration of how to develop meaningful engagement with and acknowledgement of the intellectual work of people who have often either been excluded from the "authorized shortlist," or whose work has been ignored, or merely "footnoted," in academic publications.[10] It also involves a recognition, in the words of Gloria Anzaldúa, that "an outsider is not just somebody of a different skin; it could be somebody who's White, who's usually an insider but who crosses back and forth between outsider and insider" (Anzaldúa, quoted in Lunsford, 2004, 62). In all, it requires a reconsideration of whose knowledge and what types of knowledge are viewed as knowledge to be engaged with, or as material to be "quoted" to inspire academic analysis, as I now discuss.

---

[9] On this commonality, see also Nasser-Eddin and Abu Assab (2020).

[10] On footnoting Islam in historic and contemporary studies of migration to Cuba, see Fiddian-Qasmiyeh (2016a). On the forgotten legacy of the Cuban anthropologist Fernando Ortiz, see Berg (2010), Coronil (1995), and Fiddian-Qasmiyeh (2016a).

The Politics of "Quoted" Knowledge: Rethinking the Wound

There is a long history of implicitly and explicitly dismissing the intellectual and conceptual work of people positioned outside of the northern academy. This history has been characterised by "exploiting" and "extorting," to use Paulin Hountondji's terms (1992, 242), "their" words to develop concepts and theories rather than acknowledging "their" words *as* concepts, theories, and knowledge. Indeed, as Mbembe argues (2016, 36), critiques of the "dominant Eurocentric academic model" include "the fight against what Latin Americans in particular call 'epistemic coloniality,' that is, the endless production of theories that are based on European traditions; are produced nearly always by Europeans or Euro-American men who are the only ones accepted as capable of reaching universality; a particular anthropological knowledge, which is a process of knowing about Others—but a process that never fully acknowledges these Others as thinking and knowledge-producing subjects." To illustrate such a process, I will take an example from one of the leading figures of decolonial studies who I have already cited at length above: Gloria Anzaldúa. By offering this example it is not my intention to question the integrity of the researchers under question; instead, I aim to trace the ways in which a thought, or that which marks the inception of a thought, has travelled, not in the sense of travelling theory (Said, 1983, 226–247), but travelling *as* theory. I do so as an invitation to think about the process through which theory comes to be recognised as theory, and to ask who is acknowledged as playing a significant role in the inception of theory, and who is relegated to the margins.

In her groundbreaking text *Borderlands/La Frontera*, originally published in 1987, Gloria Anzaldúa writes: "The US-Mexican border *es una herida abierta* where the Third World grates against the first and bleeds" (2002, 25). The border is *una herida abierta* (an open wound), a wound that continues to bleed due to the ongoing violence of coloniality, a colonial violence that is gendered, racialised, racist, and patriarchal in nature. And yet this wound has itself become implicated in the ongoing violence of gendered, racialised, and disciplinary hierarchies of knowledge, including when Anzaldúa has been marginalised, uncited, or merely "footnoted" in relation to what has come to be "known" as one of decolonial theory's key and foundational concepts: the "colonial wound."

Through a range of problematic citation processes forming the foundation of this example, Anzaldúa has at best been presented as inspiring the foundation for the conceptualisation and theorisation of the "colonial wound," and at worst entirely absented from publications applying this concept. These processes range from scholars introducing "what can be called *following and reformulating a bit* G. Anzaldúa, 'the colonial wound'" (Tlostanova, 2008, 1, emphasis added), to Anzaldúa's words being demoted, in a footnote, to the status of a "metaphor": "Chicana intellectual and activist, Gloria Anzaldúa, described the borders between America and Mexico as 'una herida abierta.' *We see in this metaphor*, an expression of the global 'colonial wound'" (Tlostanova & Mignolo, 2009, 143, emphasis added). From a core concept in her own text, Anzaldúa's words have travelled to other spaces: as noted above, with her words depicted as *pre*ceding theory and being relegated to a footnote; subsequently entirely absented (Mignolo, 2009); and ultimately referred to in a footnote added a full ten lines after the first use of "colonial wound" in a 2011 article, with the displaced footnote clarifying the journey that the concept has taken: "The *concept* of colonial wound *comes from* Gloria Anzaldúa, in one of her much celebrated statements: 'The US–Mexican border es *una herida abierta* where the Third World grates against the first and bleeds'" (Mignolo, 2011, 64n9, emphasis added).

Starting and ending the above brief reflection with Anzaldúa's line is a way to recentre her and her work as the origin of this "decolonial" concept, and simultaneously to argue for a careful reflection on the politics of citation and theorisation. To do so is not to speak on Anzaldúa's behalf, since she herself has reflected on these processes of appropriation in detail: "When it [*Borderlands*] was appropriated, it was taken over and used in a token way by white theorists who would … mention my name … but as an aside. They never integrated our theories into their writing. Instead, they were using us to say, 'Here I am a progressive, liberal, white theorist. I know women of colour. See? I'm mentioning these folks'" (Keating, 2009, published in Keating, 2009, 192). Indeed, rather than acknowledging Anzaldúa as an intellectual in her own right and with her own intellectual foundations, she writes that at times white theorists "would look at some of the conclusions and concepts and theories in *Borderlands* and write about them, saying that my theories were derived from their work. They had discovered these theories. They insisted that I got these theories from Foucault, Lacan, Derrida or the French feminists. But I was not familiar with these theorists' work when I wrote *Borderlands*. I hadn't read them. So what they were saying was, 'She got it from these white folks and didn't even cite them'" (ibid.). Far from taking it for granted that only white theorists have "produced" and subsequently "own" key concepts and theoretical approaches that must be cited appropriately, it is important to disrupt citational practices that have long been implicated in bordering knowledge and keeping certain people in the centre of such systems while excluding others. In line with this reflection, attention must be paid not only to the questions of who produces knowledge, when, why, and how (all of which are key for feminist and decolonial theorists alike) but also of what knowledge is acknowledged and cited as knowledge, and on whose terms.

In this regard, a further significant challenge emerges when going beyond identifying Eurocentric biases and aiming to redress gaps in knowledge. This is the importance of not only recognising but indeed centralising the knowledge and the conceptualisations of people who have migrated, been displaced, and/or who are responding to migration in different ways (Fiddian-Qasmiyeh, 2019a, 2019b).

If our starting point is (which I believe it should be) the acknowledgement that people have heterogeneous experiences of migration and are active agents whose capacity to act is restricted by diverse systems of inequality and violence, it subsequently becomes essential to go beyond collecting, or documenting, such experiences, voices, and acts (Fiddian-Qasmiyeh, 2019a, 2019b; Nasser-Eddin & Abu-Assab, 2020; Qasmiyeh, 2014). From this starting point, it becomes necessary to challenge rather than reproduce the assumption that migrants and refugees merely experience, are affected by, and/or respond to migratory processes, and that it is only through critical scholarly attention that these experiences can be analysed, for "us" to make sense of "their" lives and worlds. In the powerful words of Yousif M. Qasmiyeh, it is essential to reject the violence of projects that take ownership of migrants' and refugees' voices—"After spending hours with us, in the same room, she left with a jar of homemade pickles and three full cassettes of our voices" (Qasmiyeh, 2014, 68; also see Qasmiyeh, 2021)—even, or especially, when these projects are undertaken ostensibly to subsequently "give voice" to people from the South. It is in this context that Qasmiyeh posits that the aim should be "to embroider the voice with its own needle: an act proposed to problematise the notion of the voice; something that cannot be given (to anyone) since it must firmly belong to everyone from the beginning" (2019, n.p.; see also Qasmiyeh, 2020, 2021). Such a commitment means thinking carefully about how and why we "quote" migrants, refugees, and those responding to migration, and to recognise that analysis and theorisation are not the preserve of academics and practitioners.

People who are involved in diverse migratory processes conceptualise their own situations, positions, and responses as everyday theorists rather than as providers of "data" to be analysed to provide the materials for conceptual and theoretical scholarship (Fiddian-Qasmiyeh, 2015, 2016b). This means that it is urgent for us to focus intently on identifying and challenging the diverse structural barriers—including academic, political, economic, cultural, and social ones—that prevent certain people's understandings and worldviews from being perceived as knowledge. Anzaldúa may have written that "all … is fiction," but this is only because, firstly, "to me, everything is real" (in Keating, 2009, 108) and, secondly, words are more than "metaphors" to be "reformulated a bit" (op cit.) to be owned and subsequently mobilised by theorists. Fiction, poetry, and art is knowledge, to be read and engaged within their own right as knowledge, not "converted" into "knowledge" through the analyses of expert critics (Garb, 2019; and as argued by Walter Benjamin,[11] see Selz, 1991, 366). I use this as an analogy for the modes of research that have often underpinned our work as scholars in the field of migration, and a reminder of the importance of the arts and humanities in their own right, as forms of knowledge that sit beside (following Jarratt, 1998), rather than acting as "seasoning" for "social science" research and publications (Fiddian-Qasmiyeh, 2019a, 44–45).

Indeed (and I am fully aware of the irony of including such a statement within only a few lines of having traced Anzaldúa's erasure or footnoting), Mignolo draws attention to the need to "shift the attention from the enunciated to the enunciation" (Mignolo, 2009, 2). Equally, Gayatri Spivak famously interrogates "Can the Subaltern Speak?" (1988) in ways that focus both on the subaltern speaker (the enunciator) and the structurally unequal processes of enunciation, and Homi Bhabha conceptualises the "Third Space" as a "contradictory and ambivalent space of enunciation" by arguing, in terms that might be read as resonating in some ways with Anzaldúa's conceptualisation of *nosotras*, that "it is in this space that we will find those words with which we can speak of Ourselves and Others. And by exploring this hybridity, this 'Third Space', we may elude the politics of polarity and emerge as the others of our selves" (2006, 156–157).

As such, in addition to considering which topics, geographies, and directionalities of migration are explored, and which scholars or enunciators are being cited (i.e., women of colour, southern scholars), it is essential to remain critically attentive to the conditions under which processes of enunciation take place and are engaged with. In particular, it is a focus on the unequal process of listening and recognising speech as more than words that emerges as being pivotal here, as Hooks (1989, 5–6) argued over three decades ago: "Certainly, for black women, our struggle has not been to emerge from silence into speech but to change the nature and direction of our speech, to make a speech that compels listeners, one that is heard … the voices of black women … could be tuned out, could become a kind of background music,

---

[11] With many thanks to Yousif M. Qasmiyeh for drawing my attention to this reference.

audible but not acknowledged as significant speech." This thus involves being attentive to who is positioned as being capable of producing "significant speech," including across intersecting vectors of gender, race, sexuality, migration status, and, as discussed above, also what kinds of knowledge are viewed as significant in their own right.

Acknowledgements An earlier version of this chapter was published as the Introduction to a journal Special Issue of *Migration and Society*, and is republished here with the kind permission of Berghahn Journals. The original citation is: Fiddian-Qasmiyeh, E. (2020). Introduction: Recentering the South in Studies of Migration. *Migration and Society*, *3*(1), 1–18. https://doi.org/10.3167/arms.2020.030102. With sincere thanks to Mette L. Berg, Yousif M. Qasmiyeh, and Johanna Waters for their invaluable comments on earlier iterations of this article, which, in turn, builds upon conversations we have had on related issues over many years.

References

Achiume, E. T. (2019). Migration as decolonisation. *Stanford Law Review*, *71*(6), 1509–1574.

Adamson, F. B., & Tsourapas, G. (2019). The migration state in the Global South: Nationalizing, developmental, and neoliberal models of migration management. *International Migration Review*. https://doi.org/10.1177/0197918319879057

Álvarez Velasco, S. (2020). From Ecuador to Elsewhere: The (re)configuration of a transit country. *Migration and Society*, *3*, 34–49.

Amin, S. (1972a). *Neocolonialism in West Africa*. Penguin.

Amin, S. (1972b). Underdevelopment and dependence in Black Africa: Origins and contemporary forms. *Journal of Modern African Studies*, *10*(4), 503–524.

Amin, S. (1985) *Delinking: Towards a polycentric world*. Trans. Michael Wolfers. Zed.

Anzaldúa, G. (2002). *Borderlands/La Frontera: The New Mestiza*. 25th anniversary (4th ed.). Originally published in 1987. Aunt Lute Books.

Asad, T. (Ed.). (1975). *Anthropology and the colonial encounter*. Ithaca Press.

Bakewell, O. (2008). Research beyond the categories: The importance of policy irrelevant research into forced migration. *Journal of Refugee Studies*, *21*(4), 432–453.

Berg, M. (2010). On the social ground beneath our feet: For a cosmopolitan anthropology. *Social Anthropology/anthropologie Sociale*, *18*(4), 433–440.

Bhabha, H. (2006). Cultural diversity and cultural differences. In B. Ashcroft, G. Griffiths, & H. Tiffin (Eds.), *The post-colonial studies reader* (pp. 155–157). Routledge.

Boano, C., & Astolfo, G. (2020). Notes around hospitality as inhabitation: Engaging with the politics of care and refugees' dwelling practices in the Italian urban context. *Migration and Society, 3*, 222–232.

Boatça, M. (2018). Caribbean Europe: Out of sight, out of mind? In B. Reiter (Ed.), *Constructing the pluriverse: The geopolitics of knowledge* (pp. 197–218). Duke University Press.

Bommes, M., & Morawska, E. (2005). *International migration research: Constructions, omissions and the promises of interdisciplinarity*. Ashgate.

Brankamp, H., & Daley, P. (2020). Laborers, migrants, refugees: Managing belonging, bodies, and mobility in (Post)Colonial Kenya and Tanzania. *Migration and Society, 3*, 113–129.

Carrier, N., & Mathews, G. (2020). Places of otherness: Comparing Eastleigh, Nairobi, and Xiaobei, Guangzhou, as sites of South-South migration. *Migration and Society, 3*, 98–112.

Chakrabarty, D. (2000). *Provincializing Europe: Postcolonial thought and historical difference*. Princeton University Press.

Connell, R. (2007). *Southern theory: The global dynamics of knowledge in social science*. Allen & Unwin Australia.

Conti, R. L., Dabaj, J., & Pascucci, E. (2020). Living through and living on? Participatory humanitarian architecture in the Jarahieh Refugee Settlement, Lebanon. *Migration and Society, 3*, 213–221.

Coronil, F. (1995). Introduction to the Duke University Press Edition: *Transculturation and the Politics of Theory: Countering the Center, Cuban Counterpoint*. In *Cuban Counterpoint: Tobacco and Sugar*, by Fernando Ortiz, translated by Harriet de Onís (pp. ix–lvi). Duke University Press ed. Durham, NC: Duke University Press.

Crush, J., & Chikanda, A. (2018). South-South migration and diasporas. In E. Fiddian-Qasmiyeh & P. Daley (Eds.), *The Routledge handbook of South-South relations* (pp. 380–396). Routledge.

Dastile, N., & Ndlovu-Gatsheni, S. J. (2013). Power, knowledge and being: Decolonial combative discourse as a survival kit for Pan-Africanists in the 21st century. *Alternation, 20*(10), 105–134.

Düvell, F., & Vollmer, B. (2009). *Irregular migration in and from the neighbourhood of the EU: A comparison of Morocco*. Centre on Migration, Policy and Society (COMPAS), University of Oxford, September.

Escobar, A. (1995). *Encountering development: The making and unmaking of the third word*. Princeton University Press.

Farah, R. (2020). Expat, local and refugee: "Studying up" the global division of labor and mobility in the humanitarian industry in Jordan. *Migration and Society, 3*, 130–144.

Fiddian-Qasmiyeh, E. (2014). Gender and forced migration. In E. Fiddian-Qasmiyeh, G. Loescher, K. Long, & N. Signona (Eds.), *The Oxford handbook of refugee and forced migration studies*. OUP.

Fiddian-Qasmiyeh, E. (2015). *South-South educational migration, humanitarianism and development: Views from the Caribbean, North Africa and the Middle East*. Routledge.

Fiddian-Qasmiyeh, E. (2016a). Embracing transculturalism and footnoting Islam in accounts of Arab migration to Cuba. *Interventions: International Journal of Postcolonial Studies, 18*(1), 19–42.

Fiddian-Qasmiyeh, E. (2016b). On the threshold of statelessness: Palestinian narratives of loss and erasure. *Journal of Ethnic and Racial Studies, 39*(2), 301–321.

Fiddian-Qasmiyeh, E. (2018). Southern-led responses to displacement: Modes of South-South cooperation? In E. Fiddian-Qasmiyeh & P. Daley (Eds.), *The handbook of South-South relations* (pp. 239–255). Routledge.

Fiddian-Qasmiyeh, E. (2019a). Disasters studies: Looking forward. *Disasters, 43*(S1), S36–S60.

Fiddian-Qasmiyeh, E. (2019b). 'Exploring refugees' conceptualisations of southern-led humanitarianism. *Southern Responses to Displacement*. Retrieved October 28, 2022, from https://southernresponses.org/2019/04/08/exploring-refugees-conceptualisations-of-southern-led-humanitarianism/

Fiddian-Qasmiyeh, E., & Daley, P. (2018). Conceptualising the Global South and South-South encounters. In E. Fiddian-Qasmiyeh & P. Daley (Eds.), *The handbook of South-South relations* (pp. 1–28). Routledge.

Garb, T. (2019). Verbatim proceedings of the roundtable conversation: Writing displacements into literature. *Refugee hosts 2019 conference on politics and poetics of local responses to displacement*. https://refugeehosts.org/roundtable-stories-of-overlapping-displacement-understanding-local-experiences-and-responses/

Gardner, K., & Osella, F. (2003). Migration, modernity and social transformation in South Asia: An overview. *Contributions to Indian Sociology, 37*(1–2), v–xxviii.

Geddes, A. (2005). Migration research and European integration: The construction and institutionalization of problems of Europe. In M. Bommes & E. Morawska (Eds.), *International migration research: Constructions, omissions and the promises of interdisciplinarity* (pp. 265–280). Ashgate.

Grosfoguel, R. (2011). Decolonizing post-colonial studies and paradigms of political economy: Transmodernity, decolonial thinking, and global coloniality. *Transmodernity: Journal of Peripheral Cultural Production of the Luco-Hispanic World, 1*(1). Retrieved from https://escholarship.org/uc/item/21k6t3fq

Grosfoguel, R., Maldonado-Torres, N., & Saldívar, J. D. (2016). Latin@s and the 'Euro-American Menace': The decolonization of the U.S. empire in the twenty-first century. In R. Grosfoguel, N. Maldonado-Torres, & J. D. Saldívar (Eds.), *Latino/as in the world system: Decolonization struggles in the 21st century U.S. empire* (pp. 3–30). Routledge.

Grosfoguel, R., Oso, L., & Christou, A. (2015). 'Racism', intersectionality and migration studies: Framing some theoretical reflections. *Identities, 22*(6), 635–652.

Grovogui, S. (2011). A revolution nonetheless: The Global South in international relations. *The Global South*, special issue, *The Global South and World Dis/Order*, 5(1), 175–190.

Hester, S. L., & Squires, C. R. (2018). Who are we working for? Recentering black feminism. *Communication and Critical/cultural Studies*, 15(4), 343–348.

Hooks, B. (1984). *Feminist theory: From margin to center*. South End Press.

Hooks, B. (1989). *Talking back: Thinking feminist—Thinking black*. Sheba Feminist Publishers.

Horner, R. (2019). Towards a new paradigm of global development? Beyond the limits of international development. *Progress in Human Geography*. https://doi.org/10.1177/0309132519836158

Hountondji, P. J. (1992) [1983]. Recapturing. In V. Y. Mudimbe (Ed.), *The surreptitious speech. Presence Africaine and the politics of otherness, 1947–1987* (pp. 238–248). University of Chicago Press.

Içduygu, A., & Yükseker, D. (2012). Rethinking transit migration in Turkey: Reality and re-presentation in the creation of a migratory phenomenon. *Population, Space and Place*, 18(4), 441–456.

de Heredia, I. M., & Wai, Z. (Eds.). (2018). *Recentering Africa in international relations*. Palgrave Macmillan.

IOM (International Organization for Migration). (2013). Migration and development within the South: New evidence from African, Caribbean and Pacific Countries. *IOM Migration Research Series 46*. https://unofficeny.iom.int/sites/default/files/mrspercent2046percent20migrationpercent20andpercent20developmentpercent20withinpercent20thepercent20south.pdf

Jarratt, S. C. (1998). Beside ourselves: Rhetoric and representation in postcolonial feminist writing. *A Journal of Composition Theory*, 18(1), 57–75.

Jazeel, T. (2019). Singularity: A manifesto for incomparable geographies. *Singapore Journal of Tropical Geography*, 40(1), 5–21.

Jubilut, L. L. (2020). The role of universities in the protection of refugees and other migrants: A view from Brazil and Latin America. *Migration and Society*, 3, 238–246.

Keating, A. (Ed.). (2009). *The Gloria Anzaldúa Reader*. Duke University Press.

Koh, S. Y. (2020). Noncitizens' rights: Moving beyond migrants' rights. *Migration and Society*, 3, 233–237.

Kothari, U. (Ed.). (2005). *A radical history of development studies: Individuals, institutions and ideologies*. Zed Books.

Lunsford, A. (1998). Towards a mestiza rhetoric: Gloria Anzaldúa on composition and postcoloniality. *A Journal of Composition Theory*, 18(1), 1–27.

Lunsford, A. (2004). Towards a mestiza rhetoric: Gloria Anzaldúa on composition and postcoloniality. In A. Lunsford & L. Ouzgane (Eds.), *Crossing borderlands: Composition and postcolonial studies* (pp. 33–66). Pittsburgh University Press.

Madlingozi, T. (2018). Decolonising 'decolonisation' with Mphahlele. *New Frame*, November 15, 2019. Retrieved from https://www.newframe.com/decolonising-decolonisation-mphahlele/

Mbembe, A. (2015). Decolonizing knowledge and the question of the archive. https://wiser.wits.ac.za/system/files/Achille%20Mbembe%20-%20Decolonizing%20Knowledge%20and%20the%20Question%20of%20the%20Archive.pdf

Mbembe, A. (2016). Decolonizing the university: New directions. *Arts & Humanities in Higher Education, 15*(1), 29–45.

Medie, P., & Kang, A. (2018). Power, knowledge and the politics of gender in the Global South. *European Journal of Politics and Gender, 1*(1–2), 37–54.

Mignolo, W. D. (2009). Epistemic disobedience, independent thought and decolonial freedom. *Theory, Culture and Society, 26*(7–8), 1–23.

Mignolo, W. D. (2011). Epistemic disobedience and the decolonial option: A manifesto. *Transmodernity*, Fall, 43–66.

Migration and Society. (n.d.). Migration and society style guide. https://journals.berghahnbooks.com/_uploads/air-ms/migration-and-society_style_guide.pdf

Minh-ha, T. T. (1989). *Woman, native, other: Writing postcoloniality and feminism.* Indiana University Press.

Missbach, A., & Hoffstaedter, G. (2020). When transit states pursue their own Agenda: Malaysian and Indonesian responses to Australia's migration and border policies. *Migration and Society, 3*, 64–79.

Missbach, A., & Phillips, M. (2020). Introduction: Reconceptualizing transit states in an era of outsourcing, offshoring, and obfuscation. *Migration and Society, 3*, 19–33.

Mohanty, C. (1988). Under western eyes: Feminist scholarship and colonial discourses. *Feminist Review, 30*, 61–88.

Morreti, S. (2020). Transit migration in Niger: Stemming the flows of migrants, but at what cost? *Migration and Society, 3*, 80–88.

Nasser-Eddin, N., & Abu-Assab, N. (2020). Decolonial approaches to refugee migration: Nof Nasser-Eddin and Nour Abu-Assab in conversation. *Migration and Society, 3*, 190–202.

Natter, K. (2018). Rethinking immigration policy theory beyond 'western liberal democracies.' *Comparative Migration Studies, 6*(4), 1–21.

Nawyn, S. J. (2016a). Migration in the Global South: Exploring new theoretical territory. *International Journal of Sociology, 46*(2), 81–84.

Nawyn, S. (2016b). New directions for research on migration in the Global South. *International Journal of Sociology, 46*(3), 163–168.

Ndlovu-Gatsheni, S. J. (2018a). Against bringing Africa 'back-in.' In M. Iñiguez de Heredia & Z. Wai (Eds.), *Recentering Africa in international relations* (pp. 283–305). Palgrave Macmillan.

Ndlovu-Gatsheni, S. J. (2018b). Decolonising borders, decriminalising migration and rethinking citizenship. In H. H. Magidimisha, N. E. Khalema, L. Chipungu, T. Chirimambowa, & T. L. Chimedza (Eds.), *Crisis, identity and migration in post-colonial Southern Africa* (pp. 23–37). *Advances in African economic, social and political development*. Springer.

Ndlovu-Gatsheni, S. J. (2013). *Empire, global coloniality and African subjectivity*. Berghahn Books.

Ndlovu-Gatsheni, S. J., & Tafira, K. (2018). The invention of the Global South and the politics of South-South solidarity. In E. Fiddian-Qasmiyeh & P. Daley (Eds.), *The Routledge handbook of South-South relations* (pp. 127–140). Routledge.

Ngugi wa Thiong'o. (2009). *Re-membering Africa*. East African Educational Publishers Ltd.

Ngugi wa Thiong'o. (1986). *Writing against neo-colonialism*. Vita Books.

Pailey, R. N. (2019). De-Centering the 'white gaze' of development. *Development and Change*. https://onlinelibrary.wiley.com/doi/full/10.1111/dech.12550

Patel, S. (2018). Sociology through the 'South' prism. In E. Fiddian-Qasmiyeh & P. Daley (Eds.), *The handbook of South-South relations* (pp. 31–47). Routledge.

Peel, J., & Lin, J. (2019). Transnational climate litigation: The contribution of the Global South. *American Journal of International Law, 13*(4), 679–726.

Phillips, M. (2020). Managing a multiplicity of interests: The case of irregular migration from Libya. *Migration and Society, 3*, 89–97.

Piguet, E., Kaenzig, R., & Guélat, J. (2018). The Uneven geography of research on 'environmental migration.' *Population and Environment, 39*(4), 357–383.

Pisarevskaya, A., Levy, N., Scholten, P., & Jansen, J. (2019). Mapping migration studies: An empirical analysis of the coming age of a research field. *Migration Studies*. https://doi.org/10.1093/migration/mnz031

Qasmiyeh, Y. M. (2014). Thresholds. *Critical Quarterly, 56*(4), 67–70.

Qasmiyeh, Y. M. (2019). To embroider the voice with its own thread. *Berghahn Books blog*, January. https://berghahnbooks.com/blog/to-embroider-the-voice-with-its-own-needle

Qasmiyeh, Y. M. (2020). Engendering plural tales. *Migration and Society, 3*, 254–255.

Qasmiyeh, Y. M. (2021). *Writing the camp*. Broken Sleep Books.

Quijano, A. (1991). Colonialidad y Modernidad/racionalidad. *Perú Indígena, 13*(29), 11–21.

Quijano, A. (2007). Coloniality and modernity/rationality. *Cultural Studies, 21*(2–3), 168–178.

Richter, Chris. (2018). Promoting good migration governance through South-South cooperation. *Inter Press Service News*, 12 September. http://www.ipsnews.net/2018/09/promoting-good-migration-governance-south-south-cooperation/

Said, E. W. (1978). *Orientalism*. Pantheon Books.

Said, E. W. (1983). *The world, the text, and the critic*. Vintage.

Saleh, T. (1969). *Season of migration to the North*. Trans. Denys Johnson-Davies. Oxford University Press.

Santos, B. (2014). *Epistemologies of the South: Justice against epistemicide*. Paradigm Publishers.

Schinkel, W. (2018). Against 'immigrant integration': For an end to neocolonial knowledge production. *Comparative Migration Studies, 6*(31), 1–17.

Scholten, P. (2018). Research-policy relations and migration studies. In R. Zapata-Barrero & E. Yalaz (Eds.), *Qualitative research in European migration studies* (pp. 287–302). Springer.

Selz, J. (1991). Benjamin in Ibiza. In G. Smith (Ed.), *On Walter Benjamin* (pp. 353–366). MIT Press.

Sheppard, E., & Nagar, R. (2004). From East-West to North-South. *Antipode, 36*(4), 557–563. https://doi.org/10.1111/j.1467-8330.2004.00433.x

Sidaway, J. (2012). Geographies of development: New maps, new visions? *Professional Geographer, 64*(1), 49–62.

Smith, L. T. (1999). *Decolonizing methodologies: Research and indigenous peoples*. Zed Books.

Smith, K. (2013). International relations in South Africa: A case of 'Add Africa and Stir'? *Politikon, 40*(3), 533–544.

Spivak, G. C. (1988). Can the subaltern speak? In C. Nelson & L. Grossberg (Eds.), *Marxism and the interpretation of culture* (pp. 271–313). University of Illinois Press.

Tlostanova, M. (2008). How can the decolonial project become the ground for the decolonial humanities? A few reflections from the "vanished" second world. https://globalstudies.trinity.duke.edu/sites/globalstudies.trinity.duke.edu/files/file-attachments/reflections_Tlostanova_how_can%20_the_decolonial_project.pdf

Tlostanova, M., & Mignolo, W. (2009). Global coloniality and the decolonial option. *Kult 6*, special issue, *Epistemologies of transformation: The Latin American decolonial option and its ramifications.* http://www.postkolonial.dk/artikler/kult_6/MIGNOLO-TLOSTANOVA.pdf

Turner, S., Pham, T.-T.-H., & Hạnh, N. T. (2020). The territorialization of Vietnam's northern upland frontier: Migrant motivations and misgivings from world war II until today. *Migration and Society, 3*, 162–179.

Vanyoro, K. P. (2019). Decolonising migration research and potential pitfalls: Reflections from South Africa. *Pambazuka News*, 17 May. https://www.pambazuka.org/education/decolonising-migration-research-and-potential-pitfalls-reflections-south-africa

Vera Espinoza, M. (2020). Lessons from refugees: Research ethics in the context of resettlement in South America. *Migration and Society, 3*, 247–253.

Vogt, W. (2020). Dirty Work, dangerous others: The politics of outsourced immigration enforcement in Mexico. *Migration and Society, 3*, 50–63.

Wurtz, H., & Wilkinson, O. (2020). Local faith actors and the global compact on refugees. *Migration and Society, 3*, 145–161.

Open Access This chapter is licensed under the terms of the Creative Commons Attribution 4.0 International License (http://creativecommons.org/licenses/by/4.0/), which permits use, sharing, adaptation, distribution and reproduction in any medium or format, as long as you give appropriate credit to the original author(s) and the source, provide a link to the Creative Commons license and indicate if changes were made.

The images or other third party material in this chapter are included in the chapter's Creative Commons license, unless indicated otherwise in a credit line to the material. If material is not included in the chapter's Creative Commons license and your intended use is not permitted by statutory regulation or exceeds the permitted use, you will need to obtain permission directly from the copyright holder.

4

Writing the Refugee Camp: A Southern–Southern Correspondence

Yousif M. Qasmiyeh and Elena Fiddian-Qasmiyeh

I

Classically, the act of writing, *kitāba*, as the Arabic language contends, is premised on thinking through processes that are normally within the remit of *the far,* and for *this far* to be bridged, constant grasping is necessitated so the written would one day replace the discerning eyes as a witness. In this sense, writing is ultimately witnessing, not in order to monopolise the seen (and the scene) but rather to archive afresh what was and will be. *Writing the Camp* is then archiving by writing the refugee, myself and others, as both the observer and the observed, the guest and the host, the researcher and the researched in equal measure. The correspondence inherent in writing, the writing for and about, crosses many times of significance but also sustains its own time, that of writing in the aftermath and in anticipation at the same time.

Y. M. Qasmiyeh (✉)
University of Oxford, Oxford, UK
e-mail: Yousif.qasmiyeh@ell.ox.ac.uk

E. Fiddian-Qasmiyeh
Department of Geography, University College London, London, UK
e-mail: e.fiddian-qasmiyeh@ucl.ac.uk

II

This writing from the South reaffirms the refugee as a time-*maker* and not just a time-*seeker* in search of other times. In making time, time is sought, pondered and reassembled and not just found. For time to be made, it should be hunted down in sites where refugees are not mere wait-*ers*. The refugee camp is one of those sites where times are constantly remembered, conserved and, if necessary, resuscitated at later times. Thus the refugee is never a passive wait-*er*, or a self-proclaimed accepter of temporal indistinctness. Far from it, the refugee in writing as well as in thinking retains the initiative to exist despite existence and survive from the position of the writer with or without language. The illiterate mother is also a writer, a re-teller of her own voice, always suspicious of aid and aiding for the sake of just survival. To eat is not to consume. It is above all to dictate and calibrate the pace of the interior to match the texture of the exterior.

III

In *Writing the Camp*, 'refugees ask other refugees: who are we to come to you and who are you to come to us?'. This active engagement between refugees reaffirms what could be called *a solidarity beyond time* where suffering is not the denominator at all but instead it is humanity that has become suspicious of its humanness for spitting certain people out. To ask is to assume and in turn trigger an answer. But since it is the refugee who asks and the one who is expected to answer, both the question and the answer become embedded in their own body so much so that the coming echo, in this case from the camp's corners, is also that of those who were and will be there at one time.

IV

Since this writing is an acknowledgement *from* one South (*al-janūb*) *of* another, as complex sites and times, in this instance, embodied in this refugee-refugee correspondence, it percolates borders and on its route it gathers the will-be-written. While difference revives, the different creates *this* difference and in doing so belongs and becomes *in* difference.

V

Yes, they are seen but they can also see. Let us remember: The refugee eye is both water and narration.

The following poems were originally written and published as part of the Refugee Hosts research project, and subsequently in Yousif M. Qasmiyeh's collection, *Writing the Camp* (Broken Sleep Books, 2021).

Writing the Camp

Yousif M. Qasmiyeh

What makes a camp a camp? And what is the beginning of a camp if there is any? And do camps exist in order to die or exist forever?

Baddawi is my home camp, a small camp compared to other Palestinian camps in Lebanon. For many residents, it comprises two subcamps: the lower and the upper camps that converge at the old cemetery. As I was growing up, it was common for children to know their midwife. Ours, perhaps one of only two in the entire camp, was an elderly woman, who died tragically when a wall collapsed on top of her fragile body during a stormy day in the camp. The midwife was the woman who cut our umbilical cords and washed us for the first time. She lived by the main mosque—*Masjid al-Quds*—that overlooked the cemetery. She would always wait by the cemetery to stop those whom she delivered on the way to school, to give them a kiss and remind them that she was the one who made them.

The camp is never the same albeit with roughly the same area. New faces, new dialects, narrower alleys, newly constructed and ever-expanding thresholds and doorsteps, intertwined clothing lines and electrical cables, well-shielded balconies, little oxygen and impenetrable silences are all amassed in this space. The shibboleth has never been clearer and more poignant than it is now.

Refugees ask other refugees, who are we to come to you and who are you to come to us? Nobody answers. Palestinians, Syrians, Iraqis and Kurds share the camp, the same-different camp, the camp of a camp. They have all come to re-originate the beginning with their own hands and feet.

Now, in the camp, there are more mosques, more houses of God, while people continue to come and go, like the calls to prayer emanating at slightly varied times from all these mosques, supplementing, interrupting, transmuting, and augmenting the voice and the noise simultaneously.

Baddawi is a camp that lives and dies in our sight. It is destined to remain, not necessarily as itself, so long as time continues to be killed in its corners.

Refugees Are Dialectical Beings

Yousif M. Qasmiyeh

Only refugees can forever write the archive.
The camp owns the archive, not God.
For the archive not to fall apart, it weds the camp unceremoniously.

The question of a camp archive is also the question of the camp's survival beyond speech.
Circumcising the body can indicate the survival of the place.
Blessed are the pending places that are called camps.

My father, who passed his stick on to me, lied to us all:
I slaughtered your brother so you would grow sane and sound.
My mother, always with the same knife, cuts herself and the vegetables.
The eyes which live long are the ones whose sight is contingent upon the unseen.

God's past is the road to the camp's archive.
We strangle it, from its loose ends, so we can breathe its air.
Without its death, the archive will never exist.
In whose name is the camp a place?

It is the truth and nothing else that for the camp to survive it must kill itself. The transience of the face in a place where faces are bare signs of flesh can gather the intransience of the trace therein in its multiple and untraced forms. The unseen—that is the field that is there despite the eye—can only be seen by the hand. After all, the hand and not the eye, is the intimate part.

Green in the camp only belongs to the cemetery.
The veiled women crying at the grave are my mother and my sisters. Once, my mother wanted to bring the grave home with her.
In the solemnity of the place, faces fall like depleted birds.
In belonging to the camp, senses premeditate their senses.
The aridity of a camp presupposes the aridity of life.

The concrete is barely permanence. If you pay attention you will see the cracks in their souls.
At the farthest point in life—the point of no return—dialects become the superfluous of the body.
Camp (n): a residue in the shape of a crescent made of skin and nothing.

Time, when killed, has no mourners, only killers.
The camp has its own signature.
What it signs and countersigns is never the permanent.
The camp is what remains when the meadows of the instant desert us.
The foot without a trace is a god.
Those who are arriving at the threshold are not one of us. It will take them time to know who they are.
Nothing is as old as the archive that is yet to be written.

The archive is always written in the future. (After Derrida)
Were I in possession of an archive, I would bury it by my side and let it overgrow, upon my skin and inside my pores.
The enmity in the archive is the enmity of the intimate. By detailing the body, the archive loses its sight.
I am absent or deemed absent. The fingers that I am holding before you, in your hand—a sullen hand—are mine and nothing else.
I wish it were possible to write the camp without the self.
In the camp, we surrender the meaning of the camp in advance.
The camp is the impossible martyr attributed to the meaning of 'dying for'.
In the camp, going to the cemetery is going to the camp and going to the camp is going to the cemetery.
In Baddawi, reaching the camp only occurs through the cemetery.
Is the cemetery not another home, host and God?
In entering the camp, time becomes suspended between dialects.
The dialect that survives is never a dialect.
The dialectical subtleties in the camp are also called silence.

For the dialect to become an archive, no utterance should be uttered.
Who is the creator of dialects? Whose tongue is the shibboleth?
The dialect is a spear of noises.
Ontologically, the dialect is a being in the shape of a knife.
Only dialects can spot the silent Other.

My cousins in Nahr Al-Bared camp have always defended their dialect to the extent of preserving it in their fists.
I used to be asked to raise my voice whenever I opened my mouth. As if voices were ethereal creatures with an ability to rise.

Voices are the earthliest of creatures. Not only do they wreak havoc on earth, they remain silent in death.
What is it that makes a dialect a knife?
Is the dialect not a mythology of the silent?
To exist in the singular means the death of the Other.
'Dialects' is not a plural; it is the anomaly of a condition that should have never been one.
A ladder to God is the green in the cemetery.

In the camp, deserting the camp means summoning the certainty of the certainty. To this day, nobody has ever managed not to return.
Only in the camp do dialects outlive their people.
The untranslatability of the camp… We write it on parchments of time evermore, so it remains intact as a spectre when it is no more.

The dialect that survives on its own is that of the dead.
Dialects when uttered become spectres of time.
For us to hear ourselves we sign the covenant of the dialect.
A dialect always has a face—disfigured, a face nonetheless.
Where is the mouth in the testimony?

Those who come to us are never themselves in the same way we are never ourselves. When dialects descend upon the camp, the camp wails and ululates at the same time. In the presence of dialects, nobody knows what to do but to listen to the penetrating noise of the coming.
Is the dialect not the unavowable Other?
Refugees are dialectical beings.

Anthropologists

Yousif M. Qasmiyeh

I know some of them.
Some of them are friends but the majority are enemies.
Upon the doorstep you observe what they observe with a lot of care.
You look at them the way they look at you, curiously and obliquely.
You suddenly develop a fear of imitating them whilst they imitate you.
You worry about relapsing into one of your minds while sharing mundane details with them.
Sometimes I dream of devouring all of them, and just once with no witnesses or written testimonies.

All of us wanted to greet her.

Even my illiterate mother who never spoke a word of English said: Welcome! After spending hours with us, in the same room, she left with a jar of homemade pickles and three full cassettes with our voices.

Open Access This chapter is licensed under the terms of the Creative Commons Attribution 4.0 International License (http://creativecommons.org/licenses/by/4.0/), which permits use, sharing, adaptation, distribution and reproduction in any medium or format, as long as you give appropriate credit to the original author(s) and the source, provide a link to the Creative Commons license and indicate if changes were made.

The images or other third party material in this chapter are included in the chapter's Creative Commons license, unless indicated otherwise in a credit line to the material. If material is not included in the chapter's Creative Commons license and your intended use is not permitted by statutory regulation or exceeds the permitted use, you will need to obtain permission directly from the copyright holder.

5

Migration Research, Coloniality and Epistemic Injustice

Karl Landström and Heaven Crawley

Introduction

In this chapter, we draw on a combination of feminist social epistemology and decolonial theory to take stock of ongoing critical debates among migration scholars regarding the ethics and social epistemology of their knowledge producing practices. While most migration scholars engaging in these debates do not draw on the concepts of epistemic injustice and epistemic oppression, we argue that applying these concepts takes us beyond a description of the need to decentre migration research, towards a critique of the ways in which migration research itself contributes to epistemic injustice and oppression. Understanding the processes through which this happens, rather than just

---

K. Landström (✉)
Responsible and Sustainable Business Lab, Nottingham Business School, Nottingham Trent University, Nottingham, UK
e-mail: karl.landstrom@ntu.ac.uk

H. Crawley
United Nations University Centre for Policy Research (UNU-CPR), New York, NY, USA
e-mail: crawley@unu.edu

K. Landström
African Centre for Epistemology and Philosophy of Science, University of Johannesburg, Johannesburg, South Africa

the epistemic outcomes, can help us to identify ways to address the structural inequalities with which the production of migration knowledge is often associated.

We argue, for example, that the debates about the eurocentrism of contemporary academic migration scholarship can be fruitfully thought of as matters of epistemic oppression (see Dotson, 2012, 2014). These debates are, at their core, about systematic undue exclusions of certain perspectives, viewpoints and communities from the epistemic communities and the epistemic endeavours of migration researchers. These exclusions produce deficiencies in the shared epistemic resources among these scholars, and the practitioners and policymakers they inform. We use the debate regarding eurocentrism as one of several examples to illustrate how contemporary critiques of academic migration scholarship can be deepened by being viewed through the lens of epistemic marginalisation. This lens makes it possible to clearly analyse and spell out what is at stake, both ethically and epistemically, in these debates. Moreover, the conceptual framework of epistemic injustice not only provides the analytic tools for a deeper critique, but also enables the identification of forward-looking proposals which can be developed by migration scholars to address the socio-epistemic injustices in their field. We illustrate this potential by applying the conceptual apparatus developed around epistemic injustice to three different approaches that migration scholars have presented as potential correctives to the eurocentrism of their field.

The chapter is structured as follows. We start by outlining recent critiques of academic migration research by migration scholars themselves. In the section that follows, we argue that many of these critiques can be deepened through the application of an epistemic injustice lens, which helps us to understand how epistemic injustice and oppression take place. We then draw on the critique of eurocentrism in migration research to assess three different approaches developed by migration scholars. We argue that while two of these approaches have significant limitations in helping us to understand, and address, epistemic injustices, the third approach seems to be more promising. The chapter ends with a concluding section in which the arguments are summarised and the normative implications spelt out.

The State of Academic Migration Research

Like many other research areas across the humanities and the social sciences, topics such as eurocentrism, decolonisation and decentring have been the subject of increasing interest within the field of migration studies (Fiddian-Qasmiyeh, 2020; Mayblin & Turner, 2020). It is widely acknowledged, for example, that the study of migration has been dominated by scholarship produced in the Global North (Fiddian-Qasmiyeh, 2020, this volume; Gardner & Osella, 2003; Piguet et al., 2018; Pisarevskaya et al., 2020) and that the theoretical frameworks, methodological approaches and underlying assumptions of migration studies are primarily based on European traditions (Mayblin & Turner, 2020).

Reflecting this, it has been argued that migration research interests and priorities often align with the political and policy priorities of the Global North (Crawley & Skleparis, 2018; Scholten, 2018). A common theme among many of these critiques is their examination of the core premises for knowledge production on migration within the academy (Amelina, 2022; Nieswand & Drotbohm, 2014), and the development of alternative strategies for doing so (Raghuram, 2021). Such alternative strategies and approaches have been developed as part of calls for the denaturalisation (Amelina & Faist, 2012), demigranticisation (Dahinden, 2016) and decolonisation (Mayblin & Turner, 2020) of the production of knowledge on migration. It has also been suggested that migration research suffers from a "representation challenge", prompting calls for critical examination of the role of scientists and research in "othering" discourses both within and outside of the academy (Amelina, 2022). According to Amelina (2022), this "representation challenge" consists of three intertwined components.

Firstly, migration knowledge production reproduces a "figure of the migrant" (Nail, 2015) which reflects dominant political discourses and, in particular, discourses centred on the nation states of the Global North (Amelina, 2022). This has led some migration scholars to question the categories adopted in discourses on migration both within and outside of academic research (Bakewell, 2008; Collyer & de Haas, 2012; Koser & Martin, 2011; Zetter, 2007). Migration scholars have long questioned the possibility of clearly and easily distinguishing between different types of migrants and called for a move beyond simplistic dichotomies such as between "migrants" and "refugees" (Crawley & Skleparis, 2018). Similarly, scholars have problematised and questioned how "forced" migration is distinguished from "voluntary" migration (Betts, 2013; Long, 2013; Zetter, 2007). It has been argued that such distinctions are overly simplistic and do not reflect how migration processes actually work (Collyer & de Haas, 2012; Koser & Martin, 2011). Others have emphasised the complexity of migration processes and argued that migration scholarship needs to move beyond transnational studies (Faist et al., 2013; Levitt & Schiller, 2004) in ways that explicitly address global power asymmetries, including those whose origins can be traced back to colonisation (Amelina, 2022). The important point here is that where the boundaries are drawn between categories determines what content is subsumed under these categories, and thus has the epistemic effect of shaping understandings of migration processes and outcomes (Crawley & Skleparis, 2018). This has concomitant ethical ramifications due to how these categories are operationalised in migration governance, and in particular, in distinguishing different groups of migrants from one other.

A core concern in these debates is that politically determined categories and concepts are transformed into the analytical categories adopted in migration research practice. Such categories are drawn into research practice through a range of means, including the requirements of research funding (Amelina, 2022) and as part of the researchers' aspirations for policy relevance (Bakewell, 2008). As one of the authors has argued previously, in adopting dominant policy categories for scholarly analysis, migration scholars allow those categories to shape academic knowledge production on the topic of migration, and in so doing import the politics that underlie the creation and upholding of these categories (Crawley & Skleparis, 2018). Moreover, drawing on these dominant categories as the basis for analysis comes at a cost both epistemically and ethically, as it sets undue limitations on the understanding of the complexities of migration processes, and potentially makes the scholar complicit in political processes in which migrants have had their rights undermined and continuously been stigmatised and vilified. Thus, the categories adopted for the purposes of migration research are of both epistemic and ethical significance, as dominant policy categories fail to properly capture the complex relationships necessary to understand the complexities of migration processes, while at the same time reinforcing and upholding unjust and harmful migration governance regimes and discourses. The separation of "migration studies" from "refugee studies" and "forced migration studies" provides a further illustration of the ways in which categorical separation shapes the organisation of migration research (Hathaway, 2007; Hayden, 2006; Scholten et al., 2022).

The second component of Amelina's (2022) challenge is closely related to the first, and centres on the idea that the knowledge produced in academic migration research, particularly that produced in the Global North, adopts the viewpoints of the institutions governing migration in the countries of the Global North, and particularly of Global North nation states (Grosfoguel et al., 2015). Arguments that studies of migration closely relate and parallel the interests of states and powerful actors in the Global North are commonplace in migration studies. Bakewell (2008), for example, has argued that the emphasis on the need for academic research to be policy relevant has encouraged migration researchers to adopt the categories, concepts and priorities of policymakers and practitioners as the initial frame of reference when identifying areas of study and formulating research questions. In doing so, the worldview of policymakers and practitioners is privileged in the development of new research areas and projects, which has the epistemic effect of constraining the research questions pursued, the areas and topics studied, the methodologies adopted, and the analysis conducted. This, Bakewell (2008) argues, has led to certain groups of migrants being rendered invisible in both research and policy. Bakewell (2008) calls for migration scholars to break away from the emphasis on policy relevance, and instead challenge core assumptions that shape migration research and policymaking.

Similar arguments are made by Schinkel (2018), who argues that the categories, questions and modes of analysis of social science cannot be separated from those of the state, and that much research into immigrant integration in Western Europe comes out of particular entanglements between academic social scientists and state institutions (Schinkel, 2018). These connections have also been highlighted by Pisarevskaya et al. (2020), who trace the predominance of particular research themes and questions within the field. The authors argue that "classical questions", such as research into the challenges of integration of migrants in Europe and North America, and questions pertaining to how to manage and govern migration within and to Europe and North America, are examples of how the dominant themes of the field privilege and adopt the categories, concepts and priorities of dominant actors and institutions in the Global North. Fiddian-Qasmiyeh (2020) similarly argues that migration research has predominately consisted of studies of migration from the Global South to the Global North, despite the fact that most internal and cross-border migration takes place in the Global South. Adding further weight to these concerns is Amelina's (2022) observation that even scholars who seek to challenge these dominant narratives run the risk of equating categories of political practice with those of scientific analysis, and thus unintentionally reproduce those same narratives.

The third component of the "representation challenge", and one which is rejected by both decolonial theorists and feminist epistemologists, is that of zero-point epistemology, in other words, universalist conceptions of knowledge centred around disembodied, dislocated "neutral" subjects (Mitova,

2020). Feminist epistemologists such as Alcoff and Potter (2013), post- and decolonial scholars (Grosfoguel, 2013; Spivak, 1988) among many others, reject the notion that the knower's social and geohistorical situatedness is epistemically irrelevant, arguing that one's situatedness has epistemic implications, and that a core part of a person's situatedness as a knower is his or her positionality. The knower's positionality has implications for how the knower fares in the "power games" which determine who is credited with knowledge and who is not (Mitova, 2020). Further, an individual's positionality can have implications for the focus of his or her intellectual pursuits and interests (Mitova, 2020). Decolonial theorists such as Grosfoguel (2013) and Mignolo (2009) similarly reject zero-point epistemology, emphasising instead the epistemological importance of an individual's geohistorical situatedness.

Recent critiques, such as that of De Genova et al. (2021) challenge research in the field of migration that claims to be "neutral". As a corrective, they propose migration research underpinned by feminist epistemology that reflects both differing collective standpoints, and individual positionalities. Grosfoguel et al. (2015) have argued that migration studies reproduce Global North-centric social science views of the world. They are particularly critical of migration scholarship that purports to be universal, and that attaches itself to traditional scientific values such as neutrality and objectivity, arguing that these are a myth, particularly in the social sciences. Instead, they emphasise how everyone speaks from differing locations of gender, class, race, and sex in the hierarchies of the world. To these categories they add the notion of coloniality, arguing that colonial legacies shape not only migration but also scholarship on migration. Grosfoguel (2003), following Quijano (2000), argues that knowledge production, including migration (Grosfoguel et al., 2015), is divided by the "coloniality of power" into colonising and colonised epistemic positions, and thus not detached from colonial domination. They argue that research in migration studies has generally spoken from a non-neutral location within the colonial divide and has largely reproduced colonial epistemologies.

The final two components of the representation problem tie existing critiques of migration scholarship to feminist epistemology, and to decolonial theory. While the links between colonialism and migration run deep (see Fynn Bruey and Crawley, this volume), migration research has often obscured these connections through a focus on the present and an emphasis on individualistic and economic explanations (Collins, 2022; Mayblin & Turner, 2020). Collins (2022) argues that the occlusion of colonialism in migration studies has not only supported oppressive border and migration regimes, but also ignored the epistemic coloniality of migration studies. He further argues that addressing the complicity in the production of colonial knowledges in migration studies requires that critical attention be paid to relations of power, race, class, gender and sexuality in the exercising of mobility, as well as critical reflection on development and migration discourses as governance techniques. As Bhambra (2017) suggests, this epistemic coloniality, and particularly the limited attention paid to the colonial histories of migration patterns and governance, has shaped migration studies and provided the basis for narrow and parochial understandings of migration and responsibilities towards migrants. At the same time, migration researchers have arguably been complicit in advancing current forms of migration management through the production of knowledge of positions some, predominantly non-white, migrants as being in need of governing (Schinkel, 2019). To this extent, migration research can be seen as part in the perpetuation of epistemic injustice.

Migration Research, Epistemic Injustice and Epistemic Oppression

The idea that knowing, producing new knowledge and sharing knowledge are all social activities is widely acknowledged, and has been forcefully argued for by standpoint-theorists (Harding, 2009; Hartsock, 1983; Hill Collins, 1990), social epistemologists (Craig, 1990; Goldman, 1999) and philosophers of science (Kitcher, 1990; Koskinen & Rolin, 2019) among others. The recognition that epistemic life is social, that epistemic systems are built from and by social processes, and that certain individuals and groups may be excluded to varying degrees within this sociality and from these processes (Dotson, 2012, 2014), is a core notion in the theorisation of epistemic injustice and epistemic oppression. Theorists of epistemic injustice argue that some such exclusions not only cause epistemic harms—such as a loss of knowledge or infringements on epistemic agency—but also constitute moral wrongs (Fricker, 2007), thus, tying ethical considerations to epistemological concerns. Epistemic injustice is understood broadly as any unjust epistemic relation which disadvantages someone in their capacity as knower (Fricker, 2007). Epistemic injustice can take a range of forms (Pohlhaus, 2017), including within the sphere of academic research and its governance (Grasswick, 2017).

Closely related to the concept of epistemic injustice are the concepts of epistemic oppression, epistemic exclusion and epistemic agency. Epistemic oppression refers to epistemic exclusions afforded to certain positions and communities that in turn produce deficiencies in social knowledge and within shared epistemic and hermeneutical resources leading, in turn, to deficiencies in social knowledge and shared epistemic resources (Dotson, 2012). Epistemic exclusions are infringements on the epistemic agency of knowers that reduce their ability to participate in a given epistemic community (Dotson, 2012). Finally, epistemic agency refers to the ability to utilise persuasively shared epistemic resources within a given epistemic community, in order for the knower to participate in knowledge production and, if required, the revision of those same resources. Each of these concepts picks out dimensions of how social factors and relations of power shape epistemic lives and epistemic practices.

Many of the critiques of migration research outlined in the previous section explicitly pertain to socio-epistemological practices of undue exclusion and marginalisation, while at the same highlighting the ethical consequences of those same processes. However, despite the socio-epistemic focus of these critiques, the topic of epistemic injustice and oppression in migration research remains underexplored. Rather than examining the practices involved in their own research, scholars working on migration and epistemic injustice have instead focused on the epistemic injustices that migrants face in a range of different settings such as migration governance procedures (Hänel, 2021; Sertler, 2018; Wikström, 2014), health-care (Peled, 2018), in support programmes (Steen-Johnsen & Skreeland, 2023) and in education (Wee et al., 2023). The conceptual apparatus developed around the notions of epistemic injustice and epistemic oppression is yet to be used to explore and theorise issues in migration research processes themselves. This sets the field apart from other closely related disciplines such as development studies (Cummings et al., 2023; Koch, 2020)[1] and poverty research (Dübgen, 2020) where the conceptual apparatus developed around these two concepts has been successfully leveraged to theorise both extant ethical and epistemic issues and concrete paths to improvement.

The studies of epistemic injustice and oppression in these closely related fields offer a starting point for thinking about the intersection of existing critiques of academic migration research and matters of epistemic (in)justice. In this section, we draw on examples of critiques of migration scholarship from migration scholars that can fruitfully thought of as matters of epistemic injustice and oppression, even if those concepts are not being employed by

---

[1] The Journal of Human Development and Capabilities dedicated a whole special issue in 2022 to the issue of epistemic (in)justice called "An Epistemological Break: Redefining participatory research in capabilitarian", which was guest edited by Melanie Walker, Alejandra Boni, Carmen Martinez-Vargas and Melis Cin. See: https://www.tandfonline.com/toc/cjhd20/23/1.

the critics themselves. In so doing, we aim not only to ground these critiques on a solid normative foundation, but also deepen the analysis in a way that helps us to identify exactly what is at stake, both ethically and epistemically.

Eurocentrism in Migration Studies

Epistemic oppression can take many different forms. As noted above, a core expression of epistemic oppression is the systematic marginalisation and exclusion of particular groups of knowers, as well as certain sets of epistemic resources (Dotson, 2012, 2014). Eurocentric academic fields are characterised by such undue exclusions, and in the case of the migration studies, these undue exclusions are reflected in the emphasis placed on the epistemic resources, and priorities of dominantly situated actors and institutions in the Global North.

Many contemporary critiques of migration studies, including several of those discussed above, can easily be translated into the language of epistemic injustice and oppression. The eurocentrism of migration studies is widely acknowledged (Fiddian-Qasmiyeh, 2020, also this volume), and many of the existing critiques of migration studies explicitly target the eurocentrism of the area. It has been argued that eurocentrism, for example, constitutes both a form of epistemic oppression (Posholi, 2020), and an epistemology of ignorance (Alcoff, 2017). Research that challenges the "classical" questions, topics and themes that migration studies typically privileges and adopts, including the categories, concepts and priorities of dominant actors in the Global North, are clearly critiques of eurocentrism.

The eurocentrism of migration studies manifests itself in a number of ways, including through the existence of knowledge gaps in areas that have historically not been prioritised, such as migration between the countries of the Global South, as contrasted with migration from the Global South to the countries of the Global North (Fiddian-Qasmiyeh, 2020, this volume). Knowledge gaps that are the product of the eurocentrism of academic migration research can be thought of as a distributive form of epistemic injustice, as they are cases in which epistemically valuable goods, such as information and research findings, are unfairly distributed. Further, undue epistemic marginalisations are reflected in the dominant epistemic and conceptual frameworks that are shared within particular epistemic communities. When the shared epistemic resources in an epistemic community become unserviceable or unsuited for making sense of or conveying the experiences of marginalised individuals and groups, those groups are unfairly disadvantaged both in terms of making sense of their experiences, and also in terms of participating in the epistemic community at large (Dotson, 2012). Such gaps, or flaws in the shared epistemic resources have been identified by critical migration scholars. Such critics have argued that many of the core concepts in the field are far from universally applicable (Fiddian-Qasmiyeh, 2020, this volume) and lose their relevancy as one moves beyond the context of Western Europe and North America (Adamson & Tsourapas, 2020; Natter, 2018).

Epistemic Exploitation

The critique of eurocentrism is not the only critique that can be made sense of, or expanded upon, by drawing on the concepts of epistemic injustice and oppression. For example, a growing body of literature critiques the use and treatment of research and fieldwork assistants, particularly in the Global South, illustrating the ways in which such practices are often exploitative (Sukarieh & Tannock, 2019; Turner, 2010). Local research assistants are often subcontracted in international research collaborations to fulfil a range of important tasks in the research process. These core tasks commonly include planning field work, background literature reviews, data collection, translation, and transcriptions among other activities. In the critiques of the treatment of research and fieldwork assistants, a core argument is that while fieldwork and research assistants are doing significant epistemic labour, they are commonly rendered invisible and effectively silenced when it comes communicating the results of the research despite playing core epistemic roles in the research process (Jenkins, 2018; Molony & Hammett, 2007; Turner, 2010). Their work is often not appropriately recognised, nor are these individuals given appropriate credit for their epistemic labour (Sukarieh & Tannock, 2019). This is not only an issue in migration research, but rather spans a wide range of academic disciplines and has been argued to be a product of the increasing internationalisation of academic research (Sukarieh & Tannock, 2019).

The inadequate acknowledgement of research and fieldwork assistants can be understood as a form of epistemic exploitation (Berenstain, 2016). Epistemic exploitation, as theorised in feminist social epistemology, occurs when members of certain groups are required to systematically carry out epistemic labour to produce and transmit knowledge for the purposes and interests of the members of a dominantly situated group. The working relationships between research leads and research assistants critiqued by Sukarieh and Tannock (2019) and Turner (2010), for example, can be thought of as examples of epistemic exploitation. Epistemic exploitation is unjust in a number of ways. It is unjust in distributive terms, as credit for epistemic labour is unfairly allocated to the exploiter, rather than the "silenced" research assistant. It is also unjust in the sense that certain individuals are treated as mere means to serve the interests of others, rather than being treated as equals. Grasswick (2017), as well as Koskinen and Rolin (2019), identify the treatment of differently situated participants in epistemic endeavours such as research collaborations as a domain in which epistemic injustices are commonly perpetuated. This includes the treatment of other academics, but also other stakeholders such as research participants, non-academic research collaborators and members of the communities in which the research is being conducted, reflecting the structural forces the shape these collaborations.

Wilful Hermeneutical Ignorance

While some of the critiques discussed in the previous section map almost perfectly onto existing concepts from the epistemic injustice and epistemic oppression literature, others do not. Nonetheless, these critiques share important similarities with core concepts found in feminist social epistemology and/or decolonial theory which makes it possible to draw on those concepts for further analysis. One such instance is Crawley and Skleparis' (2018) critique of the adoption of policy categories outlined above, and which the authors argue, are based on simplistic binaries and linear understandings of migration processes and experiences which are epistemically flawed and ethically dubious. The epistemic and ethical thrust at the heart of Crawley and Skleparis' (2018) criticism shares important similarities with the notion of wilful hermeneutical ignorance. Using her conception of wilful hermeneutical ignorance, Pohlhaus (2012) picks out instances in which epistemic agents actively choose to utilise epistemic resources that are flawed or structurally prejudiced, despite alternative sets of hermeneutical resources that could be utilised being readily available to them. This seems to be the case in the instances of policy categories being adopted migration research criticised by Crawley and Skleparis (2018). These categories or sets of epistemic resources are flawed, particularly in terms of being unable to appropriately account for the complexity of the lived experiences of migrants. These flaws are acknowledged in the wider literature (see Bakewell, 2011; Collyer & de Haas, 2012; Gupte & Mehta, 2007; Koser & Martin, 2011; Scherschel, 2011; Zetter, 2007). Nonetheless, these sets of epistemic resources continue to be adopted in academic research, with concomitant negative epistemic effects.

Wilful hermeneutical ignorance is a form of epistemic injustice that includes both an agential and a structural dimension. For example, the concept of wilful hermeneutical ignorance is helpful in analysing the issues criticised by Crawley and Skleparis (2018), as it allows for the identification of both structural and agential wrongs. There are structural reasons why various sets of epistemic resources become dominant, but the epistemic agent also plays an active role in choosing to adopt these epistemic resources despite the abundant evidence of their flaws. Using the concept of wilful hermeneutical ignorance developed by Pohlhaus (2012) to think about such cases, draws attention to the structural factors which lead to the use of epistemically flawed resources, despite the existence of more epistemically sound alternatives. Further, as Crawley and Skleparis (2018) emphasise, this is not simply a question of semantics: categories such as "refugee" and "migrant" have consequences for people's lives, entitling some protection and rights while simultaneously denying others the same rights and protection.

These examples illustrate how at least some of the socio-epistemological critiques that migration scholars levy against their own field can be understood and analysed using the normative framework of epistemic injustice. In response to the existing inequities and epistemic oppression of contemporary poverty research, Dübgen (2020) calls for a redistribution of the outcomes of academic research, as well as sweeping changes to the dominant modes of knowledge production in the discipline. She argues that this would entail fundamentally rearranging the ways in which research is designed, conducted and implemented, as well as reconsidering the epistemic norms that govern and authenticate the knowledge producing endeavours of poverty researchers. Most importantly, she calls for an end to undue, and structural marginalisation of epistemic agents involved in academic knowledge production on poverty.

Addressing the Eurocentrism of Migration Research

In this section we turn our attention to the ways in which some of the issues identified in this chapter might be addressed. We have chosen to focus on how the eurocentrism of migration scholarship might be addressed, given that it has been identified as a significant issue in migration studies with concomitant epistemic and ethical consequences. Fiddian-Qasmiyeh (2020, this volume) outlines three ways in which migration researchers have tried to redress the eurocentrism of their field: firstly, by examining the applicability of classical concepts and frameworks in the Global South; secondly, by addressing the "gaps" in previous research by studying migration in the Global South and South–South migration; and finally, by engaging critically with the geopolitics of knowledge production. These approaches are often employed simultaneously.

Scholars adopting the first approach acknowledge that most concepts are not universal. These approaches commonly draw on research in countries outside of the Global North to explore and interrogate concepts and policies originally developed based on the perspectives of the Global North. An example of scholarship that engages in such examination is that of Natter (2018) who challenges the theoretical usefulness of essentialist, dichotomous categories such as Western/non-Western or democratic/autocratic, calling for a more nuanced theorising of migration policymaking that goes beyond simplistic dichotomies and instead centres structures, functions and practices. Other examples include scholars who offer critiques of the concepts of "transit migration" and transit states (Missbach & Hoffstaedter, 2020; Velasco, 2020), or concepts such as innovation and self-sufficiency (Wurtz & Wilkinson, 2020).

This first approach shares important similarities with what has been theorised as the negative programme of epistemic decolonisation, which entails eliminating undue and unreflective Western influences on knowledge supplies and production (Mitova, 2020). A core part of the negative programme consists of critically questioning the basic assumptions, theories, methodologies, categories and aims of eurocentric scholarship in order to expose undue colonial influences on existing sets of epistemic resources and knowledge production processes (Nyamnjoh, 2019). Such critical interrogation is an important part of creating a more just research environment. However, as Mitova (2020) forcefully argues, a "negative programme" on its own is not enough to advance knowledge, nor to correct the flaws of the existing sets of epistemic resources. For the existing epistemic resources to be improved, the negative programme needs to be accompanied by a positive programme that adds to or changes the existing epistemic resources in fruitful ways. Thus, there is good reason to be sceptical of the efficacy of approaches that only include a "negative programme" to appropriately address the issue of eurocentrism in migration research.

In contrast, the second approach is one that includes a "positive" programme, which attempts to "fill" the "gaps" in migration research and policy resulting from the eurocentrism of the field. This, proponents argue, is achieved by promoting and funding studies into topics and areas that have been previously understudied. One example of this is recent research into the topic of South–South migration (Crush & Chikanda, 2018; Nawyn, 2016a, 2016b), which was long neglected in comparison to the study of migration from the Global South to the Global North (Fiddian-Qasmiyeh, 2020, this volume). It is also reflected in the work of the Migration for Development and Equality (MIDEQ) Hub.[2] Fiddian-Qasmiyeh and Daley (2018) argue that filling existing knowledge gaps can function as a corrective to the historical imbalance in migration research and Global North discourses about migration, giving the approach its justification. However, they caution that the interest that policymakers and politicians in Europe and North America have shown in South–South migration raises concern that northern actors might instrumentalise and co-opt southern dynamics and people to achieve the aims of Global North states and institutions (Fiddian-Qasmiyeh & Daley, 2018).

Further, the enactment of this approach is not without its own pitfalls. As Fiddian-Qasmiyeh (2020) argues, just filling gaps is not enough for this approach to be appropriately corrective. Rather, attention must be paid to questions such as: who is producing new knowledge, when and where are they doing so, how are they doing so and why? Further, important socio-epistemic questions pertaining to whom and what knowledge is allowed to be part of these processes, and on what terms, are equally important. This clearly parallels the emphasis on the epistemic importance of positionality and geohistorical situatedness in the writings of both feminist and decolonial scholars. The normative principle at the heart of many "positive" decolonial programmes, namely, to proactively draw on marginalised sets of epistemic resources to advance knowledge across various domains, would serve well as guidance for these approaches to be able to serve the corrective function they aspire to. Adhering to this principle would ensure that the attempts to fill these "gaps" are not also based on the same eurocentric epistemologies that these approaches are aspiring to address. Additionally, these first two approaches would do well to complement each other as part of an encompassing approach consisting of both a critical dimension, and a gap filling dimension. However, such an approach would have to be appropriately reflective of socio-epistemic matters to avoid the pitfalls discussed in this section, as well as to avoid reproducing the eurocentrism of migration studies.

The third approach of engaging critically with the geopolitics of knowledge production appears the most promising, as it combines both a "negative"

---

[2] The Migration for Development and Equality (MIDEQ) Hub unpacks the complex and multi-dimensional relationships between migration and inequality in the context of the Global South. MIDEQ aims to transform the understanding of the relationship between migration, inequality, and development by decentring the production of knowledge about migration and its consequences away from the Global North towards the Global South. MIDEQ mobilises resources for partners in the Global South to define their own research questions and generate their own knowledge, producing robust, comparative, widely accessible evidence on South–South migration, inequality, and development; and engaging national and regional partners on key policy issues. More at www.mideq.org

programme and a "positive" programme. Proponents of this approach argue that addressing eurocentrism requires critical engagement with the geopolitics of knowledge production on migration, and decentring the production of knowledge away from centres of power in the Global North (Achiume, 2019; Grosfoguel et al., 2015; Pailey, 2020). Mitova (2020) has argued that epistemic decentring consists of a "negative" and a "positive" dimension. On this account, the "negative" dimension of re-centring consists of rejecting zero-point epistemology, and instead taking seriously the role of positionality, and geohistorical and social situatedness in epistemic endeavours, while the second dimension consists of correcting distorted relationships of power, and particularly those that stem from social and racial hierarchisation and restoring epistemic authority and freedom to marginalised knowers, thus facilitating a more epistemically just production and exchange of knowledge on migration.

The call to decentre knowledge production has gained increasing uptake in the scholarship on migration (Pastore, 2022; Triandafyllidou, 2022; Zardo & Wolff, 2022), with a growing number of migration scholars calling for post- and decolonial approaches as alternatives to more traditional approaches (Collins, 2022; Vanyoro, 2019, this volume). Collins (2022) argues that approaches inspired by post- and decolonial scholarship make possible critical migration scholarship that could unravel the epistemic coloniality that shapes both migration scholarship and migration governance. In order to do so, Collins (2022) emphasises the importance of both challenging undue epistemic exclusions and engaging with marginalised knowers and their knowledge. As Vanyoro (2019) argue, doing so would entail reshaping not only the processes of producing new knowledge, but also how knowledge is circulated and reproduced both in research and education. Others have called for scholars in migration studies to take seriously and incorporate the critical decolonial epistemologies of migrants and the marginalised into their knowledge production, while also cautioning against essentialist thinking and the "naïve, populist celebration" of the knowledge of oppressed groups (Grosfoguel et al., 2015).

This approach is the most promising of the three approaches discussed in this section. It includes a substantial "negative programme" of interrogating and challenging the geopolitics of migration scholarship, while at the same time emphasising an epistemically inclusive, albeit critical programme for reshaping migration scholarship. But even this approach is not without its limitations. It is important remember that many of the issues that are the subject of critique within migration studies stem from structural sources. This means that efforts to address them may well lie beyond the remit of the members of a single discipline or research area. As Anderson (2012) emphasises, structural problems need structural solutions, and eurocentrism cannot be addressed without structural change.

Conclusion

In this chapter we have taken stock of existing critiques of contemporary migration research and brought these debates into contact with ongoing debates among decolonial scholars and in feminist social epistemology. We have illustrated how some ethical and epistemic concerns voiced by migration scholars in regard to the socio-epistemic functioning of their field can be understood using the conceptual apparatus that has been developed around the notions of epistemic injustice and oppression. In so doing, we hope to have illustrated the relevance and usefulness of both feminist social epistemology and of decolonial theory for theorising the socio-epistemic challenges that migration scholars face. The conceptual framework of epistemic injustice and oppression not only offers clarity in what is at stake within migration studies both ethically and epistemically, but also elucidates moral and epistemic reasons for why these issues should be addressed. This framework both calls attention to issues of undue epistemic marginalisation, and centres these issues as a core concern as migration scholars critically reflect upon the knowledge production, and dissemination practices of their field.

So how can these concerns be addressed? The work of the MIDEQ Hub shows that the applicability of classical concepts and frameworks in the Global South needs to be addressed not just by migration scholars in the Global North but by scholars originating from, and working in, the Global South who have deep familiarity with the political, social and linguistic contexts within which migration takes places. Research on migration in the Global South and on South–South migration should not just be about "gap filling", but rather should be fundamentally concerned with the ways in which new epistemic resources are created and the conditions under which epistemic resources are shared. Epistemic justice is about allowing or enabling marginalised researchers to think about and analyse their experiences in ways that value and appropriately recognise those experiences, and particularly so when these clash with the perspectives of the dominantly situated and hegemonic discourses. Anything else would simply represent a continuation of undue epistemic marginalisation.

Acknowledgements This work has been undertaken as part of the Migration for Development and Equality (MIDEQ) Hub. Funded by the UKRI Global Challenges Research Fund (GCRF) (Grant Reference: ES/S007415/1), MIDEQ unpacks the complex and multi-dimensional relationships between migration and inequality in the context of the Global South. More at www.mideq.org.

References

Achiume, E. T. (2019). Migration as decolonization. *Stanford Law Review, 71*, 1509–1574.

Adamson, F. B., & Tsourapas, G. (2020). The migration state in the Global South: Nationalizing, developmental, and neoliberal models of migration management. *International Migration Review, 54*(3), 853–882. https://doi.org/10.1177/0197918319879057

Alcoff, L., & Potter, E. (2013). *Feminist epistemologies*. Routledge.

Alcoff, L. M. (2017). Philosophy and philosophical practice: Eurocentrism as an epistemology of ignorance. In I. J. Kidd, J. Medina, & G. Pohlhaus (Eds.), *The Routledge handbook of epistemic injustice* (pp. 397–408). Routledge.

Amelina, A. (2022). Knowledge production for whom? Doing migrations, colonialities and standpoints in non-hegemonic migration research. *Ethnic and Racial Studies, 45*(13), 2393–2415.

Amelina, A., & Faist, T. (2012). De-naturalizing the national in research methodologies: Key concepts of transnational studies in migration. *Ethnic and Racial Studies, 35*(10), 1707–1724.

Anderson, E. (2012). Epistemic justice as a virtue of social institutions. *Social Epistemology, 26*(2), 163–173.

Bakewell, O. (2008). Research beyond the categories: The importance of policy irrelevant research into forced migration. *Journal of Refugee Studies, 21*(4), 432–453.

Bakewell, O. (2011). Conceptualising displacement and migration: Processes, conditions and categories. In K. Koser & S. Martin (Eds.), *The migration-displacement nexus: Patterns, processes and policies* (pp. 14–28). Berghahn Books.

Berenstain, N. (2016). Epistemic exploitation. *Ergo: An Open Access Journal of Philosophy, 3*.

Betts, A. (2013). *Survival migration: Failed governance and the crisis of displacement*. Cornell University Press.

Bhambra, G. K. (2017). The current crisis of Europe: Refugees, colonialism, and the limits of cosmopolitanism. *European Law Journal, 23*(5), 395–405.

Collins F. L. (2022). Geographies of migration II: Decolonising migration studies. *Progress in Human Geography*.

Collyer, M., & de Haas, H. (2012). Developing dynamic categorisations of transit migration. *Population, Space and Place, 18*(4), 468–481.

Craig, E. (1990). *Knowledge and the state of nature: An essay in conceptual synthesis.* Clarendon Press.

Crawley, H., & Skleparis, D. (2018). Refugees, migrants, neither, both: Categorical fetishism and the politics of bounding in Europe's "migration crisis." *Journal of Ethnic and Migration Studies, 44*(1), 48–64.

Crush, J., & Chikanda, A. (2018). South-South migration and diasporas. In E. Fiddian-Qasmiyeh & P. Daley (Eds.), *The Routledge handbook of South-South relations* (pp. 380–396). Routledge.

Cummings, S., Dhewa, C., Kemboi, G., & Young, S. (2023). Doing epistemic justice in sustainable development: Applying the philosophical concept of epistemic injustice to the real world. *Sustainable Development.*

Dahinden, J. (2016). A plea for the "de-migranticization" of research on migration and integration. *Ethnic and Racial Studies, 39*(13), 2207–2225.

De Genova, N., Tazzioli, M., et al. (2021). Minor keywords of political theory: Migration as a critical standpoint. *Environment and Planning c: Politics and Space, 40*(4), 781–875.

Dotson, K. (2012). A cautionary tale: On limiting epistemic oppression. *Frontiers: A Journal of Women Studies, 33*, 24–47.

Dotson, K. (2014). Conceptualizing epistemic oppression. *Social Epistemology, 28*(2), 115–138.

Dübgen, F. (2020). Scientific ghettos and beyond. Epistemic injustice in academia and its effects on researching poverty. In V. Beck, H. Hahn, & R. Lepenies (Eds.), *Dimensions of poverty: Measurement* (pp. 77–95). Springer International Publishing.

Faist, T., Fauser, M., & Reisenauer, E. (2013). *Transnational migration.* Polity Press.

Fiddian-Qasmiyeh, E. (2020). Introduction. *Migration and Society, 3*(1), 1–18.

Fiddian-Qasmiyeh, E., & Daley, P. (2018). Conceptualising the Global South and South-South encounters. In E. Fiddian-Qasmiyeh & P. Daley (Eds.), *The handbook of South-South relations* (pp. 1–28). Routledge.

Fricker, M. (2007). *Epistemic injustice.* Oxford University Press.

Gardner, K., & Osella, F. (2003) Migration, modernity and social transformation in South Asia: An overview. *Contributions to Indian sociology, 37*(1–2), v–xxviii.

Goldman, A. (1999). *Knowledge in a social world.* Oxford University Press.

Grasswick, H. (2017). Epistemic injustice in science. In I. J. In Kidd, J. Medina, & G. Pohlhaus (Eds.), *The Routledge handbook of epistemic injustice* (pp. 313–323). Routledge.

Grosfoguel, R. (2003). *Colonial subjects: Puerto Rico in a global perspective.* University of California Press.

Grosfoguel, R. (2013). The structure of knowledge in Westernized universities: Epistemic racism/sexism and the four genocides/epistemicides of the long 16th century. *Human Architecture: Journal of the Sociology of Self-Knowledge, 11*(1), 73–90.

Grosfoguel, R., Oso, L., & Christou, A. (2015). "Racism", intersectionality and migration studies: Framing some theoretical reflections. *Identities, 22*(6), 635–652.

Gupte, J., & Mehta, L. (2007). Disjunctures in labelling refugees and oustees. In J. Moncrieffe & R. Eyben (Eds.), *The power of labelling: How people are categorised and why it matters* (pp. 64–79). Earthscan.

Hänel, H. C. (2021). Epistemic injustice and recognition theory: What we owe to refugees. *Migration, Recognition and Critical Theory,* 257–282.

Harding, S. G. (2009). Standpoint theories: Productively controversial. *Hypatia: A Journal of Feminist Philosophy, 24*(4), 192–200.

Hartsock, N. (1983). The feminist standpoint: Developing the ground for a specifically feminist historical materialism. In S. Harding & M. Hintikka (Eds.), *Discovering reality: Feminist perspectives on epistemology, metaphysics, methodology, and the philosophy of science* (pp. 283–310). D. Reidel.

Hathaway, J. (2007). Forced migration studies: Could we agree just to 'date'? *Journal of Refugee Studies, 20*(3), 349–369. https://doi.org/10.1093/jrs/fem019

Hayden, B. (2006). What's in a name? The nature of the individual in refugee studies. *Journal of Refugee Studies, 19*(4), 471–487. https://doi.org/10.1093/refuge/fel021

Hill Collins, P. (1990). *Black feminist thought: Knowledge, consciousness, and the politics of empowerment*. Routledge.

Jenkins, S. (2018). Assistants, guides, collaborators, friends: The concealed figures of conflict research. *Journal of Contemporary Ethnography, 47*(2), 143–170.

Kitcher, P. (1990). The division of cognitive labor. *Journal of Philosophy, 87*(1), 5.

Koch, S. (2020). "The local consultant will not be credible": How epistemic injustice is experienced and practised in development aid. *Social Epistemology, 34*(5), 478–489.

Koser, K., & Martin, S. (2011). The migration-displacement nexus. In K. Koser & S. Martin (Eds.), *The migration-displacement nexus: Patterns, processes and policies* (pp. 1–13). Berghahn Books.

Koskinen, I., & Rolin, K. (2019). Scientific/intellectual movements remedying epistemic injustice: The case of indigenous studies. *Philosophy of Science, 86*(5), 1052–1063.

Levitt, P., & Schiller, N. G. (2004). Conceptualizing simultaneity: A transnational social field perspective on society. *The International Migration Review, 38*(3), 1002–1039.

Long, K. (2013). When refugees stopped being migrants: Movement, labour and humanitarian protection. *Migration Studies, 1*(1), 4–26.

Mayblin, L., & Turner, J. (2020). *Migration studies and colonialism*. John Wiley and Sons.

Mignolo, W. (2009). Epistemic disobedience, independent thought and decolonial freedom. *Theory, Culutre and Society, 26*(7–8), 159–181.

Missbach, A., & Hoffstaedter, G. (2020). When transit states pursue their own agenda: Malaysian and Indonesian responses to Australia's migration and border policies. *Migration and Society, 3*(1), 64–79.

Mitova, V. (2020). Decolonising knowledge here and now. *Philosophical Papers, 49*(2), 191–212.

Molony, T., & Hammett, D. (2007). The friendly financier: Talking money with the silenced assistant. *Human Organization, 66*(3), 292–300.

Nail, T. (2015). *The figure of the migrant*. Stanford University Press.

Natter, K. (2018). Rethinking immigration policy theory beyond "western liberal democracies." *Comparative Migration Studies, 6*(1), 1–21.

Nawyn, S. (2016a). Migration in the Global South: Exploring new theoretical territory. *International Journal of Sociology, 46*(2), 81–84.

Nawyn, S. (2016b). New directions for research on migration in the Global South. *International Journal of Sociology, 46*(3), 163–168.

Nieswand, B., & Drotbohm, H. (2014). Einleitung: Die reflexive Wende in der Migrationsforschung. In B. Nieswand & H. Drotbohm (Eds.), *Kultur, Gesellschaft, Migration: Die reflexive Wende in der Migrationsforschung* (pp. 1–37). Springer VS.

Nyamnjoh, F. B. (2019). Decolonizing the university in Africa. *Oxford Research Encyclopedia of Politics*. https://oxfordre.com/politics/display/10.1093/acrefore/9780190228637.001.0001/acrefore-9780190228637-e-717

Pailey, R. N. (2020). De-centring the "white gaze" of development. *Development and Change, 51*(3), 729–745.

Pastore, F. (2022). The problematic decentring of migration policy studies. *Territory, Politics, Governance, 11*(4), 770–775.

Peled, Y. (2018). Language barriers and epistemic injustice in healthcare settings. *Bioethics, 32*(6), 360–367.

Piguet, E., Kaenzig, R., & Guélat, J. (2018). The uneven geography of research on "environmental migration." *Population and Environment, 39*(4), 357–383.

Pisarevskaya, A., Levy, N., Scholten, P., & Jansen, J. (2020). Mapping migration studies: An empirical analysis of the coming of age of a research field. *Migration Studies, 8*(3), 455–481.

Pohlhaus, G. (2012). Relational knowing and epistemic injustice: Toward a theory of willful hermeneutical ignorance. *Hypatia, 27*(4), 715–735.

Pohlhaus, G. (2017). Varieties of epistemic injustice 1. In I. J. In Kidd, J. Medina, & G. Pohlhaus (Eds.), *The Routledge handbook of epistemic injustice* (pp. 13–26). Routledge.

Posholi, L. (2020). Epistemic decolonization as overcoming the hermeneutical injustice of Eurocentrism. *Philosophical Papers, 49*(2), 279–304.

Quijano, A. (2000). Coloniality of power and Eurocentrism in Latin America. *Nepantla, 1*(2), 533–580.

Raghuram, P. (2021). Democratizing, stretching, entangling, transversing: Four moves for reshaping migration categories. *Journal of Immigrant and Refugee Studies, 19*(1), 9–24.

Scherschel, K. (2011). Who is a refugee? Reflections on social classifications and individual consequences. *Migration Letters, 8*(1), 67–76.

Schinkel, W. (2018). Against "immigrant integration": For an end to neocolonial knowledge production. *Comparative Migration Studies, 6*(1), 1–17.

Schinkel, W. (2019). Migration studies: An imposition. *Comparative Migration Studies, 7*, 32.

Scholten, P. (2018). Research-policy relations and migration studies. In R. Zapata-Barrero & E. Yalaz (Eds.), *Qualitative research in European migration studies, IMISCOE research series* (pp. 287–302). Springer.

Scholten, P., Pisarevskaya, A., & Levy, N. (2022). An introduction to migration studies: The rise and coming of age of a research field. In P. Scholten (Eds.), *Introduction to migration studies*. IMISCOE research series. Springer. https://doi.org/10.1007/978-3-030-92377-8_1

Sertler, E. (2018). The institution of gender-based asylum and epistemic injustice: A structural limit. *Feminist Philosophy Quarterly, 4*(3).

Spivak, G. C. (1988). Can the subaltern speak? In C. Nelson & L. Grossberg (Eds.), *Marxism and interpretation of culture* (pp. 271–313). University of Illinois Press.

Steen-Johnsen, T., & Skreland, L. L. (2023). Epistemic injustice in a parenting support programme for refugees in Norway. *Families, Relationships and Societies*, 1–16.

Sukarieh, M., & Tannock, S. (2019). Subcontracting academia: Alienation, exploitation and disillusionment in the UK overseas Syrian refugee research industry. *Antipode, 51*(2), 664–680.

Triandafyllidou, A. (2022). Decentering the study of migration governance: A radical view. *Geopolitics, 27*(3), 811–825.

Turner, S. (2010). The silenced assistant: Reflections of invisible interpreters and research assistants. *Asia Pacific Viewpoint, 51*(2), 206–219.

Vanyoro, K. P. (2019). Decolonising migration research and potential pitfalls: Reflections from South Africa. *Pambazuka News*, 17 May. https://www.pambazuka.org/education/decolonising-migration-research-and-potential-pitfalls-reflections-south-africa

Velasco, S. Á. (2020). From Ecuador to elsewhere: The (re)configuration of a transit country. *Migration and Society, 3*(1), 34–49.

Wee, H. L., Karkkulainen, E. A., & Tateo, L. (2023). Experiences of epistemic injustice among minority language students aged 6–16 in the Nordics: A literature review. *Education Sciences, 13*(4), 367.

Wikström, H. (2014). Gender, culture and epistemic injustice. *Nordic Journal of Migration Research, 4*(4), 210.

Wurtz, H., & Wilkinson, O. (2020). Local faith actors and the global compact on refugees. *Migration and Society, 3*(1), 145–161.

Zardo, F., & Wolff, S. (2022). Decentering the study of migration governance in the Mediterranean. *Geopolitics, 27*(3), 687–702.

Zetter, R. (2007). More labels, fewer refugees: Remaking the refugee label in an era of globalization. *Journal of Refugee Studies, 20*(2), 172–192.

Open Access This chapter is licensed under the terms of the Creative Commons Attribution 4.0 International License (http://creativecommons.org/licenses/by/4.0/), which permits use, sharing, adaptation, distribution and reproduction in any medium or format, as long as you give appropriate credit to the original author(s) and the source, provide a link to the Creative Commons license and indicate if changes were made.

The images or other third party material in this chapter are included in the chapter's Creative Commons license, unless indicated otherwise in a credit line to the material. If material is not included in the chapter's Creative Commons license and your intended use is not permitted by statutory regulation or exceeds the permitted use, you will need to obtain permission directly from the copyright holder.

6

Rethinking Power and Reciprocity in the "Field"

Kudakwashe Vanyoro

Introduction

Calls for decolonisation are on the rise everywhere, including in migration studies (see Achiume, 2019; Fiddian-Qasmiyeh, 2020; Teye, 2021; Vanyoro, 2019; Vanyoro et al., 2019). Criticisms of "fieldwork" with migrants as a vulnerable group are part of an ongoing and broader discussion focused on migration studies' extractive character. This chapter explores how the distinction(s) implied by the term "fieldwork" gives rise to false and misleading dichotomies that are not so useful to any decolonial migration praxis that tries to undo the bureaucratic damage of hegemonic ideas about research ethics. It argues that the dichotomies of "home" and the "field" conjured by this term negate an intermediate space between these two extremes in which social relationships, kinship ties and social value define the possible extent of the risk of migration research to further marginalise or protect migrants. These opposing possibilities arise from the interaction of these social attributes to the extent that they mediate a definition of ethical responsibility that is meaningful in particular contexts. This lends, in turn, a novel meaning to power and reciprocity that necessitates a paradigm shift in the kinds of ethics procedures as well as considerations in partnerships on migration studies that presume that power relationships are evened out when the research is undertaken by

---

K. Vanyoro (✉)
Department of Anthropology, University of the Witwatersrand, Johannesburg, South Africa
e-mail: Kudakwashe.vanyoro@wits.ac.za

African researchers working in African academic institutions. This chapter reveals that even well-meaning articulations of what characterises an extractive or unethical relationship with participants are often ominous to local meanings of social relationships, kinship ties and social value in African contexts. Without the necessary critical attention, it concludes, there is a real risk that such norms go unquestioned and contribute to the ongoing bureaucratic damage of hegemonic ideas about ethics so widely accepted in African as in other academic institutions.

The first section of this chapter problematises the "field" as the site from which data is extracted. It is suggested that the conception of migrants in "fieldwork" gives rise to a problematic ethics that is focused on certain definitions of power and reciprocity that is important to include in discussions about decolonising migration studies. The chapter then broadly discusses the term "decolonisation" as a concept that scholars use to capture the ways in which power is appropriated and negotiated in migration studies—or avoided altogether. In the third section, the chapter moves on to describe the ways in which the intermediate space between "home" and the "field" is often overlooked in trying to counterbalance power relationships between researchers and migrants. This allows the chapter to begin discussing the implications of this tension on ethical responsibility and ultimately what an ethics of reciprocity could look like. The chapter here relies on representation and Ubuntu as two key concepts that could be used to inform this ethics. This part of the chapter shows that the increase in focus on decolonising migration studies as a function primarily of North–South power relations has contributed to the neglect of social value in African communities and has contributed to the continuation of uneven relationships between indigenous researchers and migrant research participants. It has also peddled the myth that decolonisation in migration studies can be achieved by balancing power relations between North and South academic institutions through, for example, investing more financial resources in those in Africa. In the fourth section, the chapter provides examples of ethical responsibilities that are shaped by the intermediate space based upon typical experiences of the local "indigenous" researcher. While these may be related to many issues, in this chapter, those identified include the value of revealing identities of non-state actors abusing power, for the "greater good" and looking to the welfare of community members. The chapter concludes by providing suggestions about ways forward and how to do things differently.

Problematising the "Field"

The concept of "fieldwork" in social science research is synonymous with distinction. It is a separation between two zones: one of writing and teaching in one's own university and another of collecting data somewhere else, a place perceived as aloof, remote, and far removed. Putatively, it is like a piece of land to be tilled. In this sense, the field is a place of cultivating well thought through ideas, theories and methods as well as new social relationships with research participants for the germination of new knowledge. This new knowledge is "doubly mediated" in the sense that it is "shaped by the ideas and preconceptions of both ethnographer and informants" (van Beek, 1991, 139). Tantamount to this distinction is the original idea of mystery, expedition and discovery of the "ethnoscape"; that those who are going to the field are removing themselves from their homes to enter new and unexplored lands where they will interact with marginal societies, cultures and human beings. Fieldwork here also implies a separation between two identities: that of the field worker and that of the "other", who is in this case the migrant.

Within North–South relationships, the enterprise of fieldwork often sets Africa up as a foil to Europe as expressed so vividly in Conrad's (2015) *Heart of Darkness*. As with the very study of Africa, this is a text that represents "a kind of original sin in view of the objective role it played in the history of colonisation" (Hountondji, 2009, 126). Like all sorts of paradigmatic oppositions, there is nothing unique or ahistorical about the notion of "fieldwork" and its internment to a "dichotomising system" (Mudimbe, 1988) such as the one expressed in the home/field nexus. Fieldwork as a construct conjures the influences of what Mudimbe (1988) has called a "colonising structure"; a carefully crafted machine meant to "save the other" by "harvesting" knowledge about the "other's" way of life.

In Mudimbe's (1988) writing, a colonising structure is characterised primarily by the following attributes: (1) domination of physical space; (2) reformation of the natives' minds; and (3) integration of local economic histories into the Western perspective. Hence, the first way the "harvest" of data through fieldwork contributes to colonial power relations is that leaving "home" to enter the "field" symbolises the first step towards dominating a physical space, which allows researchers to learn about the "native" enough to know what needs to be reformed about them to get to the point where gathered local histories can eventually be integrated into a Western epistemology. This ultimate "harvest" is then culpable in the production of a body of knowledge as a means of exploiting colonies. It has contributed to what Mudimbe (1988) understands as a technique for "implementing structural distortions" that could aid underdevelopment in the colonies by transfer of surpluses and ensuring that colonies do not have structural autonomy to sustain their economies. Walter Rodney gives plenty of credible evidence to show that colonialism primarily aimed at developing metropoles and only gave the colonies a few scraps as accidental byproducts of exploitation (see Rodney, 2018).

The second way the ultimate "harvest" from fieldwork has contributed to inequality is through the language of characterising the "field"; broadly understood as categories. These representations tend to be shaped by anthropological discourses and indices of beings and societies that superimpose what can be called African or "oriental" characteristics, particularly through contrasts between black and white. These comparisons tell a story that likely replicates silent but potent epistemic arrangements (Mudimbe, 1988). This confirms that each paradigm reflects an assumption of the world which in turn implicates the very systems that produce epistemological stances. Such representations have become institutionalised through disciplines like migration studies that categorise migrants and refugees as vulnerable and marginalised groups. This amounts to an epistemological ordering which takes place by looking at signs in terms of arrangement of identities and differences as they would appear in ordered tables.

Definitions of those deemed vulnerable often signify figures of "a shortcoming, an impending failure" (Cole, 2016, 264). For example, vulnerable persons are defined by the University of the Witwatersrand's Human Research Ethics Committee (Non-Medical) (2022, 2–3) as people with:

> a lack of capacity or impaired ability to provide voluntary informed consent; health status; social pressures that may impact on the ability to make a free and informed decision; an inability to protect one's interest in research. Vulnerability may be considered a dynamic and specific to a particular context, and may arise as a result of power asymmetries between participants and researchers/institutions. There may be layers of vulnerability that function and interact with a person's circumstances. Being vulnerable does not necessarily imply that harm or exploitation will occur, but it does increase the risk of harm or exploitation through research.

According to this document, migrants are considered vulnerable because they are dependent on the state to maintain a legal status as documented migrants, asylum seekers or documented refugees. They can also be characterised as "individuals at increased risks" because they could be criminalised by the state as undocumented migrants.

Decolonisation and Power in Migration Studies

The colonisation of Africa is where one always starts when beginning to think about the problem with social sciences in relation to power and reciprocity; and migration studies is rightly situated in this context. To look at migration studies outside the colonial context is to overlook significant developments that relate to the establishment of a Northern-centric social science view of the world that comes from interpreting the experience of "others" in the zone of being (Grosfoguel et al., 2015). This bias can be traced back to the very foundations of a field that originated in North America and Europe, to the extent that academic and policy studies of and responses to migration have been dominated by scholarship produced in the Northern Hemisphere (Fiddian-Qasmiyeh, 2020, also this volume). Forced migration studies have been implicated in contributing to the legitimisation of the containment of refugees from the Global South outside of the Global North in "the new global apartheid' (see Mayblin, 2017, 31–32).

The obvious hegemony of particular discursive frames of reference in the field of migration studies have necessitated a paradigm shift in thinking through epistemological and conceptual considerations. Therefore, migration studies is now increasingly interested in decolonial perspectives. Briefly defined, "decolonisation" is "the process which signifies the end of rule by a foreign power and the recuperation and/or formation of an 'independent' entity, usually a nation-state, through a process often referred to as a 'transfer of power'" (Gopal, 2021, 881). There are, however, more explicit and specific calls to decolonise migration studies that have called for approaches that decentre the Global North (see Achiume, 2019; Daley, 2021; Ndlovu-Gatsheni, 2018; Vanyoro, 2019). And there are others that call to recentre the Global South, while not explicitly framing their work as decolonial or positioning it within the colonial experience or other postcolonial frameworks. These scholars rely more on poststructuralist ethics and calls for shifting power asymmetries in research partnerships (see Jacobsen & Landau, 2003; Landau, 2019; McGrath & Young, 2019). This work is also subsumed in the "reflexive turn" as the field has taken seriously the politics and ethics of the knowledge-producing process involving vulnerable groups (see Amelina, 2021; Dahinden, 2016; Nail, 2015) This is done by using participatory methods, for example, to counter-act top-down methodological approaches that have dominated the field (see Oliveira & Vearey, 2015).

The central concern for everyone here appears to be with the question "where does power lie"? What we do not see much of in these reflexive debates is engagement with the layers of coloniality that emerge from the perspective of the "indigenous researchers" identity when doing what has come to be accepted as "fieldwork". There appears to be a liberal humanitarian preoccupation with an ethics that can level the power imbalances between white European researchers and Black African migrants in research. Yet, colonial-esque identity politics have been a crucible for relationships between indigenous researchers and research participants in the field of social science since colonial times and the beginning of fieldwork in Africa. Equally, this relationship cannot be separated from the power imbalances between white European researchers and Black African migrants in research because in certain instances it is what has necessitated the involvement of "indigenous researchers". I draw on Jean-Hervé Jezequel's (2010) work as an example here. The author finds that colonial scholarly research in Black Africa made use of local informants as the administrator-ethnographers, believing that Africans were useful in terms of the collection of raw data when faced with the need to collect data for compiling ethnographic and historical records. With time, African authors mastered their own art to write and undertake ethnography to advance interests related to their own academic careers. While they could have chosen other modes of self-expression like literary studies, they did not waste time in choosing ethnography. Some colonialists appreciated these talents acting as "protectors" to allow them to publish and carry out surveys, while others were bent on stifling them. Hence the marginalisation was more predominant, and they entered research in subordinate positions. Still, in these different positions, some Africans took positions that challenged white studies, while others reinforced them.

This suggests the need to be careful about reducing the idea of "coloniality" to North–South relations, or those between Africa and Europe, when thinking about power. Not everything that is imbued within the South–South context represents decolonial possibilities and relationships. Recentring South–South migration in research and debates is thus not panacea in and of itself. It is also not in participatory or any other revolutionary methods that there lies hope to find the true meaning of decolonisation. Instead, there is a need to look elsewhere for possibilities for decolonisation in other fundamental issues that are yet to be interrogated in migration studies, even if it is now increasingly interested in decolonial perspectives. It also suggests that it is important to turn our attention towards questioning the normativity of the kinds of ethics procedures as well as considerations in migration studies undertaken by African researchers working in African academic institutions.

Tensions Between Academic and Social Meanings of Ethical Reciprocity

Ethics is about protecting participants and researchers from risks and harm. Some ethics concepts include but are not limited to anonymity; confidentiality; risks; harm; vulnerability and reciprocity. Some academic institutions on the African continent that observe ethical approaches tend to be very procedural. In trying to counterbalance power relationships between researchers and migrants, this approach determines that there is a strict separation between "home" and the "field", which risks missing the grey areas that lie in between the two. Ethics review boards of such universities may draw a rigid line between these two components, requiring postgraduate students that are planning to do their non-medical fieldwork involving human participants to emphasise, among many things African scholars would have come to expect, that participants may not receive any direct benefit from participating in their study. In trying to realise this balancing act, they must find other ways to provide some kind of indirect benefits. For example, instead of paying people for participating in their research study, they could emphasise the value of their study's contribution to knowledge and/or improved policies. At best, participants may receive some travel costs to take part in the interview capped at a certain level, although this is likely to be different across the many African academic institutions of higher learning. What is consistent though is that the sphere of economic exchange is important in formulating ethical ways to try and not "contaminate" the integrity of the research process when engaging people with direct economic needs.

Few fundamental questions are asked about the historical and geographic contexts that have given rise to this solution. The economic sphere appears to be the primary descriptor of value, which defines and sets boundaries for the kinds of reciprocity researchers should be looking to determine or avoid at the end of their research. But what understandings of the meaning of value and reciprocity underpin such understandings of what could constitute a problematic transaction in social science research? Does the epistemology that gives rise to this understanding do justice to the lived experiences of African researchers? These questions can help in probing the fact that there remain penalties for African scholars who would appear to be looking out only for themselves by "flaunting" their privilege when they arrive at research sites in flashy hired cars and retiring to lush hotel rooms. It is clear that for people who are working on their own communities, this matters more because it places certain expectations about how they should act in these situations as ethical researchers who are socially responsible. Trust building starts from the place that one should not be insensitive to the circumstances of others as people who know what it is like. It would follow that a different kind of responsibility regime arises that ethics boards need to be fully aware of when they place economic integers to what can be reasonably exchanged during research.

Kalinga (2019, 270) observes that indigenous researchers have "an additional obligation to respect social customs and codes", which are not easily visible to foreign research partners and are responsible for receiving and interpreting these codes. Given the nature of the current ethics boards in place, the dilemma for African scholars is that choosing to reset the process, build trust and address the sources of such discontent is also tantamount to "career suicide" (see Kalinga, 2019 for a more detailed analysis). The "indigenous researcher" thus finds him or herself negotiating their place within a context where colonialism usurped social value, which stripped the social sphere of its moral value and in the process its potential to be a consideration in the balancing out of unequal power relationships. For example, in an African context, the term community is inclusive of all life (bios): animals, the habitat (the land), flora and even the elements. The success of life is found in the ability to maintain a healthy relationship with all (Setiloane, 1998, 79) and not only in economic terms. This broader conception of harmony as a communal outcome and of what value looks like has implications on how we define value in research, leading to conceptions of ethical responsibility that produce an ethics of reciprocity centred on the economic exchange of goods.

Framing an Ethics of Responsibility in African Society

Having discussed the meaning of responsibility from the perspective of ethical reciprocity, this chapter now turns to a discussion of some conceptual ways to frame an ethics of responsibility in Africa that is attentive to social value as a possible source of balancing out of unequal power relationships between researchers and participants in migration studies. First, this section discusses the importance of understanding the concept of representation as it tells us how responsibility differs according to researchers' positionality. Second, it presents Ubuntu as a key concept that could be used to inform an ethics of responsibility that respects social value in ways that are meaningful for migrant communities and researchers.

Who is Responsible for Representing What?

Representation answers to how responsibility differs according to researchers' positionality. African researchers, in particular, have the difficult responsibility of retaining quite real truths about African communities that have been rendered problematic by the colonial manipulation of the culture, socialisation institutions, beliefs, economies and ways of living without also turning these representations into fetishes that reinforce racist stereotypes about the continent. This suggests that it is not enough to expect African researchers to be the ones sensitive to the question of social value, as in fact their position is tenuous to the degree that it may produce outcomes that further unequal relationships with participants.

This tenuous position results from two issues of concern to a conversation about ethics. The first one is that there arises for African researchers tasked with doing research about Africans, a tension between positioning Africa's specific characteristics as a product of history, and the historical distortions informed by its fetishisation in "African studies". As Magubane (1971, 419) writes, colonialism imposed the urban order on the "conquered indigenous societies" of Zambia, Rhodesia, Kenya and South Africa; one involving "patterns of social organisation, economy, administration, religion and culture". Africans today are rightly frustrated by images of Africa as a backward place; "predominantly represented by nature—lush savannah with beautiful animals, stunning deserts and waterfalls" (Obbo, 2006, 155). African bodies are depicted as either "dancing or starving" (Obbo, 2006, 155), walking from huts and so forth, residing in Wainaina's (2005) "Safari", "Tribal", "Timeless" continent. Certainly, some of this imagery captures a certain albeit sad reality about Africa that speaks to its own rurality, attendant economies that are largely subsistent and problems of poverty created by colonialism. Even as urbanisation has become a dominant trope in media and scholarly representations of Africa, Obbo (2006) admits that in the five African cities she visited and took photos of multistorey buildings, it was equally difficult to avoid images of street children, beggars and hawkers. If this is the case by the admission of "Africanists" themselves, what is the ethical problem with popular Western representations of this kind? My argument here is that it is the emphasis on using this imagery as a template or setting for any text on human suffering, war or strife juxtaposed to the impending benevolence of the West to save African people that cajoles racist ideas that these problems are unique to Africa alone.

This spectacle compels some "Africanists" to try to present corrective representations that can place Africa in "modernity", with its tall buildings, trains, banks, and all you could think (Obbo, 2006). Africans are said to have also entered "modernity" by becoming "a 'middle class' imbued with 'Western' values" (Obbo, 2006, 156). Their dilemma is also that it is difficult to cherish this discourse or sing the praises of "modernity" without sounding like they are demonising African heritage, tradition, infrastructure and knowledge. Yet it has become a characteristic of postcolonial African political societies that there are dual forms of governance, traditional residing alongside governments; albeit the former is more symbolic. In this society, "African and 'Western' culture are bound together in the closest co-dependence and co-recognition" (Magubane, 1971, 423). So, to some extent, it may also be that Africanists criticised for overly celebrating modernity are not necessarily aspiring to a European way of life but rather only expressing "a desire to escape from the sad condition colonialism imposed on them" (Magubane, 1971, 421). In this sad escapism, the modernisation paradigm became a sphere for Africa's "big men" to flaunt their achievements, while still expecting to return home to servile wives (Obbo, 2006). There is a danger thus that celebrating African modernity can thus easily be met with a rejection of images of "peasants" to the degree that "detribalization" or Westernisation (the "success story" of colonial education) is overly romanticised and governance issues related to colonialism are glossed over. As Obbo (2006, 158) concludes, the results can be Africans who are "unable to face sitting on mats, entering smoke-filled kitchens or hoeing for hours in the sun".

The second issue that arises that is of concern to ethics when it comes to representation is that the assumption arises that by virtue of being "insiders" to a particular group "we" either can speak for "them", or "we" know everything there is to know about "them". The "field" of ethnographic inquiry is not simply a geographic place waiting to be entered, but rather a conceptual space whose boundaries are constantly negotiated and constructed by the ethnographer and members (Fitzgerald, 2006). The notion of insider–outsider is therefore intricate to social scientists carrying out ethnographic research and entering the "field". The line between what constitutes the "inside" or "outside" in ethnographic research is often fine and blurred (Zaman, 2018). It is here that studying Africa also requires more than being an African as it raises the possibility that some "Africanists" may begin to see themselves as "the proper representatives of Africa to the outside world and their voices as the authentic conduits of social and cultural truth" (Obbo, 2006, 158). This can turn dangerous to the extent that for some fieldwork to collect empirical evidence comes to be a "waste of time" in attending to "villagers" who have "no theories, let alone the luxury of philosophical thinking" (Obbo, 2006, 158). In this regard, the insider–outsider position reveals certain damning truths about itself that make it even dangerous to the welfare and representation of participants.

These two problems of representation are related because they point to the different agendas and interests at the heart of the question of responsibility, such that it is not enough to be African to do ethical research. Rather than identity, ideally, the question of responsibility should concern itself with why researchers ask the questions they ask. In other words, why is a researcher asking about, say for example, huts? How do they perceive them and what do they assume them to represent? Because while there are real demographic issues concerning the inequality and poverty that is indeed prevalent on the continent, it cannot be acceptable that an image of the hut essentially comes to signify or index these characteristics. This is a problematic byproduct of colonialism's redefinition of the utility of the value of African social spaces like "traditional" households that rendered it deplorable to talk about huts in any "productive" conversation about economic development. As Magubane (1971, 420) adumbrates, "the possibility of political action by Africans to change the status quo has been denied implicitly by the way in which social change has been conceptualised". This means that there needs to be a deeper attention to the question informing the writing and the discourse, opinion or interest it is trying to satisfy. This exercise takes us to a place of reflecting on the different kinds of "responsibility regimes" researchers come with when they are doing research in the "field". Hence, ethics is not only about balancing North–South power relations but also about engaging the different modes of perception that are informing the social expectations about the researcher in the community and what they signify to wield differential responsibilities to identity types.

Ubuntu: A Currency for Responsibility

An understanding of the idea and social value of African community can play a central role in informing the ways researchers pose questions and the kinds of questions they ask. Community in African society, unlike Western conceptions, ties African people's well-being to that of the entire community, which is the basis of Ubuntu. This raises fundamental ontological differences between African and Western being since an African "is not just an individual person, but one born into a community whose survival and purpose is linked with that of others. Thus, the human person is first a member of a clan, a kindred or a community" (Anthony, 2013, 550–551). If Africans are to be guided by Ubuntu, they follow here "a multidimensional concept that represents the core value of African ontology's—such as respect for human beings, for human dignity and human life, collective sharedness, obedience, humility, solidarity, caring, hospitality, interdependence, and communalism" (Hailey, 2008, 5).

This is not to say that these are all values that are not recognised in the West; however, they are not emphasised to the same extent (Hailey, 2008, 5). Instead of "I think therefore I am" Ubuntu says, "I am human because I belong"; or "I am because we are", which suggests that one becomes a human being only in a fellowship with the life of others (Nel, 2008). In other words, there is a sense of community in which all the inhabitants of the cosmic order exist for each other, which suggests that no being exists for itself, but exists because others exist (Anthony, 2013). If knowledge occurs in a human context, the purpose of its creation, dissemination, and application is for the collective well-being of these humans (Martin, 2008, 962). It is not for self-aggrandisement, promotion, career advancement, good university or peer standing or feeling good about oneself. This may very well place a specific kind of responsibility on the local or so-called indigenous researchers who are expected to be a conduit of decentring migration studies yet constrained to operate according to ethics regimes conceptualised in Western knowledge systems that are more attuned to ideas of modernity, economic development and progress while seeing little value in the African social sphere.

Typical Experiences of "Indigenous Researchers" Doing Migration Fieldwork

Researchers who do not neatly fit typologies of "home" and "field" implied by the putative construct of "fieldwork", carry identities that do not make it easy for them to escape the communal obligations related to the well-being of the collective. Examples of such identities may include non-nationals conducting research on their own displaced or migrant co-nationals. These are individuals who may be doing their own research or, as is often the case, research assistants collecting data on behalf of tenured academics based in European institutions. This follows the nineteenth-century model where the emergence of the division of scholarly labour took place in West Africa based on "a network of local assistants, comprising both European administrators and indigenous public servants, who did data collection, while scholars and senior administrative officials could devote their time to producing books and articles" (Jezequel, 2010, 147). These responsibilities may be related to many issues but, in this chapter, those identified include the value of revealing identities of non-state actors abusing power, for the "greater good" and looking to the welfare of community members.

The Politics of Revealing Identities

The language of anonymity is perhaps one of the most unquestioned and unqualified aspect of ethics in the "field". Research does not always have to be anonymous as there is also room for researchers to discuss the risks associated with people's participation and how to mitigate these risks. In fact, some are happy to be identified for different reasons. However, there are instances when participants do not want to be identified by their real names and the office they hold, or even those who take issue also with the naming of the organisations they work for as it raises the possibility of them being identified by colleagues. What should be considered ethical when the community affected by the actions of such participants deems it important to expose them to the realisation of social justice? What becomes the role of the researcher and whose interests should they prioritise for their work to be considered ethical?

The conventional answer would be to consider that action which protects the welfare of the research participant in question. While such key informants do not fall under vulnerable groups (unless maybe they are a community representative), their welfare is considered under the principle of harm as they could suffer some loss of income as an outcome of their participation and divulging sensitive information. It is difficult to separate this status quo from one of the firebrands of colonialism: the distinction between public life and private life. This distinction, situated in the notion of the neo-liberal state, seeks mainly to create a dichotomy; one between the state and the non-state. Those imagined to be in power in this separation are state actors, while non-state actors are easily portrayed as benevolent and neutral, incapable of inflicting harm on others. In fact, theirs is a humanitarian mandate to save, protect and rescue. This imagination has captured the minds of many to the extent that few in ethics boards would take issue with an expose of political leaders that hold public office. Researchers might therefore write about public officials like Ministers when they endanger the lives of migrants, without a care for the risks associated with the lack of anonymity for their livelihoods. Yet, the moment one states that they intend to interview people working in NGOs or any other private office, the question arises how the researcher will ensure that they protect the identities of these actors and respective organisations. There appears here to be a reluctance to engage the decades of critique and literature on humanitarianism that clearly shows their alignment, in certain instances, with government power or "governmentality". The colonial dichotomising system between public and private/civil life has clearly led many into using ethics that accepts these distinctions by perceiving the humanitarian sphere as existing and functioning in opposition to the state.

What is sequestered in this approach is that sometimes naming plays a key part in addressing power relations between the community and non-state actors. This is the case in instances where donor money is being stolen, or humanitarian modes of categorisation are creating unethical triage regimes that perpetuate inequality and social vulnerability. These should not be reduced to "personal stories" or "intimate complaints", as Kilomba (2010) would call them, but represent serious accounts of discrimination. The ability to name represents an escape from the "brutal mask of speechlessness" which is meant to silence and elicit fear (Kilomba, 2010). Such truths could include those raised by Thomson (unpublished) who writes that, although services are supposed to be provided without charge in the camp, you cannot receive them without paying a bribe, including no resettlement or transfers for medical procedures. Refugees in her ethnographic study in Nyarugusu camp also complain that they want more access to communication with and input into management decisions. Vanyoro's (2022) ethnographic research documents the role of humanitarian actors in the waiting of Zimbabwean migrant men at a transit shelter located at the Zimbabwe–South Africa border.

There is insufficient space for such stories and experiences in considering what should be considered anonymous within ethical reason that serves the interests of migrants and refugees. "Indigenous" researchers who often return to these communities have to ask themselves or answer questions about what they have done since completing their research to expose non-state actors who abuse their authority in the public realm. This tension attests how the removed and dichotomous concept of fieldwork that does not allow sensitivity to the lives and careers of those who inhabit both "home" and "field" simultaneously has led to an unsustainable ethics that does not protect the communities they purport to represent.

Looking Out for the Welfare of Community Members

An adinkra symbol among the Akan, *funtummireku,* depicts two crocodiles sharing a common stomach accompanied by a proverb stating that the crocodiles struggle for food that goes into the same stomach (Martin, 2008). In this kind of African community, mutual aid and support through things like gifting and assisting are not only a question of economic value; they hold a moral one too. Transgressing this norm may attract ostracisation, funny looks and even worse "social death" among one's kin.

This said, it is very problematic for a researcher to simply set up interviews with struggling people and leave the rest to chance or natural unfolding. Owing to the material disjuncture that divides researchers and participants, it is unethical to simply go about conducting interviews with hungry migrants. One identifies and draws their humanity and even fullness from the relational exchange that comes from acting on this inequality, and if one does not display Ubuntu, they are not sufficiently *muntu* (a human being).

Hegemonic academic ethics lead us to think that anything that entails giving to help out in this situation is compromising. Researchers have conducted research with budgets that do not account for these incidents. Traditional conceptualisations of research emphasise that you cannot compensate participants even for their time as it compromises objectivity. This is a defence to some traces of colonial fieldwork practices that have been documented, such as ones where informants were paid and gained "not only prestige from close association with the white man but also a sizeable income in the slack season" (van Beek, 1991, 154). In this instance, it can be said that "the chance to control the information flow balanced the scales of power" (van Beek, 1991, 154). In reflecting on this limitation and possible social costs, "indigenous researchers" may end up adapting by using their own money to buy some groceries for the communities when they can. This is a cost that does not do justice and is not well suited to the intimate encounters they have as embedded kinds of fieldworkers.

Acting Differently

Reciprocity and power are imperative to achieving ethical research and protecting migrant research participants. The increase in calls for decolonisation has contributed to the increase in awareness and sensitivity to the dangers and risks uneven power relations between the Global North and South present to the further marginalisation of African migrants. With the growth of these calls, more and more conversations are skewed towards economic considerations. This chapter has shown that the increase in this kind of focus has contributed to the neglect of social value in African communities and has contributed to the continuation of uneven relationships between indigenous researchers and migrant research participants. It has also peddled the myth that decolonisation in migration studies can be achieved by balancing power relations between North and South academic institutions, through say, investing more financial resources in African ones. This neglects two important issues highlighted in this chapter. First is how African researchers' who receive these resources have to navigate their insider–outsider position as it reveals certain damning truths that make their involvement dangerous to the welfare and representation of participants. Second, indigenous researchers are expected to be a conduit of decentring migration studies yet constrained to operate according to ethics regimes conceptualised in Western knowledge systems that come with their own conceptions about modernity, economic development and progress, which see little value in Africa's social sphere.

These dilemmas are more visible because ethics boards are continuing to emphasise definitions of responsibility that create tensions for researchers who do not neatly fit typologies of "home" and "field" implied by the putative construct of "fieldwork", and these researchers are continuing to find ways to combat the social costs of their work. This chapter suggests the need for a questioning as well as transformation of the influences that colonialism and colonial ethnography have on our conception of "ethics" in situations that demand reciprocity, or the coloniality of migration studies will surely continue. More research is needed to understand beyond the power imbalances between white European researchers and Black African migrants in research. This could also help challenge the homogenous and hegemonic narrative of colonialism in migration studies to focus on particular projects and work cultures. This optic can help us to think through the role and place of African scholars themselves in using academia as a vehicle to get what they want, unveiling other hidden forms of power.

References

Achiume, E. T. (2019). Migration as decolonization. *Stanford Law Review, 71*, 1509.
Amelina, A. (2021). After the reflexive turn in migration studies: Towards the doing migration approach. *Population, Space and Place, 27*(1), e2368.
Anthony, K. I. (2013). The dimensions of African cosmology. *Filosofia Theoretica: Journal of African Philosophy Culture and Religion, 2*(2), 533–555.
Cole, A. (2016). All of us are vulnerable, but some are more vulnerable than others: The political ambiguity of vulnerability studies, an ambivalent critique. *Critical Horizons, 17*, 260–277. https://doi.org/10.1080/14409917.2016.1153896
Conrad, J. (2015). *Heart of darkness*. Alma Books.
Dahinden, J. (2016). A plea for the 'de-migranticization' of research on migration and integration. *Ethnic and Racial Studies, 39*(13), 2207–2225.
Daley, P. (2021). Reclaiming mobility: A Pan-Africanist approach to migration. *CODESRIA Bulletin, 2&3*, 17.

Fiddian-Qasmiyeh, E. (2020). Introduction: Recentring the South in studies of migration. *Migration and Society, 3*(1), 1–18.

Fitzgerald, D. (2006). Towards a theoretical ethnography of migration. *Qualitative Sociology, 29*, 1–24.

Gopal, P. (2021). On decolonisation and the University. *Textual Practice*, 1–27.

Grosfoguel, R., Oso, L., & Christou, A. (2015). 'Racism', intersectionality and migration studies: Framing some theoretical reflections. *Identities, 22*(6), 635–652.

Hailey, J. (2008). Ubuntu: A Literature Review. A Paper Prepared for the Tutu Foundation: London. *Available from: cite. seerx. ist. psu. edu/viewdoc/download/ doi, 10*(1.459).

Hountondji, P. J. (2009). Knowledge of Africa, knowledge by Africans: Two perspectives on African studies. *RCCS Annual Review. A selection from the Portuguese journal revista crítica de ciências sociais,* (1).

Jacobsen, K., & Landau, L. B. (2003). The dual imperative in refugee research: Some methodological and ethical considerations in social science research on forced migration. *Disasters, 27*, 185–206.

Jezequel, J. H. (2010). Voices of Their Own? African participation in the production of colonial knowledge in French West Africa, 1900–50. In: T. Helen & G. Robert (Eds.), *Ordering Africa: Anthropology, European imperialism and the politics of knowledge* (pp. 145–172). Manchester University Press.

Kalinga, C. (2019). Caught between a rock and a hard place: Navigating global research partnerships in the Global South as an indigenous researcher. *Journal of African Cultural Studies, 31*(3), 270–272.

Kilomba, G. (2010). *Plantation memories: Episodes of everyday racism.* Unrast Verlag.

Landau, L. B. (2019). 'Capacity, complicity, and subversion: Revisiting collaborative refugee research in an era of containment. In S. McGrath & J. E. E. Young (Eds.), *Mobilizing global knowledge: Refugee research in an age of displacement* (pp. 25–44). University of Calgary.

Magubane, B. (1971). A critical look at indices used in the study of social change in colonial Africa [and Comments and Replies]'. *Current Anthropology, 12*(4/5), 419–445.

Mayblin, L. (2017). *Asylum after empire: Colonial legacies in the politics of asylum seeking.* Rowman & Littlefield.

Martin, D. (2008). Maat and order in African cosmology: A conceptual tool for understanding indigenous knowledge. *Journal of Black Studies, 38*(6), 951–967.

McGrath, S., & Young, J. E. E. (Eds.). (2019). *Mobilizing global knowledge: Refugee research in an age of displacement.* University of Calgary.

Mudimbe, V.Y. (1988) *The Invention of Africa.* [Chapter One "Discourses of Power and Knowledge of Otherness"] (pp.1–23). Indiana University Press.

Nail, T. (2015). *The figure of the migrant.* Stanford University Press.

Ndlovu-Gatsheni, S. J. (2018). Decolonising borders, decriminalising migration and rethinking citizenship. In H. H. Magidimisha, N. E. Khalema, L. Chipungu, T.

C. Chirimambowa, & T. L. Chimedza (Eds.), *Crisis, identity and migration in post-colonial Southern Africa* (pp. 23–37). Springer.

Nel, P. J. (2008). Morality and religion in African thought. *Acta Theologica, 28*(2), 33–47.

Obbo, C. (2006). But we know it all! African perspectives on anthropological knowledge. In M. Ntarangwi, M. Babiker, & D. Mills (Eds.), *African anthropologies: History, critique and practice* (pp. 154–169). Zed Books.

Oliveira, E., & Vearey, J. (2015). Images of place: Visuals from migrant women sex Workers in South Africa. *Medical Anthropology, 34*(4), 305–318.

Rodney, W. (2018). *How Europe Underdeveloped Africa*. Verso Books.

Setiloane, G. (1998). Towards a biocentric theology and ethic — Via Africa. In: C.W. du Toit (Ed.), *Faith, Science and African Culture. African Cosmology and Africa's Contribution to Science* (pp. 73–84). UNISA.

Teye, J. (2021). Q&A: South-South migration has long been overlooked. Why? The New Humanitarian, 18 July. https://www.thenewhumanitarian.org/interview/2021/7/8/why-south-south-migration-has-long-been-overlooked

Thomson, M. (unpublished). Navigating Aidscapes: Refugee Activism in and out of a UN Camp in Tanzania.

University of the Witwatersrand's Human Research Ethics Committee (Non-Medical). (2022). HREC (Non-Medical) Risk level categories definitions (updated November 2022). University of the Witwatersrand.

van Beek, W. (1991). Dogon restudied: A field evaluation of the work of Marcel Griaule [and comments and replies]. *Current Anthropology, 32*(2), 139–167.

Vanyoro, K. (2019). Decolonising Migration Research and Potential Pitfalls: Reflections from South Africa. Pambazuka News, 17 May. https://www.pambazuka.org/education/decolonising-migration-research-and-potential-pitfalls-reflections-south-africa.

Vanyoro, K. (2022). 'This place is a bus stop': Temporalities of Zimbabwean migrant men waiting at a Zimbabwe-South Africa border transit shelter. *Incarceration, 3*(1), 26326663221084580.

Vanyoro, K P., Hadj-Abdou, L., & Dempster, H. (2019). Migration Studies: From Dehumanising to Decolonising. LSE Higher Education Blog, 19 July. https://blogs.lse.ac.uk/highereducation/2019/07/19/migration-studies-from-dehumanising-to-decolonising/

Wainaina, B. (2005) 'How to Write about Africa,' Granta 92, Available online at: www.granta.com/Archive/92/How-to-Write-about-Africa/Page-1

Zaman, S. (2018). Native among the natives: Physician anthropologist doing hospital ethnography at home. *Journal of Contemporary Ethnography, 37*(2), 135–154.

Open Access This chapter is licensed under the terms of the Creative Commons Attribution 4.0 International License (http://creativecommons.org/licenses/by/4.0/), which permits use, sharing, adaptation, distribution and reproduction in any medium or format, as long as you give appropriate credit to the original author(s) and the source, provide a link to the Creative Commons license and indicate if changes were made.

The images or other third party material in this chapter are included in the chapter's Creative Commons license, unless indicated otherwise in a credit line to the material. If material is not included in the chapter's Creative Commons license and your intended use is not permitted by statutory regulation or exceeds the permitted use, you will need to obtain permission directly from the copyright holder.

7

What Does it Mean to Move? Joy and Resistance Through Cultural Work in South–South Migration

Hyab Teklehaimanot Yohannes and Alison Phipps

Introduction

> Once I lived in a beautiful town;
> Once, I owned a beautiful house,
> with a grand garden full of flowers,
> and I was a prince of it all. Once,
> I lived in a house with a name:
> And now, I am just a number.
> Nations talked to nations
> And robbed me of myself.
> They made me
> a number among millions.

The above lines are from the poem *Where are my unnumbered days?* by a young Syrian boy, Mohamed Assaf, reflecting on his childhood (Assaf & Clanchy, 2018). Mohamed Assaf, as articulated in the above lines, appears perplexed by how his life is reduced to such a precarious form of existence that he features as just a number. It echoes the words of another refugee,

---

H. T. Yohannes (✉) · A. Phipps
University of Glasgow, Glasgow, UK
e-mail: Hyab.Yohannes@glasgow.ac.uk

A. Phipps
e-mail: Alison.Phipps@glasgow.ac.uk

© The Author(s) 2024
H. Crawley and J. K. Teye (eds.), *The Palgrave Handbook of South–South Migration and Inequality*, https://doi.org/10.1007/978-3-031-39814-8_7

from the time of the Holocaust, Simone Weil, who remarked that the lure of quantity is the most dangerous of all (Weil, 1970).

In another poem, *When my teachers asked me*, Mohamed Assaf speaks of becoming a "refugee", which for him was an unthinkable prospect, yet that was "The word the West was holding for [him]" (Assaf & Clanchy, 2018, 210). As he points out in his poem, Mohamed Assaf is only one person among many millions of displaced people. Published annually, the UNHCR Global Trends Report (2022) leads in providing the latest statistical trends of involuntarily displaced people. According to the UNHCR Global Trends report, the number of involuntarily displaced people across the world totalled over 89 million at the end of 2021, 83% of whom were hosted in the Global South, with over 72% living in immediately adjacent countries (UNHCR, 2022, 2). The report indicates that the number of displaced people has now "exceeded 100 million" as a result of the ongoing conflicts in Ukraine, Burkina Faso, and Myanmar (UNHCR, 2022, 7). These numeric measurements from UNHCR are highly reductive to comprehensively understand the lived realities of those caught up in the search for refuge from war and persecution.

The category of the forced migrant,[1] as Mohamed Assaf points out, reduces displaced people to nameless and faceless numbers. Forced migrants in general and those from the Global South in particular are often rendered nude, damned, and unwelcome persons by violent practices of (b)ordering and (dis)counting (see, for example, Agamben, 1995; Aiyar et al., 2016; Berry et al., 2016; Malkki, 1996; Mbembe, 2019). We only need to think of the branding on skin in the death camps of the Holocaust, to the use of numbers not names to refer to those held in Australian detention centres in the last decade. Practices of both quantifying and qualifying through naming can become practices of erasure, their powerful technologies largely in the hands of state actors for the purpose of control. This control may be humanitarian, or it may be exclusionary, but the legacies are similar in the intersections of both.

Over the last few decades, it has been apparent that (b)ordering and (dis)counting are deployed ubiquitously, including on the bodies of migrants, through biometric and electronic borders (Aas, 2006; Amoore, 2006; Mbembe, 2019; Salter, 2004). To draw carceral lines between the Global

---

[1] The concept of migration is mired in contested processes of labelling and categorisation of migrants into "asylum seekers", "refugees", "internally displaced persons", etc. While we recognise the contestation around these nouns which distil processes of categorisation and their use in research, policy, and practice, we focus in this chapter on the lived realities and prescencing of forcibly displaced people—forced migrants, rather than "migrants" in general—in the Global South regardless of their legal status or whether they have crossed international border or not.

North and Global South, state, and non-state (b)ordering regimes are deployed along territorial and extra-territorial borders, as well as in airports, refugee camps, hotspots, water bodies, and deserts. These violent (b)ordering structures are designed to keep the bodies and faces of forced migrants away from borders and cameras. Equipped with "smart" technologies (Salter, 2004), these (b)ordering regimes "count" and "discount"—(dis)count—those who have lost their lives and those who "sneak" across the violent borders, respectively. The goal is, as Mbembe (2019, 7) points out, "to make life itself amenable to 'datafication'". This is exactly what the settled narrative of forced migration from the Global South to the Global North boils down to in the current migration scholarship (Phipps, 2022).

Yet, the story of South–South migration cannot be reduced to the violence of (b)ordering and (dis)counting. In fact, migrants continue to move both inside and outside of the Global South. Movement allows migrants to overcome, as mobile human beings with various capabilities but also vulnerabilities, the exclusive barriers of time, space, and knowledge deployed by (b)ordering and (dis)counting regimes. Historically speaking, South–South migration is rooted in intercultural and interepistemic communication. For example, referring to the pre-colonial migration of people within the continent of Africa, Mbembe (2020, 58) observes:

> It is a history of colliding cultures, caught in the maelstrom of war, invasion, migration, intermarriage, and a history of various religions we make our own, of techniques we exchange, and of goods we trade. The cultural history of the continent can hardly be understood outside the paradigm of itinerancy, mobility, and displacement.

Despite the threat of (b)ordering and (dis)counting to "this very culture of mobility" (Mbembe, 2020, 58), similar patterns of mobility are still practised in the Global South. The migration of workers from South Asia to the Middle East and from Eastern Africa to Southern Africa are just two examples of mobility within the Global South (see Malkki, 1996; Wickramasekara, 2011). Moreover, climate-induced internal displacement continues to create new patterns of semi-nomadic life within the borders of Horn of Africa countries and beyond (see Bach, 2022). Nevertheless, as shown above, the association of these forms of migration with barriers of place, time, and (dis)counting has prevented transformative work in South–South migration. In addition to inflicting enduring violence, the regimes of (b)ordering and (dis)counting create epistemic barriers—borders between the knowable and unknowable—that obscure the fluidity, creativity, and interculturality of South–South migration. These illusive regimes of epistemic (b)ordering and (dis)counting create differential humanity in which some lives are regarded as more qualified than others, more liveable than others (see, for example, Butler, 2006; Mbembe, 2019). These are colonial predicaments of what Maldonado-Torres calls "metaphysical catastrophe", namely, "the meaning and function of the basic parameters of geopolitical, national, as well as subjective and intersubjective dynamics to the extent that it creates a world to the measure of dehumanization" (Maldonado-Torres, 2016, 12). These modalities of dehumanisation leading to the death of forced migrants are perceived, to use Mayblin's (2020, 39) blunt description, as "beneficial to the whole population, and [the forced migrants'] suffering is of little consequence to society as a whole".

One of the approaches to dealing with the necropolitics that are part of the "metaphysical catastrophe" has been to engage the arts in work for advocacy and communication of both the plight and the complexity of regimes of (b)ordering. Where research and development work engage with arts and culture, however, it typically does so to communicate findings, educate, or mediatise. This chapter considers how art and cultural works serve as methods practised daily by migrants in contexts of violent (b)ordering, (dis)counting, and survival. It opens by unpacking necropolitics of the (b)ordering and (dis)counting that are not only drawn between the here and there, the us and them, but also between the knowable and the unknowable. The intention, here, is to rebuke the creation of "death-worlds and their minions" (Schaffer, 2020, 48) with the forms of resistance which demonstrate and persist where people are manifestly, often gloriously, alive. It then moves on to conceptualise ways of destituting these violent structures of (b)ordering and (dis)counting through artistic, poetic, and cultural work. The chapter concludes by stressing the need for cultural work mediated by arts-based research to unmask not only the humanity within the South–South migration but also the potent forces of comfort and discomfort.

Necropolitics of (Dis)counting and (B)ordering

The insecurity, instability, and precarity of the South–South migration are often associated with the deployment of barriers of place, time, and (dis)counting. The inherently colonial relations of power and knowledge between the Global North and Global South (see Fynn-Bruey, Fiddian-Qasmiyeh this volume), create exclusive modes of distancing, containing, counting, and discounting. What these relations keep distant from the Global North are the discursively nude and bare bodies of the Southern migrants.

"The goal is", as Mbembe (2019, 9) asserts, "to better control movement and speed, accelerating it here, decelerating it there and, in the process, sorting, recategorizing, reclassifying people with the goal of better selecting anew who is whom, who should be where and who shouldn't, in the name of security". This confining of forced migrants in space and time is epitomised at the interstices of borders, refugee camps, torture camps, and detention facilities (see, for example, Elena Fiddian-Qasmiyeh, 2020a, 2020b; Fisseha, 2015; Malkki, 1996; Yohannes, 2021a, 2021b). As Yohannes perceptively explains, "These spaces—the coordinates of the carceral network—are where the exception is applied to ensure the complete domination, surrender, and annihilation of the [refugees]… the refugees' instincts, capacities, and potentialities are negated indefinitely" (2021b, 200).

Stranded indefinitely in these spaces of impoverishment, violability, and denigration, forced migrants, figuratively and literally speaking, appear only in the statistical schemata of international organisations, deployed as part of the (b)ordering spectacle. The UNHCR Global Trends Report details the latest trends:

> With millions of Ukrainians displaced at the time of writing, as well as further displacement elsewhere this year, notably in Burkina Faso and Myanmar, total forced displacement now exceeds 100 million people… This means 1 in every 78 people on earth has been forced to flee – a dramatic milestone that few would have expected a decade ago. (UNHCR Report, 2022, 7)

These numbers and other statistics are often used by governments and international institutions to forecast economic impacts and security risks in countries of the Global North. The International Monetary Fund (IMF), for example, predicted the following budgetary expenditure for people seeking asylum in European countries in 2015 and 2016:

> IMF staff estimate that, on a GDP-weighted basis, average budgetary expenses for asylum seekers in EU countries could increase by 0.05 and 0.1 percent of GDP in 2015 and 2016, respectively, compared to 2014… Austria (at 0.08 and 0.23 percent of GDP), Finland (at 0.04 and 0.28 percent of GDP), Sweden (at 0.2 and 0.7 percent of GDP), and Germany (at 0.12 and 0.27 percent of GDP) are expected to shoulder the largest spending increases in 2015 and 2016, respectively, relative to 2014. (Aiyar et al., 2016, 12)

These are not neutral statistics. They go beyond making purely economic assessments to create alarmist discourses of a threatening refugee "crisis", an "invasion", and of a "mass influx" of undesirable people into the Global North (see Berry et al., 2016; Heller & Pécoud, 2020). Heller and Pécoud (2020, 483) explicate:

> Migration statistics do not merely "describe," in an "objective" manner, a pre-existing social reality. They rather contribute to the very existence of "migration" by making the phenomenon visible and countable by governments. They are both the product of immigration policies and the condition for these polices to exist, thereby constituting the privileged tool through which state policies operate.

The systemic techniques used to render people (in)visible and calculable, fuelled by the mainstream media and by uncritically produced migration scholarship, including the perpetuation of state and intergovernmental serving data "extraction" processes, create an environment in which governments can establish necropolitical bordering regimes, to the detriment of people seeking refuge. For example, the European Commission, at the height of the so-called "refugee crisis" in 2015, adopted a new policy "to boost the central EU resources devoted to the refugee surge in 2015–16 by €1.7 billion (0.01 per cent of EU GDP) to €9.2 billion (0.07 per cent of EU GDP) by reallocating resources from other parts of the EU budget" (Aiyar et al., 2016, 13). These resources are used to provide "funding for the FRONTEX budgets, support to member countries for migration and border management… and support to countries outside the EU (for example, through the EU Regional Trust Fund in response to the Syrian crisis and additional funding for Turkey)" (Aiyar et al., 2016, 13). The primary goal, here, is to reinforce a "fortress Europe" whose borders are stretched beyond the continent's territorial limits so as to immobilise in precarious conditions people desperately seeking refuge and govern them through necropolitics (see Damoc, 2016; Kofman & Sales, 1992; Mainwaring, 2019; Van Avermaet, 2009).

The regimes of fortification and necropolitics enforced to contain most of the displaced people within a particular region—the Global South—threaten the very humanity of the forced migrants. The vulnerability, violability, and inaudibility of these migrants are directly associated with the regimes of bordering deployed primarily by the Global North, but also within the Global South. The bordering regimes are designed not only to institute a radical form of inhospitality but also to create necropolitical conditions in which migrants are met by violent borders, while also being preyed on by organised criminals such as smugglers and traffickers. This is why migrants from the Global South are often trapped in irregular forms of movement, such as smuggling, trafficking, and/or deportation (see Human Rights Watch,

2009; Loschi et al., 2018; Yohannes, 2021a). Stranded in the necropolitical spectacles of (im)mobility and carcerality, these migrants feature as "discounted bodies", or "bodies at the limits of life, trapped in uninhabitable worlds and inhospitable places" (Mbembe, 2019, 10). Death is normalised for these (dis)counted migrants; for example, the IOM Missing Migrants Project recorded the deaths of 49,383 people between 2014 and July 2022 (Missing Migrants Project, 2022). These are simply (dis)counted people; discounted in life and counted in death, namely, "necropolitics" or the politics of "subjugation of life to the power of death" (Mbembé, 2003, 39). The Missing Migrants project themselves also caution as to any potential claims for accuracy in their data, given that such data are notoriously difficult to obtain and to verify.

Furthermore, "stuckness" in spaces of containment, such as refugee camps and informal settlements, is another characteristic feature of migration from and within the Global South. The necropolitical violence faced by refugees in realms of immobility, inhospitality, and precarity are epitomised in regions stretching from Western and Eastern Africa to North Africa and the Middle East; from Yemen, Syria, and Iraq to Myanmar; and from South America to the US border with Mexico (see Green, 2015; Malkki, 1996; Mudawi, 2019; Yohannes, 2021a). The refugee camps and informal settlements spreading from eastern Sudan, Kenya, and Uganda to Asia–Pacific and South America are just some examples of places where refugees live for decades in impoverished and destitute states (see, for example, Bahlbi, 2016; Davies, 2020; Green, 2015; Kok, 1989). The migrants in these impoverished spaces continue are stuck in realms of destitution and necropolitics. Those without the adequate resources and ability to move (e.g., children, single mothers, and disabled people) are displaced (or mobilised) in conditions of immobility. For the resourceful and those able to move, irregular migration allows them to dodge the impoverished camps, torture camps, and violent borders. For these migrants, forced to navigate unsafe journeys, movement is necessary to overcome solitude, persecution, torture, and immobility. Theirs is a story of "survival" (Perl, 2019). Below, we discuss ways of revealing the humanity of the Southern migrants through their survival stories of cultural agency and cultural work for justice.

Revealing the Humanity in South–South Migration: "Destituting" the Practices of (B)ordering and (Dis)counting

Practices of (b)ordering and (dis)counting leave forced migrants facing a perpetual struggle to communicate their lived experiences to a world that continues to be indifferent to them. They do so "by crossing borders, dying in treacherous waters and deserts and appearing in politicised spaces" (Yohannes, 2021b, 18). The stories of Yohanna, who perished off the island of Lampedusa on 3 October 2013 with her new-born baby still attached to her by its umbilical cord, and of a nameless child, who died alongside Yohanna, (dis)counted as *No.92*, are just a few examples of the necropolitics of (b)ordering and (dis)counting. Reduced to media content and an abstract number, the lives and deaths of the many thousands of migrants who perish in the carceral spaces are rendered, respectively, "unliveable" and "ungrieveable", as Butler would argue (Butler, 2009). Their bodies perish, as if they had never existed, and they are reduced to numbers, as if they had never had names, which amounts to "epistemic and pedagogical brutality" (Maldonado-Torres, 2016, 3). The question becomes one of methodology: how to go beyond these profound structures of violence and disposability, as Butler (2006, 30) invites us to contemplate:

> If we stay with the sense of loss, are we left feeling only passive and powerless, as some might fear? Or are we, rather, returned a sense of human vulnerability, to our collective responsibility for the physical lives of one another?

"In crucial times", Lévinas (1996) reminds us, "when the perishability of so many values is revealed, all human dignity consists in believing in their return" (121). This return of human dignity cannot be achieved without restorative, reparative and regenerative works of art, of culture, of memory, and of imagination. We find such restorative, reparative, and regenerative creations primarily in the artistic work of people with lived experiences, but also in decolonial aesthetics. Michael Adony,[2] for example, has depicted Yohanna's story through his powerful artwork. Adonay's painting depicts the unheard cries of the new-born baby who never got a chance to see the light of the day, and the pain of a mother unable to welcome her new-born baby.

---

[2] Michael Adonay is an Eritrean visual artist, specialising in painting. He is a five-time winner of Eritrea's national painting competitions before he moved to Australia, where he currently lives, in 2012. Adonay's artwork discussed in this chapter are publicly available on his website at http://www.michaeladonai.net/

These cries represent not only expressions of desperate need, but also a call for humans to assume ethical responsibility for one another as part of a human family. What factors led to these calamities? What circumstances limit the ethical responsibility people feel for the refugees? What stops states from helping a drowning woman with her new-born baby still attached to her by its umbilical cord? What is possible in the moment when we "regard the pain of others" (Sontag, 2004)? What is destituting our affective registers? These are fundamental questions to address if we wish to understand both the humanity of the other and our own humanity. The "cry" constitutes a starting point for a theory that can help us answer these questions, as Maldonado-Torres (2007, 256) aptly puts it:

> The cry, not a word but an interjection, is a call of attention to one's own existence… It is the cry that animates the birth of theory and critical thought. And the cry points to a peculiar existential condition: that of the condemned.

In short, the cry can guide us towards the "truth". Michael Adonay's powerful artwork invites us to "contemplate" the truth of those whose very lives and livelihoods are perpetually at stake. It takes us beyond what Sontag has termed the "spectating" of "calamities taking place in another country". She argues that "For photography of atrocity, people want the weight of witnessing without the taint of artistry, which is equated with insincerity or mere contrivance" (Sontag, 2002, 26–27). What artists, such as Michael Adonay enable is a way of bringing continuity into the future or what has been rendered mute, controlled, enumerated, and therefore consigned within the structures of power that accompany "data collection". The image brings the stories flooding back, the stylisations which belong within orthodox forms of artistic expression troubling the controlled stories of western forms of artistic expression, the fluidity of movement of water and hair and umbilical cord refusing the stasis, the rigour mortis. As a figure is dignified by blues and golds and greens of careful, attentive brush strokes there is presence and story, the story of a painter, the story of the shipwreck, the story of the woman, her labour, her body found and both given the number 92, and ungiven that number through the silence of art.

The image appeals to us to reclaim the humanity of the other in the same way we recognise our own humanity. It reminds us that "love and rage are possible in spite of the profound wounds created by modernity/coloniality" (Maldonado-Torres, 2016, 24). We are called upon to reclaim our collective humanity by destituting the (b)ordering and (dis)counting practices that coloniality has maintained through its exclusive politicisation of life. It is an answer to Donna Haraway's questions in *Staying with the trouble:* "How can we think in times of urgencies without the self-indulgent and self-fulfilling myths of apocalypse, when every fibre of our being is interlaced, even complicit, in the webs of processes that must somehow be engaged and repatterned?" As Italian philosopher Giorgio Agamben powerfully argues, "Life is not in itself political, it is what must be excluded and, at the same time, included by way of its own exclusion" (2014, 65). In Agamben's political theory, this constitutively exclusive process of politicisation creates "human beings [who] could be so completely deprived of their rights and prerogatives that no act committed against them could appear any longer as a crime" (Agamben, 1998, 97). The cry is the language of innocent people whose lives have been rendered disposable. Attending to the cry by making room for the agency of lives and the agency of artists insistent on regenerative work, is a powerful way to resist this situation. We return to this point below.

"I Can't Bear You Being Called NUMBER 92": The Destituting Power of Poetry

While artistic image is one form which can counter the (dis)counting, the arts in general when used through ceremony and not in the service of forms of propaganda, and when bound into ethical practices of attention, can all serve to destitute the violences of erasure and silencing.

Poetry is a powerful way of resisting and "destituting" the omnipresent violence of (b)ordering and (dis)counting. Where image can work to visibilise, poetry to work to vocalise. "To destitute work means", Agamben (2014, 73) explains, "to return it to the potentiality from which it originates, to exhibit in it the impotentiality that reigns and endures there". As Agamben argues, poetry is a way of destituting the violence of the speaker. Agamben (2014, 70) asks: "What is a poem, in fact, if not an operation taking place in language that consists in rendering inoperative, in deactivating its communicative and informative function, in order to open it to a new possible use?" At this point, we now invite you to consider Selam Kidane's poem entitled *No. 92.*

> I wonder what she called you.
>   Your precious mama…
>   Maybe she called you Berhan?… My Light
>   Or did she call you Haben?… My Pride
>   She may have called you Qisanet… Rest
>   Or were you, Awet? Victory…

> Tell me, Little One, did she name you after her hope?
> Or her aspirations... her dream?
> Did she name you after the brother she lost?
> Or after her father long gone?
> Did she name you after the desert she crossed?
> Or the land she left behind...?
> Maybe she named you for the land you were to inherit?
> Tell me, Little One, what did your precious mother call you?
> For I can't bear you being called Number 92...

In contemplating these words, we invite you to contemplate those drowned, trafficked, tortured to death, and/or rendered nameless. Contemplation subsists alongside criticality. As Boaventura de Sousa Santos demonstrates (Santos, 2014, 19–20), "[a] sense of exhaustion haunts the Western Eurocentric critical tradition [...] Of there is so much to criticize, why has it become so difficult to build convincing, widely shared, powerful, critical theories that give rise to effective and profound transformative practices?".

What if, alongside Selam Kidane, we insist on *also* walking behind and looking down to see and feel the light, pride, rest, victory, hope, and dreams of those who are left behind and/or (un)buried following painful death. What if contemplation, the silence present in standing before a work of art, the softening of the mind needed as a poem plays with and entices new ways of hearing the world, is where the exhaustions of critique can meet the restorative, reparative, and regenerative possibilities of cultural work.

Kidane's words open different ways to be alongside the names, not numbers, of those whose lives humanity has failed to pronounce. These words allow us to destitute the assigning of abstract numbers and "restore" the real names, for destitution along with "restoration" are "the coming politics" (Agamben, 2014, 74). They step beyond "weak answers" (Santos, 2014, 20) which the Eurocentric critical tradition has for the "strong questions confronting us in our time". Agamben reminds us that contemplation, in operativity, and destitution, as emerging forms of politics, are operatives through which we can reclaim our collective humanity from the violent power of the state. The work of contemplative and joyful art is central to this emerging politics. The presence of joy and of contemplation, of silence and of energy in the face of the tiredness of critiques, as liberation theologian Andrade argues "are counter proof". Joy, in such circumstances, or the stillness and dignity of the poise of the figures in Adonay's image, the line from Kidane "tell me, Little One, what did your precious mother call you? For I can't bear you being called Number 92..." do the work of destituting the violence of what created the impulse to the image, the poem in the first place. And in the posing of the question by Kidane, or the unveiling of the image by Adonay, there is the first step away from the destitution and in that step is felt, however fleeting, the potential of the joy of resistance, and a understanding that "other worlds are possible" (Graeber & Wengrow, 2021).

Agamben, again, writes: "Politics and art are neither tasks nor simply 'works': they name, rather, the dimension in which the linguistic and corporeal, material and immaterial, biological and social operations are made inoperative and contemplated as such" (2014, 74). The inoperativity of violence—physical, epistemic, or otherwise—should be the goal of the meditative art and poetry.

Joy as a Form of Resistance

In addition to destituting violence, cultural and artistic works can also create the conditions for the possibility to "enjoy" life. Again, we take pains here to emphasise that this is not always the work undertaken by cultural and artistic work. Here, "enjoyment" is understood, in Lévinasian terms, as "the ultimate consciousness of all the contents that fill [our lives]" (Lévinas, 2011, 111). "The final relation", Lévinas adds, "is enjoyment, *happiness*" (2011, 113, emphasis in the original). When correctly deployed, cultural, and artistic works can exhibit the happiness contained within migrants' survival stories, or in the survival of their stories, their afterlives in narratives which refuse erasure and enact memory. For migrants, migration does not merely consist of moving from place to place; it also involves creating, dancing, mediatising, and exhibiting joy. If not joy and imaginative work, what is brought to our lives by playing with clay, making pottery, weaving, painting, decorating, music, dance, theatre, cinema, sculpture, architecture, and literature? Music, for example, has never ceased to bring joy to colonised and opposed peoples, even during the most difficult times of colonisation, as Mbembe (2015, 4) explains:

> Indeed, in Africa, music has always been a celebration of the ineradicability of life, in a long life-denying history. It is the genre that has historically expressed, in the most haunting way, our raging desire not only for existence, but more importantly for joy in existence.

A sense of joy in existing makes living thinkable for migrants in the face of unthinkable violence inflicted by (b)ordering and (dis)counting practices. As part of our restorative work with South–South migrants, we have witnessed migrants, throughout their journeys, resolutely and unapologetically celebrating their cultures, festivals, and prayers, as well as their traditional coffee, food, and attire. In addition to sustaining their own peculiar migration survival stories, these moments of celebration present us with memories and images that shape our ways of thinking about and being with the migrants. They often turn power relations upside down and enable those previously being destitute to turn the tables and become those hosting, those enabling, those even also destituting as the language and culture of the dominant group are usurped in such moments by that of those others discounted or subjugated to integration as assimilation. As can be seen in the pictures below, moments of prayer, music, poetry, and cultural celebration bind together poets, social scientists, musicians, and artists as co-producers of knowledge together with the migrants (Figs. 7.1 and 7.2).

Moments of prayer and cultural celebration can be artistic, poetic, cultural, and life affirming. They can also be awkward, uncomfortable, and strange depending on the fluency of their use. But under both circumstances these are not "weak" responses to "strong questions" but rather elicit powerful affective responses. In addition to finding opportunities to be happy in these acts of prayer, celebration, and artistic meditation, the migrants mobilise joy and fluency in cultural practice as the ultimate form of resistance to the violence of their own cultural destitution as migrants. These organised moments of joy enable the migrants to destitute violence and their fear of it at its very roots,

Fig. 7.1 Refugee-organised mass at St. Joseph's Roman Catholic Church, Cairo, Egypt

Fig. 7.2 Eritrean coffee celebration with Alison Phipps, Glasgow, Scotland

even if the shadow of violence inevitably returns in moments of despair. For the migrants, it is a way of asserting that no one can take away their capacity to be happy and enjoy life, for their capacity to be happy rests on, as Lévinas puts it, "the independence and sovereignty of enjoyment" (2011, 114). It is only by recognising this irreducible capacity to experience joy and generate discomfort and comfort, artfully, that we can come to understand that the life of a migrant, in Lévinasian terms, "is not a *bare* existence; it is a life of labor and nourishments; these are contents which do not preoccupy it only, but which 'occupy' it, which 'entertain' it, of which it is enjoyment" (Lévinas, 2011, 111, emphasis in original). In other words, this irreducible capacity to continue to be happy is an invocation of the migrants' humanity in the face of the stubborn necropolitics of the Global North. Thus, we argue that generative cultural enjoyment, as a form of resistance, is central to the work of reclaiming humanity in South–South migration.

Crucially, movement, circulation, communication, and sharing are all central to these imaginative, contemplative, and creative works within South–South migration. Such acts open possibilities for visibility, recognition, and globality. South–South migration reveals but also enables these possibilities. For the migrants, mobility has existential value; to move is to live, to survive, to connect, to resist, to exist, and to enjoy. The migrants' ability to move, despite the impediments they face, demonstrates that they will not be confined by (b)ordering practices or remain perpetually suspended in time in impoverished refugee camps and informal settlements. Despite (b)ordering regimes' acquisitions of new "smart" technologies of violence (Salter, 2004), the migrants use their collective creative powers to continue to move, survive, and be visible. They find their authentic voices in this irreducible capacity to move. Yet, when speaking of mobility as a voice, we must be mindful that this voice is neither universal nor univocal. In the complex (b)ordering regimes, some migrants are more resourceful and capable than others; some are more successful in their journeys than others (Haile, 2020; Yohannes, 2021a, 2021b). In fact, some might remain stuck in perpetual immobility and yet "keeping on the move without letting pass" (Tazzioli, 2020, 101).

The barriers of place, time, and knowledge imposed by (b)ordering and (dis)counting regimes dissolve to the point of non-existence every time these migrants are welcomed in places not far from their homes and not indifferent to their ways of life. South–South migration within the continents of Africa (e.g., Congolese migrants migrating to South Africa, the entrepreneurship of East African refugees in Uganda, South Sudan, Angola, etc.), South America (e.g., Venezuelan refugees settled within the region), and Asia (e.g., Syrian refugees settled in the Middle East, Yemeni refugees in the Gulf, etc.) are just a few examples of refugees making significant contributions to the economic and socio-cultural life of the regions in which they settle (see Crush & Ramachandran, 2014; Kibreab, 2000; Kok, 1989). These forms of movement, intersubjective encounter, intercultural communication, and skills/knowledge sharing enable the South–South migrants to turn themselves into communicative and trading "nomads", in the Lévinasian sense of the term. For Lévinas, "Nothing is more enrooted than the nomad… he or she who emigrates is fully human: the migration of man does not destroy, does not demolish the meaning of being" (1998, 117). These practices of mobility grounded in principles of "*ubuntu*" reveal the possibilities and opportunities within the region, as well as the many works of peace and hospitality that reign in invisibility (see Arthur et al., 2015).

Reclaiming the Humanity of Forced Migrants

Throughout this chapter, we insist on remembering the dismembered bodies of the displaced migrants and recognising their humanity in the same way we recognise our own humanity. And we suggest that the tasks of remembering, and recognition comprise attending to the forced migrants' pain and joy, cries, songs, and poems, as well as understanding and welcoming the migrants. These sensibilities and the ability to move from the very foundations of the forced migrants' human qualities. As Maldonado-Torres (2008,

133), for example, reminds us: "Before the word reaches the horizons of meaning, where the world is unveiled and the meaning of reality becomes clear, the cry becomes a call for the recognition of the singularity of the subject as such". That is to say that the manifestation of pain and happiness through the phenomenologies and epistemologies of crying and rejoicing against those of "blindness" (Santos, 2001) constitute the primal utterances of subjects held by (b)ordering and (dis)counting in "a *state of injury*" (Mbembé, 2003, 21, emphasis in original). These primal epistemic utterances come before the so-called participant stories, which are often obtained through extractive methods such as interviews and focus group discussions.

To put these utterances into words—that is, to transition from attending to feelings to saying and writing—is, as Qasmiyeh (2019) puts it, "to embroider the voice with its own needle". For Qasmiyeh,[3] "voice" is "a prior state of being that is initiated by and therefore intrinsically belongs to the individual herself" (2020, 254). Qasmiyeh (2020, 254) adds:

> Indeed, embroidering the voice is writing the intimate, the lived, and the leftovers in life into newer times as imagined by the writer herself; it is writing without a helping hand from anyone but rather through continuously returning to the embroidered (and what is being embroidered) and its tools, notwithstanding how incomplete and fragmentary they are.

The transition from attending to primal epistemic utterances and to embroidering the voice opens the possibility for the Southern subject to emerge "out of the impossibility of demanding anything whatsoever" (Maldonado-Torres, 2008, 136). This departure from the primordial epistemic utterances allows us to abandon the Cartesian dictum of "I think, therefore I am", in favour of harnessing the epistemic powers of "I feel, therefore I can be free" (Lorde, 2018, 4), together with ubuntu sensibilities which situate being in the collective. Feelings come before thinking and writing, and these must be attended to in their epistemic order in order to excavate the "shards of radical potential buried in the sedimentation of the political present" (Kramer, 2019, 12). The artistic and cultural works we have highlighted above as examples allow us to begin the arduous task of inviting scholars into methods which might promote "epistemic healing" (Khan & Naguib, 2019). As Mbembe (2015, para. 17) expounds:

---

[3] Qasmiyeh is a Palestinian refugee and researcher, born in a refugee camp. See also University of Oxford, Faculty of English, Spotlight on Students available at https://www.english.ox.ac.uk/article/yousif-m.-qasmiyeh.

From art, literature, music, and dance, I have learnt that there is a sensory experience of our lives that encompasses innumerable unnamed and unnameable shapes, hues, and textures that "objective knowledge" has failed to capture. The language of these genres communicates how ordinary people laugh and weep, work, play, pray, bless, love and curse, make a space to stand forth and walk, fall, and die.

As such, intercultural and interepistemic communication mediated by artistic and cultural work allows the humanity of the Global South to manifest itself in ways the Global North cannot render invisible and inferior.

Furthermore, reclaiming humanity entails the unconditional ethical responsibility to encounter the Other, in Lévinasian terms, "face-to-face" (see Lévinas, 2011). For Lévinas, the otherness of the Other is an inescapable reality. It is, fundamentally, a realisation of an ontology of being of other beings—of an existence of other humans—outside oneself. Questioning that very existence—the otherness of the Other—amounts to "an act of ontological violence" (Walker, 2004, 530).

We therefore must dissociate the face of the forced migrant from the "invented threat" that the Global North wishes to perceive. The vulnerable faces and precarised situations of the forced migrants are indications neither of threats to be feared nor inferior beings to be dominated. This reality should be the guiding principle in our attempts to destitute the violence—epistemic or otherwise—of (b)ordering and (dis)counting. Reclaiming the humanity of the forced migrants and restoring their dignity requires a radical ethical responsibility to receive them, be sympathetic to their weary faces, and be prepared to live with them. This unconditional welcome is "subjectivity as welcoming the Other, as hospitality" (Lévinas, 2011, 27). From this standpoint, Lévinas (1994) asks: "To shelter the other in one's own land or home, to tolerate the presence of the landless and homeless on the "ancestral soil", so jealously, so meanly loved—is that the criterion of humanness?" (98). Lévinas' response is: "Unquestionably so" (98). The conviction that people should gift their homes/lands/shelters to welcome the forcibly displaced constitutes the essence of a collective ethical responsibility towards one another.

Therefore, the task of reclaiming the humanity of forced migrants necessitates re/membering the names and faces of the migrants, as well as recognising their dignity, humanity, and epistemic utterances. The urgent task, we argue, is to demolish intellectually the violability and bestiality assigned to forced migrants and create a place of decolonial possibility in which to imagine new ways of knowing and being. The place from which to begin this task is "the realm of intersubjectivity", a site where the humanity of the subjects in question is recognised (Maldonado-Torres, 2008, 131). To be clear, we are not suggesting that forced migrants be humanised, because that would assume they are not already "human enough" (Maldonado-Torres, 2016, 13). In fact, the sensibilities we have outlined above are a testament to the humanity of these migrants. We are simply pointing to the lively practices of comfort and discomfort, of joy and exuberance in their manifold presences in migratory settings and practices, as manifesting what Barber describes as "the art of making things stick" (Barber, 2007). By this, she is pointing to the way cultural practices, play, ceremony, and ritual observance of seasonality are laden with heavy ways of spending time and expending energy on what seems frivolous, uneconomical, even pointless, and yet is accompanied by embodied practice of tears, laughter, silence, observation, dance, and contemplation. Ritual practices are, in Barber's view, also part of ensuring continuity of knowledge about how to reclaim humanity and such practices have, according to Graeber and Wengrow, always been part of the human archaeological and anthropological record, it is simply the narrative of Eurocentric scholarship that has assumed otherwise (Graeber & Wengrow, 2021). This humanist call, as Frantz Fanon articulates, demands "quite simple attempt to touch the other, to feel the other, to explain the other to myself" (1986, 231). These are the decolonial foundations of restorative, reparative, and regenerative cultural and epistemic praxes that allow the humanity of the South–South migration to be birthed in the intellectual endeavours.

Conclusion

In this chapter, we have demonstrated how (b)ordering and (dis)counting are deployed to create necropolitical borders between the Global North and Global South, but also within these regions, with the intention of (im)mobilising, containing, and detaining forced migrants. As Mbembe points out, these necropolitical regimes function by "deepening the space and time asymmetries between different categories of humanity while leading to the progressive ghettoization of entire regions of the world" (2019, 11). As demonstrated, the Global South has become the primary target of necropolitical (b)ordering and (dis)counting experimentation on the region's forced migrants. The Global North and Eurocentric humanitarian organisations roam the Global South with their measurement-heavy perceptions to create what Santos (2016) calls "Abyssal thinking". "Abyssal thinking", Santos (2016, 118) explains, "consists of a system of visible and invisible distinctions, the invisible ones being the foundations of the visible ones". We have demonstrated how distinctions are made between migrants' primal utterances and the Global North's measurement-heavy perceptions to maintain the abyssal thinking. The former is subordinated to the latter to obscure the humanity of the migrants by reducing them to calculable figures and rendering them unintelligible and invisible.

Despite the titrations of life and death conditions, however, the Global South continues to be a place where "a symbiotic merging of life and mobility" is possible (Mbembe, 2019, 10). For the migrants, movement is a liminal mode of living and being, in which life is lived as a journey across time and space. Indeed, as shown, South–South migration is inextricably linked to the migrants' experiences of mobility against spatial, temporal, and conceptual barriers. Thus, any attempt to understand South–South migration requires understanding the lived experience of the migrants, which includes listening to their pain, as well as their love and their rage. The Global South must be able to think, write, and theorise about South–South migration from its own geopolitical and epistemic locations, rather than relying on the measurement-heavy perceptions of the Global North. And, most importantly, the Global North must recognise that the faces and places of the Global South have an equal stake in any intersubjective, intercultural, and interepistemic interactions. Both North and South need the resources of hope which are found in resistance prayers of both joy and sorrow, widening the tired narratives of critique from their narrow moorings.

Moreover, we refuse to contemplate the colonial necropolitical projects of (b)ordering and (dis)counting—epistemically or otherwise; our only contemplation consists of their destitution, to break the carceral cage and necropolitical governance they create. There is no point in metricising people for the sake of (dis)counting; fortifying borders for the sake of (b)ordering; legislating laws for the sake of dehumanising; and waging necropolitics for the sake of "governing through death" (Mayblin, 2020, 38). We therefore suggest systemic destitution of (b)ordering and (dis)counting practices, whose prime function is to create differential levels of humanity, whereby some lives are deemed more qualified than others. We have argued for the intellectual demolition of these structurally violent regimes and suggested doing so on epistemic, conceptual, and ethical grounds. We have shown how artistic and cultural works such as poetry and music can help us contemplate, listen to, and restore sensibilities subjected to epistemic muteness. From this perspective, we have rejected the conditions and preconditions of necropolitics in favour of "sowing and growing that give root to praxis; a sowing and growing that herald life in an era of violence-death-war" (Walsh, 2021, 11). To humanise the cultural and epistemic work in South–South migration, one must consider "delinking" the cultural and epistemic work from violence—epistemic or otherwise (Mignolo, 2007). Let art be art on its own terms and culture be a way of life in its own contexts.

We have opened our discussion with a poem because, as Lorde (2018, 1) eloquently affirms, "it is through poetry that we give name to those ideas which are—until the poem—nameless and formless, about to be birthed, but already felt".

> Obedience
>   I spent the day in obedience
>   Unwriting all that has been written.
>   Unwalking the beech strewn paths.
>   Unthinking all that has been thought
>   Unfeeling all sensuous sensation.
>   I let the water lap around my skin
>   then unlapping, let the water join the mist.
>   I held only air.
>   Spoke only with silence.
>   Touched only the shadows lay.
>   I reeled in every prayer, unhooked the bait,
>   Threw the fish back into the water.
>   Decreated, I surveyed the battlefield.
>   Warriors are not warriors outwith wartime.
>   Warriors are gardeners, poets,
>   spirits of the living,
>   spirits at one
>   with the dead.
>   Decreated, I tore the many words from my lips,
>   the many thoughts from my mind,
>   the hopes from my heart.
>   Decreated, I left the dance floor.
>   And for a while
>   my land had rest from war.
>   Disobedience
>   After letting my land rest,
>   I disobeyed.
>   I could do no other.
>   It began with a poem
>   from the place of obedience.
>   The words made the clinging mist blush crimson
>   The bark in the forest burn red like cedar
>   Scented as richly and skelfing the skin.
>   The ink smudged,

the wax melted,
the carpet of leaves was moist.
The fish swam onto the hook,
onto the fire
and into the poem's wide,
wild mouth.
(Phipps, 2019).

References

Aas, K. F. (2006). The body does not lie': Identity, risk and trust in technoculture. *Crime, Media, Culture, 2*, 143–158.

Agamben, G. (2014). What is a destituent power? *Environment and Planning D, 32*, 65–74. https://doi.org/10.1068/d3201tra

Agamben, G. (1998). *Sovereign power and bare life*. Stanford University Press, Stanford, Calif.

Agamben, G. (1995). We refugees. *Symposium: A Quarterly Journal in Modern Literatures, 49*, 114–119. https://doi.org/10.1080/00397709.1995.10733798

Aiyar, M. S., Barkbu, M. B. B., Batini, N., Berger, M. H., Detragiache, M. E., Dizioli, A., Ebeke, M. C. H., Lin, M. H. H., Kaltani, M. L., & Sosa, M. S. (2016). *The refugee surge in Europe: Economic challenges*. International Monetary Fund.

Amoore, L. (2006). Biometric borders: Governing mobilities in the war on terror. *Political Geography, 25*, 336–351. https://doi.org/10.1016/j.polgeo.2006.02.001

Arthur, D. D., Issifu, A. K., & Marfo, S. (2015). An analysis of the influence of Ubuntu principle on the South Africa peace building process. *JGPC, 3*. https://doi.org/10.15640/jgpc.v3n2a4

Assaf, M., & Clanchy, K. (2018). Once, I lived in a house with a name. *Migration and Society, 1*, 209–211. https://doi.org/10.3167/arms.2018.010119

Bach, J.-N. (Ed.). (2022). *Routledge handbook of the horn of Africa*. Routledge.

Bahlbi, Y. M. (2016). Human trafficking and human smuggling to and from Eastern Sudan: Intended and unintended consequences of States' policies. *Academic Journal of Interdisciplinary Studies, 5*, 215.

Barber, K. (2007). Improvisation and the art of making things stick. In E. Hallam and T. Ingold (Eds.), *Creativity and cultural improvisation* (pp. 25-45). Berg.

Berry, M., Garcia-Blanco, I., & Moore, K. (2016). *Press coverage of the refugee and migrant crisis in the EU: A Content Analysis of Five European Countries*.

Butler, J. (2006). *Precarious life: The powers of mourning and violence*. Verso, London.

Crush, J., & Ramachandran, S. (2014). *Migrant entrepreneurship collective violence and Xenophobia in South Africa*. Southern African Migration Programme (SAMP), Oxford, South Africa.

Damoc, A.-I. (2016). Fortress Europe breached: Political and economic impact of the recent refugee crisis on European states. *Annals of the University of Oradea, 25*, 20–29.

Davies, D. (2020). Dreamlands, border zones, and spaces of exception: comics and graphic narratives on the US-Mexico border. a/b: *Auto/Biography Studies, 35*, 383–403. https://doi.org/10.1080/08989575.2020.1741187

Fanon, F. (1986). *Black Skin, White Masks*, Repr. ed, Pluto classics. Pluto Press.

Fiddian-Qasmiyeh, E. (2020a). *Refuge in a moving world: Tracing refugee and migrant journeys across disciplines*. Books at JSTOR.

Fiddian-Qasmiyeh, E. (2020b). Introduction. *Migration and Society, 3*, 254–255. https://doi.org/10.3167/arms.2020.030122

Fisseha, M. (2015). Organ trafficking of Eritreans in the Sinai: Perpetration or provision of service? *SSRN Journal*. https://doi.org/10.2139/ssrn.2609329

Graeber, D., & Wengrow, D. (2021). *The dawn of everything: A new history of humanity*. Allen Lane.

Green, P. (2015). *Countdown to Annihilation: Genocide in Myanmar*.

Haile, S. (2020). Voices to be heard? Reflections on refugees, strategic invisibility and the politics of voice. In E. Fiddian-Qasmiyeh (Ed.), *Refuge in a moving world: Tracing refugee and migrant journeys across disciplines* (pp. 32–40). UCL Press.

Heller, C., & Pécoud, A. (2020). Counting migrants' deaths at the border: From civil society counterstatistics to (inter)governmental recuperation. *American Behavioral Scientist, 64*, 480–500. https://doi.org/10.1177/0002764219882996

Human Rights Watch. (2009). *Pushed back, pushed around Italy's forced return of boat migrants and asylum seekers, Libya's mistreatment of migrants and asylum seekers*. Human Rights Watch, New York.

Khan, F. R., & Naguib, R. (2019). Epistemic healing: A critical ethical response to epistemic violence in business ethics. *Journal of Business Ethics, 156*, 89–104. https://doi.org/10.1007/s10551-017-3555-x

Kibreab, G. (2000). Resistance, displacement, and identity: The case of Eritrean refugees in Sudan. *Canadian Journal of African Studies, 34*, 249. https://doi.org/10.2307/486416

Kofman, E., & Sales, R. (1992). Towards fortress Europe? *Women's Studies International Forum, 15*, 29–39. https://doi.org/10.1016/0277-5395(92)90031-P

Kok, W. (1989). Self-settled refugees and the socio-economic impact of their presence on Kassala, Eastern Sudan. *J Refugee Stud, 2*, 419–440. https://doi.org/10.1093/jrs/2.4.419

Kramer, S. (2019). *Excluded within: The (un)intelligibility of radical political actors*. Oxford University Press.

Lévinas, E. (2011). *Totality and infinity: An essay on exteriority*, 23rd printing. ed. Duquesne Univ. Press [u.a.], Pittsburgh, PA.

Lévinas, E. (1998). *Entre Nous: On thinking-of-the-other, European perspectives*. Columbia Univ. Press.

Lévinas, E. (1996). *Proper names, Meridian : Crossing aesthetics*. Stanford University Press.
Lévinas, E. (1994). *In the time of the nations*. Indiana University Press.
Lorde, A. (2018). *The master's tools will never dismantle the master's house*. Penguin Books, London.
Loschi, C., Raineri, L., & Strazzari, F. (2018). The implementation of EU Crisis Response in Libya: Bridging theory and practice. EUNPACK Working paper. Deliverable 6.02.
Mainwaring, Ċ. (2019). *At Europe's Edge: Migration and Crisis in the Mediterranean*, 1st ed. Oxford University Press. https://doi.org/10.1093/oso/9780198842514.001.0001
Maldonado-Torres, N. (2016). *Outline of Ten Theses on Coloniality and Decoloniality*. Frantz Fanon Foundation Paris.
Maldonado-Torres, N. (2008). *Against war: Views from the underside of modernity*. Duke University Press, Durham.
Maldonado-Torres, N. (2007). On the coloniality of being: Contributions to the development of a concept. *Cultural Studies, 21*, 240–270. https://doi.org/10.1080/09502380601162548
Malkki, L. H. (1996). Speechless emissaries: Refugees, humanitarianism, and dehistoricization. *Cultural Anthropology, 11*, 377–404. https://doi.org/10.1525/can.1996.11.3.02a00050
Mayblin, L. (2020). *Impoverishment and Asylum: Social Policy as Slow Violence*, Routledge Advances in Sociology. Routledge, Milton Park, Abingdon, Oxon
Mbembe, A. (2020). Afropolitanism. *Nka Journal of Contemporary African Art, 2020*, 56–61. https://doi.org/10.1215/10757163-8308174
Mbembe, A. (2019). Bodies as borders. *From the European South, 4*, 5–18.
Mbembe, A. (2015). Achille Mbembe: The value of Africa's aesthetics. *The Mail & Guardian*. https://mg.co.za/article/2015-05-14-the-value-of-africas-aesthetics/. Accessed 20 July 2022.
Mbembé, J.-A. (2003). Necropolitics. *Public Culture, 15*, 11–40.
Mignolo, W. D. (2007). Delinking: The rhetoric of modernity, the logic of coloniality and the grammar of de-Coloniality. *Cultural Studies, 21*, 449–514. https://doi.org/10.1080/09502380601162647
Missing Migrants Project. (2022). Data | Missing Migrants Project [WWW Document]. URL https://missingmigrants.iom.int/data. Accessed 6 July 2022.
Mudawi, H. A. (2019). Refugees and forced migration from Eritrea and Ethiopia to Sudan. In E. Wacker, U. Becker, K. Crepaz, K. (Eds.), *Refugees and forced migrants in Africa and the EU* (pp. 151–159). Springer Fachmedien Wiesbaden, Wiesbaden. https://doi.org/10.1007/978-3-658-24538-2_8
Perl, G. (2019). Migration as survival. *Migration and Society, 2*, 12–25. https://doi.org/10.3167/arms.2019.020103
Phipps, A. (2022). Against capture, cleansing and extraction: Towards a new eco-social discourse of research and investigation. United Nations Research Institute for Social Development. https://www.unrisd.org/en/library/blog-posts/against-capture-cleansing-and-extraction-towards-a-new-eco-socialdiscourse-of-research-and-investig2022

Phipps, A. M. (2019). Decolonising multilingualism: struggles to decreate, Writing without borders. *Multilingual Matters*, Blue Ridge Summit.

Qasmiyeh, Y. M. (2019). To embroider the voice with its own needle. https://berghahnbooks.com/blog/to-embroider-the-voice-with-its-own-needle. Accessed 26 May 2022.

Qasmiyeh, Y.M. (2020). Introduction. *Migration and Society 3*, 254–255. https://doi.org/10.3167/arms.2020.030122

Salter, M. B. (2004). Passports, mobility, and security: How smart can the border be? *International Studies Perspectives, 5*, 71–91.

Santos, B. D. S. (2001). Toward an epistemology of blindness: Why the new forms of 'ceremonial adequacy' neither regulate nor emanicipate. *European Journal of Social Theory 4*(3): 251–279.

Santos, B. D. S. (2014). *Epistemologies of the South: Justice against Epistemicide*. Routledge.

Santos, B. S. (2016). *Epistemologies of the South: Justice against Epistemicide*. Routledge.

Schaffer, S. (2020). Necroethics in the time of COVID-19 and Black Lives Matter. In J. M. Ryan (Ed.), *COVID-19: Global pandemic, societal responses, ideological solutions*. Routledge. https://doi.org/10.4324/9781003142089

Tazzioli, M. (2020). *The making of migration: The biopolitics of mobility at Europe's Borders*. Society and space series.

UNHCR. (2022). *Global Trends Report 2021*, UNHCR. https://www.unhcr.org/publications/brochures/62a9d1494/global-trends-report-2021.html

Van Avermaet, P. (2009). Fortress Europe. Language policy regimes for immigration and citizenship. In G. Hogan-Burn, C. Mar-Molinero, & P. Stevenson (Eds.), *Discourses on language and integration*, Amsterdam, Benjamins.

Walker, P. O. (2004). Decolonizing conflict resolution: Addressing the ontological violence of westernization. *American Indian Quarterly*, 527–549.

Walsh, C. (2021). Decolonial praxis. *International Academy of Practical Theology. Conference Series* (pp. 4–12).

Wickramasekara, P. (2011). Labour migration in South Asia: A review of issues, policies and practices. International Migration Working Paper.

Yohannes, H. T. (2021a). Refugee trafficking in a carceral age: A case study of the Sinai trafficking. *Journal of Human Trafficking* 1–15. https://doi.org/10.1080/23322705.2021.1885005

Yohannes, H. T. (2021b). The realities of Eritrean refugees in a carceral age (PhD). University of Glasgow.

Weil, S. (1970). *First and last notebooks: Supernatural knowledge*. Oxford University Press.

Open Access This chapter is licensed under the terms of the Creative Commons Attribution 4.0 International License (http://creativecommons.org/licenses/by/4.0/), which permits use, sharing, adaptation, distribution and reproduction in any medium or format, as long as you give appropriate credit to the original author(s) and the source, provide a link to the Creative Commons license and indicate if changes were made.

The images or other third party material in this chapter are included in the chapter's Creative Commons license, unless indicated otherwise in a credit line to the material. If material is not included in the chapter's Creative Commons license and your intended use is not permitted by statutory regulation or exceeds the permitted use, you will need to obtain permission directly from the copyright holder.

Part II

Unpacking "the South" in South–South Migration

8

Global Trends in South–South Migration

Kerilyn Schewel and Alix Debray

Introduction

Migration is a feature of every society. Most people migrate internally, or within countries, but a smaller share moves internationally, or across country borders. Scholarship and public discourse tend to focus on international movements from the Global South to the Global North, yet as this chapter will show, over one-third of all international migration in 2020 was between countries of the Global South—a greater share than South–North migration (UN DESA, 2020). Countries in the Global South host at least 40% of all international migrants, and over 85% of refugees and asylum seekers.

Contrary to prevalent and somewhat alarmist narratives that migration is reaching unprecedented and unmanageable scales, global levels of international migration have remained surprisingly stable. Absolute volumes of international migration have increased significantly, but so too has the global

---

K. Schewel (✉)
Duke Center for International Development, Sanford School of Public Policy, Durham, NC, USA
e-mail: kerilyn.schewel@duke.edu

A. Debray
UNU-CRIS, Bruges, Belgium

Ghent University, Ghent, Belgium

A. Debray
e-mail: adebray@cris.unu.edu

© The Author(s) 2024
H. Crawley and J. K. Teye (eds.), *The Palgrave Handbook of South–South Migration and Inequality*, https://doi.org/10.1007/978-3-031-39814-8_8

153

population. According to the most recent UN Population Division estimates, international migrants constituted just 3.6% of the 7.8 billion people living on this planet in 2020—a percentage that is only one point higher than the 2.6% registered in 1960 (UN DESA, 2020). In the Global South, the share of the population who are international migrants is even smaller than the global average: 2.9% in 2020 (UN DESA, 2020).

Despite the surprising stability of the global rate of international migration, clearly much in the world has changed over this period of accelerated globalisation. In 1960, the top three destination countries of international migrants were the US, India, and Pakistan. In 2020, they were the US, Germany, and Saudi Arabia. India and Pakistan have fallen to 14th and 19th, respectively, while new European and Middle Eastern countries have moved into the top ten. The most important changes in international migration appear to be directional (see Czaika & de Haas, 2014). Global population movements track deeper geopolitical and economic changes, as people move to seize new opportunities, to respond to shifting labour markets and new inequalities, and to flee new conflicts in our global age.

This chapter presents a broad-brush overview of recent trends in South–South migration, using origin and destination international migrant stock data from the United Nations Department of Economic and Social Affairs (UN DESA). After providing more detail about the UN DESA dataset, the chapter has three main sections. The first compares volumes and gender composition of South–South migration with other types of migration (South–North, North–North, and North–South) between 1990 and 2020. The second section presents the top twenty South–South migration corridors, followed by brief regional overviews. The final section considers patterns specific to refugees and internationally displaced peoples in the Global South.

Migration Data in the Global South

To review trends in South–South migration, we faced two important decisions. First, what countries constitute the Global South? As previous chapters have explored, the categories of Global South and Global North are somewhat arbitrary and increasingly contested. No universally agreed upon list of qualifying countries exists. Definitions based on geography, income-level, or human development indicators fail to capture the remarkably diverse political, socioeconomic, and cultural realities that constitute the Global South, and treating the Global South as one entity obscures rising inequalities within it. Our primary aim in this chapter is to analyse migration trends in regions that are traditionally under-represented in migration studies—without necessarily limiting the term to a country's level of economic or human development. For our review of global trends, we used the list of 138 "Countries in the Global South" provided by the Organization for Women in Science for the Developing World (OWSD) to establish the baseline for the categories of "South" and "North" (see Fig. 8.1).

The second key decision concerned what migration data to use. There are two main types of migration data. Stock data refers to the number of people living in a destination country who were born or have citizenship elsewhere at a specific point in time. Flow data captures how many migrants are moving between two countries over a given period. Stock data tends to be more available and reliable than migrant flow data, but stock data tends to undercount population mobility. Flow data is more coveted by migration researchers, but only 45 countries report migration flow data to the United Nations, and of these, only Azerbaijan, Kazakhstan, and Kyrgyzstan are from the Global South (UN DESA, 2015). It is even more difficult to track irregular migration, smuggling, and displacement. Data on these forms of migration tend to rely on more creative data collection strategies (e.g., cell phone, social media, court documents, or tracking data collected at strategic transit locations) rather than standard statistical or administrative sources (e.g., census, household survey, visa, or border data).

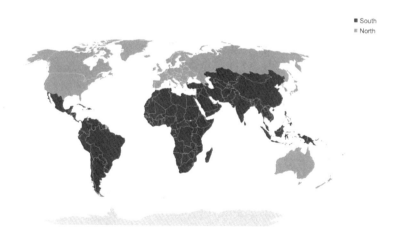

Fig. 8.1 Global South and Global North country categorisation from the Organisation for Women in Science for the Developing World (OWSD) (*Source* Map template powered by Bing © Australian Bureau of Statistics, GeoNames, Microsoft, Navinfo, OpenStreetMap, TomTom)

To map global trends and identify key South–South migration corridors, we use origin and destination international migrant stock data from UN DESA, which may be further explored by interested readers using the online Migration Data Portal run by the International Organization of Migration.[1] UN DESA provides global estimates of international migrant stocks based on national statistics on country of birth, and where data on the foreign-born were not collected in national censuses, based on country of citizenship (UN DESA, 2020a). This dataset allows us to explore differences by gender and over time (between 1990 and 2020). It also includes refugee and asylum seeker figures within the dataset, reflecting a definition of international migrants as people who change their country of residence, regardless of their reason for moving.

The UN DESA dataset is the most geographically comprehensive dataset available on international migration, including estimates of migrant stock data for 232 countries/areas. However, the dataset also has important limitations. First, stock data likely underestimates actual migration flows. Second, the dataset is built upon population census data, which can be inaccurate and unreliable in many countries where national statistical bureaus have not received sufficient investment or support. Since the 2010 round of censuses, for example, 43% of Central and Southern Asian countries and 16% in Sub-Saharan African countries do not have at least one data source on international migrant stocks (UN DESA, 2020b). Third, countries may use different criteria to identify international migrants, based on different minimum duration of stay in the country, complicating cross-country comparisons. Finally, this dataset does not attempt to measure migration flows or irregular migration. For these reasons, it is likely that the number of people moving across borders—particularly in the Global South—is higher than the estimates of international migrants based on population census data presented here.

Global Overview

South–South migration has been and remains a significant share of global population movements. Figure 8.2 shows the evolution of international migrant stocks in millions of people in 1990, 2005, and 2020. South–South migration was the predominant form of international migration in 1990, surpassed by South–North migration in 2005 and is now slightly greater than South–North migration in 2020. North–North and South–South migration show surprisingly comparable volumes of international migration in 1990

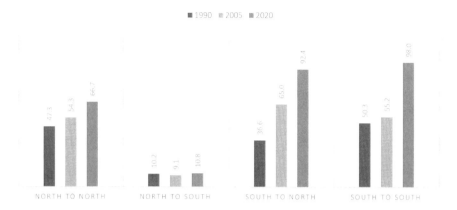

Fig. 8.2 Evolution of international migrant stocks, in millions of people (*Source* Own calculation by using UN DESA, 2020)

and 2005, before a significant rise in South–South migration in 2020. North–South migration has remained relatively small as a share of global population movements, hovering around 10 million people between 1990 and 2020. Figure 8.2 suggests that international migration within the Global South appears to be on the rise, at least in terms of absolute numbers.

Describing migration trends in terms of absolute numbers or percentages of a population gives two very different impressions. For example, the total stock of international migrants in Africa increased from 15.7 million in 1990 to 25.4 million in 2020. However, the percentage of the total population in Africa that were migrants declined from 2.5% in 1990 to 1.9% in 2020 (UN DESA, 2020). Thus, although absolute numbers of migrants rose significantly, overall population growth increased more quickly. This demographic context is important to keep in mind as young populations grow across many countries in the Global South, while many countries in the Global North face population ageing and decline.

Figure 8.3 shows international migration trends from the Global South by gender, distinguishing between South–South migration and South–North migration. Male and female migration is roughly equal (50% split) across time periods in the South–North corridor, with a slight increase in the number of females relative to males in 2020. South–South migration shows greater gender differences. As a share of total movements within the Global South, male migration increased from 55% in 1990 to 58% in 2020. Although the gender composition of migration flows varies significantly across countries and corridors, big picture trends suggest that women constitute a declining percentage of South–South migration since 1990.

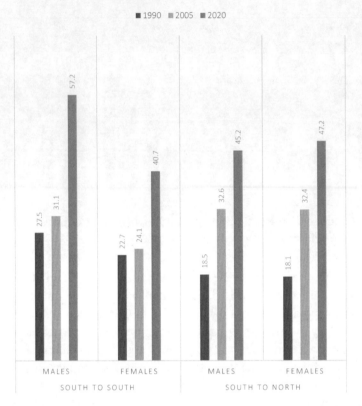

Fig. 8.3 Evolution of international migrant stock by gender, in millions of people (*Source* Own calculation by using UN DESA, 2020)

Regional and Sub-regional Trends

This section reviews international migration trends for different regions and sub-regions of the Global South. Figure 8.4 shows the countries included in each region/sub-region: Central America, South America, Sub-Saharan Africa, North Africa (excluding Egypt), the Middle East (including Egypt), Central Asia, South Asia, South-East Asia, China, and Small Island States (including the Caribbean and smaller islands in Oceania).

Table 8.1 shows the top twenty migration corridors across the Global South. Migration from South Asia to the Middle East is the largest migration corridor, and it has grown substantially in recent decades. The number of international migrants of South Asian origin in the Middle East grew from 8.4 million in 1990 to 21.5 million in 2020. The top five migration corridors that follow are all intra-regional corridors, with some of the largest movements taking place between countries of Sub-Saharan Africa, the Middle East,

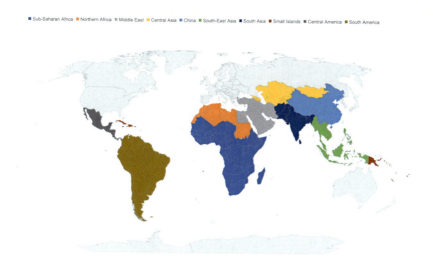

Fig. 8.4 Geographic groupings used for regional analyses (*Source* Map template powered by Bing © Australian Bureau of Statistics, GeoNames, Microsoft, Navinfo, OpenStreetMap, TomTom)

South America, South Asia, and South-East Asia, in that order. Table 8.1 also shows significant movements between regions neighbouring each other: from China to South-East Asia, for example, or between South and South-East Asia.

Intra-regional migration is the dominant trend for most of the Global South, but Fig. 8.5 illustrates important differences in the relative share of intra-regional versus extra-regional destinations by sub-region. Some sub-regions like Central America, Northern Africa, and Central Asia show low levels of intra-regional migration and high levels of extra-regional migration—a relatively stable trend since 1990. It is no coincidence that these areas border wealthy regions of the Global North: North America, Europe, and Russia, respectively.

Other areas of the Global South show greater diversity in the evolution of intra-regional versus extra-regional migration. Some regions have seen a relative rise in intra-regional movement. The Middle East, for example, had comparable levels of intra-regional and extra-regional migration in 1990 and 2005, before a large increase in intra-regional migration in 2020. This jump reflects, in part, the arrival of over six million Syrians in Middle Eastern countries over this period. South America had greater extra-regional movements to destinations outside the continent in 2005, but in 2020, sees a notable rise in intra-regional migration.

Table 8.1 Top 20 regional corridors in the Global South

#	Migration corridors in the Global South		International migrant stock at mid-year, both sexes combined		
	Origin sub-region	Destination sub-region	1990	2005	2020
1	South Asia	Middle East	8,430,184	9,908,618	21,543,951
2	Sub-Saharan Africa	Sub-Saharan Africa	11,491,413	11,723,891	17,808,594
3	Middle East	Middle East	4,707,666	7,067,549	16,930,232
4	South America	South America	2,077,128	2,894,144	8,557,503
5	South Asia	South Asia	13,805,470	9,404,692	8,218,312
6	South-East Asia	South-East Asia	1,652,270	5,072,632	7,641,267
7	South-East Asia	Middle East	1,347,646	1,951,598	4,303,417
8	China	South-East Asia	2,485,449	2,885,850	3,425,709
9	South Asia	South-East Asia	217,470	803,747	1,771,538
10	South-East Asia	South Asia	659,702	692,752	1,520,414
11	Sub-Saharan Africa	Northern Africa	1,372,517	599,161	1,489,388
12	Northern Africa	Sub-Saharan Africa	248,780	799,347	1,172,533
13	Northern Africa	Middle East	544,892	668,883	1,125,149
14	Central Asia	Central Asia	1,397,406	1,261,496	956,318
15	Small Islands	Small Islands	493,506	672,976	934,299
16	Sub-Saharan Africa	Middle East	214,251	336,788	774,124
17	Central America	Central America	1,195,652	503,647	743,476
18	South-East Asia	China	304,298	440,523	635,568
19	Middle East	Northern Africa	312,014	487,831	633,657
20	Small Islands	South America	66,386	72,844	424,637

Source Own calculation using UN DESA (2020)

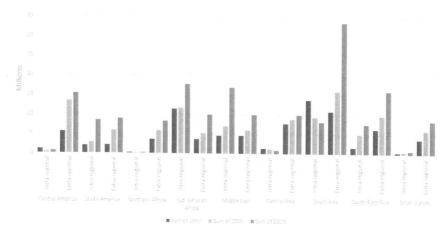

Fig. 8.5 Evolution of intra- and extra-regional migration per sub-region, in millions of people (*Source* Own calculation by using UN DESA, 2020)

Other sub-regions show the opposite trend. South Asia shows a clear decline in intra-regional migration and a sharp rise in extra-regional movements, increasingly directed towards Middle Eastern countries. South-East Asia has had higher levels of extra-regional migration since 1990, but the gap between extra- and intra-regional migration grew larger in 2020. Sub-Saharan Africa, which has the largest volumes of intra-regional mobility in the Global South, saw a jump in both intra-regional and extra-regional migration between 2005 and 2020. The following sections explore these regional dynamics in greater detail, including information on the top ten origin and destination countries for each sub-region.

The Middle East

The rise of the Middle East as a major global migration hub has been one of the more important trends over the late twentieth and early twenty-first centuries. Saudi Arabia and the United Arab Emirates (UAE) are two of the top 10 global destination countries, hosting 13.5 million and 8.7 million immigrants, respectively (MPI, 2023). When analysing immigrants as a percentage of the total population, and excluding small island or city states, the top destination societies are almost all in the Middle East. In the UAE, for example, immigrants made up 88.1% of the total population in 2020. Other notable countries with majority immigrant populations in 2020 include Qatar (77.3%), Kuwait (72.8%), and Bahrain (55.0%) (MPI, 2023).

The labour demand for immigrant workers in the Gulf States rose after the discovery of vast reservoirs of oil in the mid-twentieth century, and the 1973 oil shock that significantly increased the price of oil. This generated new financial resources to undertake major development projects and greater demand for foreign workers to carry out the work. While there were only some two million migrant workers in the Gulf region in 1975, some 68% of whom were from other Arab countries (Thiollet, 2011), the scale of migration increased dramatically over the following decades. As Table 8.2 shows, most migrant workers now come from South Asia, particularly countries like India, Pakistan, and Bangladesh. Migration from India grew from just under 2 million in 1990 to 9.6 million in 2020. There were 3.4 million migrants from Pakistan and Bangladesh, respectively, in 2020. Migration from other countries in the Middle East remains significant (36%), followed by migration from Europe and North America, Northern Africa, and Sub-Saharan Africa. Migration from Northern Africa doubled from 544,892 in 1990 to over 1.1 million in 2020, and migration from Sub-Saharan Africa more than tripled from 214,251 in 1990 to 774,124 in 2020. However, this misses significant irregular movements. Irregular migration from Ethiopia to the Middle East, for example, has been estimated to be at least double the number of formal figures (Demissie, 2018).

Different world regions show important gender differences in migration to the Middle East. South Asian and South-East Asian countries see the greatest and growing gender divergence since the 1990s. The number of South and South-East Asian women living in the Middle East roughly doubled from 3.6 million in 1990 to 7.3 million in 2020, responding to the increasing demand for domestic workers, nurses, and service staff. The number of male migrants from South and South-East Asia has historically been higher, responding to labour demand for construction workers, drivers, mechanics, or other professional positions. Mirroring global trends in South–South migration, male migration from South and South-East Asia accelerated at a faster pace than female migration, tripling from 6.2 million in 1990 to 18.6 million in 2020.

Other world regions show smaller gender differences in migration to the Middle East. Europe, North America, South America, and China are distinctive for having more female migrants in the Middle East than male migrants. There were 34,576 South American women in the Middle East in 2020, compared to 29,234 men, and 19,163 Chinese women compared to 9149 Chinese men.

Migrants leaving Middle Eastern countries are most often found in other Middle Eastern countries (62% of the 27.2 million international migrants). 32% are in Europe and North America. Top destination regions in the

Table 8.2 Top 10 countries of origin and destination to/from the middle east

Middle East Top 10 countries	International migrant stock at mid-year, both sexes combined		
	1990	2005	2020
Origin of immigrants in the Middle East			
India	1,975,728	3,741,866	9,599,189
Syrian Arab Republic	442,253	553,442	6,874,146
State of Palestine	1,587,057	2,952,323	3,585,723
Bangladesh	869,805	1,440,960	3,462,617
Pakistan	921,081	1,465,954	3,430,202
Afghanistan	4,161,055	2,611,285	3,327,155
Egypt	1,013,052	1,329,893	2,892,044
Indonesia	840,520	1,116,538	2,312,797
Philippines	406,073	691,436	1,695,969
Yemen	430,032	560,791	1,176,308
Destination of migrants from the Middle East			
Jordan	1,111,847	2,133,048	3,320,209
Germany	1,658,152	1,637,174	3,081,546
Saudi Arabia	1,139,748	1,432,174	2,956,307
Lebanon	507,755	713,223	1,694,805
United States of America	677,567	1,113,774	1,659,457
United Arab Emirates	290,782	594,462	1,544,303
Syrian Arab Republic	248,532	780,766	799,360
Kuwait	232,103	236,573	641,953
Canada	171,917	366,338	617,982
Libya	232,821	415,550	545,200

Source UN DESA (2020)

Global South are Northern Africa and South and South-East Asia, though contributions to overall migration are small, at 2.3% and 0.5%, respectively.

Central Asia

Migration from Central Asian countries is primarily towards countries that were historically part of the Soviet Union, notably the Russian Federation and Ukraine. Russia and Ukraine are also top origin countries for migration to Central Asia, suggesting these migration systems constitute more reciprocal than one-way flows (Table 8.3). The over 6 million Central Asians living in Russia are fundamental to the Russian economy, working in agriculture, construction, sanitation, transportation, and other service sectors. This movement is also central to economic development in Central Asia. Remittances from Russia to Kyrgyzstan and Tajikistan, for example, accounted for 31%

and 27% of GDP, respectively, in 2020 (UN, 2022). Migration to countries within Central Asia is also significant, particularly to Kazakhstan and Azerbaijan.

Beyond the former Soviet states and Europe, migration to and from South Korea is another notable migration dynamic. There are some 300,000 ethnic Koreans living in Central Asian countries, particularly Kazakhstan and Uzbekistan, many of whom identify as "Koryo-saram". Migration from Korea to the Russian Far East occurred as early as the 1860s and reached up to 200,000 by the late 1930s. During the Pacific War, suspicions arose that Koreans were spies for Japan, and Stalin deported all Koreans living in the Far East to Central Asian countries (Lee, 2012). Over this same period, new cohorts of migrants arrived from Korea, fleeing the forced labour imposed by ruling Japanese there. These historical movements shape present day trends.

Table 8.3 Top 10 countries of origin and destination to/from Central Asia

Central Asia	International migrant stock at mid-year, both sexes combined		
Top 10 countries	1990	2005	2020
Origin of immigrants in Central Asia			
Russian Federation	4,827,672	3,672,762	3,852,550
Ukraine	698,546	483,316	531,981
Uzbekistan	313,900	328,289	398,019
Armenia	242,326	207,593	179,557
Azerbaijan	557,925	459,675	168,014
Belarus	162,368	106,536	113,339
Georgia	86,408	97,901	94,028
Dem. People's Republic of Korea	20,894	53,664	67,390
Turkey	27,114	45,668	54,421
Kazakhstan	128,198	65,782	52,710
Destination of migrants from Central Asia			
Russian Federation	6,415,013	6,599,176	6,712,940
Germany	21,117	808,920	1,385,026
Ukraine	759,545	746,617	726,710
Kazakhstan	190,092	287,206	385,323
United States of America	81,416	145,863	277,895
Azerbaijan	306,703	257,446	214,599
Greece	93,459	123,578	136,908
Belarus	149,559	131,987	127,119
Armenia	468,862	409,298	119,061
Turkmenistan	165,850	117,815	103,116

Source UN DESA (2020)

The Republic of Korea remains one of the top ten origin countries of immigrants in Central Asia, though current numbers are far smaller than historical movements.

Labour migration from Central Asia to the Republic of Korea is also emerging as a relatively new migration dynamic. In 2007, facing a declining fertility rate and labour shortages, the Korean government enacted immigration reforms to attract more labour migrants, which included issuing work visas for ethnic Koreans from the former USSR. Between 2007 and 2017, 12,885 ethnic Koreans from Uzbekistan, Kazakhstan, and Kyrgyzstan moved to Korea, working mostly in low-skilled occupations (Lakupbaeva, 2019). Though absolute numbers of migrants remain relatively small, the financial remittances they send home are significant. Kazakhstan's National Bank notes that Kazakh citizens working in South Korea sent home 104.8 million USD in 2018 in comparison to 1.7 million USD in 2012. The same trend has been observed in Uzbekistan, where the largest number of Central Asia's ethnic Koreans reside. In 2018, Uzbek migrant workers in Korea sent home 108.3 million USD, in comparison to 49 million in 2016 (Lakupbaeva, 2019). As Russia wages a war against Ukraine, straining the security and economic benefits of migration between these countries and Central Asia, new migration destinations like Korea may play an increasingly important role in the migration and development trajectory of Central Asian countries in the coming years.

South and South-East Asia

Migration within and from countries in South Asia and South-East Asia are some of the largest population movements in the world. This region is also home to the world's most populous countries, like India, Indonesia, Pakistan, and Bangladesh. Table 8.4 shows that the largest population movements into countries in South Asia come from other countries in the same region—Bangladesh, India, and Afghanistan. The same is true for South-East Asia, where intra-regional migrants tend to come from countries like Myanmar, Indonesia, Malaysia, Lao, and Cambodia. The largest movements into South-East Asia, however, are from China.

Although intra-regional migration in South Asia and South-East Asia remains high and continues to grow, migration to destinations further afield, most notably the Middle East as well as countries in North America and Europe, is increasing more quickly. In 2020, major destinations from South Asia include the Middle East (Saudi Arabia and the UAE in particular), the US, India, and Pakistan. India and Pakistan were the top two destinations

Table 8.4 Top 10 countries of origin and destination to/from South Asia and South-East Asia

South Asia	International migrant stock at mid-year, both sexes combined			South-East Asia	International migrant stock at mid-year, both sexes combined		
Top 10 countries	1990	2005	2020	Top 10 countries	1990	2005	2020
of Origin				of Origin			
Bangladesh	4,377,309	3,319,816	2,529,809	China	2,485,449	2,885,850	3,425,709
India	3,262,078	2,614,679	2,130,244	Myanmar	235,518	1,325,023	2,214,204
Afghanistan	3,389,132	1,182,065	1,614,449	Indonesia	378,209	1,099,501	1,566,667
Myanmar	315,171	195,247	966,906	Malaysia	252,910	882,359	1,206,651
Pakistan	1,932,018	1,168,095	938,459	Lao People's Dem. Republic	170,494	545,996	949,225
Nepal	528,220	790,645	773,129	Cambodia	104,579	381,431	712,910
China	181,183	264,458	290,796	Nepal	30,814	152,072	615,603
Malaysia	104,896	206,388	214,252	Bangladesh	36,271	260,155	508,614
Sri Lanka	286,991	209,833	192,777	India	104,825	259,070	378,208
Indonesia	73,015	125,254	151,920	Philippines	201,171	231,479	310,058
of Destination				of Destination			
Saudi Arabia	2,487,058	3,272,541	6,777,653	United States of America	2,120,448	3,688,276	4,667,507
United Arab Emirates	819,653	2,141,020	5,719,387	Thailand	491,071	2,102,361	3,492,856
India	7,123,422	5,420,461	4,266,695	Saudi Arabia	964,087	1,266,999	2,621,922
United States of America	608,437	1,893,515	3,764,181	Malaysia	441,262	1,251,012	1,942,904
Pakistan	6,194,110	3,165,408	3,195,896	Singapore	245,003	994,038	1,413,482
Iran (Islamic Republic of)	3,990,232	2,394,581	2,723,176	Bangladesh	526,804	570,055	1,409,376
Oman	252,266	546,840	1,972,289	Australia	494,166	692,368	1,184,028
Kuwait	671,008	846,443	1,938,424	Canada	536,369	823,355	1,172,165
United Kingdom	771,593	1,250,683	1,831,708	United Arab Emirates	108,933	329,121	896,397
Qatar	41,403	357,364	1,608,807	Japan	72,740	312,853	738,927

Source UN DESA (2020)

of South Asian migrants in 1990 by a large margin but have experienced a notable decline in registered immigrant populations in the decades since. This decline is due in part to a decline in refugee movements. For example, following the Soviet invasion of Afghanistan from 1979 to 1989, migration from Afghanistan reached 3.3 million in 1990, the majority of whom were hosted in Pakistan. By 2020, the number of immigrants from Afghanistan had declined to 1.6 million.

The top destinations from South-East Asia are the US, followed by Thailand, Saudi Arabia, Malaysia, and Bangladesh. The rise of Thailand as a major destination country is one of the newer trends—from less than half a million in 1990 to 3.5 million in 2020.

There are significant country-level differences in the nature and drivers of movement across these large regional groupings. Myanmar, for example, experienced a notable rise in the number of people migrating internationally to neighbouring countries in South and South-East Asia. There were just over one half million migrants from Myanmar in South and South-East Asian countries in 1990, and this grew to over 3 million by 2020. Today Myanmar is second only to China in 2020 for the number of migrants it sends to other countries in the region. There was a notable rise in refugee movements from Myanmar, particularly from the Rohingya population, an ethnic minority that has been denied citizenship and faces persecution and violence in Myanmar. About one million Rohingya refugees now live in the largest refugee camp in the world in Cox's Bazar, Bangladesh. However, a larger number of migrants from Myanmar are categorised as labour migrants. According to the latest Myanmar Population Census of 2014, more than two million Myanmar citizens were abroad, over 70% of whom were working in Thailand (ILO, 2022). A smaller number were working in Malaysia, China, Singapore, the Republic of Korea, Japan, and the Gulf countries. Many migrant workers from Myanmar use licensed overseas employment agencies to migrate, but due to the costs, time, and uncertainties that it will result in better conditions, a greater share may migrate irregularly (ILO, 2022).

China

A major economic force in East Asia, China has experienced remarkable development gains in recent decades. Over the last forty years, China contributed close to three-quarters of the global reduction in the number of people living in extreme poverty. At China's current national poverty line, the number of poor fell by 770 million over this period (World Bank, 2022). Between 1990 and 2020, China's urban population grew from 26.4% of the total population to 61.4%. The number of Chinese living abroad more than doubled from 4.2 million in 1990 to 10.4 million in 2020.

Most international movement from China is to countries or territories within the region. In 2020, top destinations include Hong Kong, the Republic of Korea, Japan, and Singapore (Table 8.5). International migration to the US is also notably high, as is Chinese migration to Canada and Australia. Migration to South America has grown significantly, more than doubling between 2005 and 2020 (from 53,884 to 114,604) yet remains relatively small compared to other regional destinations.

There is growing international interest in migration between China and African countries (see also Teye et al., this volume). Formal figures of migration between these regions remain low, with UN DESA data capturing just 33,998 Chinese migrants on the African continent in 2020 and providing no data on Africans in China. However, surveys, qualitative research, and

Table 8.5 Top 10 countries of origin and destination to/from China

China Top 10 countries	International migrant stock at mid-year, both sexes combined		
	1990	2005	2020
Origin of immigrants in China			
Viet Nam	285,788	300,897	303,095
China, Hong Kong SAR	622	68,509	209,555
Republic of Korea	37,449	85,449	144,831
Brazil	3057	33,986	57,602
Philippines	7118	33,428	56,657
Indonesia	5386	18,179	30,811
United States of America	4288	12,251	20,762
China, Macao SAR	3099	9755	18,918
Thailand	1477	6950	11,779
Peru	557	6168	10,455
Destination of migrants from China			
China, Hong Kong SAR	1,659,157	2,070,537	2,408,447
United States of America	773,939	1,607,654	2,184,110
Republic of Korea	19,827	243,217	803,011
Japan	150,383	648,120	775,893
Canada	168,079	508,994	699,190
Australia	97,526	227,561	653,232
Singapore	150,447	299,651	426,434
China, Macao SAR	172,346	236,962	300,567
Italy	32,172	137,633	233,338
United Kingdom	23,384	146,994	208,229

Source UN DESA (2020)

on-the-ground observations suggest this migration corridor is far larger than these formal figures suggest (Bodomo, 2012).

Chinese migrants are moving to African countries to work in trade, infrastructure development, mining, commerce, and agriculture. Data from the China–Africa Research Initiative estimates there were 103,983 Chinese workers in Africa in 2020, down from a peak of 263,659 in 2015, mostly working in construction. These estimates do not include informal migrants such as traders and shopkeepers. In 2020, the top five destinations of Chinese workers—accounting for 46% of all Chinese workers in Africa—were Algeria, Nigeria, Ethiopia, the Democratic Republic of Congo, and Angola (CARI, 2022). More focused case studies suggest even higher numbers of Chinese immigrants than the CARI data. Botchwey et al. (2019), for example, suggest there were approximately 50,000 Chinese migrants in the informal gold mining sector in Ghana between 2008 and 2013. Because small-scale gold mining is restricted by law to Ghanaian citizens, most Chinese miners do not have legal status and are often missed in population statistics.

Africans are also migrating to China in growing numbers to pursue opportunities for higher education, trade, or tourism (see Bodomo, 2012; Cissé, 2013; Haugen, 2012). Most African traders arrive in China on short-term visas, to buy goods that they resell in African countries. Some settle in China, but they tend to stay on renewable one-year visas, and thus may not be counted in formal statistics as permanent migrants. Many other African students, traders, or workers are unable to renew their short-term visas and can become trapped in a precarious position of informality.

Africa

Despite growing interest in migration from Africa to new destinations like China, migration from African countries is still overwhelmingly directed towards other African countries (see also Setrana & Yaro, this volume). Taking Africa as a whole, the top ten origin countries and nine out of the top ten destination countries are all other African countries. Some of these movements are driven by conflict and humanitarian crises—as seen in the large growth in international migration from South Sudan (Table 8.6). As of 2020, refugees and asylum seekers comprised a striking one third of all international migration within Sub-Saharan Africa (UN DESA, 2020a). However, this should not overshadow the more significant, yet arguably more mundane forms of mobility related to demographic transitions, higher levels of education and infrastructure, economic growth and the changing aspirations of Africa's younger generations (see Flahaux & de Haas, 2016).

Sub-Saharan Africa experiences the largest intra-regional movements in the Global South, and the second highest in the world after Europe. 63% of the 28.3 million migrants from countries in Sub-Saharan Africa moved to other countries within Sub-Saharan Africa, top destinations including Côte d'Ivoire, South Africa, and Uganda. An additional 5.3% moved to countries in Northern Africa. Migration outside the continent is primarily directed towards Europe (18.1%), followed by North America (8.7%), the Middle East, and less than 2% in Australia and New Zealand, South and East Asia, South or Central America.

Migration from Northern Africa is smaller (8.7 million in 2020) and unlike migration from Sub-Saharan Africa, is predominantly directed towards Europe and North America (70.3% of total migration in 2020). This has been a relatively stable trend since 1990, and France has remained the top destination country of all African migration over this period (Table 8.6). Other regional destinations from North Africa include Sub-Saharan Africa (13.5%) and the Middle East (13.0%).

Comparisons across time suggest that migration from Africa is diversifying beyond intra-regional patterns of emigration. In 1990, for example, 83% of migration from Sub-Saharan Africa was to other African countries; this declined to 68.2% in 2020. Migration to Europe and North America captured a growing share of migrants from Sub-Saharan Africa, from 13.8% in 1990 to 26.9% in 2020.

Nevertheless, recent surveys of migrants within Africa—many of whom would not be captured in UN DESA data—find that migration remains overwhelmingly intra-regional. One study collecting migration flow data at key transit hubs in West and Central Africa found that only 10% of migrants from this region intend to travel to Europe (Allie et al., 2021). Further, despite widespread international attention on violent conflict as a driver of movement in this region, three-quarters (74%) report economic reasons for moving, such as searching for jobs or engaging in seasonal work-related migration. One quarter (25%) cite family-related factors, such as following family and friends, and only 3.5% of migrants say they are moving because they fear for their safety (Allie et al., 2021).

Table 8.6 Top 10 countries of origin and destination to/from Africa

Sub-Saharan Africa	International migrant stock at mid-year, both sexes combined			North Africa	International migrant stock at mid-year, both sexes combined		
Top 10 countries	1990	2005	2020	Top 10 countries	1990	2005	2020
of Origin				*of Origin*			
South Sudan	504,409	217,693	1,648,384	South Sudan	4753	1441	869,489
Burkina Faso	1,014,852	1,331,642	1,565,304	State of Palestine	188,859	257,762	337,162
Democratic Rep. of the Congo	324,530	934,138	1,500,845	Eritrea	65,813	198,172	226,461
Mali	593,691	818,724	1,164,370	Western Sahara	167,905	131,163	162,952
Sudan	229,704	229,704	1,107,440	Somalia	4,843	93,968	123,128
Somalia	731,909	590,237	1,033,232	Chad	197,035	81,639	103,983
Côte d'Ivoire	315,601	601,380	922,034	Iraq	5968	62,738	83,058
Zimbabwe	163,266	348,083	912,266	Ethiopia	943,913	109,217	72,125
Central African Republic	19,263	94,192	767,662	Syrian Arab Republic	20,338	26,800	57,125
Nigeria	267,662	313,024	673,280	France	29,973	24,717	53,400
of Destination				*of Destination*			
Côte d'Ivoire	1,789,579	2,196,031	2,483,381	France	1,781,618	2,535,850	3,166,741
United States of America	242,409	902,970	2,031,637	Spain	145,547	573,161	853,009
South Africa	748,376	939,136	1,839,023	Italy	251,766	487,772	620,033
Uganda	394,598	244,461	1,646,637	South Sudan	0	0	587,824
United Kingdom	430,541	907,259	1,434,404	Saudi Arabia	178,769	232,539	481,215
Sudan	1,341,832	478,568	1,324,964	Chad	10,625	248,464	374,098
Nigeria	299,556	870,507	1,177,115	United States of America	32,731	103,906	345,448
France	514,393	777,573	1,116,709	Belgium	339,682	202,676	271,701
Ethiopia	1,072,032	395,359	1,017,711	Israel	236,046	245,812	242,387
Kenya	195,916	635,707	971,029	Germany	109,796	135,738	216,988

Source UN DESA (2020)

Latin America

Like Africa, Latin America shows important sub-regional differences. Migration from Central America is primarily extra-regional, oriented towards North America, while migration from South America is equally intra-regional and extra-regional (Fig. 8.5). In 2020, there were 14.8 million Central Americans living in the US compared to 3.5 million South Americans. Over the last decade, migration from Central America to the US was primarily from Mexico and Northern Central American countries, but in recent years, those trends have changed. In 2022, there were more Nicaraguans, Cubans, and Venezuelans arriving at the US–Mexico border than migrants from El Salvador, Guatemala, and Honduras (Ruiz Soto, 2022). The migration systems that have long facilitated migration from Mexico and Central America to the US are extending southward, responding both to political, economic, and environmental insecurity in these origin countries and significant labour demand for immigrant workers in the US.

Unlike migration from Central American countries, intra-regional migration within South America has increased significantly between 2005 and 2020. This is due in part to the large increase in the number of Venezuelans fleeing their failing state, but the increase in intra-regional migration is not only due to displacement. Over the last decades, several regional integration mechanisms helped facilitate intra-regional mobility. The Andean Community of Nations (CAN) and the Southern Common Market (MERCOSUR) encouraged regular, cross-border migration in South America by facilitating entry, migratory procedures, and access to documentation and social rights for migrants (IOM, 2021). Argentina remains the top destination country in the region (Table 8.7).

Migration into South America from outside the continent is diversifying in terms of origin countries, particularly migration from Africa and Asia. Asian immigration is long-standing, particularly from the People's Republic of China, Japan, and the Republic of Korea, while new movements are observed from Bangladesh, India, Pakistan, Nepal, and Arab Syrian Republic, among others (IOM, 2022). In recent years, the African population has also increased, and the main African nationalities in the region are Angolan, Moroccan, and South African. There are small but noteworthy movements from countries in the Horn of Africa, Nigeria, Democratic Republic of the Congo, and Egypt, among others (IOM, 2020).

Table 8.7 Top 10 countries of origin and destination to/from Latin America

Central America Top 10 countries	International migrant stock at mid-year, both sexes combined			South America Top 10 countries	International migrant stock at mid-year, both sexes combined		
	1990	2005	2020		1990	2005	2020
of Origin				*of Origin*			
United States of America	232,303	556,383	861,487	Venezuela (Bolivarian Rep. of)	44,861	57,713	4,103,204
Nicaragua	257,223	296,929	395,784	Colombia	606,648	790,935	1,329,616
Venezuela (Bolivarian Republic of)	3569	12,124	218,960	Paraguay	282,471	493,113	749,084
Colombia	24,583	50,617	99,665	Bolivia (Plurinational State of)	178,252	351,466	635,043
Guatemala	99,965	61,822	93,792	Peru	72,234	281,108	534,230
Honduras	38,647	43,406	89,064	Argentina	168,593	222,994	306,242
El Salvador	730,358	45,532	79,963	Spain	455,556	269,622	301,077
Mexico	16,078	23,825	36,619	Haiti	12,050	16,468	293,827
China	13,294	19,854	36,523	Chile	288,080	248,398	292,722
Spain	31,682	25,808	34,749	Italy	498,803	290,362	280,286
of Destination				*of Destination*			
United States of America	5,425,992	13,103,628	14,758,303	United States of America	1,028,173	2,332,368	3,450,637
Costa Rica	170,970	285,726	393,034	Spain	149,497	1,473,717	2,232,483
Spain	15,873	60,070	235,745	Argentina	821,329	1,227,314	1,890,644
Canada	66,015	137,120	185,379	Colombia	54,829	59,711	1,822,273

(continued)

Table 8.7 (continued)

Central America	International migrant stock at mid-year, both sexes combined			South America	International migrant stock at mid-year, both sexes combined		
Top 10 countries	1990	2005	2020	Top 10 countries	1990	2005	2020
Mexico	407,679	52,878	113,516	Chile	59,457	190,961	1,218,287
Guatemala	252,094	42,028	60,342	Peru	27,115	37,275	1,060,437
Belize	25,130	34,220	50,564	Venezuela (Bolivarian Rep. of)	659,209	787,727	1,041,640
Panama	13,339	19,398	38,610	Ecuador	54,221	116,474	629,845
Italy	5558	20,751	36,290	Italy	99,552	330,054	544,875
El Salvador	32,718	26,789	32,303	Brazil	123,074	158,215	467,897

Source UN DESA (2020)

Small Island Nations

The majority of international migrants from small island states are found in wealthy countries of the Global North, but the second most common destination are other small island states. Of the 9 million international migrants from the Caribbean, for example, most reside in North America (74.9%), followed by other countries in Latin America and the Caribbean (14.7%), most of these going to other Caribbean islands, followed by countries in Europe (10%), and of these, predominantly Southern European countries. There are fewer residents of Caribbean origin in Africa (13,714) and Oceania (11,687).

There were over half a million migrants from islands in Oceania in 2020, including Melanesia, Micronesia, and Polynesia. Most move regionally to Australia and New Zealand (56.6%), followed by North America (27.8%), and then to other islands in Oceania (12.3%). Of the 313,069 international immigrants living on these Oceanic islands, most come from European countries (23.7%), predominantly Western European countries, followed by South-East Asian countries (21.0%), North America (8.7%), and then Australia and New Zealand (6.8%).

Small island nations face unique socioeconomic and environmental vulnerabilities related to their remote geography, small land mass, and reliance on tourism and ocean-based natural resources. In recent decades, the adverse and disproportionate consequences of climate change on small island states are of growing international concern. Small islands have been devastated by sudden-onset events like hurricanes, tropical storms, and cyclones, leading to immediate population displacements often accompanied by high rates of return. Small islands also face slow-onset events such as sea level rise or ocean acidification, which threaten to undermine local livelihoods and the long-term capability to stay in place.

Research is just beginning to tease out the implications of sudden- and slow-onset climate change on migration patterns from small island nations. For example, one study of population movements within and from Puerto Rico after Hurricane Maria in 2017 analysed data generated by mobile phones, social media, air travel records, and census data between July 2017 and 2018 (Acosta et al., 2020). They find overall population loss from Puerto Rico, but the magnitude differs by data source: 4% according to Census data and up to 17% according to social media data. Rural areas lost a greater share of their population, and movements within Puerto Rico were primarily from rural to urban municipalities.

Quantifying the effects of slow-onset climate change on migration patterns has proved more challenging. Gradual climate and environmental changes—like changes in sea level rise, temperature, or precipitation patterns—have more indirect and non-linear effects on migration trends. Environmental changes are mediated by the political, economic, technological, social, and cultural context. Even in small island settings, initial research suggests that slow-onset climate change does not have a stronger effect than other demographic or developmental drivers of migration (see, for example, Speelman et al. [2021] on the Maldives).

International Displacement in the Global South

Asylum seeking and refugee movements are a relatively small portion of global international migration (roughly 10%). However, the demands and burdens associated with displaced populations are overwhelmingly carried by countries within the Global South. Refugee movements—like other forms of population mobility—are most often intra-regional movements. In fact, 69% of refugees and other people in need of international protection live in countries neighbouring their countries of origin. Twenty-two per cent of refugees and other internationally displaced peoples are hosted in countries categorised by the United Nations as the 'least developed countries' (UNHCR, 2022)—countries including Bangladesh, Chad, the Democratic Republic of the Congo, Ethiopia, Rwanda, South Sudan, Sudan, the United Republic of Tanzania, Uganda, and Yemen. For comparison, just 17% are hosted by high-income countries in the Global North.

Although communication and transportation costs around the world are diminishing, which one might expect might facilitate greater South–North movements of refugee populations, wealthy countries across the Global North are developing increasingly sophisticated techniques of "remote control" to bar asylum seekers from spaces where they can ask for sanctuary (Fitzgerald, 2019).[2] International norms of collective responsibility and *non-refoulement* are eroding, and the result is that potential South–North refugee movements become forcibly South–South.

According to the UN Refugee Agency (UNHCR), there are three durable solutions to international displacement: voluntary repatriation, local integration, and resettlement to another country. However, according to UNHCR's most recent statistics, less than 1% of refugees are resettled each year (just 39,266 in 2021) and less than 1% of refugees are repatriated to their home countries (just 49,795 in 2021). "Over half of the refugees for whom

UNHCR is responsible", one report states, "find themselves trapped in protracted situations, where they have lived for years or even decades on end" (UNHCR, 2011). In this context, local integration can be a formal strategy of host country governments, or an informal strategy pursued by refugees trying to build a new life for themselves and their families. Most will fail to achieve full citizenship; over the past decade, only 1.1 million refugees were naturalised in their country of asylum. Some of the best examples we have of creative strategies for local integration come from countries in the Global South, like the United Republic of Tanzania and Sierra Leone (UNHCR, 2011).

These dynamics mean that countries of the Global South are shouldering responsibility for refugees and asylum seekers without sufficient international support to realise durable solutions for displaced populations. When Germany accepted one million refugees, mostly from Syria, in 2015 and 2016, the country was praised (and criticised by anti-immigrant groups) for its relative generosity. Yet, the scale of refugees resettled relative to Germany's population of over 80 million pales in comparison to other refugee-receiving nations in the Global South. Lebanon, for example, hosts some 1.5 million Syrian refugees and 13,715 refugees of other nationalities in a country with a population of just 6.8 million people. Lebanon hosts the largest number of refugees per capita and per square mile in the world.

Conclusion

South–South migration constitutes a significant share of humanity's international population movements—larger in volume than South–North migration in 2020. Most international migrants leaving the Global South move to countries within their home region, particularly in areas like Sub-Saharan Africa, the Middle East, and South America. Exceptions to this trend are regions of the Global South that neighbour wealthier countries of the Global North, like Central America, North Africa, Central Asia, or small island states in Oceania and the Caribbean. In these places, extra-regional, South–North migration is more common than intra-regional, South–South migration.

This chapter finds important shifts in the relative share of intra- and extra-regional movements across the Global South since the 1990s. In regions like Sub-Saharan Africa, South Asia, and South-East Asia, which are home to some of the largest intra-regional movements in the world, there has been a notable rise in extra-regional migration as more international migrants travel further distances. In fact, migration from South Asia to the Middle East is now the largest South–South migration corridor in the world.

The implications of these trends for migration governance are two-fold. Because most migrants in the Global South move regionally, there is a need to strengthen regional cooperation on migration governance. Many countries across the Global South are striving to do so within the framework of regional economic communities, like the Economic Community of West African States or the Southern Common Market (MERCOSUR) in South America. However, the rise in extra-regional movements requires complementary international frameworks. This is the aspiration of the Global Compact on Migration, the first UN global agreement on a common approach to international migration in all its dimensions—though its objectives and recommendations remain non-binding.

While the big picture trends presented in this chapter are clear, more specific country-level data should be taken with a dose of scepticism. This brief overview uses some of the best global and cross-nationally comparable dataset we have on international migrant stocks. However, as our introduction highlighted, capturing international migration flows and trends remains exceedingly difficult. The formal figures we present here likely underestimate the true extent of migration occurring within the Global South, and some important trends—like migration between Africa and China—are simply not reflected in the UN DESA dataset.

Improved understanding of South–South migration requires greater investment in census data collection, which requires funding and capacity-building in the statistical bureaus of many countries across the Global South—a responsibility that should be shouldered by the international community interested in reliable data on migration, not only national governments. We also need more detailed case studies and surveys of migration corridors, to better understand the nature, volume, composition, and reasons for migration within and between countries and sub-regions of the Global South. The following chapters address this need by presenting exploring South–South migration trends and experiences within and between Latin America, Africa, and Asia.

Notes

1. https://www.migrationdataportal.org/.
2. For example, at the time of writing, Australia diverts asylum seekers to an offshore processing center on the island of Nauru. The US under the Trump administration forcibly returned asylum seekers to Mexico—a policy that

continued with Venezuelan asylum seekers under President Biden. Frontex, an agency of the European Union tasked with managing its borders, has been accused of "pushbacks" or returning migrants and asylum seekers to their point of departure.

References

Acosta, R., Kishore, N., Irizarry, R., & Buckee, C. (2020). Quantifying the dynamics of migration after Hurricane Maria in Puerto Rico. *Proceedings of the National Academy of Sciences, 117*(51), 32772–32778.

Allie, F., Christensen, D., Grossman, G., & Weinstein, J. (2021). *Using IOM flow monitoring data to describe migration in West and Central Africa*. IPL Report: Immigration Policy Lab.

Bodomo, A. (2012). *Africans in China*. Cambria Press.

Botchwey, G., Crawford, G., Loubere, N., & Lu, J. (2019). South–South irregular migration: The impacts of China's informal gold rush in Ghana. *International Migration, 57*(4), 310–328.

CARI. (2022). *Number of Chinese workers in Africa, 2009–2020*. Chinese-Africa Research Initiative database, Johns Hopkins University. http://www.sais-cari.org/data-chinese-workers-in-africa

Cissé, D. (2013). South–South migration and Sino-African small traders: A comparative study of Chinese in Senegal and Africans in China. *African Review of Economics and Finance, 5*(1), 17–28.

Czaika, M., & de Haas, H. (2014). The globalization of migration: Has the world become more migratory? *International Migration Review, 48*(2), 283–323.

Demissie, F. (2018). Ethiopian female domestic workers in the Middle East and Gulf States: An introduction. *African and Black Diaspora: an International Journal, 11*(1), 1–5.

Fitzgerald, D. S. (2019). *Refuge beyond reach: How rich democracies repel asylum seekers*. Oxford University Press.

Flahaux, M. L., & De Haas, H. (2016). African migration: Trends, patterns, drivers. *Comparative Migration Studies, 4*, 1–25.

Haugen, H. Ø. (2012). Nigerians in China: A second state of immobility. *International Migration, 50*(2), 65–80.

ILO. (2022). *Labor migration in Myanmar*. International Labour Organization. https://www.ilo.org/yangon/areas/labour-migration/lang--en/index.htm

IOM. (2020). *Extraregional migration in the Americas: Profiles, experiences and needs*. Regional Office for Central America, North America and the Caribbean San José, Costa Rica. International Organization for Migration.

IOM. (2021). *Migration data in South America.* Migration Data Portal. https://www.migrationdataportal.org/regional-data-overview/migration-data-south-america

IOM. (2022). *Recent Migration Movements in South America—Annual Report 2022.* International Organization for Migration, Buenos Aires.

Lakupbaeva, Z. (2019). *Central Asia's Koreans in Korea: There and (mostly) back again.* openDemocracy. https://www.opendemocracy.net/en/odr/central-asias-koreans-in-korea-there-and-mostly-back-again/. Accessed 25 October 2022.

Lee, W. (2012). *The Koreans' migration to the Russian Far East and their deportation to Central Asia: From the 1860s to 1937.* Masters thesis, University of Oregon.

MPI. (2023). Top 25 destinations of international migrants. *Migration Policy Institute (MPI) Data Hub.* https://www.migrationpolicy.org/programs/data-hub/charts/top-25-destinations-international-migrants. Accessed 10 April 2022.

OWSD. *Countries in the Global South by region and alphabetical order.* Organization for Women in Science for the Developing World. https://owsd.net/sites/default/files/OWSD%20138%20Countries%20-%20Global%20South.pdf

Ruiz Soto, G. A. (2022). *Record-breaking migrant encounters at the U.S.–Mexico border overlook the bigger story.* Migration Policy Institute Commentaries. https://www.migrationpolicy.org/news/2022-record-migrant-encounters-us-mexico-border. Accessed 11 November 2022.

Speelman, L. H., Nicholls, R. J., & Safra de Campos, R. (2021). The role of migration and demographic change in small island futures. *Asian and Pacific Migration Journal, 30*(3), 282–311.

Thiollet, H. (2011). Migration as diplomacy: Labor migrants, refugees, and Arab regional politics in the oil-rich countries. *International Labor and Working-Class History, 79*, 103–121.

UN. (2022). Sanctions on Russia already hitting remittance-dependent countries in Central Asia: IOM. *UN News,* 15 June 2022. https://news.un.org/en/story/2022/06/1120502

UN DESA. (2015). *International migration flows to and from selected countries: The 2015 revision* (United Nations database, POP/DB/MIG/Flow/Rev.2015).

UN DESA. (2020). *International Migrant Stock 2020* (United Nations database, POP/DB/MIG/Stock/Rev.2020).

UN DESA. (2020a). *International migration 2020 highlights.* United Nations Department of Economic and Social Affairs, Population Division (ST/ESA/SER.A/452).

UN DESA. (2020b). *Methodology report: International migrant stock 2020.* United Nations, Department of Economic and Social Affairs, Population Division (United Nations database, POP/DB/MIG/Stock/Rev.2020).

UNHCR. (2011). *The benefits of belonging: Local integration options and opportunities for host countries, communities and refugees.* UNHCR: Operational Solutions and Transition Section.

UNHCR. (2022). *Refugee population statistics database*. https://www.unhcr.org/refugee-statistics/

World Bank and the Development Research Center of the State Council, the People's Republic of China. (2022). *Four decades of poverty reduction in china: Drivers, insights for the world, and the way ahead*. World Bank.

Open Access This chapter is licensed under the terms of the Creative Commons Attribution 4.0 International License (http://creativecommons.org/licenses/by/4.0/), which permits use, sharing, adaptation, distribution and reproduction in any medium or format, as long as you give appropriate credit to the original author(s) and the source, provide a link to the Creative Commons license and indicate if changes were made.

The images or other third party material in this chapter are included in the chapter's Creative Commons license, unless indicated otherwise in a credit line to the material. If material is not included in the chapter's Creative Commons license and your intended use is not permitted by statutory regulation or exceeds the permitted use, you will need to obtain permission directly from the copyright holder.

9

The Dynamics of South–South Migration in Africa

Joseph Awetori Yaro and Mary Boatemaa Setrana

Introduction

South–South migration involves the movement of individuals from one developing country to another in the Global South. Although there are significant international movements between the countries of the Global South (see Schewel and Debray, this volume) migration narratives tend to focus on migration from the Global South to the Global North. These narratives are, however, starting to change as researchers and policymakers from the Global South increasingly contribute to the migration discourse in the South. The changing global economy, growing interconnectedness, and the political landscape are contributing factors to the increasing attention given to South–South migration (see, for example, Bakewell et al., 2009; Setrana et al., 2022). Factors such as cultural attitudes, economic incentives, geopolitical realities, and international cooperation account for the increasing flows between countries of the Global South (Halperin & Heath, 2020).

The outcomes of South–South migration are diverse and contradictory; while some highlight the negatives associated with South–South migration,

---

J. A. Yaro
Department of Geography and Resource Development, University of Ghana, Accra, Ghana

M. B. Setrana (✉)
Centre for Migration Studies, University of Ghana, Accra, Ghana
e-mail: mbsetrana@ug.edu.gh

namely poverty and inequality which arise by draining resources from vulnerable countries (see, for example, Ratha et al., 2011), others are of the view that South–South migration promotes economic growth and creates new opportunities for innovation and collaboration (see, for example, Setrana & Arhin-Sam, 2022; Setrana & Kliest, 2022; Teye, 2022; Ullah & Haque, 2020). These perspectives are largely skewed towards the use of economic indicators as measurements of development and ignore the welfare and social aspects (Quartey et al., 2020). Research undertaken by the large number of Global South scholars involved in the Migration for Development and Equality Hub (MIDEQ) provides a more nuanced explanation that reflects the trends, patterns, and complexities of South–South migration.[1] This research indicates that South–South migration is essential for economic development and knowledge transfer between countries in the Global South (see also Bakewell et al., 2009). It helps bridge the gap between skilled labour and knowledge, leading to a better quality of life for the population (see also World Health Organization, 2008). It also helps improve agricultural practices and technologies in the receiving country (see also Zossou et al., 2020). Furthermore, it contributes to addressing population imbalances and reducing brain drain (see also Quartey et al., 2020).

There is a need for policymakers, scholars, and development partners to recognise the relevance of South–South migration in order to develop policies and strategies that facilitate the migration processes and ensure benefits to both sending countries and the migrants. South–South migration must be seen as a strategic and constructive approach for developing countries to work together towards a shared goal (Ratha & Shaw, 2007). By recognising the value of South–South migration and promoting policies that support the integration of migrants, developing countries can create more inclusive and prosperous societies for all (Bakewell et al., 2009). Human mobility dynamics in Africa provide one of the clearest examples of the potential benefits of South–South migration.

Migration trends and patterns in Africa have changed over time: geographical patterns have significantly changed from the colonial days through the post-colonial era to the neoliberal era (see also Fynn Bruey and Crawley, this volume). These changing patterns have been shaped by the global geopolitical context, global economic changes, international migration policies and laws, and environmental disturbances. The reasons for intra-African movements are diverse and defined by both the African context and external barriers to international migration beyond the African continent. The majority of African migration within the continent occurs due to socio-economic, political, and environmental factors (Flahaux & De Haas, 2016). Many Africans move to other regions of the continent in search of better job opportunities, higher wages, and better living conditions (Setrana & Kleist, 2022; Teye, 2022).

Drawing on academic sources, including our own studies on various dimensions of African migration, this chapter argues for a more evidence-based analysis of the African migration story.[2] The popular narrative by policymakers and academics that it is a continent plagued by mass displacement and migration, primarily due to poverty and conflict (Flahaux & De Haas, 2016; Korn, 2001; Oucho et al., 2006) with the majority of Africans fleeing across the Mediterranean to Europe, as reflected in media representations. We argue that based on the overwhelming evidence that most Africans move *within* Africa, there is a need for a corrective narrative.

Migration Trends and Patterns in Africa

The innate nature of people to change their location in response to either push or pull factors makes migration an indispensable phenomenon in Africa. In the twenty-first century, the narrative of international migration has transitioned from the practice of "forced colonial slavery" to movements that are motivated by the need to tap into better socio-economic opportunities, conducive political environments, and human-friendly environmental conditions on the continent. There are increasing numbers of movements within the African continent. This can be attributed, in part, to the concerted efforts of African states and international institutions to promote regional integration (Kayizzi-Mugerwa et al., 2014) among the regions of Africa, namely, western, southern, eastern, northern, and central Africa. The drive towards regional integration has created more opportunities for people to move freely within the continent, leading to increased migration. The growth of African economies has also contributed to increase intra-regional mobility: as more countries experience economic growth, there is a greater demand for labour, which has led to an increase in cross-border movement.

The various regional economic communities, namely, CEN-SAD, COMESA, EAC, ECCAS, ECOWAS, IGAD, and SADC (Møller, 2009) have been instrumental in promoting the movement within the continent. For example, ECOWAS has been instrumental in promoting free movement of people and goods throughout West Africa (see also Teye and Oucho, this volume), while SADC has focused on fostering agricultural development and improving infrastructure. Although there are challenges with the ratification and implementation of free movement protocols, this regional cooperation remains an important goal for many African countries as member states work together towards a more prosperous future for all their citizens and migrants.

As of mid-year 2020, the total number of international migrants stood at 280.6 million which constitutes 3.6% of the total global population.[3] The vast majority of these migrants remain within the regions from which they originated. According to the evidence, the highest rate of intra-regional migration is in Europe (70%), followed by Sub-Saharan Africa with an intra-regional migration share of 63%.

As shown in Fig. 9.1, the international migrant stock as a percentage of the total population in Africa has been dwindling, reaching its peak at 2.5% in 1990. This decreased from 1.9% in 2000 to 1.7% in 2010. Since 2015, the international migrant stock as a percentage of the total population in Africa has remained constant.

There is widespread evidence that most African migrants are not crossing oceans, but rather, there is a high level of land-border crossings within the region. The African migration report estimates that 94% of African migrants who cross the oceans do so regularly (Achieng et al., 2020). The report further indicates that 14% of migrants population globally are from Africa while 41% and 24% respectively are from Asia and Europe (Achieng et al., 2020). These figures emphasise the fact that intra-African migration is prominent and this story must be told in order to change the misconception around the irregular migration of Africans across the Mediterranean. A cursory look at migration data further shows that 4 out of 5 international migrants residing in eastern, middle, and western Africa hail from the same African region (Fig. 9.3).

This unique trend of intra-regional migration calls for unbiased academic research, policy guidelines, and measures that reflect the regional setting,

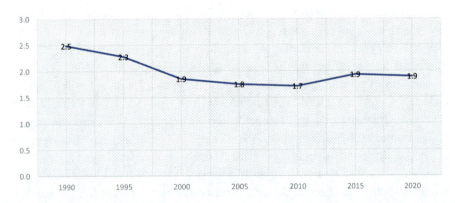

Fig. 9.1 International migrant stock as a percentage of the total population in Africa (*Source* Based on data extracted from the UNDESA database, 2020[4])

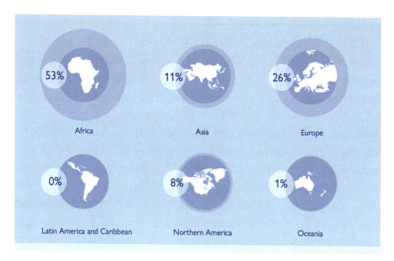

Fig. 9.2 Destination of African migrants globally

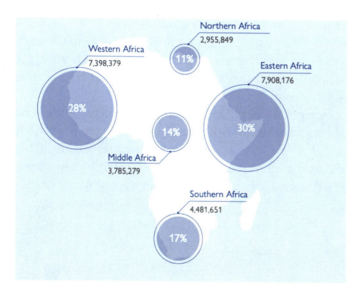

Fig. 9.3 Distribution of migrants on the continent (*Source* Retrieved from the Migration Data Portal, March 2022)

the needs of the African migrant and, ultimately, promote the aspirations of the African people. Admittedly, issues of conflicts, natural disasters, and unfavourable climatic conditions may lead to forcibly displacement of persons. For instance, the ongoing conflicts in the Ethiopian's Tigray region have led to the massive displacement of people who are crossing the

Ethiopian-Sudan border, with women and children being a highly vulnerable group (UNHCR, 2020). Apart from that, if left unabated, the impacts of climate change which are affecting agricultural activities, food supply, and the availability of potable water may not only stimulate migration and forced displacement, but also increase the proportion of distressed migrants in the future.

Nonetheless, a greater chunk of mobility in Africa is largely attributed to the high levels of trade and other socio-economic engagements that have been in existence across several centuries. Africa hosts about five million migrants from the rest of the world (Achieng et al., 2020). Aside from historical trade practices, it is anticipated that the promotion of migrant-friendly trade treaties such as the African Continental Free Trade Area (AfCTA) agreement has the potential to promote labour mobility, commerce, and investment within the region. Moreover, the outbreak of COVID-19 has reshaped the operations of global supply chains and businesses, hence, the ratification of AfCTA can be seen as a conduit for the advancement of intra-continental cross-border trade in an era of growing isolationism.

With reference to Africa, the trajectory of international migrant stock has been increasing continuously for the past decade from 1990 to 2020 (see Fig. 9.4), and this further reinforces the fact that regular intra-regional migration is a common practice in the sub-region.

As shown in Fig. 9.5, there has been an upward trend in the annual rate of change in the migrant stock with a percentage increase from 1.3% in 2000 to 5.0% in 2015. The rate of increase however slowed in 2020, and this can be partly attributed to the impact of the COVID-19 pandemic and the associated international travel restrictions that were imposed across the globe.

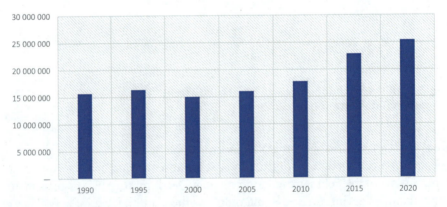

Fig. 9.4 International migrant stock in Africa (*Source* Based on data extracted from the UNDESA database, 2020)

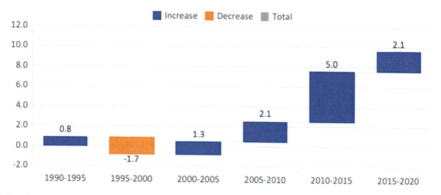

Fig. 9.5 Annual rate of change of the migrant stock in Africa (*Source* Based on data extracted from the UNDESA database, 2020)

The dynamics of migration in Africa show that countries with peaceful and robust economic environments attracted a greater proportion of the young and active migrant labour force. This confirms the general assertion that both skilled and unskilled workers move to environments that offer them better economic prospects in sectors ranging from manufacturing, agriculture, and service sectors. By mid-2020, out of a total of 6.4 million international migrants recorded in the Southern African region 45.3%, representing 2.9 million migrants, chose South Africa as their destination country (IOM).[6] This can be attributed to the disparities in economic growth and prospects between countries within the SADC economic block, where South Africa is considered as the beacon of economic growth. Precisely, the mining potentials of South Africa coupled with the existence of a good business climate has been a pull factor for migrants from Mozambique, Lesotho, Malawi, Botswana, and Eswatini, among others. A similar trend can be seen in western Africa, where migrants from Sahel countries such as Mali, Niger, and Burkina Faso head southwards to coastal countries like Ghana and Côte d'Ivoire which are relatively endowed with better economic prospects in the agriculture, mining, and fishing sectors (Dick & Schraven, 2021). Moreover, the quest to promote economic integration within the ECOWAS sub-region through visa-free travelling protocols has translated into an increase in labour mobility over the past decade.

Amid the evolving social norms that allow women to partake actively in the labour market, it appears that there has been a rise in the independent migration of females in search of better economic opportunities since 2010 after a decrease in 2005 (Setrana & Kleist, 2022).

As can be seen in Fig. 9.6, there was a decreasing trend in the percentage share of international female migrant stock in Africa (between 1995 and

2005). However, from 2005 till 2020, the trend was reversed to reveal a continuous increase in the female share of international migrants. The high volumes of daily crossings of borders by traders, most of whom are market women, illustrate the active engagement of African women in the labour market. This contemporary shift clearly communicates that cultures are undergoing a positive change in that women are no longer considered as residual and dormant partakers in the economic transformation agenda of societies. As of 2020, there was a daily estimate of at least 30,000 people moving in-between the townships of Rusizi and Goma, which happen to be border towns between the Democratic Republic of Congo and Rwanda (Achieng et al., 2020). About 75% of those moving between the border towns are women who trade in fabric, foodstuffs, and other electronic goods. Similarly, Beitbridge, the political border post between South Africa and Zimbabwe, registers an average of more than 30,000 daily crossings by people engaging in cross-border commerce and trade. This phenomenon is not particular to the aforementioned border towns but can be seen in most of the border towns within the region. The higher levels of female labour force participation associated with these border crossings have an extended impact on family earnings, consumption, and the general welfare of households.

International migrants as a percentage of the total population within the regions of southern Africa have been increasing with the highest percentages recorded from 2010 to 2020. Table 9.1 presents data on the African regional variation in the international migrant stock as a percentage of the total population from 1990 to 2020.

Table 9.1 provides data on the annual rate of change in the migrant stock from 1990 to 2020. Statistically, Table 9.1 highlights the fluctuations in the annual rate of change of the migrant stock across different sub-regions and establishes that southern Africa had consistently maintained the highest

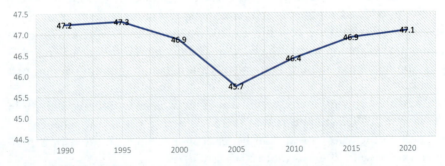

Fig. 9.6 Female migrants as a percentage of the international migrant stock in Africa (*Source* Based on data extracted from the UNDESA database, 2020)

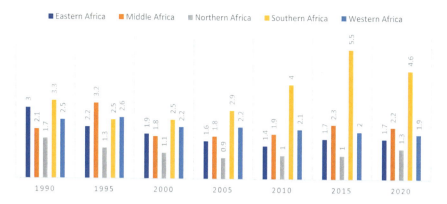

Fig. 9.7 International migrant stock as a percentage of the total population 1990–2020 (*Source* Based on data extracted from UNDESA database, 2020)

Table 9.1 Annual rate of change in the migrant stock from 1990 to 2020

	1990–1995	1995–2000	2000–2005	2005–2010	2010–2015	2015–2020
Eastern Africa	−3.6	−0.5	−0.2	−0.2	6.9	2.7
Middle Africa	12.0	−8.1	2.0	4.3	7.1	2.1
Northern Africa	−2.9	−1.8	−1.7	2.2	1.8	7.9
Southern Africa	−3.0	1.1	4.4	7.9	7.8	−2.1
Western Africa	3.9	−0.6	2.5	1.2	2.2	1.3
Total for Africa	0.8	−1.7	1.3	2.1	5.0	2.1

Source Based on data extracted from UNDESA database (2020)

annual rate of change, except for the period from 2015 to 2020 when it was surpassed by the northern African sub-region.

From 1990 to 1995, the Middle Africa sub-region exhibited the highest proportion of the annual rate of change in the migrant stock, accounting for 12.0%. Although there was a decline in this highest percentage during the period of 1995–2000 compared to 1990–1995, the sub-region with the highest annual rate of change shifted from middle Africa to southern Africa. Such migration patterns in Middle Africa are shaped by each country's unique culture, language, and economic factors (Chaudhry & Ouda, 2021). Factors that drive migration within the Middle African region include poverty, political instability, and ethnic conflict. Poverty is one of the primary drivers of migration in the region. The lack of basic necessities such as clean water, food, and access to healthcare has compelled many to seek opportunities in other countries.

In this new period, southern Africa recorded a rate of 1.1%. Subsequent time intervals displayed an increase in the highest proportion of the annual rate of change, including 2000–2005, 2005–2010, and 2010–2015, with percentages of 4.4%, 7.9%, and 7.8% respectively. Notably, southern Africa consistently held the highest annual rate of change of the migrant stock compared to the other regions under consideration throughout these specified time intervals. These trends in the southern Africa region show that it is one of the regions with the highest number of people moving within the continent (Bakewell & De Haas, 2007). The drivers of migration within the southern Africa region are multifaceted and complex, but they could be attributed to several reasons such as economic disparities, political instability, and environmental changes (Raleigh, 2011). The shortage of employment and other economic opportunities in some countries such as Zimbabwe and Malawi are forcing most people to migrate to neighbouring countries such as South Africa and Botswana.

However, from 2015 to 2020, the northern African sub-region recorded the highest annual rate of change in the migrant stock, reaching 7.9%. In the region, economic and social factors such as poverty, unemployment, and lack of basic services are some of the key drivers of migration within the region. One of the primary drivers of migration in North Africa is economic factors. High unemployment rates in the region push many people to seek employment opportunities abroad, particularly in Europe.

Demographic Overview of Migration Within the Regions of Africa

In 1990, the proportion of male migrants as part of the total population in eastern Africa was higher at 3.1% compared to their female counterparts at 2.9%. In 1995, 2000, and 2005 this trend persisted with males as a percentage of the total population representing 2.3%, 2.0%, and 1.7% respectively, indicating that male migrants were a higher percentage of the total population during those years. Nevertheless, in 2010, 2015, and 2020, both sexes had the same percentage which represented 1.4% and 1.7%, and 1.7% each in 2010, 2015, and 2020 respectively. In southern Africa, male migrants as a percentage of the total population dominated the migrant stock compared to the female in all the year intervals. The case was not different in West Africa as in all the year intervals.

With regard to sex, the data shows that males generally dominate migration within the continent and among the various regions in Africa. Eastern and western Africa record the highest migration of both males and females although the former is higher. Despite the lower proportion of female migrants on the continent, it is important to note that there is increasing independent migration of women. The increasing migration of women has been noted by feminist migration scholars because it gives autonomy and empowers migrant women when compared with traditional migration narratives where women were seen as persons accompanying husbands and fathers (Setrana & Kleist, 2022). In Western Africa, there have been slight decreases and increases, representing 45.1% to 45.7%, slightly below the average of female migrants from all over Africa. Here the changing narrative not necessarily about the percentages but about the autonomous decision-making of women for various reasons including furthering education and searching for employment among other things. In the early 1990s, the implementation of the structural adjustment programme rendered many women jobless. Many of these women gained livelihoods that empowered them to take care of their families by engaging in cross-border trading.

Table 9.2 illustrates the sex distribution of the annual rate of change of the migrant stock from 1990 to 2020. As can be seen, from 1990 to 1995, the proportion of the annual rate of change of the migrant stock in eastern Africa was the same for males and females as both sexes recorded −3.6% each. However, the annual rate of change of the migrant stock from 1995 to 2000 was higher for females (−0.4%) than the males (−0.6). In the period 2000–2005, the males overtook the females where the males accumulated an annual rate of change of the migrant stock of 0.5% as against −1.1% for females. Nevertheless, from 2005 to 2010, 2010 to 2015, and 2015 to 2020, the females had a higher proportion of the annual rate of change of the migrant stock than the males which represents 0.9%, 7.0%, and 2.9% respectively.

Regarding Middle Africa, between 1990 and 1995, both males and females had an equal annual rate of change in the migrant stock, with both sexes recording 12.0%. However, from 1995 to 2000, the annual rate of change in the migrant stock was higher for males (−7.9%) compared to females (−8.4%). In the subsequent periods of 2000–2005 and 2005–2010, females surpassed males in terms of the annual rate of change in the migrant stock. During the former period, females accumulated an annual rate of change of 2.2%, while in the latter period, it increased to 4.4%. However, from 2010

Table 9.2 Annual rate of change in the migrant stock in Africa 1990–2020, by regions and sex

	1990–1995		1995–2000		2000–2005		2005–2010		2010–2015		2015–2020	
	M	F	M	F	M	F	M	F	M	F	M	F
Eastern Africa	−3.6	−3.6	−0.6	−0.4	0.5	−1.1	−1.2	0.9	6.8	7.0	2.6	2.9
Middle Africa	12.0	12.0	−7.9	−8.4	1.8	2.2	4.3	4.4	7.7	6.5	1.1	2.1
Northern Africa	−2.1	−3.7	−0.9	−2.9	−0.2	−3.6	2.0	2.5	1.9	1.7	6.8	9.3
Southern Africa	−3.2	−2.7	0.7	1.5	4.0	5.1	7.9	7.9	6.9	9.0	−1.5	−3.0
Western Africa	3.7	4.1	−0.6	−0.7	2.7	2.3	1.2	1.2	2.0	2.4	1.3	1.4
Total for Africa	0.8	0.9	−1.5	−1.8	1.7	0.8	1.8	2.4	4.8	5.2	2.0	2.2

Source Based on data extracted from the UNDESA database (2020)

to 2015, the annual rate of change in the migrant stock for males (7.7%) exceeded that of females (6.5%). In contrast, from 2015 to 2020, females (2.1%) dominated males (1.1%) in terms of the annual rate of change in the migrant stock.

In terms of sex distribution in North Africa, there were notable differences in the annual rate of change in the migrant stock between males and females during specific time intervals. From 1990 to 1995, 1995 to 2000, 2000 to 2005, and 2010 to 2015, the males experienced a higher annual rate of change in the migrant stock, with percentages of −2.1%, −0.9%, −0.2%, and 1.9% respectively. However, during the periods from 2005 to 2010 and 2015 to 2020, the females exhibited a higher annual rate of change in the migrant stock compared to males, with percentages of 2.5% and 9.3% respectively.

With regard to sex disaggregation in Southern Africa, there were distinct patterns in the annual rate of change in the migrant stock between males and females during specific periods. From 1990 to 1995, 1995 to 2000, 2000 to 2005, and 2010 to 2015, the females exhibited a higher annual rate of change in the migrant stock, with percentages of −2.7%, 1.5%, 5.1%, and 9.0% respectively. However, from 2015 to 2020, the males displayed a higher annual rate of change in the migrant stock compared to females, with a percentage of −1.5%. Additionally, between 2005 and 2010, both males and females had an equal annual rate of change in the migrant stock, with both sexes recording 7.9%.

Concerning the sex distribution in West Africa, from 1995 to 2000, and 2000 to 2005, the males recorded a higher annual rate of change in the migrant stock than the females which represent −0.6%, and 2.7% respectively. However, from 1990 to 1995, 2010 to 2015, and 2015 to 2020, the females had a higher annual rate of change in the migrant stock than the males which constitutes 4.1%, 2.4%, and 1.4% respectively. Also, between 2005 and 2010, both males and females had the same proportion of the annual rate of change in the migrant stock, with both sexes recording 1.2%.

Generally, migrants in destination areas in Africa are found within the age bracket of 25–54 years. In terms of the sexes, in 2010, 2015, and 2020, the highest proportion of male and female migrants at destination areas was found within the age categories of 40–49 (6.2%), 35–44 (6.8%), and 45–49 (3.3%) respectively. When disaggregated by gender, out of the total male migrants in destination countries in Africa, close to one-fifth (17.3%) in the year 2010 were within the age category of 30–54 while the year 2015 and 2020 recorded (19%) and (18.1%) respectively who also fall within the same age category. Likewise, the females within the year intervals of 2010, 2015, and 2020 could also be found within the age bracket of 35–44 (5.0%), 35–39 (2.9%), and 30–34 (2.8%) respectively. One notable finding is the higher number of young migrants at destination areas within the economically active age range. This observation suggests that a significant majority of African migrants, regardless of sex, tend to be in the age group that is actively participating in the workforce of destination countries. This concentration indicates the potential economic motivations behind migration within the African continent, as individuals within this age range often seek better employment opportunities, the highest wages, and improved living standards in their destination countries.

Conclusions

The vast majority of African migration occurs within the continent, demonstrating that South–South migration in Africa is key to Africa's development agenda. Intra-migration is prominent with many African migrants crossing from one country on the continent to another country. Unlike the misconceived narratives that portray African migrants as persons moving irregularly through the Mediterranean to the Global North. Migration within and across Africa is beneficial to both sending and receiving countries. Some of the gains range from remittances, investments in education, health and housing sectors, and skills transfer, among others (Tonah & Setrana, 2017). Through South–South migration on the African continent, migrants who have acquired skills and values contribute to development in various capacities (Setrana & Tonah, 2016). There are enormous benefits of migration to both the destination and origin countries on the African continent. More positive impact is recorded on the economically active African group and the independent women migrating across the different regions and countries in Africa. Such African migrants become economically independent to support themselves and their households. For example, African migrants contribute through remittances which represent a source of foreign exchange supplementing household income for purchasing basic needs. Additionally, African migrants at both destination areas and in the home countries have established transnational businesses, created jobs, and paid taxes in the countries to which they move (Setrana & Arhin-Sam, 2022). South–South migration within the African continent has created employment for the many women who were displaced due to the implementation of the structural adjustment programme. These issues were compounded by the legacies of colonialism which shaped movements within the African continent through inequalities in development efforts, infrastructural imbalances, and deliberate forced movements.

More of the benefits of South–South migration can be achieved through strategic programmes and policies and narrating the migration realities on the African continent. To maximise the benefits of African migration within and across, many governments in Africa have implemented policies to ensure greater engagement with their citizens abroad, as well as those who make the decisions to finally return home, in order to maximise the developmental benefits of migration.

Efforts towards addressing the challenges associated with migration either to or from the sub-region and intra-regional migration are key to promoting the interlinkages between migration and development. Governments have implemented various measures, such as national migration policies, for effective migration management broadly, which have been successful to varying degrees (ICMPD & IOM, 2016). Given the importance of the African diaspora in national development across the region, it is recommended that governments harmonise policies across the sub-region to address the benefits.

Notes

1. Funded by the UKRI Global Challenges Research Fund (GCRF) (Grant Reference ES/S007415/1), the MIDEQ Hub unpacks the complex and multidimensional relationships between migration and development in the context of the Global South. More at www.mideq.org.
2. Our analysis has also benefitted from work at the Centre for Migration Studies (CMS), University of Ghana, and other local and international institutions such as UNDESA, IOM, and the Migration Data Portal. The Portal aims to serve as a single access point to timely, comprehensive *migration statistics* and reliable information about *migration data* globally. See https://www.migrationdataportal.org/.
3. See https://www.migrationpolicy.org/programs/data-hub/charts/immigrant-and-emigrant-populations-country-origin-and-destination.
4. Available at https://www.un.org/development/desa/pd/content/international-migrant-stock.
5. See https://migrationdataportal.org/regional-data-overview/southern-africa.

References

Achieng, M., El Fadil, A., & Righa, E. (2020). What is wrong with the narrative on African migration? In A. Adepoju, C. Fumagalli, & N. Nyabola (Eds.), *Africa migration report: Challenging the narrative* (pp. 1–14). IOM.

Bakewell, O., & De Haas, H. (2007). African Migrations: continuities, discontinuities and recent transformations. In L. De Haan, U. Engel, & P. Chabal (Eds.), *African alternatives* (pp. 95–117). Brill.

Bakewell, O., de Haas, H., Castles, S., Vezzoli, S., & Jónsson, G. (2009). *South–South migration and human development: Reflection on African experiences.* International Migration Institute.

Chaudhry, S., & Ouda, J. (2021). Perspectives on the rights of climate migrants in the horn of Africa: A case study of Somalia. *Journal of Somali Studies, 8*(1), 13.

Dick, E., & Schraven, B. (2021). Rural-urban migration in West Africa: Contexts, trends, and recommendations. Global knowledge partnership on migration and development (KNOMAD) Policy Brief 13. KNOWMAD, Washington, D.C., USA. https://www.knomad.org/publication/rural-urban-migration-west-africa-contexts-trends-and-recommendations

Flahaux, M.-L., & De Haas, H. (2016). African migration: Trends, patterns, drivers. *Comparative Migration Studies, 4*, 1–25.

Halperin, S., & Heath, O. (2020). *Political research: Methods and practical skills.* Oxford University Press.

ICMPD & IOM (2016). *A survey on migration policies in West Africa* (2nd ed.). ICMPD/IOM.

Kayizzi-Mugerwa, S., Anyanwu, J. C., & Conceição, P. (2014). Regional integration in Africa: An introduction. *African Development Review, 26*(S1), 1–6.

Korn, D. A. (2001). *Exodus within borders: An introduction to the crisis of internal displacement*. Brookings Institution Press.

Møller, B. (2009). Africa's sub-regional organisations: Seamless web or patchwork? Working papers series 2 (56). Crisis States Research Centre, School of Economics and Political Science.

Oucho, J., Gelderblom, D., & Van Zyl, J. (2006) *Migration in South and Southern Africa: Dynamics and determinants*. HSRC Press.

Quartey, P., Setrana, M. B., & Tagoe, C. A. (2020). Migration across West Africa: Development-related aspects. In P. Fargues, M. Rango, E. Borgnäs, & I. Schöfberger (Eds.), *Migration in West and North Africa and across the Mediterranean: Trends, risks, development and governance* (pp. 270–278). International Organization for Migration.

Raleigh, C. (2011) The search for safety: The effects of conflict poverty and ecological influences on migration in the developing world. *Global Environmental Change, 21*, S82–S93. https://doi.org/10.1016/j.gloenvcha.2011.08.008

Ratha, D., Mohapatra, S., & Scheja, E. (2011). Impact of migration on economic and social development: A review of evidence and emerging issues. *World Bank Policy Research Working Paper* 5558.

Ratha, D., & Shaw, W. (2007). *South–South migration and remittances*. World Bank Publications.

Setrana, M. B., & Arhin-Sam, K. (2022). Harnessing social and political Remittances for Africa's development: The case of skilled returnees and skilled return migrant groups in Ghana. In M. Konte & L. M. Mbaye (Eds.), *Migration, remittances and sustainable development in Africa* (pp. 138–156). Routledge.

Setrana, M. B., & Kleist, N. (2022) Gendered dynamics in West African migration. In J. K. (Ed.), *Migration in West Africa*. IMISCOE Research Series (pp. 57–76). Springer International Publishing.

Setrana, M. B., Kyei, J. R. K. O., & Nyarko, D. (2022). Beyond the binary debates in migration: Experiences of Fulani nomads, sedentary Fulani, and autochthone farmers in Agogo, Ghana. *Migration Studies, 10*(2), 152–171.

Setrana, M. B., & Tonah, S. (2016). Do transnational links matter after return? Labour market participation among Ghanaian return migrants. *The Journal of Development Studies, 52*(4), 549–560. https://doi.org/10.1080/00220388.2015.1126255

Teye, J. K. (Ed.). (2022). Migration in West Africa: An introduction. In *Migration in West Africa*. IMISCOE Research Series (pp. 3–17). Springer International Publishing. https://doi.org/10.1007/978-3-030-97322-3_1

Tonah, S. & Setrana, M. B. (2017). Introduction. In S. Tonah, M. B. Setrana & J. A. Arthur (Eds.), *Migration and development in Africa: Trends, challenges, and policy implications* (pp. 1–40). Lexington Books.

Ullah, A. A., & Haque, M. S. (2020). *The migration myth in policy and practice: Dreams, development and despair*. Springer.

UNDESA. (2020). *International migrant stocks*. https://www.un.org/development/desa/pd/content/international-migrant-stock

UNHCR. (2020). Ethiopia tigray emergency immediate regional needs (November–December 2020). https://reporting.unhcr.org/sites/default/files/UNHCR%20Requirements%20for%20Ethiopia%20emergency%20-%2022%20December%202020.pdf

World Health Organization. (2008). *Closing the gap in a generation: Health equity through action on the social determinants of health: Final report of the commission on social determinants of health*. World Health Organization.

Zossou, E., Arouna, A., Diagne, A., & Agboh-Noameshie, R. A. (2020). Learning agriculture in rural areas: The drivers of knowledge acquisition and farming practices by rice farmers in West Africa. *The Journal of Agricultural Education and Extension, 26*(3), 291–306.

Open Access This chapter is licensed under the terms of the Creative Commons Attribution 4.0 International License (http://creativecommons.org/licenses/by/4.0/), which permits use, sharing, adaptation, distribution and reproduction in any medium or format, as long as you give appropriate credit to the original author(s) and the source, provide a link to the Creative Commons license and indicate if changes were made.

The images or other third party material in this chapter are included in the chapter's Creative Commons license, unless indicated otherwise in a credit line to the material. If material is not included in the chapter's Creative Commons license and your intended use is not permitted by statutory regulation or exceeds the permitted use, you will need to obtain permission directly from the copyright holder.

10

Migration as a Collective Project in the Global South: A Case Study from the Ethiopia–South Africa Corridor

Dereje Feyissa, Meron Zeleke, and Fana Gebresenbet

Introduction

Overall, there is an individualist thrust in migration studies, whether in the earlier theories of functionalism and historical materialism or the current aspiration–capability framework. Aside from differences in nuances, these theories take individuals as the primary unit of analysis and most engage with the collective dimensions of migration either tangentially or instrumentally. Seeking to redress a knowledge gap, this chapter discusses Hadiya migration to South Africa as a collective project, its changing contours towards individualisation, and the implications of this for the viability of the Hadiya migration project.

D. Feyissa (✉)
College of Law and Governance, Ethiopian Institute of Peace, Addis Ababa University, Addis Ababa, Ethiopia
e-mail: dereje.feyissa@aau.edu.et

M. Zeleke
Centre for Human Rights, Addis Ababa University, Addis Ababa, Ethiopia
e-mail: meron.zeleke@aau.edu.et

F. Gebresenbet
Institute for Peace and Security Studies, Addis Ababa University, Addis Ababa, Ethiopia
e-mail: fana.g@ipss-addis.org

We provide ethnographic examples to substantiate our arguments. These relate to four moments in the migration process: the onset of Hadiya migration to South Africa as a collective project through a prophecy and the associated sacred imagination of South Africa as the promised land; the intensification of migration as a collective project expressed in the form of an elite-managed historical project of catching up; the role of social networks in building not only individual but also collective capabilities and the erosion of the collective nature and increasing individualisation of the Hadiya migration project under the influence of success in accumulating material wealth and associated greed. We argue that exclusive categorisation of migration as either individualist or collective at any given moment in time is a simplification of reality, suggesting that we should instead conceptualise migration as being located on a continuum with the two options taking extreme ends.

Moreover, the nature of migration could oscillate from one end to the other (and back) across time due to the influence of different factors. Migration should be viewed as a complex social change process during which the nature of the migration experience itself changes. In making this argument, we want to highlight the collectivist side of migration as a better approach to understand southern realities. However, while arguing for a greater engagement with migration as a collective project we reject a dichotomy between the individual and collective dimensions of the migration process and argue for a continuum within which the relative dominance of one or the other component varies over time.

This chapter is based on the findings of research undertaken as part of the Migration for Development and Equality (MIDEQ) Hub[1] focusing on the Ethiopia–South Africa corridor. Various qualitative research methods were used to generate the data used in this chapter: from key informant and in-depth interviews to life histories, focus group discussions, and document analysis. Fieldwork was carried out at various times from 2019 to 2022 in Addis Ababa, and Hadiya Administrative Zone in southern Ethiopia focusing on four emigration localities: Hosanna, Jajura, Fonqo and Shashogo. The chapter is also based on limited phone interviews with Hadiya migrants in South Africa and online sources of information.

The chapter is organised in five major sections. The first section situates the chapter within the main theoretical frameworks in migration studies, making a case for the need to go beyond the prevailing individualist thrust. Section two discusses the genesis of Hadiya migration to South Africa, which is part of the wider Ethiopia–South Africa migration corridor. Section three examines how Hadiya migration to South Africa as a collective project. It consists of two sub-sections. The first of these focuses on how the Hadiya have built collective capabilities by drawing on religious resources—from sacred imagination of South Africa as a promised land to spiritual negotiation of risks throughout the journey, to place making at destinations. Second, is the role of social networks in creating collective migration capabilities, evident in covering the cost of migration and mutual support mechanisms throughout the journey and in the process of settlement and adaptation at the destination. Section four discusses shifts in Hadiya migration project from collective to increasingly individualist orientation, abetted by greed and the capitalist logic that underpins material accumulation, and leading to the unravelling of the supportive social institutions as free riding and competition set in. As greed is taking precedence over the public good, Hadiya society is now going through a reflexive moment as migration is increasingly turning from a "blessing" into a "curse". We conclude by making a case for a greater engagement with migration as a collective project especially in the context of the Global South. However, in doing so, we should take the collective and the individualist in migration processes as a continuum, not as binaries.

Conceptual Framework—Beyond the Individualist Thrust in Migration Studies

The existing literature on migration can be grouped into two three main approaches, all with an emphasis on individuals as their unit of analysis albeit with some differences in terms of how far they engage with migration as a collective project. These are functionalism, historical structuralism and the aspiration-capability framework (ACF). Functionalism conceptualises migration as a rational choice that an individual makes after evaluating its socio-economic costs and benefits in order to access more secure sources of income and a wider pool of opportunities (see Hagen-Zanker, 2008; de Haas, 2021). It has the merit of bringing migrants' agency forward but provides an oversimplified version of the messiness of human nature (Feyissa et al., forthcoming; Mazzilli et al., this volume). Not only does this approach describe human beings as rational actors, but also locates them in an environment where all choices are equally possible, individuals have access to perfect information and are not embedded in structures of power other than the market (Arango, 2000; Massey et al., 1998). Functionalism acknowledges migrants' agency, but looks at just a narrow portion of the dynamics at play in the world, including how migrants' agency is situated within a collective imagination of the good life; creation of aspiration and construction of capabilities.

Historical-structuralism, by contrast, focuses on structure rather than agency, depicting migration as the result of socio-economic inequalities between individuals and states (de Haas, 2021). De Haas (2021) highlights how historical-structuralism conceives migration as an irrational process that migrants get into because of distorted information or because they are drawn into it by an exploitative macro-structure. Although this approach pays attention to the power structures individuals are embedded in—be they economic, political, class or gender—historical-structuralism conceptualises migrants as responding as these forces dictate, leaving little space for agency. For instance, it does not explain either why migrants retain agency even under difficult conditions, nor why individuals facing the same structural constraints react to them in different ways. Overall, historical-structuralism acknowledges that migrants can be constrained by multiple powers but portrays them as reacting to overbearing structures rather than agents. Like functionalism, it does not pay attention to the "collective self" which individual migrants tap into and mobilise to negotiate and muddle through the multiple constraints they face throughout the migration process.

Building on the works of Carling, de Haas (2021 but see also his earlier works) developed the ACF, which is widely considered as the state of the art in migration studies. Although ACF engages with the collective dimension of migration much more than functionalism and historical-structuralism, and it has a stronger liberal-individualist thrust as well in its understanding of both aspiration and capability. The individualist thrust in ASF's understanding of aspiration is very much reflected in the choice of agency as a central concept, while the conception of capability by Amartya Sen, whose work de Haas builds on, is also critiqued for similar biases (Gore, 1997; Robeyns, 2007; Uyan-Semerci, 2007). A liberal individualist orientation, in its atomic sense, often avows that "people are autonomous and self-contained individuals, whose rights are prior to and independent of any conception of the common good" (Howlowchak, 2006, 20). An individual liberalist framing accents that an individual is autonomous and hence cannot and shouldn't be harried by community interests. When community interests are highlighted, they are often relegated as instrumental, non-intrinsic positions (see various sources cited in Ibrahim, 2021). The ACF takes the aspiration as well as capability to migrate as a personal trait, ignoring that sending communities could aspire and collaborate in designing and effecting migration decisions over a certain period. When it comes to human rights discourse in relation to mobility, the ACF adopts Berlin's (1969) understanding of negative and positive freedoms as a "structure".

While de Hass (2021) essentially views migration as an individual project with aspirations and capabilities built by the individual and the returns being primarily individual too, he does not ignore the need to pay attention to the role of other factors such as culture, education and exposure to media in shaping people's preferences and notions of the "good life", personal life aspirations and more. These other collective factors however are not viewed as having intrinsic value. This chapter challenges the exclusive individualist thrust in migration studies from a Southern perspective and asks if migration-related decisions are really only individual. Through a case study of Hadiya migration to South Africa, we argue that relationships mattered more prominently in earlier phases of the migration processes, with later increasing importance of individualism.

As will be shown through our case study of Hadiya migrants to South Africa, the decision-making process is highly informed by local Hadiya values of communalism. Communalism in African values is partly centred on the "duties" of the individual to the "community" (Nagengast, 2015), in contrast to Berlin's position. Cobbah (1987) alludes that in the African worldview, individual rights are often balanced against the requirements of the group and individual group solidarity and collective responsibility. The African notion of family seeks a vindication of the communal well-being. In other words, the starting point is not the individual but the whole group. Such a "holist approach starts with social relationships and sees the individuals as not an independent being but rather as a one whose whole nature is constituted by the character of the social relationships in which he stands: African communalism is more than a mere life style. It is a worldview" (Cobbah, 1987, 324).

The Making of the Ethiopia–South Africa Migration Corridor

As one of the strongest economies on the continent, South Africa is among the major destination countries for migrants moving within Africa. Close to three million migrants resided in South Africa in 2020 (UN DESA, 2020). Ethiopians are among the most significant of these migrant populations, with estimates varying between 250,000 by Cooper and Esser (2018) and Yordanos (2018), and IOM (2021) stating that between 200,000 and 300,000 new Ethiopians arriving in South Africa between 2016 and 2018 alone. According to a report by the South African Department of Home Affairs (2015), Ethiopia is ranked as the second of the top 15 migrant sending countries. These Ethiopians make a smaller share of the estimated more than three million Ethiopians living abroad (Girmachew, 2019). Ethiopian migration to southern destinations has primarily been directed to the Gulf, Kenya and the Sudan. Starting from the 1990s and increasing since the 2000s, South Africa has emerged as another major southern destination.

Ethiopian migrants' journey to South Africa is perilous, involving the crossing of state borders of as many as six countries covering close to 5000 km.[2] The journey follows different routes involving different modes of transport: air, water and land. The few migrants affording the high-priced means of migration take a direct flight from Addis Ababa to Johannesburg but most combine bus, boat and foot to cross-transit countries. Typically, the land route from Ethiopia to South Africa starts in Kenya and then passes through Tanzania, Malawi, and Mozambique/Zimbabwe to South Africa. Many migrants have perished in transit countries. A recent IOM study (2021) notes that more than 7000 Ethiopian migrants have died or gone missing on irregular migration routes between 2012 and 2020.

Most Ethiopian migrants in South Africa are engaged in the informal retail trade running shops predominantly in Jeppe, the Ethiopian commercial enclave in Johannesburg, and in the nearby townships, popularly known as "locations" (Zack & Yordanos, 2016). Some of the migrants are well established, evident in the growing remittances they send to support families and the investments they have made in small and large-scale businesses. Successful migrants send collective remittances to Ethiopia supporting churches and local and national development projects.

Although the Ethiopian migrants in South Africa come from all over the country, most are from southern Ethiopia, particularly from the Hadiya–Kembata area. A report of Hadiya Zone Human Resource and Social Affairs department (quoted in Fikreab & Asrat, 2020, 10) estimated that 61,148 Hadiya youth migrated to South Africa between 2013 and 2018. A survey by Tsedeke and Ayele (2017, 3) found that nearly 40% of households in Hadiya–Kembata have at least one international migrant. Hadiya migration to South Africa is barely over two decades old but it has already left major imprints on the social fabric greatly defining the conception of the good life. This migration trajectory has been enabled by collective efforts throughout the various stages of the migration process—from the making of aspiration, decision-making, the journey, in the process of settlement and the decision to come back as well as in the pattern of migrants' investment.

Hadiya Migration to South Africa as a Collective Project

Hadiya Migration to South Africa as an Enactment of a Divine Script

One of the central social events which is deeply implicated in the process of Hadiya migration to South Africa, especially during the formative stage, is a prophecy delivered by a Canadian pastor, Peter Youngrin, who came to Hosanna in 2001. Below is the excerpt of the prophecy as told by many research participants which is intimately implicated in migration processes:

> I have a message from God to deliver to you. I saw God opening a new southern route for Hadiya. From now onwards you will see a constant flow of people; people work hard and prosper; that they will bring blessing to Hosanna and to Ethiopia more broadly. Hosanna town will be transformed beyond recognition; the time will come when three wheeled cars will fill the streets of Hosanna …. God will allow movement of people; one which will bring prosperity. (Focus group discussion with church leaders, Hosanna, December 2019)

The key message of the prophecy is how God opened a "southern door" for the Hadiya through which prosperity would come. In effect this is a prophecy which "sacralises" and endorses migration as God-sanctioned and as God's redemptive plan for the Hadiya. Pastor Youngrin did not directly say "go to South Africa", he rather prophesised the onset of a large-scale migration of Hadiya and their socioeconomic transformation. For the Hadiya, God used the Pastor as a conduit to bless them as a people and their journey. To lend the prophecy plausibility, Pastor Youngrin said "you would soon see signs". For the Hadiya, it did not take long before they started seeing the signs of the prophecy working, i.e., the onset of a massive migration of Hadiya to South Africa, which is to the South of Ethiopia anyway.

Large-scale Hadiya migration to South Africa has a strong spiritual dimension situated within the prophetic tradition of evangelical Christianity. This is linked with migration processes at various levels—from decision-making, migratory agency, and pre-departure farewells, to sense making at destinations. The prophecy operates collectively. For one thing, it is a prophecy for the Hadiya as people, not individual Hadiya. The Hadiya also claim a collective agency for the prophecy, that it is God answering Hadiya's mothers' intense prayer to help them overcome the social and economic deprivations and lack of peace, as the prophecy coincided with a major drought and political persecution of the Hadiya youth by the ruling party for supporting an opposition party. It is also construed as an affirmation of God's favour of the Hadiya as "committed" Christians, which aligns well with Hadiya's self-understanding as an avant guard of Protestantism in Southern Ethiopia, and Ethiopia more broadly. The following narrative by a Hadiya migrant indicates how aspiration is shaped by the prophecy and its invocation to negotiate and mitigate the risks of the journey to South Africa:

> Imagine, the journey from Hadiya to South Africa involves crossing more than five or six countries and is perilous in which many people might die. Notwithstanding the risks, the main news in Hadiya became *"geba"* [he has entered South Africa without much difficulty]. Not long after someone announced that he would travel to South Africa, we would hear *geba*. The blessing made the journey a lot easier than one would have expected. I left in 2004, three years after Peter came. I was a student at that time. I talked to my friends about the idea of going to South Africa. They all readily agreed. When we decided to travel it felt as if we were already in South Africa. I remember the enthusiasm and the confidence we had. We never thought of the risks we might encounter during the journey and the language difficulties we might encounter. In fact, it felt like as if we were moving from one house to another within Hadiya". (Pastor Birhanu, Wengel Amagnoch Church based in Johannesburg, interviewed in Addis Ababa, November 8, 2020)

The spiritual aspect of Hadiya migration to South Africa is very instructive. It plays out in decision-making and motivation, instancing "confidence without caution" as one of the problems of "believing" and the lack of even hesitation, as mentioned in the aforementioned narrative. Of course, the spiritual aspect also affects and fosters such things as resilience: when things are not going well, people feel the strength to persevere and are arguably better placed to cope with adversity. As Levitt (2007) alludes, the transnational lives of migrants are inextricably linked to spirituality whereby religious leaders and centres of worship are part of the multi-layered webs of connections.

In a video message that they sent to friends and relatives in Hosanna, a group of Hadiya migrants detained in transit by Tanzanian authorities and returned by IOM appeared joyful, singing loud Gospel songs with a mood of defiance mentioning it is not a question of if but when they will go back to South Africa with the help of God. Prospective migrants in Hosanna on the other hand were busy buying gospel songs with strong migration content. An example of this would be one which explicitly mentions major hurdles on transit countries such as the Tete bridge on the Zambezi River (also called Samora Michel bridge) along the border between Mozambique and

South Africa where hundreds of Ethiopian migrants perished while trying to cross through suffocating containers and other hazardous means. Here we see belief or the prophecy helping migrants manage the risks involved during migration.

More recently, this prophetic tradition has given way to more individualised prophecies. Hadiya evangelical prophets now divine the future for prospective migrants featuring as migration counsellors—further delivering God's favour at a more individual level for the service for which they get material rewards. These local prophets not only tell prospective migrants when to migrate and how, but they also persuade the parents of prospective migrants who are in the family to have a better prospect of success both during the journey as well as in the process of settlement. They also communicate with the relatives of prospective migrants in South Africa convincing them that it is worth investing in sponsoring a particular prospective migrant whose migration project is ordained by God, hence ensuring "value for money". In some instances, the prophets cum migration counsellors advise prospective migrants to drop their plan to migrate. The following story from a stayee in Hosanna throws light onto how decision-making is shaped by a prophetic tradition:

> I contemplated to migrate to South Africa when I reached grade 10, when most Hadiya youth consider it to be the right migration age. I was good at school but not sure whether I would pass the national examination. Like many of my peers I visited a local prophet in Shashogo who divined my future. She told me that my future lies here in Ethiopia, not South Africa. I went to South Africa in case I would not score a good grade. I was a bit skeptical about the prophecy but my uncle who brought me to South Africa insisted that I should go back home concerned that I might not succeed in South Africa as this would be against the will of God. It turned out that I scored the highest grade, came back and joined university. With a privilege of hindsight, I now say that her prophecy is a correct prediction of my future and good that I heeded her advice (interviewed in May 2021).

This suggests that the role the local prophets play goes beyond a mere "counselling" service and spiritual providence as they also act as spiritual entrepreneurs/mediators between migrant family members and the prospective migrants. A major dimension of the flow in the Ethiopia–South Africa corridor is also pastors and their transnational spiritual engagement with the migrants. Their sermons are increasingly filled with migration-related content, including conveying the good news for some, mentioning that they are here in South Africa to stay while advising others to go back home as soon as possible. In so doing they are being conduits of a divine message. As such, decision-making in the process of Hadiya migration to South Africa is not fully comprehensible unless we thoroughly engage with the spirituality of migration, which is above all communal. The decision to migrate or to stay operates at the collective level, in this case within the cultural repertoire of a community such as belief systems. The spiritual frame of reference for Hadiya migration to South Africa goes even deeper, as migrants and their families reflect on Hadiya migration to South Africa in relational terms situating it within the broader historically shaped regional inequality between the "core North" and "peripheral South" in the context of state formation in Ethiopia both in political representation and national wealth allocation. Historically, Hadiya belong to Ethiopia's periphery and migration to South Africa is understood as a means to renegotiate this regional inequality (see the following sub-section). In so doing the Hadiya attribute an "inherent link" between peoples of the periphery and their greater representation in South–South migration:

> How come that Amharas, Tigres and Oromos [people of the core regions] are not migrating to South Africa as much as the Hadiya and other Southerners do [people of the periphery]? Their oversight is not accidental. God has blinded them of this opportunity protecting it for us. Had they known about the opportunities in South Africa they would have taken up all the opportunities. They are everywhere. Many Ethiopians in Europe, the US and Canada are Amharas, Tigreans and Oromos. They have money, knowledge, and wider social network. And yet we [the Hadiya and other peoples from Southern Ethiopia] managed to make it to South Africa despite our apparent lack of skill and political networks. This is because God awakened us (*aberalin*). (Interview with a returnee businessman, Hosanna, February 4, 2021)

The word *aberalin* used here refers to a collective self, that God is now engaging Hadiya as a people, not individually, by opening a southern route through which prosperity comes. In this sacred narrative, Hadiya migration to South Africa features as a quintessential future-making project at the societal level displacing other avenues of socio-economic mobility.

Social Networks and Collective Capability

Hadiya migration to South Africa has been enabled by various forms of social networks and institutions both in places of origin and at destination. Although there are cases of individuals entirely paying for the cost of their migration, in most cases fundraising involves not only the nuclear but also the extended family, friends and neighbours. In fact, in some instances, families decide and prioritise who in the family should migrate and when. This depends on comparative advantages prioritising children who are more enterprising. In other instances, parents impose the migration agenda on a recalcitrant child counting on the life transformational role of migration, an instance of the intrinsic value of migration. The following story of Simba and Solomon from Queenstown, Eastern Cape Province of South Africa, demonstrates how friendship networks contribute to the building of migrants' capability, informed by the ethic of reciprocity:

> Solomon and I are not blood relatives but close friends from the same village. …. We both failed the national school leaving examination [and] felt so ashamed that we did not dare to go home that day. Instead, we wept and slept on the street. That was the day I decided to migrate to South Africa. I had a good prospect of migrating to South Africa because I had relatives there. I promised my friend that if and when I migrate to South Africa, he would be the first person that I will take. The hope of going to South Africa made us forget our sorrow. My relatives pledged to contribute 25 cows to help me pay for the migration. But none of it was materialised. Instead, Solomon's father stepped in. He sold his only ox and gave it to me hoping that I would take his son to South Africa. As I promised, Solomon was the first person I brought to South Africa, even before my brothers". (Queenstown, August 2022)[3]

The collective nature of Hadiya migration continues throughout the journey. In most cases, Hadiya migrate to South Africa in a group so that they support each other in times of needs. By contrast, most Ethiopian migrants, especially those from Addis Ababa, migrate individually and the exigencies of the journey rather force them to construct social relatedness impromptu, which is much more fragile than Hadiya migrants who travel in groups with a robust social relatedness. A returnee migrant from Addis Ababa recounted his experience during the journey as follows:

> I was alone during the journey. The day I bid farewell to my younger brother to the US I was on the move to South Africa. In Moyale I met another migrant from Addis who was also alone. We made an oath to support each other until we reach South Africa and even there. Although we parted company in South Africa, the mutual support was critical in sustaining us throughout the journey. (interviewed in Addis Ababa, December 2022)

Apart from migrants themselves as networks, there are various intermediate, self-sustaining structures. This includes the "migration industry", which involves brokers and smugglers who have an interest in, and tend to facilitate, the continuation of migration (see also Hones et al., this volume). The migration industry in the Ethiopia–South Africa corridor is based on access to information and trust given the higher risks associated with the journey. The Hadiya are fairly represented in the brokerage industry who closely cooperate with the Somali, Kenyan and Eritrean smugglers further linked with various intermediaries in southern African countries. The movement is typically organised directly from Hosanna or Nairobi. Access to the quality (effective) brokerage is very important in the Ethiopia–South Africa migration corridor which is increasingly securitised by the Ethiopian government because many of the migrants are "irregular migrants" vulnerable to manipulation by "human traffickers". Aspirant migrants have a clear preference for transnationally connected local brokers who are more trusted. Fekadu, Deshingkar and Tekalign have noted that migration brokers in Hadiya are positively signified (affectionately called *beri kefach*/door openers) and brokerage is considered as socio-culturally embedded business because:

Migration brokers live among the community, they worship with the community, and their children go to the same school as the children from the local community. Migration to South Africa is a long journey with a high risk of being intercepted and deported. Thus, for potential migrants using the services of a broker with whom they share multiple relationships, and whom they believe will respect the local values and norms, is a strategy to reduce risks. Brokers will work hard and use their own money to mitigate migration failures as these impacts on their reputation (Adugna et al., 2019, 17).

This is very different from the view of brokers as "human traffickers" by government and international development actors. There are many cases in which brokers paid back the brokerage fee for a failed migration project. Being Hadiya is thus already a social capital allowing differential access to effective and "responsible" brokerage service. Using a religious analogy, some research participants even recast the brokers as Moses who would guide the journey to "the promised land", i.e., South Africa: "As the Prophet Muse transitioned the Israelites from wandering in the wilderness to the Promised Land, so did the brokers bring us to South Africa".[4] That many of Hadiya migrants have little or no formal education make it difficult for them to comprehend how brokerage really works imbuing it with a mystic dimension: "We didn't know anything about where South Africa is and how to get there. I was a kind of person who would get lost even from one village to another in Hadiya. Tell me, isn't it then a miracle that I managed to reach South Africa. And that was possible thanks to the brokers".[5] Reflecting this, a female broker based in Kenya was considered as a matron, reputed for her brokerage service with a humane face. Her migrants' shelter in the border town of Gambo in Kenya had a place for worship, clean accommodation and good food to migrants, at times even slaughtering ox to make the migrants feel comfortable and prepare for the strenuous journey.

Hadiya have also adapted their cultural institutions and established new ones at destination places to build their individual and collective capabilities. *Iqub* and *idir* are some of these institutions which play an important role in the process of adaptation and in running their businesses. *Iqub* is a traditional rotating saving association and *idir* is a funeral association. Although these associations are used by most Ethiopian migrants, it is the Hadiya and other migrants from southern Ethiopia who use them most extensively, partly because of their wider social networks. They share not only a "southern" identity, collectively referred to by Ethiopian migrants from other parts of Ethiopia as *ye Hosanna lijoch* ("sons of Hosanna"), particularly referring to Hadiya and migrants from the neighbouring Kembatta. The Hadiya and Kembatta have managed to transcend their traditional hostility in Ethiopia,[6] and instead expanded the mutually beneficial social network that partly enabled them to carve out a particular business niche. The *Hosanna lijoch* focused on the location business, initially delivering commodities from door to door in townships and villages currently upgraded into Tuck Shops and Spazas. Hadiya migrants have also immersed in other types of social relationships and obligations, some are newly minted in response to the imperatives of life at destination. Social occasions such as wedding, birth, migrants' welcoming (*qibela*) and sending off (*shignit*) parties are also fundraising moments; part of which is used to pay for the migration to relatives. A striking feature of Hadiya migrants in South Africa, as corroborated by migrants from other parts of Ethiopia, is how a Hadiya would drive thousands of kilometres to attend a wedding or funeral. On average for a social occasion that cost 40,000 Rand the host would gather up to 40,000 Rand. So far, the highest contribution for a Hadiya migrant sending-off party was 450,000 Rand. The returnee migrant used this money to set up a business upon return to Hosanna.

A new social institution that has been invented by Ethiopian migrants in South Africa is a labour arrangement between established migrants (called *boss*) and new arrivals (*borders*). As he expands his business, a *boss* would need a partner to open additional shops in remote places. A *border* is given the goods on credit with an agreed upon amount of profit for the *boss*. A *boss* is usually based in bigger cities such as Joburg but smaller *bosses* operate from smaller towns. A *boss* supplies the *border* through truck. Usually, a *boss* hires a driver but when the transaction is higher himself distributes the goods. This contractual relation works entirely based on trust. Thus, a Hadiya *boss* prefers to work with a Hadiya *border*. A returnee migrant from Addis Ababa laments the competitive advantage of *ye Hosanna lijoch border* as compared with other Ethiopian migrants as follows:

> *Ye Hosanna lijoch* get to work soon after their arrival because a Hadiya or Kembatta boss want to work with people from their regions. They trust them and give them goods worth 30,000 Rand. This is a lot of money for a starter. It will take a longer time for migrants from Addis to reach that level. Hadiya migrants know each other or know their clans and families. This allows them to trust each other. The *boss/border* arrangement works if people are related as it is based on a high level of trust. The *boss* also does not consider this as a competition because the more their business expand the more trusted people they need. (interviewed in Addis Ababa, December 17, 2022)

As these examples demonstrate, individual Hadiya migrants' agency is situated within these self-help associations and symbiotic labour relations, shedding light on how migration capability is built through a collective effort.

Processes of Individualisation of the Hadiya Migration Project

Hadiya migrants in South Africa have benefitted from the high profit margins of the businesses they engage in, the social support and financial saving schemes which help new arrivals to stand on their feet, and the higher value of the Rand in the late 2000s and early 2010s. This newly acquired wealth was re-invested in changing business lines from door-to-door selling of commodities (i.e., "location" business) to *spaza* shops.

The same period also witnessed increasing financial remittances sent back home from South Africa. What started as remittances for household consumption evolved towards heavy investment in the transport sector (public, as well as freight) before the land speculation bonanza. This speculative land market since 2015 was free riding the local economy, to the detriment of many peri-urban farmers and increasing corruption in the governance structure. In South Africa, increasing wealth also led to higher involvement of Hadiya migrants in criminal activities, often by tipping information to others who will do the actual robbing and at times joining the gang groups in South Africa.

Thus, material success in South Africa came at the cost of eroding the very basis for the success of Hadiya migrants, i.e., the collective conception of the whole migration enterprise. Perhaps the absence of an institutional setup to direct the newfound wealth into more productive and socially useful ends led to the spiralling of dispossessive engagements with peri-urban farmers, which primarily benefits land speculators (mainly migrants), politicians, and land brokers. The zonal administration is represented as more of a bureaucratic hurdle to migrant investors than facilitators, among others the demand for bribes at different stages. We now have many cases of siblings quarrelling and fighting over wealth, and elders resolving such disputes with payments of handsome service fees. The trust in pastors and individual prayers and prophecies is dwindling also, as religious officials are suspected of being corrupt and becoming more oriented towards material success than deeper religious teachings.

The blessing inscribed in the prophecy is now also considered as a curse in the context of increasing violence that involves homicide in the destination country and rising living costs and corruption in places of origin. While commenting on these processes of excessive individualisation, a research participant surmised: "migration has mutated from being a *bereket* [blessing]' into *mergemt* [curse]". Still, the individualisation of the migration project and its social cost is interpreted through the overarching spiritual scheme of interpretation, i.e., how individuals "abused" the blessing to individually advance at the expense of the collective good, leading to God withdrawing his favour from the Hadiya, as noted by a research participant from the Mekaneyesus Church in Hosanna:

> Not all migrants have responded to God's gift in a responsible manner. Some have behaved and made good use of the blessing – they changed themselves and their family, as prophesised by Peter. However, some abused the blessing – engaged in violence, extra marital affairs, divorce etc. It seems as if God has withdrawn His favour so much so that brothers started killing each other in South Africa". (interviewed in Hosanna, December 2019)

The emergence of predatory local prophets called *ye festal agelgayoch*, i.e., amateur door-to-door spiritual service providers, throws further light onto the moral decay that surrounds the migration project. Unlike in earlier times when the blessing of church leaders was sought after, *ye festal agelgayoch* are now operating more as schemers than interpreters of God's will. Emboldened by the claim to a privileged access to divine knowledge, they extort money from the families of prospective migrants making the journey appear risk-free as long as it is endorsed by them and without adequate preparation by families.

The shift from the collective to unilateral migration decision-making by the youth is yet another instance of the individualisation of the migration project. Previously migration was a consultative process—who was prioritised to migrate was decided based on who is in a better position to contribute to the family good. There were even instances where parents would impose migration on an unruly child. Now, the material success of some of the migrants has fuelled an aspiration with a sense of immediacy—children putting pressure on parents and even blackmailing them to sell their assets and pay for their migration. There is also an increase in unilateral decisions: the youth steal initial capital that takes them up to the border with Kenya and then inform parents—changing the facts on the ground leaving and their parents with no option than paying for the migration regardless of their economic conditions.

The greed and the individualisation of the Hadiya migration project have had a corrosive impact on their collective capabilities. Brokers have become more exploitative, no longer operating under a moral framework as they did previously. In fact, some of the brokers extort money from migrant families twice: to send them to South Africa and from detention camps especially in Tanzania. Detained migrants have two options: either accept a three or four-year prison sentence or to pay 200,000 birr to be deported back to Ethiopia. Migrant families who can afford to pay brokers to bring them back home. Meanwhile, the supportive institutions that the Hadiya either elaborated on and built responding to the imperatives of migration are currently unravelling. The *boss–border* relations, for example, are turning more exploitative; the *borders* increasingly resent the much higher profit margin of their respective *bosses*. Conniving with South African brokers, some of the *bosses* are also involved in abducting *borders* (especially new arrivals without sponsors). A *boss* demands the money that he pays to the brokers once the *border* starts earning. Or he demands work for free until the service amounts to the money he paid (a form of indentured labour). The feeling of being exploited, and working under dangerous working conditions in shops in the townships has generated social tension, not just between a *boss* and a *border* in South Africa but also in places of origin as *bosses* and *borders* are caught in webs of transnational social relations. This tension in some instances resulted in the form of violence, a *boss* or a *border* conniving with South African criminal groups involving robbing or even killing. The competition over business turfs between *bosses* is also turning violent. This has a spillover effect on the viability of the mutual support institutions such as *iqub*. Resenting the business success of a fellow *iqub* member, some migrants would tip information to criminals when he receives and where he hides the *iqub* money. As undocumented migrants, the Hadiya put their money at home or in the shops until they remit it to families in Ethiopia through the hawala system. This has turned what was previously an asset into a liability, i.e., receiving *iqub* money creates a moment of vulnerability. There are also now free riders faking deaths in places of origin in order to collect the *idir* money.

Overall, there is an increase in migrants involvement in crime and migrant-on-migrant violence ranging from robbery to homicide. This has severely affected the quality of inter-personal relations. An example of this would be the souring of the bond between Simba and Solomon that we cited in the previous section. Solomon got involved in crime, robbing his fellowmen in concert with South African criminal elements. In a migrant community trial in Queenstown, Simba testified against his close friend for violating community norms in the following manner:

> The bible says "Take no part in the worthless deeds of evil and darkness; instead, expose them". I am very much disappointed to find out that Solomon is involved in crime. I was also robbed of my newly bought shop for 150,000 Rand. I do not know the identity of my robbers. I asked Solomon to work with me as a shareholder. He refused. I did not know that he was a thief. It was the Kunusten [sic Queenstown] community which helped me raise 450,000 Rand and helped me get back to business and bring my wife. Solomon borrowed from three persons and finally he took a thief with him to rob them. He ate *iqub* and run away. We need to name and shame people like Solomon regardless of our close relationships. (Queenstown, August 2022, https://fb.watch/iZWte1lcQX/)

During our research, many Hadiya returnee migrants mentioned that in fact robbing migrant businesses in South Africa was first started and encouraged by Ethiopian migrants. This is evident in the language South African robbers used to justify their act as a matter of entitlement. Initially, they would say "give me my coca" while demanding money from a shop owner but now they say "give me my *iqub* money"; adding that South Africans would not know about *iqub* money if they were not told by Ethiopians themselves. The capitalist logic and the greed that it underpins have currently undermined migration as a collective project among the Hadiya; one of the critical factors for their thriving and flourishing in South Africa despite the multiple challenges they have faced.

The changing contours of migration away from the positives and more towards the negative has induced a collective reflexive moment, around whether Hadiya migration to South Africa could ultimately become a liability given the pervasive and fragile rentier local economy, negative educational and agricultural outcomes and a looming social conflict engendered by the speculative land market unless these problems are mitigated by a visionary leadership that enhance the developmental potential of migration.

However, despite increasing individualisation and the dangers with which it is associated, all is not lost. There are some migrants and returnees who are still committed and are working towards the collective project of improving the lot of the Hadiya. This is primarily expressed in the form of investment in productive sectors in Hadiya Zone (e.g., commercial farms or dairy farms), despite the lack of cooperation and bureaucratic hurdles, risks the business model comes with, and the lower profit margins compared to speculative land investments. Moreover, there are attempts to bring in technology and insights from South Africa to improve productivity as well. All this is to ensure food security, restore Hadiya pride as self-sufficient and demonstrate to others that agriculture is a profitable sector to engage in.

Conclusion

An important factor for the success of South–South migration (as well as South–North migration in some cases) is the collective nature of migration. This collective worldview is not merely instrumental, but intrinsic to local cultures and social life. As we have argued in this chapter, this is ignored by the three dominant theories in migration studies: functionalism, historical structuralism and the aspiration—capability framework. As developed by de Haas, ACF very much takes an ahistorical assessment of migration, while the reality is that, as the Hadiya case study demonstrated, the nature of migration (i.e., location on the individual-collective continuum) changes across time with differing consequences to the migration process and its outcome.

As demonstrated in the discussion in the various sections of the chapter, the secret of Hadiya migrants' success in South Africa is large because of their collective imagination, imbued with a sense of social responsibility and mutual support as well as the urge to catch up with neighbours through the new affordances of migration. Now, their collective wellbeing is being undermined by the growing individualisation of the migration process, both in place of origin and at destination. In place of origin, this includes the emergence of a robust rentier local economy in Hadiya Zone at the top of which we find local government officials who live off the migration rent resulting in a very weak and corrupt public sector juxtaposed with a thriving private sector, a unique case in the context of Ethiopia. This rentier economy is undermining the viability of Hadiya society, not least the private sector from which its rents come in the first place. A key component of the private sector are migrants and their businesses. While the local political leadership, and the public sector more broadly, is responsive to the demands of private businesses which themselves are rent seekers it is very obstructive of the businesses set up by some visionary migrants who go out of their way to serve the public good. The Hadiya need to regain their collective imagination of migration as a public good going forward, otherwise to use their religious language, the blessing of migration will rapidly turn into a curse in which migration is increasingly devoid of its developmental potential.

At the place of destination, the increasing individualisation of the Hadiya migration project has weakened the hitherto mutual support of social institutions while labour relations between senior and more recent migrants have become more exploitative. Combined with the stiff competition over migrants' commercial spaces, the material turn in the Hadiya migration project has generated tension and conflict, including a rising homicide rate among Hadiya migrants in South Africa. The individualisation of the collective Hadiya migration project is resulting from a multitude of factors including, but not limited to, material gain and success. While paying attention to the changing nature of the "individualist-collectivist continuum" across time and space, we underscore two key points. First, one should not in any way over essentialise the trend as a complete shift from collective to individualistic one. Secondly, we need to clearly indicate that we approach the shift as an ongoing process and that we will not rule out the possibility of a return to a collective outlook.

Acknowledgements This work has been undertaken as part of the Migration for Development and Equality (MIDEQ) Hub. Funded by the UKRI Global Challenges Research Fund (GCRF) (Grant Reference: ES/S007415/1), MIDEQ unpacks the complex and multi-dimensional relationships between migration and inequality in the context of the Global South. More at www.mideq.org.

Notes

1. This work has been undertaken as part of the Migration for Development and Equality (MIDEQ) Hub, which unpacks the complex and multi-dimensional relationships between migration and inequality in the context of the Global South. More at www.mideq.org.
2. Countries typically crossed during the journey include Kenya, Tanzania, Malawi Mozambique and Zimbabwe.

3. Available at https://fb.watch/iZWte1lcQX/.
4. Interview with a returnee migrant, Hosanna, June 14, 2021.
5. Interview with a returnee migrant, Jajura, May 5, 2021.
6. This hostility was deepened by two massacres that occurred in the 1970s—the Ajura massacre where many Hadiya were killed by the Kembatta, followed by a retaliatory measure by the Hadiya in Wachemo where many Kembatta were killed. The Kembatta administrator Petros Gebre was implicated in this strained relation between the two communities.

References

Adugna, F., Deshingkar, P., & Ayalew, T. (2019). *Brokers, migrants, and the state: Berri Kefach "door openers" in Ethiopian Clandestine migration to South Africa*. University of Sussex. Working Paper 56. https://hdl.handle.net/10779/uos.23472446.v1

Arango, J. (2000). Explaining migration: A critical view. *International Social Science Journal, 52*(165), 283–296.

Berlin, I. (1969). Two concepts of liberty. In I. Berlin (Ed.), *Four essays on liberty* (pp. 118–172). Oxford University Press.

Cobbah, J. (1987). African values and the human rights debate: An African perspective. *Human Rights Quarterly, 9*(3), 309–331.

Cooper, B., & Esser, A. (2018). *Remittances in Ethiopia: exploring barriers to remittances in sub-Saharan Africa* (p. 4). Centre for Financial Regulation & Inclusion.

De Haas, H. (2021). A theory of migration: The aspirations-capabilities framework. *Comparative Migration Studies, 9*(8), 1–35.

Fikreab, M., & Asrat, W. (2020). Tragedy of rural youth out-migration and its socioeconomic consequences in Lemo Woreda of Hadiya Zone, Southern Ethiopia. *Journal of Economics and Sustainable Development, 11*(17), 9–15.

Girmachew, A. (2019). Migration patterns and emigrants' transnational activities: Comparative findings from two migrant origin areas in Ethiopia. *Comparative Migration Studies, 7*(5), 1–28.

Gore, C. (1997). Irreducibly social goods and the informational basis of Amartya Sen's capability approach. *Journal of International Development, 9*(2), 235–250.

Hagen-Zanker, J. (2008). *Why do people migrate? A review of the theoretical literature*. Maastricht Graduate School of Governance Working Paper MGSoG/2008/WP002 (January 2008), Maastricht University, the Netheralnds.

Howlowchak, A. (2006). Liberal individualism, autonomy, and the great divide. *Philosophy in the Contemporary World, 13*(1), 20–27.

Ibrahim, S. (2021). Individualism and the capability approach: The role of collectivities in expanding human capabilities. In E. Chiappero-Martinetti, S.

Osmani, & M. Qizilbash (Eds.), *The Cambridge handbook of the capability approach* (pp. 206–226). Cambridge University Press.

International Organization for Migration (IOM). (2021). *Families of missing migrants: Their search for answers, the impacts of loss and recommendations for improved support*. https://publications.iom.int/books/families-missing-migrants-united-kingdom-their-search-answers-impacts-loss-and-recommendations

Levitt, P. (2007). *God needs no passport*. The New Press.

Massey, D., Arango, J., Hugo, G., Kouaouci, A., Pellegrino, A., & Taylor, J. (1998). *Worlds in motion: International migration at the end of the millennium*. Oxford University Press.

Nagengast, E. (2015). Bookends seminar: Communalism and liberalism in the struggle for human rights in Africa. *Juniata Voices, 15*, 80–86.

Robeyns, I. (2007). The capability approach: A theoretical survey. *Journal of Human Development and Capabilities, 6*(1), 93–117.

Tsedeke, L., & Ayele. (2017). Logistic mixed modeling of determinants of international migration from the Southern Ethiopia: Small area estimation approach. *American Journal of Theoretical and Applied Statistics, 6*(3), 170–182.

United Nations Department of Economic and Social Affairs (UN DESA). (2020). *International migration 2020 highlights*. https://www.un.org/en/desa/international-migration-2020-highlights

Uyan-Semerci, P. (2007). A relational account of Nussbaum's list of capabilities. *Journal of Human Development, 8*(2), 203–221.

Zack, T., & Estifanos, Y. (2016). Somewhere else: Social connection and dislocation of Ethiopian migrants in Johannesburg. *African and Black Diaspora: An International Journal, 9*(2), 149–165.

Open Access This chapter is licensed under the terms of the Creative Commons Attribution 4.0 International License (http://creativecommons.org/licenses/by/4.0/), which permits use, sharing, adaptation, distribution and reproduction in any medium or format, as long as you give appropriate credit to the original author(s) and the source, provide a link to the Creative Commons license and indicate if changes were made.

The images or other third party material in this chapter are included in the chapter's Creative Commons license, unless indicated otherwise in a credit line to the material. If material is not included in the chapter's Creative Commons license and your intended use is not permitted by statutory regulation or exceeds the permitted use, you will need to obtain permission directly from the copyright holder.

11

Migration and Inequality in the Burkina Faso–Côte d'Ivoire corridor

Bonayi Hubert Dabiré and Kando Amédée Soumahoro

Introduction

Burkina Faso is a landlocked Sahelian country with low income and limited natural resources. With a Gross Domestic Product (GDP) in 2020 of USD 16.1 billion for a population of more than 20 million inhabitants growing at a rate of 2.9% per year (RGPH, 2019), Burkina Faso falls into the category of least developed countries (LDCs). It has a GDP/capita of around USD 768.8 compared to an average of USD 1,566.3 in Sub-Saharan Africa.

International migrants leaving Burkina Faso in 2019 chose several destinations, mainly in Africa, and particularly West Africa, which indicates that migration to the ECOWAS countries is the most important. By contrast, Europe receives only 2.6% of Burkina Faso's migrants (see also Setrana and Yaro, this volume). Most migratory movements outside the country are directed to Côte d'Ivoire, which accounted for 61.1% of migrants in 2019 (RGPH, 2019). The eight West African Economic Monetary Union (WAEMU) countries alone account for more than 75% of recent migrants leaving Burkina Faso. The two other essential destinations after Côte d'Ivoire

B. H. Dabiré (✉)
Université Joseph Ki-Zerbo, Ouagadougou, Burkina Faso
e-mail: dabire.bonayi@yahoo.fr

K. A. Soumahoro
University Felix Houphouet-Boigny, Abidjan, Côte d'Ivoire
e-mail: kandoamedeesoum@gmail.com

are Mali and Ghana, respectively, 12.5 and 8.6% (RGPH, 2019). The observation that can be made is that while the Burkinabè migrate internationally, most settle in neighbouring countries.

Indeed, migration between Burkina Faso and Côte d'Ivoire constitutes one of the largest migration flows in the world. In the 2019 census, it was found that 6 out of 10 residents have already migrated outside the country (RGPH5, 2019). People from the poorest rural areas of Burkina Faso migrate to Côte d'Ivoire for work, a journey that is facilitated by free movement and low costs. Child labour and trafficking are also common, especially in the cocoa plantations.

Despite the various disruptions observed in the Burkinabe migration space—associated with the internal mining boom within Burkina Faso and political and economic crises in Côte d'Ivoire—this major migration trend persists, even if some premises of change are emerging. Migration movements out of the country over the last five years preceding the 2019 census (RGPH, 2019) are male-dominated, with 85% of men compared to 15% of women, i.e., five times more men than women. As for migrants to Burkina Faso, in 2019, 90% of them were Burkinabè. Most of these migrants come from Côte d'Ivoire (86%), with the rest coming mainly from countries bordering Burkina Faso (RGPH, 2006, 2019). Only 10% of immigrants are non-Burkinabé. Thus, international migration (in and out) is dominated by Burkinabè.

This chapter discusses the inequalities associated with migration in the Burkina Faso–Côte d'Ivoire corridor based on a literature review and data from a survey conducted in 2020 as part of research undertaken by the Migration for Development and Equality (MIDEQ) Hub.[1] The chapter begins by explaining the historical context of Burkinabè migration to Côte d'Ivoire, as well as specific characteristics of this migration, such as the main reasons, types and forms. It then discusses the different inequalities linked to this migration in both countries including those associated with gender and childhood.

---

[1] The Migration for Development and Equality (MIDEQ) Hub unpacks the complex and multi-dimensional relationships between migration and inequality in the context of the Global South. More at www.mideq.org

Historical Background of Migration Between Burkina Faso and Côte d'Ivoire

Numerous factors have been put forward—including historical, social, demographic and economic factors—to explain the migration of Burkinabè. Historically, colonisation was a critical factor in triggering international migration, especially the numerical importance of the phenomenon and its orientation towards Côte d'Ivoire (Coulibaly, 1978; Piché et al., 1981, 1996). The magnitude of the migration of Burkinabe to Côte d'Ivoire is closely tied to the establishment of a system that, from the beginning of colonisation, tied Upper Volta (now Burkina Faso) to Côte d'Ivoire.

The literature on Burkinabè emigration shows that colonisation was the main factor that triggered the major international migration flows to Côte d'Ivoire (Coulibaly, 1986; Cordell et al., 1996; Deniel, 1968; Fynn Bruey and Crawley, this volume). This process has three main phases, each triggering a different flow type. The first was a period of conquest and pacification, the establishment of a colonial administration and the development of some local infrastructure, including roads and administrative buildings. To achieve this, the colonisers instituted a system of forced labour and taxes. The population's reaction was to "flee" before the invader (Suret-Canale, 1964; Piché et al., 1981), and these movements generally took place over short distances into the country's interior areas that were inaccessible to the colonisers. Some of these movements were also made in Ghana, with the dual objective of escaping the invader and avoiding the sums demanded by the administration.

The second phase began in 1921 with the law's adoption of the colonies' development. Indeed, in the logic of the vast colonial project, the colonies formed a whole where each one should play a role according to its natural potential. In French West Africa (AOF), "the Mossi Plateau (Upper Volta) is the most densely populated area, and according to the division of labour assigned to each colony, this country was designated as a provider of labour for work in the other colonies, particularly Côte d'Ivoire" (Coulibaly & Vaugelade, 1981, 84). It should be noted that the colony of Upper Volta, created in 1919, was abolished in 1932, and a large part of it was attached to Côte d'Ivoire. The purpose of this abolition and the attachment of a large part of the former Upper Volta to Côte d'Ivoire was to direct the migration of Burkinabè towards the Ivorian plantations. In contrast, traditionally, the Voltaic people migrated towards the Gold Coast (present-day Ghana) (Deniel, 1968). Thus, from the first years of the inter-war period, the Voltaics constituted the majority of agricultural workers on the plantations of the Lower Côte d'Ivoire.

The third phase began in 1947. After the abolition of forced labour in 1946 and the reconstitution of Upper Volta in 1947 within its current borders, the migration movement became voluntary and increased as a result of the establishment by the Ivorian planters of the Syndicat Interprofessionnel pour l'Acheminement de la Main-d'œuvre (SIAMO), a private structure for the recruitment of Burkinabe workers. According to Raymond Deniel (1968), from the 1950s onwards, approximately 20,000 people from Burkina Faso entered Côte d'Ivoire each year through these structures.

Data from the 1960/61 demographic survey indicate how Côte d'Ivoire, which was not initially the top country of emigration, gradually replaced Ghana as the source of labour. These statistics show that during the suppression of the Upper Volta, the reversal of flows took place to the detriment of Ghana (Fig. 11.1).

It can be seen from Fig. 11.1 that before 1932, migration to Côte d'Ivoire was very marginal. From 1947 onwards, Côte d'Ivoire became the leading destination for Burkinabe migrants. It was between 1932 and 1947 that the reversal occurred. It was precisely then that the Upper Volta was suppressed and that a large part of the country—notably the Mossi Plateau—was attached to Côte d'Ivoire. On the eve of independence, Voltaic emigration was exclusively to Côte d'Ivoire. Stopping the migration of Voltaic people to Ghana and redirecting them to Côte d'Ivoire was a constant concern of the colonial authorities. The dislocation of the colony of Upper Volta in 1932 and the attachment of its most populous part (the Mossi Plateau) to Côte d'Ivoire were part of this strategy (Coulibaly, 1986; Deniel, 1968).

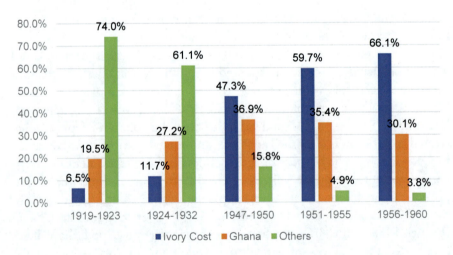

Fig. 11.1 Evolution of international migration from Upper Volta, 1919–1960

It should be noted that during the colonial period, Burkinabe migration to Ghana and Côte d'Ivoire was essentially a forced movement, especially in the period between 1919 and 1946. Indeed, during the colonial period, migration to Côte d'Ivoire involved the deportation of Burkinabè workers to Ivorian plantations (Suret-Canale, 1964). Even those who went to Ghana were essentially fugitives from the colonial invasion. Forced labour, the system of exploitation of the significant concessions held by private companies in Côte d'Ivoire, the major infrastructure works undertaken by the coloniser, conscription into the army, especially during the world wars, the "voluntary" system, and the forced recruitment of workers led to a massive emigration of Burkinabe to neighbouring countries, mainly Ghana and Côte d'Ivoire (Coulibaly, 1986; Songré, 1972). The abolition of forced labour recruitment in 1946 (Babacar Fall, 1993) ended the forced migration of Burkinabè workers to Côte d'Ivoire and opened up an era of voluntary migration (Piché & Cordell, 2015).

Factors and Characteristics of Burkinabe Migration After Independence

If colonisation is one of the primary contexts that has driven the migration dynamics towards Côte d'Ivoire, other economic, social, demographic and even political factors contribute towards maintaining, perpetuating and amplifying this migration.

After independence, Ivorian migration policy was, for a long time, very liberal, and the president of the period, Félix Houphouet-Boigny, pronounced on several occasions that foreign migrants were welcome. In addition to this favourable predisposition of the Ivorian authorities to migration, the underdevelopment situation of Burkina Faso must be emphasised. With a Human Development Index (HDI) of 0.452 and ranked 182nd out of 189 countries (UNDP, 2020), Burkina Faso is considered one of the poorest countries in the West African sub-region. As noted above, Burkina Faso is a landlocked Sahelian country, where nearly 90% of the population lives from agriculture (PNDES, 2016). However, this agriculture is dependent on the vagaries of rainfall. It cannot meet the population's needs, forcing it to migrate as part of a livelihood strategy.

Moreover, agriculture as the main, if not exclusive, activity in rural Burkina Faso, is also a subsistence activity that occupies farmers for only five to six months of the year (when the rainy season lasts). Thus, the sole recourse to agriculture to ensure the substance of household members is increasingly risky: not only is there very high variability in rural household incomes from one year to the next, but there are also fluctuations in market prices over which the farmers have no control (Marchal, 1985). This situation is identified in the literature as the main reason for the migration of Burkinabè to Côte d'Ivoire.

Drought periods, which lead to a deficit in cereal production, are also associated with outward migration. Boutillier et al. (1977) and Vaugelade (1991) establish a positive correlation between drought years and high migration periods. The authors show that intense emigration movements follow years of poor harvests. However, other authors (Coulibaly, 1980), based on a national survey conducted in 1980, believe that while the drought factor must be considered, its effects are localised and not generalised. In other words, while droughts and poor harvests are specific causes of emigration, their effects are not systematic and depend on the locality.

Other cultural factors as drivers of migration are mentioned in the literature. These include production and power relations and mechanisms for achieving economic and residential independence within Burkinabe social units, particularly among the Mossi. For several authors (e.g., Deniel, 1968; Capron & Kohler, 1976; Boutillier, 1975), the hierarchical structure of Mossi society, characterised by the domination of the younger generation by the older, is one of the main causes of migration. Thus, "this predominantly authoritarian/autocratic society attributes political, ritual and social means to the older generation, and allows the younger generation to be held in long-term dependence" (Boutillier, 1975, 155). Moreover, the accession to independence of young people follows a long and complex process. It is during this long period of dependence that the young person chooses to migrate. Migration is the search for individual autonomy, the struggle of the individual to escape from a social system in which he feels exploited, or in any case in which he does not have direct and personal access to the fruits of his labour (Ancey, 1983; Boutillier et al., 1977, 1985). It is in response to these forms of domination that young people choose to migrate as a way of acquiring their autonomy.

It is also often mentioned in the literature on the causes of migration in Upper Volta that migration is considered by society or even used by society as a "rite of passage" (Coulibaly, 1980, 65). To migrate to Côte d'Ivoire is to show courage. Very often, the migrant is presented as someone who has braved the unknown and the dangers with which migration is associated. This image is partly due to the period of compulsory recruitment under colonisation and the flight to Ghana, where migrating was a courageous act. Thus, migration would be "a rite of passage" by which the young person affirms his courage and bravery: one does not become an adult until one has made one's first migration (Deniel, 1968). People who have never migrated are often mocked by young people, especially young girls (Kohler, 1972).

It should be noted that at the domestic level, the policy of the Burkinabè authorities has been to encourage emigration, counting on remittances from migrants to boost the economy. Conventions on migration were signed with Côte d'Ivoire (March 9, 1960), Mali (September 30, 1969) and Gabon (August 13, 1973) to provide security for Burkinabè migrants and to organise their remittances to Burkina Faso. For example, in the convention with Côte d'Ivoire, Burkina Faso was to provide quotas of migrants at the request of the Ivorian planters, and in return, a portion of the migrant's wages was to be paid directly to Burkina Faso into a fund created for this purpose.

Migration Strategies

The migration observed between Burkina Faso and Côte d'Ivoire after independence (1900–1975) was essentially circular (Cordell et al., 1996). Indeed, migrants who leave for Côte d'Ivoire do not aim to settle there: migration strategies are family-based, and migrants who go to Côte d'Ivoire aim to resolve their situation and help their household in Burkina Faso. In addition, the migratory movements between Burkina Faso and Côte d'Ivoire are back and forth: a migrant's project from the outset includes their return. However, as time goes by and more and more opportunities become available to migrants, some end up settling. This is especially true of successful migrants, those who have obtained large plantations or large and successful businesses. It is also the case of first-time migrants who have previously settled in western Côte d'Ivoire and who have seen their status change from sharecroppers or workers to owners of farms, which allows them to invest in their country of origin, a situation that allows them to maintain regular contact with Burkina Faso. Thus, while the circular aspect remains an important characteristic of Burkinabè international migration, it must be recognised that more and more migrants are settling abroad on a longer-term basis, particularly in Côte d'Ivoire since 1975 (Ouédraogo and Piché, 2007).

However, what marks the migration exchanges between Burkina Faso and Côte d'Ivoire today is the importance of return migration, particularly after the Tabou events in 1999.[2] Although the return movement began in the 1970s (Piché & Cordell, 2015), it gained momentum in the 1990s. Indeed,

---

[2] In November 1999, in Tabou, 400 km from Abidjan, a dispute between an indigenous planter and a Burkinabè national degenerated into a full-blown community conflict that led to the sudden departure of more than 10,000, mostly Burkinabè, to their country of origin.

the fairly recurrent clashes between Burkinabè migrants and Ivorians accelerated the return movement from the 1990s with the Tabou events of 1999, the 2002 rebellion and the 2010 post-election crisis. As Mandé points out (2015, 342), "having become the scapegoats of political crises, the Burkinabè suffer exactions, and for many, their salvation lies in returning to their country".

Overview of Inequalities Linked to Burkinabè Migration

Traditionally, Burkinabè migrants leave the rural areas for Côte d'Ivoire (Dennis et al., 1996). Poverty, the search for an income, the degradation of agricultural land and the lack of prospects for salaried employment in rural areas have convinced Burkinabè to continue to look outside the country for ways to earn a living and support their families back home (Marchal, 1975). In other words, it is generally the poorest who migrate. However, migration has economic and social costs that are not affordable for everyone. Migration requires more effort to mobilise financial or human resources and to mobilise family social networks. The poorest often borrow money to finance their migration, forcing them to work during the first months of their migration to repay the loan. Those with a network (of relatives and friends) already established in Côte d'Ivoire have a definite advantage over those without.

To make their emigration to Côte d'Ivoire possible, Burkina Faso migrants mainly mobilise their family and friend relationships. This social capital (family and friends) is crucial in migration. Consequently, those who do not have it will have more difficulty or less chance of migrating. This means that there are inequalities in the opportunity to migrate.

Gender Inequalities in Migration

If men's migration is perceived as usual, even natural, this is not the case for women's migration. Although the situation is beginning to change, reticence or pejorative apprehensions about women's migration are still prevalent. Compared to men, the negative perception associated with women migrating alone reflects the social norms determining what a woman can or should do. According to the opinions collected during the field surveys of MIDEQ, women should not expose themselves to adventures like men. Indeed, in the eyes of Burkinabè society, it is inconceivable that a woman should migrate alone. The social justifications are that women are fragile and more vulnerable to the difficulties and vicissitudes of migration. Worse, it is thought that women are weak enough to succumb to prostitution as a profession or as a last resort since they are not supposed to be able to do the hard physical work in the plantation fields, which is what constitutes the real financial manna of Burkinabè migrants in Côte d'Ivoire:

> As for the migration of women, I find that it is not at all normal because the majority of them migrate to go and work as prostitutes. If a woman migrates, she has no strength. What kind of work will she do there? She cannot work on a plantation, or anything if it is not to sell herself, and that money is dirty. (Interview with a 45-year-old head of household, a farmer in the Southwest)

For a long time in Burkina Faso, female migrants were almost exclusively women who accompanied or joined their husbands in Côte d'Ivoire. The difficult migration conditions during the colonial period associated with forced migration, as outlined above, contributed to the marginalisation of women in migration.

Inequalities Related to Childhood

Differences in the treatment of children in Burkina Faso can be observed between the biological children of the household and those who are not, such as children whose parents have left for migration. These inequalities related to childhood are generally observed at the level of schooling. Studies conducted in Burkina Faso as part of the MIDEQ Hub show that left-behind children have a higher enrollment rate than children whose parents have not migrated. One inequality these left-behind children face is access and retention in school. On the other hand, the biological children of the household are enrolled in the best-quality schools. This may be because parents who migrate to Côte d'Ivoire and have more resources send money to send their children to school to stay in Burkina Faso, which host households must do. Nonetheless host households favour their biological children by sending them to the best schools.

Remittances and Skills Transfers of Burkinabè Migrants

An analysis by the National Institute of Statistics and Demography based on data from three series of surveys on household living conditions conducted in Burkina Faso shows that the higher the proportion of migrants in a household, the higher its standard of living and the higher its secondary school attendance rate. Thus, migration is a factor in reducing poverty.

These migrants who make money transfers to their households of origin allow the latter to improve their living conditions (BCEAO, 2011). As a result, the issue of cash transfers has become central to discussions on development and the reduction of poverty and inequality. According to the BCEAO (2011), in 2011, Burkina Faso received 96.5 billion CFA francs in remittances from migrants, 31% of which came from Côte d'Ivoire. According to data from the Harmonized Survey on Household Living Conditions (EHCVM, 2018) carried out in 2018 by the National Institute of Statistics and Demography, these remittances amounted to 81 billion CFA francs, 45% of which came from Côte d'Ivoire. Although this was a decrease compared to 2011, it is clear that remittances are significant in volume and mostly come from Côte d'Ivoire. Moreover, remittance figures are generally thought to be underestimated because of the lack of control over remittance channels.

These cash transfers contribute to poverty reduction, particularly in rural areas, because, even if there is a tendency to use the transfers in productive sectors, a large part is destined for migrant households for current consumption (food, health, education) and certain expenses, sometimes of a prestigious nature (weddings, funerals, etc.). According to the 2014 Continuous Multisectoral Survey results, the main reason for transfers is family support (88.8%), which shows that transfers are mainly aimed at fighting poverty in rural households. In Sub-Saharan Africa, migrant transfers, by increasing the disposable income of recipient households, have an impact on reducing poverty and inequality, as the work of Gupta et al. (2007) has shown. Remittances thus reduce inequalities at the household level by allowing the poor households to reduce income gaps. Households that receive remittances are envied because they have a safety valve that allows them to cope with difficult situations. These households appear to be privileged, often living the lifestyle of city dwellers.

The preponderance of households with migratory experience to be able to borrow money in case of emergency can be explained by the household's negotiating capacity, but also and above all by the relational capital available to households with migrant members. In addition, migrant households are slightly more likely to be able to find a loan in case of need compared to non-migrant households (Marc et al., 2022). This is because having someone who has migrated is a guarantee of financial capacity and repayment compared to other households.

It is important to note that migrants do not only transfer money: they also transfer skills acquired during migration, occasional or permanent returns to Burkina Faso. One idea developed in the literature is that return migrants are carriers of innovation in the rural areas to which they return after a stay in Côte d'Ivoire (Dabiré, 2017; OECD, 2017). Indeed, these migrants have acquired skills they use once they return to their country of origin. For example, research by the OECD (2017) in Burkina Faso showed that households with returning migrants are more likely to invest in agricultural assets than households without returning migrants. In addition, households with return migrants are more likely to manage a non-farm business than those without return migrants (OECD, 2017). Thus, thanks to their skills acquired in Côte d'Ivoire, migrants innovate and modernise rural work.

The study conducted by Dabiré (2017) confirms the hypothesis that migrants returning from Côte d'Ivoire are carriers of innovation. Returning migrants innovate by building on existing practices that were theirs before leaving for emigration, drawing on their experiences in Côte d'Ivoire. Even when they are in agricultural activities, migrants invest in types of crops specific to commercialisation (cashew, maize, etc.). In addition, they innovate by introducing tree farming, which was previously unknown in Burkina Faso. This study also notes that migrants are oriented towards the practice of cash crop production, while non-migrants focus on crops for consumption (Dabiré, 2017).

Inequalities Associated with Migration in Burkina Faso

Although migration is generally perceived as a positive process in terms of poverty reduction, it is clear that migration can also contribute to increased inequality in Burkina Faso by privileging some and not others. As Sidiki Coulibaly (2015) points out:

> The data from the 2000 survey seem to show, on the contrary, that this eradication of poverty in Burkina Faso is not for tomorrow……Certainly, the crumbs of development, collected here and there by a few "lucky" migrants, will give the illusion that migration is beneficial for the migrant, his or her family, or

even the entire nation and that it even allows for the social ascension of some. However, even the profitability of the migration funds transferred to Burkina Faso serves so little and so badly. The system is set up in such a way that this hard-earned money still favours the privileged and not the poor fringe of rural or urban areas. (Coulibaly, 2015, v)

One of the downsides of migration is the reduction in the supply of labour in rural areas, as highlighted in research by OECD (2017), which found that younger people (aged 15–44) represent 90% of current emigrants, a larger proportion than non-migrants (76%) and that about 60% of emigrants were employed in Burkina Faso (in agriculture-related activities and elementary trades) before they left the country. However, due to a lack of resources, these households cannot recruit agricultural labour and must compensate for the lack of human resources with additional effort from the remaining members. Migration from rural areas thus creates inequalities because households with migrants find themselves in a labour shortage situation and are thus more vulnerable.

The study conducted by the ISSP in 2020 as part of the MIDEQ Hub's research shows that households with migration experience with Côte d'Ivoire are poorer than households with no migration experience, a result that was entirely unexpected and suggests that Côte d'Ivoire. This survey is the most recent and has provided results that have never previously been observed. These results suggest that migration creates inequalities between households with migrants and households without migrants and that Côte d'Ivoire is not the El Dorado it was previously. More recently, Burkinabè migration has diversified to other countries, notably Italy, the United States, Canada and the Gulf States (General Population Census of Burkina Faso, 2019). Studies have shown that migrants to the North are more beneficial regarding economic benefits (De Vreyer et al., 2010).

This inequality between rich and poor in the face of migration is highlighted in several studies. In a study conducted in Donsin (a Mossi village located about 30 km from Ouagadougou), Smith (1977) observed that migration seems to be practised more by small, relatively well-off families and by larger families rather than by small, poor families. But once the poor overcome these obstacles and migrate, their contribution to the fight against poverty and inequality is undeniable because once in Côte d'Ivoire, the poor transfer more than the rich.

What, then can we conclude about the contribution of migration to Burkina Faso?

Migration's contribution to reducing poverty and inequality is ambivalent with outcomes perceived differently depending on the angle from which they are viewed. In the case of Burkina Faso, migration has positive effects in certain aspects. For example, in opinion surveys, households' perception of migration is more nuanced, and migration is often considered positive even if it sometimes disrupts family life. However, analysis of the impact of migration on inequalities in Burkina Faso based on empirical studies shows that it is difficult to establish a general theory on the issue. The impact of migration on inequalities is a function of context, region, time, etc., and the theoretical antagonism in the conception is not reflected in the facts of migration.

Inequalities in Côte d'Ivoire

Evidence from research conducted as part of the MIDEQ Hub shows that migration produces certain inequalities in destination countries, including Côte d'Ivoire. This section highlights the different forms of inequality linked to migration.

Inequalities in Rights Linked to Citizenship and Employment

Inequalities in rights are at the centre of the concerns that emerged in the exchanges on the ground in Côte d'Ivoire regarding South–South migration. These take shape in the inequality of rights linked to citizenship and employment: on the one hand between the social construction of statelessness and the social construction of the concept of the foreigner; and on the other hand between barriers to entry into formal and construction of monopolies in informal jobs.

Concerning the inequalities of rights linked to citizenship, these are based on the social construction of statelessness and the social construction of the concept of the foreigner. Article 15 of the Universal Declaration of Human Rights (1948) states, "Everyone has the right to a nationality. No one may be arbitrarily deprived of his nationality, nor of the right to change nationality". However, according to the data collected in the field, the question of the naturalisation of migrants and their children is creating a category of people who are effectively stateless. This category of actors is a victim of the rights inequalities attached to citizenship in the Burkina Faso–Côte d'Ivoire corridor. Burkinabè migrants are therefore weakened regarding their employment situation and socio-family sociability. This situation is the corollary of a double dynamic of precariousness and social weakening:

To become an Ivorian, you must be in Côte d'Ivoire before independence and have worked there. Some had it, and some did not. What do we do for them?" (U.J., 52, Burkinabe community leader in Soubré)

My big brother was born in Ivory Coast. He did everything here, got his diplomas, and when he started working. After six years of service, he was fired without paying his rights". (AT, 22 years old, is a young Burkinabè living in Mossikro)

Statelessness is created when the descendants of migrants are recognised neither as citizens of Burkina Faso nor as citizens of Côte d'Ivoire. This situation is a corollary of the construction of nationality. During the colonial period, it was necessary to be in Côte d'Ivoire before 1960, and to have worked in an Ivorian company or administration, justified by a work certificate or a residence certificate, to gain citizenship. After independence, another law stipulated that people born from January 1961 to January 1973 had Ivorian nationality.

The legal inequalities linked to citizenship provide a framework for analysing the notion of the foreigner. The concept of the foreigner is socially constructed from the socio-historical, contextual and biological foundations of structuring the relationships of an individual or a social group to a given space. In Côte d'Ivoire's context, those born there and claiming their social identity apply for naturalisation. They are perceived as foreigners because, most often, their request for naturalisation undergoes the effect of an administrative lethargy which consists in forcing them first to pay a stamp up to 75000fcfa and to undergo a morality investigation. This process is long and characterised by administrative complexity. This reflects an inequality of rights linked to citizenship and marks limited access to resources (education, employment, political participation, income):

We are subject to obstacles linked to our surname even if we are Ivorians. There is an instrumentalisation of nationality and the concept of the foreigner for political ends." (AT, 22-year-old young Burkinabè living in Mossikro)

In addition, Burkinabè migrants are socially constructed as Ivorians through mobilising ideological referents of land rights, seniority, heritage and heritage investments, cultural and historical traits and the activation of historical events of the participation of their parents in the construction of Côte d'Ivoire. The inequalities of rights attached to citizenship in the Burkina Faso–Côte d'Ivoire corridor constitute the basis of unequal relations in the migratory context, contributing to the poverty and vulnerability experienced by migrants. They influence income poverty, poverty of life and living conditions and poverty associated with the absence of assets and material goods. Other forms of inequality arise from this inequality in access to rights and citizenship, including inequalities in access to education, employment and health.

The cross-sectional analysis of migration between Côte d'Ivoire and Burkina Faso shows that Burkinabè migrants face unequal access to employment once in the host areas. Employment-related inequalities are visible through institutional barriers to entry into formal jobs and the construction of monopolies in informal jobs. Priority is given to nationals for formal jobs through provisions likely discouraging employers from recruiting a non-national. Burkinabè migrants suffer a social downgrading in the competition for access to employment opportunities launched by political actors, social protection structures, public administration or individuals from municipalities despite obtaining a diploma. This process operates based on identity and by excluding migrants from access to local employment niches, in particular trades such as civil servants in the sub-prefecture or town hall. For example, in Méagui, migrants denounce social exclusion in the recruitment methods around local administrative services, in particular, the sub-prefecture and the town hall.

> Some young people born here, after obtaining the baccalaureate, are forced to drop out of school to learn a trade and reintegrate because they cannot have a reserved national job. In Burkina, it is not very easy because you have to find accommodation to go to school, and some do not know any parents there. At Méagui town hall, if you are not Ivorian, you do not work there. (A consular delegate in Méagui)

Inequalities in Income, Gender and Access to Education in the Host Areas

There is evidence of inequalities in income, gender and access to education for Burkinabè in Côte d'Ivoire. Firstly, income inequalities between Burkinabè are constructed through institutional barriers to access formal jobs, as noted above. However, in rural areas, income inequality also occurs in the access to and management of land resources. Indeed, Burkinabè migrants from Côte d'Ivoire are constrained by socio-cultural norms. Specifically, because the land cannot be definitively sold, Burkinabè purchases land but then loses it:

They sell the land to the Burkinabè, and then they come and seize them. This is why the Burkinabè here in Korhogo are more involved in trade (PA, 59 years old, leader of the Burkinabè community of Korhogo)

However, income inequalities among Ivorians are built on the monopoly created by Burkinabè migrants in access to informal jobs. These forms of inequality are socially maintained by conflict and competition between migrants and institutional actors between migrants and Ivorians for access to these activities. Indeed, the circumvention of institutional barriers to entry into formal employment results in a massive insertion of Burkinabè migrants into the activities of the informal sector. The latter enter these activities by controlling the dissemination and marketing of the activity and the production of ideological references delegitimising the competence of Ivorians in this sector (flower growing, market gardening, sale of wood, sale of meat):

Ivorians are lazy; they do not like hard work; they like office work. These migrants construct themselves as courageous and legitimate for these activities". The "myth of courage and bravery" is put forward to prevent the host from carrying out the foreigner's activity. (RT, 35 years old, Ivoirian businessman in Abidjan-Yopougon)

Poverty is analysed through several dimensions of social reality. It highlights access to basic needs, including food, health, housing, security, education, etc. Beyond the poverty of income and the absence of assets and goods, we also note the poverty of living and living conditions.

In addition, gender inequalities are perceptible through the social exclusion of women in access to land resources. This translates into different access to land resources between men and women and between the youngest and the oldest. This type of inequality is found in the ability of these different categories of actors to appropriate the management and exploitation of land capital. In rural areas of Burkina Faso, the main activity is work fieldwork. The income of these social groups comes from the exploitation of the land and the sale of the various resources generated from this resource (vegetables, rice, maise sorghum, fonio, beans, etc.). Women and young children face socio-cultural pressures that prevent them from accessing and managing family land assets: local norms based on community land management make men and/or elders the legitimate and exclusive holders of the land so that they are the ones who are destined to exploit them on behalf of the whole family. As a result, the men and the elders hold the only income for the whole family. These burdens inhibit the desire to empower women and young people who do not have income-generating activities. They limit household opportunities because they are linked to the income of the head of the household.

Finally, for this part, inequalities in access to education constitute a brake on higher education. This form of inequality between the children of migrants and Ivorians is analysed based on access to secondary education after CM2.[3] Moreover, there are barriers to higher education after obtaining the Baccalaureate diploma. Although the majority of migrants who enter Côte d'Ivoire do not have a level of higher education, some of their children who were born in the country have been educated. In interviews conducted with some heads of households, there is a perception that the options available to Burkinabè children after obtaining their certificates of primary and elementary studies are unequal due to nationality. These children are often oriented towards private schools where the parents must finance their studies at 50%. By contract, some Ivorian children are referred to schools whose support is almost 100% by the State.

> From CM2, there is a problem…nationals, the State will direct them to a school where it supports 100%, while for foreigners, the child will be directed to a school where the parent takes charge at 50%. (Focus group participant in Mossikro)

Inequalities in Health and Access to Resources in Activities Involving Children

The management of health problems among migrants lifts the veil on the mobilisation of money and social capital as resources for creating inequalities. Respondents were critical of the functioning of the health system for migrants in Côte d'Ivoire. They argued that money and social connections are resources that structure care relationships between patients and physicians. According to our respondents, these two variables are factors in the creation of unequal treatment between individuals because those who have money or know certain people from medical personnel are more likely to receive health services than those who do not:

> All the health structures work like this. If you do not have the money and you have not found the right person, you will be told that there is no bed when there is. (M.Z., 46 years old, housekeeper, Soubré)

---

[3] CM2 is the last class in primary school for entry into college. This class is taken after the Certificate of Elementary Primary Studies. It is the first diploma of the primary school curriculum.

For example, in Korhogo in the North, migrants criticised the behaviour of specific social child protection structures. During discussions, some leaders said they were not in tune with the behaviour of some social services in dealing with Burkinabè cases. The consular delegate of Korhogo acknowledged that the social service of Korhogo is not sufficiently involved in the problems linked to child labour. These children often work in gold panning sites, where they consume drugs and use dangerous products for the treatment of gold which are harmful and damage their lungs. As soon as the state of health of these children deteriorates and they are taken to health centres, the community leaders note that the only activities of the social protection services are limited to questioning the Burkinabè community for cases of children abandoned in care settings. They provide no support, let alone help when these children get sick. Instead, they fall under the responsibility of their community leaders, who are then forced to mobilise community contributions to support them. These children thus remain under the responsibility of their structure throughout their transfer to Burkina Faso. This accentuates the vulnerability of associations because they are not subsidised by their supervisory structure, in particular, the consulate.

Within the framework of inequalities in access to resources in activities involving children, these inequalities oscillate between inequality of struggle in sectors of activity institutionally recognised as a transmission belt for the exercise of child labour, inequality of access to resources to combat trafficking and child labour and inequalities linked to childhood in school reception in reception areas.

Firstly, it is clear that there is inequalities in policies relating to child trafficking and child labour. Several sectors are institutionally recognised as areas of trafficking and child labour activities: cocoa farming, craft trades, street trades and domestic trades. However, our research suggests that there is a concentration of efforts to fight against this phenomenon in cocoa farming to the detriment of other sectors. This results in less awareness in areas such as handicrafts, street trades and domestic work such that many parents continue to have their children work in these industries:

> Some parents think that child labour is done in agriculture, in cocoa, they did not think that it is also done in trades. They put the children in motorcycle mechanics because the gentleman has a motorcycle, so putting his child in this job can help him solve his motorcycle breakdowns later. (P.O., 47 years old, Social welfare officer from San Pedro)
>
> Because of the chocolatiers and the fact that the GDP is based on the marketing of cocoa, economic issues surround the marketing of cocoa. Suddenly, all efforts are concentrated on cocoa farming, so there is child labour

in urban areas, in the streets (F.L., 43 years old, expert at the National Agency for Rural Development (ANADER) at Soubré)

Secondly, the unequal access to resources to fight against child trafficking and child labour that emerges from the survey observations testifies that there are many actors in the fight against child trafficking and child labour. In the department of Soubré, for example, it is possible to observe NGOs, specialised reception centres, orphanages, state structures and funding bodies. Some reception centres recognise unequal access to the resources needed to care for their residents. These legally recognised centres are often downgraded when allocating donations, equipment, and financial resources for the protection or care of children in favour of centres that are more politically accustomed and endowed with relational social capital. This weakens the fight against child labour in this social space. An inequality revealed by this actor is the abandonment by the social centres of the child referred to the orphanage:

> There is an inequality in the grants given to NGOs to deal with child trafficking and child labour as well as their care. The funds come for the children, but we do not receive them but see them in the reports that they have been shared. Officially recognised orphanages do not fall under their right to dispose of funds at the expense of certain organisations. (T.Y., 56 years old, head of the Soubré social welfare centre)

Finally, the inequalities related to childhood in school reception testify to the difficulties faced by Burkinabè children in the reception areas regarding schooling. This inequality is produced by the poverty of parents who cannot secure birth certificates and associated paperwork for their children due to parental illiteracy and religious constraints. This category of parents prefers to send their children to Koranic schools, which do not offer any opportunities at the national level in terms of recognition of diplomas and traditional professional integration.

> Parental poverty is often the cause of dropping out of school (exclusion, self-exclusion): children go to school very early, and when they drop out at age 10, they no longer go to school, can no longer return to school and becomes idle, either they are in the welds, or they accompany their parents in the field (J.K., 29 years old, an employee at the specialised reception centre in Soubré)
>
> Free education is not effective on the ground for communities. They say that the school is free, but it is the notebooks that we give, but the books are not free. (G.H., 36 years old, Secretary of the Soubré orphanage)

Conclusion

Even though colonisation was an essential factor that contributed to the increased migration of Burkinabè migrants towards Côte d'Ivoire, the end of colonisation did not slow down the process. On the contrary, migration between Burkina Faso and Côte d'Ivoire was maintained and amplified given the benefits that Côte d'Ivoire derived from this migration and the contribution that these migrants made to their families back in Burkina Faso.

On a macro level, the contribution of migration to the reduction of poverty and inequality in Burkina Faso is ambivalent. In some respects, migration has positive effects and provides invaluable support to poor households whose migrants are a safety valve, especially for food. In this regard, households have a positive perception of migration. However, migration creates inequalities in Burkina Faso because it is not possible for everyone to migrate; those with social networks, financial resources and relationships migrate more easily. The impact of remittances creates significant disparities between households that receive remittances and those that do not. Moreover, migration creates a deficit of workers in the country of departure, especially in rural areas.

Seen from Burkina Faso, the migrant in Côte d'Ivoire is perceived as someone who has succeeded and lives in pleasant conditions. The situation is quite different because Burkinabè migrants living in Côte d'Ivoire are victims of inequalities. The study conducted in Côte d'Ivoire within the framework of the MIDEQ Hub highlights the different forms of inequality linked to migration. These inequalities are mainly related to access to rights, exclusion and xenophobia. Once they arrive in Côte d'Ivoire, Burkinabè migrants face inequalities in access to work through institutional barriers to entry to formal employment opportunities. This barrier is manifested by the priority given to nationals in jobs.

Acknowledgements This work has been undertaken as part of the Migration for Development and Equality (MIDEQ) Hub. Funded by the UKRI Global Challenges Research Fund (GCRF) (Grant Reference: ES/S007415/1), MIDEQ unpacks the complex and multi-dimensional relationships between migration and inequality in the context of the Global South. More at www.mideq.org

References

Ancey, G. (1983). Monnaie et structure d'exploitation en pays Mossi. *Ouagadougou, Paris, ORSTOM* (p. 240).

Babacar Fall. (1993). *Le travail forcé en Afrique Occidentale Française 1900–1945, édition Karthala*. ISBN :978_2_86537_372_7.

BCEAO. (2011). Banque Centrale des Etats de L'Ouest, Direction nationale pour le Burkina Faso, Enquête sur les envois de fonds des travailleurs migrants au Burkina Faso, Rapport final, 46.

Boutillier, J.-L. (1975). « Données économiques concernant les migrants de main d'oeuvre voltaïque» in Les migrations de travail mossi : évolution récente et bilan des migrations de travail. Les migrants et la société Mossi. Copyright, Ministère du travail et de la Fonction Publique Haute Volta, Fascicule 1 (pp. 147–203).

Boutillier, J.-L. et al. (1977). "Système socio-économique Mossi et migrations", Cahiers ORSTOM, série Sciences Humaines vol. XIV, n°4. (pp. 361–381).

Boutillier, J.-L. et al. (1985), « La migration de la jeunesse du Burkina », in Cahiers ORSTOM, série Sciences Humaines vol. XXI, n°2–4. (pp. 243–249).

Capron, J., & Kohler, J-M. (1976). *Migrations de travail vers l'étranger et développement national*. Communication présentée lors du Séminaire sur les méthodes de planification du développement rural, Ministère du Plan et de la Fonction publique et du Travail, Ouagadougou (mars).

Cordelll, D., Gregory, J.W., & Piche, V. (1996). *Hoe and wage. A social history of a circular migration system in West Africa*. Westview Press.

Coulibaly, S. (1978). *Les migrations voltaïques : Les origines, les motifs et les perceptions des politiques*. Thèse de doctorat, Université de Montréal.

Coulibaly, S. (1980). "Vers une explication des courants migratoires voltaïques", Labour, Capital and Society/Travail, Capital et société, vol. 13, n°1. (pp. 77–104).

Coulibaly, S., & Vaugelade, J. (1981). Impact de la sécheresse de 1969–1974 sur les migrations en Haute Volta. Communication au congrès général de Manille 9–16 décembre 1981, UIESP.

Coulibaly, S. (1986). Colonialisme et migration en Haute Volta (1896–1946). Dans: D. Gauvreau et al. (Éds.). *Démographie et Sous-Développement dans le Tiers-Monde* (pp. 73–110). Mc GILL University.

Coulibaly, S. (2015). *Préface in « entre le mile et le franc, un siècle de migrations circulaires en Afrique de l'Ouest »* Victor Piché Dennis Cordell, Press Universitaire du Quebec, 380p.

Dabiré, B. H. (2017). L'innovation économique et sociale introduite par les migrants de retour dans la zone frontalière du Burkina Faso d'avec la Côte d'Ivoire ? *Revue Ahoho* (19), 38–51. Lomé/Togo.

De Vreyer, P., F. Gubert, & A. Robilliard (2010). Are there returns to migration experience? An empirical analysis using data on return migrants and non-migrants in West Africa. *Annales d'Economie et de Statistique* 97/98, 307–328.

Deniel, R. (1968). De la savane à la ville, essai sur les migrations des Mossi vers Abidjan et sa Région. Collection des travaux du CASHA.

Dennis, C. et al. (1996). *Houe and wage. A social history of circular migration system in West Africa.* Westview Press, Colorado, United Kingdom, 384 p.

Enquête Harmonisée sur les Conditions de Vie des Ménages (EHCVM). (2018). *Institut national de la statistique et de la démographie (INSD), Rapport général.* 160p.

Gupta, R., & Pandey, D. P. (2007). Threatening factors for critically endangered White-rumped and Slender-billed Vultures in Chitwan district. *Nepal. Environmental Biology and Conservation, 12,* 1–7.

Kohler J.-M. (1972). Les migrations des Mossi de l'Ouest, Paris, O.R.S.T.O.M., Travaux et documents, n°18, 106 p.

Mandé, I. (2015). Le transnationalisme et la mondialisation des flux migratoires Burkinabè face aux crises identitaires en Côte d'Ivoire, de 1990 à nos jour. Dans : V. Piché & D. Cordell (Eds.) *Entre le mil et le franc : un siècle de migrations circulaires en Afrique de l'Ouest, le cas du Burkina Faso* (pp. 338–348).

Marc, M. et al. (2022). Understanding inequalities in the context of Burkina-Faso Côte d'Ivoire Migration. *Zanj: The Journal of Critical Global South Studies, 5*(1/2). https://doi.org/10.13169/zanjglobsoutstud.5.1.0008.

Marchal, J. Y. (1975). "Géographie des aires d'émigration en pays Mossi" in Enquêtes sur les mouvements de population à partir du pays Mossi (Haute-Volta) : les migrations de travail mossi, tome II, fasc. 3, O.R.S.T.O.M. (pp. 29–71).

Marchal, J. Y. (1983). Yatenga, nord Haute-Volta : la dynamique d'un espace rural soudano-sahelien. - Paris, ORSTOM, (travaux et documents de l'ORSTOM), 873p.

OCDE, Paris. [Consulté le 20/01/2023]. disponible sur. https://doi.org/10.1787/9789264275003-6-fr.

OECD. (2017). Interactions entre politiques publiques, migration et développement au Burkina Faso, les voies de développement, Editions OCDE, Paris, 2017,140p.

Ouédraogo & Piché. (2007). (sous la direction de) avec la collaboration de Stéphanie Dos Santos, Dynamique migratoire, insertion urbaine et environnement au Burkina Faso. Au-delà de la houe. L'Harmattan Burkina Faso/Presses universitaires de Ouagadougou/Paris, Harmattan, 328 p.

Piché, V., & Cordell, D. D. (2015). *Entre le mil et le franc. Un siècle de migrations circulaires en Afrique de l'Ouest : Le cas du Burkina Faso.* Presses de l'Université du Quebec.

Piché, V., Gregory, J., & Desrosiers, D. (1981). Migration et sous-développement en Haute-Volta : Essai de typologie. *Cahiers Québécois De Démographie, 10*(1), 87–120.

PNDES. (2016). Plan National de développement économique et social, Burkina Faso, 89 p.

RGPH. (2006). Institut National de la Statistique et de la Démographie du Burkina Faso Rapport final sur le recensement de la population.

RGPH5. (2019). Institut National de la Statistique et de la Démographie du Burkina Faso 5ème RGPH : Résultats définitifs.

Smith-Thibodeaux, J. (1977). Les Francophones de Louisiane. Paris, Éditions Entente, 134p

Songré, A. (1972). "Réflexions sur l'émigration voltaïque après le séminaire sur les migrations modernes en Afrique occidentale" in Notes et Documents Voltaïques, vol.V, (pp. 57–65).

Suret-Canale. (1964). L'Afrique noire occidentale et centrale - l'ère coloniale (1900–1945), Editions Sociales, Paris, 637 p.

UNDP. (2020). Programme des Nations Unies pour le Développement, Rapport annuel 2020.

Vaugelade, J. (1991). "Les unités collectives dans les enquêtes statistiques africaine: Pour la traduction et pour l'utilisation du concept de ménage agricole" in Cahier Sciences Humaines vol. XXVII n° 3-4 (pp. 389–394).

Open Access This chapter is licensed under the terms of the Creative Commons Attribution 4.0 International License (http://creativecommons.org/licenses/by/4.0/), which permits use, sharing, adaptation, distribution and reproduction in any medium or format, as long as you give appropriate credit to the original author(s) and the source, provide a link to the Creative Commons license and indicate if changes were made.

The images or other third party material in this chapter are included in the chapter's Creative Commons license, unless indicated otherwise in a credit line to the material. If material is not included in the chapter's Creative Commons license and your intended use is not permitted by statutory regulation or exceeds the permitted use, you will need to obtain permission directly from the copyright holder.

12

Unequal Origins to Unequal Destinations: Trends and Characteristics of Migrants' Social and Economic Inclusion in South America

Victoria Prieto Rosas and Gisela P. Zapata

Introduction

This chapter provides an overview of the trends and characteristics of recent migration flows in South America. Specifically, we examine the size of the migrant population, its socio-demographic profile, and selected indicators of social and economic inclusion in six countries: Argentina, Colombia, Chile, Ecuador, Peru, and Uruguay. In recent years, these countries have undergone radical transformations in their migration profile, either by witnessing rising levels of intraregional migration, diversification in the origins and motivations of flows, and/or suddenly becoming immigration and transit countries. For instance, the stock of the foreign-born population in South America grew by around 75% between 2015 and 2020 (UNDESA, 2020), while the number of asylum applications increased sixfold during the same period (UNHCR, 2023). These transformations have added a layer of complexity to our understanding of the historic and persistent socioeconomic inequalities that characterise the region, posing additional challenges to migrants' social and economic inclusion (Zapata & Prieto Rosas, 2020).

V. P. Rosas (✉)
University of the Republic, Montevideo, Uruguay
e-mail: victoria.prieto@cienciassociales.edu.uy

G. P. Zapata
Federal University of Minas Gerais (UFMG), Belo Horizonte, Brazil
e-mail: gpzapata@cedeplar.ufmg.br

The analysis is based on national household surveys and census data available before the COVID-19 pandemic.[1] The countries included in this analysis were chosen on the basis of their diverse migration experience, with countries such as Argentina and Chile having long-term experience as destinations for regional migrants, while Colombia, Ecuador, Peru, and Uruguay, have recently emerged as attraction nodes in the region's changing migration landscape.

Although South and other Latin American[2] countries have been widely praised for their progressive discursive and policy approach to migration and refugee protection in the last quarter century (Acosta, 2018; Jubilut & de Oliveira Lopes, 2018), these have been put to the test by the growing recent flows of people in need of international protection, especially from Haiti, Cuba, and Venezuela. The political-institutional emergency, exceptional ad hoc responses adopted by many countries of the region have made evident the gap between the (blunt) progressive discourse—in part to make a political statement vis-a-vis the (lack) of rights of the region's emigrant populations in the Global North—and the implementation of the progressive legal frameworks (Gandini et al., 2019; Zapata et al., forthcoming). In particular, mass displacement has unveiled many countries' poor administrative and institutional capacity, low budgets, and, in many cases, lack of political will to honour national, regional, and international commitments (Gandini et al., 2019).

In this context, we understand social inclusion as the process of acquiring well-being, defined as the full exercise of social, economic, political, and cultural rights (Sainsbury, 2012). Inclusion processes consider "participation in social life, access to education, healthcare, as well as basic infrastructure and the availability of material resources such as income and housing. Thus, refers to a process of improvement of the economic, social, cultural and political conditions for the full participation of people in society, which has both objective and subjective dimensions" (CEPAL, 2017, 92).

For migrant and refugee populations, the legislation concerning their entry and permanence in the societies of destination affects this process by shaping their "modes of incorporation" (Sainsbury, 2012). These modes of incorporation are as diverse as the social protection matrixes of host countries, which include the state, international agencies, and civil society as providers

---

[1] We used 2018/2019 household surveys for Argentina, Ecuador, and Uruguay, and Census data for Colombia (2018), Chile (2017), and Peru (2019).

[2] Here, Latin America encompasses nations where Romance languages are commonly spoken, despite the various denominations used to group these countries. This typically comprises most South American nations, except for Guyana and Suriname, as well as Central American countries and Mexico.

of services; as well as social structures and regulatory frameworks including migrants' access and type of documentation. As has been previously documented, in South and other Latin American countries, there is a broad spectrum of exclusion/inclusion of migrant and refugee populations in social protection schemes, which reflect different assemblages of actors in the provision of services, as well as modes of protection and incorporation, which are often mediated by access to documentation (Vera Espinoza et al., 2021; Zapata et al., 2022). These dynamics pose serious limits to the conventional assimilationist perspective on migrant integration (Portes, 1981). Thus, we propose to analyse observed outcomes against normative frameworks, which in South America are, in principle, generally sufficiently advanced to render migrants as subjects of civil, social, and economic rights, on par with nationals. To this end, we ask: are migrants effectively accessing health, labour, housing, education, and social protection rights on equal conditions to native populations?

As we show throughout the chapter, there are significant gaps with respect to migrants' and refugees' access to social and economic rights, which also intertwine with pre-existing intersectional inequalities—in terms of gender, age, race/ethnicity, among others—and an array of other contingent (to crisis) and pre-existing social, political, and economic inequalities that result in the limited or lack of effective social inclusion of these populations across the region.

This chapter is organised into four sections. First, we discuss the historical and long-lasting inequalities in South America in terms of income, gender, and race/ethnicity. Second, we unpack the main migration trends with regard to their magnitude and composition, and migrants' sociodemographic profile for six countries in the region: Argentina, Colombia, Chile, Ecuador, Peru, and Uruguay. Third, we examine the normative social and economic inclusion of migrant populations in countries' migration and refugee legal framework, while highlighting the gaps in effective inclusion for some selected dimensions. Finally, we conclude with a discussion on the challenges and opportunities for the social inclusion of migrant and refugee populations in this region of the Global South.

Pre-existing Inequalities in the Americas

Latin America is one of the most unequal regions in the world. Its matrix of socioeconomic inequality is conditioned by the economic structure of the region. That is, the labour market acts as the link between the unequal economic structure, especially in terms of access and quality of employment, and the highly unequal distribution of income and, thus, socioeconomic status. Inequality manifests in an array of social indicators—poverty, education, employment, and social protection gaps—and intertwines along the life cycle, disproportionately affecting certain population groups. In addition to socioeconomic status, gender, race/ethnicity, age, and intra and inter rural–urban inequalities are structuring axes of the matrix of social inequality in Latin America (ECLAC, 2016).

Despite the reductions in inequality observed across Latin America in the first two decades of the twenty-first century, with poverty falling from an average of 42.3% in 2002 to 23.1% in 2018, and the Gini coefficient dropping 6.5 points during this period, from 0.528 to 0.463, the systemic lack of equal opportunities for all have rendered these gains fragile. Before the pandemic, the richest 10% of the region's population had an income 22 times higher than that earned by the bottom 10%, and the richest 1 and 10% took, respectively, 21 and more than 50% of pre-tax national income,[3] (Busso & Messina, 2020). These disparities in income are partly explained by the high levels of informality in the region, with informal workers comprising, on average, around half of the employed population. Informality, in turn, is associated with job insecurity, low earnings, lack of benefits and pension, and, thus, higher levels of vulnerability. In fact, accessing a job is not so much of a problem, as effective inclusion once in the labour market. Partial inclusion and exclusion take place in highly segmented labour markets where informality and other poor working conditions rule (Weller, 2012). For example, in Colombia, Ecuador, and Peru, informal employment accounts for over 60% of total employment (Table 12.1).

Women and other minorities are disproportionately impacted by these dynamics: women have lower rates of labour force participation than men, are overrepresented in the informal labour market and earn 13% less than men; while adjusting for education, afro-descendants and indigenous people earn wages that are, on average, 17 and 27% lower than the rest of the population, respectively (Busso & Messina, 2020, 117). For instance, in the countries analysed, women have rates of labour participation between 17% (Peru) and 31% (Ecuador) lower than men; and the gender gap in terms of unemployment can be as high as close to 50% in Ecuador and Uruguay and 66% in Colombia (Table 12.1).

---

[3] These statistics include four of the six countries under analysis (Argentina, Chile, Colombia, and Uruguay). In OECD countries with similar levels of development, the income accrued by the top 10% is 12 times the income earned by the bottom 10%, and the top 1 and 10% garnered, respectively, 12% and about 40% of the entire economy.

Table 12.1 Activity, unemployment, and informal employment rates by sex in urban areas for selected countries, circa 2018

	Argentina	Chile	Colombia	Ecuador	Peru	Uruguay
Activity rate						
A. Male	71.01	70.79	80.49	79.28	84.6	72.13
B. Female	49.52	49.30	57.01	54.63	69.81	55.96
Sex Gap (B/A)	0.70	0.70	0.71	0.69	0.83	0.78
Unemployment rate by sex						
A. Male	8.20	6.68	7.09	2.92	3.17	6.86
B. Female	10.51	7.96	11.79	4.38	3.88	10.07
Sex Gap (B/A)	1.28	1.19	1.66	1.50	1.22	1.47
Informal employment by sex						
A. Male	48.10	28.30	62.90	60.60	64.50	25.10
B. Female	48.90	30.90	61.60	65.40	73.30	22.60
Sex Gap (B/A)	1.02	1.09	0.98	1.08	1.14	0.90

Source ILOSTAT (2022)

When inequalities, in terms of gender and ethnicity are considered, the evidence points to a significant divide in education and labour affecting indigenous and afro-descendent women. On average in Brazil, Ecuador, Peru, and Uruguay, afro-descendent women have 2 years of education less than non-afro non-indigenous women, and 1.4 years of education less than non-afro non-indigenous men. Also, average monthly earnings for afro-descendent women are 36% lower than the earnings of non-afro non-indigenous women, and 60% lower than earnings for non-afro non-indigenous men (ECLAC, 2016, 35).

As we show in the third section, the migrant/refugee condition adds an additional layer of social and economic disadvantage for these populations, complexifying these dynamics and rendering mobile women and ethnic minorities as particularly vulnerable groups. However, there are differences in the way that states administer these diverse inequalities. As Sainsbury has pointed out, the very nature of welfare state regimes affects migrants' access to social rights. Thus, countries such as Argentina and Uruguay seem to have less tolerance for high levels of inequality, while Andean countries such as Colombia, Ecuador, and Peru seem to be more tolerable (Vera Espinoza et al., 2021). Although all countries analysed in this chapter are unequal, on paper, they display relatively similar patterns in terms of inclusion, even though they are rather heterogeneous in the way they effectively guarantee access to social rights (Blofield et al., 2020; Midaglia et al., 2017).

Migration Trends and Socio-demographic Profile of Migrant Populations

In this setting of structural inequalities, South American countries[4] have experienced intense regional migration flows since the 1950s—especially between bordering countries, which at times seemed to be an extension of internal migration dynamics—with nodes of attraction historically centred around the most advanced economies of Venezuela, Argentina, and, since the late 1990s, Chile (Bengochea, 2018). Extraregional emigration to the United States (US) and Europe has also been an important feature of South American migration dynamics since the 1970s, reaching its highest point in the 1990s and early 2000s. However, after the 2008 Global Economic Crisis and up to 2015, the return of South Americans accompanied by their families, especially from the United States and Spain, and Colombian intraregional migration have dominated the region's international mobility landscape (Cerrutti & Parrado, 2015; Martínez-Pizarro & Rivera-Orrego, 2016; Prieto-Rosas & Bengochea, 2022). Another important long-term feature of the region's migration pattern is the fact that extraregional migration flows have consistently been losing ground (Masferrer & Prieto, 2019).

Since 2015, intraregional migration in South America has displayed unprecedented growth rates (Fig. 12.1). Between 2015 and 2020, the stock of the foreign-born population in the region grew by around 75%. Most of this growth is attributable to Venezuelan displacement, which represented 39% of all immigration in South America in that five-year period. According to the UN Population Division, in 2020, the number of Venezuelans that had settled in another South American country since 2015 was around 4.1 million, an equivalent to the total stock of regional migrants recorded in South America in the decades of the 1990s or the 2000s (Fig. 12.1). All other flows originating in the South American region have shown modest growth rates in this period, except for Colombia, whose emigrant stock in the region grew 50% from 2005 to 2010.

The Venezuelan exodus has transformed the landscape of international migration in South America, turning countries such as Colombia, Ecuador, and Peru into net immigration countries for the first time since records exist (1950), and Venezuela itself—which was the second major destination of regional migrants in South America—into a net emigration country with —22 emigrants per thousand inhabitants in the 2015–2020 period (Prieto-Rosas & Bengochea, 2022).

---

[4] The South American region includes Argentina, Bolivia, Brazil, Chile, Colombia, Ecuador, French Guiana, Guyana, Paraguay, Peru, Suriname, Uruguay, and Venezuela.

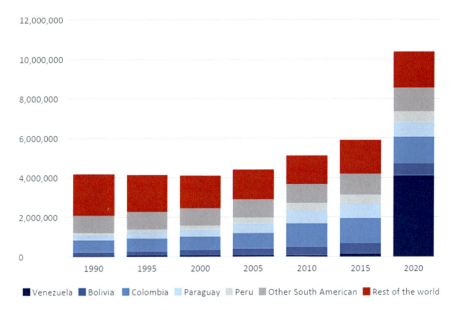

Fig. 12.1 Estimated stock of the foreign-born population in South America by origin, 1990–2020 (*Source* United Nations Department of Economic and Social Affairs, Population Division [UNDESA, 2020]. International Migrant Stock 2020)

In addition to these transformations in the magnitude and composition of the foreign-born population in South America, the expansion in the number of people in search of international protection has been another remarkable change produced by the mass displacement from Venezuela, but also by the incorporation of Caribbean flows into the South American migration system. In fact, the number of annual asylum applications from citizens of Venezuela, Cuba, and Haiti surpassed that of Colombians for the first time since 2000 (Fig. 12.2). Cuban nationals have mainly sought refuge in Ecuador and Uruguay, while Haitians headed to Brazil, in both cases either settling permanently into these countries or spending long periods of time in transit to Mexico and the United States (Correa Alvarez, 2013; Freier et al., 2019; Prieto Rosas et al., 2022; Trabalón, 2019).

As a result of the above-mentioned transformations, around 2018, all South American countries, even those with no previous experience of immigration, had seen their foreign-born population increase, representing about 2% of the total population in Colombia, Ecuador, and Uruguay, 4.5% in Chile, 5.5% in Argentina, and 0.6% in Peru. In all these countries, except Chile, which along with Argentina, has a longer tradition as a magnet for regional flows, Venezuelans are by far the largest national origin among recent migrants. In all countries, recent flows are also composed either by migrants

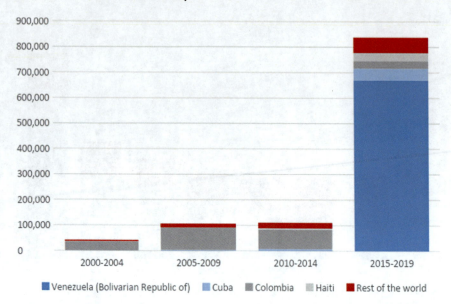

Fig. 12.2 Number of asylum applications received in South American countries by claimant's nationality, 2000–2019 (*Source* United Nations High Commissioner for Refugees [UNHCR, 2023]. *Note* Values for five-year periods show accumulated annual figures)

from neighbouring countries, returnees from Spain and the United States, or by Caribbean migrants from Cuba, the Dominican Republic, and Haiti (Table 12.2).

The socio-demographic profile of recent migrants differs from that of long-term migrants in the region, in terms of age and/or education. In some countries such as Argentina and Uruguay, recent immigration has rejuvenated a population stock that had not been renewed since the mid-twentieth century, after European immigration ceased. Also, better-qualified Venezuelan migrants have somewhat transformed the pre-existing pattern dominated by less skilled border migrants. As shown in Table 12.2, it is remarkable that in Peru, Argentina, and Uruguay, between 45 and 67% of recent immigrants have university degrees. This contrasts with the relative distribution of recent migrants by educational attainment observed in Colombia, where 59% had not completed secondary education.

Table 12.2 Main sociodemographic characteristics of recent immigrants in selected South American countries, circa 2018

	Argentina[1]	Chile[2]	Colombia[3]	Ecuador[4]	Peru[5]	Uruguay[6]
Percent of foreign-born population (%)	5.5	4.5	2.0	2.0	0.6	2.6
Main origins among recent immigrants* (%)	NA	Peru (20.2)	Venezuela (77.8)	Venezuela (69.4)	Venezuela (26.5)	Venezuela (54.6)
	NA	Colombia (18.2)	United States (1.1)	Colombia (12.6)	Argentina (9.5)	Cuba (16.5)
	NA	Venezuela (15.3)	Ecuador (0.55)	Spain (5.9)	Chile (7.8)	Dominican Rep. (7.5)
	NA	Haiti (11.6)	Spain (0.51)	Cuba (4.3)	Colombia (7.6)	Peru (5.8)
Percent of women among recent immigrants (%)*	51.7	51.8	49.1	49.4	48.8	50.2
Educational attainment of recent immigrants* (%)						
Less than Secondary completed	17.0	35.5	59.1	19.8	9.0	4.4
Secondary completed	28.4	46.5	34.6	49.0	45.5	27.9
University completed	54.6	18.8	6.3	31.2	45.6	67.7

Source (1) Permanent Household Survey (EPH for its acronym in Spanish), 2nd semester 2018 (INDEC); (2) Population Census 2017 (INE); (3) Population Census 2018 (DANE); (4) National Employment, Unemployment and Underemployment Survey 2019 (ENEMDU for its acronym in Spanish); (5) Population Census 2018 (INEI); (6) Continuous Household Survey 2018 (ECH for its acronym in Spanish) (INE)

Note (*): recent immigrants are those who arrived five years before the survey or census date, except in Ecuador, where we include people arriving from 2010 to 2019, as there is no information on the previous residence on a fixed date

Migrants' Formal vs. Effective Social and Economic Inclusion

Since the turn to the twenty-first century, LAC countries have witnessed a shift towards a more 'liberal' discursive and policy approach to migration and refugee protection. This progressive turn can be attributed to the confluence of a series of factors, such as the political-ideological changes brought about by the rise to power of centre-left governments in many countries of the region, especially in South America, the intensification of the process of regional integration, the ripening of historical demands made by civil society, and the rapidly changing dynamics of mobility in this traditionally emigrant-sending region (Acosta & Freier, 2015; Ceriani & Freier, 2015; Freier, 2015). This shift can be elucidated, for instance, by the fact that, in the past two decades, 17 LAC countries ratified the 1990 International Convention on the Protection of the Rights of All Migrant Workers and Their Families; all countries, except Barbados, Cuba, and Guyana, had ratified the 1967 Protocol on the Status of Refugees, and 15 countries had, fully or partially, incorporated the 1984 Cartagena Declaration[5] into their national legislations (Table 12.3) (Acosta & Harris, 2022; Zapata & Prieto Rosas, 2021).

Latin American countries have also signed a series of subregional binding instruments for the free movement and equal treatment of its citizens: the 2002 Residency Agreement for Nationals of the MERCOSUR States, Bolivia, and Chile; the 2006 Central American Free Mobility Agreement; and the 2021 Andean Migration Status. Since it came into force in 2009, the MERCOSUR agreement has conferred the right to free mobility, as well as social and economic rights to citizens of the bloc and associated members, all South American countries except Guyana, Suriname, and Venezuela that did not ratify it.

They have also made efforts to work collectively in the area of migration through the establishment of non-binding regional forums and consultative bodies such as the 1996 Regional Conference on Migration (*Proceso de Puebla*) and the 2000 South American Conference on Migration[6] (*Proceso de Lima*). These were established as spaces for inter-state coordination, debate, and exchange of information and best practices, to promote migrants' rights

---

[5] In addition to the causes contained in the 1951 Geneva Convention on the Status of Refugees and its 1967 Protocol, the Declaration broadened the definition of refugee to include situational elements in the claimant's country of origin, to also contemplate "persons who have fled their countries because their lives, safety or freedom have been threatened by generalised violence, foreign aggression, internal conflicts, massive violation of human rights or other circumstances that have seriously disturbed public order" (Cartagena Declaration, 1984).

[6] All 12 South American countries are members of this process, with Mexico acting as an observer.

Table 12.3 Main characteristics of migration and refugee legal frameworks in selected countries, 2022

Country	Human rights oriented legislation ([1, 2])	Refugee concept includes expanded definition of Cartagena (1984) ([1])	Social and Economic Rights afforded to migrants and refugees ([2, 3])
Argentina	Law 25,871/2004	Law 26,165/2006	Health, education, and social assistance for all migrants and refugees. Labour rights only for regular migrants
Chile	Ley de Migración y Extranjería 21,325/ 2021	Refugee Law 20,430/ 2010	Civil rights, health, and education for all migrants and refugees. Labour rights and social protection only for regular migrants
Colombia	Limited (Law 1465/ 2011 and Law 2136/2021)	Decree 2840/2013	Civil rights only
Ecuador	Organic Law of Human Mobility 2017	Executive Decree 3301 / 1992	Health, education, labour, and social protection for all migrants and refugees
Peru	Migration Law, Legislative Decree 1350/2017	Refugee Law, 27,891/ 2002	Health, education, and labour rights for migrants and refugees. Social protection only for regular migrants
Uruguay	Migration Law (18,250/2008);	Law on the Right to Refuge and Refugees (18,076/ 2006)	Civil, health, education, housing, and labour for all migrants and refugees. Social protection rights only for regular migrants

Source: ([1]) Zapata and Prieto Rosas (2021), p.68; ([2]) Ley de Migración y Extranjería N° 21,325/2021;
([3]) Migration and Refugee Laws of each country

and an integral approach to mobility in the framework of the economic and social development of the region (IOM, 1996, 2000).

Furthermore, 38 countries belonging to the United Nations Economic Commission for Latin America and the Caribbean (ECLAC) signed the 2013 Montevideo Consensus on Population and Development. The Consensus, a follow-up to the 1994 Cairo Conference, has among its priority actions, the assistance and protection of migrants, regardless of migration status, and guaranteeing the inclusion of international migration in national, regional, and global agendas and strategies (Zapata & Prieto Rosas, 2021).

More recently, building on the regional framework of Cartagena, 28 countries and 3 territories in LAC adopted the 2014 Brazil Declaration and Plan of Action, agreeing to work together to uphold the highest international and regional protection standards, implement innovative solutions for refugees and other displaced people and end the plight of stateless persons throughout the region in the following decade (Brazil Declaration, 2014).

In South America, Argentina was a pioneer in passing a human rights-oriented legislation in 2004 (25,871) recognising a person's right to migrate as 'essential and inalienable', which the country pledged to guarantee on the basis of the principles of equality and universality. On the heels of this law, the country incorporated the Cartagena Declaration's expanded definition in its 2006 General Law for the Recognition and Protection of Refugees (Law 26,165). Under these laws, all migrants and refugees are afforded access to basic rights such as health, education, and social assistance, while labour rights are reserved for regular migrants who hold residency permits (see Table 12.3).

Uruguay also took similar measures with the passing of the Law on the Right to Refuge and Refugees (18,076) in 2006 and Law 18,250 in 2008, which also guaranteed due process and equal rights on par with nationals, regardless of sex, race, language, religion, economic and legal status, etc. With one of the most progressive laws in the region, migrants and refugees in Uruguay are guaranteed access to civil, basic health, education, housing, labour rights, and social protection, regardless of migratory status.

Ecuador was the first country in South America to include the expanded definition of the Cartagena Declaration into its refugee legislation in 1992 (Executive Decree 3301). In 2008, it passed a constitutional reform recognising the 'universal right to migrate', and although its Organic Law of Human Mobility was only enacted in 2017 (and amended in 2021), it extends health, education, and social protection rights to all migrants and refugees, regardless of migration status. Access to the labour market is limited to residence permit holders (Acosta & Harris, 2022).

In Peru, Law 27.891/2002 recognised the rights of refugees according to the international instruments ratified by the country and adopted the expanded definition of Cartagena. More recently, Legislative Decree 1350/2017 aligned the country's migration framework with the principles of international law, guaranteeing basic rights for all migrants and special protections for vulnerable populations such as LGBTI, victims of smuggling, trafficking, and gender-based violence (Blouin and Button, 2018). Under these normative instruments, migrants and refugees are guaranteed basic access to health and education, while social protection and labour rights are reserved for regular migrants holding residence permits.

In contrast, Colombia, an important sending country in the region, with around 10% of its population residing abroad (Zapata, 2019), has historically lagged behind in terms of immigrant legislation. A coordinating mechanism, a National Migration System (SNM), was created in 2011 (Law 1465). Although it aims to support the government in the design, implementation, and evaluation of migration policies, it focuses primarily on the Colombian diaspora (Zapata, 2021). Only in 2021, the country sought to align its Integral Migration Policy (PIM) with its political constitution and international Human Rights obligations. Law 2136 is centred, among others, on the principles of sovereignty, reciprocity, equality, and the recognition of migrants as subjects of rights, to promote safe, orderly, and regular migration. This law reaffirmed that migrants and refugees should enjoy the (civil) rights and guarantees granted by the Constitution, with access to emergency healthcare, education, and the labour market reserved for some residence permit categories (Acosta & Harris, 2022).

Similarly, although Chile enacted a Refugee Law, which incorporated Cartagena's expanded definition of refugee in 2010, the country's security-oriented migration law from the dictatorship era (Decree 1094/1975), was only changed in 2021. Although Chile's Ley de Migración y Extranjería 21.325/2021 frames migration in a language of inclusion and protection of human rights, it retains part of its national security focus by setting limits and restrictions for accessing these protections (Doña-Reveco, 2021). As such, the law guarantees equal treatment on par with nationals with regard to access to civil rights, and basic health and education for all migrants and refugees, while housing and labour rights and social protection are afforded only to regular migrants who hold residence permits.

In addition, Argentina, Ecuador, Peru, and Uruguay also contemplated measures for the state's promotion of migratory regularisation as a central principle of their migration laws (CELS and CAREF, 2020).

However, as has been widely documented, these progressive laws have been put to the test by the recent mass influx of migrants and displaced persons, primarily from Haiti, Cuba, and Venezuela (Gandini et al., 2019; Zapata & Tapia Wenderoth, 2022; Freier & Doña-Reveco, 2022). Two main trends can be identified with regard to the political-institutional responses to these flows. First, there is broad heterogeneity across countries in terms of the full implementation of these progressive laws, with Argentina and Uruguay using the legal frameworks in place. Meanwhile, Colombia, Chile, Ecuador, and Peru have relied on ad hoc instruments such as visas or temporary residence permits to welcome these populations. Second, the response has been characterised by high levels of discretionary and the absence of a coherent and coordinated regional response, comprising instead the adoption of a mosaic of 'exceptional', temporary measures to manage these mixed flows. In most countries, these implementation gaps may be the result of lack of administrative capacity or unfavourable political conditions, and the coexistence of a plethora of restrictive practices—resulting from incomplete transitions from security-oriented dictatorship era to human rights-based legislations—that ultimately limit protections and rights (Acosta et al., 2019; Ceriani, 2018; Gandini et al., 2019). For instance, the region's initial widely praised open and generous response to Venezuelan displacement has morphed into increasing levels of xenophobia, stricter entry restrictions, militarisation and/or closure of borders, and the production of 'irregularity' in countries such as Ecuador, Peru, and Chile (Acosta et al., 2019).

This is not surprising given the many peculiarities and contradictions that characterise Latin America's mobility dynamics, especially with regard to forced migration. On the one hand, the region both produces and receives a substantial number of migrants and refugees, legal frameworks have incorporated multiple humanitarian international and regional instruments of protection, and many countries have advanced in establishing resettlement programmes and humanitarian entry visas to guarantee safe access to potential refugees, such as Argentina, Chile, and Uruguay (Jubilut et al., 2021). In addition, some countries, especially in South America, have used the state's discretionary power to implement complementary protection alternatives such as humanitarian stay visas, the Union of South American Nations' citizenship (for now just a proposal), and the aforementioned Mercosur Residence Agreement. On the other hand, a multiplicity of challenges to Refugee Status Determination (RSD), such as curtailed access to the territory, inadequate RSD procedures, and/or lack of institutional capacity vis-a-vis growing demands, have proliferated in recent years (Ceriani, 2018; Jubilut & de Oliveira Lopes, 2018).

As recent studies have shown, there is a gradient of effective inclusion/exclusion of migrants and refugees in social protection policies and programmes, across the region, which was exacerbated during the COVID-19 pandemic. At one end, there are countries with clear legal frameworks that guarantee full inclusion, where migrants and refugees are seen as subjects of rights (Brazil and Uruguay). At the other end, there are countries such as Chile, Colombia, Mexico, and Peru, characterised by legal ambiguity and partial inclusion, where migrants and refugees are considered humanitarian subjects, with protection resting upon ad hoc, contingent measures. Somewhere in the middle of the gradient, Ecuador stands out by its legal ambiguity, full inclusion on paper but outright exclusion in practice, with migrants and refugees also seen as humanitarian subjects (Vera Espinoza et al., 2021; Zapata et al., 2022). Thus, even though in all countries, either constitutions and/or migration laws guarantee equal treatment on par with nationals, in practice, regular migration status acts as a barrier to the access and effective exercise of certain social and economic rights. For instance, in Colombia and Ecuador, irregular migrants only have effective access to emergency health services, and Decree 804/2019 forbids access to existing cash transfer programmes for non-Ecuadorian nationals. Meanwhile, in Argentina and Uruguay, access to non-contributory social transfers such as old-age and disability pensions, is limited to those with legal residency (CAREF, 2020). In short, we are witnessing a process of limited social inclusion, where the migrant/refugee condition is superimposed and intertwines with pre-existing inequalities, adding an additional layer of social and economic disadvantage for these populations. In addition, states' inability to adequately guarantee migrants' basic rights, especially in times of crisis, has brought to the fore the fact that many rights are contemplated only on paper but not in practice.

Gaps in the Effective Access to Social and Economic Rights

The highly uneven implementation of the country-case's progressive legal frameworks, along with the magnitude and velocity of unprecedented migration flows, resulted in a puzzle for social inclusion. To what extent did migrants effectively access health, labour, housing, education, and social protection rights on equal conditions to native populations? In this section we examine a selection of indicators to address this question. Still, it is important to note that appropriate data on the well-being of migrants is scarce and is hardly comparable between the different contexts of arrival, which challenges our comparative understanding of the process of social inclusion in South America. Household surveys are the timeliest instrument to examine the living conditions of migrant populations but not all of them include representative samples of these populations. For example, the number of migrants included in survey samples tends to be very small to produce valid estimates disaggregated by sex, race/ethnicity, and national origin. Also, household surveys do not include collective dwellings in their samples which challenges the study of newly arrived migrants often living in hostels, *pensiones*, and other types of non-private housing. Despite these limitations, we can still produce some indicators that point to the gap between migrants and native populations on housing and labour conditions using data from household surveys and, when possible, censuses—a preferable data source given the nature of its universal coverage. Yet, these indicators may underestimate the number of migrants in a given population, and thus, overestimate the well-being of migrant populations (Fig. 12.6).

The analysis indicates that, except for Peru, recent migrants[7] tend to have higher labour participation rates than natives, ranging from 20% in Argentina, Colombia, and Ecuador to 40% in Chile (Fig. 12.6). In terms of unemployment, the magnitude of the gap between recent migrants and natives is quite high, with extreme cases such as Peru, where the unemployment rate is four times higher for immigrants (Fig. 12.6). Given the pre-existing gender gaps found in these countries (Fig. 12.1), presumably such differences in access to the labour market between recent migrants and natives may be larger for migrant women. Previous research, based on census and survey data from 2010 to 2015, showed that unemployment affects female migrants to a greater extent than male migrants. Also, the gender gap was found to be larger among migrants than natives in countries such as Argentina, Brazil, Costa Rica, Chile, the Dominican Republic, Mexico, and Uruguay (Carrasco & Suárez, 2018).[8] Labour market gaps also manifest in (poorer) working conditions for migrants. For example, in Uruguay, inequalities in wages by gender and race/ethnicity are superimposed on migratory status, with recent Afro-descendant immigrants working in low paid jobs, making 80% less than non-migrant white natives (Márquez et al., 2020).

---

[7] Recent immigrants are those who arrived five years before the survey or census date, except in Ecuador, where we include people arriving from 2010 to 2019, as there is no information on the previous residence on a fixed date.

[8] We were unable to analyse the interplay between gender and migration status on unemployment because of the small number of migrants found in the available household surveys used for the analysis. Because of the pandemic, some of these countries are yet to undertake their census for the 2020 round and/or sought their ability to capture migrants and other vulnerable populations limited in household surveys.

This precarious labour incorporation also manifests in (poorer) access to adequate housing, with recent immigrants being generally more exposed to overcrowding,[9] and other inadequate conditions such as lack of ventilation and irregular and unfair tenancy (Bengochea & Madeiro, 2020; Marcos & Mera, 2018; Mera, 2020). As shown in Fig. 12.6, Chile and Colombia have the largest gaps between recent migrants and the native population, with overcrowding affecting, respectively, 60 and 40% more recent immigrants than natives. These remarkable differences may be explained by the fact that the data sources for these two countries (census) include private and collective dwellings. In contrast, for other countries where the gap is smaller, the data comes from household surveys, which, oftentimes, exclude collective dwellings, plagued with inadequate housing conditions.

In addition to the above-mentioned gaps in migrants' effective access to housing and labour rights, it is worth highlighting that there are other inequalities within this group related to stratification on the basis of national origins and/or the implementation of national legal frameworks. The discretionary misuse and implementation of migration and refugee laws (Jubilut et al., 2021; Zapata et al., *forthcoming*) and the interplay between migration laws and regional agreements—e.g. Mercosur (CAREF, 2020) translates into a wide and complex array of migrant categories which determine different conditions of access to rights with regard to health, education, labour, and social protection, an important particularity when speaking of inequality in this region. A clear example of these trends is the proliferation of migrant categories that confer different rights and thus, lead to a variety of documentation trajectories among Venezuelan displaced populations in Colombia and Peru (Gandini et al., 2019).

Conclusions

As has been shown throughout the chapter, South America is a unique setting to study the interplay between mobility and inequality. Given the multiple pre-existing layers of inequality that characterise the region, the influx and settling of populations originating in other highly unequal societies challenge the classical understanding of the drivers of migration (why people move) and the incorporation or integration of migrant populations into host societies. On the one hand, South–South migration does not fit into the rationale of the neoclassical perspective, given that the benefits of migrating would barely

---

[9] There are several definitions of overcrowding. Here, we refer to living in accommodations with more than two people per dormitory (Lentini and Pelero, 1997).

compensate for the costs, in the context of migration from unequal origins to unequal destinations, or mobility between "transnational third worlds" (Santos, 2004). On the other hand, the conventional assimilationist perspective on migrant integration (Portes, 1981) overlooks destination settings where even the desired standard (native's living conditions) would be less than optimal.

The analysis presented in this chapter has shown that in many countries of the region, significant portions of the population (immigrant and native alike) face very high levels of labour informality, and women and ethnic minorities in particular, are confronted by several difficulties in materialising their education, housing, and labour rights. Despite the limited inclusion of migrants and refugees into the host societies, there is evidence pointing to relative improvements but also worsening in some dimensions of well-being with respect to the origin country. For instance, for many Dominicans and Peruvians, working in Uruguay represented the first time that they held a formal job (Prieto Rosas et al., 2022); while Venezuelans, accustomed to enjoying a certain level of social protection before the country's grave socio-political and economic crisis, have experienced a process of pauperisation after migrating to countries such as Colombia, Peru, Ecuador, and Chile (Blouin & Freier, 2019; Gandini et al., 2020). Therefore, it is imperative to not only recognise that migration status introduces an extra layer of inequality and thus, of social differentiation, but that this occurs in already highly segmented contexts with multiple layers of inequality that feed on each other.

To overcome these limitations, we employed an alternative way of analysing migrants' effective integration by comparing observed outcomes against normative frameworks, which in South America are, in principle, generally sufficiently advanced as to render migrants as subjects of civil, social, and economic rights, on par with nationals. Despite the region's highly praised progressive legal framework, there are serious implementation gaps that not only make it difficult to guarantee migrants' effective social inclusion but also produce new—and reproduce the region's long entrenched and persistent—inequalities. This may be the result of the lack of migration policies and programmes to address the specific needs of the migrant population, as well as the legal and documentation stratification that results from the discretionary—at times arbitrary—implementation of the migration and refugee laws already in place. This particular kind of stratification mediates these population's effective access to social and economic rights.

The recent large influx of migrants and refugees has worsened existing dynamics and has provoked a normative backlash, exacerbated by the pandemic. This has been expressed through the use of hierarchically inferior legal instruments, which have weakened the progressive nature of the laws and made it harder for these populations to access certain rights, resulting in exclusion. This backlash is partially a response to the (worrying) rising levels of xenophobia in the region. For instance, in 2020, respectively, over half of the population in Uruguay, Colombia, and Ecuador agreed with the proposition that "immigrants come to compete for our jobs", while just around a third of the population of these countries agreed with this statement in 2015. In addition, between 40 and 80% of the population believed that the arrival of immigrants harmed their country (Latinobarómetro, 2020). Thus, these trends reflect the recent proliferation of additional legal and symbolic barriers, as well as overt and covert discrimination by the state or members of society to be overcome by migrants and refugees in South America.

References

Acosta, D. (2018). *The National versus the Foreigner in South America: 200 Years of Migration and Citizenship Law*, 1–278. https://doi.org/10.1017/9781108594110

Acosta, D., Blouin, C., & Freier, L. F. (2019). *La emigración venezolana: respuestas latinoamericanas*, 30.

Acosta, D., & Freier, L. F. (2015). Turning the immigration policy paradox upside down? Populist liberalism and discursive gaps in South America. *International Migration Review, 49*(3), 659–696. https://doi.org/10.1111/imre.12146

Acosta, D., & Harris, J. (2022). *Migration policy regimes in Latin America and the Caribbean immigration, regional free movement, refuge, and nationality*. IADB. https://publications.iadb.org/publications/english/document/Migration-Policy-Regimes-in-Latin-America-and-the-Caribbean-Immigration-Regional-Free-Movement-Refuge-and-Nationality.pdf

Bengochea, J. (2018). *Los movimientos migratorios de población sur-sur en América Latina: características del sistema migratorio y factores asociados a la migración, 1960–2010*. El Colegio de México. https://colmex.userservices.exlibrisgroup.com/view/delivery/52COLMEX_INST/1285041560002716

Bengochea, J., & Madeiro, V. (2020). *Acceso a la vivienda adecuada de las personas migrantes en la ciudad de Montevideo* (No. 1). Montevideo. www.omif.cienciassociales.edu.uy

Blofield, M., Giambruno, C., & Filgueira, F. (2020). *Policy expansion in compressed time: Assessing the speed, breadth and sufficiency of post-COVID-19 social protection measures in 10 Latin American countries*. Santiago de Chile. https://www.cepal.org/en/publications/46016-policy-expansion-compressed-time-assessing-speed-breadth-and-sufficiency-post

Blouin, C., & Button, E. (2018). Addressing overlapping migratory categories within new patterns of mobility in Peru. *Anti-Trafficking Review*, (11). https://doi.org/10.14197/ATR.201218115

Blouin, C., & Freier, L. F. (2019). Población venezolana en Lima: entre la regularización y la precariedad. In L. Gandini, F. Lozano-Ascencio, & V. Prieto Rosas (Eds.), *Crisis y migración de población venezolana. Entre la desprotección y la seguridad jurídica en Latinoamérica* (pp. 157–184). UNAM.

Busso, M., & Messina, J. (2020). *The inequality crisis: Latin America and the Caribbean at the crossroads*. https://doi.org/10.18235/0002629

CAREF, C. (2020). *Laberintos de papel*. CELS. https://www.cels.org.ar/web/wp-content/uploads/2020/10/CELS_Migrantes_digital_Final-1.pdf. Accessed 23 October 2020.

Carrasco, I., & Suárez, J. I. (2018). *Migración internacional e inclusión en América Latina: Análisis en los países de destino mediante encuestas de hogares*. Comisión Económica para América Latina y el Caribe. https://www.cepal.org/es/publicaciones/43947-migracion-internacional-inclusion-america-latina-analisis-paises-destino

Ceriani, P. (2018). *Migration policies and human rights in Latin America: Progressive practices, old challenges, worrying setbacks and new threats*. https://globalcampus.eiuc.org/handle/20.500.11825/629

Ceriani, P., & Freier, L. F. (2015). Migration policies and policymaking in Latin America and the Caribbean: Lights and shadows in a region in transition. In D. J. Cantor, L. F. Freier, & J.-P. Gauci (Eds.), *A liberal tide? Immigration and asylum law and policy in Latin America* (pp. 10–32). ILAS. https://core.ac.uk/download/pdf/33337715.pdf

Cerrutti, M., & Parrado, E. (2015). Intraregional migration in South America: Trends and a research agenda. *Annual Review of Sociology, 41*(1), 399–421. https://doi.org/10.1146/annurev-soc-073014-112249

Correa Alvarez, A. (2013). Inserción laboral y producción de espacios: la migración cubana en Ecuador. *Questiones Urbano Regionales, 1*(3), 39–65. www.institutodelaciudad.com.ec

Doña-Reveco, C. (2021). La reforma de la ley migratoria de Chile ofrece más restricciones, menos bienvenida. *Portal sobre Migración en América Latina y el CariBE*. https://www.migrationportal.org/es/insight/reforma-ley-migratoria-chile-ofrece-mas-restricciones-menos-bienvenida/

ECLAC. (2016). *The social inequality matrix in Latin America* (Economic Commission for Latin America and the Caribbean (ECLAC), Ed.). ECLAC. https://repositorio.cepal.org/bitstream/handle/11362/40710/1/S1600945_en.pdf

Freier, L. F. (2015). A liberal paradigm shift? A critical appraisal of recent trends in Latin American Asylum legislation. In J.-P. Gauci, M. Giuffré, & E. Tsourdi (Eds.), *Exploring the boundaries of refugee law: Current protection challenges*. Brill.

Freier, L. F., Correo, A., & Aron, V. (2019). The suffering of the migrant: Cuban migration and the Ecuadorian dream of free human mobility. *Apuntes, 84*, 83–110.

Freier, L. F., & Doña-Reveco, C. (2022). Introduction: Latin American political and policy responses to Venezuelan displacement. *International Migration, 60*(1), 9–17.

Gandini, L., Lozano-Ascencio, F., & Prieto Rosas, V. (2019). *Crisis y migración de población venezolana. Entre la desprotección y la seguridad jurídica en Latinoamérica* (Vol. 111). UNAM. https://doi.org/10.1192/bjp.111.479.1009-a

Gandini, L., Prieto Rosas, V., & Lozano-Ascencio, F. (2020). Nuevas movilidades en América Latina: la migración venezolana en contextos de crisis y las respuestas en la región. *Cuadernos Geograficos, 59*(3), 102–120. https://doi.org/10.30827/cuadgeo.v59i3.9294

International Labour Organization. ILO modelled estimates database, ILOSTAT. (2022). https://ilostat.ilo.org/data/. Accessed 14 February 2022.

IOM. (1996). *Regional conference on migration (RCM or Puebla process)*. IOM. https://www.iom.int/es/conferencia-regional-sobre-migracion

IOM. (2000). *Conferencia Suramericana sobre Migraciones (CSM)*. IOM. https://www.iom.int/es/conferencia-suramericana-sobre-migraciones

Jubilut, L. L., & de Oliveira Lopes, R. (2018). Forced migration and Latin America: Peculiarities of a peculiar region in refugee protection. *Archiv Des Völkerrechts (AVR), 56*(2), 131–154. https://doi.org/10.1628/avr-2018-0008

Jubilut, L. L., Vera Espinoza, M., & Mezzanotti, G. (2021). Introduction. Refugee protection in Latin America: Logics, regimes and challentes. In L. L. Jubilut, M. Vera Espinoza, & G. Mezzanotti (Eds.), *Latin America and refugee protection*. Berghahn.

Latinobarómetro. (2020). *Encuestas de opinión pública del Latinobarómetro*. Ronsa 2020. Santiago de Chile.

Lentini, M., & Pelero, D. (1997). El Hacinamiento: la dimensión no visible del déficit habitacional. *Revista INVI, 12*(31). https://doi.org/10.4067/invi.v12i31.220

Marcos, M., & Mera, G. (2018). Migración, vivienda y desigualdades urbanas: Condiciones socio-habitacionales de los migrantes regionales en Buenos Aires. *Revista INVI, 33*(92), 53–86. https://doi.org/10.4067/S0718-83582018000100053

Márquez, C., Prieto Rosas, V., & Escoto, A. (2020). Segmentación en el ingreso por trabajo según condición migratoria, género y ascendencia étnico-racial en Uruguay. *Revista Migraciones, 2020*(48).

Martínez-Pizarro, J., & Rivera-Orrego, C. (2016). *Nuevas tendencias y dinámicas migratorias en América Latina y el Caribe*. CEPAL. http://repositorio.cepal.org/bitstream/handle/11362/39994/1/S1600176_es.pdf. Accessed 3 May 2016.

Masferrer, C., & Prieto, V. (2019). El perfil sociodemográfico del retorno migratorio reciente. Diferencias y similitudes entre contextos de procedencias y de acogida en América Latina. In L. Rivera-Sánchez (Ed.), *¿Volver a casa? Migrantes de retorno en América Latina. Debates, tendencias y experiencias divergentes* (pp. 67–126). Colegio de México.

Mera, G. (2020). Migración y vivienda en la Aglomeración Gran Buenos Aires: un estudio sobre condiciones habitacionales a partir de una tipología de áreas residenciales. *Territorios*, (43), 1–32. https://doi.org/10.12804/REVISTAS.URO SARIO.EDU.CO/TERRITORIOS/A.8177

Midaglia, C., Antía, F., Carneiro, F., Castillo, M., Fuentes, G., & Villegas Plá, B. (2017). *Orígenes del bienestar en Uruguay: explicando el universalismo estratificado* (No. 1). Montevideo.

Portes, A. (1981). *1991.* Modes of structural incorporation and present theories of labor immigration. Staten Island New York Center for Migration Studies of New York.

Prieto-Rosas, V., & Bengochea, J. (2022). International migration in South America. *The Routledge History of Modern Latin American Migration, 62–77*. https://doi.org/10.4324/9781003118923-6

Prieto Rosas, V., Bengochea, J., Fernández Soto, M., Márquez Scotti, C., & Montiel, C. (2022). *Informe de resultados de la Etnoencuesta de Inmigración Reciente en Montevideo (ENIR 1, 2018). Udelar. FCS-UM. PP.* (No. 7). Montevideo. https://www.colibri.udelar.edu.uy/jspui/bitstream/20.500.12008/31715/1/DTUM-PP.07.pdf

Sainsbury, D. (2012). Welfare states and immigrant rights: The politics of inclusion and exclusion abstract and keywords Sweden: The inclusive turn and beyond. In *Chapter 10.*

Santos, B. S. (2004). Transnational third worlds. In J. Friedman & S. Randeria (Eds.), *Worlds on the move: Globalization, migration and cultural security* (pp. 293–316). Tauris.

Trabalón, C. (2019). Estrategias de movilidad, visados y fronteras Trayectorias de haitianos y haitianas hacia la Argentina. *Estudios Fronterizos, 2019*(20).

United Nations Department of Economic and Social Affairs, Population Division. (2020). *International Migrant Stock 2020.* https://www.un.org/development/desa/pd/content/international-migrant-stock

United Nations High Commissionate for Refugee. (2023). *UNHCR's Refugee Population Statistics Database.* https://www.unhcr.org/refugee-statistics/download/?url=2bxU2f

Vera Espinoza, M., Prieto Rosas, V., Zapata, G. P., Gandini, L., Fernández De La Reguera, A., Herrera, G., et al. (2021). Towards a typology of social protection for migrants and refugees in Latin America during the COVID-19 pandemic. *Comparative Migration Studies, 9*(1), 52. https://doi.org/10.1186/s40878-021-00265-x

Weller, J. (2012). Vulnerabilidad, exclusión y calidad del empleo: Una perspectiva latinoamericana. *RDE Revista Internacional De Estadística y Geografía, 3*(2), 82–97.

Zapata, G. P. (2019). Epicentros de emigración: un análisis comparativo de la evolución de sus dinámicas socioeconómicas y demográficas en Colombia y el Brasil. *Notas de Población, 108*, 133–165. https://www.cepal.org/es/publicaci

ones/44680-epicentros-emigracion-un-analisis-comparativo-la-evolucion-sus-din amicas

Zapata, G. P. (2021). Diaspora engagement policies and transnational financialisation in Colombia. *Environment and Planning a: Economy and Space, 54*(4), 722–743. https://doi.org/10.1177/0308518X211045396

Zapata, G. P., Vera Espinoza, M., & Gandini, L. (Eds.). (2022). *Movilidades y COVID-19 en América Latina: Inclusiones y exclusiones en tiempos de "crisis."* Universidad Nacional Autónoma de México, Secretaría de Desarrollo Institucional.

Zapata, G. P., Gandini, L., Vera Espinoza, M., & Prieto Rosas, V. (*forthcoming*). Weakening practices amidst progressive laws: Refugee governance in Latin America during COVID-19. *Journal of Immigrant and Refugee Studies. Special Issue 'Towards a New Migration and Asylum Research Agenda for the Americas'*.

Zapata, G. P., & Prieto Rosas, V. (2020). Structural and contingent inequalities: The Impact of COVID-19 on migrant and refugee populations in South America. *Bulletin of Latin American Research, 40*(1), pp. 1–7. https://onlinelibrary.wiley.com/journal/14709856

Zapata, G. P., & Prieto Rosas, V. (2021). La migración internacional y la protección de los derechos humanos de todas las personas migrantes. In *La implementación del Consenso de Montevideo sobre Población y Desarrollo en América Latina y el Caribe: avances y desafíos*. Montevideo. https://lac.unfpa.org/es/publications/la-implementación-del-consenso-de-montevideo-sobre-población-y-desarrollo-en-américa

Zapata, G. P., & Tapia Wenderoth, V. (2022). Progressive legislation but lukewarm policies: The Brazilian response to Venezuelan displacement. *International Migration, 60*(1), 132–151.

Open Access This chapter is licensed under the terms of the Creative Commons Attribution 4.0 International License (http://creativecommons.org/licenses/by/4.0/), which permits use, sharing, adaptation, distribution and reproduction in any medium or format, as long as you give appropriate credit to the original author(s) and the source, provide a link to the Creative Commons license and indicate if changes were made.

The images or other third party material in this chapter are included in the chapter's Creative Commons license, unless indicated otherwise in a credit line to the material. If material is not included in the chapter's Creative Commons license and your intended use is not permitted by statutory regulation or exceeds the permitted use, you will need to obtain permission directly from the copyright holder.

13

The Making of Migration Trails in the Americas: Ethnographic Network Tracing of Haitians on the Move

Louis Herns Marcelin and Toni Cela

Introduction

It is widely acknowledged that migration has the potential to contribute to human development and reduce social inequality, as codified in the UN's Sustainable Development Goals (Crawley et al., 2017; Czaika & de Haas, 2014). However, migrants can also be subject to entrenched complex vulnerabilities resulting from social exclusion, marginalisation, climate-related disasters, wars, human rights abuses, and violence, at home and in destination countries. Haiti, in many ways, epitomises this continuum of intersectional inequities which create a path dependency for vulnerability. Path dependency shapes people's movements, and for many Haitians, these paths have been framed and reframed by history, from captivity to the middle passage, from enslavement to the Haitian revolution. Today, serial disasters, socioeconomic crises, social neglect, racist Western policies, and political cynicism have synergistically driven young people to urban slums or to destinations outside of Haiti altogether (Marcelin & Cela, 2017). For the largely undocumented Haitian population trekking across the Americas in search of a new life, the vulnerability they experienced—and are attempting to escape—in

---

L. H. Marcelin (✉) · T. Cela
University of Miami, Miami, FL, USA
e-mail: lmarcel2@miami.edu

T. Cela
e-mail: toni.cela@inured.org

© The Author(s) 2024
H. Crawley and J. K. Teye (eds.), *The Palgrave Handbook of South–South Migration and Inequality*, https://doi.org/10.1007/978-3-031-39814-8_13

their homeland signals to social actors on these trails and in destination countries that those migrating are not protected by their own government and can be exploited.

This chapter reports on a multidisciplinary study that included a household survey and ethnographic network tracing to capture how educated youths, the human resources Haiti so desperately needs to rebuild its institutions, are caught on different migration trails in South and Central America on the way to the US–Mexico border. We use the concept of "circulation" to frame these fluid patterns of migration and the cultural experiences of those who move through them (Lee & Lipuma, 2002; Marcelin & Cela, 2017). On these trails, Haitians—already deprived of basic rights at home—carry their path dependency into a systemic vulnerability, compounded by unequal access to rights and social protections, and the unwillingness of many states and institutions across the Americas to adopt mitigating steps.

This chapter provides a contextual understanding of network formation among people on the move that potentially shapes their vulnerabilities in the Americas. Although the increasing presence of Haitians in Latin America has been widely acknowledged since 2010, government data are often limited. Some scholars have drawn attention to the role networks play in the formation of communities primarily through ethnographic investigation or, to a lesser extent, secondary data analysis (Cárdenas, 2014; Carrera, 2014; de Oliveira, 2017; Gomez & Herrera, 2022; Joseph, 2017, 2020; Montinard, 2019; Sá, 2015; Vieira, 2017). These studies confirm that circulatory movement is at the core of Haitian migration in Latin America, often blurring the lines between transit and destination countries for Haitians on the move (Audebert, 2017; Audebert & Joseph, 2022; Joseph, 2020). In this chapter, we provide a brief overview of the sociohistorical processes that have combined with environmental factors, including disaster events, to create path dependency to vulnerability for Haitians on these migration trails. Then, we discuss the study's methodological approach and data sources. We outline key findings and conclude by elaborating on the vulnerabilities that force many Haitians to leave their homeland, vulnerabilities they also experience, in varying degrees, on these migration trails.

Haiti's Unending Crises and Broken Social Contract

Since independence in 1804, Haiti has experienced and continues to be shaped by, a succession of political and social crises: state vs. society, urban vs. rural, rule of law vs. impunity, and extractive authoritarian political governance vs. democratic participation. In addition, crises have been imposed by external corrosive forces such as the coerced indemnity paid to France, US occupation, and continual socio-political interference from the US and its allies (Anglade, 1982; Bellegarde, 2013; Dupuy, 1997; Fatton, 2002; Gamio et al., 2022; Heinl & Heinl, 1996; Lundahl, 1982; Marcelin, 2012; Plummer, 1988; Schmidt, 1971; Trouillot, 1990, 1995). Compounding societal fragility are cascading natural and man-made disasters, such as hurricanes, earthquakes, and epidemics, and associated environmental risks that make complex emergencies an existential threat for Haitian society and its core institutions (Marcelin et al., 2016).

Further exacerbating the plight of Haitians is the rampant political dysfunction characterising the post-dictatorship period (1986 to present) leading to the pervasive political and institutional capture model that has taken a unique form in Haiti: minimal level equilibrium, a game in which powerful, parasitic networks of vested interests bleed various institutions and sectors to the brink of death (Marcelin, 2015; World Bank, 2022). In this perverse model, socio-political and economic institutions are sources of rent rather than means to creating opportunities, promoting well-being, and/or providing services for the public good (World Bank, 2022). Institutional destabilisation has fragmented Haiti's social fabric and eroded public trust at all levels, as the state has been unable to provide its citizens with even the most basic services, such as birth certificates and identification cards (Immigration & Refugee Board of Canada, 2015; INURED, 2017). To navigate daily life and access basic services, most of the population relies on informal personal networks. It is within this context of despair and lost hope in the country's future that the pathways for circulatory migration have been formed.

Haitian Migration Trails in Latin America

Contemporary Haitian migration must be understood in the context of US interventionist policy and its economic interests in the Caribbean, as these migration flows were partly driven by the US occupation of Haiti

(1915–1934) and its Dominican neighbour (1916–1924) when the land was expropriated from hundreds of thousands of Haitians who were then forced into labour on large plantations (Lundahl, 1979, 2011; Millet, 1978). Large-scale Haitian migration dates back to the early twentieth century, when agricultural labourers worked on sugarcane plantations in Cuba (Casey, 2012, 2017; Castor, 1988; Fouron, 2020; Laguerre, 1984; Millet, 1978; Schmidt, 1971) and the Dominican Republic (DR) (Martinez, 1999). Estimates suggest that during that time 200,000 Haitians worked in the DR and twice as many in Cuba (Audebert, 2011). Labour migration to the DR would eventually outpace migration to Cuba, fomenting periodic, and at times violent, anti-Haitian sentiment and culminating with the 2013 denationalisation and subsequent expulsion of Dominicans of Haitian origin (Joseph & Louis, 2022; Marcelin, 2017; OECD & INURED, 2017).

In the 1960s and 1970s, the Duvalier regimes' socio-political transformations led many upper- and middle-class Haitians to migrate to the US and Canada as these countries adopted immigration policies targeting non-European professionals (Fouron, 2020; Laguerre, 1984; OECD & INURED, 2017; Portes & Stepick, 1993) while others sought employment opportunities, primarily through the United Nations, in recently independent nations of sub-Saharan Africa (Jackson, 2014; OECD & INURED, 2017). Neoliberal policies introduced and promoted by USAID and the World Bank in the 1980s prioritised the development of the agro-industrial and manufacturing industries in the capital, intensifying rural-to-urban migration over investments in local agriculture (DeWind & Kinley, 1988). The Duvalier regime's eventual fall in 1986 gave way to urban and rural poor seafaring migration to neighbouring Caribbean nations and the US (Audebert, 2022; Cela et al., 2022; OECD & INURED, 2017).

In the aftermath of the 2010 earthquake in Haiti, Latin America would emerge as a choice destination, as newly restrictive immigration policies in the US, Canada, and France drove Haitians to alternative destinations. Less restrictive policies of some Latin American countries offered a solution for those searching for a new home (INURED, 2020; Joseph, 2017, 2020; Montinard, 2019; OECD & INURED, 2017; OIM, 2015). However, it must be noted that in Latin America, Haitians have not benefitted from the protections of international humanitarian law as they are seldom classified as refugees (Bilar et al., 2015). Nonetheless, contextual factors such as the Brazil-led United Nations Stabilisation Mission in Haiti (MINUSTAH) and the demand for low-skilled labour to build infrastructure for the 2014 FIFA World Cup and 2016 Summer Olympics made Brazil an ideal destination for thousands of young Haitians, some encouraged by smuggling networks (Audebert, 2017; Carrera, 2014; Joseph, 2017; INURED, 2020; de Souza e Silva et al., this volume). By 2014, as Brazil faced one of its worst economic recessions and rising anti-immigrant and anti-Black sentiment led to deadly attacks against Haitians and other migrant populations, Chile, a regional economic powerhouse, emerged as an alternate destination (BBC, 2017; INURED, 2020; Morley et al., 2021). But by 2018, Chile's conservative government had launched a voluntary return initiative targeting Haitians (INURED, 2020), only to be followed by migrant regularisation policies adopted in 2021 that made it nearly impossible for Haitians to obtain legal status (Bartlett, 2021). These unhospitable measures frame the contexts for Haitian migration northward towards the US–Mexico border (OECD & INURED, 2017; INURED, 2020).

On these constantly changing trails, Haitians—unprotected and marginalised at home—carry a path dependency for vulnerability, compounded by unequal access to rights and social protections, and the unwillingness of many state and institutional actors across the Americas to adopt mitigating steps.

Methodology and Survey Demographics

This study includes data from three sources collected between May 2019 and May 2022 as part of the MIDEQ Hub[1]: (1) the MIDEQ origin survey administered in Haiti; (2) an ethnographic study of a sub-sample of the MIDEQ origin survey participants; and (3) a network survey tracing 181 Haitians in Brazil and Chile. The objective was to capture data on network compositions, migration costs, routes, and modalities of movement within and between countries. The study protocol was reviewed and approved by the Interuniversity Institute for Research and Development's (INURED's) US Department of Health and Human Services recognised Institutional Review Board, authorization number MD-S-020/1–2019-223.

The MIDEQ Haiti origin survey contains 11 sections, divided into two main parts: part one (Sections 1 to 6) for all households and part two (Sections 7 to 11) for households with migrants in Latin America only. The survey consisted of 949 households from five (out of ten) departments in Haiti: 33% (309) in the Ouest department, 20% (189) in Artibonite, 20%

---

[1] The Migration for Development and Equality (MIDEQ) Hub unpacks the complex and multi-dimensional relationships between migration and inequality in the context of the Global South. More at www.mideq.org

(188) in Nord, 16% (150) in Centre, and 12% (113) in Grande-Anse. Forty-five per cent (424) of households are urban and 55% (525) rural. The average number of people per household is 4.9 and the average age of household head is 40. Household size data is consistent with Haiti's national statistics bureau, where the reported average was 4.5 (IHSI, 2015).

More than half (57%; 543 of 949) of all households participating in the MIDEQ Haiti origin survey had a family member living in Brazil or Chile (hereafter referred to as "households with people migrating in Latin America") and 43% (406 of 949) were households without members living in Latin America (hereafter referred to as "non-migrant households"). 58% (313 of 543) of households with family members in Latin America were urban and 42% (230 of 543) rural. Households with family members in Latin America were oversampled so that a representative profile could be achieved, allowing for profile comparisons between households with family members in Latin America and those without. Of the 761 current people who have migrated[2] within the sample, 41% (309) had some secondary schooling and 26% (200) had completed secondary school, the former representing the most common level of educational attainment among them. 13% (100) had some (6%; 49) or completed (7%; 51) post-secondary or university education.[3] There were no notable differences in educational attainment by gender.

Ethnographic social network tracing is able to research interacting groups of people who are highly mobile and, in many instances, hard to reach (Brownrigg, 2003; Marcelin and Marcelin, 2003). The method uses purposeful or respondent-driven sampling (Heckathorn, 1997; Khoury, 2020) whereby eligible participants help reach or recruit other participants in the same network. Using this approach, we gathered data on mobility, itineraries, and transitional settlements, inventorying genealogically connected households in participant communities. An interacting ("whole" or "sociocentric") social network has multiple actors and requires different collection and analysis methods than single networks. Tracing requires that researchers obtain locations of participants' "place or domiciles", identify their "co-residents", and record the duration of each participant's stay with each set of co-residents for each domicile. Researchers explored migration histories, mobility, and the dynamics of social identities through in-depth interviews

---

[2] Each of the 543 households could report up to three family members living in Latin America accounting for the 761 total number.

[3] It is important to acknowledge that the migrating party was not interviewed. The individual-level migrant data (n = 761) was collected by proxy through the head of household.

with selected participants and informal focus groups with subsets of participants. Quantitative and qualitative data were analysed separately and later triangulated with ethnographic data sources.

The social network survey contains data on 181 individuals who migrated to Brazil or Chile obtained from a sample of 109 participants who were asked to provide details on up to 3 participants per household. These participants were all members of the networks we traced. Participants were asked basic household information including the relationships between those who migrated. For each study participant, basic sociodemographic and migration information was obtained: gender, year and location of birth, educational attainment, current country of residence, returnee status, and how many times they had left Haiti. Then, the interviewee was asked to provide data on each migration endeavour attempted by the destination country. Participants were allowed to provide up to three destinations for each relative or member of the group, including themselves. The series of indicators organised by destination country included information on the destination country, year of migration, reasons for migrating, and sources of funding.

Of the total sample, 63% (114) were male and 37% (67) female. The average and median age was 25. Haitians migrating to Latin America were relatively well educated, with 60% of respondents completing secondary school or higher (including technical/vocational school or university). 15% of study participants had only some primary school education or completed their primary school studies.

Findings

The Trajectories of Haitians on the Move

More than half (56%, 102) of participants in the social network survey reported living in Brazil, one-quarter (46) in Chile, and 14% (25) in Mexico. The remaining eight (4%) lived elsewhere. 46% (84) left Haiti only once while 41% reported leaving Haiti multiple times. Specifically, 29% (52) left Haiti twice, and 12% (21) three or more times (see Fig. 13.1 for migration routes).

Approximately half (90) of all respondents reported Brazil as their first destination, followed by Chile (27%; 49), and the Dominican Republic (20%; 37). Most (92%; 166) reported migrating to their first country in 2010 or later.

Fig. 13.1 Haitian migration to the Latin American and Caribbean (LAC) region

Migration and Brain Drain in the LAC Region

According to study participants, the principal objective of migration was to secure employment and seek new opportunities to fulfil their lives. 57% (103) reported work as their principal objective for migrating to the first destination country, followed by family reunification (18%; 32). Notably, all except for three of those who reported family reunification were women although the frequency of women migrating for work was nearly as high as men at 43% (26). Notably, in the MIDEQ country of origin survey, male migration for employment was viewed positively by a larger share of participants (72%)

than female migration for the same purposes (50%), with no notable difference in responses by gender. The third most cited reason for migrating to the first country was education (12%; 21).

During qualitative interviews, study participants reinforced the idea that Haitians migrate for host of reasons, which they describe as a search for a better life, or as they often say, "*kote lavi a fe kwen* [where life has a corner[4]]". A study participant in Mirebalais, Haiti, explains why her family member migrated: "That person decides that they can't live in Haiti because they have so many needs that are enormous and they have nothing to do". They decide to go to the Dominican Republic, Brazil, Chile, they also go to the Caribbean to find "*kote lavi a fe kwen*".

Another participant explained his reason for migrating to Brazil, "first of all so that I could study and to have a life that was more or less better than the one I had in Haiti". A family member provided the rationale for the recent migration wave towards Latin America, suggesting that "they didn't know that people could go there without visas, so they started putting USD $1,000 in their pockets and going where it was easiest".

While these data reinforce the dominant public narrative that Haitians leaving their homeland do so for economic reasons, this framing belies a very important fact: a significant portion of the youth migrating to and through Latin America are among Haiti's most educated. As data from both the MIDEQ origin and social network surveys illustrate, Haitians on the move in Latin America are relatively well educated when compared to Haiti's local population, with a significant percentage, 39% and 60% in the respective surveys, having completed their secondary school education. Prior studies of Haitian migration (Lemay-Hébert et al., 2019; OECD & INURED, 2017) corroborate this fact. In fact, the national study of migration conducted in 2014 found a positive relationship between higher levels of educational attainment and the desire to migrate, with public sector employment identified as the only potential mitigating factor (OECD & INURED, 2017). We argue that these youths are often better positioned to build on institutional networks—established in schools, universities, and/or through employment—that will serve as the capital they need to migrate.

The low absorptive capacity of Haiti's labour market (World Bank, 2015, 2022), the systemic institutional crisis that has affected all aspects of daily life in Haiti, the country's rule of law failure (Marcelin & Cela, 2021), climate-driven cascading disasters and calamities (Marcelin & Cela, 2017; World

---

[4] This expression generally means a place where one can live. However, in the Haitian rural imaginary a corner represents a space one can occupy undisturbed, therefore the expression suggests a desire to find a place to exist and pursue one's hopes and dreams in peace.

Bank, 2015, 2022), and the endemic structural and interpersonal violence that make human security and safety fragile (UNODC, 2023) converge in contributing to disillusionment and despair, particularly among its educated youth, fostering a desire to migrate. This calls our attention to the need for further scientific scrutiny of the impact of migration on Haiti's ability to rebuild its institutions and infrastructure (after disasters), and develop a true participatory democracy given the mass exodus of critical human resources.

Path Dependency, Circulation, and Intermediations in Migration

Haiti's precarious archives and registry system leave many citizens "undocumented" at birth. Some will remain that way until they decide to migrate. Cascading disaster events have exacerbated this phenomenon as the destruction of official records is common in times of disasters, particularly during the 2010 earthquake, and families regularly lose documents as they try to survive these events (Marcelin et al., 2016). Therefore, many Haitians legally come into existence through migration that requires official documentation to obtain legal status elsewhere. As in prior studies (Handerson, 2015; Montinard, 2019) our data reveal that securing official documentation in Haiti compels many Haitians to enlist the services of intermediaries who are often inefficient and/or corrupt.

While significant attention is paid to the expanding role of smugglers in migration, which, in 2016, was an industry estimated between US $5.5 and $7 billion globally (UNODC, 2018), the role intermediaries play in facilitating global migration is much more complex (see also Jones et al., this volume). Government bureaucracy, inefficiency, and graft are key features of vulnerability in Haitian society (Dias et al., 2020; INURED, 2020; Montinard, 2019) as all Haitians, irrespective of class, location, or political level, must use their personal or intermediary networks to secure timely services. The most vulnerable rely on paid intermediaries; others rely on the intervention of well-placed family members, friends, or former classmates. Thus, intermediaries of all sorts facilitate the international mobility of Haitians and influence their destinations and outcomes (Jones & Sha, 2020). Haitians migrating through multiple countries where there may not be a Haitian consulate or embassy experience serious practical challenges in accessing justice (OAS and IOM, 2016). Haitians on the move—marginalised by their own government—have little expectation that their human rights will be recognised by host governments.

More than half (56%) of MIDEQ country of origin survey participants reported using an intermediary to facilitate their trip. Similar results were obtained through the social network survey; however, as there were up to three destinations given per participant, this question was asked for each country. In the latter survey, almost half (49%; 89) of all migrants used the services of an intermediary for destination country one. Interestingly, the proportion increases to 63% (43 of 68) for the second destination and remains relatively high for the third country at 55% (12). Of those who used the services of an intermediary,[5] two-thirds (67) required assistance with document preparation; half (44) used their services to purchase airline or bus tickets; and 27% (24) paid for guides. Further, the social network survey captured the migrating party's aggregate experience across all destinations. One participant explained how the migration enterprise created demand for intermediary services of various kinds, including supplying invitation letters which this participant who lived in multiple destinations explained became "a business in itself". Thus, intermediaries are integral to facilitating international migration in Haiti.

Migration Capital: The Role of Social Networks in Haiti and Abroad

When asked why one country was selected over another, over one-third (35%; 64) reported being influenced by family or friends in the destination country; 27% (49) reported better employment opportunities and/or salaries; 18% (32) reported ease of migration. A non-negligible amount (8%, 15) reported migrating to pursue educational opportunities. When asked where they obtained the most important information needed to migrate to their first destination, almost two-thirds (64%; 116) reported family members or friends already in the destination country. These findings are consistent with those from the MIDEQ origin survey where almost half (45%; 243) reported receiving the most important information for their trip from family members or friends at destination. The remaining responses included information obtained from the migrant him/herself (10%; 18); family and/or friends in Haiti (7%; 13); and others (not family or friends) at destination (6%; 11). These data illustrate the importance of social networks (family and friends), particularly those already in the host country, in facilitating migration and how these networks serve as "migrant capital" (Busse & Vasquez Luque, 2016).

---

[5] As this was a multiple response indicator the total exceeds 100%.

One respondent shared how he was influenced "to go to Brazil because of family [he] had in Brazil. [His] uncle there... said Brazil is a bit better than the situation in Haiti". Another shared how a friend who had migrated before him influenced his decision:

> I have a friend who had a travel agency, and he was always visiting Chile...every person he helped migrate [to Chile] worked and after a short time, 6, 7, 8 months I saw that they were able to save USD $2,000 to send for their wife or child or another family member. Imagine if you are working in Haiti, you could never do that. [In Chile] ...when their family needs USD $300, USD $400, USD $500 they can get it and send it. I wanted to find out for myself.

However, the qualitative data also revealed other sources influencing decision-making, including local media in Haiti:

> ... in Haitian culture there is something called, *radyo djòl* [radio mouth], something from the mouth to ears, that's how information circulates. Once people hear ... there's an opportunity ... they just leave!... In Haiti, *"they"* make everything happen, that *"they"* you hear about...it's an entity you can't identify but it's an entity that says a lot in Haiti. *"They!"*

Thus, the decision to migrate does not always entail rational choice but may reflect one's hopes, if not their desperation.

Participants were asked about the *two* main sources of financing for their journey to their first destination, with most citing household resources (57%; 103), followed by their own resources (53%; 96). 41% (74) also reported financing their trip through family or friends outside the household. Just 7% (13) reported having financed their first trip with a loan.[6] This study participant explains how family members in Haiti support their ambition to migrate:

> Sometimes you have a family member who says, "I would like to leave the country, how can you help me?" ...When you look at the country, young men, young women are struggling they have nothing to do... you tell them: don't start no mess, go there, be disciplined, work. ... if they don't have a passport...you will give them the money to get their passport. Or you can give them some money to hold in their hands[7]....

---

[6] Since this indicator allowed for up to two responses, the reported proportions do not add up to 100%.

[7] The expression, "*bal yon ti kob pou l kenbe nan men l* [give them some money to hold in their hands]" is equivalent to giving them spending or pocket money to cover additional or unforeseen expenses.

When asked about the role of family members or friends living abroad, the participant elaborated:

> Sometimes when you have people in the diaspora… [those aspiring to migrate] make more demands of the diaspora asking them to send money.

As Haiti has the lowest Gross Domestic Product (GDP) per capita in the LAC region, Haitians find it costly to migrate to Latin America. In the MIDEQ origin survey, participants reported spending between USD $2500 and USD $3500, two- and three-times Haiti's per capita GDP, on their journey to Brazil or Chile. Notably, in both surveys the proportion of "don't know" responses to questions concerning migration expenses was slightly higher for female participants, many of whom were unaware of the full costs of migration as it had been organised by a male, usually at destination. Females migrating to Chile as "tourists" were the few exceptions.[8]

Migration: A High-Risk, High-Reward Investment

In the post-disaster context, the decision to migrate has been influenced by social networks, perceived economic opportunities abroad, the host country's migration policies, and intermediaries facilitating the process. Haitians choose to leave their homeland despite the significant challenges posed by such a decision.

The exploitation of Haitians desperate to leave the country has created markets for formal and informal intermediaries. Just over one-third (35%; 63) of participants in the social network survey reported encountering difficulties before migrating. A significant portion (83%, 52) experienced problems obtaining travel documents; many family members reported that: "Rakètè te manje kòb li plizyè fwa [Intermediaries took his/her money many times]!", intimating that they paid for services that were never rendered. During interviews, one study participant living in Brazil recounted facing a series of delays while working with an informal intermediary to secure criminal background checks for him and his brother. Eventually, he received the documents and explained that he was helping his brother migrate: "because he can help me help my family back home…it's a chain, one pulls the other [to the host country]".

---

[8] Tourist migration to Chile required demonstration that one had sufficient funds for the trip. Therefore, women, in this instance, would have those funds on their person. However, Haitian women migrating to Chile were similarly unaware of the overall costs of migration, such as airline tickets and/or document preparation.

In 2020, when Panama adopted a new migration policy (Executive Decree 451) requiring tourist visas for Haitians in transit, those migrating chose the less expensive option of transiting through the DR, which also required a tourist visa. Dominican visa fees range between USD $40 and USD $60, depending on the type of visa sought. With increased demand, one participant explained that "the [Dominican Consulate] takes their passport for USD $250 but the [intermediaries] receive USD $450…for one visa". Based on this participant's allegation, Haitians are paying several hundred dollars simply to transit through the DR while intermediaries and Dominican officials pocket approximately USD $200 each. Among other challenges faced before departing Haiti, 10% of survey participants (5) reported that they did not have enough money for the journey; and 5% (3) were victims of corruption at the airport.

The proportion of participants experiencing difficulties while in transit to their first destination country was lower, at 14% (24). The nature of the difficulties experienced was distributed as follows: five (21%) reported insufficient funds; four (17% each) reported intermediary abandonment or theft by an official. One family member explained: "While in transit, the intermediary asked for more money and threatened that if he did not pay, he would be deported to Haiti". The proportion of respondents reporting difficulties during transit to countries two and three was much higher, at 43% and 41%, respectively. In the following example, two brothers migrating to Mexico, their third destination, are barred from boarding an aircraft in the DR.

> …I think this is serious racism because the people who were checking us in were done and let us go then a supervisor, a Black one at that, said we must have a transit visa. He stopped us…we asked them to cancel our tickets for us…but they said no, they didn't have the authority to do that…the ticket was purchased in France and France is not on the same time [zone]…we sent an email and tomorrow we will see what will happen [with the travel agency]. We will see if they can re-issue the ticket or reimburse us, but I don't know.

In this example, we see the importance of social networks, and the critical role family plays in the migration endeavour. The tickets were purchased in France by a family member. Unable to have their tickets re-issued or obtain a refund, family members had to purchase new tickets departing 6 days later while incurring the costs of the two brothers remaining in the DR for an additional week.

The proportion of difficulties encountered at destination was much higher, at 73% (131); most of the challenges were attributed to securing employment:

> The first thing [they try] to find out is whether there is work available…if there is work, they say, "My friend, I am going!" Sometimes they get there and the work that they did in Haiti they can't find it [there]. They may find other work that is worse than what they were doing in Haiti. Sometimes the person goes to work on a farm whereas when they were [in Haiti] they never worked on a farm. They worked in masonry, but they never did that before, but they must because they are now somewhere where if they don't work, they won't eat. They have to work in a profession that is not theirs which is unfortunate, but they do it, nonetheless.

Therefore, for youth looking for opportunities to make a living abroad, many are disappointed by the real challenges of labour market integration (Cárdenas, 2014; Sá, 2015). However, work, even under the most precarious circumstances, allows them to support themselves while pulling other family members into an extensive network of migrating Haitians now better positioned to support their families, and Haiti, from abroad.

Discussion

Haitian circulatory migration is a complex, collective project that encompasses multiple migrations from the homeland as well as onward migration—towards better opportunities and/or in response to the challenges of host country integration. Deprived of human rights and facing vulnerability at home (Human Rights Watch, 2023; INURED, 2017), Haitians carry their path dependency on these trails, where they face unequal access to rights and social protections and systemic vulnerability as they travel to and through South and Central America. However, this path dependency is framed and exacerbated by historic, hemispheric anti-Haitianism which "consists of ideologies, outcomes, policies, political strategies, and practices that reify the negative connotations associated with Blackness and Haitian nationality" (Joseph & Louis, 2022, 388). In spite of these challenges, migration remains a core strategy of Haitian survival.

In order to migrate, Haitians tap into existing social networks—what Busse and Vasquez Luque (2016) refer to as "migrant capital"—and may activate new ones (de Oliveira, 2017; Joseph, 2020; Sá, 2015). These networks provide pre-departure knowledge and information, financial resources, contacts, and the emotional support crucial to transforming migration aspirations into reality. These networks are sources of both reliable and questionable information, which significantly influences migration decision-making through word of mouth, social media, and other platforms (Joseph, 2017; Sá, 2015).

Migration to Latin America is a high-risk, high-reward investment in an expensive endeavour that network members make in the hopes that as one successfully migrates, s/he will help others migrate or support those remaining in the homeland through remittances (Montinard, 2019; Nieto, 2014).

In migration studies, analyses of migrant decision-making processes are often reductive, focusing in time and space on the origin country, failing to capture what occurs as people are on the move. Ours and other studies (Sá, 2015) reveal that Brazil may be the destination of choice today and become a transit country or one of multiple destinations in the future. Haitian migration in the LAC region is contextual, subject to decision-making processes in different geographic spaces at different points in time.

The demographics of Haitians migrating to Latin America is in many ways misleading in terms of what it will reveal upon their arrival in the host country. While the principal motivation for migrating in this study was employment, this was also the most cited challenge encountered at destination. Some found the information they had received in Haiti misleading or false or that the reality at destination had since changed (Cárdenas, 2014). As has been noted elsewhere (Cárdenas, 2014; Sá, 2015), countries in the region tend not to recognise Haitian university diplomas, contributing to decreasing socioeconomic status and underemployment for educated Haitians. This illustrates how the path dependency one attempts to escape in the homeland, unemployment, and underemployment, can re-emerge in the host country. Despite these challenges—exorbitant costs, exploitation, limited employment opportunities—Haitians continue to migrate and encourage family members and friends—male or female—to follow suit.

Consistent with prior studies (INURED, 2020; OECD & INURED, 2017), we found that Haitian women are more likely to migrate under family reunification processes, though they are increasingly migrating on their own (INURED, 2020). Their dependence on a partner at destination was further reflected in their lack of knowledge of the processes or costs associated with their own migration. Haitian women's "restricted" mobility is consistent with the structural violence and gender inequality suffered in Haiti that fosters dependence on men (Cela, 2017; Cela et al., 2023; INURED, 2017). Hence, migration—even for the purposes of securing employment—was viewed less favourably for women than men. And, the migration of single women is generally viewed with suspicion, if not outright disdain, presuming that the trip is financed (or official documents secured) through *quid pro quo* relationships with a paramour or intermediary (Cela et al., 2023). Both assumed scenarios reflect the gender-based dependency intrinsic to Haitian society in which a woman's mobility must be facilitated by a man in Haiti, in transit, or at destination.

With few exceptions, migration within the Global South carries risks prior to, during, and/or at destination for Haitians. Those migrating with undocumented status rely on networks at home and destination to finance an often-unpredictable journey (Dias et al., 2020; IOM, 2014; Kenny, 2013; Nieto, 2014). At the end of that journey is the hope of survival, which they understand as a space where one can support themselves and live in peace, *kote lavi fe kwen*. Largely influenced by their social network, "a better life" is reduced to the mere ability to secure employment (Joseph, 2017, 2022; Cárdenas, 2014; INURED, 2020), even for those with tertiary degrees. While this process has been well documented, the cost of these human capital losses to a homeland in perpetual crisis remains unquantifiable.

For Haitians, the search for a better life may lead to one or multiple destinations (INURED, 2020). For the undocumented, circumstances may prevent them from taking a direct route even when there is one intended destination (Audebert, 2017, 2022; Busse & Vasquez Luque, 2016; Cavalcanti & Tanhati, 2017; Hagen-Zanker & Mallett, 2020). Educational and economic status, as well as social and migrant networks, determine which routes (direct or indirect) are available to them (Handerson, 2015). Therefore, the characterisation of migration as merely a movement from origin to destination countries obscures people's experiences of journeying to and residing in multiple countries over time (Crawley & Jones, 2021; Audebert, 2022; Audebert & Joseph, 2022; Joseph, 2020; INURED, 2020). As economic, political, and/or social contexts change in host nations, Haitians may decide to migrate onwards. Undocumented Haitians may take alternate routes to their destination to avoid detection. Transit migration renders them vulnerable in contexts where laws, systems, cultural practices, and languages are different.

Changes in migration policies also re-route the paths of Haitians on the move. A threefold increase in migration of Haitians through Peru, between 2010 and 2011, substantially decreased in 2012 when Peruvian immigration laws were revised to require tourist visas (Busse & Vasquez Luque, 2016; Cárdenas, 2015). Similarly, before June 2020, many Haitians took advantage of low-cost flights to Panama (Busse & Vasquez Luque, 2016; Dias et al., 2020) to transit onwards to Latin America or north to the US–Mexico border

(Abdaladze, 2020). However, changes in Panamanian policies (Dubuisson, 2020) introduced an expensive and complex transit visa requirement, re-routing Haitians through the Dominican Republic (INURED, 2020). Policy changes create new markets, with some intermediaries adapting their services while new ones emerge to meet the demand. Such was the case with representatives from Dominican Consulates in Haiti, collaborating with local *raketès* (intermediaries), charging more than ten times the value of visas without the knowledge of their central government (Listín Diario, 2022). Yet, the Haitian government perpetuates its citizen's vulnerability through inaction and silence, failing to protect them from the predatory practices of local and foreign intermediaries or the human and labour rights abuses they suffer in transit or at destination. It is reminiscent of the abandonment Haitians—denationalised in the DR and expelled to Haiti—experienced from the Haitian government. Officially welcomed by the government in word but not in deed, they would eventually become stateless in Haiti as well (Joseph & Louis, 2022).

Conclusion

The vulnerability Haitians experience at home creates a path dependency that informs their migratory experiences in the Global South. Mirroring their experiences at home, Haitian migration in the LAC region has been largely characterised by precariousness, volatility (Gómez and Herrera, 2022), and anti-Haitian sentiment (Joseph & Louis, 2022; OECD & INURED, 2017). In Latin America, where they are seldom classified as refugees, Haitians do not enjoy the protections afforded by international humanitarian law. Although at various times since 2010, they have received complementary protection by states in the region, these mechanisms have been based on states' goodwill and can be withdrawn at any time.

The failure of the Haitian government to uphold a social contract with its citizens propels many to leave home. Its failure to defend its citizens' rights abroad signals to formal and informal intermediaries, host communities, and foreign governments that Haitians are vulnerable and unprotected. Haitians on migrant trails, thus, depend on the benevolence of foreign governments, advocacy efforts and support of migrant-serving organisations, and solidarity within their social networks to survive. Therefore, Haitians on the move must remain nimble to respond to evolving and often unstable contexts they encounter in their search for a place where they can live in peace, *kote lavi fe kwen*, and reach their full potential as human beings.

Acknowledgements We thank INURED's field researchers in Haiti; Kéthia Charles, Pierre Rigaud Dubuisson, Dabouze Estinvil, Olriche Fortin, and Catherine Hermantin, and in Brazil; David Jean-Bart, Vitor Jasper, and Marie Florence Thélusma. We also thank our data analyst and geographer, Mario da Silva Fidalgo, for helping us triangulate the different data sources used for this chapter. We are grateful to April Mann for editing several iterations of this chapter. The research for this chapter was undertaken as part of the UKRI GCRF South–South Migration, Inequality and Development (MIDEQ) Hub, grant reference ES/S007415/1.

References

Abdaladze, N. (2020) *Haitians make long continental transit in hope for a better future*. Available at https://cronkitenews.azpbs.org/2020/07/20/haitians-continental-transit/.

Anglade, G. (1982) Les Haïtiens dans le monde. Les Journées Internationales du Congrès Mondial Haïtien à Montréal. Montréal, CA.

Audebert, C. (2011). *La diaspora haïtienne: vers l'émergence d'un territoire de la dispersion?* L'Harmattan.

Audebert, C. (2017). The recent geodynamics of Haitian migration in the Americas: Refugees or economic migrants? *Rev Bras De Est De Pop, 34*(1), 55–71.

Audebert, C. (2022). Reconceptualizing the Haitian migration system in the Caribbean basin: A Spatial approach to multi-local fields. *Journal of Latin Am and Carib Anth, 27*(3), 309–327.

Audebert, C. & Joseph, H. (2022). El sistema migratorio haitiano en América del Sur: recientes desarrollos y nuevos planteamientos. In H. Joseph & C. Audebert (Eds.), *El sistema migratorio haitiano en América del Sur CLASCO 17–50* (pp. 1–30). CLASCO.

Bartlett, J. (2021). *Why Haitians are fleeing Chile for the US border*. Available at https://www.washingtonpost.com/world/2021/09/26/chile-haitian-border-migrants/

BBC. (2017). *Brazil's recession worst on record*. Available at https://www.bbc.com/news/business-39193748.

Bellegarde, C. (2013). *L'occupation américaine d'Haïti: Ses conséquences morales et économiques*. Les Editions Fardin

Bilar, A. B., et al. (2015). Mudanças climáticas e migrações: Reflexões acerca dos deslocamentos de nordestinos e haitianos no território brasileiro. *Revista Brasileira De Geografia Física, 8*(6), 673–1691.

Brownrigg, L. A. (2003). *Ethnographic social network tracing of highly mobile people. Census 2000 Evaluation J.2*. US Census Bureau, Statistical Research Division.

Busse, E., & Vasquez Luque, T. (2016). The legal illegal nexus: Haitians in transit migration deploying migrant capital. *International Journal of Sociology, 46*, 205–222.

Cárdenas, I. C. (2015). Migraciones haitianas en la región andina. Boletín del Sistema de Información Sobre Migraciones Andinas. FLASCO.

Castor, S. (1988). *L'Occupation Américaine d'Haïti*. Société Haïtienne d'Histoire.

Carrera, G. B. (2014). Pourquoi migrer? Notes sur les vieilles et nouvelles blessures d'Haïti. In OIM (Ed.), *La migration Haïtienne vers le Brésil: Caracteristiques, opportunités et enjeux* (pp. 33–50). IOM Publications.

Casey, M. (2012). *From Haiti to Cuba and back: Haitians' experiences of migration, labor, and return, 1900–1940*, dissertation, University of Pittsburgh.

Casey, M. (2017). *Empire guest workers; Haitian migrants in Cuba during the age of US occupation*. Cambridge University Press.

Cavalcanti, L., & Tanhati, T. (2017) 'Características sociodemográficas e laborais da imigração haitiana no Brasil', In L. Cavalcanti & B. Feldman-Bianco (Eds.), *Dossiê: Imigração Haitiana no Brasil: Estado das Artes* (pp. 68–71). PERIPLOS: Revista Investigación sobre Migraciones

Cela, T. (2017). Negotiating education: Gender, power and violence in Haiti's higher education institutions. In L. H. Marcelin, T. Cela, & H. Dorvil (Eds.), *Haitian youth in the Americas* (pp. 1–24) Presses de l'Université du Québec. https://doi.org/10.2307/j.ctt1z27hmd.9

Cela, T., et al. (2022). Migration, memory and longing in Haitian song. *Zanj, Journal of Critical Global South Studies, 5*(1/2), 193–227.

Cela, T. et al. (2023). Crises and the continuities of structural violence: Gender-based violence in Haiti before and during COVID-19. *Caribbean Conjunctures*.

Crawley, H., & Jones, K. (2021). Beyond here and there: (re)conceptualising migrant journeys and the 'in-between". *Journal of Ethnic and Migration Studies, 47*(14), 3226–3242.

Crawley, H., et al. (2017). *Unravelling Europe's migration crisis': Journeys over land and sea*. Policy Press.

Czaika, M., & de Haas, H. (2014). The globalization of migration: Has the world become more migratory? *International Migration Review, 48*(2), 283–323.

de Oliveira, M. (2017). Haitianos no Paraná: Distinção, integração e mobilidade. In B. Feldman-Bianco & L. Cavalcanti (Eds.), *Dossiê*: Imigração Haitiana no Brasil: Estado das Artes (1st edn.). PERIPLOS: Revista Investigación sobre Migraciones.

DeWind, J., & Kinley, D. H. (1988). *Aiding migration: The impact of development assistance on Haiti*. Routledge.

Dias, G., Jarochinski Silva, J. C., & da Silva, S. A. (2020). Travellers of the Caribbean: Positioning Brasília in Haitian migration routes through Latin America'. *Vibrant, 17*, 1–19.

Dubuisson, P. R. (2020). *Politiques migratoires en Amérique Latine entre 2010 et 2020 et choix du Brésil comme pays de destination par les migrants haïtiens*. Available at https://www.mideq.org/fr/blog/politiques-migratoires-en-am%C3%A9rique-latine-entre-2010-et-2020-et-choix-du-br%C3%A9sil-comme-pays-de-destination-par-les-migrants-ha%C3%AFtiens/. Accessed November 2, 2022.

Dupuy, A. (1997). *Haiti in the new world order*. Westview Press.

Fass, S. M. (1988). *Political economy in Haiti: The drama of survival*. Transaction Publishers.

Fatton, R. (2002). *Haiti's predatory republic: The unending transition to democracy*. Lynne Rienner Publishers.

Fouron, G. E. (2020). *Haiti's painful evolution from promised land to migrant-sending nation*. Available via https://www.migrationpolicy.org/article/haiti-painful-evolution-promised-land-migrant-sending-nation. Accessed September 2, 2020.

Gamio, L. et al. (2022). *Haiti's lost billions*. Available at https://www.nytimes.com/interactive/2022/05/20/world/americas/enslaved-haiti-debt-timeline.html.

Gomez, C., & Herrera, G. (2022). State and "mixed migrations": Migration policies towards Haitians, Colombians and Venezuelans in Ecuador. In G. Herrera & C. Gómez (Eds.), *Migration in South America* (pp. 77–95). Springer.

Hagen-Zanker, J., & Mallett, R. (2020). *Understanding migrant decision-making: Implications for policy*. MIDEQ.org.

Heckathorn, D. (1997). Respondent-driven sampling: A new approach to the study of hidden populations. *Social Problems, 44*(2), 174–199.

Heinl, R. D., & Heinl, N. G. (1996). *Written in blood: The story of the Haitian people, 1492–1995*. University Press of America.

Human Rights Watch. (2023). *Haiti events of 2022*. Available at https://www.hrw.org/world-report/2023/country-chapters/haiti

Immigration and Refugee Board of Canada. (2015). *Haiti: The availability of official documents since the 12 January 2010 earthquake*. Available at https://www.refworld.org/docid/5595341e4.html

Institut Haïtien de Statistiques et d'Informatique (IHSI). (2015). *Population totale de 18 ans et plus. Ménages et densités estimés en 2015*. Gouvernement d'Haïti.

International Organization for Migration (IOM). (2014). *Haitian migration to Brazil: Characteristics, opportunities and challenges*. IOM.

Interuniversity Institute for Research and Development (INURED). (2010). *The challenge for Haitian higher education: A post-earthquake assessment of higher education institutions in the Port-au-Prince metropolitan area*. Available at http://www.inured.org/uploads/2/5/2/6/25266591/the_challenge_for_haitian_higher_education.pdf

Interuniversity Institute for Research and Development (INURED). (2017). *Republic of Haiti: Country of origin information paper*. Available at http://www.inured.org/uploads/2/5/2/6/25266591/unchr_coi_haiti_final_redacted_report_inured.pdf.

Interuniversity Institute for Research and Development (INURED). (2020). *Impact of COVID-19 on families in urban and rural Haiti*. Available at http://www.inured.org/uploads/2/5/2/6/25266591/impact_of_covid-19_on_haitian_families_eng.pdf.

Jackson, R. O. (2014). The failure of categories: Haitians in the United Nations Organization in the Congo, 1960–1964. *Journal of Haitian Studies, 20*(1), 34–64.

Jones, K., & Sha, H. (2020). *Mediated migration: A literature review of migration intermediaries* (MIDEQ Working Paper).

Joseph, H. (2015) *Diaspora: As Dinâmicas da Mobilidade Haitiana no Brasil, no Suriname e na Guiana Francesa*. Dissertation, Universidade Federal do Rio de Janeiro (UFRJ)- Museo Nacional.

Joseph, H. (2017). Diaspora, circulation et mobilité: Jeunes Haïtiens au Brésil. In L. H. Marcelin, T. Cela, & H. Dorvil (Eds.), *Haitian Youth in the Americas* (pp. 1–24). Presses de l'Université du Québec. https://doi.org/10.2307/j.ctt1z27hmd.9.

Joseph, H. (2020). The Haitian migratory system in the Guianas: Beyond borders. *Dialogos, 24*(2), 198–227.

Joseph, D., & Louis, B. M., Jr. (2022). Anti-Haitianism and statelessness in the Caribbean. *Journal of Lat Am and Carib Anthro, 27*(3), 387–407.

Kenny, M. L. (2013). The emerging Haitian diaspora in Brazil. *Wadabagei: A Journal of the Caribbean and its Diaspora, 14*(1/2), 99–114.

Khoury, R. (2020). Hard-to-survey populations and respondent-driven sampling: Expanding the political science toolbox. *Perspectives on Politics, 18*(2), 509–526. https://doi.org/10.1017/S1537592719003864

Lee, B., & LiPuma, E. (2002). Cultures of circulation: The imaginations of modernity. *Public Culture, 14*(1), 191–213.

Laguerre, M. (1984). *American Odyssey: Haitians in New York City*. Cornell University Press.

Lemay-Hébert, N., et al. (2019). Internal brain drain: Foreign aid, hiring practices and international migration. *Disasters, 44*(4), 621–640. https://doi.org/10.1111/disa.12382

Listín Diario. (2022). *Visas domincanas en Haití: 3,700 millones de pura discrecionalidad*. Available at https://listindiario.com/la-republica/2022/04/18/717634/visas-dominicanas-en-haiti-3700-millones-de-pura-discrecionalidad. Accessed November 1, 2022.

Lundahl, M. (1979). *Peasant and poverty in Haiti*. Croom Helm.

Lundahl, M. (1982). A note on Haitian migration to Cuba: 1890–1934. *Cuban Studies, 12*(2), 21–36.

Lundahl, M. (2011). Some economic determinants of Haitian migration to the dominican republic. *Iberoamericana, 39*(1), 37–64.

Marcelin, L. H. (2012). In the name of the nation: Ritual, blood, and the political habitus of violence in Haiti. *American Anthropologist, 114*(2), 253–266.

Marcelin, L. H. (2015). *Haiti laid bare: Fragility, sovereignty, and delusional recovery*. World Bank.

Marcelin, L. H. (2017). Les jeunes, la migration et les solidarités Haïtiano-Dominicaines: Une entretien avec Colette Lespinasse. In L. H. Marcelin, T. Cela, & H. Dorvil, (Eds.), *Haitian Youth in the Americas* (pp. 123–172). Presses de l'Université du Québec. https://doi.org/10.2307/j.ctt1z27hmd.9.

Marcelin, L. H., & Cela, T. (2017) Introduction: Haitian youth in the Americas: Generations, identity and transnational circulation. In L. H. Marcelin, T.

Cela, & H. Dorvil, (Eds.), *Haitian Youth in the Americas* (pp. 1–24). Presses de l'Université du Québec. https://doi.org/10.2307/j.ctt1z27hmd.9.

Marcelin, L. H., & Marcelin, L. M. (2003). Haitian migrant farm workers in the south of the United States. In *Ethnographic social network tracing of highly mobile people. Census 2000 Evaluation J.2*. US Census Bureau: Statistical Research Division.

Marcelin, L. H., Cela, T., & Shultz, J. (2016). Haiti and the politics of governance and community responses to Hurricane Matthew. *Disaster Health, 3*(4), 1–11.

Martinez, S. (1999). From hidden hand to heavy hand: Sugar, the state, and migrant labor in Haiti and the Dominican Republic. *Latin American Research Review, 31*(1), 57–84.

Millet, K. (1978). *Les paysans haïtiens et l'occupation américaine d'Haïti, 1915–1930*. Collectif Paroles.

Montinard, M.V.L. (2019). *Pran wout la: Dynamiques de la mobilité et des réseaux Haïtiens*. Dissertation, Universidade Federal do Rio de Janeiro Museu Nacional.

Morley, S. P., et al. (2021). *A journey of hope: Haitian women's migration to Tapachula, Mexico*. Center for Gender and Refugee Studies.

Nieto, C. (2014). *Migración haitiana a Brasil: Redes migratorias y espacio social transnacional*. CLACSO.

OECD and INURED. (2017). *Interactions entre politique publiques, migration et développement en Haïti*. Organisation for Economic Cooperation and Development (OECD) and the Interuniversity Institute for Research and Development (INURED).

Organisation internationales pour les migrations (OIM). (2015). *Migration en Haïti Profile migratoire national 2015*. OIM.

Organization of American States (OAS) and International Organization for Migration (IOM). (2016). *Irregular migration flows to/within the Americas from Africa, Asia and the Caribbean*. OAS/IOM.

Portes, A., & Stepick, A. (1993). *City on the edge*. University of California Press.

Plummer, B. G. (1988). *Haiti and the great powers: 1902–1915*. Louisiana State University Press.

Sá, P. R. C. (2015). As redes sociais de haitianos em Belo Horizonte: Análise dos laços relacionais no encaminhamento e ascensão dos migrantes no mercado de trabalho. *Cadernos Observatórios Das Migrações, 1*(3), 99–127.

Schmidt, H. (1971). *The United States occupation of Haiti, 1915–1934*. Rutgers University Press.

Trouillot, M.-R. (1990). *Haiti: State against nation; the origins and legacy of Duvalierism*. Monthly Review Press.

Trouillot, M.-R. (1995). *Silencing the past: Power and the production of history*. The Beacon Press.

United Nations Office on Drug and Crime (UNODC). (2023). *Haiti's criminal markets: Mapping trends in firearms and drug trafficking*. Available at chrome-extension://efaidnbmnnnibpcajpcglclefindmkaj/https://www.unodc.org/documents/data-and-analysis/toc/Haiti_assessment_UNODC.pdf

United Nations Office on Drug and Crime (UNODC). (2018). *Global study on smuggling of migrants*. Available via https://www.unodc.org/documents/data-and-analysis/glosom/GLOSOM_2018_web_small.pdf

Vieira, R. (2017). O Governo da mobilidade Haitiana no Brasil. *MANA, 23*(1). https://doi.org/10.1590/1678-49442017v23n1p229

World Bank. (2015). Haiti: *Toward a new narrative*. Available at https://elibrary.worldbank.org/doi/epdf/https://doi.org/10.1596/22580

World Bank. (2022). *Haiti: Pathways to responding to recurrent crises and chronic fragility*. Available at Haiti-Systematic-Country-Diagnostic-Update-Pathways-to-Responding-to-Recurrent-Crises-and-Chronic-Fragility.pdf (worldbank.org).

Open Access This chapter is licensed under the terms of the Creative Commons Attribution 4.0 International License (http://creativecommons.org/licenses/by/4.0/), which permits use, sharing, adaptation, distribution and reproduction in any medium or format, as long as you give appropriate credit to the original author(s) and the source, provide a link to the Creative Commons license and indicate if changes were made.

The images or other third party material in this chapter are included in the chapter's Creative Commons license, unless indicated otherwise in a credit line to the material. If material is not included in the chapter's Creative Commons license and your intended use is not permitted by statutory regulation or exceeds the permitted use, you will need to obtain permission directly from the copyright holder.

14

Migrant Labour and Inequalities in the Nepal–Malaysia Corridor (and Beyond)

Seng-Guan Yeoh and Anita Ghimire

Introduction

Like many countries in the Global South, both Nepal and Malaysia are deeply entangled with the kinetics of a neoliberal capital-intensive globalisation regime promoted and lubricated by an array of transnational institutions (Walby, 2009; MoLESS, 2023), nation-state bureaucracies, and local socio-economic networks. Among its many intersectional dimensions is a growing and expansive multi-scalar articulation of transnational finance capital with futuristic national planning policies and the varied involvement of local industries, businesses, and rent-seeking entrepreneurial activities (Graeber, 2011; Harvey, 2007, 2019; Smith, 2008; Walby, 2009).

At least for the last three decades, this trend has moreover mutated to include what could be characterised as an international division of mobile and flexible labour. The export of citizens from poorer countries to richer host countries of comparatively cheaper and more flexible and pliable migrant labour has been facilitated by a host of state and non-state intermediaries (Baas, 2020; Gammeltoft-Hansen & Sorensen, 2013; Henaway, 2023; Rodriguez 2010, 2023). What drives these citizens to go abroad for work

---

S.-G. Yeoh
School of Arts and Social Sciences, Monash University, Bandar Sunway, Malaysia
e-mail: yeoh.seng.guan@monash.edu

A. Ghimire (✉)
Nepal Institute for Social and Environmental Research, Kathmandu, Nepal
e-mail: bhattarainitu@gmail.com

is a mixed bundle of motivations. Among others, personal hopes of socio-economic uplift, adventure in a foreign country, escape from domestic travails, and the fulfilment of aspirations viewed as somewhat lacking or unobtainable in their own countries. However, in the host countries, foreign migrant workers (together with refugees) are categorised, surveilled, and governed in ways that are closely related to their precarious position within the capitalist value regime in extracting value (Rajaram, 2018). As non-citizens of Malaysia, this surplus population experience daily the logic and force of a differentiated "hierarchy of rights" (Nah, 2012) and bordering practices that resonate with the figure of Giorgio Agamben's *homo sacer* (Garces-Mascarenas, 2015; Rajaram & Grundy-Warr, 2004).

At the time of writing, there are a least 15 different nationalities forming a significant part of the Malaysian labour force. Nepal migrant workers are estimated to be the third highest population after Indonesian and Bangladeshi citizens. This chapter draws from the concept of "migration infrastructure" (Xiang & Lindquist, 2014) as a point of departure to elaborate on how the different logics of operation and spaces of mediation found in the five dimensions of the migration infrastructure—the commercial, the regulatory, the technological, the humanitarian, and the social—work incommensurately to produce and modulate various kinds of migration inequalities. Based on fieldwork data collected on the life–work conditions and aspirations of Nepalis,[1] we begin by highlighting various everyday migration inequalities encountered and negotiated by them in deciding to leave their home country to work in Malaysia. From there, we address broader structural migration inequalities faced by Nepali and non-Nepali foreign migrant workers in Malaysia as identified, monitored, and globally reported by an influential agency with transnational reach, the US State Department, in ostensibly addressing the aforesaid. Finally, we review how the COVID-19 global pandemic brought into sharp relief and public view everyday and structural inequalities that were relatively ignored or underplayed in the past in Malaysia. Said differently, we elaborate on how the colliding and contradictory logics of operation of the migration infrastructure as found in Malaysia became accentuated by a highly mobile and non-discriminating actant that both compounded

---

[1] This chapter is based largely on fieldwork conducted in the Nepal–Malaysia migration corridor. This included interviews with Nepali migrant workers, intermediaries (recruitment agencies and employer federations), migrant workers civil society groups as well as a monitoring of events unfolding in both countries were conducted between 2019 and 2022. With respect to migrant workers per se, in Nepal, 30 interviews with returnee migrants, 12 focus group discussions with wives of migrants, and 20 interviews were conducted with aspiring migrants who were at different stages of the migration proces were conducted. In Malaysia, semi-structured interviews and focus group discussions with 145 Nepali migrants were accomplished. In total, the views of 145 Nepali males and 50 females were garnered from both ends of the Nepal–Malaysia corridor.

and confounded ascribed differences between citizens and non-citizens of the country.

Nepalis Migrant Workers in Malaysia: An Overview

According to the World Bank, Malaysia is an upper middle-income country (GNI per capita of US$10,570 in 2020) with a population of around 32.4 million. By comparison, Nepal is a lower middle-income country (GNI per capita of US$1,120) with a population of 29.1 million. Foreign employment plays a strong role in Nepal's economy—contributing to 25% of GDP by latest estimates (MoLESS, 2023). Moreover, the latest population census reveals that around 7.5% of the citizens are out of the country (NPC and CBS, 2022).

Before the COVID-19 global pandemic struck, Malaysia was recorded to have a labour force of 15.8 million, the majority of whom (53%) were employed in the service sector. Various sectors in Malaysia depend heavily on foreign migrant labour (both the 2.2 million documented and estimated 2–4 million undocumented non-citizens) to function (see Figs. 14.1 and 14.2). About 70% of them were found in the plantation, manufacturing, and construction sectors (see Fig. 14.4).

Fig. 14.1 Total number of foreign migrant workers holding valid temporary work permits (PLKS) in Malaysia (*Source* Malaysian Parliamentary Report, 2014–2020)

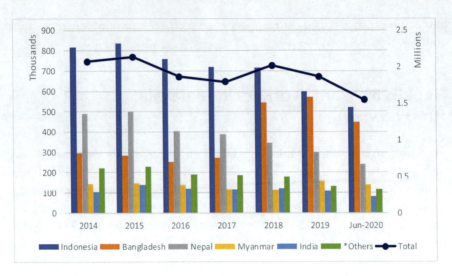

Fig. 14.2 Total number of foreign migrant workers according to nationalities (*Source* Malaysian Parliamentary Report, 2014–2020)

In 2020, it was estimated by the Ministry of Human Resources that there were about 241,106 documented Nepali migrant workers in the country. Of this figure, 97% are men. Nepalis are mostly employed in the manufacturing (73%) sector followed by services (21%) and the remaining in agriculture and plantation as well as construction sectors (see Fig. 14.4). Noteworthy is that 95% of all Nepali migrant women are concentrated in the manufacturing sector (see Fig. 14.3). Except for a short period between 2020 and 2021 when a temporary ban and the COVID-19 pandemic impeded Nepalis from moving abroad for employment, Malaysia has been among the top five destination countries of choice for Nepali men since 2008 when the government started keeping records of outbound Nepali workers. In 2019–2020, 23% of Nepali migrant workers applied for labour permits in Malaysia making it the third most popular country. During COVID-19 (2021–2022), this dropped to 8% and placed Malaysia in fourth position. By comparison, while Malaysia is not the popular destination for Nepali female labour migrants, what is interesting in that they are mainly employed in the formal manufacturing sector unlike in the Gulf Cooperation Council (GOC) countries where they are found only in the informal domestic sector.

Fig. 14.3 Number of Nepali migrant workers (with PLKS) by gender (*Source* Malaysian Parliamentary Report, 2014–2019)

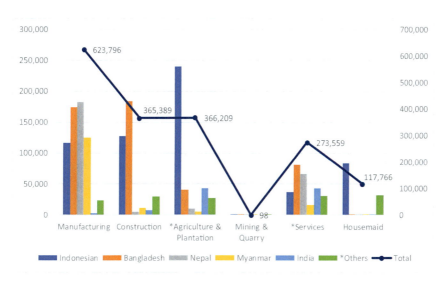

Fig. 14.4 Total number of migrant workers by sectors and nationalities (with PLKS) (*Source* Malaysian Parliamentary Report, April 2020)

Becoming a Nepali Migrant Worker in Malaysia

Like many other foreign migrant workers in Malaysia, the primary motivation propelling Nepalis to leave their families behind and venture into a foreign land for waged labour is the hope of securing better livelihoods and futures for their respective households. In other words, these individuals are already entangled in an array of pre-existing inequitable socio-cultural, economic, and political structures and circumstances not of their making.

For example, some of the Nepalis' experiences of inequality in the migration process are manifested in language. The official Nepali language used for facilitating the migration process is not the mother tongue of many migrants of plains origin (hereafter, Madhesi). This already creates a dependency on several layers of intermediaries for these migrants in helping them navigate the cumbersome process of getting government permits for labour migration. When combined with a lack of or little formal education—another common attribute of aspiring Madheshi migrants—the cost of migration becomes much higher compared to that for aspiring migrants of hills origin (hereafter, Pahadi). Thus, a Madhesi migrant who has primary education usually paid US$1,170 to a local broker while a Pahadi migrant who had completed lower-secondary education, for whom the mother tongue and the processing language are the same, would have paid as little as US$390 for going to Malaysia to perform the same kind of work. While language manifests as a tangible barrier in this particular instance, this distinction reflects the long history of marginalisation of the Madhesi people in Nepal.

Aspirations for migration are also transnationally generated and mediated by larger historical forces. In effect, these vectors provide the aspiring migrant with a larger migration frame beyond the local and nation-state imaginaries to evaluate their personal and collective circumstances (Carling & Collins, 2017; Xiang & Lindquist, 2014). Exposure to the outside world through media and easier communicational flow related to migration, education, and the different histories of labour migration in the origin country influences how these vectors act upon these aspirations and how aspiring migrants are able to conduct reality checks before investing in the migration process. Here, we see the interplay of the technological dimension with other dimensions of the migration infrastructure. For the Madhesis, labour migration beyond India is a current phenomenon dating only to around 10 years back while for the Pahadis, migration to the Gulf Cooperation Council states and countries of South-East Asia started more than 30 years ago. Well-established social networks to these destinations have often meant that for aspiring Pahadis, there are easy and reliable reference points to check for job security and the cost of migration as well as possible sources for support during times of difficulties.

Besides the aforementioned social networks, the migrants' own skillsets, educational backgrounds, and prior migration experiences also shape their respective migration trajectories. According to the Nepal government records, only 0.002% of migrants going to Malaysia fall into the high-skill category compared to 53.2% in the skilled category and 38% in the unskilled category in 2021–2022 (MoLESS, 2023). Our Nepali interviewees came mainly from rural farming or semi-urban working-class backgrounds. Most live in extended and intergenerational family settings. Very few had education beyond Grade 10. The older ones, especially men, would have worked for some years in Nepal or in neighbouring India before deciding to try their luck further afield. A smaller number of men and women said they had worked in Gulf countries like Dubai or the United Arab Emirates before choosing Malaysia as an alternative destination.

Mobility and migration experiences are also shaped by prevailing gender norms found in Nepali society. Some of the older married women we interviewed had already small family businesses like local sundry shops (*kirana*) or sewing shops in the localities they reside in. They decided to go abroad to work for the purpose of generating additional income for their households. By comparison, younger married women often come to Malaysia to work to be with their husbands who were already in the country and usually at their husbands' requests. But this was pursued if it was fairly certain that they be working for the same company or at least in the same town. Their children would be left behind under the care of their grandparents. Another category of Nepali women who sought work abroad were widowed, divorced, estranged from their husbands or were experiencing domestic violence. Some also migrated as their husbands could not be the breadwinner for their families after being disabled due to injury or long-term illness. Like their male counterparts, young single women shared similar aspirations in wanting to see and experience the world beyond Nepal even while earning to provide better educational prospects for their younger siblings (like attaining a college degree and professional qualifications) and subsidise their parents' daily expenses back home. However, before leaving their homes for work abroad, young single women have to seek the permission and blessings of their male guardians because of socio-cultural perceptions and government requirements. The parental fear that their daughters will not be able to find a willing spouse after several years abroad is a constraint that has to be assuaged by the aspiring female migrant worker before the next step can be taken. But, once successfully negotiated and over time, our interviewees tell us that their parents have usually become grateful for how their regular remittances have made their lives less difficult.

Apart from the reasons already cited, pre-existing economic inequalities found in Nepal also generate the motivation for migration. Migrants who choose to work in Malaysia and the Gulf Cooperation Council states usually come from financially poor backgrounds. Similarly, social customs such as dowry systems, low wages, lack of employment opportunities, and the difficulty of accessing capital in Nepal prevented them from producing enough funds to pursue some of their aspirations like buying land, upgrading their dwellings, and setting up small businesses like sundry shops, animal husbandry, and restaurants. Nepal is thus perceived by our interviewees as a country that was lacking in tangible opportunities that would help them improve their livelihoods and futures. In some cases, this lack was seen as more severe because of their historically marginalised social-economic, gender, class, and caste backgrounds. People of lower economic status and women, in particular, have no collaterals to secure loans from both formal and informal sources for their local entrepreneurship activities. Moreover, better-off neighbours would not usually trust them with loans if they wanted to start a small local business. Instead, these informal funding sources would prefer to give loans to these individuals if they opted to work abroad because of the anticipated high income of migrant labour and the high interest rates (in some cases, even up to 60%). In short, local financial systems help to promote migration over local entrepreneurships for economically less well-off Nepalis. Aspirations to climb up the social hierarchy of caste through the accumulation of wealth also drive migration. Nepalis, particularly from the so-called "low caste" groups, often see remittances as a way of helping to resettle away from their place of origin where they face caste-related discrimination (Chaudhary, 2020).

To be sure, the capacity to aspire and drive to pursue these dreams was often encouraged, if not prompted, by local recruiting agents (who can sometimes be their relatives) and residents from their own villages who had already taken the step to work abroad earlier, thus involving the social networks of the migration infrastructure characterised by Xiang and Lindquist. In some cases, local agents (occasionally involving human resource personnel from Malaysia) will target specific localities for regular recruitment drives especially if these places have garnered a reputation for producing residents with a good and reliable work ethic. Moreover, if siblings or relatives were already working in Malaysia, the pull is even stronger because of the knowledge that there will be someone physically close at hand to turn to in times of need or emergency. Interestingly, one of the oft-cited reasons by our interviewees for their preference for Malaysia was its apparent similar and favourable climate in comparison to the extreme weather conditions of Gulf countries. This viewpoint reflected the geographical origins of most of our interviewees who came from the lowland Terai region rather than the hilly or mountainous parts of the country. Some men also joked that the promise of freer access to alcohol and women companions was an additional powerful attractive draw.

Translating these aspirations into reality requires engaging further with another dimension of the expansive and labyrinthine migration infrastructure for the purpose of becoming a duly certified and legible foreign migrant worker as recognised and understood by state authorities (Scott, 1999). The first obstacle to overcome—with respect to the regulatory dimension of the migration infrastructure—is having to raise enough funds to secure an array of documents (passport, medical examination report, work visa, and so forth) that will certify and enable their onward mobility to Malaysia. For Nepalis, the choice of Malaysia among the other 153 labour destination countries is also a reflection of pre-existing socio-economic inequalities. As people of Pahadi origin can afford to get higher education, invest in learning the local language and acquiring skills, and pay higher migration costs, the common destinations are South Korea, Japan, Malta, Dubai, Romania, Poland, Spain, and other European countries where salaries and working conditions are better.

Almost all the interviewees took loans from relatives and friends, and, if there was enough collateral, from local banks and creditors. Only a tiny minority did not resort to this approach as they dipped into savings generated from a previous stint of working abroad. The median debt among our interviewees was US$800 with interest rates ranging from 14 to 18%. After securing work in Malaysia, they took between 6 months to 5 years to repay their debts. This is based on an average monthly salary of US$280 with interviewees spending very little on themselves for the purpose of remitting as much money as possible to their families and repaying back loans; some as much as two-thirds of their salaries. To earn more, almost all our interviewees opted to work overtime (12 hours) daily. While typically they have one day off in a week (in some cases, only one day off in a month) security guards, however, have no such benefits given the nature of their work. Even on public holidays, they are required to be on duty.[2]

The racialised discrimination between Nepali migrant workers noted earlier does not stop even when they are on the verge of leaving their country. Madhesi migrants shared how the Pahadi recruitment agents often make

---

[2] During the initial stages of the COVID-19 pandemic when the Movement Control Order (MCO) was enforced by the authorities and work was stopped for several weeks, our interviewees shared they were provided with basic salaries plus two meals a day. In less favourable situations, they were just provided with meals without any salaries. In the case of the latter, many had to dip into their savings and borrow from friends. When the MCO was partially lifted for specific industries, some of the interviewees were required to work longer hours so as to meet high export demands and the shortage of labour.

fun of them when they asked for explanations or when they were unable to understand the many rules the agents narrated in a brisk manner. They also feel discriminated against during the pre-employment orientation classes where the language used is the national Nepali language and not their mother tongue and local dialects. They are often put together with Pahadi migrants who already have a previous migration experience or have better information on the migration process. The training modules and the *modus operandi* of these trainings do not accommodate differences between novices and returnee migrants as well as Nepalis whose main language is not Nepalese. Due to this language barrier and a culture of racism against the Madheshi people, our interviewees shared how Madheshis were often herded into separate groups and spoken in a harsh and derogatory manner in the Nepal immigration checkpoints.

In situations where the Madheshi/Pahadi distinction is irrelevant, a foretaste of their collective enforced status as a lowly foreign migrant worker was palpably experienced at the border checkpoint of the Kuala Lumpur international airport. Many of our interviewees can still vividly remember experiencing cultural shock and embarrassment at the hands of Malaysian immigration officials in their first trip to the country. They were spoken to in harsh tones in a language they could not understand. When slow to act on their verbal commands, some were even slapped or kicked. While waiting to be processed by the officials, they had to squat on the floor in long rows.[3] After being processed, the wait may extend into several hours (even stretching overnight if they arrived in the evening) without any food or water being supplied before local recruiting agents or their employers came to collect and whisk them to various destinations throughout the country. Eventually, a majority of Nepali migrant workers would find themselves concentrated in the highly urbanised and industrialised states of Selangor and Johor.

Having to quickly gain a basic and practical oral familiarity with the Malay language (the national language of Malaysia) was essential to navigating through their working lives and everyday existence in a foreign country. Nepali migrant workers either learnt this by themselves through trial and error or, more quickly, through the help of other Nepalis who have been working in Malaysia longer. With basic Malay, their life-worlds intersected not only with their immediate supervisors and co-workers of other nationalities but also with an array of Malaysians like salespersons, market vendors, policemen, and so forth. While some interviewees said they were able to make friends with co-workers of other nationalities, nevertheless, the norm

---

[3] A few years ago, the lead author was prevented by an official from filming foreign migrant workers being processed in this manner while he walked past them near to the immigration counters.

is to stick to and rely on fellow Nepalis for support and camaraderie. This segmented sociality is reinforced by employers typically segregating their dormitories to house different nationalities as a way of building group morale. However, Madhesi interviewees shared that Pahadis who have been working in Malaysia for a longer time often do not readily extend their support and camaraderie to them. Instead, the latter continue their discriminatory attitudes even in a foreign land. Some said that while they had initially stayed with Pahadis, the distinctive differences in food, culture, etiquette, and languages between them became an additional burden to cope along with having to adjust to the new environment in Malaysia. Because of this, many eventually chose to live in separate accommodation.

Some of our interviewees were able to relate of the numerous "injustices" that they had personally faced or have heard about happening to their countrymen/women. These include being treated unfairly and harshly by employers, having to pay bribes when stopped by policemen, and being robbed by local gangs after payday. In particular, migrants with low skills, less exposure, and less formal education, and female migrants face higher risks of being cheated. They usually land in jobs that are more difficult than promised and have less benefits. Wage theft and workplace violation of rights are also more common among this group. Such difficult and exploitative circumstances often push migrants to run away from their original employers. A few of our interviewees admitted to being "runaways"—absconding from their legally designated workplace—and hence automatically becoming "undocumented" or "irregular" migrant workers as defined by the Immigration Act 1959. This excludes them from any protection and services from the state and further deepens their state of vulnerability.

This section has highlighted an array of everyday and structural migration inequalities encountered by Nepali migrant workers as an index of the collisions and contradictions between primarily the relational social, commercial, and regulatory dimensions of the migration infrastructure as found in Nepal and Malaysia. The next section looks at how the regulatory and humanitarian themes as embodied in the annual globalist Trafficking in Persons Report published by the US State Department frames and evaluates a selection of these migration inequalities in Malaysia and how they were, in turn, disputed by commercial and regulatory stakeholders in Malaysia.

Forced Labour in Malaysia: The Trafficking in Persons Report[4]

On 23 March 2022, local newspapers reported Malaysia formally ratified the International Labour Organisation's (ILO) forced labour convention known as Protocol 29 (P29).[5] The then Minister of Human Resources, M. Saravanan, described it as "a historic moment for the country" and noted that Malaysia is only the second country in the 11-member states of the Association of Southeast Asian Nations (ASEAN) after Vietnam to ratify the protocol. In November of the previous year, the same ministry had launched the National Plan on Forced Labour (NAPFL) 2021–2025, developed with ILO, with the objective of eliminating the stigma of forced labour in Malaysia by 2030.

Five years earlier, Malaysia had ratified an ILO convention on the issue of minimum wage. In May 2022, during the Labour Day celebrations, the Ministry of Human Resources had announced that the minimum wage has been raised from RM1,200 (US$270) to RM1,500 (US$340) for all workers irrespective of their nationalities. This was met with widespread reservations from employers who felt that the move was ill-timed given that the country's economy was still slowly recovering from the debilitating effects of the COVID-19 pandemic. Some warned that the increased labour costs will filter down to consumers to bear. By contrast, trade unions and migrant workers civil society groups welcomed this long overdue readjustment to keep up with the rising costs of living faced by low waged workers especially in urban centres.

A few confluent vectors have accounted for this apparent benevolent course of action, some propelled by the policing gaze of international peer pressure and others more contextually generated. Paradoxically, it was the global COVID-19 pandemic which had singularly exposed an array of inequities experienced by many foreign migrant workers in Malaysia to the public eye and subsequently hastened widely publicised efforts in redressing them, however belated they may be.[6]

---

[4] Other reports highlighting the mistreatment and vulnerability of migrant workers in Malaysia over the years include Human Rights Watch (2004), Amnesty International (2010), Bhutta (2021), Verite (2014), Fair Labour Association (2018), and SOMO (2013). For a study of migrant workers' access to redress options in Nepal, see Paoletti et al. (2014).

[5] In 2015, Malaysia participated in the ILO's Global Bridge Project funded by the US Department of Labour. This obliged the country to ratify the Forced Labour Protocols as part of the Trans-Pacific Partnership (TPP) conditions.

[6] For academic studies on foreign migrant workers in Malaysia, see (Anderson 2021; Devadason and Chan 2014; Frank & Anderson 2019; Kaur 2014; Low 2020; Nah 2012).

At the international level, for several years Malaysia had been lowly categorised in the US State Department's annual report of the Trafficking in Persons (TIP). In 2021 (and again in 2022), Malaysia's status was downgraded to Tier 3 after being placed on the Tier 2 Watch List for the previous 3 years, an unflattering position last occupied in 2014. The highest achieved was Tier 2 in 2017. These ratings have financial implications as a Tier 3 position would restrict the country's ability to receive foreign aid, loans from multilateral banks, and foreign investments. Moreover, items believed to be made through forced labour would be denied entry into the US market.

The 2021 (and 2022) TIP reports said the reason for the downgrade was because "the Government of Malaysia does not fully meet the minimum standards for the elimination of trafficking and is not making significant efforts to do so even considering the impact of the COVID-19 pandemic on its antitrafficking capacity" (US Department of State, 2022, 369). It further noted that while the government took some steps to address trafficking through the prosecution and conviction of traffickers, provided protection services to trafficking victims, and conducted victim identification training to relevant officials like labour inspectors and immigration officials, and so forth, there were nevertheless still serious structural vulnerabilities to overcome.

Most were recurring and unresolved issues highlighted in earlier TIP reports. Among others, and more directly related to forced labour, it noted that the authorities continue to conflate human trafficking with migrant smuggling which subsequently impeded anti-trafficking law enforcement and victim identification efforts. By relying on victims to "self-identify" and not implementing SOPs to proactively identify victims during law enforcement raids, the authorities continued to inappropriately penalise victims for immigration and prostitution violations. This occurred even in raids on factories suspected of having forced labour, considered "the more prevalent trafficking problem in Malaysia" (US Department of State 2022, 371). Moreover, authorities often relied on reports of abuse from embassies representing foreign workers or from workers' complaints of non-payment of wages and other violations rather than proactive screening efforts. During raids, trafficking victims were often treated like criminals (e.g., the wearing of handcuffs), and this inhibited them to speaking candidly to law enforcement officials. The report further noted that:

Employers utilise practices indicated of forced labour, such as restrictions on movement, violating contracts, wage fraud, assault, threats of deportation, the imposition of significant debts, and passport-retention—which remained widespread—to exploit some migrant workers in labour trafficking on oil palm and agricultural plantations; at construction sites; in the electronics, garment, and rubber-product industries; and in homes as domestic workers. Malaysian law allows employers to hold workers' passports with the workers' permission, but it is difficult to determine if workers have freely given permission, and some employers retain the passports to prevent workers from changing jobs (US Department of State 2022, 373).

Trafficking cases typically operate through criminal syndicates assisted by corrupt police and immigration personnel. Even when traffickers were caught and prosecuted, TIP reports noted that the results of investigations on high-ranking government officials complicit with forced labour crimes were not made public in the interest of transparency. A noteworthy exception was what transpired after the seismic political shift in 2018 when the first regime change in Malaysian political history happened at the 13th General Elections.[7] A year later, the deposed former deputy prime minister, who also served as the minister of home affairs then, was charged with 40 counts of corruption on allegations of receiving kickbacks in visa issuance contracts for foreign workers. The COVID-19 pandemic stalled the court proceedings and is unresolved at the time of writing. The report also highlighted that in December 2020, the Malaysian government filed 19 charges against a disposable glove manufacturing company under the Workers' Minimum Standards of Housing and Amenities Act (Act 446) for "inhumane living conditions" in migrant workers' dormitories (US Department of State, 2022, 370). Nevertheless, it also observed that the government did not report investigating or prosecuting this company for human trafficking crimes despite credible evidence of debt-based coercion.

Key industry players in Malaysia were unhappy with the TIP 2022 report which maintained the Tier 3 status for the country. They questioned the credibility of the individuals engaged in preparing the report as well as the methods of assessment adopted and the nature of the empirical evidence gathered to arrive at their conclusion. For instance, the president of the Malaysian Small & Medium Enterprises Association said that despite a significant number of SMEs (about 80%) having embarked on making changes to comply with Act 446 as well as improving their remuneration packages for foreign workers, this "overall improvement" was not factored into the report and "does not reflect the reality on the ground".[8] In an editorial piece for the

---

[7] In 2019, the Government of Malaysia together with its tripartite partners, the Malaysian Employer Federation (MEF) and Malaysian Trade Union Congress (MTUC) signed an MoU with the International Labour Organization (ILO) on the Decent Work Country Programmes (DWCP) 2019–2025.

[8] "Industry players cry foul: TIP Report did not reflect reality on the ground", *The Star*, 24 July, 2022.

largest English daily in Malaysia, the writer opined that "something's wrong" with the report since several of the countries placed in Tier 1 and Tier 2 were places where "human lives mean nothing" in comparison to Malaysia.[9] In a parliamentary session, the Home Minister commented that the TIP Report was "subjective and not factual" given that the government has already taken many initiatives including improving present laws on anti-human trafficking and labour the past year.[10]

In Nepal, the main policy frameworks related to migrant protection are the Foreign Employment Act (currently being reviewed at the time of writing), the Labour Act, Human Trafficking and Control Act, and the Foreign Employment Policy. The Ministry of Labour Employment and Social Security has the primary responsibility for overall management and policy guidance, the Department of Foreign Employment regulates the migration process, the Foreign Employment Board takes responsibility for migrants' welfare and protection, and the Foreign Employment Tribunal for justice and legal protection. The new Foreign Employment Information and Management System keeps data related to labour migration. There is also a national committee for controlling human trafficking in addition to the above. Other actors include the Department of Passports, diplomatic missions and labour attaché in destination countries, Department of Consular Support, and the Ministry of Women. The government works with private and public stakeholders such as the Nepal Association of Foreign Employment Agents and the Federation of Nepal Foreign Employment Orientation Agencies, I/NGOs, and UN Agencies. Although the policy on labour migration in Nepal is regarded as among the most progressive in South Asia, nevertheless, criticisms have been levelled on the efficacy of some Nepali embassies in providing sufficient support and protection to Nepali workers. In Malaysia, apart from the assistance of a handful of Malaysian NGOs, a small array of concerned Nepali individuals and community groups have turned to social media (particularly Facebook) to partially fill this lack by providing information, counselling, and emergency support. In sum, observers have highlighted how the severe lack of implementation and enforcement has impeded effective service delivery to Nepali migrants in Malaysia.[11]

As assessed by Lee and Pereira (2023, 8), this is because:

---

[9] "Punishing persecution", *The Star*, 31 July, 2022.
[10] "TIP Report is 'subjective'", *The Star*, 3 August, 2022.
[11] For example, all of the MIDEQ study respondents in Nepal had paid much more than the government declared fees cap of 10,000 NPR (75.44 USD) to the recruitment agency for arrangement of their migration.

Vested interests of recruitment agencies and commercial entities in the labour supply industry prevail in both the receiving and sending countries, sometimes in joint ventures of nationals of both countries. The prospects of combatting forced labour ride significantly on the design, harmonization, and enforcement of bilateral arrangements.

Disease, State, and Labour in Malaysia

In the past, the migration infrastructures of both Nepal and Malaysia functioned in the absence of severe disruptions. However, under the extraordinary global reach of the COVID-19 pandemic, much of what was taken-for-granted was reconfigured. The humanitarian became more foregrounded even as the commercial and regulatory dimensions tussled in addressing the contagion while trying to keep the economy afloat in the face of a debilitated migrant labour force.

The outbreak of the first recorded COVID-19 case in Malaysia occurred in January 2020. After a significant spike in reported cases following a large Muslim religious gathering in late February, the first lockdown—the Movement Control Order (MCO)—was put in place in mid-March. This measure was partially relaxed in subsequent months when double-digit figures were reached. But this changed again after a state by-election in October 2020 produced a large spike in infections and another prolonged cycle of lockdown imposed.

At the beginning of the MCO, the Senior Minister for Security had urged Muslim Rohingyas who had attended the religious gathering to come forward voluntarily for testing regardless of their legal status because the government was "concerned about their wellbeing". Rohingya community leaders responded that their alleged large presence at the said gathering was overestimated. Subsequently, those who had gone for testing reported not being treated well at the clinics and hospitals.

This early and apparent benevolent stance towards undocumented noncitizens changed drastically in a matter of days. A series of crackdowns were carried out in places where migrant workers and refugees were known to reside. Those rounded up and detained included women and children. Undocumented migrant workers found to be COVID-19 positive were kept in separate make-shift hospitals while COVID-19 negative cases were detained elsewhere to await deportation. High COVID-19 infection rates were subsequently reported in the detention centres. In July 2020 when Al-Jazeera broadcasted an investigative documentary on the nature of these detentions, the Malaysian government did not take kindly to it. Among other punitive actions, the authorities revoked the work permit of the Bangladeshi migrant worker featured in the story and deported him, and raided the Al-Jazeera office.

In early April 2020, local media attention focused on South Asian (including Nepali) migrant workers residing in the old precinct of Kuala Lumpur popularly known as "Masjid India" (Indian Mosque). Because of high infection rates among them, the buildings where these workers stayed were placed under enhanced lockdown for a couple of weeks. The unhygienic and cramped living conditions of these buildings were publicly exposed and became viral talking points among concerned Malaysians and civil society groups. In the following months, more media exposes of this type were made alongside reports of high infection rates in the dormitories of factory migrant workers and make-shift accommodation at construction sites. The then Minister of Human Resources, M. Saravanan, accompanied a few of these raids and was reported as saying that the living conditions were "deplorable" and resembled "modern slavery". This led quickly to the enforcement of Act 446 (amended in 2019) on the Workers' Minimum Standards of Housing and Amenities. These standards adhered more closely to those set by the ILO. Failure to adhere to these standards would result in defaulters having to pay a fine of RM 50,000 (USD11,364) for every worker affected. In response, industry pleaded for a one-year extension to set their house in order given the dire economic situation they were mired in, a plea which was subsequently repeated two years later. In a Parliamentary sitting in December 2020, the Minister of Human Resources reported that more than 90% of foreign workers (estimated at 1.4 million) accommodation provided by their employers did not comply with Act 446.[12]

High infection rates and clusters among foreign migrant workers prompted the government to proclaim mandatory testing for all foreign workers, and the costs to be borne by their employers. The business sector, especially the Small Medium Enterprises (SMEs), chorused the government to provide subsidies for testing. They cited greatly depressed cash flows and the spectre of bankruptcy should this directive be pushed through without any offer of financial aid. The government relented by allowing the state-run SOSCO (Social Security Organisation) funds to be used by employers for this purpose. However, it was later revealed that a significant number of documented foreign workers (between 30 and 40%) were not even put on this scheme by their employers in the first place. For the testing of undocumented migrant

---

[12] "Provide decent accommodation or face legal action", *The Star*, 17 December, 2020.

workers, employers also suggested that the government should pay for them as they did not want to face criminal action by revealing that they have this category of workers in their payroll. This tug-of-war about costs, responsibility, and the frequency of testing would persist for the remaining part of the year.

A similar exchange between the captains of industry and government officials was also evident in the debate between having to balance lives and livelihoods in the context of a pandemic. In the case of foreign migrant workers, the crucial role they play in keeping the wheels of industry and business turning in Malaysia became evident. When international borders opened briefly in the middle of 2020, tens of thousands of foreign migrant workers, mainly those from neighbouring Indonesia, had decided to return home given the uncertainty of the job situation and they wanting to spend precious time with their families during this difficult period. Moreover, as new hires were not allowed to come into the country, industry players lamented of severe labour shortages in the construction, manufacturing, and plantation sectors.

Because of persistent pleas from the captains of industry in Selangor, the most industrialised state in the country, the state authorities eventually allowed 50% of the workforce, mainly in the construction sector, to resume work by the end of April 2020. Rising unemployment figures[13] had prompted the government to suggest that these shortages be filled by Malaysian citizens. In response, employers assessed Malaysians as either unsuitable or disinterested in these 3D ("dirty, dangerous and difficult") jobs. Severe labour shortages translated to massive loss in profits for the industry and, by extension, lower tax revenues for the government. For instance, in the palm oil sector, decade high prices meant literally millions of dollars of unpicked oil palm fruits were left to rot away every day. Similarly, rubber gloves manufacturers pleaded that the assembly line production needed workers to feed the extraordinary demand for their products as protective wear for COVID-19 frontliners.

By early June 2020, this economic conundrum was severe enough for the Malaysian Employers Federation (MEF) to suggest that the government should forsake enforcing issues of legality/illegality with regard to foreign migrant labour. Instead, the huge reservoir of undocumented foreign workers could be re-categorised as legally permissible labour. This would not only mitigate labour shortages but also have the additional benefit of generating much-needed revenue for the government coffers. At the end of

---

[13] By June 2020, this was reported at about 5.5% unemployment rate (750,000), an increase of 2% above the previous figure before the COVID-19 pandemic struck.

2020, the Malaysian government launched the Labour Recalibration Plan with a target of 250,000 undocumented migrant workers to be recruited by employers. Additionally, for every undocumented migrant worker recalibrated, the authorities required that a similar ratio of individuals be deported as a way to resolve overcrowding and reduce high COVID-19 infection rates in the detention centres. The authorities decided that the costs of deportation would be financed by the prospective employer.[14]

By early 2021, it was reported that only 8.5% of documented foreign workers in six high risk states in the country were sent by their employers to be mandatorily screened for COVID-19 despite the provision of free test kits supplied by SOSCO to clinics throughout the country.[15] Moreover, local media exposed a scam involving several clinics selling fake results for a fee of between RM300–500 each (USD68–114). When the government announced intentions of imposing a total lockdown again because of high rates of infections, SMEs rallied together to plea for targeted lockdowns (conditional MCO) and more financial aid. Despite the provision of numerous stimulus packages in the previous year by the government, SMEs lamented this was not enough and thousands of businesses would continue to fold up as they had already exhausted most of their savings in the previous year to pay for rentals, salaries, and so forth. They counselled for closer consultations between government and industry stakeholders before any firm decisions are made.[16]

During this time, the Nepal government arranged for repatriation flights to bring Nepali workers back home. More than 51,000 Nepalis returned between 15 June and the end of August 2019. However, there were still around 250,000 migrants registered for return in Nepal embassies who were left on their own to find their way back home. The Nepali government could not do much to resolve numerous reported cases of abuse of migrant workers during the pandemic.

Up to the first half of 2022, the complaint by SMEs and large businesses of a severe shortage of labour (estimated to be around 1.2 million) persisted and remained largely unresolved.[17] This was amplified by a brief diplomatic tiff between Indonesia and Malaysia. As noted earlier, Indonesians currently constitute a large majority of foreign migrant labour in Malaysia. While this

---

[14] "Technology vs corruption", *The Star*, 27 December, 2020; "Not all eligible for recalibration plan", *The Star*, 5 December, 2020; "Conditions set to hire foreign workers", *The Star*, 4 December, 2020.

[15] However, employers still had to pay for the screening costs imposed by clinics or hospitals.

[16] "SMEs request for additional assistance", *The Star*, 12 January, 2021.

[17] This desperate state-of-affairs led the MEF to suggest to the government to consider recruiting workers from refugees, illegal immigrants, and paroled prisoners to offset some of the labour shortage in key sectors. See "Costly labour crunch", *The Star*, 20 July, 2022.

impasse was eventually resolved, it underscored the strong bargaining position of a labour sending country in an extraordinary time involving the intersections between disease and capital.[18] In the case of Nepal, after a major cross-border investigation exposing collaborated corruption and charging of exorbitant fees to workers by Nepali and Malaysian officials and private companies, the then Minister, Mr Gokarna Bista, banned Nepalis from going to Malaysia for employment in May 2018. The investigation revealed that Malaysian businesses and Nepali middlemen in Kathmandu were allegedly working under the political protection of the former deputy Prime Minister of Malaysia and influential politicians and bureaucrats in Kathmandu to cheat Nepali workers. It revealed that they had illegally taken more than USD450 million from aspiring Nepali workers between September 2013 and April 2018. Following the ban, the two governments signed a Memorandum of Understanding (MoU) which among others required employers to pay for visa fees and air tickets when taking Nepali workers. It was decided that salaries be paid in the first week of every month. The MoU also called for a joint working group to work out the technical details of implementation. Unfortunately, some points of disagreements, such as the devolution of medical testing institutions to provincial level, could not be resolved even after September 2019 when the Nepal government had removed the ban. Moreover, the MoU failed to work on important issues specific to the corridor such as high number of workplace accidents, unidentified deaths, and high suicide rates as well as issues of inequality related to class, gender, and skill levels.

Conclusion

In the last three decades, the closely intertwined migration infrastructures of Nepal and Malaysia have worked efficiently to facilitate the transnational flow of labour and remittances. On the one hand, the import of cheap, pliable, and flexible labour from Nepal into Malaysia has helped to drive the national economy in Malaysia. Similarly, it has also contributed substantially to the household economy in Nepal. Nevertheless, together with migrant labour from other Asian countries, Nepali migrant workers occupy a precarious surplus position within the capitalist value regime of extracting value. Moreover, as the non-citizens of Malaysia, they experience daily the logic and force of a differentiated "hierarchy of rights" and "bordering practices" in

---

[18] "23,000 maids coming soon", *The Star*, 6 August, 2022; "Indonesia lifts workers' entry ban", *The Star*, 29 July 2022.

reminding and keeping them in their place, a manifestation of what we have called structural migration inequalities.

As noted, for the aspiring Nepali migrant worker, the decision to go to Malaysia is itself a manifestation of a pre-existing set of socio-economic inequalities already inherent in Nepali society. Much of the current migration policies, though important for migrants, do not adequately address or take into serious account these long-standing inequalities. Both in the country of origin and in the host country, these prevailing kinds of discrimination have been perpetuated in the daily life of the Nepali migrant. Similarly, the dominant migration-for-development discourse largely focuses on economic benefits and undervalues the social and mental wellbeing of the migrant worker. Moreover, these issues are currently not prioritised as policy and implementation goals in the national, regional, and global migration policy frameworks such as the Global Forum for Migration and Development and the Global Compact on Migration.

In terms of the migration infrastructure concept, it is evident that the commercial dimension currently dominates and cause all other dimensions to orbit around its logic of operation and spaces of mediation, notwithstanding the periodic interventions of the regulatory, humanitarian and even the social, and its wake constituting the range of everyday and structural migration inequalities discussed in this chapter. Ironically, it is COVID-19, an unanticipated vector that sits outside the migration infrastructure, that has exposed this appalling state-of-affairs to public view, a perspective hitherto largely confined to civil society groups and concerned politicians and academicians. As to whether the attitudinal and policy changes set in motion in recent times to address some of these migration inequalities can be sustained to bear tangible and equitable outcomes for Nepali migrant workers in particular and other foreign migrant workers in Malaysia in general for the foreseeable future remains to be seen.

Acknowledgements Research for this chapter was funded by the Migration for Development and Equality (MIDEQ) Hub (Grant Reference ES/S007415/1). The MIDEQ Hub unpacks the complex and multi-dimensional relationships between migration and inequality in the context of the Global South. The authors would like to thank the research assistance of Nadiah Ahmad, Sharmini Nathan, and Yvonne Khor, and the logistical support of North–South Initiative in facilitating access to Nepali migrant workers in Malaysia.

References

Amnesty International. (2010). *Trapped: The Exploitation of Migrant Workers in Malaysia*. Amnesty International.

Anderson, J. T. (2021). Managing labour migration in Malaysia: Foreign workers and the challenges of 'control' beyond liberal democracies. *Third World Quarterly*, 42(1), 86–104.

Baas, M. (ed.) (2020). *The migration industry in Asia: Brokerage, gender and precarity*. Palgrave.

Bhutta, M. et al. (2021). Forced labour in the Malaysian medical gloves supply chain during the COVID-19 pandemic. Research summary, Modern Slavery and Human Rights Policy and Evidence Centre, London.

Carling, J., & Collins, F. (2017). Aspiration, desire and drivers of migration. *Journal of Ethnic and Migration Studies*, 44(6), 909–926.

Chaudhary, D. (2020). Case study: Influence of remittances on socio-economic development in rural Nepal. *Remittance Review*, 5(1), 83–96.

Devadason, E. S., & Chan, W. M. (2014). Policies and laws regulating migrant workers in Malaysia: A critical appraisal. *Journal of Contemporary Asia*, 44(1), 19–35.

Fair Labour Association. (2018). *Assessing forced labour risks in the palm oil sector in Indonesia and Malaysia*. A research report for the Consumer Goods Forum. https://www.theconsumergoodsforum.com/wp-content/uploads/2018/11/201811-CGF-FLA-Palm-Oil-Report-Malaysia-and-Indonesia_web.pdf

Frank, A. K., & Anderson, J. T. (2019). The cost of legality: Navigating labour mobility and exploitation in Malaysia. *International Quarterly for Asian Studies*, 50(1–2), 19–38.

Gammeltoft-Hansen, T., & Sorensen, N. N. (eds.) (2013). *The migration industry and the commercialization of international migration*. Routledge.

Garces-Mascarenas, B. (2015). Revisiting border practices: Irregular migration, borders, and citizenship in Malaysia. *International Political Sociology*, 9(2), 128–142.

Graeber, D. (2011). *Debt: The first 5,000 years*. Melville House.

Harvey, D. (2007). *A brief history of neoliberalism*. Oxford University Press.

Harvey, D. (2019). *Spaces of global capitalism. A theory of uneven geographical development*. Verso.

Henaway, M. (2023). *Essential work, disposable workers: Migration*. Fenwood Publishing.

Human Rights Watch. (2004). *Help wanted. Abuses against female migrant domestic workers in Indonesia and Malaysia*. https://www.hrw.org/report/2004/07/21/help-wanted/abuses-against-female-migrant-domestic-workers-indonesia-and-malaysia

International Labour Organisation. (2020). *Promoting decent work for sustainable development: Malaysia Decent Work Country Programme (DWCP)*. ILO.

Kaur, A. (2014). Managing labour migration in Malaysia: Guest worker programs and the regularization of irregular labour migrants as a policy instrument. *Asian Studies Review, 38*(3), 345–366.

Lee, H. A., & Pereira, A. (2023). *Can Malaysia eliminate forced labour by 2030?* ISEAS Yusof Ishak Institute.

Low, C. C. (2020). De-commercialisation of the labour migration industry in Malaysia. *Southeast Asian Studies, 9*(1), 27–65.

MoLESS (Ministry of Labour Employment and Social Security). (2023). *Nepal labour migration report 2022*. MoLESS.

Nah, A. (2012). Globalisation, sovereignty and immigration control: The hierarchy of rights for migrant workers in Malaysia. *Asian Journal of Social Science, 40*(4), 486–508.

National Planning Commission and Central Bureau of Statistics. (2022). Preliminary report of census 2021. Singhadurbar; National Planning Commission and Central Bureau of Statistics.

Paoletti, S., Taylor-Nicholson, E., Sijapati, B., & Farbenblum, B. (2014). *Migrant Workers' Access to Justice at Home: Nepal*. Open Society Foundations.

Rajaram, P. K. (2018). Refugees as surplus population: Race, migration and capitalist value regimes. *New Political Economy, 23*(5), 627–639.

Rajaram, P. K., & Grundy-Warr, C. (2004). The irregular migrant as homo sacer: Migration and detention in Australia, Malaysia and Thailand. *International Migration, 42*(1), 33–64.

Rodriguez, N. P. (2023). *Capitalism and migration: The rise of hegemony in the world system*. Springer.

Rodriguez, R. M. (2010). *Migrants for export: How the Philippine state brokers labour to the world*. University of Minneapolis Press.

Scott, J. C. (1999). *Seeing like a state: How certain schemes to improve the human condition have failed*. Yale University Press.

Smith, N. (2008). *Uneven development: Nature*. University of Georgia Press.

SOMO (Centre for Research on Multinational Corporations). (2013). *Outsourcing labour: Migrant labour rights in Malaysia' electronic industry*. SOMO.

US Department of State. (2022). *Trafficking in Persons Report. July 2022*. US Department of State.

US Department of State. (2021). *Trafficking in persons report: Malaysia*. https://www.state.gov/reports/2021-trafficking-in-persons-report/malaysia/. Accessed 10 September, 2022.

Verite. (2014). *Forced labour in the production of electronic goods in Malaysia: A comprehensive study of scope and characteristics*. Verite, Amherst, MA.

Walby, S. (2009). *Globalization and inequalities: Complexity and contested modernities*. Sage.

Xiang, B., & Lindquist, J. (2014). Migration infrastructure. *International Migration Review, 48*(S1), S122–S148.

Newspapers

"Industry players cry foul: TIP Report did not reflect reality on the ground", *The Star*, 24 July, 2022.
"Punishing persecution", *The Star*, 31 July, 2022.
"TIP Report is 'subjective'", *The Star*, 3 August, 2022.
"Provide decent accommodation or face legal action", *The Star*, 17 December, 2020.
"Technology vs corruption", *The Star*, 27 December, 2020.
"Not all eligible for recalibration plan", *The Star*, 5 December, 2020.
"Conditions set to hire foreign workers", *The Star*, 4 December, 2020.
"SMEs request for additional assistance", *The Star*, 12 January, 2021.
"Costly labour crunch", *The Star*, 20 July, 2022.
"Indonesia lifts workers' entry ban", *The Star*, 29 July 2022.
"23,000 maids coming soon", *The Star*, 6 August, 2022.

Open Access This chapter is licensed under the terms of the Creative Commons Attribution 4.0 International License (http://creativecommons.org/licenses/by/4.0/), which permits use, sharing, adaptation, distribution and reproduction in any medium or format, as long as you give appropriate credit to the original author(s) and the source, provide a link to the Creative Commons license and indicate if changes were made.

The images or other third party material in this chapter are included in the chapter's Creative Commons license, unless indicated otherwise in a credit line to the material. If material is not included in the chapter's Creative Commons license and your intended use is not permitted by statutory regulation or exceeds the permitted use, you will need to obtain permission directly from the copyright holder.

15

Inter-regional Migration in the Global South: Chinese Migrants in Ghana

Joseph Kofi Teye, Jixia Lu, and Gordon Crawford

Introduction

There has been a Chinese presence in Africa for many centuries, with a rise and fall in numbers at particular historical periods (Merli et al, 2016; Wang, 2022). For instance, the European colonial powers introduced Chinese labourers, especially in the post-slavery period, to work on their African colonial possessions as a captive labour force in the eighteenth and nineteenth centuries (Snow, 1988, 42–6, cited in Harris, 2013, 176). Additionally, after the Chinese Revolution in 1949, China provided support to various liberation movements in Africa, and then post-independence assisted with material and technical support to selected newly independent countries (Harris, 2013, 176). From the start of the twenty-first-century Chinese migration to Africa has become increasingly significant (Brautigam, 2009; Broadman, 2007;

J. K. Teye (✉)
Centre for Migration Studies, University of Ghana, Legon, Ghana
e-mail: jteye@ug.edu.gh

J. Lu
College of Humanities and Development Studies, China Agricultural University, Beijing, China
e-mail: lujx@cau.edu.cn

G. Crawford
Centre for Trust, Peace and Social Relations, Coventry University, Coventry, UK
e-mail: gordon.crawford@coventry.ac.uk

© The Author(s) 2024
H. Crawley and J. K. Teye (eds.), *The Palgrave Handbook of South–South Migration and Inequality*, https://doi.org/10.1007/978-3-031-39814-8_15

Cardenal & Araujo, 2014; Mohan & Tan-Mullins, 2009), in line with the dramatic increase in Chinese trade and investment throughout the continent (Taylor, 2006, 1). However, while there is consensus that numbers have increased rapidly in recent years (Li, 2012, 62–64), estimates vary considerably and there remains a paucity of data about Chinese migrant flows to Africa (Mohan & Tan-Mullins, 2009, 591). Nonetheless, the increased diversity of Chinese migrants is clear, with increasing numbers of independent and unregulated migrants in addition to those official migrants connected to Chinese state-related projects, often in the construction sector (Wang, 2022).

While the increased movement of Chinese migrants to Africa has received attention in the literature in recent times, there is little understanding of the drivers and impacts of this migration (Merli et al., 2016; Teye et al., 2022). Research has suggested that while the increasing presence of Chinese migrants in informal sectors in African countries has created employment for low-skilled African workers, it has also led to growing resentment and opposition from some low-income Africans, often resulting in the vilification of Chinese migrants in various countries (Abid et al., 2013; Ajakaiye & Kaplinsky, 2009; Wang & Elliot, 2014), including Ghana (Tschakert, 2016).

This chapter examines the drivers and impacts of Chinese migration to Ghana, a West African country which has been a significant destination for Chinese migrants for several decades. The Chinese presence in this country is recorded from the late nineteenth century when indentured Chinese labourers were brought to the former Gold Coast by the British colonial government, including in 1897 a small group of 16 Chinese miners and technicians to work in the gold mines (Li, 2012, 74–75). After independence in 1957, a relatively small Chinese business community established itself in Ghana, for instance, in the catering and casino sectors, and more latterly in small-scale agriculture (Cook et al., 2016). In the twenty-first century, the number of Chinese non-resident migrant workers has increased, associated with the large-scale government-to-government infrastructure projects that have been undertaken, such as the construction of roads, the Bui dam, and football stadiums for the Africa Cup of Nations tournament in 2008. However such migration was usually short-term and regulated through being tied to official construction projects. Official numbers of Chinese citizens entering Ghana remained relatively small until the latter half of the 2000s. Sautman and Yan (2007) estimated the number of Chinese migrants in Ghana, in 2004, was about 6,000, but numbers have increased substantially since then, including an increased number of irregular migrants. Sources at the Chinese Embassy in Ghana reported that, as of 2018, there were about 30,000 Chinese migrants in Ghana (Zurek, 2018).

The Chinese in Ghana work in several sectors, including wholesale and retail trade, construction, manufacturing, mining, education and healthcare activities, and agriculture (Teye et al., 2022). Of all these sectors, it is Chinese involvement in the retail trade and artisanal mining sectors that has generated the most public debate. Although the artisanal mining and retail trade sectors are legally reserved for Ghanaians, an increasing number of Chinese migrants are working in these sectors (Teye et al., 2022). While we examine the impacts of Chinese migrants with particular focus on these sectors, examples have also been taken from other sectors, where appropriate.

This chapter is based on primary data as well as a review of relevant literature. The primary data was largely collected in 2020 and 2021, as part of the Migration for Equality and Development (MIDEQ) Hub.[1] The MIDEQ team in Ghana collected quantifiable data through a questionnaire survey of 1,268 Chinese immigrants, of which 855 respondents were male and the rest were female. The chapter also draws on qualitative data generated through in-depth interviews with 62 Chinese migrants and some Ghanaians. Qualitative data collected on return migrants in China was also used, as well as earlier interviews with Ghanaian small-scale miners with experience of working with Chinese miners. In line with the guarantee of anonymity, pseudonyms have been used throughout this paper. The chapter is structured in five sections. This introductory section is followed by an overview of conceptual issues, including a discussion of the drivers of Chinese migration to Ghana. The third section discusses the impacts of Chinese migration in Ghana, with the fourth section then analysing the impact of Chinese migration in China. We draw out the main conclusion in the last section of the chapter.

Conceptualising Drivers of Migration from China to Ghana

Given the increased flow of Chinese migrants to various parts of the world, some researchers have drawn on existing migration theories or proposed new frameworks to explain the drivers of migration from China to other parts of the world (Mohan et al, 2014; Wang, 2022; Xiang & Lindquist, 2014). The push–pull theory, social networks theory, and migration infrastructure framework have all previously been used to explain the reasons behind the flow of Chinese migrants to Ghana (Sparreboom et al., 2018; Teye et al.,

---

[1] The Migration for Development and Equality (MIDEQ) Hub unpacks the complex and multi-dimensional relationships between migration and inequality in the context of the Global South. More at www.mideq.org.

2022). This chapter relies heavily on insights from the conceptualisation of migration drivers by Van Hear (2012, 1), who defines drivers of migration as "the factors which get migration going and keep it going once begun". Van Hear identified four migration drivers, namely: predisposing/underlying/ drivers; proximate drivers, precipitating drivers, and mediating drivers.

The *predisposing/underlying drivers* are structural inequalities (especially between migrants' places of origin and destinations) which create the context in which migration is desirable. Structuralist migration theorists (see Morawska, 2012; Wallerstein, 1974) have traditionally attributed international migration to inequalities in the global distribution of economic and political power. The *proximate drivers* are the macro-economic factors that have a direct bearing on migration. At migrants' sending areas, these factors include a poor economic environment, political instability, and environmental degradation, driving people away from their usual places of residence. At migrants' destinations, they include good economic conditions and peaceful environments that may attract migrants (Teye et al., 2015). The *precipitating drivers* of migration are the conditions that directly trigger departure or migration. At migrants sending areas, these include unemployment, low wages, and poverty (Van Hear, 2012) while at migrants' destinations, these may include the availability of job opportunities and high wages. The *mediating drivers* are made up of factors which facilitate or constrain migration. These include the quality of transportation facilities, improved communications, access to economic resources, and social networks required for migration.

What Factors Drive Chinese Migrants to Ghana?

Our analysis shows that all the various categories of drivers influence migration flows from China to Ghana. Although the literature does not comprehensively focus on the role of *predisposing or underlying drivers* in shaping migration from China to Ghana, there is enough evidence to suggest that structural inequalities between the two countries contribute to migration flows along the corridor. As Ghana does not have adequate economic resources, it relies on loans and grants from the government of China for infrastructure development. In most cases, these loans come with conditional agreements which call for the services of Chinese firms and expatriates. Most of the migrants that migrate as part of such agreements are either highly skilled or low-skilled single men who migrate to Ghana to work for Chinese firms involved in the construction of roads, buildings, hydropower plants, railroad, and telecommunications networks (Cook et al., 2016). For instance, about 110 Chinese nationals worked on the Bui hydroelectric power project in Ghana (Aryee, 2015). Similarly, more than 100 Chinese citizens worked in Tamale during the construction of Tamale airport. While the Chinese who move to Ghana to work with Chinese construction firms tend to go back at the end of the contracts signed in China, some have remained in Ghana for several years to work in the trade sector or lucrative mining sector (Teye et al., 2022).

Apart from Chinese migrants who initially moved to Ghana as a result of Chinese government grants to the government of Ghana, economic and political changes in China have also enhanced Chinese firms' competitive advantage, which in turn promotes the migration of independent Chinese entrepreneurs to Ghana and other African countries. Chinese entrepreneurs are increasingly able to access loans for investments in the trade and manufacturing sectors in African countries (Wang, 2022, 2).

With regard to the role of *proximate and precipitating drivers*, some scholars who use the traditional "push–pull theory" to discuss the flow of migrants have discussed the combined effects of both the proximate and precipitating factors in shaping migration flows (see Sparreboom et al., 2018; Wang, 2022). Our MIDEQ study showed that the low earnings of some people and high cost of living in China were among the factors that pushed people to migrate from China. For instance, GHGPm23, a middle-aged male Chinese migrant from Hefei reported that he was employed in China but the salary was inadequate to meet the needs of his household. He migrated to Ghana with the help of his brother who was already in Ghana. Similarly, GHGPm28, a young male Chinese from Henan Province, reported that he migrated to Ghana in 2018 because the cost of living in China was very high. He feels working in Ghana is less difficult and more profitable:

> In China, the cost of living is expensive and we work very hard there. We work for twelve hours, which is difficult. But when I came to Ghana, working here is not really difficult and I can also make money that is why I came here
> (GHGPm28, a male Chinese migrant from Henan Province, China)

The above statement shows that while wages in China are generally higher than wages in Ghana, the high cost of living in China makes life difficult for low-income earners. Migrants are pulled to Ghana because of the possibility to make huge profits in the trade and mining sectors. As shown in Table 15.1, 65% of male migrants and 48.7% of female migrants who took part in the MIDEQ study, mentioned better job/wages in Ghana as the main reason for migrating to Ghana. Some small-scale entrepreneurs also reported that it is very difficult to climb up the social ladder in China because the big companies "control" the market. However, there are more opportunities for them to grow their businesses and improve social status in Ghana, as highlighted below:

> In China, the market is controlled by big firms so I heard that there is more profits in Ghana. So, I moved here to start gold business. Now I am highly respected here and if I go back to China, my friends respect me more because of the things I am doing with the money from Ghana (GHGPm21, a 38-year-old male Chinese migrant from Zheijiang province)

As Wang (2022, 2) has argued elsewhere, Chinese migrants in similar situations as the above case view "the fairer opportunity structure and more flexible

Table 15.1 Reasons for migration to Ghana by gender (multiple response)

Reasons for migrating to Ghana	Male		Female		All	
	Frequency	%	Frequency	%	Frequency	%
Better job opportunities/wage in Ghana	556	65.0	201	48.7	757	59.7
Ghana is safe(r)	331	38.7	161	39.0	492	38.8
Had family/friends in Ghana	198	23.2	179	43.3	377	29.7
Low cost of moving to Ghana	88	10.3	39	9.4	127	10.0
Easy to access Ghana (geography, migration policy)	83	9.7	28	6.8	111	8.8
Advised by recruiter	72	8.4	27	6.5	99	7.8
I was brought here (not choice)	49	5.7	28	6.8	77	6.1
Better education opportunities in Ghana	33	3.9	37	9.0	70	5.5

space for career and identity transitions" as a major reason to move to Ghana and other African countries. Apart from economic drivers related to employment and wages, the fact that Ghana is a relatively safer place to live was mentioned by 38.7% of the males and 39% of the females as the reason for coming to Ghana (see Table 15.1).

The role of *mediating or facilitative drivers* in shaping migration flows from China has also been discussed in the literature. While some studies have highlighted how Chinese migrants rely on social networks to migrate (Mohan et al., 2014; Teye et al., 2022), Xiang and Lindquist (2014, S124) has called for the need to focus more broadly on migration infrastructures, defined as "the systematically interlinked technologies, institutions, and actors that facilitate and condition mobility". These authors have identified five dimensions of migration infrastructure, namely: "the commercial (recruitment intermediaries), the regulatory (state apparatus and procedures for documentation, licencing, training and other purposes), the technological (communication and transport), the humanitarian (NGOs and international organizations), and the social (migrant networks)" (Xiang & Lindquist, 2014, S124). In our MIDEQ research, we found that migration infrastructures were generally relied upon by the migrants to move to Ghana. As shown in Table 15.1, social networks, in particular, played a pivotal role in the migration of many of the Chinese in Ghana. Among female migrants, joining family and friends was the second most prominent reason for migrating (43.3%), while for male migrants, this was the third most important reason (23.2% of respondents mentioned this reason). Females were more likely to rely on social networks for migration as many of them came to join their spouses, as shown by the case of GHGPm12, a female Chinese migrant:

> My husband was already here, and it was time to join him. When I gave birth, my salary was no longer enough for us. My husband was the one sending money to us every month. So, we decided that it would be wise to live together in one place and to help our child grow. He processed my documents and gave me money to come with our child (GHGPm12, a female Chinese in her 30s from Shandong Province.)

Consistent with the literature (Awumbila et al., 2017; Massey et al., 1993), social networks were also relied upon for information on Ghana. GHGPm21, a 38-year-old male Chinese who deals in gold, migrated to Ghana based on information provided by his friend:

> My final decision was out of a conversation with a friend who was already in Ghana and works in the mining sector. He told me about the opportunities in

the mining sector because he knew my interest to establish my own business dating back to when we were still in college (GHGPm21, a 38-year-old male Chinese from Zheijiang province.)

As shown in Table 15.1, 21% of male and 44% of female Chinese migrants relied on information from family or relatives in Ghana to plan their migration. Some migrants also relied on friendship and kinship ties to process travel documents and funding the cost of migration, as highlighted by GHGPm18, a Chinese young man:

> My uncle helped me to go through all the processes easily because he had helped many people to travel to Africa. My uncle was the one who guided me through what to do, where to go, among other things. He helped me to arrive in Ghana without any difficulties. (GHGPm18, a Chinese young man from Wuhan in Hubei Province.)

Another facilitative driver which contributed to reliance on social networks was having family/friends in Ghana (cited by 29.7% of respondents). Perhaps as a result of the facilitative role of social networks, the low cost of moving to Ghana was mentioned by 10.3% of males and 9.4% of females as another reason for moving to Ghana.

With regard to the commercial dimension of migration infrastructures, 28.3% of the migrants interviewed during our MIDEQ research reported that they contacted a broker or registered with a recruitment agency as part of preparations to migrate to Ghana. With reference to the regulatory regime, some of the migrants mentioned that it was quite easy to get an initial visa to travel to Ghana. The recruitment agencies assisted some of the migrants to navigate through the regulatory regimes. About a quarter (25.5%) of migrants had pre-departure training before leaving China. The technological dimension of migration infrastructures was also highlighted by some of the migrants. Nearly three quarters (70.8%) of the migrants reported that they used internet to get information about Ghana prior to leaving China.

Economic Activities of Chinese Migrants in Ghana

Chinese migrants in Ghana and elsewhere in Africa work in several sectors. As shown in Table 15.2, the MIDEQ data shows that the major sectors where our Chinese respondents work include, wholesale or retail trade

(20.6%), construction, demolition or site preparation (13.5%), manufacturing (12.6%), accommodation and food (10%), mining (9.7%), education and healthcare activities (7.5%), and agriculture (5.9%). The Chi-square test shows that the distribution is gendered. For instance, a higher proportion of females (28.1%) work in the wholesale and retail sector than males (17%). The mining sector, on the other hand, is dominated by males (13.3% of males as against 2% of females). Chinese migrants in the mining sector are not linked to the government.

Chinese traders tend to work in the retailing of textiles, electrical appliances, medicines, food items, and agricultural products. Most Chinese entrepreneurs are involved in illegal retail because petty trading is legally reserved for only Ghanaians. In most cases, the Chinese shops are registered in the names of Ghanaians so as to avoid being arrested by security officials. Thus, although Ghana's Investment Promotion Act (2013) (Act 865) does not allow foreigners to engage in petty trade, Chinese enterprises are able to operate illicitly by relying on networks with Ghanaian traders (Teye et al., 2022). Since 2007, local traders in Ghana have been organising demonstrations against Chinese nationals due to their perceived take-over of the retail trade business. Studies by Sparreboom et al. (2018) reveal that many Ghanaian citizens, however, like the trading activities of Chinese citizens because their goods are cheaper. Some Ghanaian traders also have mutual networks with the Chinese as they get a cheap supply of goods from them.

Chinese involvement in small-scale gold mining in Ghana can be traced back to 1998 when a small number of miners from Hunan province were involved in fairly unsuccessful ventures (Crawford et al., 2015). However,

Table 15.2 Sector of main work of Chinese migrants in Ghana by gender

	Male	Female	All
Agriculture, forestry, or fishing	6.4	4.7	5.9
Wholesale or retail trade	17	28.1	20.6
Construction, demolition, or site preparation	18	4.2	13.5
Manufacture or repair products	15.7	6	12.6
Accommodation or food services	5.6	19.2	10
Mining	13.3	2	9.7
Education or healthcare activities	2.9	17.2	7.5
Office administration or support activities	3.1	4.5	3.5
Infrastructure related (water, electricity)	3.9	0.2	2.7
Other	14.1	13.9	14.1
Total	100 (841)	100 (402)	100 (1243)

Pearson chi 2 = 251.7172, Pr = 0.000

the substantial increase in the gold price from 2008 onwards led to a new wave of Chinese miners migrating to Ghana. Another driver was the ongoing economic boom in China, enabling lower-class Chinese citizens to borrow sums of approximately US $25,000 from banks in China for investment in small-scale gold mining activities in Ghana. At the height of Chinese involvement in this small-scale gold mining boom in Ghana in 2012 and 2013, the Chinese media reported that almost 50,000 Chinese nationals had migrated to Ghana for purposes of small-scale gold mining, mostly from Shanglin County in Guangxi Province, a traditional area of small-scale gold mining. Such high numbers are particularly striking given that small-scale gold mining in Ghana is restricted to Ghanaians by law (see Minerals and Mining Act 2006, Act 703, Section 83a) and therefore Chinese involvement in actual mining was illegal. However, it is important to understand the context of this involvement of Chinese migrants in illegal mining. Firstly, the majority of small-scale mining undertaken by Ghanaians is actually illegal, although very prevalent, the phenomenon of *galamsey*, where unregistered miners dig for gold. Chinese miners found ways to integrate themselves into the widespread illicit gold mining sector (Crawford & Botchwey, 2017; Hilson et al., 2014; Teschner, 2012). Secondly, Ghanaian state officials, politicians, and traditional authorities (chiefs) have long tolerated and benefited from illegal mining. For instance, politicians' election campaigns have been financed by "*galamsey* kingpins", with the implication that any attempt by the government to stop illegal mining is thereby compromised (Abdulai, 2017). Evidence suggests that Chinese miners were able to tap into this "culture of impunity" through the provision of bribes to officials, chiefs, politicians, and security personnel who then "looked the other way" concerning their mining activities (Botchwey et al., 2019, 12). However, the Chinese miners did not simply integrate themselves into the existing small-scale mining sector, rather they transformed it. They introduced capital, technology, and equipment into an informal sector that had hitherto used rudimentary methods. This led to the mechanisation and intensification of production, enabling much larger sums of money to be made, especially at a time when gold prices were historically high. However, such mechanisation also caused widespread environmental destruction. This led to a media outcry against illegal mining in general and, initially, against Chinese miners in particular. Ultimately this forced the government's hand, leading to a crackdown on the Chinese miners. These latter points are discussed in the impact section below.

As previously explained, apart from trading and small-scale mining, Chinese have historically worked in the construction sector. Most of the migrants in this sector are either highly skilled or low-skilled single men who have migrated to Ghana to work for Chinese firms involved in the construction of roads, buildings, hydropower plants, railroad, and telecommunications networks (Cook et al., 2016). The migration of these persons is directly linked to the Chinese government's financial support to Ghana. In most cases, loans given by the Chinese to the Government of Ghana come with contract agreements that require the engagement of the services of Chinese firms and expatriates (Sparreboom et al., 2018). Chinese involvement in the manufacturing sector has not attracted much attention but it is significant. Chinese employers are involved in the manufacture of a wide variety of goods, including medicines, clothing, cooking utensils, etc. (Teye et al., 2022). Their involvement in the accommodation and hospitality sector is also significant. There are a number of Chinese hotels and restaurants in Ghana (Sparreboom et al., 2018).

Impacts of Chinese Migration in Ghana

Economic Impacts

The Chinese presence in Ghana has positively contributed to economic transformation in some sectors. Chinese involvement has transformed small-scale gold mining in Ghana from a traditional and indigenous activity that had used rudimentary tools for centuries into a highly mechanised industry that can no longer be called artisanal and often is more medium-scale than small-scale. In particular, the Shanglin miners introduced specialist equipment from China—wash plants, crushing machines, and water platforms with mechanised suction equipment for river dredging—as well as the use of heavy machinery (such as excavators and bulldozers). Collaboration between Chinese and Ghanaian miners led to business relationships and processes of technology and skills transfer that resulted in Ghanaian miners adopting the same mechanised techniques. A common practice by licenced Ghanaian miners was to form a partnership with Chinese miners, to whom they (unlawfully) sub-let their concessions, taking between 10 and 15% of the value of the gold produced, while the Chinese who financed and undertook the mining activities took 85–90%. Ghanaian miners also benefited from the know-how of the Shanglin miners. After such agreements expired, the Ghanaian miners had gained the capital to continue with mechanised production without direct Chinese involvement. Mechanisation has significantly intensified production and areas of land are now mined in weeks that previously would have taken years using traditional methods (Crawford et al.,

2015). The intensification of gold production is reflected in the phenomenal increase in production from small-scale mining, increasing almost nine-fold from 2005 to 2018, and from 11% of total production to 41%.

The technology transfer discussed above is not limited to the gold mining sector. In the construction sector, Chinese construction companies have been bringing into Ghana heavy machinery to construct roads, dams, and bridges. The Ghanaians who work with the Chinese gain skills in managing the heavy equipment. The presence of Chinese migrants, in the trade sector, has also positively contributed to the transformation of the sector. A number of Ghanaian traders get their goods "on credit" from Chinese businesses (See Sparreboom et al., 2018). However, some Ghanaian businesses have been highlighting competition with Chinese traders as a challenge to business growth and their desire to make good profits.

Incomes and livelihoods have also improved substantially for those who work with the Chinese in the various sectors. Some of the local labourers who work with the Chinese earn substantial amounts of money. Small-scale mining has, for instance, become big business, at least for those Ghanaian and Chinese miners in ownership and financing roles. A Ghanaian miner collaborating with Chinese miners on his small-scale concession indicated that his 15% amounted to an income of 15,000 to 25,000 Ghanaian cedis per week (approximately USD $6,000 to USD $10,000 per week in 2013). However, the state benefits little: this is an informal sector, with no taxes on incomes paid by miners. One benefit to the state is through increasing sales of gold to the Precious Minerals Marketing Company (PMMC), the official government gold buying and exporting agency. It should be noted that individual chiefs, state officials, and politicians have also benefited through bribery and corruption, with such benefits being private and illicit (Crawford & Botchwey, 2017). Similarly, traders who have partnerships with the Chinese benefit from the higher profits.

Chinese entrepreneurs sometimes built up roads and schools for the community in order to create a more harmonious relationship with local communities, and sometimes they donated money or goods to local people, thus directly or indirectly helping local economic development. The wider local economy has also benefited, notably local women traders from whom migrant workers who buy vegetables, chickens, and other foodstuff for their daily consumption, thereby helping local families improve their livelihoods. This concurred with interviews conducted by Crawford and Botchwey with Ghanaian miners in 2014 in Dunkwa-on-Offin, a town that was a centre of Chinese mining in the mid-2010s, one of whom stated that "the town was hot, very busy" and local people "had money in their pockets" (Botchwey et al., 2019: 110). Similarly, research by Liu (2014), also undertaken in Dunkwa, revealed that local traders had been upset when the Chinese miners were forced to leave (see below), with the consequent decline in sales. However, MIDEQ research participants noted that in some communities the Chinese do not do much as far as social responsibility is concerned:

> The Chinese presence has benefitted this community marginally. They have created jobs for a few people, of which most of them are members of Amanfro, the nearby community. However, the Chinese have not engaged in any corporate social responsibility activities such as building of schools and clinics. They have not contributed any medical equipment to the clinic…. They have also not helped the community to get potable water. (GHGPRk01, a male key informant in a host community)
>
> Between the year 2010 and 2011, the Chinese bought for NM DA JHS [Junior High School] and Methodist JHS some computers, jerseys and footballs. But during the same period, they destroyed a lot of the water bodies in the community. … Generally speaking, apart from the employment the Chinese offered the people in this community, they haven't done much to better the lives of the people in the community. (Male focus group discussion, GHGPRFGD02)

The above statements show that while people in the study communities have benefitted from employment opportunities, there is a general belief that the Chinese migrants have not helped to provide social amenities.

Environmental Impacts

Many of the environmental impacts of the Chinese economic activities in Ghana are associated with gold mining. One negative consequence of mechanisation of production has been the intensification of environmental degradation, impacting both land and water resources. Extensive destruction of farmland occurred due to the scramble to acquire land for small-scale mining in the gold rush from 2008 onwards, especially by Chinese miners who came with capital to buy land, as highlighted during a male focus group discussion:

> The mining company has taken possession of all the lands in the community that were used for farming. They have also cut down all the shea nut trees in the town. So, we no longer get shea nut to extract the shea oil for sale to help in the development of the community. The sad thing is that, the owners of

the land that they took possession of are not even employed in the company. (GHGPRFGD13, male focus group discussion in host community)

Environmental and economic impacts are intermingled, with the loss of farmland affecting both cocoa production and food crop production, and having an adverse effect on both food security and the country's foreign currency earnings (Crawford & Botchwey, 2017, 12). The destruction of river systems has emerged as another serious form of environmental degradation, particularly through direct mining in rivers, despite such practices being illegal. As noted, Chinese miners introduced water platforms and suction equipment for river dredging, with Ghanaian miners then adopting this practice. As a result, rivers have become severely polluted, with high levels of water turbidity and loss of aquatic life. Additionally, drinking water has become increasingly contaminated, with increased cost of treatment to make such water potable (CSIR - Water Research Institute, 2013). A focus group participant in a mining community highlighted some of these challenges in the statement below:

> Their presence has affected us negatively because we normally dig gold but in bits. They are doing it in large quantities, destroying our water bodies….Prior to the arrival of the Chinese, our *galamsey* people mined the gold and took it home to wash it. However, the Chinese came to show us that excavators could be used to dig so deep and changfan machines to wash it in large quantity to enable them get more money (GHGPRk03, a female key informant in a mining host community in Ghana)

Such environmental destruction finally led the government to take action against illegal mining, with some targeting of Chinese miners, as discussed below.

Political and Security Impacts

Concern about the scale of environmental destruction associated with mechanised small-scale gold mining has led to considerable disquiet among the populace and media pressure that has forced the government to act. This has occurred on two occasions, both involving a militarised crackdowns, with the first focusing on "illegal Chinese miners". Initially in May 2013, President Mahama established an Inter-Ministerial Task Force aimed at "flushing out" illegal miners in a military-style operation. Although this was officially aimed at all illegal mining, the spotlight on Chinese miners was evident. The operation led to the deportation of 4,592 Chinese nationals, along with small numbers of other foreign nationals from Russia, Togo, and Niger (Modern Ghana, 12 July 2013), while many other foreign miners fled the country. It was notable that no Ghanaian miners were arrested despite their involvement in illegal mining, often in collaboration with Chinese miners. Subsequently, in April 2017, President Akufo-Addo declared a moratorium on all small-scale mining, enforced by a military taskforce (Operation Vanguard) from July 2017. Initially in place for six months, this moratorium was extended for 20 months until December 2018, when it was lifted but only for those registered miners who had successfully renewed their licences. By late January 2018, Operation Vanguard had resulted in the arrest of 983 miners, this time overwhelmingly Ghanaian, and only including 12 Chinese and four Burkinabé miners. There have also been clashes between Chinese miners and local youth in some communities. The local youth sometimes attack Chinese miners for destroying their lands.

Inequalities

The presence of the Chinese in Ghana has contributed to both a reduction in inequality as well as a widening of it. In the gold mining sector, the transformation in small-scale mining due to the techniques and equipment introduced by the Chinese miners has led to a huge increase in incomes for those at the top of the industry, but has also brought about a widening of inequalities, with stratification among Ghanaians involved in small-scale mining having significantly increased, inclusive of a gender dimension. Those miners that have accumulated capital (invariably males) have been able to substantially increase their incomes, and also to diversify their sources of income through investment in hotels, for instance. Yet with mechanisation replacing unskilled labour, many women, children and young people are now left to extract small remnants of gold by re-washing the gravels that remain in heaps of "tailings" at abandoned pits after intensive mining has been completed. Among Chinese miners, outcomes were varied, often influenced by class position in Shanglin. Again, those able to mobilise capital to invest in mining machinery and pay for travel tended to do much better than those that had to take on loans and incur debt (Botchwey et al., 2017: 315). The same situation was observed by the MIDEQ team in the trading sector. Ghanaian traders who have partnerships with the Chinese earn more income.

At the same time, there are reports of exploitation of Ghanaian employees by Chinese employers. In some cases, wages paid to Ghanaians are reportedly far lower than what is paid to Chinese at the same levels. There have also been reports of exploitation of the Ghanaians who "front" for the Chinese business entrepreneurs to register their businesses. The case of a 44-year-old male Ghanaian illustrates this level of exploitation. He was approached by a Chinese who wanted to set up a retail shop in 2016. MUGU's documents were used to register the shop "as the owner". Currently, MUGU works as a salesperson who is paid 1400 Cedis per month. He is scared that he would be sacked if he demands more benefits:

> In the Registrar General's office, I am the owner of the business. [But] in reality, I am just a sales boy for them. Even his nephew earns higher than me. He [the nephew] has a car but I don't even have a bicycle. I receive just 1400 [cedis] as salary… I am scared that if I ask for more salary, he will sack me and get another Ghanaian's documents to register (a 34 year old male Ghanaian)

The above scenario demonstrates exploitation within social networks. As Awumbila et al (2017) have noted, even in situations where individuals are cooperating for a common goal, exploitation may occur within networks due to unequal power relations.

Benefits of Migration to Chinese Migrants and Household Members Left Behind

Improved Incomes and Livelihoods

Except for few individuals, the majority of Chinese who migrated to Ghana reported improved incomes. In the trading sector, the migrants reported higher profitability and improved living conditions compared with working in China, as highlighted below by a Chinese in the trading sector:

> My living condition is better now than when I was in China due to my profitable business. I live in a two-bedroom house at Adenta; I have a car and a fiancée. Although I was not poor, I did not have some of these things when I was in China. I had my own business back in China but not as profitable as the new one in Ghana. I did not have a car in China and lived in a one-bedroom after the divorce. (GHGPm09, a middle aged Chinese young man from Beijing)

Chinese migrants engaged in small-scale gold mining particularly earn higher amounts than they would have earned in China. For the average employees in the mining sector, 100 thousand Yuan (CNY) per year is the basic level in addition to reimbursement of their costs on visas and travels. However, it is widely agreed that for those gold mining bosses, the income from gold mining is much more than 100 thousand Yuan (CNY) per year (approximately US$14,000), although it is quite difficult to know the exact amount they earn. Before migrating to Ghana, the miners were engaging in agricultural production, trucks for transport, small-scale factories, and so on. The economic benefits of all these livelihood activities cannot be compared with gold mining in Africa no matter whether he is an employee or a boss. And this is the strongest driver for many Chinese people to migrate to Ghana for small-scale gold mining. Traders in Ghana also reported that they earn more in Ghana than in China. This can be seen with their newly built houses, expensive brand cars, and expenditures on children's education in China.

Remittances and Local Development

The migration and economic activities of Chinese migrants generally benefit their left-behind family members and local communities with remittances including financial and social ones. Data from the MIDEQ survey in Ghana indicates that 65.6% of male and 49.1% of female Chinese migrants sent remittances to their relatives within the twelve months prior to the study. Financial remittances generally flow between Chinese groups through bank transfers and the remittances are generally used for the improvement of houses, children's education, and health care. Especially when the profit is quite high, the migrants will invest in housing in the rural areas, and even the big cities. Besides, social remittances also are observed in some areas of the counties where the migrants come from. One typical case is the "Gold Mining Garden", an investment by one returned gold miner in Shanglin County, which includes many African culture elements including sculptures, grass-roofed houses, photos of Ghanian attractions, etc. This has played a role in the dissemination of African cultures and enables more Chinese to learn and understand Africa.

While migration and remittances obviously contribute to local development through building of houses and acquisition of cars, they also have negative effects on some aspects of local development. Interviews in China revealed that migrating for gold mining in Africa has become a popular culture in the traditional mining communities and this quick way to make money has greatly shaped the youth's values and weakens their aspirations for any other industry investment. Thus migration to Africa for work in the gold mining sector, to some extent, is harmful for local entrepreneurship and industry development.

Inequalities in Areas of Origin

About 20 years ago, all of the households in the research sites in China were similar, with their livelihood activities being mainly related to agriculture production. There is evidence that gold mining opportunities in Ghana have deepened inequalities in the communities of origin at both the household and community levels. In the fieldwork, it was observed that not all of the migrants have brought earnings and wealth back to their families: The wealth and money brought home strongly depends on when the migrants entered Ghana and engaged in the gold mining activities. Early migrants could access high-quality mines with more possibilities while the later ones, especially those who went to Ghana after 2012, actually lost more than they earned. In the three years since the start of the COVID-19 pandemic, the situation has become worse for some migrants. Some interviewees in the left-behind families responded that their husbands/sons are afraid of coming back to China because they borrowed a lot of money which they could not pay because of the economic challenges associated with COVID-19. Some traders also reported similar inequalities. In some cases, the pioneer migrants made huge profits but those they helped to migrate in recent years do not have the same profits. Thus while the literature often discusses inequalities between migrant households that receive remittances and households that do not receive any remittances (Bragg et al., 2017; Pickbourn, 2016), we have seen that there are inequalities among different families depending on migration status and the time-period that the migrant travelled to Ghana.

Psychological and Health Impacts

While financial remittance and benefits are given more attention in the literature (Bajra, 2021) than health and psychological impacts of migration, some returned migrants mentioned that it could be frightening to work in the gold mines, especially when they experienced robbery and other attacks. A few returned migrants said they even have experienced an exchange of gunfire with those robbers which brought long-term psychological impact on their current life. Finally, some returned migrants told us that Chinese migrants whose visas expired were sometimes captured by policemen and detained in dark rooms until some local prominent people or Chinese friends came to bail them. One respondent said that as a result of these incidents, he has been having nightmares and will therefore never go back to any African country.

Malaria is also an inevitable challenge for all Chinese migrants in Ghana. Nearly all the returned migrants we interviewed have been affected by malaria, with some of their fellow villagers having died due to malaria. Another health risk for the Chinese migrants is HIV which is high due to sexual promiscuity among the miners. In some villages, more than 10 migrants have been infected with HIV which also brings the risk to their wives.

Conclusion

Chinese migration to Ghana has increased considerably in recent decades, and this chapter focuses on the drivers and impact of such migration in Ghana, with particular reference to the trading and small-scale mining sectors. Relying on Van Hear's (2012) conceptualisation of the drivers of migration, we have demonstrated that migration flows from China to Ghana are driven by an interaction of underlying, precipitating, proximate, and mediating factors. With regard to underlying factors, structural inequalities between the two countries provide a context for the flow of Chinese government financial grants with conditionalities which facilitate the migration of skilled and unskilled migrants to Ghana. Precipitating and proximate drivers include high costs of living in China and limited opportunities for upward social and economic mobility. As argued elsewhere (see Wang, 2022), high profit margins, especially in the small-scale gold mining and trade sectors, attract Chinese migrants to Ghana because these factors provide opportunities for social mobility.

The migration of Chinese people to Ghana has both positive and negative impacts. In the mining sector, Chinese migrants have introduced new equipment and techniques which has led to a transformation of small-scale mining into a mechanised and intensive operation. Positively, incomes and livelihoods of both Ghanaian and Chinese miners have improved with the overall increase in efficiency of production, and there has been a spill-over effect into the wider local economy that serves the small-scale miners. However, financial rewards from intensified production have benefited some more than others, with increased income inequalities along social class lines, largely determined by ownership of capital. There has also been a gender dimension to such increased inequalities, with poor women's situation in the sector worsening as they become marginalised or excluded by mechanised production. Such differential economic benefits were also very evident among the Shanglin miners, with the fortunes of some contrasted with the debt bondage of others. Negative impacts include greater environmental degradation of both water bodies and land, including the loss of agricultural land for the production of both food and cash crops. Such pollution also brings with it a cost to the state in reclaiming land and cleaning-up water sources, while tax incomes from small-scale gold production remain limited and often evaded. An additional negative impact is on the legitimacy of the state in the eyes of its citizens, given the evidence of state collusion in unlawful activities and its hypocrisy in undertaking a military-style crackdown in a selective manner. Similarly, in the trade and manufacturing sectors, Ghanaians that are in partnership with Chinese entrepreneurs benefit in terms of employment and higher incomes. However, there have been cases of exploitation of some Ghanaians by Chinese migrants. While migrants and their families left behind benefit through improved incomes and remittances, migration and associated financial flows contribute to a deepening of inequalities in migrants' sending areas. Migration and working in illegal mines in Ghana are also associated with a number of psychological and health problems that continue to affect returned migrants.

Acknowledgements This work has been undertaken as part of the Migration for Development and Equality (MIDEQ) Hub. Funded by the UKRI Global Challenges Research Fund (GCRF) (Grant Reference: ES/S007415/1), MIDEQ unpacks the complex and multi-dimensional relationships between migration and inequality in the context of the Global South. More at www.mideq.org

References

Abid, R. Z., Manan, S. A., & Amir, Z. A. (2013). 'Those nation wreckers are suffering from inferiority complex': The depiction of Chinese miners in the Ghanaian press. *International Journal of Society, Culture and Language, 1*(2), 34–49.

Abdulai, A. G. (2017). The galamsey menace in Ghana: A political problem requiring political solutions? *Policy Brief, 5,* June. University of Ghana Business School.

Ajakaiye, O., & Kaplinsky, R. (2009). China in Africa: A relationship in transition. *European Journal of Development Research, 21*(4), 479–484. https://doi.org/10.1057/ejdr.2009.3

Aryee, E. T. K. (2015). *International migration: An evaluation of irregular Chinese migrants in contemporary Ghana.* Doctoral dissertation, Thesis, University of Ghana.

Awumbila, M., Teye, J. K., & Yaro, J. A. (2017). Social networks, migration trajectories and livelihood strategies of migrant domestic and construction workers in Accra, Ghana. *Journal of African and Asian Studies, 52*(7), 982–996.

Bajra, U. Q. (2021). The interactive effects of remittances on economic growth and inequality in western Balkan countries. *Journal of Business Economics and Management, 22*(3), 757–775.

Botchwey, G., Crawford, G., Loubere N., and Lu, J. (2019). South-South irregular migration: The impacts of China's informal gold rush in Ghana, *International Migration*, 57 (4), 310–328. https://doi.org/10.1111/imig.12518

Bragg, C., Gibson, G., King, H., Lefler, A. A., & Ntoubandi, F. (2017). Remittances as aid following major sudden-onset natural disasters. *Disasters, 42*(1), 3–18.

Brautigam, D. (2009). *The Dragon's gift: The real story of China in Africa.* Oxford University Press.

Broadman, H.G. (2007). *Africa's silk road: China and India's new economic frontier.* World Bank.

Cardenal, J. P., & Araujo, H. (2014). *China's silent army: The pioneers, traders, fixers and workers who are remaking the world in Beijing's image.* Penguin.

Cook, S., Lu, J. X., Tugendhat, H., & Alemu, D. (2016). Chinese migrants in Africa: Facts and fictions from the agri-food sector in Ethiopia and Ghana. *World Development, 81,* 61–70.

Crawford, G., Agyeyomah, C., Botchwey, G., & Mba, A. (2015). *The impact of Chinese involvement in small-scale gold mining in Ghana. Research Report.* International Growth Centre, London School of Economics. https://www.theigc.org/project/the-impact-of-chinese-involvement-in-small-scale-gold-mining-in-ghana/#outputs

Crawford, G., & Botchwey, G. (2017). Conflict, collusion and corruption in small-scale gold mining: Chinese miners and the State in Ghana'. *Commonwealth and Comparative Politics,* 55(4), 444–470. https://doi.org/10.1080/14662043.2017.1283479

Council for Scientific and Industrial Research (CSIR)—Water Research Institute. (2013). Impact of small-scale mining on the water resources of the Pra River basin. CSIR.

Harris, K.L. (2013) The Chinese in South Africa: Five centuries, five trajectories. In Chee-Beng Tan (Ed.) *Routledge Handbook of the Chinese Diaspora* (pp.176–190). Routledge.

Hilson, G., Hilson, A., & Adu-Darko, E. (2014). Chinese participation in Ghana's informal gold mining economy: Drivers, implications and clarifications. *Journal of Rural Studies, 34,* 292–303.

Li, A. S. (2012). *A history of overseas Chinese in Africa to 1911.* Diasporic Africa Press.

Liu, S. N. (2014). Ghanaians. *Perception of Chinese migrants in Ghana.* Unpublished mimeo.

Massey, D. S., Arango, J., Hugo, G., Kuoaouci, A., Pellegrino, A., & Taylor, J. E. (1993). Theories of international migration: A review and appraisal. *Population and Development Review, 19*(3), 431–466.

Merli, M. G., Verdery, A., Mouw, T., & Li, J. (2016). Sampling migrants from their social networks: The demography and social organization of Chinese migrants in Dar es Salaam, Tanzania. *Migration Studies, 4*(2), 182–214.

Mohan, G., Lampert, B., Tan-Mullins, M., & Chang, D. (2014). *Chinese migrants and Africa's development. New imperialists or agents of change?* Zed Books.

Mohan, G., & Tan-Mullins, M. (2009). Chinese migrants in Africa as new agents of development? An analytical framework. *European Journal of Development Research, 21*(4), 588–605. https://doi.org/10.1057/ejdr.2009.22

Morawska, E. (2012). Historical-structural models of international migration. In Martiniello, M. and J. Rath (Eds.), *An introduction to international migration studies: European perspectives* (pp.176–190). Amsterdam University Press.

Pickbourn, L. (2016). Remittances and household expenditures on education in Ghana's northern region: Why gender matters. *Feminist Economics, 22*(3), 74–100.

Sautman, B., & Yan, H. R. (2007). Friends and interests: China's distinctive links with Africa'. *African Studies Review, 50*(3), 75–114.

Snow, P. (1988). *The star raft: China's encounter with Africa.* Weidenfeld and Nicolson.

Sparreboom, T., Badasu, D. B., Teye, J. K., Kandilige, L. and Setrana, M.B. (2018). Immigration and economic growth in Ghana. In OECD/ILO *How immigrants contribute to Ghana's economy* (pp.176–190). OECD Publishing. https://doi.org/10.1787/9789264302037-en.

Taylor, I. (2006). *China and Africa: Engagement and compromise.* Routledge.

Teschner, B. A. (2012). Small-scale mining in ghana: The government and the galamsey. *Resources Policy, 37*(3), 308–314.

Teye, J. K., Awumbila, M., and Benneh, Y. (2015). Intra-regional migration in the ECOWAS region: trends and emerging challenges. In Akoutou, A., B., Sohn, R., Vogl, M. and D. Yeboah (Eds.), *Migration and civil society as development drivers—A Regional perspective* (pp.176–190). Zei Centre for European Integration Studies.

Teye, J. K., Kandilige, L., Setrana, M. B., & Yaro, J. A. (2022). Chinese migration to Ghana: Challenging the orthodoxy on characterizing migrants and reasons for migration. *Ghana Journal of Geography, 14*(2), 203–234.

Tschakert, P. (2016). Shifting discourses of vilification and the taming of unruly mining landscapes in Ghana. *World Development, 86*, 123–132.

Van Hear, N. (2012). Forcing the issue: Migration crises and the uneasy dialogue between refugee research and policy. *Journal of Refugee Studies, 25*(1), 2–24.

Wang, J. (2022, April 7). What drives Chinese migrants to Ghana: it's not just an economic decision. *The Conversation.* https://theconversation.com/what-drives-chinese-migrants-to-ghana-its-not-just-an-economic-decision-177580

Wang, F. L., & Elliot, E. A. (2014). China in Africa: Presence, perceptions and prospects. *Journal of Contemporary China, 23*(90), 1012–1032.

Wallerstein, I. (1974). *The modern world-system I: Capitalist agriculture and the origins of the European world-economy in the sixteenth century.* Academic Press.

Xiang, B., & Lindquist, J. (2014). Migration infrastructure. *International Migration Review, 48*(s1), S122–S148.

Zurek, K. (2018). Ghana has the highest number of African students in China. https://www.graphic.com.gh/news/general-news/ghana-has-the-highest-number-of-african-students-inchinaenvoy.html

Open Access This chapter is licensed under the terms of the Creative Commons Attribution 4.0 International License (http://creativecommons.org/licenses/by/4.0/), which permits use, sharing, adaptation, distribution and reproduction in any medium or format, as long as you give appropriate credit to the original author(s) and the source, provide a link to the Creative Commons license and indicate if changes were made.

The images or other third party material in this chapter are included in the chapter's Creative Commons license, unless indicated otherwise in a credit line to the material. If material is not included in the chapter's Creative Commons license and your intended use is not permitted by statutory regulation or exceeds the permitted use, you will need to obtain permission directly from the copyright holder.

16

Inter-regional Migration in the Global South: African Migration to Latin America

Luisa Feline Freier, Leon Lucar Oba, and María Angélica Fernández Bautista

Introduction

In April 2018, a rather unbelievable migratory journey caught the attention of international media when a Brazilian fishing boat rescued a group of twenty-five men from West Africa, who risked their lives crossing the Atlantic in a dilapidated catamaran from Cape Verde to Brazil.[1] Their survival was close to miraculous: their engine failed, their mast broke, and they had to resort to fishing and drinking their own urine to survive. Finally, they were rescued after spending thirty-one days at sea. The ordeal these men went through illustrates the extreme risks some African migrants are willing to take in the pursuit of a better life (Parent et al., 2021).

---

[1] See https://www.theguardian.com/world/2018/may/22/african-migrant-brazil-boat-rescue-atlantic-crossing

---

L. F. Freier (✉)
Political Science and International Development Research Centre (IDRC), Universidad del Pacífico, Lima, Peru
e-mail: lf.freierd@up.edu.pe

L. Lucar Oba
Pontificia Universidad Católica del Perú, Lima, Peru

M. A. Fernández Bautista
Pontificia Universidad Católica del Perú, Lima, Peru

© The Author(s) 2024
H. Crawley and J. K. Teye (eds.), *The Palgrave Handbook of South–South Migration and Inequality*, https://doi.org/10.1007/978-3-031-39814-8_16

While images of African nationals trying to reach Europe dominate popular perceptions and media coverage, African migrants are also taking longer and riskier journeys in the search of new destinations and improved opportunities (Yates & Bolter, 2021), including China (Bork-Hüffer et al. 2014; Mulvey, 2021), Israel (Orr & Ajzenstadt, 2020), and Latin America (Cinta Cruz, 2020; IOM, 2015).[2] Latin America-bound African migrants have profited, in many cases, from both relatively liberal immigration policies and border porosity, moving with the intention of settlement and transmigration towards North America (Baeninger et al., 2019; Freier & Holloway, 2019).

Although African migration to Latin America plays a relatively small role in absolute numbers, it has significantly increased in the past decade. Consequently, the corresponding literature has significantly gained momentum, yet it remains little noticed in mainstream migration studies, partly because it is predominantly written in Spanish. At least four factors make African migration to Latin America especially worth academic analysis: first, its stark increase; second, its relatively new and pioneer character; third, the vast geographical and cultural distances travelled; and fourth, the diversity of migrants characteristics, aspirations, and capabilities (see De Haas, 2021). The questions that the literature has raised include why African migrants choose Latin American host or transit countries, and how they are received in both political and sociocultural terms.

In this chapter we seek to showcase what has been discovered and also what remains unknown regarding these questions, based on the secondary literature and empirical population data. In the first section, we provide a review of the existing literature. The second section offers an empirical exploration of the patterns of African asylum seekers and refugees in Latin America based on UNHCR data, as well as Mexican apprehension data. In the third section, we discuss the socio-political reception of African migrants in three main receiving countries: Argentina, Brazil, and Mexico. We then conclude by the highlighting main takeaways and avenues for further research.

---

[2] Of course, most African international migrants continue to move within their own region (Flahaux and De Haas, 2016).

Latin America as a New Destination of African Migrants

Africa has long been seen as a "continent on the move" based on three partial misconceptions: first, African migration has been seen as high and increasing; second, as almost exclusively directed towards Europe; and third as predominantly driven by poverty, violence, and environmental crises factors (Flahaux & De Haas, 2016; Setrena & Yaro, this volume). Although some of these assumptions go back to journalistic observations and biases rather than empirical evidence, the migration literature has long built on them, developing push–pull explanatory models that point to African migration as a South–North dynamic driven by poverty and income gaps, especially vis-a-vis Europe, underpinning the idea of the failure of development in African countries (Bakewell, 2008; Collier, 2013; De Haas, 2007).

According to the IOM, in 2020 around 21 million Africans were living in another African country, a significant increase from 2015, when around 18 million Africans were estimated to be living within the region. The number of Africans living outside of Africa, also grew during the same period, but less, from around 17 million in 2015 to over 19.5 million in 2020, with 11 million (56.4%) residing in Europe, and 5 million (25.6%) and 3 million (15.4%) living in Asia and North America, respectively.[3] In global comparison, of the 281 million international migrants in 2020, 14.4% were African migrants. This constitutes an increase of only 0.3% in five years, from 14.1% in 2015.[4]

In the past twenty years, the field of African migration studies has grown, addressing this increasing diversity of African migration that is far from exclusively directed to Europe, but mainly to other African countries (Beauchemin et al., 2015; Sander & Maimbo, 2003), and also to other regions such as the Gulf countries and the Americas (Bakewell & De Haas, 2007), including Latin America (Freier, 2011; Freier & Holloway, 2019; Yates & Bolter, 2021). There is a growing refutation of classical "push–pull" models that focus on migrants as passive objects that are pushed by external factors such as poverty, demographic pressure, violent conflict, or environmental degradation. Indeed, just as other migrants, Africans migrate for a variety of reasons, such as family, work, educational reasons, and other personal aspirations (Bakewell & Jónsson, 2011; Beauchemin et al., 2015; Feyissa et al., this volume).

---

[3] See https://publications.iom.int/system/files/pdf/WMR-2022.pdf.
[4] https://www.iss.europa.eu/sites/default/files/EUISSFiles/Brief_8_Imagine%20Africa%204.pdf.

Contradicting the mainstream assumption that African migration is somewhat "exceptional" in that it is mainly driven by myriad "crises", De Haas and co-authors have stressed that people only migrate if they have the ambition and resources—or aspirations and capabilities—to do so, thus focusing on the agency of migrants (Castelli, 2018; De Haas, 2011, 2014, 2021; Flahaux & De Haas, 2016). From this, it follows that "development", and not the absence of it, is a main driver of migration, as aspirations and capabilities to migrate tend to increase progressively as countries grow richer (De Haas, 2011, 2014; Flahaux & De Haas, 2016). Although poor people also migrate, they tend to do so less frequently and over shorter distances; while the more skilled and relatively wealthy are more likely to turn into long-distance international migrants (Flahaux & De Haas, 2016; McKenzie, 2017).

Against this backdrop, the literature on African migration to Latin America significantly increased in recent years, ranging from earlier policy reports (IOM, 2015) to a number of special issues (Requene, 2021), covering a range of topics from the drivers of migration and choice of destination to sociopolitical reception and integration. In Argentina and Brazil, some African migrants have successfully integrated locally through—often informal—commercial activities (Kleidermacher, 2013; Wabgou, 2016; Zubrzycki, 2019), while intersectional discrimination is a continuous challenge for African migrants across the continent (see also de Souza e Silva et al., this volume on the experience of Haitians in Brazil).

The receiving countries of African migration that have been most studied include Argentina, with migrants coming mostly from Senegal, Nigeria, Sierra Leone, Congo, and Angola (Maffia, 2014); Brazil, with migrants coming mostly from Senegal, Eritrea, Somalia, the Democratic Republic of the Congo, Cameroon, and Ghana (Álvarez Velasco, 2016; JRS, 2023; OIM, 2012; Yates & Bolter, 2021); and Mexico, with migrants coming mostly from Eritrea, Somalia, the Democratic Republic of the Congo, Cameroon, and Ghana (Ray & Leyva, 2020).

African transmigrants to the United States tend to pass through many Latin American countries such as Brazil, Argentina, Bolivia, Peru, Ecuador, and Colombia (Cinta Cruz, 2020; Kyle & Ling, 2001). These journeys imply many (irregular) border crossings, and extensive treks through the deadly Darien jungle, in the border area between Colombia and Panama, which serves as the gateway for both intra- and extra-regional migrants to Central America and from there to the United States and Canada (Amahazion, 2021; Miraglia, 2016).

In this context, for many authors, a key concern is the increased securitisation of the US–Mexican border, which has resulted in policies that restrict the entry and lead to the detention of African migrants—such as the case of the detention of thousands of African migrants in the "Siglo XXI" migrant detention centre in Tapachula (Requene, 2021). The risks of these journeys include the lack of legal protection, exposure to human trafficking, the threat of deportation, and the ill-treatment African migrants receive from authorities in both the United States and Mexico, where instances of discrimination and mistreatment are widespread (Gibney, 2021; Mercada, 2021; Requene, 2021; Winters & Mora Izaguirre, 2019).

Regarding the determinants of African migration to Latin America, these have been seen in the liberalisation of Latin American migration policies in contrast to the North America and Europe, including the relaxation of entry visa regimes, and relatively stable economic development in the aftermath of the 2008 financial crisis (Freier, 2011; Freier & Holloway, 2019; Maffia, 2010; Zubrzycki & Agnelli, 2009). Here Ecuador's extreme policy of "open doors"—the abolishment of all visa requirements for all nationals in 2008 (which was soon partially reversed) has received special attention (Freier & Holloway, 2019; Álvarez Velasco, 2020; Sector, 2016). Aspirations and capabilities of African migrants in Latin America, of course, are diverse. In the Ecuadorian case, Freier and Holloway (2019) show how socio-economic and educational background vary across different groups of African migrants who chose Ecuador as a visa-free safe haven fleeing persecution, for the sake of settlement (based on relatively improved opportunities), or as a gateway for transmigration to North America.

Despite their legislative liberalisation, in practice, Latin American host countries are ill equipped for the integration of African migrants, partly because African immigrants were long considered transit migrants (Álvarez Velasco, 2016; FLACSO, 2011; GS/OAS, IOM, 2016; Yates & Bolter, 2021). In this sense, policy implementation faces major challenges due to legislative loopholes and bureaucratic deficiencies that end up creating difficulties for migrants to regularise their status (Acosta & Freier, 2015; Castles, 2004a, 2004b; Lahav & Guiraudon, 2006). At the same time, Latin American governments struggle to provide adequate humanitarian protection and services to those in need (Langberg, 2005; Moncayo & Silveira, 2017; Yates & Bolter, 2021). Such difficulties also arise in the context of considerable asylum procedure drop-out rates, as both migrants and refugees seek asylum to regularise their stay, often only being in transit.[5]

---

[5] This scenario is different in the Caribbean where asylum seekers tend to stay for several years waiting for a permanent resolution (Cinta Cruz, 2020).

African migrants in Latin America often find themselves in situations of vulnerability, due to linguistic and informational barriers regarding migration rules in the region (Pavez-Soto et al., 2019), the dangers involved in transregional travel (CEPAL, 2021), the presence of structural racism and other forms of discrimination in the host countries (Espiro, 2019). The literature has paid special attention to realities such as discrimination (Espiro et al., 2016); education (Pavez-Soto et al., 2019); religious practices (Henao, 2009; Parent et al., 2021);poverty and its links with the socio-economic crisis, gender, and evolving social, economic, and political processes, among other aspects (Wabgou, 2016).

As in other regions, "race" is an indispensable analytical category for the study of African migration and socio-economic integration in Latin America (see also de Souza e Silva et al., this volume). Its reception has to be understood in terms of the socio-psychological heritage of slavery and structural racism, for example in Brazil where race still operates as a "hierarchical criterion in various legal norms on migration, nationality and citizenship" (de Souza Silva & Borba de Sá, 2021; de Souza Silva et al., this volume). Racist representations of African migrants perpetuate dynamics of racialisation and segregation and are linked to confinement in immigration detention centres and surveillance by the countries migrants are trying to cross or reach (Requene, 2021). At the same time, discrimination is intersectional with pregnant African migrants facing special stigmatisation (Muñoz et al., 2021; Wabgou, 2016).

Research has also shown that, while migrants often face discrimination and vulnerability, they can also demonstrate resilience in the face of such challenges. This resilience can manifest in various ways, such as through civic activism and empowerment, which tends to increase with legal status (Espiro et al., 2016; Freier & Zubrzycki, 2019). In addition, studies have explored the religious coping strategies of migrants, such as those who risked their lives crossing the Atlantic in a dilapidated catamaran from Cape Verde to Brazil (Parent et al., 2021). Understanding the resilience and coping strategies of migrants can help policymakers and practitioners support their well-being and integration into their new communities.

Mapping African Migration to Latin America

In order to map the trends in African migration flows to Latin America,[6] in the following section we discuss UNHCR data on African asylum seekers and refugees, as well as apprehension data on African nationals in Mexico. Although the numbers of asylum seekers do not allow us to measure the overall numbers of migrants and refugees moving towards and through the region, they likely mirror trends in African migration, in terms of both origin and destination countries, as both Africans in need of international protection and economic migrants tend to file asylum claims as a way of migratory regularising (IOM, 2015). The numbers of refugees, on the other hand, indicate which nationalities are granted protection, and consequently are likely to form communities. Finally, data on apprehended migrants at the US–Mexican border indicate which nationalities tend to transmigrate towards North America.

Figure 16.1 shows the stark increase of African asylum seekers in the past ten years, from 1,840 in 2012 to 38,459 in 2022. In 2015, African asylum seekers represented more than 30% of all pending asylum claims in the region, which led to significant political concerns (Freier, 2011). However, with the intensification of the Venezuelan displacement crises since 2015, and 6 million displaced and over 700,000 asylum seekers in the region by 2023 (R4V, 2023), the percentage and political salience of Sub-Saharan African asylum claimants in the region subsided, even though numbers of pending African asylum claims are at a historic high (Fig. 16.2).

According to UNHCR figures as of 2022, most African asylum seekers in Latin America come from West and Central Africa. The countries of origin with the highest number of asylum seekers are Senegal, Angola, Nigeria, Ghana, and the Democratic Republic of Congo (see Table 16.1). Regarding refugees, Southern Africa sends the largest number of refugees to Latin America, with the Democratic Republic of Congo and Angola standing out, followed by countries in the West and Central Africa region (see Table 16.1). In terms of both sending and receiving countries, the main flows of asylum seekers are: Senegalese, Nigerians, Ghanians, Bissau-Guineans, Angolans, and Congolese in Brazil; Senegalese in Argentina; and Senegalese and Angolans in Mexico (in both cases with a significant increase in 2022).

---

[6] For the purposes of this study, we consider Latin America as the region made up of the following countries: Argentina, Bolivia (Plurinational State of), Brazil, Chile, Colombia, Costa Rica, Cuba, Dominican Republic, Ecuador, El Salvador, Guatemala, Haiti, Honduras, Mexico, Nicaragua, Panama, Paraguay, Peru, Uruguay, and Venezuela (Bolivarian Republic of).

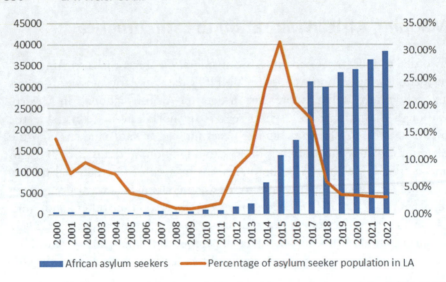

Fig. 16.1 African asylum seeker population in Latin American countries (2000–2022)

In terms of protection granted, we see a small but steady increase from 2015, with overall numbers nevertheless remaining extremely low. The number of African refugees in Latin America increased from 4128 in 2012 to 5948 in 2022. In terms of the percentage of African refugees in the region, it dropped from a high of 12% in 2004 to 2% in 2022. The main host countries of both African asylum seekers and refugees in Latin America are Argentina, Brazil, and Mexico, with Brazil standing out with a high number of asylum seekers from West and Central Africa and refugees from Southern Africa (see Table 16.2). In 2022, Brazil hosted 78,4% of the total number of African refugees in Latin America (Fig. 16.3).

Another way to measure migration flows from Africa to Latin America is by looking at the number of apprehensions of Africans in Mexico. Although in absolute terms the number of African migrants in Latin America remains low compared to citizens of other regions—especially in comparison with South American transmigration—the increase of African migration to and through the region is undeniable. As Yates and Bolter point out (2021), in fiscal year 2019, Mexico made nine times as many (800%) more detentions of African migrants than in 2014, while in Europe the number of arrests decreased by half for the same period. In the case of the number of African asylum seekers in Latin America, 2022 marks an increase of more than 8000% over the number of asylum seekers in 2000 (83 times as many).

According to official Mexican migration statistics, in the last 15 years, the number of detentions of African migrants varied with an upward trend until 2019, when it reached a peak of 7.065 irregular African migrants detained,

Fig. 16.2 African asylum seeker population in Latin American countries (2022)

which represented 3,9% of the total number of irregular migrants presented to Mexican migration authorities. Despite the sharp drop in the number of apprehensions of Africans in 2020 due to the outbreak of the COVID-19 pandemic, in 2022 the number of African apprehended had again increased to 5437, suggesting an increasing trend in the number of African migrants attempting to reach the United States via Mexico. Looking at the main nationalities of African migrants detained, in 2019, Cameroon led with 3124 detentions, followed by the Democratic Republic of Congo with 1822 detentions. In 2022, the top-5 nationalities detained in Mexico were Senegalese (939), Cameroonians (649), Angolans (599), Ghanaians (563), and Somalis (537) (Figs. 16.4 and 16.5).

Table 16.1 Major African countries of origin of asylum seekers and refugees in Latin America, 2022

Major African countries of origin of asylum seekers and refugees in Latin America

Asylum seekers		Refugees	
Country	Number of asylum seekers in 2022	Country	Number of refugees in 2022
Senegal	9155	Democratic Republic of the Congo	1835
Angola	7591	Angola	1219
Nigeria	3635	Nigeria	375
Ghana	3306	Liberia	326
Democratic Republic of the Congo	3267	Sierra Leone	236
Guinea-Bissau	1580	Cameroon	203
Cameroon	1215	Guinea	180
Guinea	1105	Mali	166
Morocco	850	Ghana	145
Somalia	702	Burkina Faso	113
Togo	687	Sudan	109
Egypt	506	Somalia	94

Table 16.2 Main host countries for African asylum seekers and refugees in Latin America

Main host countries for African asylum seekers and refugees in Latin America

Asylum seekers		Refugees	
Country of asylum	Number of asylum seekers in 2022	Country of asylum	Number of refugees in 2022
Brazil	29,974	Brazil	4665
Mexico	5653	Mexico	385
Argentina	1830	Argentina	365
Uruguay	341	Ecuador	170
Costa Rica	328	Peru	67

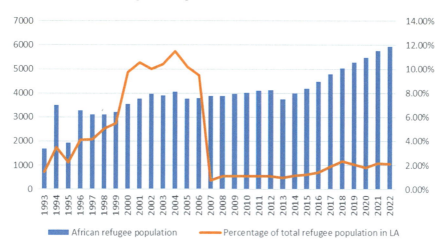

Fig. 16.3 Total African refugee population in Latin American countries (1993–2022)

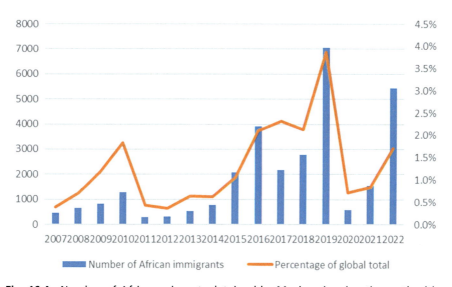

Fig. 16.4 Number of African migrants detained by Mexican immigration authorities (2007–2022)

Socio-political Reception and Integration of African Migrants

In the following section, we will describe the dynamics of the socio-political reception and integration of African migration in three of the most important host countries, namely Argentina, Brazil, and Mexico, embedded in their political and socio-psychological context. The process of discursive and legal

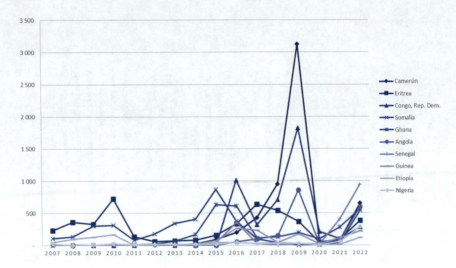

Fig. 16.5 Top-10 irregular African migrant nationalities presented before Mexican immigration authorities

immigration policy liberalisation in Latin America that scholars identified as one of the determinants of African migration to the region, began at the turn of the century and was a response to the restrictive migration policies implemented by the United States and European Union (EU). This liberalisation led to the *de jure* protection of migrants' rights, in terms of regularisation and decriminalisation of irregular migration (Acosta & Freier, 2015; Caicedo Camacho et al., 2020; Cantor et al., 2015; Melde & Freier, 2022).

Ironically, the literature has pointed out lacking policy implementation and loopholes precisely when it comes to extra-regional and phenotypically diverse, such as African migrants (Finn & de Reguero, 2020; Freier & Castillo Jara, 2021; Santi Pereyra, 2018; Stang, 2016). The stigmatising and criminalising of migrants and refugees in Latin America flourished in the context of the massive displacement of Venezuelan and Central American citizens in recent years (Vera Espinoza et al., 2020).

In socio-psychological terms, it has been pointed out that there are profound historical and structural conditions that impact the reception and socio-economic integration of migrants in Latin America. Here, socio-racial hierarchies are the fluid and context-dependent ranking of individuals and groups, based on their perceived physical and socio-economic characteristics, within a broader system of socio-racial relations in which ethno-racial groups occupy different levels of political, economic, and cultural power (Freier & Bird, 2020; Freier & Lucar Oba, 2023). In some countries, such as Brazil, there is evidence of continuing explicit discrimination and racism towards Afro-descended and indigenous peoples, despite national consciousness construction as "mestizo nations" (Beck et al., 2011; Telles, 2014; de Souze e Silva et al., this volume). In others, such as Argentina, racism has come to show in immigration policy-making practices by prioritising white European immigration and rendering Afro-descendants invisible (Frigerio, 2008).

Argentina

Mirroring the broader regional trend, Argentina has witnessed a gradual growth in the number of asylum seekers from the West and Central Africa region, with Senegalese asylum seekers standing out, especially since 2015. In 2022, UNHCR registered 1.801 African asylum seekers in Argentina, of which 1.386 were Senegalese representing 76.9% of the total number of applicants from Africa in Argentina and 3.6% of all African asylum seekers in Latin America. The majority of Senegalese in Argentina are not formally registered, and the 2010 census only recorded 459 Senegalese nationals, although estimates suggest that the Senegalese community in Argentina was made up of between 2000 and 10,000 people (Cybel, 2018), compared to a total of 1.8 million of foreigners residing in the country in 2010.

Argentina has been a pioneer in immigration policy liberalisation. Its 2004 migration law guarantees all migrants (including irregular migrants) socio-economic rights, such as education, healthcare, and the right to claim unpaid wages, and facilitates migrant regularisation (Melde & Freier, 2022). Its 2006 Refugee Law is the most progressive in the region, and thus likely in the world (Cantor et al., 2015). Despite this, there are practical barriers to regularisation and protection for certain groups of migrants, including African migrants, who entered the country irregularly (Acosta & Freier, 2015; Freier & Zubrzycki, 2019). It is noteworthy that the small yet relatively substantial increase in Senegalese immigration and asylum applications since the early 2000s led to concerns among the Argentine authorities about the "exploitation" of its asylum system (Freier, 2011).

Argentina's socio-racial hierarchy is reflected in the symbolic erasure of Black individuals from society and the growing prevalence of whiteness in the population (at least in the capital Buenos Aires), especially throughout much of the twentieth century (Freier & Lucar Oba, 2023; Frigerio, 2008). During the Argentine nation-building-process in the late nineteenth century, successive governments strove to make ethnic and "racial" diversity invisible (Zubrzycki, 2019), for which they encouraged large-scale European immigration, often based on openly racist motivations (Bastia & Vom Hau, 2014).

These migration policies led to the creation of a national myth according to which "there are no blacks in Argentina" (Cullenward, 2009), with the consequent assumption that "there is no racism" in Argentina (García, 2009).

Against this background, 97.2% of Argentines self-identify as European (mostly Italian and Spanish descendants) (INDEC, 2010). The growing presence of migrants from sub-Saharan Africa in the Argentine cities has led to their exoticisation based on stereotypes and attention paid to their physical and body traits (Freier & Zubrzycki, 2019; Morales, 2010; Zubrzycki, 2019). Although especially Senegalese migrants have integrated locally through, often informal, commercial activities (Kleidermacher, 2013; Zubrzycki, 2019), and with the support of ethnic networks and brotherhoods (Kleidermacher & Murguía-Cruz, 2021), discrimination and police violence directed against immigrants of colour persist (Freier & Zubrzycki, 2019).

Brazil

Brazil is the Latin American country that hosts the largest number of African asylum seekers and refugees −29.974 and 4.665, respectively. This means that Brazil receives 77.9% of asylum applications from Africans in Latin America, and hosts 78.4% of African refugees in the region. According to UNHCR data, most asylum seekers come from West and Central Africa (17.519 in 2022). The main sending countries of asylum seekers are Senegal (6.256), Nigeria (3.276), Ghana (2.462), Guinea-Bissau (1.556), Togo (572), and Cameroon (566); followed by Southern Africa with 9.657 asylum seekers, with Angolans standing out with 6.444 and Congolese with 2.506 applicants; North Africa with 1.745 asylum seekers with Morocco standing out with 796 applicants; and, finally Eastern Africa with 1.053 applicants.

Between 2003 and 2010, African migration to Brazil increased significantly, including from Lusophone countries that do not tend to seek asylum, such as Angola, Cape Verde, Mozambique, and Sao Tome and Principe (Uebel, 2021). This growth was experienced during the Lula Da Silva administration (2003–2011), who repeatedly stated his openness towards migration and the ties between Africa and Brazil (Silva, 2023; Uebel, 2021). The drivers for African migration to Brazil are linked to the motivations of both transmigration and settlement—Brazil's strategic geographic location as a common entry point to the Americast (Yates & Bolter, 2019); the cultural and linguistic proximity (in the case of Lusophone countries); as well as Brazil's foreign policy, which promoted scholarships and professional exchanges (Erthal & Marcondes, 2013; Rizzi & da Silva, 2017; Uebel, 2021).

Under Dilma Rousseff's government (2011–2016), African immigration in Brazil continued to increase, by 38%, with a growth of 226% in annual flows between 2003 and 2016 (Uebel, 2020a). The influx of African immigrants brought about significant changes in political, academic, and institutional debates in Brazil concerning issues such as racial quotas, recognising vulnerable communities, and the formulation of specific refugee admission policies (Uebel, 2020b). In the context of the World Cup in 2014 and its visa exemption for all nationalities, Senegalese and West African migration to Brazil increased (Campbell, 2018).

Brazil has a comprehensive legal framework to protect the rights of migrants and refugees, including its 1997 Refugee Law, which is considered the second most progressive in the region (Freier & Gauci, 2020), its Migration Law (Law No. 13.445/2017), and the National Plan for the Reception and Integration of Refugees. The Migration Law, enacted in 2017, replaced the 1980 Aliens Act and aims to promote the integration of migrants into Brazilian society by granting them access to basic rights such as healthcare, education, and employment. The law also establishes a regularisation programme for undocumented migrants, which allows them to obtain documentation and protection from exploitation. The National Committee for Refugees (CONARE) is responsible for the recognition of refugee status and the protection of refugees.

Despite the legal framework, refugees and migrants in Brazil still face significant challenges, including xenophobia and discrimination (Nemitz, 2022). In particular, refugees and migrants from Haiti, Venezuela, and Syria have faced challenges in accessing basic services and integrating into Brazilian society (Caetano, 2022). Civil society organisations have played an essential role in advocating for the protection of refugees and migrants in Brazil, and the government has taken steps to improve the situation. The National Plan for the Reception and Integration of Refugees, established in 2019, aims to improve the integration of refugees into Brazilian society and increase their access to services (Fischel de Andrade & Marcolini, 2019).

In terms of its socio-racial hierarchy, a defining feature of Brazilian society is its diverse socio-racial composition and the significance of "race" in the structural inequalities that are reproduced to this day (de Albuquerque, 2010; Hordge-Freeman, 2013; de Souza e Silva et al., this volume). Despite the myth of Brazil being a "racial democracy" (Hasenbalg & Huntington, 1982), Brazilian politics and social relations have been characterised by a long history of structural racism that is rooted in the colonial legacy of the slave labour economy of Black Africans, which was the socio-economic foundation on which modern Brazil was built. As the last country in the Western Hemisphere, slavery in Brazil was only abolished in 1888.

More recent African migration has captured the attention of the Brazilian government and its institutions, with some actors actively working to receive and integrate the new immigrants (Uebel, 2020b), while law enforcement is used—as in Argentina—to harass and intimidate informal and irregular merchants (Tendayi et al., 2022). Parts of the Brazilian media have engaged in sensationalism in regard to the African immigration, especially in the case of Senegalese nationals (Araújo & da Silva Freitas, 2022), provoking a rise in episodes of xenophobia and aversion to immigrants, including physical aggression and hate speech by politicians (Nemitz, 2022; Saglio-Yatzimirsky, 2017).

Mexico

In the Mexican case, based on apprehension data, the flow of African migrants has increased over the span of the last 15 years, peaking with 7.065 apprehensions in 2019, which represented 3.9% of the total irregular migrant population detained in Mexico in that year. After the abrupt drop in the number of migrants in 2020 due to the COVID-19 pandemic, there was a significant growth in 2022, when 5.437 African migrants were recorded in Mexico. In 2022, the main African nationalities detained in Mexico were Senegalese, Cameroonians, Angolans, Ghanaians, and Somalis. According to UNHCR figures, in 2022, Mexico registered 3.381 asylum seekers from West and Central Africa, 1.866 from Southern Africa, 283 from East and Horn of Africa, and 22 from North Africa.

As other countries in the region, Mexico liberalised its migration policies, embodied in the decriminalisation of irregular migration in Mexico in 2008—through an amendment to the 1974 General Population Law, which decriminalised irregular migration (CALDERÓN CHELIUS, 2012; Casillas, 2015; Gall, 2018)—and the enactment of its migration and refugee laws in 2011, which replaced the 1974 General Population Law. According to Freier and Gauci (2020), Mexico's refugee law ranks third in the region (with Costa Rica) in terms of rights granted to asylum seekers and refugees. However, despite important advances in the protection of migrants' human rights, the migration law maintains a securitising and criminalising approach to irregular migration (Gall, 2018).

A key measure included in the 2011 migration legislation was the *oficio de salida* (exit permit), which authorised migrants without legal status to leave Mexico within a period of 20–30 days, through any border. These *oficio de salida* were granted to African migrants to legally reach the US–Mexico border and be able to apply for asylum in the United States. As of June 2019, Mexican authorities stopped issuing these permits, preventing many African migrants from reaching the US–Mexico border and forcing them to remain in Tapachula (Averbuch, 2020). This was part of a US refoulement policy to reduce the daily number of asylum seekers, also known as the "metering" policy of the US Department of Homeland Security (Smith, 2019), next to Article 42 expulsions and the Migration Protection Protocols (MPP).

In terms of its socio-racial hierarchy, since the Mexican Revolution of 1910, *mestizaje* is a central notion of "mexicanness" as a national identity that defines belonging to the imaginary of the Mexican nation in contrast to the immigrant and/or foreigner (Yankelevich, 2017). *Mestizaje* also defines interethnic relations among Mexicans themselves, based on the idea of a racial mixture based on Spanish primacy and indigenous subordination, largely excluding the African contribution to the Mexican nation. Similar to Argentina, in the first half of the twentieth century, assimilationist and eugenic policies aimed at integrating indigenous and foreigners into the "mestizo" national society to "improve the race" (Yankelevich, 2012), At the same time restrictive and racist immigration policies were applied against black populations (Cunin, 2015); in addition to deportations of Mexicans of Chinese descent; and anti-Semitism against the Jewish community in Mexico (Carlos Fregoso, 2016; Pescador, 2017; Yankelevich, 2015). These racist, eugenic, and nationalist policies led to the enactment of the General Population Law of 1936, which led to prohibition and the closing of Mexico to immigration for the following decades (Gall, 2018; Yankelevich, 2012).

African migrants, who began to arrive in more visible numbers along with Haitian migrants from around 2015, are not only confronted with the lack of institutional capacity of Mexico's immigration authorities, but also face racism and stigmatisation (e.g. based on the hoax of African migrants as potential Ebola transmitters), rendering them more vulnerable for the exploitation of migrant smugglers (MANDUJANO, 2016; Gall, 2018). Molla (2021) analyses the experience of black African and Haitian migrants in Mexico based on intersectional identities (being a migrant, being black, and being a non-Spanish speaker) and how these identities confront them with the physical, verbal, and psychological violence of being black in a *mestizo* or, in other words, predominantly "non-black" country. Intriguingly, unlike their Central American peers, migrants of African descent have been well-received in the northern state of Tijuana, where they are provided with shelter, food, and economic aid (Gall, 2018).

Conclusions

The literature on African migration to Latin America has significantly increased in recent years, covering a range of topics from the motivations of migrants to their socio-political integration. The most important receiving countries are also among the most studied: Argentina, Brazil, and Mexico. In this chapter we use data on asylum seekers, refugees, and migrants detained in Mexico to map trends in African migration to, and transmigration through Latin America. The stark increase in African asylum applications across the region and African detentions in Mexico suggest that African migration is growing and much larger than official statistics suggest. Refugee numbers, which are largely concentrated in Brazil, remained stable, suggesting that Latin American countries are not expanding protection to African migrants—despite the trend of legislative policy liberalisation.

This, despite the fact that African migrants to and through Latin America are willing to take immense risks. African transmigrants to the United States pass through many Latin American countries including the deadly Darien Gap between Colombia and Panama. On this route, migrants move in speedboats between rivers and mangroves, and others walk through the dense jungle until they reach Panamanian territory, facing criminal groups dedicated to human, arms, and drug trafficking, which translates into insecurity, violence, abuse, and, in some cases, the death of migrants (Requene, 2021).

Overall, African migration to Latin America is a complex and multifaceted phenomenon that requires both further in-depth, qualitative research on migrant aspirations, capabilities, and challenges faced, as well as efforts to collect more reliable data on migrant flows and stocks. Persisting knowledge gaps likely have negative implications for the development of effective policies and programmes to protect and integrate African migrants in the region, especially in the context of their socio-racial vulnerability and marginalisation. African migration also invites us to deepen our understanding of the region's socio-racial hierarchies and sociocultural identities shaped by the colonial imprint racism, often perpetuated after the processes of independence, also vis-a-vis other migrant groups.

References

Acosta, D., & Freier, L. F. (2015). Turning the immigration policy paradox upside down? Populist liberalism and discursive gaps in South America. *International Migration Review, 49*(3), 659–696.

Álvarez Velasco, S. (2016). Control y violencia ante la migración irregularizada por la región. *Seguridad y Sociedad, 6*(14), 30–38.

Amahazion, F. F. (2021). Long voyage: African migration through Latin America to the US. *Open Journal of Social Sciences, 9*(7), 280–300.

Araújo, G. A., & da Silva Freitas, G. M. (2022). A review on discourse studies concerning migrants in media publications from Brazil and South Africa: Towards more Afro-Latin perspectives. Index. comunicación: *Revista científica en el ámbito de la Comunicación Aplicada, 12*(1), 309–333.

Arcarazo, D. A., & Freier, L. F. (2015). Discursos y políticas de inmigración en Sudamérica: ¿Hacía un nuevo paradigma o la confirmación de una retórica sin contenido? *REMHU: Revista Interdisciplinar da Mobilidade Humana, 23*, 171–189.

Averbuch, M. (2020). Mexico's other migrant standoff. *NACLA Report on the Americas, 52*(1), 13–19. https://doi.org/10.1080/10714839.2020.1733218

Baeninger, R., Demétrio, N. B., & Domeniconi, J. (2019). Imigração internacional na macrometrópole paulista: Novas e velhas questões. *Cadernos Metrópole, 22*, 17–40.

Bakewell, O. (2008). 'Keeping them in their place': The ambivalent relationship between development and migration in Africa. *Third World Quarterly, 29*(7), 1341–1358.

Bakewell, O., & De Haas, H. (2007). African migrations: continuities, discontinuities and recent transformations. *African Alternatives*, 95–117

Bakewell, O., & Jónsson, G. (2011). *Migration, mobility and the African city*.

Bastia, T., & vom Hau, M. (2014). Migration, race and nationhood in Argentina. *Journal of Ethnic and Migration Studies, 40*(3), 475–492.

Beauchemin, C., Nappa, J., Schoumaker, B., Baizan, P., González-Ferrer, A., Caarls, K., & Mazzucato, V. (2015). Reunifying versus living apart together across borders: A comparative analysis of sub-Saharan migration to Europe. *International Migration Review, 49*(1), 173–199.

Beck, S., Mijeski, K. J., & Stark, M. M. (2011). ¿Qué es racismo? Awareness of racism and discrimination in Ecuador. *Latin American Research Review, 46*(1), 102–125.

Bork-Hüffer, T., Rafflenbeul, B., Kraas, F., & Li, Z. (2014). Global change, national development goals, urbanisation and international migration in China: African migrants in Guangzhou and Foshan. *Megacities: Our global urban future*, 135–150.

Caetano E. (2022). The marginalization of Non-White refugees in Brazil. *Rio on Watch*.

Caicedo, C. N., Malapeira, D. M., Juárez, K. C., & Díez, A. A. (2020). Evolución, rasgos comunes y tendencias de las políticas y reformas migratorias en América Latina. In C. N. Caicedo (Ed.), *Políticas y reformas migratorias en América Latina* (pp. 1–13). Fondo Editorial de la Universidad del Pacífico.

CALDERÓN CHELIUS, L. (2012). Cambios en la agenda migratoria: entre el nuevo marco jurídico y las nuevas formas de migración en México. In: RAMÍREZ GARCÍA, Telésforo; CASTILLO, Manuel Ángel (coords.). *México ante los recientes desafíos de la migración internacional* (pp. 19–50). CONAPO.

Campbell, J. (2018). West African migrants arrive in Brazil after weeks adrift at sea. *Council on Foreign Relations (CFR)*.

Cantor, D. J., Freier, L. F., & Gauci, J. P. (2015). *A liberal tide? Immigration and asylum law and policy in Latin America*. University of London Institute of Latin American Studies.

Carlos Fregoso, G. (2016). Racismo y xenofobia en México. Diálogos sobre educación. *Temas actuales en investigación educativa, 7*(3), 1–4.

Casillas, R., & Rodolfo. (2015). Notas para entender la migración: Instituciones gubernamentales y política migratoria mexicanas en los albores del siglo XXI. *Migración y Desarrollo, 13*(24), 47–80.

Castelli, F. (2018). Drivers of migration: Why do people move? *Journal of Travel Medicine, 25*(1), tay040.

Castles, S. (2004a). The factors that make and unmake migration policies. *International Migration Review, 38*(3), 852–884.

Castles, S. (2004b). Why migration policies fail. *Ethnic and Racial Studies, 27*(2), 205–227. https://doi.org/10.1080/0141987042000177306

CEPAL, N. (2021). *Report of the regional review meeting on the implementation of the global compact for safe, orderly and regular migration in Latin America and the Caribbean*.

Cinta Cruz, J. H. (2020). *Movilidades extracontinentales. Personas de origen africano y asiático en tránsito por la frontera sur de México*. Universidad de Ciencias y Artes de Chiapas.

Collier, P. (2013). *Exodus: How migration is changing our world*. Oxford University Press.

Cullenward, L. K. (2009). La inmigración africana a España y Argentina en la época de la globalización. *Hispanic Studies Honors Projects, 3*.

Cunin, E. (2015). ¿México racista? Las políticas de inmigración en el territorio de Quintana Roo, 1924–1934. En Yankelevich, P. (Comp.), *Inmigración y racismo. Contribuciones a la historia de los extranjeros en México*. El Colegio de México.

Cybel, Y. (2018, June 15). De Senegal a Argentina. *El Grito del Sur*.

de Albuquerque, C (2010). *Eugenics and the myth of white racial superiority: Racism in modern Brazil*.

De Haas, H. (2007). Turning the tide? Why development will not stop migration. *Development and Change, 38*(5), 819–841.

De Haas, H. (2011). *The determinants of international migration*. DEMIG Working Paper 2. International Migration Institute, University of Oxford.

De Haas, H. (2014). *Migration theory: Quo vadis?* DEMIG, Working Paper, International Migration Institute, University of Oxford.

De Haas, H. (2021). A theory of migration: The aspirations-capabilities framework. *Comparative Migration Studies, 9*(1), 1–35.

de Souza Silva, K., & de Sá, M. B. (2021). Do Haitianismo à nova Lei de Migração: Direito, Raça e Política Migratória brasileira em perspectiva histórica. *Revista nuestrAmérica, 9*(17), 1–23.

Erthal Abdenur A., & Marcondes De Souza D. (2013). Brazil's development cooperation with Africa. *SUR, 19.*

Espiro, M. L. (2019). Trayectorias laborales de migrantes entre África y Latinoamérica: el caso de los senegaleses en Argentina. *REMHU: Revista Interdisciplinar Da Mobilidade Humana, 27*(56), 81–98. https://doi.org/10.1590/1980-85852503880005605

Espiro, M. L., Voscoboinik, S., & Zubrzycki, B. (2016). Enfrentando el racismo institucional. Análisis de dos casos de migrantes senegaleses en Argentina (2012–2016). *REMHU, Revista Interdisciplinar da Mobilidade Humana, v. XXIV, N., 48*, 63–78.

Finn, V. J., & de Reguero, S. U. (2020). Inclusive language for exclusive policies: Restrictive migration governance in Chile, 2018. *Latin American Policy, 11*(1), 42–61.

Fischel de Andrade, N., & Marcolini, J. (2019). Brazil's response to displacement: Opportunities and challenges. *Forced Migration Review, 60*, 25–28.

FLACSO. (2011). *Diagnóstico sobre la situación actual, tendencias y necesidades de protección y asistencia de las personas migrantes y refugiadas extracontinentales en México y América Central*. Facultad Latinoamericana de Ciencias Sociales.

Flahaux, M. L., & De Haas, H. (2016). African migration: trends, patterns, drivers. *CMS* 4, 1. https://doi.org/10.1186/s40878-015-0015-6

Freier, L. F. (2011). Crossing the Atlantic in search of new destinations: Contemporary African migration to Latin America IV Congreso de la Red Internacional de Migración y Desarrollo. Crisis Global y Estrategias Migratorias: Hacia la redefinición de las políticas de movilidad. 18, 19 y 20 de Mayo del 2011. Flacso-Quito, Ecuador.

Freier, L. F., & Bird, M. (2020). Seeing "Race" through a prism: Relational socio-racial hierarchies and immigration. *Open Edition Journal, 51*(1), 251–253.

Freier, L. F., & Castillo Jara, S. (2021). Movilidad y políticas migratorias en América Latina en tiempos de COVID-19. *Anuario CIDOB De La Inmigración, 2020*, 50–65.

Freier, L. F., & Holloway, K. (2019). The impact of tourist visas on intercontinental South-South migration: Ecuador's policy of "open doors" as a quasi-experiment. *International Migration Review, 53*(4), 1171–1208.

Freier, L. F., & Gauci, J. P. (2020). Refugee rights across regions: A comparative overview of legislative good practices in Latin American and the EU". *Refugee Studies Quarterly, 39*(3), 321–362.

Freier, L. F., & Lucar Oba, L. (2023). Immigration, policies, and socioracial hierarchies In E. Shizha, & E. Makwarimba (Eds.), *Immigrant lives*. Oxford University Press.

Freier, L. F., & Zubrzycki, B. (2019). How do immigrant legalization programs play out in informal labour markets? The case of Senegalese street hawkers in Argentina. *Migration Studies*, 1–30.

Frigerio, A. (2008). De la desaparición de los negros a la reaparición de los afrodescendientes: Comprendiendo las políticas de las identidades negras, las clasificaciones raciales y de su estudio en Argentina. *Consejo Latinoamericano de Ciencias Sociales*.

Gall, O. (2018). Racismos y xenofobias mexicanos frente a los migrantes: 1910–2018. REMHU, *Rev. Interdiscip. Mobil. Hum.*, Brasília 26, 53, ago., 115–134

García, M. I. (2009). *Notas para repensar el racismo en la Argentina. XXVII Congreso de la Asociación Latinoamericana de Sociología. VIII Jornadas de Sociología de la Universidad de Buenos Aires*. Asociación Latinoamericana de Sociología, Buenos Aires.

Gibney, M. (2021). The Global North is closing its doors to migration. *World Politics Review* (2021).

GS/OAS; IOM (2016). *Regional report: Irregular migration flows to the Americas from Africa, Asia, and the Caribbean*. The General Secretariat of the Organization of American States (GS/OAS) and the International Organization for Migration (IOM).

Hasenbalg, C., & Huntington, S. (1982). Brazilian racial democracy: Reality or myth? *Humboldt Journal of Social Relations*, 129–142.

Henao L. A. (2009). *African immigrants drift toward Latin America*. Reuters.

Hordge-Freeman, E. (2013). What's love got to do with it? *Racial Features, Stigma and Socialization in Afro-Brazilian Families, Ethnic and Racial Studies, 36*(10), 1507–1523. https://doi.org/10.1080/01419870.2013.788200

Instituto Nacional de Estadística y Censos (INDEC). (2010). Grupos poblacionales. *INDEC*.

International Organization for Migration (IOM). (2015). Cuadernos Migratorios n° 5, Migrantes extracontinentales en América del Sur: Estudio de casos.

International Organization for Migration (IOM). (2022). *Recent migration trends in the Americas*. Buenos Aires.

JRS USA. (2023). *Global: African migration across the Americas*.

Kleidermacher, G. (2013). Entre cofradías y venta ambulante: una caracterización de la inmigración senegalesa en Buenos Aires. *Cuadernos de antropología social*, 38, 109–30.

Kleidermacher, G., & Murguía-Cruz, N. (2021). Senegaleses en Buenos Aires: Estrategias comunitarias pre y durante la pandemia. *Huellas De La Migración*, 6(11), 45–80. https://doi.org/10.36677/hmigracion.v6i11.16018

Kyle, D., & Ling Z. (2001). Migration merchants: Human smuggling from Ecuador and China to the United States. In V. Guiraudon & C. Joppke (Eds.), *Controlling a new migration world*. Routledge.

Lahav, G., & Guiraudon, V. (2006). Actors and venues in immigration control: Closing the gap between political demands and policy outcomes. *West European Politics, 29*(2), 201–223.

Langberg, L. (2005). A review of recent OAS research on human trafficking in the Latin American and Caribbean region. *International Migration, 43*(1–2), 129–139.

Maffia, M. M. (2010). Una contribución al estudio de la nueva inmigración africana subsahariana en la Argentina. *Cuadernos De Antropología Social, 31*, 7–32.

Maffia, M. M. (2014). The new immigration from Sub Saharan Africa in Argentina. *Rev. Faculdade Direito Universidade Federal Minas Gerais, 64*, 539.

MANDUJANO, I. (2016). *La oleada migratoria destapa los horrores mexicanos*. Proceso.

McKenzie, D. (2017). Involuntary migration, inequality, and integration: National and subnational influences. *Journal of Ethnic and Migration Studies, 43*(3), 13–28. https://doi.org/10.1080/1369183X.2016.1231801

Melde, S., & Freier, L. F. (2022). When the stars aligned: Ideational strategic alliances and the critical juncture of Argentina's 2004 migration law. *Third World Quarterly, 43*(7), 1531–1550.

Mercada, T. (2021). African Migrants and the American Dream: So close and yet so far. *Revista nuestrAmérica, 9*(17), 1–13.

Miraglia, P. (2016). The invisible migrants of the Darién Gap: Evolving immigration routes in the Americas. *Council on Hemispheric Affairs, 18*.

Molla, Z. A. (2021). A treacherous journey through Latin America: The plight of Black African and Haitian migrants forced to remain in Mexico [Master of Arts in Migration Studies, University of San Francisco].

Moncayo, Á., & Silveira, A. C. (2017). Current epidemiological trends of Chagas disease in Latin America and future challenges: Epidemiology, surveillance, and health policies. *American Trypanosomiasis Chagas Disease*, 59–88.

Morales, O. G. (2010). Nuevas dinámicas migratorias globales y representaciones locales sobre los negros en Argentina. El caso de las percepciones de agentes de la Policía bonaerense sobre recientes migrantes africanos. *Sociedad y Discurso, 18*, 121–148.

Mulvey, B. (2021). "Decentring" international student mobility: The case of African student migrants in China. *Population, Space and Place, 27*(3), e2393.

Muñoz, Y. R., Tessini, K. G., Muñoz, V. R., & Sánchez, P. M. (2021). Maternidades negras en Chile: Interseccionalidad y salud en mujeres haitianas. *Revista Nuestramérica, 9*(17), 1–13.

Nemitz, E. (2022). African Migrants in Brazil Speak Out. Fair Planet. https://www.fairplanet.org/story/african-migrants-in-brazil-speak-out/#:~:text=Rosy%20Ngalula%20Kamayi%20was%20born,them%2C%22%20she%20told%20FairPlanet.

OIM. (2012). *Panorama migratorio de América del Sur*. Buenos Aires: Organización Internacional para las Migraciones (OIM).

Orr, Z., & Ajzenstadt, M. (2020). Beyond control: The criminalization of African asylum seekers in Israel. *International Review of Sociology, 30*(1), 142–165.

Parent, N., Freier, F., & Dawson, W. (2021). Lost at sea, saved by Allah: Religious coping on a migrant journey from Cape Verde to Brazil. *Mental Health, Religion and Culture, 24*(7), 659–669. https://doi.org/10.1080/13674676.2021.1919069

Pavez-Soto, I., Ortiz-López, J. E., Sepúlveda, N., Jara, P., & Olguín, C. (2019). Racialización de la niñez migrante haitiana en escuelas de Chile. *Interciencia, 44*(7), 414–420.

Pescador, J. (2017). [Review of the book Inmigración y racismo: contribuciones a la historia de los extranjeros en México ed. by Pablo Yankelevich]. *The Americas, 74*(4), 573–575.

Ray, M., & Leyva Flores, R. (2020). Undocumented African Migration in Mexico: Implications for Public Health. *Frontera norte, 32*, e2058. https://doi.org/10.33679/rfn.v1i1.2058

Requene, A. Y. O. (2021). Presentación al Dossier: "Migraciones africanas y afrodescendientes en nuestra América: Tránsitos, rutas y destinos." *Revista nuestrAmérica, 9*(17), 1–7.

R4V (2023). Map: Venezuelan Refugees and Migrants in Latin America and the Caribbean. August 2023. https://www.r4v.info/en/document/r4v-latin-america-and-caribbean-venezuelan-refugees-and-migrants-region-aug-2023

Rizzi, K. R., & da Silva, I. C. (2017). A CPLP como mecanismo de atuação do Brasil no Atlântico Sul: a ampliação da cooperação,os desafios e a possibilidade de liderança. *Revista Brasileira de Estudos Africanos, 2*(4), 32–63. https://seer.ufrgs.br/index.php/rbea/article/view/79143/47055

Saglio-Yatzimirsky, M. C. (2017). *New African and Asian migrations in Brazil: Issues on identities and racism.* INALCO.

Sander, C., & Maimbo, S. M. (2003). *Migrant labor remittances in Africa: Reducing obstacles to developmental contributions.*

Santi Pereyra, S. E. (2018). Biometría y vigilancia social en Sudamérica: Argentina como laboratorio regional de control migratorio. *Revista Mexicana De Ciencias Políticas y Sociales, 63*(232), 247–268.

Sector, P. O. (2016). *Labor and human rights risk analysis of Ecuador's Palm oil sector.* https://verite.org/wp-content/uploads/2016/11/Risk-Analysis-of-Ecuador-Palm-Oil-Sector-Final.pdf

Silva, L. (2023). *Comunicado Conjunto da Visita Oficial de sua Excelência Luiz Inácio Lula da Silva, Presidente da República Federativa do Brasil à República Democrática de São Tomé e Príncipe.*

Smith, Hillel R. (2019, 6 August). The Department of Homeland Security's Reported 'Metering' Policy: Legal Issues.

Stang, M. F. (2016). De la doctrina de la Seguridad Nacional a la gobernabilidad migratoria: La idea de seguridad en la normativa migratoria chilena, 1975–2014. *Polis, 15*(44), 83–107.

Telles, E. E. (2014). *Pigmentocracies: Ethnicity, race and color in Latin America.* University of North Carolina Press.

Tendayi, E. Tidball-Binz, M. & Namakula, C. (2022). *Brazil: UN experts decry acts of racialised police brutality*. United Nations Human Rights office of the high commissioner.

Uebel, R. R. G. (2020a). Perfil da imigração africana no Brasil durante o governo Dilma Rousseff (2011–2016): o caso dos senegaleses e oeste-africanos. FORUM. *Revista Departamento Ciencia Política, 18*, 91–123. https://doi.org/10.15446/frdcp.n18.79574

Uebel, R. R. G. (2020b). Brazilian foreign policy for immigrants and refugees: New concepts and ethical issues. *Revista Brasileira De Sociologia, 8*(19), 80–97.

Uebel, R. R. G. (2021). African migration to Brazil in the twenty-first century: New trajectories and Old Paradigms. *African Migrants and the Refugee Crisis*, 187–218.

Velasco, S. Á. (2020). From Ecuador to elsewhere: The (re) configuration of a transit country. *Migration and Society, 3*(1), 34–49.

Vera Espinoza, M., Zapata, G., & Gandini, L. (2020). *Mobility in immobility: Latin American migrants trapped amid COVID-19*. Open Democracy.

Wabgou, W. (2016). Migraciones de origen africano y sus conexiones diaspóricas: Impactos socioculturales, económicos y políticos. *Ciencia Política, 11*(22), 67–98.

Winters, N., & Mora Izaguirre, C. (2019). Es cosa suya: Entanglements of border externalization and African transit migration in Northern Costa Rica. *Comparative Migration Studies, 7*(1), 1–20.

Yankelevich, P. (2015). *Inmigración y racismo. Contribuciones a la historia de los extranjeros en México*. El Colegio de México.

Yankelevich, P. (2012). Mexico for the Mexicans: Immigration, national sovereignty and the promotion of Mestizaje. *The Americas, 60*(3), 405–436.

Yankelevich, P. (2017). Migración, mestizaje y xenofobia en México (1910–1950). *Jahrbuch Für Geschichte Lateinamerikas - Anuario De Historia De América Latina, 54*, 129–156.

Yates, C., & Bolter, J. (2019). *African Migration through the Americas: Drivers, Routes, and Policy Responses*. Migration Policy Institute (MPI). https://www.migrationpolicy.org/sites/default/files/publications/mpi-african-migration-americas-eng_final.pdf

Yates, C., & Bolter, J. (2021). African migration through the Americas: Drivers, routes, and policy responses. *Migration Policy Practice, 9*(1), 4–14.

Zubrzycki, B., & Agnelli, S. (2009). "Allá en África, en cada barrio por lo menos hay un senegalés que sale de viaje". La migración senegalesa en Buenos Aires. *Cuadernos De Antropología Social, 29*, 135–152.

Zubrzycki, B. (2019). Ser africano en Argentina. Las dinámicas de la migración senegalesa. *Nueva Sociedad*. Nuso No. 284, November–December.

Open Access This chapter is licensed under the terms of the Creative Commons Attribution 4.0 International License (http://creativecommons.org/licenses/by/4.0/), which permits use, sharing, adaptation, distribution and reproduction in any medium or format, as long as you give appropriate credit to the original author(s) and the source, provide a link to the Creative Commons license and indicate if changes were made.

The images or other third party material in this chapter are included in the chapter's Creative Commons license, unless indicated otherwise in a credit line to the material. If material is not included in the chapter's Creative Commons license and your intended use is not permitted by statutory regulation or exceeds the permitted use, you will need to obtain permission directly from the copyright holder.

Part III

Inequalities and South–South Migration

17

Poverty, Income Inequalities and Migration in the Global South

Giulia Casentini, Laura Hammond, and Oliver Bakewell

Introduction

The relationships between migration, income levels, poverty and income inequalities are a common and widespread theme of discussion in migration studies. International agencies often stress this entangled connection, by highlighting how evidence indicates that migration reduces poverty (Murrugarra et al., 2011), and that migration represents an important coping mechanism for shocks, such as natural disasters, deforestation, economic turbulence (Murrugarra et al., 2011; UNDP, 2021; Kóczán & Loyola, 2018). Moreover, in the last decades the attention on remittances and their role in reducing poverty and potentially levelling income inequalities has been widely considered. In the United Nations 2030 Agenda for Sustainable Development, one of the constitutive points to reach Goal Number 10, which is dedicated to

---

G. Casentini · L. Hammond (✉)
Department of Development Studies, SOAS University of London, London, UK
e-mail: laura.hammond@soas.ac.uk

G. Casentini
e-mail: gc32@soas.ac.uk

O. Bakewell
Global Development Institute, University of Manchester, Manchester, UK
e-mail: oliver.bakewell@manchester.ac.uk

L. Hammond
Directorate, SOAS University of London, London, UK

the reduction of inequalities within and among countries, refers to migration, and in particular to the facilitation of "orderly, safe, regular and responsible migration and mobility of people, including through the implementation of planned and well-managed migration policies" (UN, 2030 Agenda, 23).

In this chapter we discuss whether migration can play a role in reducing income inequality, by helping increase incomes and contribute to poverty alleviation, or whether it is a very selective phenomenon that tends to exacerbate inequalities. South–South perspectives are included in the analysis, albeit through a critical approach, drawing attention to the vast existing literature on the topic and focusing on migration dynamics seen in three corridors that represent our case study (Burkina Faso–Côte d'Ivoire, Ethiopia–South Africa, Ghana–China).[1]

The corridor perspective can help in disclosing some questions that may arise while producing a theoretical work on mobility. Carling and Jolivet (2016) define corridors as "frames of observation devoid of empirical assumptions and independent of the level and direction of activity within them" (Carling & Jolivet, 2016, 44). This means that they are useful conceptual frameworks to analyse both the presence and the absence of migration, its stagnation. Corridors don't have a predetermined direction, and consequently they also involve returns in the analysis. A temporal dimension is central in defining the changing characteristics of a migration corridor (Carling & Jolivet, 2016). We must underline, though, how this corridor perspective should be problematised: it is important to critically reconsider the absence of "empirical assumptions" (Carling & Jolivet, 2016, 44), by recognising the constitutive contributions made by different experiences in the corridors, made by people's lives, choices, challenges.

Our review of the literature suggests that the relationships between migration and poverty and/or income inequality are complex and highly variable. In fact, as mentioned by McKenzie (2017, 13), "contrary to simple theories of income maximization and popular perceptions, migrants are not overwhelmingly drawn from the poorer households within a country, or poorest countries". This is to say that poverty and income inequalities influence in various and contradicting ways the decision to migrate, due to a myriad of variables that we will analyse here. Also, the effects of remittances and returnees in the areas of origin have sometimes unexpected outcomes. As we will see, in fact, while remittances can often reduce poverty, for example at the household level, they have a less clear and straightforward relation with income inequality.

Who Migrates?

While trying to unpack the relationship between migration, poverty, and income inequality it has become clear that we need to focus attention primarily on those who make the decision to move, with the aim of untangling how this decision is often a collective one, even if this aspect can be sometimes relegated to the background. Migration, indeed, is a family, community, collective decision even if the migrant is only one person (see also Mazzilli et al., this volume). Often this first move can be followed by the migration of other family members, or of other co-villagers, highlighting once again the collective dimension of the migration experience.

In asking the question "who migrates", we have found out that those who move are, normally, not the poorest. But what does this mean in analytical terms?

The poorest of the poor seldom have the possibility to migrate (Crawley, 2018). As noted by Carling, "migration is restricted by poverty, illiteracy, lack of education and the absence of long-term planning in the lives of people that live from hand to mouth" (Carling, 2002, 5). This may be seen as a factor increasing inequality because access to migration is not evenly distributed (Black et al., 2005; Carling, 2002). This perspective is supported by various scholars, asserting that migration from the poorest countries is normally directed towards neighbouring countries (Flahaux & de Haas, 2016), and that the poorest are likely to maintain a local mobility, or regional at most, and primarily within a country (Skeldon, 2002). In this sense, a focus on South–South mobility can help provide a better understanding of these dynamics.

Other studies support this point, by providing examples that relate to the so-called inverse U-shaped pattern between income levels and emigration rates, which have proven to be low in the poorest countries, and rise until an income per capita of around $6000, and then start to fall (de Haas, 2010; McKenzie, 2017). Indeed, as noted by de Haas, migration is a strongly patterned choice, because people's individual choices are constrained by structural factors, and because migration processes themselves cannot follow a conventional equilibrium model following functionalist theory (de Haas, 2010, 5). The cross-sectional relation represented by the inverse U-shaped pattern suggests that reducing poverty may actually induce more people to migrate (McKenzie, 2017).

There are several explanations for the existence and persistence of this migration pattern in relation to poverty. We elaborate on this pattern through the analysis of crucial variables, which can help to build a critical approach on the reading of the profile of the migrant, that can be read also in relation to poverty and income inequality.

Migration is always *costly*. The project to move in search of a better job and better life opportunities always involves an economic effort that can vary greatly in relation to contexts and personal conditions, but that always exists. That is to say that the poor are more likely to move when migration costs are low (Bakewell, 2009). Households experiencing an increase in income due to, for example, remittances, can see their members migrating more. *Aspirations* are also considered an important variable by many scholars; de Haas (2010) has been particularly attentive in connecting them to capabilities and making them a substantial element that characterise the decision to migrate. More complicated is determining whether, and how, aspirations are related to poverty and income inequality, and how this eventual connection is developed. Doquier et al. (2014, in McKenzie, 2017) found that poorer and less educated people are partially less motivated to migrate, but much less able to turn eventual aspirations to migrate into reality, due to migration costs but also to other variables, like *education*.

Another important factor of connection between migration, poverty and inequality, education and aspirations are represented by *family networks* and the possibility of gaining *information* about opportunities abroad and routes to take. If poorer people migrate less, they will have a lower level of access to a well-structured network abroad that can not only provide reliable information, but also imagination and dreams: migration decision-making process is highly informed also by intangible and subjective factors (Hagen-Zanker & Hennessey, 2021).

We shall try to understand, now, what is distinctive of income inequalities in shaping migration, by providing reflection, critical readings and practical examples from our three migration corridors.

How Do Poverty and Inequality Influence Who Migrates, and Why?

Is the mere presence of income inequality able to affect an individual's desire to migrate? It is clear that relative deprivation matters (Bakewell, 2009; Stark & Taylor, 1989), and that inequalities within sending areas are crucial in generating migration (Black et al., 2005).

McKenzie (2017) provides a straightforward equation to combine these aspects: high inequalities and the increase of inequalities in a certain area are going to create more poor people, and this dynamic is most probably going to decrease the migration rate because poor people cannot afford/do not prefer to migrate.

These reflections are supported by some of the findings of our analysis of migration dynamics in the Burkina Faso–Côte d'Ivoire corridor, where several scholars assert that poverty is a constraint to migration, because costs and risks can be faced normally by those who have a certain economic security, people need money and information to move (Dabiré, 2007; Mouhoud, 2010; Wouterse, 2008). Nevertheless, there can also be positive effects of poverty and inequality as migration drivers, as demonstrated for example by Piché and Cordell (2015) in analysing migration patterns in the same corridor: the authors note that recognising the condition of poverty and deciding to change could act as a driver for migration. In this case, the role of aspirations in changing or ameliorating one's own personal/group condition is quite relevant. At the same time Lachaud (1999) affirms that those who move from Burkina Faso are normally peasants coming from poor rural areas, often young men (Black et al., 2005), who undertake a labour migration journey that is quite common in the historical relation between the two countries involved in this corridor (Tapsoba et al., 2022).

The Burkina Faso–Côte d'Ivoire corridor operates in the short distance, and therefore is more likely to involve "poorer" migrants. This corridor represents a long-standing practice of migration: moving to Côte d'Ivoire is a common strategy to improve one's economic situation, a trajectory that has its roots during colonial times (see also Dabiré and Soumahoro, this volume). Indeed, present-day Burkina Faso served as a labour reservoir for the more developed Côte d'Ivoire during the implementation and development of cocoa plantations (see Piché & Cordell, 2015). This historical practice of mobility has survived and adapted during time, representing also today a viable solution for many Burkinabè workers. This corridor could represent a good way forward for poorer migrants. Nevertheless, we must acknowledge the historical dimensions of this corridor and consider the colonial and postcolonial labour mobility process as inherently caused, and perpetuated, by economic inequalities between the two countries. One critical reflection that could arise from the reading of the specificities of this corridor, still vital and vibrant, and of the persistence of economic inequalities between Burkina Faso and Côte d'Ivoire, is that migration between the two countries could act as a leveller of poverty, at the micro-level, but not necessarily as a leveller of economic inequalities.

The Ethiopia–South Africa corridor represents another, different migration dynamic. This is an intra-continental, medium distance migration corridor that is relatively recent compared to other more rooted migration phenomena

(Ethiopians to Europe, North America, Middle East) (see Estifanos & Zack, 2019), and it stems from the collapse of both regimes, apartheid in South Africa and the end of Derg's military rule in Ethiopia. It involved, at the beginning, mainly men searching for a secure place during political oppression and, subsequently, election turmoil, but then it became a viable destination because of economic opportunities both in the formal and the informal market (Estifanos & Zack, 2020; Landau et al., 2018). This corridor offers many examples of the crucial role played by intermediaries, namely smugglers (providing security, protection, border crossing), but also social networks (which reduce risks and costs of migration, finance the trip, pay ransoms and provide emotional support and social connections) (see Adugna et al., 2019; Jones et al., this volume). It is possible to observe that income inequality intersects with irregularity: in a context of relative wealth, one can better confront with the possibility (often the need) to undertake irregular roads. Capabilities and aspirations must also be understood in relation to spirituality and the role of local churches in the country of origin, which have contributed to the creation of a "spiritually animated migration agency" (Feyissa, 2022, 37) that has proven to be relevant in determining migration decision-making and risk assessment (see also Feyissa et al., this volume).

Migration between Ghana and China is a long distance, intra-continental route and a corridor that requires a more expensive migration investment. As a result, those who move between the two countries are normally well educated and highly skilled people. Obeng (2019) for example notes that at least 40% of African migrants in Guangzhou (China) have had a tertiary education (see also Bodomo & Ma, 2010). Another peculiarity of this corridor is its double direction: we can observe both Ghanaians moving to China, and Chinese moving to Ghana, which can help us unpack some crucial questions on the relationship between income inequality and migration. Chinese started moving to Ghana in late 1950s (Ho, 2008), while Ghanaians initiated to migrate to China in the late 1990s–early 2000s (Obeng, 2019). For this corridor, there is evidence that highlights how the role of the household and the social network is fundamental in overcoming income inequality for those who want to leave, but also in increasing income inequality in relation to those "left behind", because there is the tendency in investing in the migration of only one individual or only one group of people, due to the high cost of the experience (trip, documents, accommodation). Indeed, this is rarely an irregular route. As noted by a recent study (Teye et al., 2022), even if Chinese migration to Ghana is initially motivated by the possibility of prosperous economic opportunities for investments and employment, then many Chinese migrants decided to stay, or to return after a period back to China due to a combination of factors, in which other variables count: the presence of a social network, the peaceful environment, the ease in accessing the migration route due to Ghana's geography and its favourable migration policy (ibid; see also Teye et al., this volume). This means that migration dynamics related to income inequality can be fully understood in their intersection with other forms of inequalities and other variables.

A Reflection on South–South Migration in Relation to Inequality

A South–South perspective has proven to be an insightful way to understand and problematise the developmental effects of migration in both countries of origin and destination (Crawley et al., 2022), especially because new patterns are observable and new data are available (De Lombaerde et al., 2014).

Nevertheless, the Global South, and South–South migration, are complex and potentially misleading definitions, which may be useful if understood and used while taking into account the historical dimensions involved in their creation (i.e. colonial period), the political construction of these categories and the limitations embedded in their theoretical application (see also Fiddian-Quasmiyeh and Carella, this volume). It is very difficult, indeed, to identify what is distinctive of South–South migration, because it involves a huge variety of movements, and the "South" is constituted by highly diverse countries, as demonstrated by our focus on three profoundly different corridors. We can identify the South with developing regions, but still the definition remains problematic (see Bakewell, 2009). Probably, South–South movements can be better understood when we focus the attention on a regional dimension, as highlighted by some critical theoretical approaches (Bakewell, 2009) and also by other works that may not be so openly critical about the definition, but ultimately use a regional perspective while talking about South–South mobility (Hossain et al., 2017).

While carefully considering the delicate and complex nature of this categorisation, we can use it to understand if there are specific features that pertain South–South migration, and if this theoretical effort can help us unpack some dynamics concerning inequalities.

In addressing South–South mobility, we must recognise that migration is a characteristic of people's livelihood, especially when we analyse cross-border migration, seasonal migration (Bakewell, 2009). Other important elements characterising Global South livelihoods are connected to the relative high level of informality, low incomes, uncertainty, and limited rights for workers (see Stark & Teppo, 2022). It seems plausible that South–South migration, that is generally less remunerative compared to South–North mobility but also less costly, can be accessible to a higher number of poor people (World Bank, 2019; see also Schewel and Debray, this volume), and consequently enhance livelihood security through income diversification (Bakewell, 2009).

Many analyses underline the importance of the role played by porous borders in the South in characterising people's movements (Campillo-Carrete, 2013; De Lombaerde et al., 2014; Hujo & Piper, 2007). Still, we need to unpack why the role of borders may be so relevant. As stated elsewhere, especially in reference to African borders (Bakewell, 2009), we are not referring to a supposedly volatile, artificial, inconsistent nature of borders created during colonial times, but to the dynamics of weak border control, and the relatively low state capacity in monitoring and registering movements (see also Campillo-Carrete, 2013). Borders do matter: it may be easy to cross borders among neighbouring countries of the Global South, but it may be also difficult to live outside one's country of citizenship (Bakewell, 2009), as demonstrated for example by the condition of exclusion from basic rights (*apartidie*) lived by a consistent number of Burkinabè migrants in the neighbouring Côte d'Ivoire. Moreover, various recent South–South migration patterns are taking place over a longer distance, such as the case of Ethiopians choosing South Africa (which has proven to be more and more irregular due to lack of documentation and stricter border control), or the migration in the Ghana–China corridor (which can normally happen regularly with a consistent economic investment). This means that, in conditions of limited options for regular movement, people will rely more on informal networks and ways of moving, searching for the assistance of families and intermediaries. The condition of uncertainty and the high level of informality in border crossing could also enhance the potential for smuggling and, ultimately, for trafficking in persons.

In this context of relatively weak regional governance and weak regional organisation with respect to the facilitation/regulation of people's mobility (De Lombaerde et al., 2014), the condition of migrants is often neglected, together with the respect of their human rights and labour rights in countries of destination. In spite of a growing interest in migration across the Global South, there is still a need for a systematic consideration and a comparative reading of the politics of state migration management (Adamson & Tsourapas, 2019). Inequalities, indeed, can also result from increased barriers to migration, including poor labour conditions and a lack of rights for migrants and their families (Crawley et al., 2022), both in countries of origin and destination.

Lastly, we would like to underline another aspect that connects South–South migration flows to poverty and income inequality. The context of political instability, insecurity and, potentially, conflict can definitely represent an incentive to migrate, and can add important variables to the increase of income inequalities among people on the move, but also among people who receive migrant communities. We refer especially to refugees, who often move to nearby developing countries (see Bakewell, 2009; Hammond, 2004; Hujo & Piper, 2007) and often settle in precarious, unorganised, and destitute spatial and social conditions.

How Does Migration Influence Poverty and Inequality in Countries of Origin?

Impacts of Remittances

Remittances play a crucial role in changing pre-existing patterns of inequalities, even if the impact that they can have at different levels (individual, household, national) and the relevance of the temporal dimension (former/recent migrants) in the same household/village requires a critical approach and a multidimensional analytical perspective. While talking about remittances, we must recognise that an important role is played also by the mechanisms through which resources are remitted in South–South migration dynamics (see also Asiedu et al., this volume). Ratha and Shaw (2007) observe that the cost of remittance transfers among countries in the Global South is higher than those of resources remitted from the Global North to the Global South, due to a lack of competition in the remittances market. This critical factor involves a wide range of social institutions, including hometown, religious, ethnic and village associations that can play a crucial role in channelling remittances not only to individual and families, but also to community-level investments and initiatives (e.g. *mouride* in Senegal, see Riccio, 2005). So, financial institutions (formal and informal) have a great weight in influencing the inequality-reducing or reinforcing effect of migrant remittances (Black et al., 2005), especially if the expenses are high.

In general, there is clear evidence that remittances can reduce poverty (de Haan & Yaqub, 2010). It is more complicated, however, to understand whether, and under what circumstances, remittances can effectively lead to investments in education and health (e.g. de Haas, 2007; Hujo & Piper, 2007; Ratha et al., 2011) and so produce tangible macro-level effects.

McKenzie (2017) affirms that even if reported remittances have soared over the last three decades, no noticeable changes in economic growth or poverty rates are apparent for the countries that send the most migrants and receive most remittances. The largest impacts of migration occur for the migrants themselves and their families, and the gains from moving to a more developed country (South–North migration) are immediate and large (McKenzie, 2017). The absolute gains are even larger for highly skilled workers (ibid.). Kóczán and Loyola (2018) report that while there is a large literature on the poverty-alleviating impact of remittances in countries of origin (e.g. Acosta et al., 2006; Loritz, 2008), their effects on inequality are much less clear (Kóczán & Loyola, 2018, 4). For example, Margolis et al. (2015) find that remittances have no significant impact on inequality, but that they reduce poverty by 40% in Algeria.

Evidence from the Burkina Faso–Côte d'Ivoire corridor can help explain this trend. Zourkaléini and Kaboré (2007) affirm that Burkina Faso has a high number of migrants per household. This permits, through remittances, the amelioration of various aspects of the household's living standards through investments in construction, schooling, facilities (e.g. construction of new latrines). Lachaud (1999, 2005) provides analysis on the importance of remittances coming from workers who have migrated to Côte d'Ivoire, in reducing rural and urban poverty, especially in the urban contexts, by reducing the exposure to economic vulnerability of the weakest social groups (unemployed, independent workers, farmers) (Lachaud, 1999). Furthermore, he underlines that in rural areas remittances can help reduce poverty and also inequalities, but that due to the resources remitted inequalities can actually widen in urban context (ibid.). Another variable that Lachaud introduces is the Ivorian conflict: by considering the political upheaval that happened in 1998 and 2003, it was possible to determine how this had caused an increasing loss of remittances coming from Côte d'Ivoire, due to the change and, sometimes, the arrest of the migratory flow of the Burkinabè (Lachaud, 2005). This means that the contribution of remittances can be variable and contradictory.

Temporal dimensions can help us to understand the impact of remittances on income inequality: remittances can exacerbate existing inequalities if they are sent to the wealthier families, which "pioneer" migrants normally come from; they can increase feelings of deprivation among those left behind (Skeldon, 2002). Findings from the Ethiopia–South Africa corridor confirm this trend, suggesting that remittances are creators of income inequality in the country of origin, because families receiving remittances can invest in new activities, in education (especially to private schools), in building new houses (see also Feyissa et al., this volume). This possibility enhances inequalities, giving rise to episodes of land speculation that entail exclusion from access to land and decent housing solutions (Feyissa, 2022). Early migrants from Ethiopia could benefit from a more regularised transit, and are normally better established so can invest more, especially in the country of origin, by sending back a growing amount of remittances, and investing in land acquisition and construction. When they go back home, they have the economic and social influence to organise a better network, that can have a relevant impact also in political terms. Moreover, they can go back and forth from Ethiopia to South Africa much more easily than later migrants, because the latter often do not have regular permits and papers (Estifanos & Freeman, 2022; Feyissa, 2022).

Inequality in the area of origin can also depend on a combination of generational approach, aspirations, and the cost of migration. Among the youngest, "not migrating" could be perceived and represented as a stain of exclusion and even shame (Estifanos & Zack, 2020). In this case, inequality can increase due to the mechanism of migration and remittances of resources. Some of these young people, in what Estifanos and Zack (2020) significantly describe as a "desperation to migrate", stole money from their family members, or sought help from micro-credit associations through loans, that must be given back. And, finally, there is a tendency to consider migration and especially remittances as a marker of social status (ibid.).

Remittances may also feed into desire for further migration. Increased households' income (due to remittances) seems to facilitate the financing of some of the costs related to out-migration of a family member (Hagen-Zanker & Leon Himmelstine, 2014). There may be remittance dependence at the household level (Hujo, 2013; Hujo & Piper, 2007), as demonstrated by evidence from the Ethiopia–South Africa and Burkina Faso-Côte d'Ivoire corridors. In poorer economies, those left behind may experience "chronic poverty" (Khotari, 2002 in Skeldon, 2002). So, poverty can be influenced in positive ways by migration, especially at the micro level, while the evaluation of the impact of migration on inequality is much more complex and challenging. In other words, we must consider that remittances can give rise to new inequalities and exacerbate existing ones.

Impacts of Outmigration on Poverty and Income Inequality

While reflecting on the impact of outmigration, we confront once again the need to incorporate a temporal dimension, or the "generational" approach, into our reading. Migration can increase and then decrease inequality in sending countries over time, because "pioneer" migrants can come from relatively richer households than later migrants, who can benefit from falling costs of migration (Kóczán & Loyola, 2018). There can be a positive link between outmigration and inequality in sending countries with a more recent migration history (Stark et al., 1988 in Kóczán & Loyola, 2018): people can be stimulated to migrate due to the various factors already mentioned in connection with remittances (facilitation in covering migration costs, sharing aspirations and information on the migration routes), and their remittances, in a first phase, can help in reducing inequalities. Afterwards, as we have seen, inequalities can increase: those who move first, gain most, and the divide between them can intensify. But how far does this inequality become structural? By interrogating Ethiopia–South Africa corridor dynamics, we can see that "these inequalities, which partially emanate from the differences in the migration experiences of former and recent migrants, are reinforced by a combination of socio-economics, cultural and structural factors prevailing in the present day informal economy in South Africa" (Estifanos & Freeman, 2022, 69). So, we might suppose that it is exactly this set of combination that can make income inequality structural. Some groups, like recent migrants and in general the youngest, find themselves in a position of vulnerability and dependence, which might exclude them from overcoming their condition of poverty.

Immediate gains brought by migration in the country of origin must be compared with the impact in the economic setting of the absence of the person who has migrated, that is to say that we have to take into consideration the income that migrants would have earned if they had not left (McKenzie, 2017). It is useful to consider other possible negative effects, such as labour shortages in the community of origin (Hujo, 2013). Evidence from the Burkina Faso-Côte d'Ivoire corridor demonstrates that migration could have negative effects on the availability of agricultural labour in the country of origin, especially if migrants stay away during the rainy season (Black et al., 2005). It might be relevant to distinguish between seasonal and more permanent migration, and their possible outcome in the country of origin. In South–South mobility dynamics, long-term migration can undermine the demographic and economic viability of the community (Skeldon, 2002), but it can also enhance it, for example by reducing pressure on the youth labour market and improving possibilities for those who stay. For example, migration from Burkina Faso does not necessarily result in remittances but reduces consumption pressures faced by sending households (Black et al., 2005).

More recent analysis on the same corridor highlights the fact that migrant households are not necessarily better off than non-migrant ones (Tapsoba et al., 2022). Even if the local perception of migration experiences is generally positive, the fieldwork results seem to demonstrate the contrary: migrant households are less able to cope with daily basic expenses (ibid.).

How Does Migration Influence Poverty and Inequality in Countries of Destination?

Socio-Economic Conditions of Migrants

Often South–South migration dynamics are characterised by higher levels of informality (Bakewell, 2009). Many of these movements are identified as irregular, sometimes in terms of the journey, but more often in terms of the permission to reside in the destination. The possibility of migrants accessing services, rights and legal protection can have an important impact on income inequalities among themselves, and between migrant and non-migrant communities. As suggested by Hujo (2013), the absence of social policy towards inclusion can enhance poverty among migrants. Social policy is, in fact, recognised as a powerful tool for poverty reduction and social development, especially in Global South countries which are dealing with more entrenched poverty and higher levels of inequality (ibid.). Studies on Côte d'Ivoire as a country of immigration highlight how the introduction of programmes of professional training could develop a viable social policy towards inclusion, that can enhance the access to decent employment, and the development of agricultural policies. Burkinabè and other migrants, indeed, are mainly directed towards the agricultural sector, which is revitalising after years of conflict (OCDE/CIRES, 2017). Notwithstanding, migrants in Côte d'Ivoire still lack citizenship rights, and this is also true for those residing in the country for generations. Due to political upheaval that happened in various phases of the post-independence history of the country, and the rise of anti-immigrant sentiments in connection with the political manipulation of the *ivoirité* (see Cutolo, 2010), the Constitution had been frequently amended through the Nationality Code, preventing a rising number of people born in Côte d'Ivoire, especially those who have Burkinabè ancestor, to acquire Ivorian citizenship (Adjami, 2016). This condition of *apatridie* causes harsh inequalities related to access to social services, education, political life and regular work, so much so that migrants often get stuck into the informal sector. The issue of *apatridie* can be the cause of a condition of structural poverty suffered by migrants. Their consequent exclusion from the formal sector can create competition with locals for the access to the informal one, increasing income inequalities between migrants and non-migrants (see Soumahoro & Bi, 2022).

The Ethiopia–South Africa corridor provides similar evidence regarding access to rights: migrants without the possibility of acquiring regular status and/or regular residence permit cannot access the formal labour market and are often forced to rely on the informal sector.

This raises the question of whether the informal sector is necessarily less remunerative than the formal one. There are studies that suggest that informality is not necessarily less remunerative, and international organisations like International Labour Organization (ILO) have recognised that the informal sector is a real, valuable source of income for many African countries because it provides after agricultural sector the greatest number of jobs (Traoré & Ouedraogo, 2021). Even if informal economy has been defined as "the *real* economy in Sub-Saharan Africa" (Stark & Teppo, 2022, 2 emphasis in original), it is always presented and managed by governments as a state of exception, raising issues about privilege, exclusion and inequality (Stark & Teppo, 2022). Indeed, it is evident from our analysis that informality is almost always associated with vulnerability and a lack of social and political rights, which makes it a potential source of an entire set of other inequalities. Another interesting issue is whether informality itself is a generator of income inequalities. It might be argued that the two variables are not necessarily correlated, especially if most migrants, or the vast majority of workers (both migrants and non-migrants) in a specific sector rely on informality. New evidence from the corridors, especially in relation to migration between Ethiopia and South Africa, can help understanding this. Recent Ethiopian migrants also always work in the informal sector and find themselves in a condition of vulnerability and income inequality compared to early settled migrants, because the latter have better access to rights, together with the better access to capital (Estifanos & Zack, 2020). Early settlers/newcomers' relations are often based on income inequality, and this can increase income inequality inside migrant communities: Ethiopian migrants often rely on ethnically based networks of settlement in South Africa (borders/bosses relation) where economic exploitation of late comers takes place (see Estifanos & Freeman, 2022; Estifanos & Zack, 2020).

When migrants have a better economic condition when compared to locals, their presence in the country of destination can almost certainly increase income inequality. In the Ghana mining sector, for example, Chinese migrants find themselves in a relative better situation compared to Ghanaian workers, they can assert themselves and gain access to resources easily (Botchwey et al., 2019). They have the economic possibility of exploiting the high levels of corruption among officials in Ghana to secure access to mines and avoid fines; they often pay lower daily rates to Ghanaians employed in the mines controlled by them (ibid.). This creates inequalities with local miners and local communities, both from an economic point of view and also in social terms. There is evidence of the Chinese capacity of constructing a powerful social and economic network that has an impact on the possibility of manipulating local laws in Ghana, regarding, for example, the import of equipment and forex exchange, that make Chinese migrants earn additional economic power (Ho, 2008).

Inequalities between earlier settlers and newcomers, who often lack sufficient funds to start their own business and work as paid labourers (Botchwey et al., 2019) are present, and the relationship between earlier and recent Chinese migrants in Ghana can also be critical due to prejudice and suspicious attitude of the former towards the latter (Lam, 2015).

On the other hand, migrants can represent a potential leveller of local inequalities, as demonstrated by the case of Chinese migrants and their relationship to the *kayayei*, young Ghanaian female migrants coming from the North of the country, who work as head porters in the capital city, Accra, in a condition of exploitation and vulnerability. Chinese entrepreneurs and workers employ them, and the *kayayei*, from their side, try to take advantage of this space of action granted by other "foreigners" to expand their role and construct their social space and place (Giese & Thiel, 2015). Recent work on this corridor (Teye et al., 2022) challenges misconceptions and myths of the Chinese presence in Ghana, highlighting that the profile of Chinese migrants in Ghana today does not conform with the common stereotype of the single men working with Chinese constructors or in manufacturing, nor with the Ghanaian media representation of single, young, lone men coming for "short-term economic gains through illicit trade or exploitation of natural resources" (Teye et al., 2022, 206). As noted in this work, the profile of Chinese migrants has profoundly changed through time, "from male-dominated and state-propelled to individual independent migrants of all ages and gender distributed in all sectors of the economy" (ibid., 231).

Consequences of Migration on Socio-Economic Conditions in Countries of Destination

The migration corridors considered in this chapter demonstrate that there can be very different outcomes of South–South migration in countries of destination. As already noted, migration between Burkina Faso and Côte d'Ivoire illustrates that migrants can stimulate the economy, can boost the labour market, and help increase production especially in the agricultural sector. Complex social consequences for the life of migrants and their families do exist and have been analysed in the previous section.

Migration between Ethiopia and South Africa has controversial outcomes, especially from a social perspective. Often migrants find themselves competing with the local poor population to access the labour market, especially the informal one, potentially worsening poverty and income inequalities. Episodes of xenophobia against migrants coming from other African countries are rising, together with insecurity and violence. Gebre et al. (2011) report a growing pressure on foreigners who try to establish themselves in the local market. There is, indeed, a widespread belief that income-generating opportunities for South Africans would lessen if resources had to be shared with migrants (ibid.).

Findings from the Ghana–China corridor, however, portray a very different situation. While we must consider that a small number of migrants moving with limited resources can have only a minimal impact on poverty and income inequality, as in the case of Ghana–China migration, it is useful to consider how the China-Ghana trajectory involving migrants coming in with some resources can represent a real chance for job creation and the increase of local business. Botchwey et al. (2019) find that collaboration in between Chinese and Ghanaian miners has resulted in mutual benefit: Chinese bring the technology and have access to mines through concessions or bribery, and from their side Ghanaians with license can work more and better.

Chinese entrepreneurs are often acknowledged as those who economically exploit the condition of general poverty in Ghana, and incidentally allow low-income households to buy new and low-cost goods. Marfaing and Thiel (2013) point out, however, that is seldom recognised how opening access to this kind of low-cost items can allow aspiring entrepreneurs to enter this market, by lowering the entry barriers. Unemployed and youth who were normally excluded from this kind of entrepreneurship can now afford to purchase goods from Chinese stores and re-sell them in the streets (ibid.). Moreover, these authors note that Chinese entrepreneurs' migrants often employ young people, who are normally less able to enter relevant network that facilitate employment opportunities. Even if these chances to enter the job market are clearly perceived by Ghanaians as volatile and seldom represent a decently paid opportunity, it must be recognised that by doing so Chinese entrepreneurs are providing new pathways into urban markets' strategies (ibid.).

If scholars report a positive and mutually benefitting relation between Chinese entrepreneurs and their employees in Ghana, in terms of reduction of income inequalities and the possibility of ameliorating social position, the same can be said of the relationships between same-level entrepreneurs. As noted by Opoku Dankwah and Valenta (2019, 1), relations between Ghanaian traders and their Chinese counterparts in Ghana may be described as "complementary, collaborative and competitive".

There are, of course, several difficulties in this relationship, especially in terms of prejudice, stereotypes, and the production of narratives of "otherness". Mohan and Tan-Mullins (2009), for example, report that different Chinese businessmen affirm that the biggest problem with Ghanaian productivity is "culture", since Ghanaian workers are perceived as unreliable ("they always disappear for funerals"), and poor infrastructures like regular power failures and the lack of public transportation can only exacerbate it (Mohan & Tan-Mullins, 2009, 596).

Conclusion

In this chapter we have proposed a critical reading of South–South migration and its relation to poverty and income inequality, by highlighting the main problems, challenges, and possibilities in relation to different dynamics happening in three migration corridors (Burkina Faso–Côte d'Ivoire, Ethiopia–South Africa and Ghana–China). Despite the difficulties in tracing some commonalities in South–South corridors, which are characterised by very different historical, social, economic, political and historical conditions, we suggest some critical analysis and points for discussion.

Our main analytical question, that of whether migration can play a role in reducing income inequality or whether it is a selective phenomenon that tends to exacerbate it, has been answered critically by providing different views and readings on forms of mobility, the profile of the migrant, the transit, conditions in the countries of origin and destination, and the role of remittances. We suggest that poverty and income inequalities can be better understood in their intersection with other variables and other forms of inequality, like age, gender, access to education, access to social networks, access to safe routes and rights in the country of destination.

This contribution provides a multifaceted and complex image of South–South migration dynamics in relation to poverty and income inequality, which could help in developing new theoretical and empirical questions for future research.

Acknowledgements This work has been undertaken as part of the Migration for Development and Equality (MIDEQ) Hub. Funded by the UKRI Global Challenges Research Fund (GCRF) (Grant Reference: ES/S007415/1), MIDEQ unpacks the complex and multi-dimensional relationships between migration and inequality in the context of the Global South. More at www.mideq.org.

Notes

1. The research has been undertaken as part of a Migration for Development and Equality (MIDEQ) Hub work package on Poverty and Income Inequality, which has involved research fieldwork completed in three South–South migration corridors: Burkina Faso–Côte d'Ivoire, Ethiopia–South Africa and China–Ghana. More at www.mideq.org.

References

Acosta, P., Caldéron, C., Fajnzylber, P., & Lopez, H. (2006). Remittances and development in Latin America. *The World Economy, 29*(7), 957–987. https://doi.org/10.1111/j.1467-9701.2006.00831.x

Adamson, F. B., & Tsourapas, G. (2019). The migration state in the Global South. *International Migration Review, 54*(3), 853–882.

Adjami, M. (2016). *L'apatridie et la nationalité en Côte d'Ivoire*. UNHCR.

Adugna, F., Deshingkar, P., & Ayalew, T. (2019). *Brokers, migrants and the State: berri kefach "door openers" in Ethiopia clandestine migration to South Africa*. MOOP working paper, 56.

Bakewell, O. (2009). *South–South migration and human development: Reflection on African experiences*. IMI working papers 15.

Black, R., Natali, C., & Skinner, J. (2005). *Migration and inequality*. World Bank. http://hdl.handle.net/10986/9172

Bodomo, A. B., & Ma, G. (2010). From Guangzhou to Yiwu: Emerging facets of the African diaspora in China. *International Journal of African Renaissance Studies, 5*(2), 283–289. https://doi.org/10.1080/18186874.2010.534854

Botchwey, G., Crawford, G., Loubere, N., & Lu, J. (2019). South–South irregular migration: The impacts of China's informal gold rush in Ghana. *International Migration, 57*(4), 310–328. https://doi.org/10.1111/imig.12518

Campillo-Carrete, B. (2013). *South–South migration: A review of the literature*. ISS working paper 570. International Institute of Social Studies.

Carling, J. (2002). Migration in the age of involuntary immobility: Theoretical reflections and Cape Verdean experiences. *Journal of Ethnic and Migration Studies, 28*(1), 5–42. https://doi.org/10.1080/13691830120103912

Carling, J., & Jolivet, D. (2016). Exploring 12 migration corridors: Rationale, methodology and overview. In O. Bakewell et al. (Eds.), *Beyond networks*. Palgrave Macmillan.

Crawley, H. (2018). *Why understanding the relationship between migration and inequality may be the key to Africa's development*. OECD-development-matters.org

Crawley, H., Garba, F., & Nyamnjoh, F. (2022). Migration and (in)equality in the Global South: Intersections, contestations and possibilities. *Zanj: The Journal of Critical Global South Studies, 5*(1/2), 1–13.

Cutolo, A. (2010). Modernity, autochthony and the Ivorian nation: The end of a century in Côte d'Ivoire. *Africa (IAI), 80*(4), 527–552.

Dabiré, B. H. (2007). Les déterminants familiaux de la migration rurale au Burkina Faso. *African Population Studies, 22*(1), 107–135.

de Haan, A., & Yaqub, S. (2010). Migration and poverty: Linkages, knowledge, gaps and policy implications. In K. Hujo & N. Piper (Eds.), *South–South migration: Social policy in a development context* (pp. 190–219). Palgrave Macmillan. https://doi.org/10.1057/9780230283374_6

de Haas, H. (2007). Turning the tide? Why development will not stop migration. *Development and Change, 38*(5), 819–841. https://doi.org/10.1111/j.1467-7660.2007.00435.x

de Haas, H. (2010). *Migration transitions: A theoretical and empirical enquiry into the developmental drivers of international migration*. International Migration Institute (IMI), University of Oxford.

De Lombaerde, P., Huo, F., & Povoa Neto, H. (2014). South–South migrations: What is (still) in the research agenda? *The International Migration Review, 48*(1), 103–112.

Estifanos, Y., & Freeman, L. (2022). Shifts in the trend and nature of migration in Ethiopia–South Africa migration corridor. *Zanj: The Journal of Critical Global South Studies, 5*(1–2), 59–75.

Estifanos, Y., & Zack, T. (2019). *Follow the money: Tactics, dependencies and shifting relations in migration financing in the Ethiopia–South Africa migration corridor*. MOOP working paper, 63.

Estifanos, Y., & Zack, T. (2020). *Migration barriers and migration momentum*. Research and evidence facility working paper.

Feyissa, D. (2022). Beyond economics: The role of socio-political factors in Hadyia migration to South Africa. *Zanj: The Journal of Critical Global South Studies, 5*(1–2), 35–58.

Flahaux, M.-L., & de Haas, H. (2016). African migration: Trends, pattern, drivers. *Comparative Migration Studies, 4*(1), 1–25.

Gebre, L. T., Maharaj, P., & Pillay, N. K. (2011). The experiences of immigrants in South Africa: A case study of Ethiopians in Durban. *Urban Forum, 22*(1), 23–35. https://doi.org/10.1007/s12132-010-9105-6

Giese, K., & Thiel, A. (2015). Chinese factor in the space, place and agency of female head porters in urban Ghana. *Social and Cultural Geography, 16*(4), 444–464. https://doi.org/10.1080/14649365.2014.998266

Hagen-Zanker, J., & Hennessey, G. (2021). *What do we know about the subjective and intangible factors that shape migration decision-making?* PRIO paper, Oslo, Prio.

Hagen-Zanker, J., & Leon Himmelstine, C. (2014). *What is the state of evidence on the impacts of cash transfers on poverty, as compared to remittances?* ODI working paper.

Hammond, L. (2004). *This place will become home: Refugee repatriation to Ethiopia.* Cornell University Press.

Ho, C.G.-Y. (2008). The "doing" and "undoing" of community: Chinese networks in Ghana. *Journal of Current Chinese Affairs, 3*, 45–76.

Hossain, M., Khan, M. A., & Short, P. (2017). An overview of South–South migration: Opportunities, risks and policies. In Short et al (Eds.), *South–South migration* (pp. 1–10). Routledge.

Hujo, K. (2013). Linking social policy, migration and development in regional context: The case of Sub-Saharan Africa. *Regions and Cohesion, 3*(3), 30–55.

Hujo, K., & Piper, N. (2007). South–South migration: Challenges for development and social policy. *Development, 50*(4), 19–25.

Kóczán, Z., & Loyola, F. (2018). *How do migration and remittances affect inequality? A case study of Mexico.* IMF working paper. International Monetary Fund. https://www.imf.org/-/media/Files/Publications/WP/2018/wp18136.ashx

Lachaud, J. P. (1999). Envois de fonds, inégalité et pauvreté au Burkina Faso. *Tiers-Monde, 40*(160), 793–827. https://doi.org/10.3406/tiers.1999.5346

Lachaud, J. P. (2005). Crise ivoirienne, envois de fond et pauvreté au Burkina Faso. *Tiers-Monde, 46*(183), 651–673.

Lam, K. N. (2015). Chinese adaptations: African agency, fragmented community and social capital creation in Ghana. *Journal of Current Chinese Affairs, 44*(1), 9–41. http://nbnresolving.org/urn/resolver.pl?urn:nbn:de:gbv:18-4-8149

Landau, L. B., Wanjiku Kihato, C., & Postel, H. (2018). *The future of mobility and migration within and from Sub-Saharan Africa, Foresight reflection paper.* The European Political Strategy Centre.

Loritz, J. (2008). *The incidence of remittances in Latin America and effects on poverty and inequality.* Master of Public Policy Dissertation, Maryland School of Public Policy.

Marfaing, L., & Thiel, A. (2013). The impact of Chinese business on market entry in Ghana and Senegal. *Africa (IAI), 84*(4), 646–669.

Margolis, D., Miotti, L., Mouhoud, E. M., & Oudinet, J. (2015). *"To have and have not". Migration, remittances, poverty and inequality in Algeria*. IZA Discussion Paper No. 7747.

McKenzie, D. (2017). Poverty, inequality and international migration: Insights from 10 years of migration and development conferences. *Revue D'économie Du Développement, 3*(25), 13–28.

Mohan, G., & Tan-Mullins, M. (2009). Chinese migrants in Africa as new agents of development? An analytical framework. *European Journal of Development Research, 21*, 588–605. https://doi.org/10.1057/ejdr.2009.22

Mouhoud, E. M. (2010). Migrations, transferts et inégalités. Apports de travaux microéconomiques: Introduction. *Revue économique, 6*(61), 973–979. www.cairn.info

Murrugarra, E., Larrison, J., & Sasin, M. (2011). *Migration and poverty: Toward better opportunities for the poor*. World Bank. http://hdl.handle.net/10986/2535

Obeng, M. K. M. (2019). Journey to east: A study of Ghanaian migrant in Guangzhou, China. *Canadian Journal of African Studies, 53*(1), 67–87. https://doi.org/10.1080/00083968.2018.1536557

OCDE/CIRES. (2017). Interactions entre politiques publiques, migrations et développement en Côte d'Ivoire. Le voies de Développement. Editions OECD, Paris. https://doi.org/10.1787/9789264277090-fr

Opoku Dankwah, K., & Valenta, M. (2019). Chinese entrepreneurial migrants in Ghana: Socioeconomic impacts and Ghanaian trader attitudes. *Journal of Modern African Studies, 57*(1), 1–29.

Piché, V., & Cordell, D. (2015). *Entre le mil et le franc: un siègle de migrations circulaires en Afrique de l'Ouest, le cas du Burkina Faso*. Presses de l'Université du Québec.

Ratha, D., Mohapatra, S., Ozden, C., Plaza, S., Shaw, W., & Shimeles, A. (2011). *Leveraging migration for Africa: Remittances, skills and investments*. World Bank. http://hdl.handle.net/10986/2300

Ratha, D., & Shaw, W. (2007). *South–South migration and remittances: Development prospectus group*. World Bank.

Riccio, B. (2005). Talkin' about migration: Some ethnographic notes on the ambivalent representation of migrants in contemporary Senegal. *Stichproben. Wiener Zeitschrift Für Kritische Afrikastudien, 8*, 99–118.

Skeldon, R. (2002). Migration and poverty. *Asia-Pacific Population Journal/United Nations, 17*(4), 67–82.

Soumahoro, K. A., & Bi, S. T. (2022). Inequalities in access to land and strategies of resilience in the Burkinabe migrants in Northern Côte d'Ivoire. *Zanj: The Journal of Critical Global South Studies, 5*(1/2), 116–130.

Stark, O., & Taylor, J. E. (1989). Relative deprivation and international migration. *Demography, 26*(1), 1–14.

Stark, L., & Teppo, A. (2022). *Power and informality in Urban Africa*. Zed Books.

Tapsoba, T. A., Meda, M. M., Sangli, G., & Dabiré, B. H. (2022). Un panorama des inégalités liées à la migration entre le Burkina Faso et la Côte d'Ivoire. *Zanj: The Journal of Critical Global South Studies, 5*(1/2), 93–115.

Teye, J., Kandilige, L., Setrana, M., & Yaro, J. A. (2022). Chinese migration to Ghana: Challenging the orthodoxy on characterizing migrants and reasons for migration. *Ghana Journal of Geography, 14*(2), 203–234.

Traoré, J. A., & Ouedraogo, I. M. (2021). Public policies promoting the informal sector: Effects on incomes, employment and growth in Burkina Faso. *Journal of Policy Modeling, 43*(1), 56–75.

UNDP. (2021). *Annual report.* https://annualreport.undp.org/assets/UNDP Annual-Report-2021-en.pdf

United Nations. (2030). *Transforming our world: The 2030 Agenda for sustainable development.* https://sdgs.un.org/sites/default/files/publications/21252030% 20Agenda%20for%20Sustainable%20Development%20web.pdf

World Bank Report. (2019). *The changing nature of work: International Bank for Reconstruction and Development.* https://www.worldbank.org/en/publication/wdr 2019

Wouterse, F. S. (2008). *Migration, poverty and inequality: Evidence from Burkina Faso* (Vol. 786). IFPRI Discussion Paper. International Food Policy Research Institute. https://ebrary.ifpri.org/digital/collection/p15738coll2/id/12445

Zourkaléini, Y., & Kaboré, T. S. (2007). *Etudes des interrelations en population et pauvreté, le cas du Burkina Faso.* UNFAJISSP.

Open Access This chapter is licensed under the terms of the Creative Commons Attribution 4.0 International License (http://creativecommons.org/licenses/by/4.0/), which permits use, sharing, adaptation, distribution and reproduction in any medium or format, as long as you give appropriate credit to the original author(s) and the source, provide a link to the Creative Commons license and indicate if changes were made.

The images or other third party material in this chapter are included in the chapter's Creative Commons license, unless indicated otherwise in a credit line to the material. If material is not included in the chapter's Creative Commons license and your intended use is not permitted by statutory regulation or exceeds the permitted use, you will need to obtain permission directly from the copyright holder.

18

Gendered Migration in the Global South: An Intersectional Perspective on Inequality

Tanja Bastia and Nicola Piper

Introduction

From being predominantly framed as "associational migrants", women have come to be recognised as migrants in their own right, as primary migrants who are moving to new countries in search of work and new economic opportunities. Huge advancements have been made in achieving a deeper understanding of migration as a gendered process but despite the early publication of Morokvasic's seminal paper on "women are birds of passage too" in 1984, there are still gaps to be filled and issues to be explored (see also Donato et al., 2006). Although migration is undeniably a global phenomenon, it remains geographically concentrated, partly in response to the existence of centres of economic (re-)production and regulatory frameworks directing migration, many of which are pitched at bilateral rather than regional, let alone global, level. In some regions, we can observe greater fluidity in the South–South context where migratory flows tend to be larger than in the South–North context. Nonetheless, the latter has been the basis for most theorising of international migration in general, and gendered migration in particular.

T. Bastia
Global Development Institute, University of Manchester, Manchester, UK
e-mail: Tanja.Bastia@manchester.ac.uk

N. Piper (✉)
School of Law, Queen Mary University of London, London, UK
e-mail: n.piper@qmul.ac.uk

In this chapter we focus on intra- and trans-regional migration in a South–South context and explore what this means for women migrants.[1] In particular, while feminist scholars have highlighted care and the ways in which migration challenges social reproduction as an important issue, migration policies continue to tend to focus on just the 'productive' lives of migrant workers. Migration theories are still mostly built on the experience of South–North migration, and there continues to be relatively little understanding of South–South migration dynamics, despite the fact that most migration occurs intra-regionally. While the development literature has paid some attention to countries of origin, particularly through research linked to the so-called migration-development nexus, most of this research continues to mainly take into account South–North migrations. This is partly so because funders largely reside in the Global North (Europe, the US, Singapore) and are interested in understanding the development implications of the migrants that arrive—and potentially then return to 'their' countries of origin. There is far less funding available in migration destination countries in the Global South and the regional poles of attraction for regional migrants, such as Argentina, South Africa or Malaysia. Language is sometimes a barrier in regard to the circulation of knowledge, as in the case of South America, where a rich and diverse literature and migration research history exists on its regional migrations, but it is generally not known or disregarded in research published in English (see Asis & Piper, 2008; also Bastia and Kofman, forthcoming, for a fuller discussion).

We start this chapter by providing a brief overview of where we are at in terms of understanding gendered migration within the context of economic centres of (re-)production, polycentrism and global efforts to govern migration, and then move on to addressing some of the key challenges women migrants face in the context of current trends, including the feminisation of migration, temporary migration, transnationally split families and cross-generational issues.

Intersectional, Gendered Migrations

As feminist scholars have advanced critiques of hetero-normative social science research, this has also led to greater attention paid to gender disaggregation of migration flows. To those who have been attentive to the role paid by women in migration as well as to the changes in global and national economies, it came as no surprise that women actually played an important role in various migration streams long before it was formally acknowledged (see Morokvasic, 1984). Globally, women have increased their share of the overall number of international migrants from 46.6% in 1960 to 48.8% in 2000 (Zlotnik, 2000). However, most of this increase is the result of women displaying greater participation in South–North migration streams towards higher-income countries. Women's share of total migrants in more developed countries increased from 47.9% to 50.9% during this period, while it remained constant in less developed countries at 45.7% (Zlotnik, 2000). More recent figures indicate that the share of women migrants increased slightly from 51 to 52% between 1990 and 2013 in the Global North. However, it decreased quite significantly from 46 to 43% in developing regions during the same period (UN, 2013). There are also significant regional variations. In Europe and North America, women make up the majority of international migrants, while Oceania, Eastern/ South-eastern Asia and Latin America have achieved gender parity (in terms of numbers) (UN, 2013).

It is clear, therefore, that the term 'feminisation of migration' does not represent migration across all regions. It relates only to the experiences of higher-income countries in the Global North as well as South America and Oceania (see also Tittensor & Mansouri, 2017). Demographic trends and women's longer life expectancy also contribute to a larger share of women among the total migrant population in terms of the stock of migrants (Donato & Gabaccia, 2015). Clearly these figures only refer to international migration. As we know, internal migration is often much more significant, at least numerically, than cross-border migration. Internal migration is generally cheaper and more accessible, so more people engage in this kind of movement. The Human Development Report on human mobility (2009) highlights the relative weight of internal migration. For some countries, internal migration is eight times larger than international migration (HDR, 2009, 22). From this point of view, internal migration is often more significant than international migration for poverty alleviation, because moving within national borders is generally more accessible to poorer people than longer and more expensive moves across international borders (Bastia, 2013). A study on migration in and from Burkina Faso, for example, shows that internal migration was more likely to reduce poverty while international migration had a positive contribution for those households that were already better off and, as such, contributed to increasing income inequalities in places of origin (Wouterse, 2008).

The term "feminisation of migration" also fails to take into account the intersectional nature of migrations. As we have argued elsewhere, migrants are by definition "intersectional subjects", whose positionality alters as soon as they move from one geographical area to another (Bastia et al., 2022). This change is often even more pronounced when they move across international borders, because ethnic, race, class dimensions that influence gendered identities are then compounded by those of migration status. Any discussion of migration and inequality, therefore, requires an intersectional perspective, given that gender relations are always also classed, racialised and ethnicised (Anthias, 2020).

Some early work on the gendered composition of internal migration streams showed how gendered labour markets and the gendered division of labour within rural households influenced decisions about migration. Sarah Radcliffe (1986) researched internal migration in a village in Southern Peru and concluded that men tended to migrate shorter distances and for shorter periods of time during the slack season in the agricultural cycle, while young women migrated longer distances, usually to the capital Lima, and they did so for much longer periods of time (often years as opposed to months) because their labour was considered 'surplus' in their native rural households.

This example might seem far removed from our discussion about the "global economy" but it is not. It illustrates how gender roles and the households' organisation of labour along gender lines influence who migrates, where to and for how long. As we have seen, as higher-income countries in Europe, North America and Asia face rapidly ageing societies while at the same time experiencing greater labour market insertion by native women, they start to rely more heavily on other women, usually (though not exclusively) international migrants, for filling in care gaps within their households. The domestic and care sectors in these regions are now dominated by women migrants, who sometimes travel thousands of miles, to take up insufficiently or even unregulated, insecure and generally low-paid jobs, while leaving behind their own families (see section below on transnational family life). Various labour market sectors as well as migration more broadly have also been subject to "governing" attempts. Given the array of institutional actors involved at the local, regional and global level, coordinating policy responses ('migration governance'), as well as advocacy efforts to influence those, are faced with the challenge of multi-layered and multi-sited character of migration regulation.

Gendered Migration, Temporality and Precarity

Cross-border migration has been an important dimension of economic development throughout the world, alongside increased demand for low-wage labour needed to sustain global and regional re/productive chains. As a result, many migrants remain within the region when migrating and their migration is proactively shaped by states. Most governments in Asia, for instance, have come to actively promote outflows or inflows of migrant workers as a key economic strategy, and they have primarily done so on the basis of strictly temporary visa policies. This is so because origin countries typically seek remittance inflows and skill transfers, while destination countries use temporary migrant labour as "disposable" inputs for jobs shunned by the local workforce. National, regional and global policy-makers have reached a consensus on mutually beneficial economic outcomes of temporary labour migration, thus spreading such policies around the world. This understanding has resulted in the subordination of migrants' legal and working rights as lesser considerations to the economic 'management' paradigm of migration flows (Piper, 2022).

Intra-regional migration in the form of temporary visa arrangements has become a distinct pattern especially in Asia since the mid-twentieth century, a period during which temporary labour migration had also risen to its prominence in the "West". In Asia, this type of migration was boosted by neoliberal economic globalisation (Gills & Piper, 2002) with its specifically gendered forms of labour supply and demand. The highly feminised migration of domestic workers is one distinct feature of such trend. Many temporary migrants take up domestic work in countries of destination. At least 53.6 million women and men above the age of 15 are reported to be in domestic work as their main job, with some source suggesting a figure as high as 100 million (ILO, 2010). Domestic worker employment constitutes at least 2.5% of total employment in post-industrialised countries and between 4 and 10% of total employment in developing countries. In gender terms, women are the overwhelming majority of the domestic workforce (at 83%), which represents 7.5% of women's employment worldwide (ILO, 2010). Moreover, the women who enter this sector of work, often belong to racialized and ethnicised social groups, not just migrant workers, but are often also of indigenous descent or of lower socio-economic class.

Temporary contract migration schemes mean that legal migration takes almost exclusively place on the basis of strictly fixed term contracts. Such contracts typically tie the worker to one specific employer, an example being the notorious Kafala system as practiced in the Gulf countries (Iskander,

2021). Breaking the contract to seek employment elsewhere—for instance in the case of abuse or contract violation on the part of the employer—can turn a migrant into an 'illegal' worker and resident. In this sense, there is no free access to the 'labour market'. Because of the strictly temporary nature of migration, the nature of employer-tied contracts and the frequent occurrences of undocumented migration as the result of absconding or overstaying, return migration can be a natural consequence of this arrangement.

The practice of restrictive policies in the form of strictly temporary migration is particularly evident in the case of migrant domestic workers who are sometimes violently prohibited from any measure that can be seen as developing intimate ties to the destination countries. Migrant domestic workers are prohibited from marrying locals and restricted from marrying migrant workers in Singapore. In these cases, marriage has to take place after departure. Female migrant domestic workers, who make up the majority, have to undergo regular pregnancy tests by the authorities, and pregnant domestic workers face being deported (Xiang, 2013; Constable, 2014). Gendered discrimination is here compounded by nationality, as states aim to preserve the national ethnic make-up by prohibiting marriage with non-nationals. Since the employers are de facto penalised when their domestic worker becomes pregnant, employers take on the role of surveillance to impose curfew or interfere with the workers' day-off, often in the name of gendered morality and 'protection' (Constable, 2014; Yeoh & Huang, 2010). In Hong Kong, migrant domestic workers are excluded from eligibility to apply for permanent residency, which is available for expatriates after seven years of residence (Constable, 2014).

The case of temporary employer-tied migration requires us to note that any development "agency" on the part of individual migrant women is hampered by ever more restrictive and selective migration policy frameworks. Restrictions are driven by barricaded access to labour markets, types of work, and length of stay; and the 'selectiveness' of workers based on their gender and/or country of origin. A migrant's agency for development is, therefore, not only restrained by the restrictive and selective nature of prevalent migration policies, but also due to gendered norms, flexible labour markets, high competition for jobs and the fraudulent practices of intermediaries (resulting in economic precarity) as well as socio-political non-commitment to newcomers and politically disenfranchised migrant-(non)citizens. These processes are not only gendered, but also racialized and marked by considerations for preserving national 'purity'. It has been shown that countries of destination tend to have the upper hand in determining the substance of bilateral negotiations (Wickramasekara, 2011). However, in recent years some countries of origin such as the Philippines have also become more selective, albeit often in the form of instituting bans on female migrants only, rather than blanket bans on everyone's migration to a specific country of destination where conditions are particularly unfavourable or exploitative.

Migrants' expectations, planning and understanding of temporality attached to space, shape their behaviour and membership practices in destination countries, most notably their participation in the labour market. Piore's study (1979, as quoted in Levitt & Rajaram, 2013) found migrants more willing to accept lower wages and comparatively worse employment conditions when they expect their stay to be temporary. The temporary nature of migration shapes or rather reflects the kind of institutional understanding that destination and origin states have of migration. Migrants are not perceived as members, or potential citizens, but rather as flexible low-wage labour that supplies manpower in areas where the destination country is experiencing short- and (usually) long-term shortage, while providing much needed monetary flows to sustain their own families. Martin (2006, 4) explains this process by using an aphorism that "there is nothing more permanent than temporary migration". Despite permanent labour shortages, temporary migration provides labour at the expense of human rights such as the right to family life, mobility, social protection and other basic rights to one's life and well-being (Castles, 2004; Sharma, 2007), affecting migrants' ability to function as agents of their own, their families' or communities' and national development.

The predominance of temporary contract migration leads inevitably to return migration. The promise of the "development effect" even for individual migrants does not usually materialise after just one stint abroad. Re-migration often occurs, and the suggested positive 'development effect' of 'circular migration' is more the manifestation of many migrants being captive to, or falling back into, the situation of precarity which they were hoping to escape.

Social Reproduction and Transnational Family Life

As (married or unmarried) women migrate to seek better opportunities elsewhere, they typically leave behind their families which in turn need to adjust to the absence of the person who usually acts as the main carer. Migrants are often unable to take their families with them because of restrictive migration regimes, as discussed above. In the past, when migration was not so strictly regulated and countries of destination actively recruited comparatively large numbers of migrants to populate their countries, it was easier to reconcile migration with family reunification or formation with spouses who hailed from the migrants' country of origin. Migration was aimed at settlement and the best way to ensure that migrants settle is for them to have their families with them. Today, however, migration regimes actively discourage settlement, except for a very small proportion of highly skilled migrants, who are deemed 'desirable' by countries of destination, in what has become the 'race for talent'. Most migrants, especially those entering informal, insecure and low-paid work, are however not welcomed, but tolerated by allowing them to stay for the duration of the performance of their key role as 'cheap and disposable labour', as discussed above. Destination countries typically want to appear able to respond quickly to economic downturns and changing political mood among their voting public. In addition, they also want to avoid bearing the costs of educating, caring for and providing a safety net for migrants' families. They therefore actively discourage or prohibit the reunification of migrant families. As we have seen, in some cases, they also control and police women migrants' bodies through pregnancy tests and deport them in the event of them falling pregnant.

Even when migration policies do not explicitly prohibit family reunification, the types of jobs available to most women migrants mean that they cannot reconcile their migration journeys with family life. Long working hours, low pay and no or limited access to benefits are contributing factors to their inability to work while also looking after their own dependents. For example, one of the sectors where women migrants predominate is care work, particularly elderly care. Migrant women working as live-in elderly carers are often on call for 24 hours a day and work six to six-and-a-half days a week. Employers will sometimes allow women to work with very small babies, but for the great majority of these women it is impossible to work and also care for dependents. Those working as cleaners for multiple households paid by the hour manage such a busy schedule in order to be able to cover their basic necessities (food, rent, transport) while at the same time trying to save as much money as possible, that they also find it impossible to reconcile work and family life (Bastia, 2015, 2019).

Some women are able to access carer programmes set up by destination countries, such as Canada, which gives them the option to apply for permanent residency and subsequently reunite with their families after they have fulfilled a two-year contract. However, as Geraldine Pratt shows, to access this programme, Filipino women have often had to work abroad in Singapore or Hong Kong, before gathering sufficient social and financial capital to apply for the programme in Canada. By the time they are able to bring their families to Canada, years have gone by, the young children they left behind meanwhile grown into teenagers or young adults, and their husbands sometimes found other partners. So even when available in theory, reunification in practice is marred by practical and emotional difficulties (Pratt, 2012). These migrant women use their migration within their region to build finances, skills and networks to eventually reach their preferred destinations in the Global North.

One of the costs associated with women's access to the global economy is, therefore, related to the split families it engenders (see Haagsman & Mazzucato, 2020). Besides the emotional pain associated with being separated from loved ones for long periods of time (Pratt, 2009; Bastia, 2019), others have also drawn attention to the unequal distribution of care labour globally as a result of migrant women performing care duties in higher-income countries. Hochschild (2000) has termed this process the 'global care chains' to highlight how families at destination that employ women migrant carers are intrinsically linked with the migrant woman's families of origin. She argued that as women migrate, they leave a "care vacuum" in their families of origin that is usually filled in by another woman who might be another family member or somebody employed by the family to undertake care duties. She might be an internal migrant, who is unable to access the more lucrative cross-border migration so might be poorer and more disadvantaged, generally of a lower socio-economic class, sometimes of indigenous descent, than the woman who moved internationally. The destination family, on the other hand, is able to benefit from a surplus of care. This might be a dual-earner family, who is able to have more income and more quality leisure time, as a result of the care that the migrant woman is contributing to their household. Globally, therefore, the migration of women carers contributes to a "care deficit" (or "displaced care", see Withers & Piper, 2018) in countries of origin and a "care surplus" in countries of destination (see also Yeates, 2004).

The analytical framework of "care chains" has contributed to highlighting the importance of care and the costs associated with low-paid, temporary and insecure migration. It has also done much to draw attention to what happens in countries of origin as a result of global migration. Some of the critiques of this way of thinking about women's migration have centred around the fact that: (i) it puts forward a zero sum game between households of origin and destination; (ii) it conceptualises care as a physical resource; (iii) it draws on a very specific experience of migration (Philippines to Canada/ US) and (iv) it does not address how care is reconfigured for migrants working in sectors other than the care sector (see Pearson & Kusakabe, 2012). Its conclusions are therefore, by necessity, quite pessimistic. More recently, scholarship emerging from South America has highlighted the multiple ways in which households of origin are able to accommodate the absence of the main carer (Gioconda Herrera, 2013, 2020). The "Asian" experience reinforces this and further underpins the supporting role that families have always played (Asis et al., 2019).

Cross-Generational Issues

The splitting of migrant families therefore raises concerns related to the care arrangements of those family members who stay in countries of origin. Most of the policy and research concern to date has focused on the migrants' children (e.g. Parreñas, 2005). This has been a particular concern that has been linked to the feminisation of migration. That is, the care of children who remained in the countries of origin was not raised in relation to men's migration because it was assumed that the main carer, i.e. the mother, remained in the country of origin and continued to care for her children. Policy-makers and researchers have started paying attention to what happens to children in contexts of migration only when they started realising that a large number of older, married women, who were also mothers, were also deciding to migrate for long distances and over long periods of time (as discussed above). The absence of fathers is not usually seen as a problem for children's well-being in policy-makers' views.

While policy-makers and the media usually refer to the migration of migrant mothers in terms of "moral panics", the research in this area is a bit less conclusive. While children (and mothers) generally suffer emotionally as a result of long separations, some research suggests that as long as children are included in their mothers' migration projects, then the consequences are they generally come to better understand their decisions and how their migration benefits the family as a whole (Parreñas, 2005). Current migration decisions also need to be placed within longer historical accounts of migration, in which the notion of the stable, nuclear family might not be as normative as in policy-makers' (or researchers') assumptions. In Bolivia, for example, there is a lot of talk of the current disruptions to family life resulting from high levels of women's emigration but in the not so distant past, it was not uncommon for children to be raised by their grandparents or uncles and aunts, when the need arose (Bastia, 2019).

Moreover, migrants generally also have parents, who might also have care-needs of their own but are often left to look after grandchildren. The literature on the migrants' parents who stay behind in the migrants' countries of origin is, however, only just beginning to emerge (Bastia et al., 2021; Vullnetari & King, 2008). Grandparents might also travel to countries of destination to care for their grandchildren and migrants, will, indeed, travel back to countries of origin to provide care for their ageing parents, if the means allow (King et al., 2017).

Much of this concern for what happens to the care of vulnerable family members in the absence of migrants, particularly mothers and the women in the family, is premised on the assumption that physical proximity is required for people to provide care and care for one another. The literature on transnational care has shown, however, that people provide care from afar in a myriad of ways: through regular phone calls, by sending remittances, arranging for substitute care, providing emotional support in times of need and, when required, visiting (Baldassar et al., 2007). Whether this is available to people in lower-income countries, for migrants with insecure jobs or in setting where access to modern communication technologies is still challenging, is still to be seen.

Missing from this discussion and of particular relevance for those women migrants who enter insecure, low-paid jobs, is the question of "caring for self". While policy-makers and researchers grapple with the consequences of women's migration for vulnerable family members in countries of origin, of paramount importance to us seems to be the well-being of the women migrants themselves. Much of the development-talk around migration raises questions about the extent to which migration can deliver development for countries, communities or families of origin. But, what about the women who undertake these journeys? In the final section we focus on migration governance and show how macro-level migration policy-making is also highly gendered and is at the root of some of the unequal processes we have discussed so far.

(Re-)production, Polycentrism and Migration Governance

Women migrants engaged in global labour markets are subjected to the dictates of 'neoliberal governmentality' through feminised forms of flexibilisation and informalisation of work, which underpin macro-economic development projects (Oksala, 2013; Peterson, 2012). Temporary migration has also been analysed as a specific form of disciplining practice for migrant subjectivity (Robertson, 2014). Given the highly-gendered labour markets and restrictive migration policies practiced around the world, female migrant workers are differently situated within labour migration dynamics in comparison to men. Gender can operate as an additional governing code (Hennebry et al., 2018). However, in migration and development policies at both national and international levels, gender is not often considered a separate analytical category. Moreover, migration policies are mostly gender-blind, ignore the power dynamics and implications of gender-segregated labour markets, and the socio-economic/cultural structures in both origin and destination countries (Piper, 2006).

In the "migration-development nexus" discourse which has greatly influenced the global governance debate in both scholarly and policy terms, the prime focus is on monetary gains measured through women migrants' contributions, i.e. the remittances they sent, in relation to national economies. This development paradigm ignores women migrants' personal experiences and the costs involved in migration, thereby failing to pay attention to their rights, protections and unique subjectivities (Piper & Lee, 2016; Walsham, 2022). Government policy frameworks are predominantly concerned with controlling migration (i.e. the exit and entry of individuals and their access to labour markets or jobs) and extracting economic benefits from foreign workers while "paying mere lip service to the human rights of migrants" (Piper, 2015, 792).

There is much greater recognition about the need to cooperate and coordinate with other states, as reflected in global migration governance, despite its multi-actor character, having become a much more concerted effort. However, the predominant regulatory framework to date—especially in the South–South context—still takes the form of bilateral agreements (BLAs), where destination countries tend to have the upper hand. The various bilateral agreements which exist on domestic worker migration, for instance, rarely include clauses on workers' rights or are gender-sensitive, let alone gender-responsive, but tend to be about technicalities (Hennebry et al., 2022). In most migrant-sending countries, in turn, women migrants' remittances make significant contributions to national economies. Separation from their families ensures a steady flow of remittances, so there is little incentive to negotiation for family unification provisions. A governmental discourse that focuses on remittances alone, however, serves to instrumentalise migrants' contributions and ignores the social costs of migration to families.

States generally refrain from formulating gender-sensitive migration policies that facilitate women's cross-border labour mobility, including across the Global South. Rather, some countries impose legal restrictions on women's labour migration, typically under the guise of protection (Hennebry, 2017). Moreover, labour laws in most host countries often poorly protect the rights of women migrants, who are subject to intersecting structural factors and discriminations based on gender, class, age, ethnicity and nationality. These factors further compound the challenges they confront (Hennebry, 2016). As a result, women migrants who are concentrated in highly gendered sectors at the low-wage end (e.g. domestic work, garment manufacturing) cannot access the same labour rights and social protections as workers in other sectors. Structural inequalities, gender discrimination in labour markets in countries of origin, and restrictive immigration controls coalesce so that women generally have fewer pathways to migrate, will be more likely to turn to recruiters and to migrate via lower skilled temporary worker schemes or undocumented channels—and as such are particularly politically disenfranchised (Hennebry, 2017; Piper, 2010). Socio-economic precarity, geographic isolation and political disenfranchisement extend to recent ideas around refugee employment in the Middle East where manufacturing has emerged as the key sector where refugee women work under Export Processing Zones conditions and without trade union representation (Lenner & Turner, 2018).

Yet, there have been some promising developments in recent years as far as the global governing framework is concerned. The great success story concerns the ILO Convention No. 189 on Decent Work for Domestic Workers. The convention was adopted in 2011 after a two-year negotiation process and several years of concerted advocacy alliances by trade union and other civil society organisations around the world. These efforts emanated particularly strongly from those civil society organisations situated in the Global South (Piper, 2015).

UN Women is also doing important work on securing better rights for migrant domestic workers, targeting in particular the migration corridor between the Middle Eastern countries and South Asia. There are now good practice examples of BLAs between some countries in the Middle East and South Asia, promising unified contracts and minimum standards. Moreover, the SDGs have specifically recognised gender as an important factor in migration, particularly stated through SDG 5.5, SDGs 5.6, 8 and 10.4. The SDGs have normative value, and it is through diverse actors and appropriate mechanisms that these goals could be achieved. The research by Hennebry et al. (2018) shows that both in terms of issues covered and the process in which they were developed, the SDGs are considerably more participatory and inclusive than their predecessor, the MDGs. Although it might be an overstatement to say that the agenda of women migrants is at the forefront of SDGs, the fact that migrant *women* are acknowledged as a specific category and target group within the SDGs constitutes a major achievement (ibid.; Datta & Piper, forthcoming).

The latest development at the global level concerns the negotiations around the Global Compact of Migration (GCM) where gender issues were also flagged up and pushed high up on the agenda by civil society organisations, supported by international organisations such as UN Women and the ILO. Implementation is a huge challenge and a space to watch. Furthermore, although decent work is mentioned in the GCM, key issues related such as decent wages and freedom of association are sidelines. Addressing migrant worker precarity in gendered and racialised labour markets, thus, remains a challenge. The existence of an ever greater number of CSOs and their expanding regional and global networks, however, are a promising factor that will continue to remind governments of their commitments.

Conclusion

We are at a critical junction in our understanding of women migrants in the global economy. Huge advancements have been made to further our understanding of migration as a gendered process, including as one that is shaped by the intersectional nature of the challenges that migrants encounter in their migration journeys. However, as we have argued, there is a continued need to keep focusing on women migrants and the way they fare in the changes that are taking place in the global, regional and national economies. This is because a focus on gender alone, especially at the individual micro level, can lead to de-politicisation, or it can re-draw attention to male migrants only, albeit one where they are understood as gendered beings.

Moreover, most of the theories that are generally drawn on for understanding gendered migration processes are based on the experience of South–North migration. As we have shown, almost half of all cross-border migration (and probably much more) is made up of South–South, intra- and trans-regional migration streams, which often have different characteristics compared to South–North migration. Temporary migration features more prominently in some regions such as Asia, for example, where it is more tightly regulated than elsewhere. Such regulation relates to migrant women's working lives but also their bodies, in cases where their reproductive lives are under surveillance by national authorities. In other regions, there is a relative ease for moving across national borders, such as among MERCOSUR member states,[2] but the precarity and insecurity associated with the type of jobs that women migrants have access to continue to be a cause of concern. Xenophobic and racist attitudes further impinge on migrants' daily lives, their socio-economic and psychological well-being. These attitudes are always also gendered.

While the development literature has paid some attention to countries of origin, most of the examples it draws on continue to include South–North migrations. Destination countries in the Global South, such as Argentina, South Africa or Malaysia, need to feature much more prominently in migration research in the future, if we are to build a truly global picture of migration and its relationship with intersectional inequalities. We also need to find ways to overcome language barriers and fully recognise migration research arising in the Global South.

As we have demonstrated in this chapter, a focus on South–South migration raises different issues for migrant workers, including women migrants, to those covered in the mainstream literature on gender and migration. A re-orientation in focus can shed new light to existing research questions. Examples from South America, for example, provide a less stark and more grounded understanding of how social reproduction is re-organised as a result of the migration of women, as compared to the negative conclusions of the global care chains literature. However, we still need a better understanding of the cross-generational effects of migration, given that most of the concern, both in research and in policy, has been on children. Last but not least, going beyond domestic and care work by conducting cross-sectoral research, especially from a comparative perspective, would be important for broadening the knowledge base on gendered migrant precarity. So, there is a strong case to be made for more research on South–South and inter-regional migration.

Notes

1. This chapter is an updated version of the article that we have co-written and was published in *Gender & Development* 27(1) Migrants in a Global Economy, March 2019, pp. 15–30, with the following title 'Women migrants in the global economy: a global overview (and regional perspectives)', which is available here https://www.tandfonline.com/doi/full/10.1080/13552074.2019.1570734?needAccess=true.
2. Argentina, Brazil, Paraguay, Uruguay and Venezuela are State Parties. Bolivia, Chile, Colombia, Ecuador, Guyana, Peru and Surinam are Associated States (https://www.mercosur.int/en/about-mercosur/mercosur-countries/).

References

Anthias, F. (2020). *Translocational belonging: Intersectional dilemmas and social inequalities*. Routledge.

Asis, M. B. A., Piper, N., & Raghuram, P. (2019). Asian contributions to global migration research: Current contributions and future avenues'. *Revue Européenne Des Migrations Internationales, 35*(1/2), 13–37.

Asis, M. B. A., & Piper, N. (2008). Researching international labor migration in Asia. *The Sociological Quarterly, 49*(3), 423–444. https://doi.org/10.1111/j.1533-8525.2008.00122.x

Baldassar, L., Baldock, C. V., & Wilding, R. (2007). *Families caring across borders: Migration, ageing, and transnational caregiving*. Palgrave Macmillan.

Bastia, T. (2013). Migration and inequality: An introduction. In T. Bastia (Ed.), *Migration and inequality* (pp. 3–23). Routledge.

Bastia, T. (2015). 'Looking after granny': A transnational ethic of care and responsibility. *Geoforum, 64*, 121–129.

Bastia, T. (2019). *Gender, migration and social transformation: Intersectionality in Bolivian itinerant migrations*. Routledge.

Bastia, T., & Kofman, E. (forthcoming). Unequal knowledge production and circulation in migration studies: Feminist perspectives. In J. Dahinden, & A. Potts (Eds.), *Reflexivities in migration studies: Pitfalls and alternatives*.

Bastia, T., Valenzuela, C. C., & Pozo, M. E. (2021). The consequences of migration for the migrants' parents in Bolivia. *Global Networks, 21*(2), 393–412.

Bastia, T., Datta, K., Hujo, K., Piper, N., & Walsham, M. (2022). Reflections on intersectionality: A journey through the worlds of migration research, policy and advocacy. *Gender, Place and Culture*. https://doi.org/10.1080/0966369X.2022.2126826

Castles, S. (2004). Why migration policies fail. *Ethnic and Racial Studies, 27*(2), 205–227.

Constable, N. (2014). *Born out of place: Migrant mothers and the politics of international labor*. University of California Press.

Datta, K., & Piper, N. (forthcoming). *Migration and the SDGs*. Edward Elgar.

Donato, K., & Gabaccia, D. (2015). *Gender and international migration*. Sage.

Donato, K. M., Gabaccia, D., Holdaway, J., Manalansan, M. I. V., & Pessar, P. R. (2006). A glass half full? Gender in migration studies'. *International Migration Review, 40*, 3–26. https://doi.org/10.1111/j.1747-7379.2006.00001.x

Gills, D. S., & Piper, N. (Eds.). (2002). *Women and work in globalizing Asia*. Routledge.

Haagsman, K., & Mazzucato, V. (2020). The well-being of stay behind family members in migrant households. In T. Bastia & R. Skeldon (Eds.), *Routledge handbook of migration and development*. Routledge.

Hennebry, J. (2017). *At what cost?: WMWs remittances and development*. UN Women.

Hennebry, J., Hari, K. C., & Piper, N. (2018). Not without them: Realising the sustainable development goals for women migrant workers. *Journal of Ethnic and Migration Studies* (JEMS) (preview online).

Hennebry, J., Grass, W., & McLaughlin, J. (2017). *WMWs' Journey through the margins: Labour, migration and trafficking*. UN Women.

Hennebry, J. (2016). *Women working worldwide: A situational analysis of women migrant workers*. UN Women.

Hennebry, J., Piper, N., Hari, K. C., & Williams, K. (2022). Bilateral Labor Agreements as Migration Governance Tools: An Analysis from a Gender Lens. *Theoretical Inquiries in Law, 23*(2), 184–205.

Herrera, G. (2013). *Lejos de tus pupilas. Familias transnacionales, cuidados y desigualdad social en Ecuador*. Onu-Muejres, FLACSO.

Herrera, G. (2020). Care and migration. In T. Bastia & R. Skeldon (Eds.), *Routledge handbook of migration and development*. Routledge.

Hochschild, A. (2000). Global care chains and emotional surplus value. In W. Hutton & A. Guiddens (Eds.), *On the edge: Living with global capitalism* (pp. 130–146). Johathan Cape.

Human Development Report. (2009). *Overcoming Barriers: Human mobility and development*. UNDP.

ILO. (2010). *ILO global estimates on migrant workres: Results and Methodology*. Special focus on migrant domestic workers, ILO.

Iskander, N. (2021). *Does skill make us human? Migrant workers in 21st century in Qatar and beyond*. Princeton University Press.

King, R., Lulle, A., Sampaio, D., & Vullnetari, J. (2017). Unpacking the ageing–migration nexus and challenging the vulnerability trope. *Journal of Ethnic and Migration Studies, 43*(2), 182–198.

Lenner, K., & Turner, L. (2018). Making refugees work? The Politics of Integrating Syrian Refugees into the Labor Market in Jordan. *Middle East Critique*. https://doi.org/10.1080/19436149.2018.1462601

Levitt, P., & Rajaram, N. (2013). The migration-development nexus and organizational time. *International Migration Review, 47*(3), 483–507.

Martin, P. (2006). Immigration reform: Implications for agriculture. *Update–Agricultural and Resource Economics, 9*(4), 1–4.

Morokvasic, M. (1984). Birds of passage are also women…'. *International Migration Review, 18*(4), 886–907.

Oksala, J. (2013). Feminism and neoliberal governmentality. *Foucault Studies*, 32–53.

Parreñas, R. S. (2005). *Children of global migration: Transnational families and gendered woes*. Stanford University Press.

Pearson, R., & Kusakabe, K. (2012). Who cares? Gender, reproduction and care chains of Burmese migrant workers in Thailand. *Feminist Economics, 18*(2), 149–175.

Peterson, V. S. (2012). Rethinking theory: inequalities, informalization and feminist quandaries. *International Feminist Journal of Politics, 14*(1), 5–35.

Piper, N. (2006). Gendering the politics of migration. *International Migration Review, 40*(1), 133–164.

Piper, N. (2010). All quiet on the Eastern Front? Temporary contract migration in asia revisited from a development perspective. *Policy and Society, 90*, 1–13.

Piper, N. (2013). Resisting inequality: Global migrant rights activism. In T. Bastia (Ed.), *Migration and inequality* (pp. 45–64). Routledge.

Piper, N. (2015). Democratising migration from the bottom up: The rise of the global migrant rights movement. *Globalizations, 12*(5), 788–802.

Piper, N. (2022). Temporary labour migration in Asia: The transnationality-precarity nexus. *International Migration, 60*, 38–47. https://doi.org/10.1111/imig.12982

Piper, N., & Lee, S. (2016). Marriage migration at the intersection of crisis and development: Migrant precarity and social reproduction. *Critical Asian Studies, 48*(4), 473–493.

Pratt, G. (2009). Circulating sadness: Witnessing Filipina mothers' stories of family separation, *Gender, Place amp; Culture, 16*(1), 3–22, https://doi.org/10.1080/09663690802574753

Pratt, G. (2012). *Families apart: Migrant mothers and the conflicts of labor and love.* Minnesota University Press.

Radcliffe, S. (1986). Gender relations, peasant livelihood strategies and migration: A case study from Cuzco, Peru. *BLAR, 5*(2), 29–47.

Robtertson, S. (2014). The Temporalities of International Migration: Implications for Ethnographic Research, ICS Occasional Paper Series vol. 5, no. 1 University of Western Sysdney

Sharma, N. (2007). Global apartheid and nation-statehood: Instituting border regimes. In J. Goodman & P. James (Eds.), *Nationalism and global solidarities: Alternative projections to neoliberal globalisation.* Oxon; Routledge.

Tittensor, D., & Mansouri, F. (2017). The feminisation of migration? A critical overview. In D. Tittensor & F. Mansouri (Eds.), *The politics of women and migration in the global south.* Palgrave.

UN. (2013). *International migration report.* New York.

UNDP. (2009). *Human development report. Overcoming barriers: Human mobility and development.* UNDP.

Vullnetari, J., & King, R. (2008). 'Does your granny eat grass?' On mass migration, care drain and the fate of older people in rural Albania. *Global Networks, 8*(2), 139–171.

Walsham, M. (2022). *Gender and global, migration governance for South–South migration.* MIDEQ Working paper series. https://southsouth.contentfiles.net/media/documents/Gender_and_Global_Migration_Governance_for_South-South_Migration_Working_Paper.pdf

Wickramasekara, P. (2011). Circular migration: A triple win or a dead end? *Global union research network discussion paper,* No. 15, ILO.

Withers, M., & Piper, N. (2018). Uneven development and displaced care in Sri Lanka. *Current Sociology, 66*(4), 590–601. https://doi.org/10.1177/0011392118 87652

Wouterse, F. S. (2008). *Migration, poverty and inequality: Evidence from Burkina Faso*. IFPRI discussion paper. http://www.ifpri.org/publication/migration-poverty-and-inequality

Xiang, B. (2013). Transnational encapsulation: Compulsory return as a labor-migration control in East Asia. In B. Xiang., B. S. A. Yeoh, & M. Toyota (Eds) *Return: Nationalizing transnational mobility in Asia* (pp. 83–99). Duke University Press.

Yeates, N. (2004). Global care chains. *International Feminist Journal of Politics, 6*(3), 369–391.

Yeoh, B. S. A., & Huang, S. (2010). Transnational domestic workers and the negotiation of mobility and work practices in Singapore's home-spaces. *Mobilities, 5*(2), 219–236.

Zlotnik, H. (2000). The global dimensions of female migration. *Migration Information Source*. http://www.migrationinformation.org/Feature/display.cfm?ID=109

Open Access This chapter is licensed under the terms of the Creative Commons Attribution 4.0 International License (http://creativecommons.org/licenses/by/4.0/), which permits use, sharing, adaptation, distribution and reproduction in any medium or format, as long as you give appropriate credit to the original author(s) and the source, provide a link to the Creative Commons license and indicate if changes were made.

The images or other third party material in this chapter are included in the chapter's Creative Commons license, unless indicated otherwise in a credit line to the material. If material is not included in the chapter's Creative Commons license and your intended use is not permitted by statutory regulation or exceeds the permitted use, you will need to obtain permission directly from the copyright holder.

19

Haitian Migration and Structural Racism in Brazil

Jailson de Souza e Silva, Fernando Lannes Fernandes, and Jorge Luiz Barbosa

Introduction

Since 2010, Brazil has received a regular and growing number of Haitian immigrants, a process which is still ongoing. There are many reasons for the arrival of this population. Brazil is seen as a reference country by Haitians since 2004 when Brazil commanded the UN mission to help stabilise the country.[1] Despite that, until 2010 the number of Haitian migrants in the Brazil was very small. The 2010 earthquake can be seen as the trigger behind the greater migration process observed in the 2010s (Silva, 2013). It is worth noting that the Brazilian government's openness to them, followed by easy legal registration of migrants, and an identification between the Haitian and Brazilian peoples are central factors encouraging Haitian migration to Brazil.

Once they arrive in Brazil, Haitian migrants face a set of challenges to achieve a dignified insertion into Brazilian society. The pattern of inequality

---

J. de Souza e Silva · F. L. Fernandes (✉) · J. L. Barbosa
UNIPeriferias, Rio de Janeiro, Brazil
e-mail: f.l.fernandes@dundee.ac.uk

J. de Souza e Silva
e-mail: jailson@imja.org.br

J. L. Barbosa
e-mail: jorgebarbosa390@gmail.com

F. L. Fernandes
University of Dundee, Dundee, UK

in Brazilian society—for which racism is foundational—is a central element in understanding the difficulties experienced by Haitians, the vast majority of whom are Black. Understanding the impact of racism on the conditions under which Haitian migrants come into Brazil, then, is a relevant element to understanding our own patterns of inequality, how they are expressed and how we can face them.

It is a well-known fact that Brazilian society is one of the most unequal in the world (Lima & Prates, 2019; Pimentel, 2023). This inequality has been produced since the beginning of the colonisation process by Portugal, from the control of the various forms of economic, political, cultural, educational, military, technological and symbolic capital (Bourdieu, 1995) by a specific social group: white, enriched, heteronormative men (Alencastro, 2000; Ellsworth, 1999; Nascimento, 2006). Its reproduction process is supported, in turn, by three central elements: patriarchy/sexism; institutional patrimonialism[2] and structural/institutional racism. In this chapter, we focus on this third element and its role in the (re)production of inequality, and how it relates with Haitian migration in particular.[3] Our aim is to provide a comprehensive reflection on the phenomenon of Haitian migration to Brazil and how the country's characteristic structural racism impacts the experiences of Haitians living in the country. The first part of this chapter contains an analysis of the socio-historical conditions delineating structural racism in Brazil and the racist structures that sustain inequality in contemporary Brazil. In the second part we present the perceptions of Haitian populations living in Rio de Janeiro on racism in Brazil and how they feel impacted by it, drawing on a vast collection of data from Haitian migrants gathered as part of the Migration for Development and Equality (MIDEQ) Hub.[4]

The Historical Context of Racism in Brazil

The Portuguese invasion and occupation of the territory that became known as Brazil began in 1500, and agricultural colonisation began in 1554 with the institution of *hereditary captaincies* and *sesmarias*—the primary forms of division of the land between white men graced by royalty (De Carvalho, 2015). That is how patrimonialism and patriarchy became the origin of Brazil's unequal social structure. The economic structure was formed by landowners developing strategies based initially on the exploitation of indigenous labour and then, on a much larger scale, of slaved Black African labour. Through that process, a genocide took place against the original population, with the death of about 90% of the indigenous population, according to historians' estimates, either through murder, intense exploitation or diseases brought by the colonisers (Garcia, 2017).

In the process of building the colony, first a sovereign Empire and then a Republic, a state dominated by male owners was established with two basic central functions: firstly, to appropriate the collective wealth and distribute it within the dominant social group and, secondly, to control the bodies and desires of subaltern populations namely women, Black and Indigenous peoples. This process continues today. The ideological/symbolic element that sustains the reproduction of Brazilian social, economic and cultural inequality is meritocracy.[5] Naturalised meritocracy then is used in Brazil as primary justification and evidence that white people, especially men, should take up the main economic, political, cultural and educational positions in the social world. These men—and white women, to a lesser extent—are the vast majority of people in public universities, in the company's directive and management boards, in the most valued and prestigious government jobs, in the cultural field and in sports institutions' leaderships, even in activities where there is a higher percentage of Black men and women (Schucman & Melo, 2022).

Meritocracy becomes an ideology—in this case, an effect that is asserted as cause or explanation, creating an illusion about reality—when Brazilian society fails to recognise its unequal structure as the true basis for maintaining the dominant positions of white people, and not the other way around. This markedly ideological argument is meant to explain how Black people, who constitute the majority (about 55%) of Brazilian society, did/do not have the proportional space in universities, the judiciary, diplomatic institutions, business management and so on. For example, among the top 500 Brazilian companies, only 4% of executives are Black (Haje, 2017); the judiciary system is comprised of about 16% *pardos* (mixed Black African background) and Black people make up just under 2% (Valente, 2018). At the same time, almost 70% of the 820,000 people incarcerated in the country are Black.[6]

Migrant populations also suffer from the prevalence of a racist logic: white migration—especially from the United States and Europe—has historically been seen as positive and valued by dominant groups, since it fits into the logic of *whitening* local societies, whereas South American and African migration is viewed by dominant groups with contempt and distrust. In the case of Haitian migration, which constitutes the largest contingent of Black migrants in the country, the process is aggravated by racism and the stigmatisation of Haiti as a country dominated by misery, political instability and natural disasters (Balaji, 2011; Clerge, 2014; Pyles et al., 2017).

Race and Racism in Brazilian Society

Critically examining racism in Brazilian society requires overcoming the idea that it is something particular to interpersonal relationships or even a localised episode of prejudicial practices. Racism is a structuring structure—to employ the famed conceptualisation by Pierre Bourdieu (1995)—or, as we prefer to call it, a complex socio-political system that creates, reproduces and updates racialised relations of social inequality and bodily distinction of rights.

For Quijano (2010), race has become a basic criterion for classifying the world population, which establishes a humanness hierarchy in social, cultural and aesthetic corporeity. As such, racism can be recognised as a regime of power based on subordinating bodies, identities and practices, underlying the capitalist mode of (re)producing social relations, and thus implies a globalised order of peoples, nations and territories:

> The new historical identities created from the idea of race were associated with the nature of roles and places in the new global structure of labour control. Both elements (race and division of labour) are structurally associated and mutually reinforcing, even though neither was necessarily dependent on the other to exist or to transform itself. (Quijano, 2010, 118)

Racism as a social regime of globalised power has established distinctive links between ways of life, social subjects and territories of existence. It is also responsible for the general and specific trajectories of the histories of societies that reproduce the very modern-colonial capitalist relations that sustain a civilisational hierarchy of being, knowing and living whose absolute centre is the Western European rationality.

Legacy of Colonialism on Racialised Relations

According to Grosfoguel (2010), racism as a power-complex system won the world over through mercantile colonisation, as geographical expansion arranged a set of combined unequal social relations: (i) a class hierarchy; (ii) an international centre/periphery division of labour; (iii) an interstate system of political-military organisations; (iv) a global ethno-racial hierarchy privileging Europeans over non-Europeans; (v) a sexual hierarchy that puts men above women and European patriarchy above other forms of man-woman relationships; (vi) a sexual hierarchy that disqualifies homosexuals in relation to heterosexuals; (vii) a spiritual hierarchy that places Christians above non-Christians; (viii) an epistemic hierarchy that places Western cosmology and knowledge above non-Western ones; and (ix) a linguistic hierarchy that privileges European languages—as well as communication and knowledge and theories produced from them—considering that others produce folklore or a smaller culture.

This system of power might be defined as coloniality. It was inaugurated with the mercantile colonialism of the fifteenth century but exceeded it and persists to this day. Despite its modern features, its anima remains colonial, since racism takes on a form that subordinates social subjects in oppressive, discretionary and humiliating work relations, in the non-recognition of subjectivities and the denial of cultural practices, in disrespect for religious beliefs, in gender constraints and violence and in the limited possibilities of insertion in public and private institutions. This is why we fully agree with the following statement of Silvio Almeida when he says:

> Racism is always structural, i.e., (…) an element that integrates the economic and political organization of a society. In short, what we seek to demonstrate is that racism is the normal manifestation of a society, not a pathological phenomenon or one expressing any kind of abnormality. Racism provides meaning, logic, and technology to the forms of inequality and violence that shape contemporary social life. (Almeida, 2018, 15–16)

We are in the face of a society construction paradigm whose main operator is racism, which we understand as a negative order of classification that, above all else, imposes a subordination condition on social subjects considered as inferior.

The fact that racism, when operating on more general scales of society, implies deep body markings, must be acknowledged. In addition to the markings of phenotypes (skin colour, hair type, nose shape), the conversation must include, as Kimberlé Crenshaw (2002) says, the intersectional relations of race and gender in the processes of reproducing social inequalities, as well as in recognising them as the cause of oppression, discrimination and lack of protection for Black women.

In Brazil, according to Munanga's (2004) teachings, racism is a social and historical construction that encompasses prejudice and discrimination by people who naturalise inequalities imposed on Black and Indigenous populations at different stages of the life cycle. Racism, therefore, is reinforced by common language, feeding on the hegemonic conditions of a culture of social privilege, and is sustained by it, while influencing everyday life and how institutions organise and interact with each other, as well as how social groups and classes are welcomed and treated.

Institutionalised Structural Racism in Brazil

In a society marked by mercantile slavery and governed by racism from its inception, as in the case of Brazil, the state takes on an instrumental role in the reproduction of racialised relations, especially in the institutionalisation of inequality and the non-recognition of rights, which perversely impact daily life. That leads to the notion that racism reveals itself as an important part of the debate around intertwining racial, cultural, sexual and gender hierarchies within the very functioning of Brazilian State institutions:

> When the public power, by means of the political elite, seems to favour, or disfavour certain groups identified by their ethnicity, race, (...) it denies the legitimacy of many other segments existing and expressing themselves, leaving the doors open to prejudicial and discriminatory practices. In other words, it denies others (the different) the possibility to have access either to the legal arsenal of equality and equity, as a dominant ideological trait, or to recognition and political participation. (Bandeira & Suarez, 2002, 1)

Our historical sociability experience confirms the racialised organisation of social relations, whose implications are manifested in multiple dimensions, contexts and events involving social subjects in unequal conditions that reiterate the privileges of classes, groups and individuals to the detriment of justice and law as organising principles in relations between citizens. This is the scenario in which repertoires of representation and oppressive and conservative identity narratives materialise to prevent the coexistence of different people and to radicalise forms of exploitation and racial subordination. These are experiences of permanently reinventing unequal conditions of existence and reiterating invisible racialised positions:

> Brazil constructs a particular notion of race according to which mixed-race and lighter-skinned people who display symbols of Europeanness – Christian formation and a mastery over language – can be considered white. By this rule, social acceptance and value become greater, the closer someone's skin pigmentation is to European-white. The attribution of colour to individuals, a common practice in Brazil which underlies the identification of colour groups by sociologists, far from dispensing with the notion of "race", presupposes a very peculiar racial ideology and racism. (Guimarães, 1999, 96)

Race is maintained as a symbol of subordination in the hierarchical division of labour, housing conditions and access to services (including public ones), and therefore continues to produce a perverse logic of maintaining members of racial groups subordinate to what the racial code of a society defines as their appropriate place of being, as individuals and groups in societal settings.

Different spatial settings constitute experiences of relationships that form and conform the subjectivities of individuals and social groups, bringing to light debates about racism in their socio–spatial conditions, their inequality markers—from *favelas*[7] to universities or from *quilombos*[8] to large city squares—with profound implications on people's life trajectories. We can understand racism in the racialisation of individuals, communities and groups, as well as practices, experiences and territories.

According to a major global study conducted by IPEA (2007), Black newborns are underweight compared to white babies, as well as more likely to die before reaching the age of one, less likely to attend day-care, and suffer from higher failing rates in school, which leads them to drop out of school with lower educational levels than white children. As a result of low education, Black individuals are less able to find a formal, qualified job. And when they do find a job, they are paid less than half the salary received by their white counterparts, which leads to them retiring later and with lower pensions, if at all. Throughout their lives, they suffer the worst attention in the healthcare system and end up living less and in greater poverty than white people (IPEA, 2007, 281). It is worth including the lethal violence that takes the lives of thousands of young Black men each year (in the past ten years, there has been a variation between 50,000–60,000 homicides per year, 75% of which are Black men) in this cognitive map. The concept of Brazil as a racial democracy does not hold in the face of the daily life of Black populations.

Whitewashing as Strategy of Reproduction of Brazilian Structural Racism

As Andrews (1997) states, the Brazilian model of race relations works very efficiently to reduce racial tension and competition, while keeping Black people in a subordinate political, social and economic position. Systemic racism is therefore created to rationally structure the functioning of society and elaborate institutional models as their socio-political disciplinary management and territorial control support. The political and aesthetic instrumentalisation of the ideology of whitewashing was, so to speak, one of the first and most brutal devices of racism in Brazil, whose harmful and perverse effects are still evident in our society.

Whitewashing became a strategy to erase black presence in Brazilian society in favour of an alleged white Christian demography with the directed European migration policy during the last quarter of the nineteenth century (Santos, 2002). Eugenics soon became more effective and lasting, however, systematically erasing the creation of memories, celebration of religions, aesthetic experiences, work practices and sociability experiences, especially to deny Black territories and bodies in strategies of socio-spatial segregation.

> (...) besides causing a sense of inferiority and self-rejection, the non-acceptance of one's ethnic fellow and the search for whitewashing lead light-skinned people to internalize a negative image of Black, which leads them to distance themselves from Black people, while most of the time looking at their situation of penury and physical and cultural extermination with indifference and insensitivity, often attributing to them the very causes of their situation. (Silva, 2007, 97)

Cida Bento (2002) argues that dominant groups consider themselves—or even create themselves—as reference for all humanity, and by doing so engage in the symbolic appropriation that elevates the white body to a condition of superiority in relation to others. This appropriation eventually legitimises their economic, political and cultural supremacy in society as a whole. Here, we are faced with yet another device of the visceral racism of Brazilian society: whiteness. The construction of whiteness is the political-ideological building of extremely negative imagery around black people, which undermines their racial identity, damages their self-esteem, blames them for the discrimination they suffer and, finally, justifies racial inequalities (Bento, 2002). Ruth Frankenberg states that whiteness is a place from which white subjects see others, and themselves, a position of power from which she attributes to the other what they do not attribute to themselves (Frankenberg, 1995).

But the subordination of Black men and women in Brazil has never been passively experienced. On the contrary, struggles for freedom forged a path of Black movements fighting for the right to education, health, work, housing and culture that greatly contributed to the achievements of our incomplete, fragile democracy. Since their enslavement, the Black population has devised modes of resistance and rebellion that have shaped social struggles and spaces to affirm their existence. From *quilombos* to *favelas* and peripheries, we battle against socio-spatial segregation. From culture and arts to African and Afro-Brazilian religions, we reinvent memories to update traditions of Black identities and belonging in the face of a distinctive order of rights. A fundamental political issue of Brazilian society hence emerges: the confrontation with racism as a possibility of overcoming social inequality and, above all, class, race and gender power relations that (re)produce the non-recognition of individual and collective rights to full citizenship.

As noted above, whiteness plays an important role in structuring perceptions of different subjects living in Brazil. This is reflected in the way migrant populations living in the country are perceived and treated. The same receptive, hospitable behaviour towards white immigrants remains widespread in social fields, while Black migrants—generally from Haiti and African countries—suffer material and symbolic violence similar to that experienced by Black Brazilians. This also results from a specific trait of Brazilian racism: its individual expression centre around phenotypical elements. The darker someone's skin colour is, the higher the level of discrimination they can suffer directly. However, Brazilian structural and institutional racism has a broader spectrum of discrimination: it affects Black and indigenous populations in general, and inflicts a series of restrictions upon them which prevents them from achieving positions of power or socioeconomic distinction, regardless of whatever professional qualifications and repertoire they may have.

What follows is a general profile of the Haitian population in Brazil and some specific evidence gathered within the scope of the MIDEQ Hub's work. This evidence allows us to envision the conditions under which the Haitian population perceives racism in Brazil and its role in preventing due access to the set of rights required to affirm their human dignity.

The Data on Haitians in Brazil

To build a systemic reading of the universe of Haitian nationals in Brazil, we chose to first establish some general data on this group of migrants, which was extracted from microdata available through SISMIGRA, an immigration Portal by the Ministry of Justice and Public Security of the Brazilian Government.[9] Haitians started migrating in significant numbers to Brazil in 2010, a movement which continued to increase until 2016 (Fig. 19.1). According to spoken accounts from Haitian researchers at MIDEQ Brazil and interviews with Haitians,[10] since 2017, in the face of an economic crisis, many began to leave the country, heading, especially, to the USA. There are no means of knowing what number of migrants have left the country or have died here, because state agencies do not have consolidated records of it.[11] However, the fluctuating inflow and its distribution in terms of numbers, gender and age groups from early in the migration to 2021—the last year the federal system accounts for in its database—allows a better understanding of the dynamics of Haitian mobility. This data, in association with information collected in

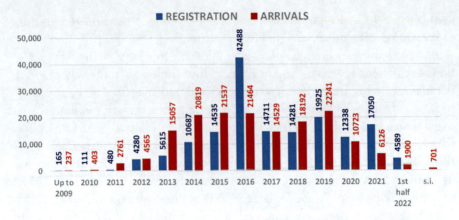

Fig. 19.1 Haitian migration to Brazil (*Source* Haitian Migrants per National Migration Record Year and Year of Entry Informed; Brazilian Government, Ministry of Justice and Public Security. Portal da Imigração (Immigration Portal). Microdata from 2000 to 2022)

our survey and focus group, become the means to broaden our perspective of the Haitian migrant population's perceptions, choices and strategies upon and after selecting Brazil as their destination.

According to official data[12] provided by SISMIGRA, there were 158,383 Haitian migrants in Brazil as at June 2022. The peak of the Haitian migration into the country was the period from 2014 to 2016, when the entry of about 21,000 migrants was recorded each year. The number declined soon after, despite a new high in 2019, when, at their peak, over 22,000 arrivals were recorded in a single year. After 2019, the number of Haitians entering Brazil has been gradually decreasing to the levels recorded in pre-2014. Although entry registration presents a more general overview of the flow of immigrants into the country, we should note that their registration as formal migrants by Brazilian entities points to a process of creating roots, from the pursuit of formal recognition and with it access to rights such as, for example, access to formal work.[13] In that sense, 2016 was when Brazil registered the largest number of Haitians—with over 42,000 registrations. The large increase from previous years and the gradual process of rooting in the country are largely responsible for this.

There is a remarkably disproportionate number of men compared to women within this group of Haitians who entered the country before 2016. This has changed more recently: in the period prior to 2016, the proportion of men fluctuated in the range of 60–80% but from 2017 onwards, there was a new trend of more balanced distribution between men and women. From then on, the entry of men oscillates in the range of 54–57%, and of women, of 43–46%. These data reveal a phenomenon whereby male family members migrate in search of security and livelihood opportunities, and through a gradual process of consolidating life in their country of destination, create the conditions for their spouse to join them. This is a very complex process, however, as it also involves the need to analyse gender relations in the sociocultural and political contexts of Haitian society, as well as an understanding of how these relations are resignified throughout the migration process. There is, furthermore, a subsequent process in which family units start migrating together—the result of elements that offer more welcoming and less hostile conditions to migrants, i.e. a welcoming support network of Haitians already established in the country, as well as more well-prepared and mature institutional mechanisms. In this context, however, gender and racial dynamics in the Brazilian cultural context and how Haitian migrants relate to them must be considered. We will address this issue along with statements made in the focus groups conducted for our study.

A change in age patterns of migrants is also observed. Whereas before 2016 there was still a greater number of men entering the country, after this period there is not only a more balanced flow of men and women, but also a gradual increase in younger people entering the country, which points an even greater rooting process where family members move to meet with the men who arrived first, as data shows. The stories told in our focus groups reinforce this narrative, as seen below.

Haitian Migrants' Perceptions of Race and Racism in Brazil

Methodological Note

Between September 2021 and February 2022, the MIDEQ team in Brazil team collected a significant amount of primary data—through a survey, in-depth interviews and focus groups—pertaining to the universe of Haitian immigrants in Brazil. A total of 101 in-depth interviews were conducted in five Brazilian states and five focus groups were conducted in three states. This method offered regional diversity in a country of continental proportions and reflected the geography of Haitian migration in Brazil. A survey of almost 900 participants was also conducted.[14] This research process was approved by Plataforma Brasil, an entity that oversees research ethical conduct in Brazil. Hiring Haitian researchers was one strategy employed by the team to facilitate the recruitment of research participants and to ensure the quality of the collected data with respect to cultural translations. These researchers were then trained and supervised by the IMJA/MIDEQ team coordinators. As a result, all of the primary data collection had the participation and agency of Haitian researchers and interviewers. This was not an accidental decision but rather derived from an epistemological and methodological perspective. Any research with social groups must recognise their subjectivity, before anything else, and ensure agency for their standpoint not only as respondents, but also as authors of instruments and analysts of the data obtained. This epistemological perspective allows participants to break with the usual hierarchical forms that tend to characterise academic investigations.

From a methodological point of view, the decision to employ Haitian researchers and to allow respondents to complete the questionnaires in Haitian Creole allowed a more comprehensive, in-depth access to this population. With that, deeper answers were attained than would have been possible by conducting a questionnaire and interviews in Portuguese. Moreover, the identity of the respondents was preserved at all levels, according to the ethical commitments adopted.

Data Analysis

Adopting a thematic framework, we have extracted some evidence from a focus group conducted specifically on racial issues to illustrate Haitian perceptions on the issue of racism and existing inequalities in Brazil. The group included six men and one woman, all Haitians.[15] It was held in Rio de Janeiro in the first half of 2022.

The participants were prompted to convey their perception of racism in Brazil, similarities, and differences in relation to Haitian society, as well as situations that they have suffered and interpreted as racial discrimination.

> Being Black in Brazil as a Haitian, from Haiti, because I have a white wife, I am received one way when I'm with my wife and another alone. And I have a way of acting when I'm alone and another when I'm with my wife. (Person A, adult male)

Regarding the perception of racism, there is a widespread understanding that Black people are discriminated against in Brazil and that they are considered inferior.

> I'll give you an example. Once I went to get my hair done in a salon in Ipanema and there were a lot of people before me. So, I went to lunch. I went into a

more or less fancy restaurant - in Haiti there is better – and said I was going to have lunch. The girl who worked there and was at the door said, "This is a la carte. I'm letting you know because you can only know how much you owe after you ate." I questioned the receptionist: "are you saying I can't eat here just because I'm Black?" I asked to call the manager and he apologised to me. (Person B, adult female)

Discussions and reflections on the issue of racism are not as frequent in Haiti as they are in Brazil.

There, rare cases of racism happen. In Brazil, it is daily. It is not that racism does not exist in our society, but it does not happen in the same way, because 94% of the population is Black – there are another 5% whites and Lebanese, who dominate society and control financial institutions. Racism is a system. When you arrive in Brazil, the vast majority do not understand racism, since it's veiled, unlike the Dominican Republic, where racism is open. There are laws in Brazil that forbid racism, but also a system that turns a blind eye to it to reduce punishment against racism and reduces its penalties.

One respondent recalls that he did not understand what racism was, as a child, but remembers being punished for speaking Creole in the classroom in Haiti. It was written in the room "no speaking Creole here"

What 12-year-old can speak French? The children of white or rich people in Haiti, Lebanese Syrians, Americans who do business in Haiti and marry Haitians. Because you come from the countryside and can't speak anything, your haircut is mocked because you don't look like people from the capital. You are submitted to that for coming from a community, which is considered inferior. In Haiti we don't see these things as racism, I began to understand that in Brazil. I don't know a Black movement in Haiti, in Brazil it is a trend to be a militant, that is a potent thing for Brazil.
(…)
In Haiti, you can't open a car dealership overnight, you'll die the next day. Because you are Black, and your origin is the countryside. If you are descended from important people and politicians, if you are born in Pétion-Ville, then you can, but if you come with knowledge from outside, you are executed. Besides, a white person in Haiti is never well-regarded: if my wife, who is white, rides a motorcycle with me on the street, she will always be cursed at. On the other hand, if a person asks me and my wife for directions and we answer differently, they will go with her answer. This is an after-effect of slavery: for them, a white person would not be lying, a white person would not be late, a white person's plans have more power. (Person A, adult male)

As Black individuals, Haitians suffer the effects of this racist stance, in addition to specific discrimination due to the widespread stigmatised representation of Haiti in Brazil: Haiti is seen as a country dominated by misery, political instability and natural disasters. Beyond that, there is a sense that their skin colour is a determinant on the way they are perceived in Brazilian society opposed to other migrants.

> In college, when I say I'm Haitian, people turn away from me and don't want to do group work with me. Brazilians have no information about Haiti, they think it's all misery and natural disasters. There are many Haitians who hide their nationality, say they are Caribbean. And that causes hurt. (Person F, young male)
>
> Brazilian society has planned racism, and it is everywhere in society. There are a 54% Black population, but the big professions, like doctors and judges, are mostly white people. So, your skin colour indicates your trajectory, because institutions outline your path and telling you how far you will go. For Haitian migrants this is visible through the enrichment of white migrants, as opposed to Black migrants. For example, when the Syrians arrived in Brazil, they were included in the Bolsa Família programme. If it weren't for the Catholic Church and pastors, who would help Haitians? (Person D, adult male)

Regarding personal experiences, respondents narrated examples of discriminatory situations in different spaces—Universities, restaurants, workspaces. There is an understanding that there is a strong correlation between being Black and being discriminated against, even as migrants (an aggravating factor), and especially for Haitians. Something that was noted by respondents was the fact that Brazil has strict legislation to criminalise racism—as well as racial harassment—while Haiti has no such legislation.[16] It was noted by others, however, that in practice there are many ways to avoid compliance with that legislation, and that it does not account for structural racism. Participants were asked what measures they believed should be taken in relation to racist practices in Brazil. Regarding possible ways to confront racism, the legal pathway was pointed out as the most appropriate.

> Anti-racism laws need to be toughened, and public policies created to raise awareness so that people fight and strengthen movements. (Person E, adult male)
>
> Toughen laws because, even if it does not destroy it, it will create respect between people. (Person D, adult male)

There is, however, a critical understanding on the limits of law, the struggles for implementing legislation in practice and the need for more structural changes in society.

> I believe that some laws are only on paper, because when it's time to enforce them, (nothing) is done. If the person knows they are going to be punished, they will not do it. (Person B, adult female)
>
> This being a structural problem, it's bigger than the laws, because when it comes to enforcing those laws, the police and judges are racist, and for this reason, Brazil needs a revolution to fight racism. It does not need weapons, but a social revolution. This revolution must promote equality. There are no Black people in leadership in Brazil… (Person A, adult male)

One noteworthy statement emerging from the group, which had been expressed previously and has been repeated in subsequent face-to-face meetings with Haitian groups as well as in-depth interviews, is the idea that racism is only real if the victim cares about it. Their self-esteem and self-worth have the power to ensure that there will be no racist practices towards them, or, at least, that they will not be affected by these practices.

> Most of all, I don't care about racism, because I believe in myself and I know who I am. Someone who is dealing with racism and believes in themselves will not care about it, because they know that they have plenty of value, plenty of power to fight life and get to where they want. That's it. (Person F, adult male)

This statement reflects how it can be difficult for members of Haitian society to understand Brazilian racial dynamics and how they structure social and economic inequalities, with a tendency to individualise experiences of racism rather than articulating them within wider structural issues. A similar process was seen in relation to the issues of skin colour. According to the participants, declaring racial identity itself produces racialisation, since we are, above all, humans and not more than one "race". Coincidentally, this is the argument used in Brazil by people—almost always white—who want to avoid any debate or policies to address the race issue.

Conclusions

The aim of this chapter was to introduce the basis of Brazilian racism and how it structures, together with sexism and institutional patrimonialism, the inequalities of Brazilian society and the particular experiences of Haitian migrants. What is evident from the evidence presented is that the markings of Black phenotypes amplify the conditions of discrimination experienced by the Haitian population in Brazil. In addition to the Black skin markers, migrant populations from Haiti need to create more sophisticated mechanisms than migrants from other countries, especially white migrants, to overcome the barriers imposed by Brazilian structural inequalities. In that sense, the Brazilian democratic forces are facing a challenge, particularly in the field of knowledge production and public management, with the creation epistemological, social, economic and legal responses to affirm the principle of human dignity of the Black population—both Brazilian and migrant alike. This is especially true in this moment of hope, with the defeat of the far-right government under Bolsonaro and the victory of the democratic forces in the 2022 elections. We expect that the studies and actions developed within the scope of the MIDEQ Hub and its work in Brazil, in partnership with other study groups in the South, will contribute to these advances, in a plural and comprehensive way.

A set of reflections emerge from this work, which we outline below.

Firstly, experiences of racism and discrimination are built from the social, historical and cultural context of each country, and this fact must be acknowledged. Indeed, in studies and writings that contribute to an understanding of the phenomenon of racism and its impact on the lives of migrants, the latter's views on racism must be understood in context. This will avoid a supposedly "naive" interpretation of their experiences of racism and allow a more in-depth analysis of their inclusion (or otherwise) in a new social context. Any formulation or design of public policies needs to take this into account.

Secondly, the strategies adopted by Haitian migrants within the specific context of their experiences must also be understood, as they differ from other groups of migrants, by their racial condition, which exposes them to situations similar to those experienced by the Black population in Brazil, but also imbues them with a different outlook and attitude towards the racialisation of social relations. These strategies emerge from the potency/inventive power (*potência*) of Haitian migrants, in their ability to devise solutions and responses within their life context. After all, we look to a peripheral epistemology because of a need to recognise the power of these people, and their own ability to navigate a new social context with tools that often had to be adapted, readapted and invented.

Acknowledgements We want to thank Cassia da Rosa e Oliveira for translating this text from Portuguese and Daniel Stefani for final revisions. We also wanted to thank the MIDEQ Brazil team, in particular Dalcio Marinho and Natalia Guindani for their support on project data management. This work has been undertaken as part of the Migration for Development and Equality (MIDEQ) Hub. Funded by the UKRI Global Challenges Research Fund (GCRF) (Grant Reference: ES/S007415/1), MIDEQ unpacks the complex and multi-dimensional relationships between migration and inequality in the context of the Global South. More at www.mideq.org.

Notes

1. More information on the United Nations Stabilization Mission in Haiti (MINUSTAH) can be found at https://peacekeeping.un.org/en/mission/minustah.
2. This is the process of systematically transferring economic resources and power to privileged social groups, with legal support and especially through the state. It materialises through tax structures, credit and interest policies, the allocation of urban equipment and services to more enriched areas of the city and through privileged access to well-valued public offices by white men, especially. These are at the heart of the thinking underpinning the work of UNIPeriferias/Instituto Maria e Joao Aleixo. UNIPeriferias is a civil society organisation working to produce alternative knowledge emerging form peripheral epistemologies. We aim to work together with peripheral groups to address their struggles and contribute on the proposition of public policies that accommodate the voice and needs of peripheral groups. More about UNIPeriferias can be found at www.uniperiferias.org.br.
3. The reason for choosing Haitian migration as the topic of this article derives from the fact that it is, first and foremost, a migration of Black people, a characteristic of that country's population, as well as the fact that, through the MIDEQ Hub and the Maria and João Aleixo Institute, we developed a research and intervention project with the Haitian migrant population in Brazil. The research consisted of a survey conducted with almost 900 Haitians living in Rio de Janeiro and São Paulo, with focus groups on specific topics, as well as interviews with the same population living in the two states, in addition to Santa Catarina, Paraná and Rondônia. Due to space limitations, for this chapter we chose to use some statements from a focus group on issues of access to the justice systems and perceptions of racism in Brazil, conducted in the city of Rio de Janeiro with members of the Haitian community.
4. The Migration for Development and Equality (MIDEQ) Hub unpacks the complex and multi-dimensional relationships between migration and inequality in the context of the Global South. More at www.mideq.org.
5. As an illustration, the French Revolution, as the greatest expression of bourgeois revolutions, accomplished a great historical feat by making the feudal principle that people would be naturally unequal, because of their social

origin, one that could be overcome. The idea that all are created equal—even if that equality is restricted to the law and state power—represented a true revolution from Western conceptual, legal and social points of view. The discourse of personal merit then came about as an element justifying the social condition of each subject, recognised in their differences from biology, from an ethos of hard work and even morals. "Self-made men" became an ideal type of capitalist hero—in typically sexist language, man would be the maker of himself.

6. According to a survey conducted by the Brazilian Public Security Yearbook, released in June 2020, 820,689 people have been put into the Brazilian prison system. 67.4% of them are black, which is a 3.4% increase from 2020. These data show a current scenario of mass incarceration in Brazil.

7. A favela is a constituent territory of the city characterised, in part or in its entirety, by the following references: (i) historical insufficiency of investments by the State and the formal market, especially real estate; (ii) financial and services (iii) strong socio-spatial stigmatisation, especially inferred by residents of other areas of the city; (iv) high levels of underemployment and informality in labour relations; (v) buildings predominantly characterised by self-construction, which are not guided by the parameters defined by the State; (vi) social appropriation of the territory with predominant use for housing purposes; (vii) educational, economic and environmental indicators below the average of the city as a whole; (viii) occupation of urban sites marked by a high degree of environmental vulnerability; (ix) degree of sovereignty on the part of the State lower than the average of the city as a whole; (x) high density of dwellings in the territory; (xi) population density rate above the average of the city as a whole; (xii) neighbourhood relations marked by intense sociability, with a strong appreciation of communal spaces as a meeting place; (xiii) high concentration of black people and descendants of indigenous people, according to the Brazilian region; (xiv) degree of victimization of people, especially lethal, above the city average. For an extensive discussion on the terminology and its socio-political implications see Silva et al. (2009).

8. "Quilombo is the denomination for communities of black slaves who resisted the slavery regime that prevailed in Brazil for over 300 years and was abolished in 1888. Quilombos were formed from a wide variety of processes that include the escape of slaves to free and generally isolated lands. However, freedom was also acquired through inheritance, donations and land revenues as payment for services rendered to the state or for stays on the lands they occupied and cultivated. There are also cases of land purchase both during the term of the slave regime and after its abolition. What characterized the quilombo was the resistance and the acquisition of autonomy. The formation of the quilombos represented the transition from the condition of slave to that of free peasant. (…) The quilombos continued to exist even after the end of slavery. Data from the Brazilian government indicates that today there

are 3495 quilombola communities spread across all regions of the country, from southern Brazil to the Amazon" (CPISP, SD).
9. Official government data on migration can be found at SISMIGRA https://portaldeimigracao.mj.gov.br/pt/dados.
10. The MIDEQ team in Brazil—a group researching the Haiti-Brazil migration corridor—collected three sets of primary data on this migrant population: a survey, qualitative interviews and focus groups. Information on the departure of a significant number of Haitian migrants to other countries, such as the United States, Canada and Chile, do not include official figures, but reflects the struggles faced by Haitians since 2015, with the economic, political and social crisis that took over Brazil.
11. Official data from the Brazilian government concern a record of the arrival of this foreign population into the country, but there is no systematised data on their exit, just as there is none on the deaths of members of the migrant population.
12. The National Migration Registry (which is mandatory to attain temporary or permanent resident permits and/or work permits) is kept by federal migration control agencies. Migrants must register in it with those agencies, but not necessarily upon arrival. Because of that, records show both the year of registration and of entry.
13. The qualitative interviews conducted by the MIDEQ Brazil team recorded that access to formal work is one of the central strategies of the Haitian migrant population to ensure their stay in the country.
14. For the survey, a single questionnaire was applied in all six migratory corridors included in the MIDEQ project, amounting to 12 countries. The questions for the in-depth interviews and focus groups were prepared by the national teams. Unfortunately, it was impossible to include the data collected through these instruments in this chapter due to space limitations, but they available by contact the authors.
15. With the exception of one gender focus group of only women and the survey—which we had previously decided would have gender parity—we struggled to find female participants for the in-depth interviews and other focus groups. This is a result of lower female presence in migration scenarios and of restrictive gender roles and relations within the Haitian migrant population.
16. Brazilian Anti-Racism Law which took place in 1989 (Brazilian Act 7.716/89).

References

de Alencastro, L. F. (2000). *O trato dos viventes. Formação do Brasil no Atlântico Sul*. Companhia das Letras.

Almeida, S. (2018). *O Que é Racismo Estrutural*. Letramento.

Andrews, G. R. (1997). Democracia racial brasileira 1900–1990: Um comportamento americano. *Estudos Avançados, 11*(30), 95–115.

Balaji, M. (2011). Racializing pity: The Haiti earthquake and the plight of "others." *Critical Studies in Media Communication, 28*(1), 50–67.

Bandeira, L., & Suarez, M. (2002). A politização da violência contra a mulher e o fortalecimento da cidadania. In C. Bruschini & S. G. Uunbehaum (Orgs.), *Gênero, democracia e sociedade brasileira*. FCC.

Bento, M. A. S. (2002). Branqueamento e branquitude no Brasil. In M. A. S. Bento (Org.), *Psicologia social do racismo: Estudos sobre branquitude e branqueamento no Brasil*. Vozes.

Bourdieu, P. (1995). *Coisas Ditas*. Brasiliense.

De Carvalho, B. (2015). The modern roots of feudal empires: The donatary captaincies and the legacies of the Portuguese Empire in Brazil. In S. Halperin & R. Palan (Eds.), *Legacies of empire: Imperial roots of the contemporary global order* (pp. 128–148). Cambridge University Press. https://doi.org/10.1017/CBO978 1316271674.006

Clerge, O. (2014). Balancing stigma and status: Racial and class identities among middle-class Haitian youth. *Ethic and Racial Studies, 37*(6), 958–977.

CPISP (SD) Quilombolas communities in Brazil. https://cpisp.org.br/direitosquilombolas/observatorio-terras-quilombolas/quilombolas-communities-in-brazil/

Crenshaw, K. (2002). Documento para o encontro de especialistas em aspectos de discriminação racial relativas à relações de gênero. *Revista De Estudos Feministas, 10*(1), 171–188.

Ellsworth, K. H. (1999). *Racial and ethnic relations in the modern world-system: A comparative analysis of Portuguese influence in Angola and Brazil*. International Studies Assoc. Conference, Arizona State University, 19th February 1999. https://citeseerx.ist.psu.edu/document?repid=rep1&type=pdf&doi=3689b851305e06019cfbf4b802a00d9d701f106d

Frankenberg, R. (1995). *The construction of white women and race matter*. University of Minnesota Press.

Garcia, M. F. (2017). Massacrada, população indígena representa menos de 0.5% do país. *Observatório do Terceiro Setor*. https://observatorio3setor.org.br/noticias/populacao-indigena-representa-menos-de-meio-por-cento-do-pais/

Grasfoguel, R. (2010). Para descolonizar os estudos de economia política e os estudos pós-coloniais: Transmodernidade, pensamento e fronteira e colonialidade global. In B. De Sousa Santos & M. P. Meneses (Orgs.), *Epistemologias do Sul*. Cortez.

Guimarães, A. S. (1999). *Racismo e Anti-racismo no Brasil*. Editora 34.

Haje, L. (2017). Apenas 4% das 500 maiores empresas brasileiras têm negros no corpo executivo, aponta ativista. *Agência Câmara de Notícias*. https://www.camara.leg.br/noticias/521027-apenas-4-das-500-maiores-empresas-brasileiras-tem-negros-no-corpo-executivo-aponta-ativista/

IPEA. (2007). Políticas sociais acompanhamento e análise. Edição especial. Vol 13. Available at https://repositorio.ipea.gov.br/handle/11058/4164

Lima, M., & Prates, I. (2019). Racial inequalities in Brazil: A persistent challenge. In M. Arretche (Eds.), *Paths of inequality in Brazil*. Springer. https://doi.org/10.1007/978-3-319-78184-6_6

Munanga, K. (2004). Uma abordagem conceitual das noções de raça, racismo, identidade e etnia. In Programa de educação sobre o negro na sociedade brasileira. Niterói: EDUFF. Recuperado de https://biblio.fflch.usp.br/Munanga_K_UmaAbordagemConceitualDasNocoesDeRacaRacismoIdentidadeEEtnia.pdf

Nascimento, E. L. (2006). *The sorcery of color: Identity, race, and gender in Brazil*. Temple University Press.

Pimentel, R. (2023). "Equal before the law," but not in practice: Brazil's social inequality crisis. *Harvard Political Review*, 22nd March 2023. https://harvardpolitics.com/brazil-social-inequality/

Pyles, L., Svistova, J., & Ahn, S. (2017). Securitization, racial cleansing, and disaster capitalism: Neoliberal disaster governance in the US Gulf Coast and Haiti. *Critical Social Policy, 37*(4), 582–603.

Quijano, A. (2010). Colonialidade do Poder. In B. de Sousa Santos & M. P. Meneses (Orgs.), *Epistemologias do Sul*. Cortez.

Santos, I. A. A. (2002). Democracia e racismo. In *Seminário nacional discriminação e sistema legal brasileiro, 2001, Brasília. [Anais...]*. TST.

Schucman, L. V., & Da Costa Melo, W. (2022). White supremacy, Brazil style. *NACLA Report on the Americas, 54*(2), 197–202.

da Silva, S. A. (2013). Brazil, a new Eldorado for immigrants? The case of Haitians and the Brazilian immigration policy. *Urbanities, 3*(2), 3–18.

de Souza Silva, J., et al. (2009). *O que é a favela, afinal?* Observatório de Favelas.

Valente, J. (2018). Oito em cada dez juízes no Brasil são brancos, aponta pesquisa do CNJ. *Agência Brasil*. https://agenciabrasil.ebc.com.br/justica/noticia/2018-09/oito-em-cada-dez-juizes-no-brasil-sao-brancos-aponta-pesquisa-do-cn

Open Access This chapter is licensed under the terms of the Creative Commons Attribution 4.0 International License (http://creativecommons.org/licenses/by/4.0/), which permits use, sharing, adaptation, distribution and reproduction in any medium or format, as long as you give appropriate credit to the original author(s) and the source, provide a link to the Creative Commons license and indicate if changes were made.

The images or other third party material in this chapter are included in the chapter's Creative Commons license, unless indicated otherwise in a credit line to the material. If material is not included in the chapter's Creative Commons license and your intended use is not permitted by statutory regulation or exceeds the permitted use, you will need to obtain permission directly from the copyright holder.

20

Climate Change and Human Mobility in the Global South

Ingrid Boas, Animesh Gautam, and Ademola Olayiwola

Introduction

The Global South has long been a focal point of research that examines the nexus between climate change and human mobility (Piguet et al., 2018; Wiegel et al., 2019).[1] The dominant assumption often is that the Global South is most vulnerable to the impacts of climate change and subsequent implications for human mobility, given lower adaptive capacities, higher geographical vulnerabilities to climate change, and other socio-economic inequalities that are already feeding pressures to migrate. This assumption tends to be generalised for the whole of the Global South, resulting in often stereotypical and simplified understandings of local vulnerabilities and of the subject of climate mobility more generally informed by "the post-colonial imagination… [of the climate migrant]… as a poor peasant from the South" (Piguet et al., 2018, 359).

In the context of this critique, several studies have aimed to critically expose pre-assumptions held about the figure of the migrant, to overcome environmental deterministic accounts of mobility in the Global South, and to show how im/mobilities that are now impacted by climate change are shaped by local contexts or may have a different meaning than sometimes is assumed

---

I. Boas (✉)
Hollandseweg 1, 6706KN Wageningen, Netherlands
e-mail: ingrid.boas@wur.nl

A. Gautam · A. Olayiwola
Wageningen University and Research, Wageningen, Netherlands

(for useful overview studies see Askland et al., 2022; Borderon et al., 2019; Hoffmann et al., 2020; Klepp, 2017; Wiegel et al., 2019; Zickgraf, 2021). The objective of this chapter is to highlight and discuss the findings and key arguments made by some of these studies, to add to a political and historical understanding of the ways in which the nexus between mobility and climate change unfolds in several regions of the Global South. For this, we will draw examples from a wide range of regions, mostly the Pacific, South Asia, and Western Africa.

We start with a general recap of the literature. Afterwards we present an overview of studies giving a more political and historical understanding of the relationships between human mobility and climate change as taking shape in the Global South. A brief note on terminology: in referring to the climate change-human mobility nexus, we will often use the term climate mobility, or in plural, climate mobilities.

Climate Change and Human Mobility: A Recap of the Debate

There exists a large body of empirical literature examining the relations between environmental change, and climate change in particular, vis-à-vis human mobility. The early accounts of this research field concentrated mostly on debating whether or not the environment has a role to play in migration decision-making (e.g. Black, 2001; Castles, 2002; Suhrke, 1994). There were some, largely environmental scholars, that tended to emphasise the impact of the environment, including global warming, on migration (see Gemenne, 2009, for a history of this debate). This was mainly out of a concern over the fast-deteriorating climate and its impact on human societies. Others, often migration and human geography scholars, have tended to critique such studies for being overly deterministic, not taking into account the highly multi-causal ways in which migration takes shape (see Gemenne, 2009 for a full account of this debate).

Research from the mid-2000s onwards has moved beyond debating towards actively examining the climate change-human mobility nexus empirically. These efforts have evolved into a fast-growing scholarship (Piguet, 2022), of which the vast majority concentrates on the Global South (Piguet et al., 2018), most often Sub-Saharan Africa and South Asia (Piguet et al., 2018; Zickgraf, 2021),[2] and most studies have a case study approach (Piguet, 2022). This empirical line of research demonstrates how migration, or human mobility more broadly, is inherently multi-causal, yet it also shows that environmental changes do have a significant role to play in that equation (Piguet, 2013). The way in which this relation plays out is contextual and dependent on other factors such as the role of social network and kinship ties, experiences with mobility, the availability of support systems, the type of environmental event, etcetera (Black et al., 2011; Borderon et al., 2019; Hoffmann et al., 2020). In taking this view, most scholarship takes a "pragmatist" stance in the debate which "questions the role and weight of environmental factors in already-occurring displacements" (Piguet, 2013, 155).

Central to this line of work is the model designed by Richard Black and colleagues (Black et al., 2011). It shows how decisions to stay or move are shaped by an intersecting set of push and pull factors, including socio-economic and political ones as well as environmental drivers. They created this model as part of a Foresight Study conducted for the UK Government (Foresight, 2011) in response to then often-heard claims of so-called future floods of climate refugees, moving from the Global South to the Global North. Their work largely debunked such claims for being too environmentally deterministic and for lacking a political and socio-economic sense of how migration processes originate and develop. Their report has become amongst the most cited and used works in this field.

To further enhance the conceptual starting points of climate-mobility research, researchers have sought more analytical and theoretical rigour, to build on, but also to move beyond, the famous drivers model produced by Black and others. In that context, Sherbinin et al. (2022) published a plea for the greater use of established migration theories, to bring greater depth to the field's initial empirical interest. In a similar context, we see a conceptual turn to the theory of mobilities originating from human geography and sociology (Sheller & Urry, 2006), applied to the fields of climate change and migration with newly emerging concepts such as Anthropocene mobilities or environmental and climate mobilities (Baldwin, 2014; Baldwin et al., 2019; Boas et al., 2022; Cundill et al., 2021; Parsons, 2019; Wiegel et al., 2019). This conceptual turn argues for a need to study the plurality, unevenness, and relationality of human mobilities in the context of a changing climate. It builds on a recent surge of works delving into the politics of the relation between climate change and human mobility, examining issues of race (Baldwin, 2016), biopolitics (Turhan et al., 2015), gender (Ayeb-Karlsson, 2020; Lama et al., 2021), or intersectionality more broadly (Cundill et al., 2021), in shaping or restricting mobility outcomes.

These studies have also expressed concern that the political has long been overlooked in the scientific and policy search for environmental causes of people's movement. An initial interest in the field has for instance been to explain different human mobilities through differences in the environmental and climate change events themselves, namely by examining fast-onset and slow-onset events and environmental changes and their consequences for human mobility (Warner 2010). Fast-onset events are environmental and climate change impacts that happen suddenly, which can take extreme forms in a short period of time, often with devastating effects. Think of a cyclone or storm surge. Research shows how these impacts often lead to temporal displacement from homes as people return home when areas are safe (Black et al., 2013). But they may also lead to situations where people are stuck and not able to move away (Black et al., 2013; Zickgraf et al., 2018). Slow-onset dynamics often lead to gradual forms of movements (Zickgraf, 2021)—slow-onset changes such as land degradation, erosions or sea-level rise may take a long period of time. It gradually becomes worse. The decision to move and stay therefore may also take a longer period of time (Boas, 2020). Zickgraf (2021) also points out how especially permanent land changes due to slow-onset climate impacts could lead to more permanent forms of out-migration, but that there yet exists insufficient literature that explores the temporality of mobility—in the sense of it being temporary or permanent.

Whilst these accounts are of high relevance and give a good starting point to understand the impact of different environmental changes, they are not as able to further deepen the explanation as to why people react differently to for example similar slow-onset changes. Whilst some people engage in rural–*urban* migrations, others engage in rural-*rural* movements, and again others do not want to move or are not able to do so, whilst again others may be temporally displaced and later return (for examples of such varied instances see e.g. Black et al., 2013; Blondin, 2020; Farbotko, 2022; Greiner & Sakdapolrak, 2013; Mallick & Schanze, 2020; Wiegel et al., 2021). To account for such differences, several studies have complemented environmental explanations with socio-political ones (see Wiegel et al., 2019, for an overview). Drawing on De Haas' aspirations-capabilities framework and mobilities literature, these studies for instance refer to differences in mobility capital or capacities to move, such as differences in resources to move, physical abilities to move, or social network connections to rely on that shape decisions and possibilities as to where and how to move (on these concepts, see Kaufmann et al., 2004; Haas, 2021; Sherbinin et al., 2022; Sheller, 2018).

An analysis of capacities to move can help to explain why some people are not able to move at all despite climate risk; often referred to as being "trapped" or "involuntary immobile" (Black et al., 2013; Blondin, 2020).

Some may be disabled limiting options to move when a disaster strikes, again others may not have social connections needed to find another place to stay, and there are differences in how well different areas and or groups are supported by government and other agencies in getting to safety (Blondin, 2020; Zickgraf et al., 2018). A recent focus in this debate has been the role of gender dynamics in explaining limited capacities to move. In Bangladesh, for example, women are often not able to stay in cyclone shelters, as they feel harassed or men perceive the presence of an unmarried woman in the shelter as a sign of dishonour (Ayeb-Karlsson, 2020). This can lead to pressures for women to stay home or outside when a disaster strikes, leaving them potentially trapped in dangerous situations.

In addition to differentiated capacities, studies have examined the differences in aspirations to move or stay (Haas, 2021). Adams (2016), in her 2016 paper, was amongst the first to highlight that people may not want to move, despite climate risks, due to attachment to place. Literature often refers to such decisions as voluntary immobility (Blondin, 2021; Farbotko, 2022; Zickgraf et al., 2018). Since Adam's paper, there have been several case studies demonstrating how identities that people have in relation to their places shape decisions to stay and can even result in active resistance against external pressures to relocate. Wiegel and colleagues for instance show this through a case of a small village in Patagonia in Chile (Wiegel et al., 2021). This village was destroyed by a mudslide and was therefore offered the option to relocate to a nearby area. The villagers however refused, in part as they identified themselves as being able to live with risk, with risk being inherent to the place they lived and grew up in. This well exemplifies how the nexus between climate change and decisions to move or stay is highly political. Residents do not simply want to give up their places and fight for their right to stay and to shape their climate futures.

The Politics of Climate Mobilities

Building on the burgeoning field of climate-mobility literature as outlined above, this next section further elaborates on the political and historical dimensions of climate mobilities that are taking shape in the Global South. We focus on ways in which global agendas and discourses frame the relations between climate change and human mobility and how this is actively being contested and reframed by several climate-impacted communities in different regions around the world. In these contestations, these communities draw from historically rooted understandings of their im/mobilities, their relations with the environment, and their attachment to place.

Recent studies show a wave of resistance amongst local communities towards often externally created narratives of inherent displacement and relocation. This resistance is visible in places such as the Pacific islands or Bangladesh threatened by the rising seas (Farbotko, 2022; Kitara, 2020; Paprocki, 2019; Suliman et al., 2019), the drylands in Kenya (Gross & Grauw, 2017), or the mountainous areas in Patagonia experiencing glacial melt and mud slides (Wiegel et al., 2021). Studies have demonstrated how people locally perceive their im/mobilities and relations with climate change, emphasising historical affinities with place or with mobility practices, and the right to self-determine one's climate future (Farbotko et al. 2023). They voice a critique of how the debate about climate mobility is largely being determined by a coalition of scientists (often from the Global North), media, development banks, and humanitarian agencies, rather than by affected communities themselves (see in particular Paprocki, 2019; Suliman et al., 2019; Whyte et al., 2019; Farbotko, 2022).

This has particularly been well put by activists and scholars who study the Pacific Island States, or more appropriately termed the Large Ocean States.[3] They express concerns about the global imagining of the Large Ocean States as sinking islands and therefore exposed to inherent displacement. This, so they argue, is preventing people from the islands to design their own climate futures. This constrained self-determination was well exemplified in a recent study by Bordner et al. (2020). They demonstrate that the Marshall Islands face difficulties in attracting adaptation funds for inhabitants to stay in place and strengthen their livelihoods on the Marshall Islands, as donors define the Marshall Islands as lost to the sea. They argue that "Marshallese decision-makers in this study perceive that aid institutions discount the existential implications of failing to pursue aggressive adaptation, assuming instead that migration is inevitable, economically rational, and even desirable" (Bordner et al., 2020, 1). In similar contexts, Farbotko (2022), and other scholars such as Suliman et al. (2019), have pointed towards voluntary immobilities in the Large Ocean States. They argue that these immobilities should be seen as political acts, seeking to reshape global imaginaries of islanders as future climate refugees by showing how people find ways to stay in place, often drawing on indigenous knowledge and their lived experiences to do so. In this way, decision to move or stay is not just seen as a process determined by external push and pull factors, but as a political act in itself (Samaddar, 2020), rooted in historical understandings of mobility and immobility in relation to surrounding environments (Suliman et al., 2019). For the islanders, debates and concerns of climate change go to the heart of their identity as a nation, as peoples. As argued by Kitara (2020, n.p.), an activist from Tuvalu: "We all know that Pacific Islanders are fighting against climate change as a direct threat to our land and our ocean. But how many of us realise that climate change means we must also fight for our political independence and our identity? This is our sovereignty; we cannot let it be taken away from us, even if our land is highly at risk".

Though scholars from, or studying, the Large Ocean States have been very vocal, they are not unique in ventilating concerns about climate refugee narratives and in pointing to the political nature of climate mobilities. For instance, a similar dynamic of dominating global agendas is visible in Bangladesh; equally portrayed as a center of climate disaster. As shown in the work by Paprocki (2019), a discourse of inevitable destruction by global warming has been put forward by development banks and (non-)governmental agencies to further transform some of Bangladesh's coastal regions from being based on rice-cultivation systems to shrimp aquaculture systems.[4] She does not deny the severe risk of climate change for these regions, but critiques policy to pre-emptively label the region as "lost" without actively exploring alternative climate adaptation scenarios and without involving local communities in the decision-making processes. The resulting transformation of the region to one of shrimp aquaculture has led to much salt intrusion into the area and loss of labour—as less labour is needed in shrimp aquaculture production compared to rice cultivation. As a consequence, there has been a large outflow of people to find jobs in neighbouring regions and cities. As Paprocki demonstrates, this migration has been reframed by policy and development agencies as an effective adaptation strategy for moving out of a region highly vulnerable to a changing climate. Yet, also here we see resistance movements, fighting against such frames and for the maintenance of local culture, and associated economies of rice cultivation and climate protection thereof (Cons, 2018; Paprocki, 2018; Paprocki, 2019).

Taken together, such examples show a problematic narration of several populations in the Global South as mere victims subject to displacement or relocation. It also demonstrates how such an imagining is actively being contested by these populations, signalling the political nature of climate im/mobilities and debates thereof. In this context, an increasing amount of empirical studies, of which some has been cited above, is adopting a politically and historically rooted view to better study the nexus between climate change and human mobility. This literature is particularly critical of environmental deterministic accounts for risking to conceal dominant power structures—such as dominant discursive frames or governance regimes as exemplified above—that depict the relationship between climate change and mobility in a particular manner without this per se resonating with local experiences and understandings of these climate risks and mobilities.

Cross-Border Climate Mobilities in the Global South

The majority of climate-mobility research poses that most movement will take place on relatively local or at most regional scales (e.g. from affected rural areas to nearby urban centres) (Boas et al., 2019; Foresight, 2011; Rigaud et al., 2018). This does, however, not mean we should lose sight of borders or of cross-border mobilities (McLeman, 2019). A postcolonial approach invites us to examine the political nature of climate mobilities, which includes a critical look at im/mobilities in relation to borders. It is about how these borders reshape im/mobility dynamics, by making new connection points or by breaking off flows (Samaddar, 2020; Sheller, 2020). This means that a mere country focus may limit our understandings and make us understand climate mobilities through Western-centric concepts of the nation state. Indeed, when we zoom into many of the cases, also local human mobilities do not per se stop at the border, or if they do physically (because of hard border controls), they are still influenced by broader dynamics and social relations that take place in the context of border politics (Spiegel et al., 2022).

One typical example concerns pastoralist mobilities, being historically a highly mobile group crossing vast regions that later in (post)colonial times turned into a landscape of different nation states. In the Eastern Himalayan Borderlands for example, where the world's third highest mountain peak of Mt. Khangchendzonga is situated, pastoralists have historically in nonlinear ways transcended political boundaries between Nepal, India and even Tibet in China. The Eastern Himalayan region has become classified as a climate-vulnerable region prone to more frequent climate-related disasters like landslides, water insecurities, and rising threats of glacial outbursts (IMI, 2019); risks which are also impacting pastoralist practice. For instance, grazing sites in the mountain regions are becoming warmer in temperature, leading to more diseases amongst the livestock, and creating risks for the herders as they have to find rangelands in higher altitudes (Feroze et al., 2019). At the same time, climate risks are not alone in impacting pastoralist cross-border mobilities and cannot be seen as separate from long ongoing pressures towards sedentarisation and criminalisation that these pastoralists have faced. Ever since the political integration of the Himalayan Kingdom of Sikkim into the state of India, state-driven postcolonial conservation narratives have assumed and framed pastoralist communities and their mobile practices as a prime threat to the environment (Tambe et al., 2005). In both Sikkim and Darjeeling, policy measures took drastic shape as a state-wide ban on grazing was imposed in 1998 followed by physical evictions of pastoralists from environmental protected areas in 2002 (Singh et al., 2021). These policy developments have drastically reduced pastoralism in these areas. Those who remain are facing ongoing stereotyping, restricted access to grazing grounds, topped with newly emerging climate risks. In this context, pastoralists have adopted various coping and adaptation strategies, including forms of resistance (Singh et al., 2021). For some on the Indian side, this has meant tapping onto cross-border social ties by making informal arrangements of transferring herds to ensure continued practice (Rai, 2021). Again others have just continued grazing practices, though in higher altitudes, and still others have been pushed into other livelihood options, such as tourism, whilst facing social exclusion in their communities for abandoning their cultural practices (Singh et al., 2021).

A similar story applies to the Fulani pastoralists in West Africa; as increasingly affected by the impacts of climate variability in West Africa, and who are culturally and linguistically related and spread across a vast area of the region, mainly in the Sahel zone. The Fulani (also called Fulbe, Fula, and Peul) people constitute one of the most mobile groups in West Africa, moving southward to coastal countries with the onset of the dry season, then back northward during the rainy season (Bruijn & Dijk, 2003; Driel, 2001). In the context of climate change, urbanisation, sedentarization pressures and rising political insecurities in the region, pastoralists today are facing increasing spatial mobility restrictions and pressures over water, pasture, and grazing routes which they have been using for many years (Alidou, 2016). A recent study suggests that environmental changes such as fluctuating rainfall patterns and frequent droughts, especially from the 1980s onwards, have led to more frequent transhumance between the Sahel and the coastal States, with pastoralists migrating further and further south (Leonhardt, 2019). However, movement across these rangelands is neither free nor unregulated. For example, pastoralists crossing Ilara borderlands between Benin and Nigeria negotiate through social networks and economic exchanges with the local communities to gain access to water points and pastures (Diogo et al., 2021). Over the years, this cross-border mobility has become increasingly complex. The expansion of farming in these areas, which heightened the pressure on land and water resources, often brought pastoralists in conflict with sedentary farmers along their transhumance routes (Bukari et al., 2020; Tonah, 2000). As a response to these violent contestations and rising geopolitical insecurities in West Africa, some governments have become even more restrictive towards the movements of the Fulani pastoralists within nations and across borders, with policies that either ban or restrict their mobility to a fixed space and time (Leonhardt, 2019). These interventions are not politically neutral. Rather, they constitute a discourse that constructs transhumance practices as archaic and perceptions that pastoralists are problematic and terrorists (Bukari & Schareika, 2015; Bukari et al., 2020; Leonhardt, 2019). Under these conditions, some pastoralists are forced to consider permanent settlement or pursue wage-labour occupations outside pastoralism in urban centers (Ducrotoy et al., 2018). However, in other cases it is not an end to their transhumance lifestyle, as pastoralists also seek to resist such government policies and frames (Bukari & Schareika, 2015; Leonhardt, 2019; Tonah, 2022).

Overall, these two examples show how pastoralist mobilities—as historically highly adaptive mobilities to environmental variability and seasonality—are being impacted by a combination of historical marginalisation and new climate risks and associated discourses. Most importantly, the examples demonstrate how their movement has become highly political, which is on the one hand driven by state politics and border controls, but also by environmental policies themselves and climate change discourse.

Beyond these examples of nomadic groups, cross-border climate mobilities are also relevant to consider in other borderland regions, where people are not per se nomadic but do cross borders in the context of work or social network connections (Spiegel et al., 2022). For instance, in the delta region located on the borders of Bangladesh and India, inhabitants have historically been moving in search of new land in the context of river and sea erosion, and for seasonal labour (Blackswan, 2018; Van Schendel, 2004). Given these lands, prior to the partition of 1947, used to be united as the great Bengal region, many of its inhabitants still have work and family ties on other sides of the border. This Bengal borderland's low-lying delta is amongst the worst affected by climate change (Shaw et al., 2022). It is impacted by cyclones and sea-level rise that intermix with natural processes of erosion and the way the delta is managed (Boas, 2020; Paprocki, 2019). The strict border regime between India and Bangladesh and ongoing efforts by the Indian government to deport Bangladeshi immigrants has severely restricted mobility. Still, cross-border mobility labelled as "illegal" remains part of daily borderland life and is therefore also one of the ways in which inhabitants seek to cope with social, economic, and climate risks (Shwely & Nadiruzzaman, 2017).

Moreover, the protest activities of people from Large Ocean States, such as Tuvalu, against narratives of inevitable relocation in the context of rising sea levels, cannot be seen as separate from cross-border mobilities. Through postcolonial ties and trade arrangements, Tuvaluans for example have been able to migrate to other states, in particular New Zealand and Australia (Farbotko et al., 2016; Hezel, 2013). This diaspora is highly vocal in seeking to regaining power over Tuvalu's climate future. To exemplify, the famous activist group the Pacific Climate Warriors is a transnational network of young pacific islanders, living on the islands (incl. Tuvalu) and abroad, but also with many residing in New Zealand and Australia. They contest the victimised image of pacific islanders into one of peaceful warriors who "fight" instead of "drown" (McNamara & Farbotko, 2017). Initiatives include journeys of traditional canoes to Australia, to raise awareness of their climate debt, their restrictive border status, whilst showing the resilience of the islanders' culture. As translocality research has argued for (Sakdapolrak et al., 2016), these dynamics show the importance of taking note of translocal connections that transcend borders as to how these shape climate im/mobility dynamics, policies, and discourses.

Conclusions and Ways Forward

This chapter has offered a modest review of a growing scholarship on the climate change-mobility nexus in the Global South that seeks to provide a critical and socially embedded understanding of this nexus. In short, we can draw three key lessons from this literature:

Firstly, an environmental deterministic account of the climate-mobility nexus in the Global South risks to conceal underlying socio-economic causes of grievance or inequalities that in addition to environmental factors shape im/mobilities. Im/mobilities are embedded within existing, often highly uneven, societal patterns which shape how people respond to and are able to adapt to climate risks. This means that researching how climate change affects capacities and aspirations to move or stay, needs to be done in relation to questions of socio-economic inequality, gender, race, or other (or collectively through a lens of intersectionality).

Secondly, it is clear that the climate change-mobility nexus is political. The policy agenda is largely determined by powerful players, such as the UN, World Bank, media, climate science. It is important to seek resonance with the views and lived experiences of affected communities, to account for indigenous perspectives and for these communities to self-determine or co-shape their climate futures.

Finally, a postcolonial understanding of climate mobilities can be helpful to think critically and reflexively about the climate change-mobility nexus. It would, amongst others, entail a critical perspective of borders (and their creation) vis-à-vis human mobilities and ask what this means for how we define climate mobilities. While there has been much recent work showing climate mobilities are largely local, this does not entail that borders are no longer relevant to climate mobilities scholarship. Categorising climate migrants as internal migrants, or as international migrants, risks to perpetuate political categories without exploring how climate im/mobilities are shaped by bordering processes or translocal dynamics transcending national borders.

We conclude this chapter with a recommendation for climate mobilities scholarship to open up its scope of research towards all parts of the world. This can help to more firmly move beyond a postcolonial imagination of the climate migrant (Piguet et al., 2018). There is ample research being done within Europe for example, whilst it is also increasingly facing climate risks, such as floods or droughts impacting on people's homes and livelihoods. Interesting also is how climate mobilities in the Global North—e.g. in the United States in the context of forest fires or sea-level rise risks—appear, when compared to the Global South, less often discussed through terms of climate mobility, migration and climate refugees. Instead, these climate mobilities are increasingly discussed through the lens of "managed retreat", as a "purposeful, coordinated movement of people and assets out of harm's way" (Siders, 2019).[5] This discursive difference—assuming climate mobilities are coordinated and managed in the Global North, whilst unregulated and crisis-like in the Global South—needs further scrutiny. It demonstrates a need to continue reflecting on the terms we use (Bettini, 2013), why we use them, and whether or not they are shaped or influenced by particular postcolonial imaginaries that need rethinking.

Acknowledgement The chapter was written in the context of Ingrid Boas' Vidi project on climate change-related mobility in the borderlands, grant number VI.Vidi.201.138.

Notes

1. We acknowledge that the term "Global South" may contribute to further stereotypical imaginings of migrants and of different geographical areas in the

world, whilst at the same it can be a force for political mobilisation in the context of debates of climate and mobility justice. See also Crawley and Teye, and Fiddian-Qasmiyeh, this volume, for a wider discussion on the concept of "Global South".
2. Zickgraf (2021) concentrated her review on slow-onset changes (such as sea-level rise) and noted that most studies on this subject concentrate on Asia. Piguet et al. (2018) had a broader focus (also including rapid-onset events such as floods) and found most studies in Sub-Saharan Africa and South Asia.
3. As a postcolonial critique, the term Large Ocean States reflects the view of a "sea of islands", contesting the frame of the Pacific Islands as "tiny isolated dots in a vast ocean" (Hau'ofa, 1993, 2017).
4. This trend had already started in the 1980s to enhance the export economy of Bangladesh but is increasingly rephrased as a climate adaptation strategy (Paprocki, 2019).
5. This argument needs further evidence-building; it is a preliminary conclusion we draw based on a preliminary reading of the debate and based on a master thesis project by Isa van Malenstein, supervised by Ingrid Boas.

References

Adams, H. (2016). Why populations persist: Mobility, place attachment and climate change. *Population and Environment, 37*(4), 429–448.

Alidou, S. M. (2016). *Cross-border Transhumance Corridors in West Africa*. https://www.shareweb.ch/site/Agriculture-and-Food-Security/aboutus/Documents/pastoralism/pastoralism_brief_couloirs_transhumance_e.pdf

Askland, H. H., Shannon, B., Chiong, R., Lockart, N., Maguire, A., Rich, J., & Groizard, J. (2022). Beyond migration: A critical review of climate change induced displacement. *Environmental Sociology, 8*(3), 267–278.

Ayeb-Karlsson, S. (2020). When the disaster strikes: Gendered (im)mobility in Bangladesh. *Climate Risk Management, 29*, 100237. https://doi.org/10.1016/j.crm.2020.100237

Baldwin, A. (2014). Pluralising climate change and migration: An argument in favour of open futures. *Geography Compass, 8*(8), 516–528.

Baldwin, A. (2016). Premediation and white affect: Climate change and migration in critical perspective. *Transactions of the Institute of British Geographers, 41*(1), 78–90.

Baldwin, A., Fröhlich, C., & Rothe, D. (2019). From climate migration to Anthropocene mobilities: Shifting the debate. *Mobilities, 14*(3), 289–297.

Basu, M., Roy, R., & Samaddar, R. (Eds.). (2018). *Political Ecology of survival: Life and labour in the river lands of east and northeast India*. Orient Blackswan.

Bettini, G. (2013). Climate barbarians at the gate? A critique of apocalyptic narratives on 'climate refugees.' *Geoforum, 45*, 63–72.

Black, R. (2001). *Environmental refugees: Myth or reality?* New issues in refugee research working paper 34. UNHCR.

Black, R., Adger, W. N., Arnell, N. W., Dercon, S., Geddes, A., & Thomas, D. (2011). The effect of environmental change on human migration. *Global Environmental Change, 21*, S3–S11.

Black, R., Arnell, N. W., Adger, W. N., Thomas, D., & Geddes, A. (2013). Migration, immobility and displacement outcomes following extreme events. *Environmental Science and Policy, 27*, S32–S43.

Blondin, S. (2020). Understanding involuntary immobility in the Bartang Valley of Tajikistan through the prism of motility. *Mobilities, 15*(4), 543–558.

Blondin, S. (2021). Staying despite disaster risks: Place attachment, voluntary immobility and adaptation in Tajikistan's Pamir Mountains. *Geoforum, 126*, 290–301.

Boas, I. (2020). Social networking in a digital and mobile world: The case of environmentally-related migration in Bangladesh. *Journal of Ethnic and Migration Studies, 46*(7), 1330–1347.

Boas, I., Wiegel, H., Farbotko, C., Warner, J., & Sheller, M. (2022). Climate mobilities: Migration, im/mobilities and mobility regimes in a changing climate. *Journal of Ethnic and Migration Studies, 48*(14), 3365–3379.

Boas, I., Farbotko, C., Adams, H., Sterly, H., Bush, S., van der Geest, K., Wiegel, H., Ashraf, H., Baldwin, A., Bettini, G., Blondin, S., de Bruijn, M., Durand-Delacre, D., Fröhlich, C., Gioli, G., Guaita, L., Hut, E., Jarawura, F.X., Lamers, M., Lietaer, S., Nash S.L., Piguet, E., Rothe, D., Sakdapolrak, P., Smith, L., Tripathy Furlong, B., Turhan, E., Warner, J., Zickgraf, C., Black, R., and Hulme, M. (2019). Climate migration myths. *Nature Climate Change, 9*(12), 901–903.

Borderon, M., Sakdapolrak, P., Muttarak, R., Kebede, E., Pagogna, R., & Sporer, E. (2019). Migration influenced by environmental change in Africa. *Demographic Research, 41*, 491–544.

Bordner, A. S., Ferguson, C. E., & Ortolano, L. (2020). Colonial dynamics limit climate adaptation in Oceania: Perspectives from the Marshall Islands. *Global Environmental Change, 61*, 102054. https://doi.org/10.1016/j.gloenvcha.2020.102054

Bukari, K. N., Bukari, S., Sow, P., & Scheffran, J. (2020). Diversity and multiple drivers of pastoral Fulani migration to Ghana. *Nomadic Peoples, 24*, 4–31.

Bukari, K. N., & Schareika, N. (2015). Steorotypes, prejudices and exclusion of Fulani Pastoralists in Ghana. *Pastoralism: Research, Policy and Practice, 5*(20), 1–12.

Castles, S. (2002). *Environmental change and forced migration: Making sense of the debate.* New issues in refugee research working papers, no. 70. United Nations High Commissioner for Refugees.

Cons, J. (2018). Staging climate security: Resilience and heterodystopia in the Bangladesh borderlands. *Cultural Anthropology, 33*(2), 266–294.

Cundill, G., Singh, C., Adger, W. N., de Campos, R. S., Vincent, K., Tebboth, M., & Maharjan, A. (2021). Toward a climate mobilities research agenda: Intersectionality, immobility, and policy responses. *Global Environmental Change, 69*, 102315. https://doi.org/10.1016/j.gloenvcha.2021.102315

De Bruijn, M., & Van Dijk, H. (2003). Changing population mobility in West Africa: Fulbe pastoralists in central and south Mali. *African Affairs, 102*(407), 285–307.

De Haas, H. (2021). A theory of migration: The aspirations-capabilities framework. *Comparative Migration Studies, 9*(1), 1–35.

De Sherbinin, A. M., Grace, K., McDermid, S., Van Der Geest, K., Puma, M. J., & Bell, A. (2022). Migration theory in climate mobility research. *Frontiers in Climate. Section Climate Mobility.* https://doi.org/10.3389/fclim.2022.882343

Diogo, R. V. C., Dossa, L. H., Vanvanhossou, S. F. U., Abdoulaye, B. D., Dosseh, K. H., Houinato, M., Schlecht, E., & Buerkert, A. (2021). Farmers' and herders' perceptions on rangeland management in two agroecological zones of Benin. *Land, 10*(4), 425. https://doi.org/10.3390/land10040425

Ducrotoy, M. J., Majekodunmi, A. O., & Welburn, S. C. (2018). Pattern of passage into protected areas: Drivers and outcomes of Fulani immigration, settlement and integration into the Kachia Grazing Reserve, Northwest Nigeria. *Pastoralism: Research, Policy and Practice, 8*(1). https://doi.org/10.1186/s13570-017-0105-1

Farbotko, C. (2022). Anti-displacement mobilities and re-emplacements: Alternative climate mobilities in Funafala. *Journal of Ethnic and Migration Studies, 48*(14), 3380–3396.

Farbotko, C., Stratford, E., & Lazrus, H. (2016). Climate migrants and new identities? The geopolitics of embracing or rejecting mobility. *Social and Cultural Geography, 17*(4), 533–552.

Farbotko, C., Boas, I., Dahm, R., Kitara, T., Lusama, T. & Tanielu. T. (2023). Reclaiming open climate adaptation futures. *Nature Climate Change 13*, 750–751. https://doi.org/10.1038/s41558-023-01733-1

Feroze, S. M., Ray, L. I. P., Singh, K. J. et al. (2019). Pastoral yak rearing system is changing with change in climate: an exploration of North Sikkim in Eastern Himalaya. *Climatic Change, 157*, 483–498. https://doi.org/10.1007/s10584-019-02551-1

Foresight. (2011). *Migration and global environmental change: Future challenges and opportunities.* The Government Office for Science.

Gemenne, F. (2009). *Environmental changes and migration flows. Normative frameworks and policy responses.* Doctoral dissertation. Université de Liège, Institut d'Études Politiques de Paris. https://orbi.uliege.be/handle/2268/137601

Greiner, C., & Sakdapolrak, P. (2013). Rural–urban migration, agrarian change, and the environment in Kenya: A critical review of the literature. *Population and Environment, 34*(4), 524–553.

Gross, E., & Grauw, S. (2017). *Rainmakers II: A seed of change.* Ajustdiggit Documentary. https://www.youtube.com/watch?v=vlgeKRoQsXI

Hau'Ofa, E. (1993). Our sea of islands. In E. Waddell, V. Naidu, & E. Hau'Ofa (Eds.), *A New Oceania: Rediscovering Our Sea of Islands* (pp. 1–17). University of the South Pacific.

Hau'Ofa, E. (2017). Our sea of islands. In P. D'Arcy (Ed.), *Peoples of the Pacific* (pp. 429–442). Routledge. https://doi.org/10.4324/9781315247175

Hezel, F. X. (2013). *Micronesians on the move: Eastward and upward bound*. East-West Center.

Hoffmann, R., Dimitrova, A., Muttarak, R., Crespo Cuaresma, J., & Peisker, J. (2020). A meta-analysis of country-level studies on environmental change and migration. *Nature Climate Change, 10*(10), 904–912.

IMI. (2019). *Understanding Mountain Peoples' approach and practices to combating climate change in the Indian Himalayan Region: Research to renewal to reforms*. Study Report. Integrated Mountain Initiative. https://inmi.in/images/Report_Final_Correction_June_02_2021.pdf

Kaufmann, V., Bergman, M. M., & Joye, D. (2004). Motility: Mobility as capital. *International Journal of Urban and Regional Research, 28*(4), 745–756.

Kitara, T. (2020). *Climate change and sovereignty*. Blog for Toda Peace Institute Global Outlook. https://toda.org/global-outlook/global-outlook/2020/climate-change-and-sovereignty.html

Klepp, S. (2017). Climate change and migration. In *Oxford Research Encyclopaedia of climate science* (pp. 1–37). https://doi.org/10.1093/acrefore/9780190228620.013.42

Lama, P., Hamza, M., & Wester, M. (2021). Gendered dimensions of migration in relation to climate change. *Climate and Development, 13*(4), 326–336.

Leonhardt, M. (2019). *Regional policies and response to manage pastoral movements within the ECOWAS region*. International Organisation for Migration.

Mallick, B., & Schanze, J. (2020). Trapped or voluntary? Non-Migration despite Climate Risks. *Sustainability, 12*(11), 4718.

McLeman, R. (2019). International migration and climate adaptation in an era of hardening borders. *Nature Climate Change, 9*(12), 911–918.

McNamara, K. E., & Farbotko, C. (2017). Resisting a 'doomed' fate: An analysis of the Pacific Climate Warriors. *Australian Geographer, 48*(1), 17–26.

Paprocki, K. (2018). Threatening dystopias: Development and adaptation regimes in Bangladesh. *Annals of the American Association of Geographers, 108*(4), 955–973.

Paprocki, K. (2019). All that is solid melts into the bay: Anticipatory ruination and climate change adaptation. *Antipode, 51*(1), 295–315.

Parsons, L. (2019). Structuring the emotional landscape of climate change migration: Towards climate mobilities in geography. *Progress in Human Geography, 43*(4), 670–690.

Piguet, E. (2013). From 'primitive migration' to 'climate refugees': The curious fate of the natural environment in migration studies. *Annals of the Association of American Geographers, 103*(1), 148–162.

Piguet, E. (2022). Linking climate change, environmental degradation, and migration: An update after 10 years. *Wiley Interdisciplinary Reviews: Climate Change, 13*(1), e746. https://doi.org/10.1002/wcc.746

Piguet, E., Kaenzig, R., & Guélat, J. (2018). The uneven geography of research on 'environmental migration.' *Population and Environment, 39*(4), 357–383.

Rai, P. (2021). *Finding the secret passage: Conservation in the High Himalayas.* Blog post. Sikkim Project. https://www.sikkimproject.org/finding-the-secret-passageconservation-in-the-high-himalayas/

Rigaud, K. K., de Sherbinin, A., Jones, B., Bergmann, J., Clement, V., Ober, K., Schewe, J., Adamo, S., McCusker, B., Heuser, S., & Midgley, A. (2018). *Groundswell: Preparing for internal climate migration.* The World Bank.

Sakdapolrak, P., Naruchaikusol, S., Ober, K., Peth, S., Porst, L., Rockenbauch, T., & Tolo, V. (2016). Migration in a changing climate. Towards a translocal social resilience approach. *DIE ERDE–Journal of the Geographical Society of Berlin, 147*(2), 81–94.

Samaddar, R. (2020). *The postcolonial age of migration.* Routledge.

Sheller, M. (2018). *Mobility justice.* Verso.

Sheller, M. (2020). *Island futures. Caribbean survival in the anthropocene.* Duke University Press.

Sheller, M., & Urry, J. (2006). The new mobilities paradigm. *Environment and Planning A, 38*(2), 207–226.

Shewly, H. J., & Nadiruzzaman, M. (2017). Invisible journeys across India-Bangladesh borders and bubbles of corrupt networks: Stories of cross-border rural-urban migration and economic linkages. In F. Chiodelli, T. Hall, & R. Hudson (Eds.), *Corrupt places: The illicit in the governance and development of cities and regions.* Routledge.

Siders, A. R. (2019). Managed retreat in the United States. *One Earth, 1*(2), 216–225.

Singh, R., Sharma, R. K., Bhutia, T. U., Bhutia, K., & Babu, S. (2021). Conservation policies, eco-tourism, and end of pastoralism in Indian Himalaya? *Frontiers in Sustainable Food Systems, 5*, 613998.

Shaw, R., Luo, Y., Cheong, T. S., Abdul Halim, S., Chaturvedi, S., Hashizume, M., Insarov, G. E., Ishikawa, Y., Jafari, M., Kitoh, A., Pulhin, J., Singh, C., Vasant, K., & Zhang, Z. (2022). Asia. In H.-O. Pörtner et al. (Eds.), *Climate change 2022: Impacts, adaptation and vulnerability. Contribution of working group II to the sixth assessment report of the intergovernmental panel on climate change* (pp. 1457–1579). Cambridge University Press. https://doi.org/10.1017/9781009325844.012

Spiegel, S. J., Kachena, L., & Gudhlanga, J. (2022). Climate disasters, altered migration and pandemic shocks:(im)mobilities and interrelated struggles in a border region. *Mobilities.* https://doi.org/10.1080/17450101.2022.2099756

Suhrke, A. (1994). Environmental degradation and population flows. *Journal of International Affairs, 47*(2), 473–496.

Suliman, S., Farbotko, C., Ransan-Cooper, H., McNamara, K. E., Thornton, F., McMichael, C., & Kitara, T. (2019). Indigenous (im)mobilities in the anthropocene. *Mobilities, 14*(3), 298–318.

Tambe, S., Bhutia, N. T., & Arrawatia, M. L. (2005). *People's opinion on the impacts of "Ban on Grazing" in Barsey Rhododendron Sanctuary, Sikkim, India*. Report, The Mountain Institute. http://www.sikkimforest.gov.in/docs/Wildlife/wwfbarsey.pdf

Tonah, S. (2000). State policies, local prejudices, and cattle rustling along the Ghana-Burkina Faso Border. *Africa, 70*(4), 551–567.

Tonah, S. (2022). *Pastoral Fulani livelihood in Contemporary Ghana*. University of Ghana.

Turhan, E., Zografos, C., & Kallis, G. (2015). Adaptation as biopolitics: Why state policies in Turkey do not reduce the vulnerability of seasonal agricultural workers to climate change. *Global Environmental Change, 31*, 296–306.

Van Driel, A. (2001). *Sharing a valley: The changing relations between agriculturalists and pastoralists in the Niger Valley of Benin*. Doctoral Dissertation. University of Amsterdam.

Van Schendel, W. (2004). *The Bengal Borderland*. Anthem Press.

Warner, K. (2010). Global environmental change and migration: Governance challenges. *Global Environmental Change, 20*(3), 402–413.

Whyte, K., Talley, J. L., & Gibson, J. D. (2019). Indigenous mobility traditions, colonialism, and the Anthropocene. *Mobilities, 14*(3), 319–335.

Wiegel, H., Boas, I., & Warner, J. (2019). A mobilities perspective on migration in the context of environmental change. *Wiley Interdisciplinary Reviews: Climate Change, 10*(6), e610. https://doi.org/10.1002/wcc.610

Wiegel, H., Warner, J., Boas, I., & Lamers, M. (2021). Safe from what? Understanding environmental non-migration in Chilean Patagonia through ontological security and risk perceptions. *Regional Environmental Change, 21*(2). https://doi.org/10.1007/s10113-021-01765-3

Zickgraf, C. (2018). Immobility. In R. McLeman & F. Gemenne (Eds.), *Routledge handbook of environmental displacement and migration* (pp. 71–84). Routledge.

Zickgraf, C. (2021). Climate change, slow onset events and human mobility: Reviewing the evidence. *Current Opinion in Environmental Sustainability, 50*, 21–30.

Open Access This chapter is licensed under the terms of the Creative Commons Attribution 4.0 International License (http://creativecommons.org/licenses/by/4.0/), which permits use, sharing, adaptation, distribution and reproduction in any medium or format, as long as you give appropriate credit to the original author(s) and the source, provide a link to the Creative Commons license and indicate if changes were made.

The images or other third party material in this chapter are included in the chapter's Creative Commons license, unless indicated otherwise in a credit line to the material. If material is not included in the chapter's Creative Commons license and your intended use is not permitted by statutory regulation or exceeds the permitted use, you will need to obtain permission directly from the copyright holder.

21

Why, When and How? The Role of Inequality in Migration Decision-making

Caterina Mazzilli, Jessica Hagen-Zanker, and Carmen Leon-Himmelstine

Introduction

For a long time, migration decision-making was seen as a one-off decision concerning whether to leave or to stay based on individual cost–benefit calculations, usually monetary ones (Harris & Todaro, 1970; Massey et al., 1993). Gradually, this concept has expanded to focus much more on the "journey" of decision-making, both in the literal and figurative sense, encompassing types and modes of travel, trajectories and destination preferences (Crawley & Jones, 2021; Hagen-Zanker & Mallett, 2016). This expansion more accurately reflects the complexity of migration decision-making, since migration does not "just" correspond to a one-time decision or even journey, but rather starts much earlier on—that is, in personal mental processes such as imagining and planning. At the same time, there is no certainty on when migration and its effects end, if they ever do (Chambers, 2018; Hagen-Zanker et al., forthcoming), even after the arrival in the place of destination.

C. Mazzilli · J. Hagen-Zanker (✉) · C. Leon-Himmelstine
Great Surrey House 203 Blackfriars Rd, London SE1 8NJ, United Kingdom
e-mail: j.hagen-zanker@odi.org.uk

C. Mazzilli
e-mail: c.mazzilli@odi.org.uk

C. Leon-Himmelstine
e-mail: c.leon-himmelstine@odi.org.uk

Until recently, two competing theoretical models tried to make sense of migration decision-making. On the one side, functionalism (Harris & Todaro, 1970) considered migrants as rational agents who decide to move in order to maximise their income and in response to "push–pull factors" (Lee, 1966). Income inequality plays a large part in this theory, as wage differentials are seen as the key factor driving migration decisions and migration is predicted to continue until wages have equalised. This approach assumes that individuals have perfect access to information, make rational decisions based on measurable, mostly economic, factors and are free to move, should they wish to. Moreover, it ignores the manifold costs of migration. Before individuals can access the higher wages resulting from migration, they first have to pursue certain investments such as the material costs of travelling, the living costs while moving and looking for work, the difficulty in adapting to a new labour market and the psychological costs—not to mention that they interact with other actors through this journey, such as employers, who can refuse to give them work for reasons other than economic ones. On the other side, the historical-structuralist model focused on the macro-structure migrants are embedded in, seeing migration as both producing and reproducing socio-economic inequalities between individuals and states (de Haas, 2021). Yet, this model does not leave any space to individual agency, portraying migrants as victims of the circumstances or as irrational beings who move even when it is not beneficial to do so. De Haas (2021) and others, such as Carling and Schewel (2020), moved towards filling the gap between these two approaches through the "aspirations-capabilities framework", which conceptualises migration decision-making as "a function of aspirations and capabilities to migrate in a given set of perceived opportunity structure" (de Haas, 2021, 31). A focus on aspirations and capabilities helps to integrate both concepts of agency and structure, considered to be one of the main challenges for advancing migration theory (de Haas, 2011). By highlighting the role of aspirations, de Haas has paved the way for the inclusion of intangible factors in decision-making, which we explore in detail below.

Both tangible and intangible inequalities play a role in migration decision-making. We approach this theme from a theoretical perspective, grounding our analysis on the current literature on inequalities as drivers of migration within the so-called Global South. As for South–North migration, South–South migration too is tightly connected to inequality, as Cela et al. (2022) argue when describing it as a phenomenon that "often perpetuates inequalities across borders" (194). The entanglement of inequality and migration is also a reason why policy-makers focus on tackling poverty and inequality as a way to reduce migration, with containment strategies intended to prevent populations from the Global South from migrating to the Global North becoming increasingly normalised (Landau, 2019).

The United Nations defines inequality as "the state of not being equal, especially in status, rights, and opportunities" (UN, DS and UNPAU, DPAD, and DESA, n.d.). Despite being a crucial concept for social justice, the breadth of inequality as a concept makes it still prone to confusion. Many authors have been singling out "economic inequality", mostly referring to income, wealth and general living conditions, while others have been focusing on access to rights (UN, DS and UNPAU, DPAD, and DESA, n.d.). Currently, there is some consensus on the definition of inequality as unequal "access to opportunities" (UN, DS and UNPAU, DPAD, and DESA, n.d.). This perspective, which we embrace, shows the pervasiveness of the factors determining inequality of opportunities both within and between countries (UN, DS and UNPAU, DPAD, and DESA, n.d.).

Throughout the chapter, we distinguish between tangible and intangible inequalities. Tangible inequalities are those inequalities that can be clearly defined and measured. In other words, they have a quantifiable impact on someone's life, such as socio-economic inequality, education and skill levels or unequal access to rights. Intangible inequalities, instead, are individually perceived, such as subjective feelings of discrimination or injustice. Being mental processes, they are less visible, more complicated to grasp, and, as such, have been studied less. Both in theory and in everyday life, telling tangible and intangible inequalities apart is not simple, as they often coexist. For instance, someone might feel discriminated against (intangible inequality) as a result of unequal economic structures (tangible inequality). Therefore, our classification does not aim at separating them, as much as presenting them more clearly, while shining light on those elements that have not been adequately explored so far.

Tangible Inequalities—Socio-Economic and Right-Access Inequality

Although economic inequality between countries has improved over the past 25 years, the gap between them is still considerable (World Bank Group, 2016), while inequality within many countries is increasing (Piketty, 2018). The UN (n.d.) indeed reports that, "today, 71% of the world's population live in countries where inequality has grown". As the UN rightly points out, this figure is particularly important because inequalities within countries are those that people feel day after day: "this is how people stack up and compare themselves with their neighbours, family members, and society" (UN, n.d.) The COVID-19 pandemic has no doubt exacerbated this polarisation, as "globally the top 1% took 38% of all additional wealth accumulated since the mid-1990s" (World Inequality Database, 2021). The World Inequality Report 2021 divides inequalities into wealth, gender and ecological—as global inequality more and more fuels, and is fuelled by, climate change and ecological emergencies (Chancel & Piketty, 2021). While the literature considers socio-economic inequality, it has not yet considered ecological inequalities in relation to migration decision-making—apart from a few exceptions (e.g., see McLeman et al., 2016). In line with these definitions, in this section we consider the impact of a broad range of tangible inequalities on migration decision-making.

A high number of studies focuses on the links between economic inequality (i.e. wealth or income differentials) and migration, although research on South–South migration appears to be comparatively less nuanced than that focused on South–North migration (see also Casentini et al., in this volume). Already in 1980, Lipton noted that economic inequality is a driver of migration. Grounding his observation on a number of rural villages in India, Lipton (1980) argues that more unequal villages present a higher likelihood of rural–urban migration. Those who leave are predominantly young men between 15 and 30 years old, which means that, with their departure, villages are deprived of the fresh ideas and energy often fuelled by young people and capable of challenging inequality.

Inequality is in its very nature a relative assessment—how people's (economic) status relates to others—and keeping this in mind makes the link to decision-making clearer. In the 1980s, a set of influential papers known as the New Economics of Labour Migration broadened existing economic theories from a sole focus on income differences between source and origin countries to economic stability, risk and social status—the latter is defined as a household's absolute income in relation to the income of others in the community, also known as relative deprivation (Stark, 1991). As Massey et al. (1993) explain, "people may be motivated to migrate not only to increase their absolute income or to diversify their risks, but also to improve their income relative to other households in their reference group" (452).

Still nowadays, economic inequalities are reflected on who is able to migrate. International migrants tend not to come from the most deprived sections of society, given the often-high costs involved in international migration (Massey et al., 1993). Access to finances supporting migration is often "sourced from migrants' savings, financial resources received from family members, remittances from successful relations and friends abroad and their connections" (Dinbabo et al., 2021, 221). Moreover, those coming from wealthier families often go through less risky migration journeys and/or land better-paid jobs once at destination. This in turn impacts on the remittances sent back to the place of origin, which both reflects income differentials between migrants and reproduces or potentially aggravates inequalities in the sending country. However, Black et al. (2006) warn that this conclusion is only partially accurate, because it frames remittances as a substitute to home earnings rather than an additional cash inflow. Indeed, even if this literature focuses on international migration, internal migration may also be costly, as it involves initial expenses and/or depends on social networks and job availability.

Rather than establishing whether migration increases or decreases economic inequality, Black et al. (2006) argue that "any overarching conclusion about impacts of inequality is unlikely to be very robust at a global or even regional level" (2). On the contrary, they state, inequalities are always context-specific and should be analysed as such. In addition, and most importantly for this chapter, Black et al. (2006) urge scholars to approach inequalities with a broader understanding than income and wealth. They write: "there are socio-cultural dimensions to inequality, as well as inequalities in access to power, whilst all aspects of inequality are highly gendered" (2)—and all these concur to shape migration decision-making. In the context of West Africans' migration to the Maghreb (Libya and Morocco) and Europe, Dinbabo et al. (2021) define inequality as "limited access to opportunities, poverty and unemployment amidst precarious development challenges", which go together with lack of "realistic expectations for a better life" (223).

Approaching inequality as more than just income and wealth, Cela et al. (2022) discuss Haitian emigration as driven by persistent structural inequalities, that is, a conjunction of economic and political instability originated during the nation's colonial past and the 1791–1804 revolution, to be then sharpened by invasion threats, diplomatic isolation, occupation, authoritarian governments, and natural catastrophes. The harsh living conditions generated by these factors have pushed "its urban poor, rural peasants, middle class, and even its educated youth to flee" (Cela et al., 2022, 194). This work reveals how far back the roots of inequality can reach, and that they impact several areas of social life at once.

Another well-explored area of study concerns the role of unequal gender norms affecting migration decision-making, which sit at a unique intersection between intangible and tangible. Evidence suggests that for men, migration often has an added social and normative component, making it a "rite of passage" where migration is seen as a path to adulthood and economic independence (Massey et al., 1994; Tucker et al., 2013). For instance, Monsutti (2007) writes that young Hazara males migrating from Afghanistan to Iran see migration as an instrument to achieve both safety and social recognition while providing for their family, and, as such, as a pivotal step towards manhood. For women, however, their migration decision can be interlinked more to what they think is expected of them as women, to their position in the household, and to their perceived family responsibilities (e.g. to reunite with partners or to marry) (Hidrobo et al., 2022). Gender norms around kinship and care are also important factors influencing the decision to migrate or to stay put (Kanaiaupuni, 2000). Scalettaris et al. (2019) conducted a study with young Afghan men at the south-eastern border of Europe, revealing the complex network of mutual obligations between them and their stayed-behind families, and the high pressure they are under. On the one side, they are pushed to "succeed" in their migration by a "quest for autonomy and recognition" (Scalettaris et al., 2019, 519), while on the other side they gradually understand that the chances of settling in Europe are slim—this driving them to become more competitive with and jealous of their peers.

However, other studies have observed that some women do not only follow the conventional gender roles of migrating as daughters or wives but migrate with the purpose to continue studying or simply pursuing a better life (Hondagneu-Sotelo, 1992). Further evidence has shown that gender norms are not static: they can and do change, with migration (and other processes) being a potential trigger of change (Marcus et al., 2015). Values and behaviours in the place of destination influence the set of norms that migrants have acquired at home, for example, when women increase their income, their confidence, their independence and their aspirations (Bastia, 2013; Leon-Himmelstine, 2017). Alternatively, migration can reinforce conservative or discriminatory gender norms (Tuccio & Wahba, 2018). Summarising, Fechter (2013) argues that migration in and of itself is neither oppressive nor liberating in gender terms, but that it rather has variegated outcomes for women and men alike,[1] which depend on the broader socio-economic context they are part of.

As mentioned in the introduction, migration policies in the Global North have increasingly focused on containing migration from the Global South. The stream of policy measures focusing on reducing inequalities in the places where migrations originate grounds on the assumption that, if development and inequalities within countries are improved, out-migration will go down. For instance, employment and education policies/programs carried out in Global South countries are framed as a tool to potentially mitigate economic, educational, but also gender inequality by providing training and/or entrepreneurship skills needed to get a (better-paid) job, and hence reducing the need to migrate. However, most studies examined in a recent literature review find these programmes actually *increase* out-migration (Hagen-Zanker & Hennessey, 2021b). For instance, the OECD (2017) reports that participants in Technical and Vocational Education and Training (TVET) programmes in the Global South are statistically significantly more likely to plan to emigrate than non-participants. This is due to the challenges that migrants face in employing their newly acquired skills in the local market, but also to their aspirations to put their training to use in a context where there are more possibilities to profit from it. This research demonstrates that, if a programme is not designed with reference to the local labour market, it will not succeed in reducing socio-economic inequality via new skills provision, simply because participants will not have the chance to apply them locally. Finally, Hagen-Zanker and Hennessey (2021b) point at individual and structural factors as complementary to employment and education programmes. Beyond the programme itself, inequality at the individual level (for instance, inequality in terms of wealth and class, gender or education) and at the collective one (socio-economic opportunities, right to work) greatly influence migration decision-making, and are often much more important than small-scale short-term policies that do not result in any structural changes.

Connecting both to this and to Cela's et al. (2022) discussion of structural inequalities, we conclude this section with some further reflections on the influence of policies on inequality and migration. In their work on the efficacy of migration policies, Hagen-Zanker and Mallett (2022) discuss how, over the past years, policies aimed at preventing irregular migration from Global South countries have worked either through the building of physical and bureaucratic obstacles or through the creation of alternative "favourable" conditions to reduce the desirability and need for migration (as discussed in the example above). Yet, they highlight that nation-states have only limited capacity to influence population movements as long as they do not tackle broader dynamics such as North–South, South–South or rural–urban inequalities and exploitative relations, such as labour market imbalances, opportunity differentials, conflicts and colonial legacies (Castles, 2004; Hagen-Zanker & Mallett, 2022; Lyberaki, 2008; Thielemann, 2004; Wiklund, 2012). In conclusion, the existence of a causal relation between migration-related policies and people's movement is debatable, since the impact of policies issued by faraway countries, regardless of how powerful, is overshadowed by the daily force of global structural inequalities on people's lives.

Intangible Inequalities—Perception of, and Feelings About, Inequality

We now move on to "intangible" inequalities, namely those referring to a person's own *perception*, rather than to a straightforward measurement.

There are several important reasons for spotlighting perceptions of and feelings about inequalities. Firstly, this is very much an understudied area. For instance, while it is now well established that income differentials are a key driver of migration, only recently the literature has started exploring how people experience and feel about inequality, inequities and discrimination, and how this in turn affects migration decision-making (Hagen-Zanker & Hennessey, 2021a).

A study conducted in Latvia by Ķešāne (2019) shows that Latvian emigrants were very sensitive to vertical inequality and income differences in their country of origin, and they expressed this through anger, disappointment, and resentment towards their government. However, they were less sensitive to inequality in the country of destination. Their emotional reactions did not correspond one–one to absolute difference in deprivation levels within each country, but rather to the migrants' *perception* of opportunities available to them in their country of origin and in the country of destination (Eade et al., 2007). Although Ķešāne's work (2019) is not based on research in the Global South, we find it provides a useful understanding of migrants' different perceptions of inequality in countries of origin versus in countries of destination and of the potentially unexpected ways this influences migration decision-making. In this context, migration is an emotionally charged decision that can have an emancipatory function—or that can be perceived as such.

The literature on the migration-emotion nexus too has, in recent years, become more substantial. Work within this stream of literature has been focusing on, for instance, feelings of entrapment, jealousy and frustrations of one's life situation (Belloni, 2019; Kalir, 2005). There is also some relevant work on the connection between migration and shame (Bredeloup, 2017), guilt (Constable, 2014) or hope (Grabska, 2020; Hernandez-Carretero, 2016), as there is relevant research on love and attachment to either people or places (Mai & King, 2009), and on belonging (Schewel, 2015). Yet, these accounts very rarely include considerations on perceived inequality.

A second reason to focus on perception is that, while some aspects of someone's life are easily measurable, others are "inherently hard to measure" (Wolton, 2022), thus, focusing on how perceptions shape up and are experienced instead of attempting at objectively measuring them can foster our understanding of the intricacies of decision-making. Discrimination is one of these aspects. Wolton (2022) explains that we can use a broad or a narrow approach when trying to quantify discrimination. While the broad approach to discrimination tends to "look at simple differences in outcomes between different groups", such as wage gaps, the narrow approach "recognizes that groups differ in more than one dimensions" (i.e. living in different locations, being from different socio-economic backgrounds, etc.), and highlights that all those dimensions can affect the outcome of the analysis. Wolton's (2022) argument also reminds us that categories of disadvantage (e.g. discrimination based on class) do not function in isolation and intersect with other differences (such as race, ethnicity, age, sexuality and so on), usually having a profound effect on migrant's decision to migrate and their experience (Bastia, 2013). Obviously, the fact that discrimination or other elements are hard to measure is not a justification to stop measuring them altogether. Rather, exactly because measurement can hardly grasp the full extent of the impact on discrimination on someone's life, it is important to *also* enquire about how people perceive, make sense and feel about it.

Third, sometimes it is *perception* of inequalities, rather than objective differentials, that triggers (or discourages) migration. For instance, as it emerges from Ķešāne's study (2019), it is misleading to label economic inequality in the country of origin as key for migration decision-making, since comparative levels of income and wealth differentials are found in many countries of origin and of destination. This means that, at times, frustration, as well as perceived lack of recognition and respect compared to more privileged groups in one's society, can constitute a driver of migration much more than monthly earnings.

Having illustrated why it is important to focus on perceptions of inequality, we move onto defining some of the ways in which it can be perceived, as identified from existing research. Inequality is multidimensional and intersectional, thus people's perception of it can draw from various elements (i.e. gender, ethnicity and class just to name a few): however, it must be remembered that most of the time perceptions of inequality in different realms of life overlap and it is hard to separate the impact of one over another. For instance, Vacchiano (2018) conducted a longitudinal study with North African youth who had emigrated and found that they had done so equally to get out of what they perceived as material marginality—i.e.

economic inequality—and to be able to enjoy "a good life"—a desire stemming for a perception of social inequality. Vacchiano (2018) argues that their migration experience is marked by "a sense of lack that derives from the exposure to normative benchmarks of good life and the simultaneous exclusion from the actual means of achieving it" (82).

Gereke's (2016) research with young men in Thailand and Mo's (2018) work in Nepal reached similar conclusions, showing that perceiving to suffer from comparative material deprivation makes some people keener to take risks. This in turn increases their likelihood of migration, including through irregular channels. In her study with young Eritrean migrants, Belloni (2019) reports that images coming through the media convey a specific image of what modernity is, and the comparison of these with the goods and services available in Eritrea, represented for the migrants a "gap between their misery and the opportunities offered by the outside world" (Belloni, 2019, 344). Precisely, "the lack of petrol, the continual power cuts as well as the low quality of products in the local market were interpreted as expressions of Eritrea's backwardness and a metonym of my informants' existential stuckedness" (Belloni, 2019, ibid.).

According to Dinbabo et al. (2021), it is the perception of a lack of local opportunities and expectations of a better life that underlies the decision of many West African migrants to cross the Mediterranean. As before, this stems not only from an objective lack of opportunities—which we do not want to downplay—but also from a reflection on which are perceived to be valuable opportunities. Perception of opportunities and, indirectly, of the chances to reduce inequality, lie at the core of the migration decision, the selection of the destination (Baláž et al., 2016) and the prospects for return (Achenbach, 2017).

Contrary to the assumption that migration is a family decision, especially when young people are involved, Belloni's (2019) study shows that young Eritrean migrants often migrate to pursue their own aspirations, even contravening the family's plans, and/or to adhere to cultural values of moral worthiness and provision for the family. Grabska (2020) focuses instead on the journeys of Eritrean girls and young women to Khartoum. Her research (2020, 22) exposes the "interplay between aspiration and desire of becoming an adult linked to a specific geographical location, dreams of being elsewhere, impossibilities of returning, and realities of uncertainties and being-stuck in between". The results of Grabska's study (2020) are particularly rich and support our argument in that they show that aspirations are mediated by age, gender, culture, religion and geographical location. In addition, they show that aspirations rarely emerge in isolation, but are rather paired with other feelings, such as stuckedness, restlessness and/or frustration. Importantly, Grabska (2020) also shows that, even in situations where migrants perceive to be forcibly kept in an intermediate destination and/or in a phase of their life (i.e. adolescence), migration is a way to expand their own decision-making and to take charge of their own life.

Aspirations can also be mediated by social caste and ethnicity, which can direct not only decisions on whether to migrate but also destination preferences. In a study on rural Nepal, Fischer (2022) finds that socially accepted destination choices are linked to caste and gender. For instance, a low-caste, male migrant might aspire to migrate to India, whereas a high-caste female migrant might aspire to travel to Australia. Of course, these aspirations are also tied in with the cost of migration and capacity to migrate to such places and as such crossing over with tangible inequalities. In addition, the returns from these different types of migration also differ, reproducing and potentially worsening existing inequalities.

A small number of studies consider the perception of inequalities and associated feelings of discrimination, leading to the decision to migrate. For instance, Alloul (2020) examines the decision-making process of European citizens of North African descent who had moved to Dubai to escape what he defines as a sense of "racial stuckedness" (313). While at home they had to cope with a stagnant socio-economic position and to face "racial ceilings for holding an immigrant and Muslim heritage" (Alloul, 2020, 352), in Dubai they found more opportunities for self-realisation and social mobility. Feelings of discrimination do not exclusively encourage outward migration but can also be the trigger for return. As an example, some studies on Turkish migrants in Western Europe look at how perceived discrimination influences return migration. Kunuroglu et al. (2018) find that perceived discrimination in the country of destination, along with a strong sense of belonging to Turkey, played a decisive role in migrants' decision to leave Germany, France and the Netherlands to move back to Turkey. Similarly, Tezcan (2019) investigates the main factors accelerating or postponing return migration for Turkish immigrants living in Germany and finds that they are a combination of economic and non-economic elements, including discrimination. More specifically, "difficult economic conditions, stigmatisation in both countries, social networks, commitment to the homeland, and perceived discriminatory attitudes" (Tezcan, 2019, 1) are found to accelerate return migration. Feelings of being discriminated against are often considered strong predictors of return aspirations (Groenewold & de Valk, 2017). Yilmaz Sener (2019) discusses the differences between the perception of discrimination and reasons for return of Turks who had migrated back to Turkey from Germany and the United

States. While those who had lived in Germany mentioned discrimination and identified it as a reason to return to Turkey, those who had lived in the United States did neither mention it nor state it was a trigger for return. Yilmaz Sener (2019) argues this depends on the presence in the country of destination of either bright or blurred ethnic boundaries, the former leaving no ambiguities on memberships while the latter being less clear cut.

Another stream of literature analyses the influence of perceived gender discrimination on people's aspirations to migrate and/or onto actual migration. Ruyssen and Salomone (2018) explore worldwide female "intentions and preparations to migrate" (224) relying on micro-level Gallup World Poll data from 148 countries collected between 2009 and 2013. Their study concludes that, while women who "do not feel treated with respect and dignity have a higher incentive to migrate abroad" (224). Concrete migration plans and journeys instead depend on a wider array of factors that are greatly "traditional", such as family obligations, but also on economic imbalances between men and women resulting in men globally having more tools and freedom to migrate. Nisic and Melzer (2016) reach similar conclusions, arguing that establishing direct causalities between gender and migration can easily become misleading if researchers do not account for macro-economic factors such as pay gaps, strict gender norms, expectations or discrimination. It is crucial to remember that migration in and of itself does not lead to a univocal outcome: if in certain cases migration can be (imagined as) "a way out of discrimination" (Ruyssen & Salomone, 2018), in others it can also preserve gender inequality (Riano et al., 2015). This happens when, for instance, the decision to migrate is not equally shared between members of a family, or the environment and values in the place of destination reproduce the same gender imbalances of the place of origin.

Research also finds that both aspirations to migrate and migration itself can be tied to the feelings of isolation, discrimination and stigma based on sexual orientation. Asencio and Acosta (2009) highlight this dynamic with respect to the case of sexual minorities in Puerto Rico. They find that, "for most participants, sexuality was not the reason they left Puerto Rico, but it was a factor in their decision to not return" (34). Importantly, Asencio and Acosta (2009) also state that ethnic identity contributes to sharpening sexual minorities' decision to migrate and/or not to return. Similarly, Del Aguila (2013) identifies a trigger towards migration in the experiences of discrimination based on sexual orientation reported by Peruvian gay men in their country of origin.

In addition, some scholars shed light on discrimination and perceived lack of belonging grounding on political elements. For instance, Charron (2020) reports that the alienation felt by Crimean IDPs in Ukraine after the Russian occupation of Crimea in 2014, together with socio-economic and emotional factors, strengthened their decision to migrate elsewhere. In this context, Charron (2020, 432) defines Crimeans' migration as neither "exclusively forced not entirely voluntary" but running along a blurred line. Similarly, in their study conducted in the Adi Harush refugee camp in Northern Ethiopia, Mallett et al. (2017, 21) report, that "social inequality and (perceived) differential treatment by Ethiopians cause many Eritreans to feel that they will never become full member[s] of the Ethiopian society".

Besides inequality perceived as discrimination, another significant element is the perception of political and policy-related inequalities. Hagen-Zanker and Mallett (2022) have shown that, regardless of what is established in formal national and international policies, individuals' decision-making is more influenced by personal, cultural and social factors than by the content of policies. This is the reason why, in the encounter between (potential) migrants and migration policies, "outcomes cannot be taken for granted" (12). Paying attention to these dynamics allows to shed some light not only on the intricacies of migration decision-making, but also onto (the limits of) migration policies' impact. For instance, Mallett et al. (2017) write that "the lack of faith in formal [migration] channels [in Ethiopia] is also heightened by perceptions of unfairness and patronage in how the various [resettlement] programmes are managed" (27).

In this section, we have highlighted some intangible inequalities emerging from existing literature. However, this is by no means an exhaustive list, as inequalities are multi-dimensional, context-dependent, and—most importantly—connected to individual perceptions.

Conclusion

This chapter has underlined the importance of inequalities for various stages of migration decision-making. We have done this by giving particular attention to tangible inequalities—namely, those that can be measured such as wealth, differences in education, skill levels or health, as well as intangible inequalities—that is, those that are less observable and more personal such as imagination, personality traits, emotions, feelings, beliefs and values based on individual's perceptions (Hagen-Zanker & Hennessey, 2021a). We also consider the role that policies intended to address inequalities play in migration decision-making, given that such policies are often designed to deter migration from the Global South.

Examining the role of tangible inequalities in shaping migration decision-making helps us to understand the influence of economic and the macro-structure factors which migrants are embedded in. The literature shows that economic inequalities are important (Lipton, 1980), but migration decision-making seems to be more the result of migrants' desire to improve their economic status. This desire is in fact combined with, and fuelled by, perceptions of relative deprivation, rather than outcomes of absolute poverty (Massey et al., 1993; Stark, 1991). However, income differentials do matter when considering which migrants can fund their own migration, access the safest routes and obtain better jobs at destination. It is also undeniable that structural inequalities, originated in part by Global South's colonial past and sharpened by current economic inequalities, *do matter* and push individuals to migrate (Cela et al., 2022).

Another important aspect of tangible inequalities is the role of unequal gender norms and relations affecting migration decision-making. While men often experience migration as a "rite of passage" and a path towards economic independence, women consider what is socially expected from them when deciding whether to migrate or stay put, although the literature has shown that women also take decisions based on their desires to improve their material situation and to pursue a better life (Hondagneu-Sotelo, 1992). Gender norms are dynamic and keep changing. This change is in part driven by migration, although its direction (either towards tighter or more egalitarian norms) seems to be context-specific (Fechter, 2013).

We also examined the literature on migration policies from the Global North to deter migration from the Global South, highlighting that such policies are not necessarily designed with reference to the structural factors that drive migration, thus usually struggling to accomplish their intended deterrence goals.

Moving forward, the chapter reviewed the ways that intangible inequalities shape migration decision-making. We stressed the important role that *perception* of inequalities plays to our understanding of the migration decision-making process: it can offer valuable insights regarding the place of emotions (Ķešāne, 2019), the aspects in migrants' lives that are "hard to measure" (Wolton, 2022), and the role of such perceptions regarding decisions to migrate or to stay put. There are many intangible inequalities involved in the decision-making process among migrants. By means of example, the desire to achieve one's aspirations for a better life plays a key role (Belloni, 2019). While these aspirations and decisions can be shaped by potential migrant's intended goals, Grabska (2020) showed that other factors are important to consider, such as individual characteristics (class, gender, age), personal values (influenced by culture or religion) or caste and ethnicity, as shown by Fischer (2022). Other intangible inequalities influencing the decision to migrate are those associated with feelings of discrimination—which can also influence return decisions—based on race and ethnicity (Alloul, 2020; Tezcan, 2019), gender (Ruyssen & Salomone, 2018), sexual orientation (Asencio & Acosta, 2009; Del Aguila, 2013) or political grounds (Charron, 2020). Another important factor is the perception of migration policies as unequal and unfair, which is one reason why many migrants disregard or interpret policies according to their needs.

The key contribution of this chapter is to amplify emerging literature in the Global South on the synergies between migration and intangible inequalities, including personal and emotional dimensions (Hagen-Zanker & Hennessey, 2021a). We have shown that perceptions of inequality are multidimensional, intersectional and overlapping. Therefore, exploring how they are shaped and experienced by migrants at different stages of the migration trajectory is important to deepen our understanding of the decision-making process. Nevertheless, we want to reiterate that tangible inequalities also matter as economic, wealth and structural inequalities are decisive factors in the decision to migrate.

Despite the evolution of the literature on tangible and intangible inequalities and their influence in shaping migration decisions, important evidence gaps stand out. The literature on tangible inequalities between the Global South and the Global North is much richer than the one looking at internal inequalities between and within Global South countries and how they influence migration decisions. In the case of intangible inequalities, the "socio-cultural dimensions to inequality" highlighted by Black et al. (2006) are also less understood. For example, broader socio-cultural norms may influence migration decisions, as for instance migrating to fulfil community expectations to work or study abroad in order to improve the economic conditions of the individual and their community, or to comply to expectations to contribute to social and religious events with remittances. Likewise, the literature linking feelings of discrimination and decisions to migrate, although growing, deserves more attention. New research is also needed regarding the mutual relationship between tangible and intangible inequalities in the Global South equally covering the different phases of people's migration trajectories—since at present most studies still concentrate on the pre-migration phase. An excellent example of such research is Silva, Barbosa and Fernandes's chapter (this volume), which illustrates the inequality and structural racism experienced by Haitian migrants in Brazil.

Further research should look into the connection between intangible inequalities and policies, aiming at fostering a dialogue between scholars and policy-makers. The literature looking at the role of policies shows that nation-states usually assume there is a linear relationship between higher skills and economic development linked to a lower desire to migrate. However, individuals may also consider their families' and communications' expectations of them, what social mobility means in their context, and how this could be achieved, along with their personal aspirations and capabilities to migrate. Another example of the gap between intangible factors and policies is the current anti-migrant discourses in some parts of the Global North and the resulting legal uncertainty for some Global South migrants already settled in Global North countries. These discourses and legal barriers are probably exacerbating individual's feelings of discrimination, affecting decisions to further migrate or to return. We encourage other scholars and practitioners to look into these less analysed dynamics in order to broaden the understanding and fair applicability of migration decision-making.

Acknowledgements This work has been undertaken as part of the Migration for Development and Equality (MIDEQ) Hub. Funded by the UKRI Global Challenges Research Fund (GCRF) (Grant Reference: ES/S007415/1), MIDEQ unpacks the complex and multi-dimensional relationships between migration and inequality in the context of the Global South. More at www.mideq.org.

Note

1. Although this specific study only mentions women and men, we are mindful that gendered experiences are not limited to these two categories.

References

Achenbach, R. (2017). Return migration decision making: Theoretical considerations. In R. Achenbach (Ed.), *Return migration decisions: A study on highly skilled Chinese in Japan* (pp. 27–77). Springer.

Alloul, J. (2020). Leaving Europe, aspiring access: Racial capital and its spatial discontents among the Euro-Maghrebi minority. *Journal of Immigrant and Refugee Studies, 18*(3), 313–325. https://doi.org/10.1080/15562948.2020.1761504

Asencio, M., & Acosta, K. (2009). Migration, gender conformity, and social mobility among Puerto Rican sexual minorities. *Sexuality Research and Social Policy, 6*(3), 34–43. https://doi.org/10.1525/srsp.2009.6.3.34

Baláž, V., Williams, A. M., & Fifeková, E. (2016). Migration decision making as complex choice: Eliciting decision weights under conditions of imperfect and complex information through experimental methods. *Population, Space and Place, 22*(1), 36–53. https://doi.org/10.1002/psp.1858

Bastia, T. (2013). Migration as protest? Negotiating gender, class and ethnicity in urban Bolivia. In T. Bastia (Ed.), *Migration and inequality*. Routledge, London. https://doi.org/10.4324/9780203067925

Belloni, M. (2019). *The big gamble: The migration of Eritreans to Europe*. University of California Press.

Black, R., Natali, C., & Skinner, J. (2006). *Migration and inequality*. World Bank. https://openknowledge.worldbank.org/handle/10986/9172

Bredeloup, S. (2017). The migratory adventure as a moral experience. In Hope and uncertainty in contemporary African migration. In N. Kleist & D. Thorsen (Eds.), *Hope and uncertainty in contemporary African migration* (pp. 134–153). Routledge.

Carling, J., & Schewel, K. (2020). Revisiting aspiration and ability in international migration. In *Aspiration, Desire and the Drivers of Migration* (pp. 37–55). Routledge.

Castles, S. (2004). Migration, citizenship, and education. *Diversity and citizenship education: Global perspectives* (pp. 17–48).

Cela, T., Charles, K., Dubuisson, P. R., Fortin, O., Estinvil, D., & Marcelin, L. H. (2022). Migration, memory and longing in Haitian songs. *Zanj: The Journal of Critical Global South Studies, 5*(1/2), 193–227. https://doi.org/10.13169/zanjglobsoutstud.5.1.0013

Chambers, T. (2018). Continuity in mind: Imagination and migration in India and the Gulf. *Modern Asian Studies, 52*(4), 1420–1456. https://doi.org/10.1017/S0026749X1700049X

Chancel, L., & Piketty, T. (2021). Global income inequality, 1820–2020: The persistence and mutation of extreme inequality. *Journal of the European Economic Association, 19*(6), 3025–3062. https://doi.org/10.1093/jeea/jvab047

Charron, A. (2020). 'Somehow, we cannot accept it': Drivers of internal displacement from Crimea and the forced/voluntary migration binary. *Europe-Asia Studies, 72*(3), 432–454. https://doi.org/10.1080/09668136.2019.1685649

Constable, N. (2014). *Born out of place: Migrant mothers and the politics of international labor*. University of California Press.

Crawley, H., & Jones, K. (2021). Beyond here and there: (re)conceptualising migrant journeys and the 'in-between.' *Journal of Ethnic and Migration Studies, 47*(14), 3226–3242. https://doi.org/10.1080/1369183X.2020.1804190

de Haas, H. (2011). *The determinants of international migration*. International Migration Institute Working paper. https://ora.ox.ac.uk/objects/uuid:0b10d9e8-810e-4f49-b76f-ba4d6b1faa86

de Haas, H. (2021). A theory of migration: The aspirations-capabilities framework. *Comparative Migration Studies, 9*(1), 1–35. https://doi.org/10.1186/s40878-020-00210-4

de Souza e Silva, J., Barbosa, J. L., & Lannes Fernandes, F. (2023). Haitian migration and structural racism in Brazil. In H. Crawley & J. Teye (Eds.), *The Palgrave handbook of south-south migration and inequality*. Palgrave, London.

del Aguila, E. V. (2013). *Being a Man in a transnational world: The masculinity and sexuality of migration*. Routledge.

Dinbabo, M. F., Badewa, A., & Yeboah, C. (2021). Socio-economic inequity and decision-making under uncertainty: West African migrants' journey across the Mediterranean to Europe. *Social Inclusion, 9*(1), 216–225. https://doi.org/10.17645/si.v9i1.3663

Eade, J., Drinkwater, S., & Garaphic, M. (2007). *Class and ethnicity: Polish migrant workers in London*. Centre for Research on Nationalism, Ethnicity and Multiculturalism, 2007. (ESRC End of Award Report, RES-000-22-1294). Centre for Research on Nationalism, Ethnicity and Multiculturalism.

Fechter, A. M. (2013). Mobility as enabling gender equality? The case of international aid workers. In T. Bastia (Ed.), *Migration and Inequality* (pp. 167–186). Routledge.

Fischer, K. (2022). *Opportunities to migrate: Temporary windows to an imagined future*. Paper presented at the 19th IMISCOE annual conference, 29 June–1 July 2022, Oslo.

Gereke, J. (2016). *Deciding to migrate: The role of social preferences, biased beliefs, and superstition in a risky choice*. Doctoral dissertation, European University Institute

Grabska, K. (2020). 'Wasting time': Migratory trajectories of adolescence among Eritrean refugee girls in Khartoum. *Critical African Studies, 12*(1), 22–36. https://doi.org/10.1080/21681392.2019.1697318

Groenewold, G., & de Valk, H. A. G. (2017). Acculturation style, transnational behaviour, and return-migration intentions of the Turkish second generation: Exploring linkages. *Demographic Research, 37*, 1707–1734.

Hagen-Zanker, J., & Hennessey, G. (2021a). *What do we know about the subjective and intangible factors that shape migration decision-making?* A Review of the Literature from Low- and Middle-income Countries. PRIO, Oslo. https://legacy.prio.org/utility/DownloadFile.ashx?id=2292&type=publicationfile

Hagen-Zanker, J., & Hennessey, G. (2021b). *Can employment and training policies and programmes influence migration decision-making in low- and middle-income countries?* MIDEQ Working Paper. https://southsouth.contentfiles.net/media/documents/WP4-employment-paper_Final_hz83ghj.pdf

Hagen-Zanker, J., & Mallett, R. (2016). *Journeys to Europe: The role of policy in migrant decision-making*. Insights report. Overseas Development Institute.

Hagen-Zanker, J., & Mallett, R. (2022). 'Inside the 'efficacy gap': Migration policy and the dynamics of encounter. *International Migration*. https://doi.org/10.1111/imig.13028

Hagen-Zanker, J., Mazzilli, C., & Hennessey, G. (forthcoming). Why we should talk about subjective and intangible factors when discussing migration decision-making. *Migration Studies*.

Harris, J. R., & Todaro, M. P. (1970). Migration, unemployment and development: A two-sector analysis. *The American Economic Review, 60*(1), 126–142.

Hernández-Carretero, M. (2016). Hope and uncertainty in Senegalese migration to Spain: Taking chances on emigration but not upon return. In N. Kleist & D. Thorsen (Eds.), *Hope and uncertainty in contemporary African migration* (pp. 113–133). Routledge, London. https://doi.org/10.4324/9781315659916

Hidrobo, M., Mueller, V., & Roy, S. (2022). Cash transfers, migration, and gender norms. *American Journal of Agricultural Economics, 104*(2), 550–568. https://doi.org/10.1111/ajae.12261

Himmelstine, C. L. (2017). *The linkages between social protection and migration: a case study of oportunidades and migration in Oaxaca, Mexico.* Doctoral thesis (PhD), University of Sussex.

Hondagneu-Sotelo, P. (1992). Overcoming patriarchal constraints: The reconstruction of gender relations among Mexican immigrant women and men. *Gender & Society, 6*(3), 393–415. https://doi.org/10.1177/089124392006003004

Kalir, B. (2005). The development of a migratory disposition: Explaining a 'new emigration.' *International Migration, 43*(4), 167–196. https://doi.org/10.1111/j.1468-2435.2005.00337.x

Kanaiaupuni, S. M. (2000). Reframing the migration question: An analysis of men, women, and gender in Mexico. *Social Forces, 78*(4), 1311–1347. https://doi.org/10.2307/3006176

Ķešāne, I. (2019). The lived experience of inequality and migration: Emotions and meaning making among Latvian emigrants. *Emotion, Space and Society, 33*, 1–8. https://doi.org/10.1016/j.emospa.2019.100597

Kunuroglu, F., Yagmur, K., Van De Vijver, F. J. R., & Kroon, S. (2018). Motives for Turkish return migration from Western Europe: Home, sense of belonging, discrimination, and transnationalism. *Turkish Studies, 19*(3), 422–450. https://doi.org/10.1080/14683849.2017.1387479

Landau, L. B. (2019). A chronotope of containment development: Europe's migrant crisis and Africa's reterritorialisation. *Antipode, 51*(1), 169–186. https://doi.org/10.1111/anti.12420

Lee, E. S. (1966). A theory of migration. *Demography, 3*(1), 47–57. https://doi.org/10.2307/2060063

Lipton, M. (1980). Migration from rural areas of poor countries: The impact on rural productivity and income distribution. *World Development, 8*(1), 1–24. https://doi.org/10.1016/0305-750X(80)90047-9

Lyberaki, A. (2008). The Greek immigration experience revisited. *Journal of Immigrant & Refugee Studies, 6*(1), 5–33.

Mai, N., & King, R. (2009). Love, sexuality and migration: Mapping the issue(s). *Mobilities, 4*(3), 295–307. https://doi.org/10.1080/17450100903195318

Mallett, R., Hagen-Zanker, J., Majidi, N., & Cummings, C. (2017). *Journeys on hold: How policy influences the migration decisions of Eritreans in Ethiopia*. ODI, London. https://odi.org/en/publications/journeys-on-hold-how-policy-influences-the-migration-decisions-of-eritreans-in-ethiopia/

Massey, D. S., Arango, J., Hugo, G., Kouaouci, A., Pellegrino, A., & Taylor, J. E. (1993). Theories of international migration: A review and appraisa'. *Population and Development Review, 19*(3), 431–466. https://doi.org/10.2307/2938462

Massey, D. S., Arango, J., Hugo, G., Kouaouci, A., Pellegrino, A., & Taylor, J. E. (1994). An evaluation of international migration theory: The North American case. *Population and Development Review, 20*(4), 699–751. https://doi.org/10.2307/2137660

McLeman, R., Schade, J., & Faist, T. (Eds.). (2016). Environmental migration and social inequality. Springer International Publishing.

Mo, C. H. (2018). Perceived relative deprivation and risk: An aspiration-based model of human trafficking vulnerability. *Political Behavior, 40*(1), 247–277. https://doi.org/10.1007/s11109-017-9401-0

Monsutti, A. (2007). Migration as a rite of passage: Young Afghans building masculinity and adulthood in Iran. *Iranian Studies, 40*(2), 167–185. https://doi.org/10.1080/00210860701276183

Nisic, N., & Melzer, S. M. (2016). Explaining gender inequalities that follow couple migration. *Journal of Marriage and Family, 78*(4), 1063–1082. https://doi.org/10.1111/jomf.12323

Organization for Economic Cooperation and Development (OECD). (2017). *Interactions entre politiques publiques, migrations et développement en Haïti*. OECD. https://read.oecd-ilibrary.org/development/interactions-entre-politiques-publiques-migrations-et-developpement-en-haiti_9789264278844-fr

Picketty, T. (2018). Capital in the 21st Century. In D. B. Grusky, J. Hill (Ed.), *Inequality in the 21st century* (pp. 43–48). Routledge, London. https://doi.org/10.4324/9780429499821-9

Riano, Y., Limacher, K., Aschwanden, A., Hirsig, S., & Wastl-Walter, D. (2015). Shaping gender inequalities: Critical moments and critical places. *Equality, Diversity and Inclusion: An International Journal, 34*(2), 155–167. https://doi.org/10.1108/EDI-12-2013-0112

Ruyssen, I., & Salomone, S. (2018). Female migration: A way out of discrimination? *Journal of Development Economics, 130*, 224–241. https://doi.org/10.1016/j.jdeveco.2017.10.010

Scalettaris, G., Monsutti, A., & Donini, A. (2019). Young Afghans at the doorsteps of Europe: The difficult art of being a successful migrant. *The Journal of Ethnic and Migration Studies, 47*(3), 519–535. https://doi.org/10.1080/1369183X.2019.1618250

Schewel, K. (2015). *Understanding the aspiration to stay: A case study of young adults in Senegal*. COMPAS Working Paper 107, University of Oxford.

Schewel, K. (2021). *Understanding the aspiration to stay: A case study of young adults in Senegal*. International Migration Institute Working Paper, Oxford: University of Oxford. https://ora.ox.ac.uk/objects/uuid:6b94a8a2-e80c-43f4-9338-92b641753215

Stark, O. (1991). *The migration of labour*. Blackwell Publishers.

Tezcan, T. (2019). What initiates, what postpones return migration intention? The Case of Turkish Immigrants Residing in Germany. *Population, Space and Place, 25*(3), 1–13. https://doi.org/10.1002/psp.2175

Thielemann, E. R. (2004). Why asylum policy harmonization undermines refugee burden-sharing. *European Journal of Migration & Law, 6*, 47.

Tuccio, M., & Wahba, J. (2018). Return migration and the transfer of gender norms: Evidence from the Middle East'. *Journal of Comparative Economics, 46*(4), 1006–1029. https://doi.org/10.1016/j.jce.2018.07.015

Tucker, C. M., Torres-Pereda, P., Minnis, A. M., & Bautista-Arredondo, S. A. (2013). Migration decision-making among Mexican youth: Individual, family, and community influences. *Hispanic Journal of Behavioral Sciences, 35*(1), 61–84. https://doi.org/10.1177/0739986312458563

United Nations (UN) – Development Strategy and United Nations' Policy Analysis Unit (DS and UNPAU) with Development Policy and Analysis Division (DPAD) & Department of Economic and Social Affairs (DESA). (n.d.). *Concepts of Inequality (Development Issues, 1)*. https://www.un.org/en/development/desa/policy/wess/wess_dev_issues/dsp_policy_01.pdf#:~:text=Inequality%E2%80%94the%20state%20of%20not%20being%20equal%2C%20especially%20in,to%20different%20people.%20Some%20distinctions%20are%20common%20though

United Nations (UN). (n.d.). *Inequality—Bridging the divide*. United Nations; United Nations. https://www.un.org/en/un75/inequality-bridging-divide

US Census Bureau. (n.d.) *Gini Index*. https://www.census.gov/topics/income-poverty/income-inequality/about/metrics/gini-index.html

Vacchiano, F. (2018). Desiring mobility: Child migration, parental distress and constraints on the future in North Africa. *Research Handbook on Child Migration*, 82–97.

Wolton, S. (2022). To fight discrimination, first you must understand how to measure it | *LSE Online*. https://www.lse.ac.uk/study-at-lse/online-learning/insights/to-fight-discrimination-first-you-must-understand-how-to-measure-it

World Bank Group. (2016). *Taking on inequality (Poverty and shared prosperity)*. The World Bank. https://openknowledge.worldbank.org/bitstream/handle/10986/25078/9781464809583.pdf?sequence=24&isAllowed=y

World Inequality Database. (2021). *World inequality report 2022*. WID—World Inequality Database. https://wid.world/news-article/world-inequality-report-2022/

Yilmaz Sener, M. (2019). Perceived discrimination as a major factor behind return migration? The return of Turkish qualified migrants from the USA and Germany. *Journal of Ethnic and Migration Studies, 45*(15), 2801–2819. https://doi.org/10.1080/1369183X.2018.1524292

Open Access This chapter is licensed under the terms of the Creative Commons Attribution 4.0 International License (http://creativecommons.org/licenses/by/4.0/), which permits use, sharing, adaptation, distribution and reproduction in any medium or format, as long as you give appropriate credit to the original author(s) and the source, provide a link to the Creative Commons license and indicate if changes were made.

The images or other third party material in this chapter are included in the chapter's Creative Commons license, unless indicated otherwise in a credit line to the material. If material is not included in the chapter's Creative Commons license and your intended use is not permitted by statutory regulation or exceeds the permitted use, you will need to obtain permission directly from the copyright holder.

22

Overcoming and Reproducing Inequalities: Mediated Migration in the "Global South"

Katharine Jones, Heila Sha, and Mohammad Rashed Alam Bhuiyan

Introduction

Contemporary patterns of international migration would not happen without migration intermediaries. In Mexico, migrants seek help from *coyotes* to embark on the process of migration (Spener, 2009); in Eritrea, from *delaloch* (Ayalew, 2018); in West Africa, would-be migrants speak of lines, connections and *dokimen* (Alpes, 2017); in Asia, Syrians may refer to *muharrib* and *hajj* (Achilli, 2018); in Bangladesh and Nepal, to *dalals* (Rahman, 2012). In all these places, engaging with one or more intermediaries to assist with migration projects is a highly normalised and entirely legitimate practice. The dependence of migrants on them is not new. All over the world, friends and

K. Jones (✉) · M. R. A. Bhuiyan
Centre for Trust, Peace and Social Relations, Innovation Village, Cheetah Road, Coventry IV5CV1 2TL, UK
e-mail: katharine.jones@coventry.ac.uk

M. R. A. Bhuiyan
e-mail: bhuiyanm2@uni.coventry.ac.uk

H. Sha
Centre for Research in Ethnic Minority Entrepreneurship, Aston University, Aston Triangle, Birmingham B4 7ET, UK
e-mail: saheira.haliel@gmail.com

M. R. A. Bhuiyan
Department of Political Science, University of Dhaka, Dhaka, Bangladesh

© The Author(s) 2024
H. Crawley and J. K. Teye (eds.), *The Palgrave Handbook of South–South Migration and Inequality*, https://doi.org/10.1007/978-3-031-39814-8_22

kinship networks have long been recognised as pivotal to helping migrants organise their journeys, find jobs and homes, as well as to friendship and civic structures (Massey et al., 1987; also see Sha, 2021b for a review of this literature). Fee-charging recruiters have continued—since colonial times—to serve as an important mechanism by which employers move workers across national borders (Burawoy, 1976). "Smugglers" who help people escape from war, dictatorship and even genocides such as the Holocaust are often feted in books and films as heroic rescuers (Fogelman, 1995; Merriman, 2019).

However, from the late twentieth century onwards, there have been dramatic transformations in the scale, types and embeddedness of intermediaries engaged in facilitating migration, especially from the Global South (Ayalew et al., 2018; Lindquist et al., 2012). Scholars have increasingly attributed late twentieth-century increases in migration flows—as well as the directions and destinations involved—to intermediaries' activities (Goss & Lindquist, 1995). Today, intermediaries are significant actors in influencing how migration happens, in shaping developmental outcomes as well as individual migrants' experiences of migration. In certain parts of the world, what were once informal cultural practices have gradually transformed into marketised activities in the formal economy. Consequently, the costs to migrants of migrating have risen exponentially (Goh et al., 2017). However, the biggest impacts of intermediaries' involvement in migration, including the highest costs, have tended to fall disproportionately on the poorest whose migrations are the most regulated, usually those in the Global South. Moreover, intermediaries in the Global South are also increasingly problematised within international policy agendas. These (partially artificially) distinguish between those deemed to be smugglers (which facilitate irregular migration) and labour recruiters (regulated migration) (Jones, 2021), again with disproportionate consequences of international policy felt by those in the Global South.

This chapter poses the question: how are global inequalities in relation to migration mediated by intermediaries? Notably, few studies specifically address South–South migration, which as this introduction to this volume notes, constitutes a significant and growing proportion of all global movements (Crawley & Teye, in this volume). To date, research has primarily addressed the roles of intermediaries in facilitating migration from Global South countries to richer, more powerful states in the Global North. In the Americas, scholars have tended to focus on the movement of migrants from Mexico and southern Americas to the United States (Hernández-León, 2013; Massey et al., 1987; Sanchez & Natividad, 2017). In Africa, studies document the recruitment of female domestic workers from countries such as

Ghana and Ethiopia, to the Gulf region and Europe (Awumbila et al., 2019). In Asia, scholars have predominantly analysed recruitment from South Asia and Southeast Asia into North America, the Gulf and East Asia (Constable, 2003; Jones, 2021; Lan, 2018). In this chapter, we have opted to use the term "Global South" as an analytical category rather than a geographical container (Haug et al., 2021, see also Fiddian-Quismayeh, in this volume). The term provides, we believe, an entry point to conceptualise the contributions of intermediaries within the complex, messy realities and inequalities of international migration.

In what follows, we first undertake the task of defining what intermediaries do. Our attention is directed at the role of intermediaries in *enabling* migration rather than those which are deployed on behalf of the state to prevent migration, such as security firms (Gammeltoft-Hansen & Sorensen, 2013). The remainder of the chapter is organised in three sections which review the relationships between intermediaries, mediated migration and inequalities associated with: (1) borders, (2) income and poverty and (3) living in new destinations.

Roles and Functions of Intermediaries

The term "intermediaries" includes individuals who might be current or former migrants, friends and kin or small-scale petty entrepreneurs, or all of these at the same time. It also includes formal recruitment businesses, visa consultancies and travel agencies. Migrants often engage concurrently with all these actors, which makes studying them complex. Unsurprisingly, intermediaries' actions can be both ambiguous and contradictory depending on one's perspective (Awumbila et al., 2019). Some are viewed by migrants as helpful service providers (Spener, 2009), others as violent extortionists (Vogt, 2016). In this section we focus on what intermediaries do rather than attempting to explain intermediaries' behaviours or motivations; a fruitless task as this is influenced by the context rather than being inherent to the act of intermediation itself (Spener, 2009).

First and foremost, intermediaries facilitate migrants' physical journeys. Travel agencies book transportation and accommodation for ordinary business and tourist travellers. Others—guides, drivers, boat pilots—assist migrants who need to travel through dangerous terrain (De León, 2015). However, only the latter are regarded as problematic by states because they also often help irregular migrants circumvent immigration policies in Global North countries (Crawley et al., 2018).

Secondly, intermediaries commonly help migrants obtain the documents required by states to legitimate travel and residency. This includes passports and visas, as well as the documents required to procure these, including birth, marriage and qualification certificates. Through "document dispatch" intermediaries secure "legal" or 'official' statuses for migrants. The documents may be either counterfeit or legitimate depending on the context (Alpes, 2017). Intermediaries may also help irregular migrants regularise their status after their arrival in a new place through assisting with applications for new documents (Anderson, 2021). They also support highly paid migrants secure citizenship, and/or business and investment visas (Cranston, 2018).

Thirdly, intermediaries organise jobs for migrants, sometimes connecting people in one country with employers in another or after migrants' arrival in the new place. The former forms of intermediaries are most associated with the temporary labour migration schemes in place in Southeast and South Asia, and the Gulf region (Lindquist et al., 2012). They are also common in Europe and North America (Schling, 2022). As part of the process of arranging employment, intermediaries may assess migrants' skills and offer job-specific training (Jones, 2014) or 'cultural' training aimed at helping migrants adapt to their new workplace (Lan, 2018). Finally, intermediaries also help migrants settle and navigate life in their new homes whether these are short-term or more permanent (Wessendorf, 2022). This includes helping with finding places to live, accessing services such as healthcare, finding information or simply providing friendship (Boyd, 1989).

Whatever the role and the function, intermediaries are always deeply rooted in the local places where migrants live and work. Nevertheless, they are also transnational actors, integrated into global economic circuits (Jones, 2021) and facilitating links back to migrants' home countries (Sha, 2021a). From the 1990s, inspired by the "transnational turn" in migration studies, many scholars embarked on theorising the wider contexts to intermediaries' activities. Fawcett (1989) visualised intermediaries as connecting migrants, employers, and states, constituting an additional state-to-state "flow" alongside interconnecting flows of capital, goods, services and knowledge. A decade later, Findlay and Li (1998) emphasised that to fully understand intermediaries' actions necessitated analysis of state regulations, organisational practices and migrants' own decisions; each influenced the other and could not be understood alone. Castles and Miller (2003) depicted a 'meso-level' through which intermediaries connected the 'micro agency' of migrants' decision-making, practices and beliefs with global macroeconomic and political structures, including state regulations. For these scholars, the global and local contexts form more than mere backdrop to intermediaries' actions;

they are a fundamental part of the explanation. Nevertheless, these early explanations largely addressed migration as "state-to-state". They ignored its more relational and dynamic aspects and the attention of migration scholars turned once again away from the 'grand theory' explanations to more micro explorations of migration.

Subsequently, Lindquist et al. (2012) notably asserted that migration could be more clearly conceptualised through a focus on "infrastructure" rather than on state policies or migrant social networks alone. This signalled a shift away from state-centric approaches to the study of intermediary actors. Moreover, this approach allowed for more complex, nuanced, analyses of multiple actors with potentially competing or contradictory motivations, but which nevertheless all worked together to make it happen. Xiang and Lindquist (2018) categorised the migration infrastructure within the temporary labour migration schemes in Asia as (1) commercial (recruitment intermediaries), (2) regulatory (state apparatus and procedures for documentation, licensing, training and other purposes), (3) technological (communication and transport), (4) humanitarian (NGOs and international organisations) and (5) social (migrant) networks. However, in practice these infrastructural approaches have at times tended towards the heuristic, under-analysing or even ignoring underlying issues of power and materiality in international migration (Jones, 2021). Notably, intermediaries may additionally be closely intertwined with the state (Xiang, 2017) or they may be directly engaged in acting on behalf of the state (Jones et al., 2022). Consequently, as well as being subject to—and hence influenced by—state regulation, intermediaries are themselves regulatory actors (Goh et al., 2017).

Infrastructural and regulatory approaches derive primarily from research conducted on migration in particular geographies, namely, Southeast and East Asia and in Europe. Other scholars have drawn on post-colonial and decolonial development literatures to depict intermediary *practices*—rather than individual intermediary actions—as brokerage (Deshingkar, 2019; Spener, 2009). Scholars working in and from the Global South emphasise that intermediaries engage in cultural practices which are normalised in many geographical contexts, especially where burdensome requirements for documentation imposed by sluggish state bureaucracies require assistance (Deshingkar, 2019; Spener, 2009). In many places, having access to networks, connections and brokers is essential to navigating everyday lives (Alpes, 2017). In these contexts, migration brokerage is just one type of multiple varieties of brokerage that have long been documented by scholars of development. Brokers of all kinds strategically mediate knowledge, expertise and contacts (Koster & van Leynseele, 2018), functioning as an entirely acceptable, legitimised and collective survival mechanism for people in the Global South (Majidi, 2018). Scholars of brokerage deliberately adopt a positionality drawn from migrants' own perspectives, rejecting state-centric categorisations and the politics of migration control. Consequently, the position and power of state actors to be the *only* legitimate arbiter of migration is challenged (Spener, 2009). The chapter turns now to outline intermediaries' roles in navigating the inequalities of states' bordering practices.

Intermediaries and Unequal Transnational Borders

> To facilitate orderly, safe, regular and responsible migration and mobility of people, including through the maintenance of planned implementation of migration policies. (Sustainable Development Goal 10, Reducing Inequality, Target 10.7)

In the Hollywood film, Elysium, Earth is overpopulated and polluted with its people enduring extreme poverty, disease and violence, while the rich and powerful live in Elysium, an orbiting space station (Mirrlees & Pederson, 2016). Spider, a hacker intermediary who organises shuttle flights to help people escape to Elysium and to steal essential medicine for those unable to access it on Earth, is portrayed to the audience as a hero, albeit a flawed one. We—the audience—root for Spider and the people he helps because we clearly see the injustice of the spatial "border" between the poverty and chaos on Earth and the riches of Elysium. Sustainable Development Goal 10 Reducing Inequality within and among countries depicts a world in which carefully planned and implemented migration policies (by 'Elysium') can contribute to reducing (income) inequalities (on 'Earth'). Yet, in so doing, the SDG drafters opted to ignore one of the most fundamental and racialised global inequalities: that of state-constructed borders (Sharma, 2006; Walia, 2021).

States construct militarised walls and fences as physical borders to deter or prevent freedom of mobility. This includes the securitisation of naturally dangerous environments on their doorsteps (De León, 2015). States also use bureaucracy and technology to regulate entry (Torpey, 1998). Yet, these practices are disproportionately experienced by citizens of poorer and less powerful states. The 2022 Global Ranking of World Passports visualises such inequalities in terms of freedom to easily access travel documents (Henley, 2022). States in East Asia, Western and Northern Europe, and

North America—often referred to as the global 'North'—rest comfortably at its top. Holders of passports from those countries can freely enter between 93% and 99% of the 195 countries in the world without applying for a visa in advance. In contrast, citizens of the states which endure the most conflict, sustained socio-economic marginalisation and susceptibility to natural disasters—those usually referred to as the "Global South"—enjoy the least freedom of mobility, including most African states as well as poorer states in Asia and South America. Citizens of these states are denied the right to freely access and participate in international circuits of work, business or leisurely travel in ways which those from Global North countries can (Jansen, 2009).

However, borders are not natural and fixed; they are an "ordering regime" which is produced by contemporary racialised capitalist rules and practices, and historic and contemporary colonial relations (Walia, 2020, 2). In practice, securitised bordering practices, including restrictive visa regimes, have increasingly been adopted by many richer Global South states. De Genova (2002) emphasises that "illegality" in migrants' statuses is produced by states' mediation of laws and policies. Its corollary is also true. Namely that the more securitised, militarised, and bureaucratised states' borders are, the more likely it is that people need to seek out—and pay for—assistance from one or more intermediaries to navigate them (Ayalew et al., 2018).

Intermediaries and the Bureaucracy of Migration

Nationals of richer, more powerful, states ordinarily need do no more than purchase a flight ticket and queue for a low-cost visa at the arrival airport. The experiences of citizens from poorer, less powerful states, are somewhat different. Many migrants often have friends or family members who either lived or who still live abroad and who play important advisory roles, inspiring migrants to migrate, connecting them to jobs and lives in the new place (Muanamoha et al., 2010). However, any travel abroad, including for tourist or family visits, often necessitates completing significant volumes of paperwork to access visas (Azad, 2019). Kern-Müller and Boker (2015), for example, describe in some detail the bureaucracy required to migrate legally out of Nepal for a job abroad. Individuals must first secure a valid passport and birth certificate, which for those who have not previously migrated or travelled abroad, can be a lengthy process via local officials. Thereafter, and once a job is secured, the individual must apply for an entry visa and work permit from the destination country consulate or embassy, sign a copy of the employment contract which should be certified by the relevant Nepali consul in the country in which the employment will take place, obtain a medical certificate, certify qualifications (if required) and/or training certificates, and obtain health insurance. All these completed, signed and completed documents are then required to be submitted in person to the Ministry of Labour in Kathmandu, the capital city of Nepal. For this reason, paying intermediaries is a popular choice for migrants; intermediaries make the process easier, including smoother and quicker.

Furthermore, intermediaries can increase migrants' chances of success in the migration process. Submitting all the required documents to the right places does not guarantee a successful outcome, as visa applications of all kinds can be unpredictable. Rules frequently change (Žabko et al., 2018) and decisions by immigration officials may in any case be entirely arbitrary regardless of what documentation is submitted (Alpes, 2017). In Cameroon, Alpes (2017) describes how fewer than one in ten of the young people she spoke to received positive visa outcomes despite multiple visits to the relevant Embassy or Consulate. Reasons for refusal which were provided by immigration officials in these places were often opaque and sometimes illogical. She writes that it was therefore unsurprising that people are therefore more likely to depend upon the services of a variety of intermediaries to help. For migrants, finding an intermediary who has the necessary connections and expertise lessens the risks of failure and makes the process more predictable. In other words, intermediaries are a necessity of life where ordinary official channels are not accessible or do not deliver what would-be migrants need (Alpes, 2017). As such, intermediaries and migrants are often united in a common strategic project to overcome state-officiated barriers to mobility (Spener, 2009).

Nevertheless, multiple studies on international labour recruitment in Asia highlight the propensity of intermediaries to "deceive" migrants through producing false documents, including false passports, contracts and visas. In practice, other scholars working within the brokerage epistemology explain that whether the paperwork is "legal" or not often matters less to the migrants than whether it "works" in securing a visa (Spener, 2009). This is partly because intermediaries are often deeply embedded in the same communities from which migrants originate (Ayalew et al., 2018). Migrants' trust lies in those within their communities rather than the distant government bureaucracies which are regarded as barriers to their desire to move (Kern-Müller & Boker, 2015). Moreover, from migrants' perspectives, officials *also* interpret, perform and *mediate* the migration rules for a fee payable for the visa and there is not necessarily a clear moral distinction between what intermediaries (from their communities) do and what the state does (Alpes, 2017). In other words, for migrants in the Global South, the state is no more a legitimate arbiter of migration rules than intermediaries. Intermediaries simply form part of the human and social capital which migrants draw on as part of the social process of migration (Singer & Massey, 1998).

Intermediaries as "Protection from Below"

People fleeing conflict and persecution are usually not able to apply for visas in advance. In these cases, different types of intermediaries—guides, drivers, pilots as well as document dispatchers—are engaged to help people reach places of safety that they would not otherwise be able to get to (Ayalew, 2018). Viewed through this light, intermediaries provide alternative sources of knowledge to migrants (Sanchez & Natividad, 2017). In addition to guiding and driving, intermediaries often also help migrants secure work along the way so they can pay for onward travel as well as arrange housing whilst in transit. This may include helping—and charging—other migrants to travel (Achilli, 2018). Others may also help in other ways such as providing food and water, shelter and clothing to migrants on their journeys or selling lifejackets if the journey is via sea (Crawley et al., 2018).

Intermediaries who organise and facilitate irregular migration are often labelled by journalists, researchers and policymakers in the 'Global North' as "smugglers" or "human traffickers" (Achilli, 2018). In contrast, migrants in the Global South themselves often view such intermediaries as a form of protection from the violence they face at home, repressive border regimes, criminality and violence they face on their journeys. Intermediaries can be, as Sanchez and Zhang (2018, 45) describe it, "a primal attempt to preserve life" and a "passport" to a better life (Majidi, 2018). Intermediaries may also be deeply vested in the survival of their charges (Ayalew, 2018). Yet, intermediaries are neither wholly good nor wholly bad, since their motivations are not discernible nor inherent to the act of intermediation (Spener, 2009). Vogt (2016) reflects on the duality of the 'protector' and 'perpetrator' roles. Intermediary guides on the, sometimes dangerous, migrant trails in the Americas often risk their own lives to do what they do, whilst being responsible for peoples' care. At the same time, migrants also endure gendered forms of violence from these guides, including physical and sexual assaults and kidnapping. However, she notes—as do others—that such incidents cannot be explained by merely the bad and 'criminal' smuggler, but instead derive from the wider structural violence generated by state policies, including border regimes (see also De León, 2015). Structural violence and inequalities caused by state-bordering practices need not only involve direct and indirect acts of physical harm experienced by migrants. It can also constitute the poverty and hunger experienced by people in the Global South in the context of global 'economic apartheid' inequalities (Sharma, 2006). The next section turns to explore the role and function of intermediaries in relation to global income inequalities.

Intermediaries and Income Inequalities

> At a time when the world faces an extremely challenging outlook, remittances are a vital lifeline for households in developing countries, especially the poorest… (Malpass, World Bank Blog, 2022)
>
> Global inequality has exploded, and there is no better way to tackle inequality than by redistributing wealth. (Oxfam, 2023, 6)

The activities of intermediaries in enabling migration from low-income countries to richer countries can alleviate poverty through remittances (Sha, 2021a). To follow this point, remittances also improve nutritional outcomes and birth weights, lead to higher enrolment rates in schooling migration and facilitate skills and knowledge transfer to Global South countries whilst providing a buffer against economic shocks and environmental disasters (Malpass, 2022). Therefore, in making it possible for people in low-income countries to migrate, intermediaries can be conceived of as "development agents" (Agunias, 2009). Together, social networks and fee-charging intermediaries reduce the risks and costs of migration, help migrants access overseas employment and generate income which they are unable to make at home (Sha, 2021a). Through advising people when and where to migrate, brokering employment and offering or organising job-specific training, it can therefore be argued that intermediaries perform a critical function in helping migrants redress global income inequalities.

Historically, only those with savings, who have something to sell or who can leverage cash contributions from family have been able to migrate (De Haas, 2007). Cash, and often significant amounts, is needed to pay for the migration documentation and to travel and settle in the new location(s). However, in addition to facilitating travel and providing advice, intermediaries also commonly provide or organise access to credit to enable would-be migrants to pay for their journeys (Zack et al., 2019). Through extending lines of credit, intermediaries make migration feasible for even the poorest migrants (Goh et al., 2017). This is especially important for women who lack access to mainstream credit sources. This consequently helps women overcome gender inequality at home that may otherwise be further entrenched by being "left behind" as husbands, brothers and fathers migrate (Torres & Carte, 2016).

Furthermore, intermediaries also indirectly enable migrants to contribute to their families' schooling, housing, and general welfare through remittances (for a review see Sha, 2021b). Informal fund transfer systems and underground banking systems established by intermediaries are especially important for those unable to access formal money transfer services (Zhao, 2013). In these cases, high levels of trust between underground bank proprietors and migrants derive from ethnic solidarity. In a further, albeit tangential way, intermediaries contribute to the ability of migrants to start businesses upon their return home. This facilitates the transfer of human capital, knowledge, ideas and practices (Sørensen & Gammeltoft-Hansen, 2012). In other words, intermediaries which facilitate migration are therefore key actors in the development project since they enable movement to happen in the first place, whilst also facilitating financial and other transnational connections (Sha, 2021a). Put simply, intermediaries serve to expand the life-choices and economic opportunities of people living in poverty and situations of income inequality at home (Kern-Müller-Boker, 2015).

Migrants themselves often view intermediaries as critical to their bids to improve their socio-economic status (Awumbila et al., 2019). Alpes (2017) notes that young Cameroonians recognise that the high unemployment, poverty and even starvation, which they and their families face is produced by colonialism and structural adjustment policies imposed by the International Monetary Fund and other international institutions. Seen through this lens, seeking out intermediaries that can help them connect to opportunities outside Cameroon, even if the process will be risky and uncertain, is a legitimate and even rational decision. In this context, migrating can be viewed as much as a collective political action as well as an economic one. Thus, Spener (2009) situates the actions of migrants in migrating—and the intermediaries who make it happen—as political acts of working-class, decolonial, resistance to global economic apartheid.

Intermediaries as Drivers of Inequalities

Nevertheless, intermediaries also contribute to and reproduce inequalities. As noted above, their actions, motivations and the differences they make can be contradictory (Awumbila et al., 2019). For instance, migrants may view—and accept—being in debt to intermediaries who help finance their migration as a legitimate cost (Lainez, 2020). On the other hand, such loans are notorious in many regions, especially Southeast and South Asia for being a source through which migrants are extorted by intermediaries. In Bangladesh, interest rates on the loans taken from the informal money lenders for paying "recruitment fees"—can be as high as 120% per annum (Bangladesh Bank, 2019). It can take migrants up to 18 months of working in the destination country to repay the fees due to these extreme interest rates. This generates what Moniruzzaman and Walton-Roberts (2018) refer to as 'resource backwash', the idea that migrants do not work to economically advance their families' wellbeing or future lives. Instead, they work primarily to pay back the credit they received that enabled them to migrate in the first place. This means they continue to live in poverty or in the worst cases find themselves in even worse economic situations because of the debt generated by the migration project. High levels of debt to intermediaries have more than only financial implications for families. To service extreme interest rates, migrants feel desperate to work whatever the conditions are (Rahman, 2012). In addition to adding quite extreme pressure on migrants, this also creates an opportunity for employers to exploit their desperation as to complain or leave would mean not servicing the debt.

Intermediaries also contribute to other forms of inequalities experienced by migrants, especially in relation to employment. In Asia, recruiting intermediaries often teach departing migrants to be "docile", to accept any working conditions whilst abroad no matter how bad these are and to not complain (Guevarra, 2010). In research conducted with Bangladeshi migrant domestic workers in Jordan and Lebanon, Jones et al. (2022) elaborate how intermediaries, in addition to teaching migrants to be compliant, coach employers to discipline and control workers to prevent them "running away". Where migrants did complain or opt to leave, intermediaries stepped in a more direct way, threatening women financially and physically. However, this was because intermediaries were financially penalised by state officials and risked being denied state permission to operate if their recruits "ran away". In other words, it was driven by the wider context of governmental rules.

Scholars of labour migration have emphasised that intermediaries often reproduce and can even amplify gendered and racial inequalities. Studies show how intermediaries which operate within state-regulated temporary labour migration schemes engage in sex-based discrimination, specifically hiring only women or only men for specific jobs even where this may be illegal under national legal frameworks (Parrenas, 2012). Intermediaries may also discriminate by nationality, channelling specific nationality—or ethnicity—groups to specific jobs (Jones, 2021). This can lead to discriminatory pay structures in countries of employment whereby migrants of one nationality may be paid significantly less than those of another. Through their discourse as well as their actions, intermediaries can influence migrants' "value" to employers and hence the wages they are paid (Jones, 2021; Sha & Bhuiyan, 2021). However, ultimately, migrants are made vulnerable by state policies which do not allow them access to the same rights and freedom of movement as citizens. The chapter turns now to outline how intermediaries mediate the inequalities faced by migrants in their new homes, including through lack of access to citizenship.

Intermediaries and the Inequalities in Their New Destinations

In the Undocumented Americans, the journalist Karla Cornejo Villavicencio relates her visit to a community pharmacy in Miami in which those who lack an official immigration status and therefore access to formal healthcare can purchase prescription medication at low cost. Corenjo Villavicencio, herself lacking an official status in the United States, quotes Julieta, a fellow "undocumented" South American who accompanies her to the pharmacy: "They know they're doing something they shouldn't, but they understand the human necessity. I have gone to them with my face swollen because of molar pain and they have given me something for the pain. I have gone to Walgreens and they won't give me something even if I'm dying in front of them" (Villavicencio, 2020, 63–64). This example emphasises the importance of already arrived migrant communities in helping others in less settled circumstances.

Many migrants face discrimination and marginalisation in their new homes. When entering a new country, even with an official status, migrants experience unequal access to the rights and protections due to citizens. In effect, migrants, especially those who lack an official status in their new home, find themselves in an extremely unequal relationship with the state and with citizens. When migrants move somewhere new, whether they stay for days, months or years, and no matter what the intention in being there is, a series of intermediaries are likely to assist (Garapich, 2008; Groutsis et al., 2015). More settled migrants may offer new arrivals advice in the job market, negotiate working conditions or assist migrants to find new, better jobs (Awumbila et al., 2019, for a review of this literature also see Sha, 2021b). Urban studies researchers and sociologists working in European and North American settings have increasingly adopted a relational, infrastructural, approach to analyse the "from the below" constellation of actors and institutions which help migrants navigate life 'after arrival' (Meeus et al., 2019; Wessendorf, 2022). This literature emphasises the significance of informal, non-state activities, including the socio-material practices of the previously arrived migrants in assisting newcomers. Arrival infrastructures comprise a variety of (non-state) housing, shops as information hubs, religious sites, facilities for language classes, hairdressers, restaurants, libraries, international shipping and call centres. They also include local and international NGOs.

This emerging body of literature provides a counterbalance to the state-centric "integration" literature. It emphasises the informal, socio-material practices of a multitude of actors, including previously arrived migrants in assisting newcomers to navigate their new environment. Exploring the constitution of and relationships between infrastructures of arrival enables consideration of a wide constellation of actors in helping migrants settle. It also (re-) places the spotlight on the special role played by long-established migrants in helping new arrivals (Wessendorf, 2022). As with those who facilitate migrants' physical journeys, at times such intermediaries may be altruistic, in others, people and organisations from within the community may charge a fee for assistance. As in the example provided by Villavicencio, some operate 'underground', informally, out of sight of officialdom as a way of expressing solidarity to migrants who are unable to access state-provided services (Zhao, 2013). Local citizens of the new state may also offer support and assistance also in a spirit of solidarity (Bauder, 2021). However, other literatures identify that such solidarity practices are most evident where co-nationals are involved because the trust between co-nationals enables these practices (Portes, 1998). Co-nationals often offer practical assistance in migrants' new homes, such as access to informal banking and remittance services, which are otherwise denied to migrants through mainstream financial services. Businesses established by settled migrants are also sometimes more likely to hire co-nationals who are more newly arrived (Zhao, 2013). Prior generations of scholars in the United States therefore emphasised the significance of 'ethnic enclaves' in providing various types of support (Portes, 1998). This included start-up capital; information on setting up businesses, or tips about business opportunities, strategies, contacts and markets (Werbner, 1987). Such enclaves provided a secure context for arriving migrants, providing both employment and a familiar cultural environment (Massey et al., 1987). In this context, intermediaries, including migrants from within their own communities, provide a counterbalance. This may take the form of making up for a deficiency where the state does not provide services or other types of assistance to migrants. Their survival requires migrants to have knowledge, contacts and networks. On the other hand, Bhimji and Wernet (2021) highlight how such practices can also be viewed as a subtle resistance to state power amidst migrants' struggle to rebuild and embed their lives in the new locale, in which the state fails to care for them, imposes internal border regimes and threatens them with deportation.

The assistance offered by intermediaries in new places does not, however, exist in a vacuum or derive from a surfeit of altruism in migrant communities. In studying recently arrived Polish communities in the United Kingdom, Garapich (2008) shows how the traditional agents of civil society which provided services for free—voluntary organisations, state policies, the Polish church or advocacy networks—were not especially prominent sources of help to the newly arrived. Instead, it was the fee-charging service providers from within the communities, including remittance services, immigration advisors, tax refund offices, 'ethnic' media, food economies, banks, travel agents, recruitment agencies, which quickly mobilised.

Conclusion

In the past half century, intermediaries of migration have become more directly and indirectly implicated in all aspects of international migration. Intermediaries perform numerous practical functions in making migration happen. They may inspire the decision to migrate and advise on where to live, how to live and how to earn money (Massey et al., 1987). They also facilitate the journey through acting as guides, drivers and pilots (Achilli, 2018) or through simply acting as a travel agency through booking transportation and accommodation *en route*. They help migrants of all backgrounds apply for visas, work permits and asylum (Alpes, 2017). They help migrants find jobs, either before leaving home or after arrival in a new place (Jones, 2014). They are transnational actors; deeply embedded in global economic circuits whilst also rooted in (migrants') places. They are also thoroughly implicated in global inequalities in relation to borders, income and citizenship. Most essentially, intermediaries (per)form the essential infrastructure which makes mobility happen in a world in which immobility is the norm (Lindquist et al., 2012). Intermediaries provide a potential alternative, a framework for resistance to inequalities generated by states whilst also sometimes reproducing, or even amplifying, them. Despite this, research on the role of intermediaries in South–South migration is as yet sadly lacking. To address—or even redress—the unbalanced content and epistemology of the existing volume of studies on intermediaries, more research on their specific contributions within South–South migration is needed.

Acknowledgements This work has been undertaken as part of the Migration for Development and Equality (MIDEQ) Hub. Funded by the UKRI Global Challenges Research Fund (GCRF) (Grant Reference: ES/S007415/1), MIDEQ unpacks the complex and multi-dimensional relationships between migration and inequality in the context of the Global South. More at www.mideq.org.

References

Achilli, L. (2018). The "good" smuggler: The ethics and morals of human smuggling among Syrians. *The ANNALS of the American Academy of Political and Social Science, 676*(1), 77–96.

Agunias, D. R. (2009). *Guiding the invisible hand: Making migration intermediaries work for development*. Migration Policy Institute.

Alpes, M. J. (2017). *Brokering high-risk migration and illegality in West Africa: Abroad at any cost*. Routledge.

Anderson, J. T. (2021). Managing labour migration in Malaysia: Foreign workers and the challenges of 'control' beyond liberal democracies. *Third World Quarterly, 42*(1), 86–104.

Awumbila, M., Deshingkar, P., Kandilige, L., Teye, J. K., & Setrana, M. (2019). Please, thank you and sorry—Brokering migration and constructing identities for domestic work in Ghana. *Journal of Ethnic and Migration Studies, 45*(14), 2655–2671.

Ayalew, T. (2018). Refugee protections from below: Smuggling in the Eritrea-Ethiopia context. *The Annals of the American Academy of Political and Social Science, 676*, 57–76.

Ayalew, T., Adugna, F., & Deshingkar, P. (2018). Social embeddedness of human smuggling in East Africa: Brokering Ethiopian migration to the Sudan. *African Human Mobility Review, 4*(3), 1333–1358.

Azad, A. (2019). Recruitment of migrant workers in Bangladesh: Elements of human trafficking for labor exploitation. *Journal of Human Trafficking, 5*(2), 130–150.

Bangladesh Bank. (2019). *A survey report on loans for expatriates: Its uses and impact*. Special Research Work 1902, Research Department, Bangladesh Bank, January 2019.

Bauder, H. (2021). Urban migrant and refugee solidarity beyond city limits. *Urban Studies, 58*(16), 3213–3229.

Bhimji, F., & Wernet, N. (2021). Supporting searchers' desire for emplacement in Berlin: Informal practices in defiance of an (im)mobility regime. *Migration Letters, 18*(2), 189–199.

Boyd, M. (1989). Family and personal networks in international migration: Recent developments and new agendas. *International Migration Review, 23*(3), 638–670.

Burawoy, M. (1976). The functions and reproduction of migrant labour: Comparative material from Southern Africa and the United States. *The American Journal of Sociology, 81*(5), 1050–1087.

Castles, S., & Miller, M. J. (2003). *The age of migration.* Guilford Press.

Constable, N. (2003). *Maid to order in Hong Kong: Stories of migrant workers.* Cornell University Press.

Cranston, S. (2018). 'Calculating the migration industries: Knowing the successful expatriate in the global mobility industry. *Journal of Ethnic and Migration Studies, 44*(4), 626–643.

Crawley, H., Duvell, F., Jones, K., McMahon, S., & Sigona, N. (2018). *Unravelling Europe's 'Migration Crisis': Journeys over Land and Sea.* Policy Press.

De Genova, N. P. (2002). Migrant "illegality" and deportability in everyday life. *Annual Review of Anthropology, 31*(1), 419–447.

De Haas, H. (2007). Turning the tide? Why development will not stop migration. *Development and Change, 38*(5), 819–841.

De León, J. (2015). *The land of open graves: Living and dying on the migrant trail.* University of California Press.

Deshingkar, P. (2019). The making and unmaking of precarious, ideal subjects—Migration brokerage in the Global South. *Journal of Ethnic and Migration Studies, 45*(14), 2638–2654.

Fawcett, J. T. (1989). Networks, linkages, and migration systems. *The International Migration Review, 23*(3), 671–680.

Findlay, A., & Li, E. L. N. (1998). A migration channels approach to the study of professionals moving to and from Hong Kong. *International Migration Review, 32*(3), 682–703.

Fogelman, E. (1995). *Conscience and courage: Rescuers of Jews during the Holocaust.* Anchor Books.

Gammeltoft-Hansen, T., & Sorensen, N. N. (Eds.). (2013). *The migration industry and the commercialization of international migration.* Routledge.

Garapich, M. P. (2008). The migration industry and civil society: Polish immigrants in the United Kingdom before and after EU enlargement. *Journal of Ethnic and Migration Studies, 34*(5), 735–752.

Goh, C., Wee, K., & Yeoh, B. S. A. (2017). Migration governance and the migration industry in Asia: Moving domestic workers from Indonesia to Singapore. *International Relations of the Asia-Pacific, 17*(2017), 401–433.

Goss, J., & Lindquist, B. (1995). Conceptualizing international labour migration: A structuration perspective. *International Migration Review, 29*(2), 317–351.

Groutsis, D., Broek, D. v. d., & Harvey, W. S. (2015). Transformations in network governance: The case of migration intermediaries. *Journal of Ethnic and Migration Studies, 41*(10), 1558–1576.

Guevarra, A. R. (2010). *Marketing dreams, manufacturing heroes: The Transnational labor brokering of Filipino workers.* Rutgers University Press.

Haug, S., Braveboy-Wagner, J., & Maihold, G. (2021). The 'Global South' in the study of world politics: Examining a meta category. *Third World Quarterly, 42*(9), 1923–1944.

Henley. (2022). *The official passport index ranking*. Available at: https://www.henleyglobal.com/passport-index/ranking. Accessed on 2 Mar 2023.

Hernández-León, R. (2013). Conceptualizing the migration industry. In T. Gammeltoft-Hansen & N. N. Sorensen (Eds.), *The migration industry and the commercialization of international migration* (pp. 42–62). Routledge.

Jansen, S. (2009). After the red passport: Towards an anthropology of the everyday geopolitics of entrapment in the EU's "immediate outside." *Journal of the Royal Anthropological Institute, 15*, 815–832.

Jones, K. (2021). 'Brokered discrimination for a fee. The Incompatibility of Domestic Work Placement Agencies with Rights-Based Global Governance of Migration. *Global Public Policy and Governance, 1*, 300–320.

Jones, K., Ksaifi, L., & Clark, C. (2022). 'The biggest problem we are facing Is the running away problem': Recruitment and the paradox of facilitating the mobility of immobile workers. *Work, Employment and Society, 0*(0). https://doi.org/10.1177/09500170221094764

Jones, K. (2014). 'It was a whirlwind. A lot of people made a lot of money': The role of agencies in facilitating migration from Poland into the UK between 2004 and 2008. *Central and Eastern European Migration Review, 3*(2), 105–125.

Kern, A., & Müller-Böker, U. (2015). The middle space of migration: A case study on brokerage and recruitment agencies in Nepal. *Geoforum, 65*, 158–169.

Koster, M., & van Leynseele, Y. (2018). Brokers as assemblers: Studying development through the lens of brokerage. *Ethnos, 83*(5), 803–813.

Lainez, N. (2020). Debt, trafficking and safe migration: The brokered mobility of Vietnamese sex workers to Singapore. *Geoforum, 137*, 164–173.

Lan, P. C. (2018). Bridging ethnic-differences for cultural intimacy: Production of migrant care workers in Japan. *Critical Sociology, 44*(7–8), 029–1043.

Lindquist, J., Xiang, B., & Yeoh, B. S. A. (2012). Opening the black box of migration: Brokers, the organisation of transnational mobility and the changing political economy in Asia. *Pacific Affairs, 85*(1), 7–19.

Majidi, N. (2018). Community dimensions of smuggling: The case of Afghanistan and Somalia. *The ANNALs of the American Academy of Political and Social Science*, 697–113.

Malpass, D. (2022). *Remittances are a critical economic stabilizer*. World Bank Blog 06 December 2022. Available at https://blogs.worldbank.org/voices/remittances-are-critical-economic-stabilizer

Massey, D. S., Alarcón, R., Durand, J., & González, H. (1987). *Return to Aztlan: The social process of international migration from Western Mexico*. University of California Press.

Meeus, B., Arnaut, K., & Van Heur, B. (2019). *Arrival infrastructures*. Palgrave Macmillan.

Merriman, H. (2019). *Tunnel 29: The true story of an extraordinary escape beneath the Berlin Wall*. Hodder and Stoughton.

Mirrlees, T., & Pederson, I. (2016). Elysium as a critical dystopia. *International Journal of Media & Cultural Politics, 12*(3), 305–322.

Moniruzzaman, M., & Walton-Roberts, M. (2018). Migration, debt and resource backwash: How sustainable is Bangladesh-Gulf circular migration? *Migration and Development, 7*(1), 85–103.

Muanamoha, R. C., Maharaj, B., & Preston-Whyte, E. (2010). Social networks and undocumented Mozambican migration to South Africa. *Geoforum, 41*, 885–896.

Oxfam. (2023). *Survival of the rich: How we must tax the super-rich*. Oxfam.

Parrenas, R. S. (2012). The reproductive labour of migrant workers. *Global Networks, 12*(2), 269–275.

Portes, A. (1998). Social capital: Its origins and applications in modern sociology. *Annual Review of Sociology, 24*(1998), 1–24.

Rahman, M. M. (2012). Bangladeshi labour migration to the Gulf states: Patterns of recruitment and processes. *Canadian Journal of Development Studies, 33*(2), 214–230.

Sanchez, G., & Natividad, N. (2017). Reframing migrant smuggling as a form of knowledge: A view from the US- Mexico border. In C. Günay & N. Witjes (Eds.), *Border politics: Defining spaces of governance and forms of transgression* (pp. 67–83). Springer International Publishing.

Sanchez, G. E., & Zhang, S. X. (2018). Rumors, encounters, collaborations, and survival: The migrant smuggling–drug trafficking nexus in the US Southwest. *The ANNALS of the American Academy of Political and Social Science, 676*(1), 135–151.

Schling, H. (2022). 'Just-in-time' migrant workers in Czechia: Racialisation and dormitory labour regimes. In E. Balioni, L. Campling, N. M. Coe, & A. Smith (Eds.), *Labour regimes and global production* (pp. 301–316). Agenda Publishing.

Sha, H. (2021a). *Intermediaries and inequalities: A literature review*. MIDEQ Working Paper. Available at: https://www.mideq.org/en/resources-index-page/intermediaries-and-inequalities-literature-review/

Sha, H. (2021b). *Migrant networks as social capital: The social infrastructure of migration*. MIDEQ Working Paper. Available at: https://www.mideq.org/fr/resources-index-page/migrant-networks-social-capital-social-infrastructure-migration/

Sha, H., & Bhuiyan, M. R. A. (2021). "Amar beton khub e kom"—The role of commercial recruitment intermediaries in reinforcing gendered and racialised inequalities. *Zanj: The Journal of Critical Global South Studies, 5*(1/2), 164–192.

Sharma, N. (2006). Global apartheid and nation-statehood: instituting border regimes. In J. Goodman & P. James (Eds.), *Nationalism and global solidarities: Alternative projections to neoliberal globalisation* (pp. 81–100). Routledge. https://doi.org/10.4324/9780203085981

Singer, A., & Massey, D. S. (1998). The social process of undocumented border crossing among Mexican migrants. *International Migration Review, 32*(3), 561–592.

Sørensen, N. N., & Gammeltoft-Hansen, T. (2012). Introduction. In T. Gammeltoft-Hansen & N. N. Sorensen (Eds.), *The migration industry and the commercialization of international migration* (pp. 1–23). Routledge.

Spener, D. (2009). *Clandestine crossings: Migrants and Coyote on the Texas-Mexico Border*. Cornell University Press.

Torpey, J. (1998). Coming and going: On the state monopolization of the legitimate 'means of movement.' *Sociological Theory, 16*(3), 239–259.

Torres, R. M., & Carte, L. (2016). Migration and development? The gendered costs of migration on Mexico's rural 'left behind.' *Geographical Review, 106*(3), 399–420.

Villavicencio, K. C. (2020). *The undocumented Americans*. One World.

Vogt, W. (2016). Stuck in the middle with you: The intimate labours of mobility and smuggling along Mexico's migrant route. *Geopolitics, 21*, 366–386.

Walia, H. (2021). *Border and rule: Global migration, capitalism, and the rise of racist nationalism*. Haymarket Books.

Werbner, P. (1987). Enclave economies and family firms: Pakistani traders in a British city. In J. S. Eades (Ed.), *Migrants, workers and the social order* (pp. 213–233). Tavistock Publishers.

Wessendorf, S. (2022). 'The library is like a mother': Arrival infrastructures and migrant newcomers in East London. *Migration Studies, 10*(2), 172–189.

Xiang, B. (2017). The base: A case of infrastructural governance of labour outmigration in China. *Mobilities, 12*(2), 175–187.

Xiang, B., & Lindquist, J. (2018). Infrastructuralization: Evolving sociopolitical dynamics in labour migration from Asia. *Pacific Affairs, 91*(4), 759–773.

Žabko, O., Aasland, A., & Endresen, S. B. (2018). Facilitating labour migration from Latvia: Strategies of various categories of intermediaries. *Journal of Ethnic and Migration Studies, 44*(4), 575–591.

Zack, T., Matshaka, S., Moyo, K., & Vanyoro, K. P. (2019). *My way? The circumstances and intermediaries that influence the migration decision-making of female Zimbabwean domestic workers in Johannesburg*. University of Sussex Migrating out of Poverty RPC Working Paper 57.

Zhao, L. S. (2013). Ethnic networks and illegal immigration. *Sociological Focus, 46*(3), 178–192.

Open Access This chapter is licensed under the terms of the Creative Commons Attribution 4.0 International License (http://creativecommons.org/licenses/by/4.0/), which permits use, sharing, adaptation, distribution and reproduction in any medium or format, as long as you give appropriate credit to the original author(s) and the source, provide a link to the Creative Commons license and indicate if changes were made.

The images or other third party material in this chapter are included in the chapter's Creative Commons license, unless indicated otherwise in a credit line to the material. If material is not included in the chapter's Creative Commons license and your intended use is not permitted by statutory regulation or exceeds the permitted use, you will need to obtain permission directly from the copyright holder.

23

The Design and Use of Digital Technologies in the Context of South–South Migration

G. Harindranath, Tim Unwin, and Maria Rosa Lorini

Introduction

Migrants are people, little different from you the reader, and we the authors. Across the world, migrants use digital technologies for a wide range of purposes and in a variety of ways, just as "we" do. Two of the authors of this chapter are long-term migrants, and we therefore draw on our own individual experiences of migrating as well as recent research within the Migration for Development and Equality (MIDEQ) Hub[1] to craft a review of relevant English language literatures on migration between countries in Africa, Asia and Latin America (including the Caribbean). This introduction provides an overview of our approach. The chapter is subsequently divided into five sections summarising our review of the literature, and then compares and contrasts this briefly with the findings of our empirical research, mainly in

G. Harindranath (✉) · M. R. Lorini
School of Business & Management, Royal Holloway, University of London, London, UK
e-mail: G.Harindranath@rhul.ac.uk

M. R. Lorini
e-mail: MariaRosa.Lorini@rhul.ac.uk

T. Unwin
ICT4D & Department of Geography, Royal Holloway, University of London, London, UK
e-mail: Tim.Unwin@rhul.ac.uk

© The Author(s) 2024
H. Crawley and J. K. Teye (eds.), *The Palgrave Handbook of South–South Migration and Inequality*, https://doi.org/10.1007/978-3-031-39814-8_23

Brazil, Ghana, Nepal, Malaysia and South Africa. A final section highlights neglected areas of research that we believe are of importance.

It is difficult to generalise about migrant behaviour (see also Mazzilli et al., in this volume). Migrants are a diverse group of people, with different demographic, economic, ethnic, social, cultural and political statuses and interests. The context in which migration occurs also matters very significantly for any analysis of how and why migrants use digital technology (tech). Moreover, migrants' uses of these technologies also often vary at different stages in their journeys, and it is important to recognise that although migrants are often marginalised and peripheral in their host countries, they and their families can frequently be privileged in their countries of origin. Furthermore, although much of the literature and practice addresses the positive benefits and potential of digital tech, it is also essential to explore the negative and unintended effects of its use.

This chapter draws on a review of existing literature on the use of digital technologies by migrants specifically between countries in Africa, Asia and Latin America (including the Caribbean). We adopt a structured approach to identifying and analysing the literature but did not aim to undertake a formal systematic review, not least because of the problems of interpretation with such reviews, especially in the social sciences (Hammersley, 2020). Although we explored the possibility of reviewing in multiple languages, we ultimately focused just on English, in part since we found rather few directly relevant papers in other languages. We acknowledge that some very useful material is published in other languages but have chosen to focus on English alone here because our sample size was already quite large, and we wished to have a consistent body of literature to review. In essence, we focused on analysing material identified in Web of Science Core (in Clarivate), supported by Google Scholar and our own knowledge of the literature. These were searched online using combinations of the following terms: Africa, Asia, Caribbean, global south, ICT, digital technolog*, Latin America, migra*, migrant, migration, mobile, refugee, South–South and tech. We then reduced the total number (>1500) of results to 74 that we agreed were most relevant and important.[2] There were two steps in the subsequent analysis: first, we categorised each publication according to a 33-point classification, and then all the material was reviewed in detail by at least one of us.

Eight overarching observations about these 74 papers were revealed through our categorisation process. First, the papers were from a rich diversity of disciplinary backgrounds, with first authors being from 37 differently styled departments,[3] and from 36 countries.[4] The most frequent disciplines represented were Communication (8, with 7 further jointly named),

Anthropology and Geography (each with 6). They were also published in 40 different journals or proceedings. Second, there was a considerable increase in the number of publications through time, from the first in 2006 to 9 in 2020 to 14 in 2021. Third, research has been conducted across the world, with South-East Asia (23) and Sub-Saharan Africa (17) dominating. The most common single origin countries were the Philippines (8) and the Syrian Arab Republic (8), whilst the most common single destinations were Singapore (15) and Jordan (8). Fourth, about half of the papers (39) had little clear theoretical framing, and many others were vague on theory, mentioning for example only that the paper was an "Ethnographic study" or an "Inductive Study". The papers that were clearer about their theoretical framing used a wide range of theoretical approaches drawn from the many disciplines of their authors. Fifth, the majority (56) of papers used qualitative methods; a further 12 claimed to be mixed methods. Sixth, almost half (36) of the papers focused on mobile phones with a further 22 papers addressing multiple technologies. Seventh, 71 of the papers examined social aspects of the use of digital tech, whereas only 32 explored political or legal issues. Around half explored economic issues (40) and cultural or religious factors (36). Finally, most (69) of the papers focused on the positive impacts and benefits of digital tech, with fewer (50) also addressing the negatives.

The remainder of this chapter examines the substantive content of these papers, and what they reveal about how and why migrants use digital tech. As an introductory overview to this, Fig. 23.1 provides a word map of the combined abstracts of all the papers and reflects several of the above generalised observations.

Fig. 23.1 Word Art derived from the abstracts of the 74 papers reviewed

Transnational Families and Digital Tech

A substantial proportion of the literature, particularly from the Southeast Asian region, focuses on how digital technologies are implicated in the lives of both migrants and their left-behind families. Papers in this category resonate with issues related to social and emotional aspects as well as caring at a distance and the rhythms of mundane family life affected by spatial and temporal boundaries. Although there is much focus on benefits from digital tech, there is also evidence of the pressures arising from constant digital connections and the strategies employed by migrants to cope with them.

Wellbeing vs Pressure

Digital technologies in general, and smartphones in particular, are often discussed in the literature as a lifeline for transnational migrant families. However, this can be a blessing and a curse for migrants. Much of the literature focuses on the benefits from digital tech for the continuation of family life (Meyers & Rugunanan, 2020), intimacy-at-a-distance (Acedera & Yeoh, 2019) and the wellbeing benefits for connected migrants (Benitez, 2012; Netto et al., 2022). Here, digitally mediated communications become embedded into the everyday helping overcome distance and sustain family life and social bonds.

However, the constant connectivity enabled through digital technologies such as smartphones also comes at a cost to migrants living precarious lives in their host countries. These include the pressure for remittances from families back home (Porter et al., 2018) as well as the relentless pressure to connect with loved ones online which in turn can lead to superficial interactions lacking in intimacy as shown by the work of Acedera and Yeoh (2018). The evidence is antithetical: while digital tech can facilitate constant co-presence, when migrants are online for long periods at a time taking part virtually in daily family rituals, such intense and prolonged digital interaction can also create unreasonable demands on migrants, especially women, irrespective of time differences and work expectations in the host country. Thus, both digital and offline relationships seem to be subject to the same power geometries that characterise the social milieu of the migrant wherever they are based.

Another interesting feature of the literature is that it is overwhelmingly focused on adult migrants. We found only one study by Acedera and Yeoh (2022) that examined the implications of digital tech use by children of migrant parents and how this might impact their lives. However, even here the focus is very much on the politics of caring at a distance involving the migrant parent and the proximate carers rather than the dynamics of digital tech use by children per se.

Care vs Control

Most of the literature on digital tech use by migrants tends to focus on how smartphones facilitate care at a distance and in particular, long-distance mothering. There is relatively less focus on the implications of such virtual caring for the migrants involved and the communication strategies that they adopt as a result. A series of studies from Southeast Asia form the exception in this regard. Acedera and Yeoh (2018) not only highlight the double burden on female migrants from having to care for loved ones back home at the same time as holding down often precarious jobs in the host countries, but also shine a light on their strategic use of digital tech which includes regular but mundane conversations with spouses and carefully curated social media presence to maintain relationships with left-behind family and limiting the use of digital tech to avoid surveillance and control from family members. Acedera and Yeoh's (2022) study on "digital kinning" practices also notes such strategic use of digital tech by left-behind children to limit or avoid the "moral gaze" of their migrant parents.

In addition, there is evidence that employers can seek to control migrant workers (especially female domestic workers) by restricting their access to digital tech (Platt et al., 2016). This further adds to the emotional pressures faced by migrant workers who are then dependent on employers for their limited access to family members back home and friends in the host countries.

Gendered Use and Effects of Digital Tech

The possibilities offered by digital technology for agency and empowerment are closely related to socio-cultural issues including gender, class, economic context, ethnicity and educational level of the users (Le-Phuong et al., 2022). The literature showcases how some of these power geometries can be amplified through the use of digital tech.

Acedera and Yeoh (2018) thus warn about how technological "solutions", particularly social media, help to reify existing gender norms and structures while preventing the emergence of more progressive gender identities in transnational spaces. Through specific digital-mediated practices such as the policing of migrant women's sexuality and public posts, and through carefully curated online presence, migrant or left-behind women are subject to the continuation of patriarchal tensions and expectations of an unequal power structure (Meyers & Rugunanan, 2020).

Similar power dynamics and social norms are visible in the case of left-behind children and their online world mirrors the offline space where girls are often subject to stricter moral control. However, there is also some evidence of digital mediation allowing for different ways of "doing family" and a limited renegotiation of social expectations (Acedera & Yeoh, 2022).

There is also evidence of the gendered effects of increasing digital tech use in the humanitarian sector such as increased domestic violence when female refugees are identified and designated as heads of household reinforcing extant power dynamics, as highlighted by the work of Schoemaker et al., 2021. Nevertheless, they also show that refugees can exercise agency in such situations through selective registrations or by choosing not to register at all where possible to avoid perceived negative consequences of such identification. Indeed, Chib et al. (2021) show that the non-use of digital technologies can be seen as a form of agentic expression by vulnerable migrants, as in the case of trans- and cis-feminine sex workers in Singapore, rather than the passive result of socio-structural factors.

Other studies of vulnerable migrants, such as foreign brides (Chib & Nguyen, 2018), show how digital technologies can be used to break their marginalisation and to strengthen their cultural identities. Digital communications are used to maintain the culture of origin, and proudly to disseminate and enjoy it. Both the consumption and production of cultural products of their country of origin are seen as strategies of resistance against alienation and powerlessness that characterise their lives in the host countries.

Information practices

Acculturation

There is an overwhelming focus in the literature on the positive aspects of mobile phone use in most acculturation studies, despite Aricat's (2015) warnings about the need to include analysis of their negative impacts. Mobile phone use is usually credited with helping migrants navigate new societies through the support of applications available for moving around, learning a language, understanding local cultures and customs, as well as for developing new social ties within the host society (Vuningoma et al., 2021). This can in turn enable migrants' acculturation strategies and the creation of a hybrid transnational space (Aricat et al., 2015).

Mobile phones are also key to maintaining links with the culture of the country of origin. However, the easy availability through digital technologies of home country news, entertainment and spiritual support from abroad can reduce exposure to the new environment in the host society, increasing dependence on co-ethnic social networks and hindering new opportunities for bridge building (Chib & Nguyen, 2018). Indeed, constant social media communication with co-nationals and family back home has been shown to create cultural isolation from the host society even as digital tech enables migrants to better understand host nationals' attitudes towards migrants (Lim & Pham, 2016).

Migrants' acculturation efforts can also be undermined by discriminatory discourses and practices that underpin their digital tech usage in the host country. As Aricat's (2015) study shows, such discourses often characterise migrants as lazy and unproductive leading to many employers restricting the use of mobiles at workplaces.

Skills and Employment

Lack of access combined with a lack of digital skills are the main factors seen as limiting the use of digital tech (Hechanova et al., 2011). In particular, specific groups, such as women and low-skilled workers face multiple digital inequalities, derived from the wider social and economic inequalities that they experience. Overcoming these inequalities through learning and skills development, and reaching a state of self-pride in using digital tech can nevertheless trigger new entrepreneurial aspirations for engaging in online business activities. The literature discusses the benefits associated with the possibilities offered by digital tech for sharing information, developing new skills, starting new business activities (Ritchie, 2022), finding jobs (Grant et al., 2013; Thomas & Lim, 2010) and developing income generation activities (Hussain & Lee, 2021). At the same time, studies point to systemic political and cultural biases in the host countries (Vuningoma et al., 2021) and the potential reinforcement or creation of social divisions through digital tech (Ritchie, 2022) as often restricting migrants from using digital technologies to seek out employment opportunities.

The literature also suggests that digital tech is essential for fostering business entrepreneurship among refugees and migrants more generally. Digital tech use positively influences migrants' entrepreneurship skills and even if extensive quantitative data are scarce, the qualitative data represented mainly through case studies, suggest that these technologies often benefit skills development, coordination and business cooperation (Ritchie, 2022).

The main constraints on migrants' skills uptake and business development appear to be limited infrastructural access combined with cultural (inequalities), political (regulatory environments that limit use by migrants and refugees), gendered social dynamics (Canevez et al., 2021) and social restrictions (including patriarchal and hierarchical structures). As Dutta and Kaur-Gill (2018) argue digital technologies do not change these problematic social structures and their power dynamics.

Advocacy and Collective Action

COVID-19 and the lockdowns introduced during the pandemic highlighted a new role for social media. WhatsApp, in particular, helped people on the margins of society such as migrant women to mobilise and respond to challenges while requesting legal support and information (Muswede & Sithole, 2022). This is not, though, the first time that digital tech solutions have been used for advocacy and collective action. The aid sector has long used social media to raise awareness on sensitive topics, to raise funds, to share information and to achieve political influence, particularly regarding working conditions and salaries of migrants (Molland, 2021). Social media furthermore contribute positively to scalability and connectivity between migrant groups and state actors.

Certain collective experiences of marginality shared on social media can also be an opportunity for bonding and mobilisation. For instance, Raheja (2022) reports that Hindu migrant-refugee men in Pakistan bond across castes through the exchange of posts and images that seek to highlight their vulnerability and strengthen their political claims for Indian citizenship. Another example of mobilisation facilitated by digital tech is presented by Hussain and Lee (2021) in relation to Rohingya women who use digital technologies such as smartphones to push back against socio-religious restrictions within refugee settlements in Bangladesh where social and political leaders also employ similar technologies for political and religious mobilisation.

The literature points to linguistic skills, education and a lack of time in addition to access as key reasons that limit participation in social media (Le-Phuong et al., 2022). As seen in relation to the use of digital tech for business improvement, socio-cultural issues connected with gender, class, economic situation and educational divide further affect their uptake.

(Digital) Inequalities

Digital tech use in the migration context often comes with new risks as well as new digital inequalities in relation to differential outcomes from such usage, often determined by limited digital literacy and inadequate understanding of digital safety and security.

The literature has long identified that access to digital tech is but one layer of inequality and that there are further layers of divide such as those associated with usage deriving from social inequalities and those related to outcomes from such usage with the digitally literate benefiting more than others (van Dijk, 2020). There are multiple layers and intersections of inequality, and the use of digital tech all too frequently exacerbates them. The evidence suggests that various socio-economic and cultural factors such as age, gender, communication preferences, linguistic proficiency, familiarity with digital tech and income levels all affect access to and use of digital tech, and therefore influence outcomes (Ritchie, 2022). For instance, Netto's (2022) study of the use of digital tech by Rohingya refugees in Malaysia, highlights how language and literacy play a crucial role in not just the ability to use digital tech but more importantly, to access a range of resilience strategies through that use. Female refugees, particularly older women, are generally less literate both in terms of language and digital literacy and therefore have more barriers to using smartphones to build resilience as well as transnational and intergenerational solidarity.

While poorer migrants often face digital inequalities, female migrants from more well-off backgrounds can also face a variety of "digital asymmetries" (Wang & Lim, 2021) such as competency asymmetry (i.e. dependency on their children to teach them digital skills), expectation asymmetry (when expected messages from loved ones are late or do not arrive) and autonomy asymmetry (when migrant mothers are required to schedule digitally mediated activities to suit their family members' schedules rather than their own). Such digital asymmetries are a key feature of digitally mediated communications within a context of entrenched social and gender-based inequalities. Indeed, the gendered surveillance often seen in digital interactions serves to exacerbate pre-existing inequalities related to gender and social norms. Our review finds that such gendered power dynamics and inequalities persist irrespective of geographical location and despite various digital coping strategies employed by migrants as discussed in the previous sections.

Digital communications have often been hailed as a facilitator of hybrid, transnational identities, particularly in the case of South–North migration. In the Southern context, however, there are fewer such studies examining issues around identity and transnationalism. While Benitez's (2012) study highlights the potential for digital communication to foster hybrid transnational identities, it also highlights the effect of digital inequalities and their socio-economic, knowledge, gender, generational, ethnic, language and disability dimensions in relation to access to, use of and outcomes from the use of digital tech. Indeed, there is evidence to suggest that marginalised migrants often retreat into their own culture and identity as a form of resistance which in turn increases social isolation from the host society (Chib & Nguyen, 2018).

Digital Humanitarianism

An important but under-addressed theme that emerges from the literature on digital tech use in African, Asian and Latin American migration contexts is a critique of the use of digital tech in humanitarian situations without regard for data justice. Remote visual technologies are increasingly used to govern refugee camps from a distance, creating what Rothe et al. (2021) call a "visual assemblage" that aims primarily to satisfy the humanitarian care and control needs of public and private actors. While the use of digital tech in this regard is often driven by efficiency considerations, Madianou's (2019) study is an exemplar in this category for its critique of the efficiency logic. Instead, she frames the datafication of humanitarianism as technocolonial extraction for ensuring project funding rather than refugee welfare while biometric data are used to entrench inequalities and power asymmetries between refugees and the humanitarian agencies/government. Thus, data and digital tech are shown to help entrench inequalities through problematic datafication efforts aimed at ensuring accountability, the privileging of digital impact data and efficiency measures for the benefit of donors, the increasing roles for the private sector in the humanitarian field, the rise of solutionism inherent in the accelerating use of hackathons to develop easy fixes for complex social problems and the widespread use of digital tech for border control and surveillance.

The datafication of displaced people is particularly problematic given the lack of regulatory safeguards that are often available in the economically richer countries of the world. This issue is highlighted by Lemberg-Pedersen and Haioty (2020) who argue that the marketisation of refugee data and the designation of the displaced as "unbanked" facilitate their integration into the global financial system. Humanitarian financialisation then serves the multiple interests of aid agencies, international organisations, private data companies and financial services providers all at the expense of "the surveillance refugee body" whose compliance is a pre-requisite for access to services. A key feature of such datafication is that the migrants whose data are being extracted have no understanding of their data rights nor do they have any knowledge of who has access to their data and how it is used.

The increased visibility caused by the use of digital tech and datafication is a double-edged sword for migrants and refugees. While access to services demands visibility, it also opens up migrants to surveillance by a variety of actors, including governments. While digital visibility enables access to services within refugee camps it also facilitates surveillance, potential denial of service and other harms such as increased personal safety implications for politically active refugees (Schoemaker et al., 2021). Although some migrants may attempt to evade visibility through selective (non)use of digital technologies, the lack of data justice in such humanitarian contexts, particularly the inability to challenge or change data held by others about refugees, further exacerbates such inequalities.

Evidence from MIDEQ Research on Migrant Use of Digital Tech

Our research and practice programme, as part of the MIDEQ Hub,[5] on the use of digital technologies by migrants and family members in multiple migration corridors (Nepal-Malaysia, Ghana-China, Haiti-Brazil and Ethiopia-South Africa) show that while migrants depend on digital tech for many aspects of their daily lives, they seldom use "migrant apps"[6] designed specifically for them. Instead, they tend to use digital tech with which they are already familiar, such as Facebook, WhatsApp or Imo (a free app for voice and video calls), depending on the context despite the proliferation of migrant apps funded by international organisations and well-meaning agencies. We also note contradictory influences of digital tech on migrants and family members characterised by the co-existence of increased digital use alongside persisting digital inequalities relating to access, use and outcomes. A key related issue is the pervasive lack of knowledge regarding issues of digital safety and security, and this is concerning given that migrants are increasingly subject to digital interventions from states, employers, and even humanitarian organisations across many South–South migration corridors.

Our findings point to some antithetical influences of digital technologies on the life and wellbeing of the migrants and their families. In the countries of origin, while access to technology increases post-migration, challenges continue to exist due to connectivity costs that are often higher than in host countries. This is particularly true in the case of remote, rural locations such as those in Nepal. The generally low level of digital skills prior to migration also affects access and use.

In the more affluent destination countries access to modern devices and the Internet is often easier and more affordable, leading to the development of digital skills, incentivised by the necessity to stay in touch with family and friends and to access information, regarding both host society and potential future destinations. Digital technologies, furthermore, help build new bridges in the host country, learn new skills, search for business opportunities and discover local culture as well as maintain links with the culture of origin.

However, our findings also provide evidence for the more dangerous and harmful side of the digital world such as increased pressure from family to be connected or to return home, the challenges associated with social media such as fake news and hacking, and the higher risk of surveillance. Many migrants are aware of the potential harm of using certain digital technologies, for themselves and their families. At the same time, they remain mostly unaware of the range of migrant apps designed specifically to support migrants orient themselves, to access labour and government information and services, to rate employers and recruitment agencies or to register complaints. Where there is some knowledge of such apps there is often a reluctance to download and/or use them due to lack of trust and an overwhelming preference for peer-to-peer support. Moreover, as with Ghanaian migrants in China, there is also evidence of migrants exercising agency by switching between regional dialects when discussing sensitive topics or while using apps that they do not trust.

The research findings disclosed further contradictions connected with the migration journey. Migrants are often balanced in their appraisal of the use of digital technologies and cite both positive and negative aspects. A word used by many migrant interviewees that rarely appears in the literature is "happiness". Migrants find happiness in their ability to support their family through remittances that improve their economic, and consequently social, circumstances. They are also able to provide better access to educational opportunities for their children or siblings. The other element of satisfaction is represented by the possibility for employment in the host country compared with the lack of such opportunities in the country of origin. Digital technologies offer new means of accessing training, for instance via YouTube that can be helpful for migrants planning to return home to set up small business ventures.

At the other end of the spectrum, there is "sadness" due to the physical distance from the family. Digital technology is cited as a source of great relief and support as it helps bridge distance from family, culture and opportunities. Nevertheless, virtual proximity is not seen as comparable to the tangibility of physical presence. Migrants express similar sentiments in relation to the limited potential of digital tech, at least in their eyes, to address the insecurity they often face in the host country. In Malaysia, Nepalese migrants state that they need to maintain a low profile and be attentive to their movements as they go about their daily lives due to fear of personal attacks from locals. In South Africa, migrants often recall xenophobic attacks and hate speech. The most common frustration is the feeling of powerlessness to fight and change the systemic discrimination they face. While many migrants do not see digital technologies as a panacea for the intractable challenges associated with migration, there is evidence to show that some migrant networks in host countries are harnessing the power of social media for advocacy and building resilience.

Under-Addressed Themes in the Literature

Our review suggests that there are numerous aspects that require further research on the use of digital technologies in the context of South–South migration and its often paradoxical implications. Most of the literature we explored was derived from qualitative research, and illustrates a rich diversity of migrant experiences. However, there is a distinct opportunity to undertake more studies using quantitative methods. Just three out of the 74 papers focused exclusively on quantitative methods and seven combined surveys alongside qualitative methods. The lack of social network type analysis of migrant flows and digitally mediated networks is also intriguing in a field that is increasingly characterised by datafication.

Very little existing research applies rigorous theoretical approaches to scaffold their studies or use them as analytical or interpretive lenses, although numerous social science theories were mentioned briefly in many of the reviewed papers. The multidisciplinary nature of the subject and the sociotechnical complexity surrounding migration and digital tech both introduce challenges in finding theories that have the scope to help interpret the findings. However, this also implies opportunities for future theory building in the field.

The focus of much of the literature thus far has been on migrants and their families, particularly on familial relations mediated by digital tech. There remain opportunities further to investigate the nuances, including the depth or superficiality, of digital interactions between migrants and family members as well as their strategic use of digital tech and even digital disconnection. An overarching theme in the literature pertains to persisting gender-based inequalities and power dynamics between female migrants and their left-behind family members. Longitudinal studies could explore if such dynamics change with the passing of time and as migration and caring roles become more firmly established within the family.

There is also a need to examine further the more negative aspects of digital tech in relation to its impact on mental wellbeing among migrants. While our research has highlighted this as an issue, there is limited coverage of wellbeing implications of digital use within the migrant literature. There is also a rather limited focus on children and youth, and there is scope here further to explore the socio-psychological implications of digital parenting. The theme of religious and cultural use of digital tech is also an area that is ripe for further investigation given the rapid expansion of e-religion.

The current literature does not adequately account for the distinction between different types of migrants, and in particular, undocumented migrants and migrants of all genders (including LGBTIQ+). It is also crying out for greater diversity in terms of coverage of regions and countries with Southeast Asia dominating the current English language research landscape. A lack of diversity is also evident in the range of themes addressed. For instance, despite the significance many scholars attach to digital inequalities, it is surprising to see very few studies focused on digital literacy and e-learning in the migration context. There is also limited literature on the use of digital tech for political mobilisation and advocacy by migrant networks in host countries despite the important work they undertake in many regions. In this regard, given the fractured nature of globalisation and rising anti-migrant sentiment across the world, it would also be instructive to (re)examine the nature of online identity formation among migrants in the host country context.

Lastly, given the march towards a "digital first" approach in many parts of the world, there is an urgent need for studies to revisit the use of so-called migrant apps not merely from the point of view of their efficacy but also from the perspective of migrants who are encouraged or required to use them but, as our research suggests, seldom do.

Conclusions: The Promises and Perils of Digital Tech

This chapter has provided an overview of English language publications on migration between countries in Africa, Asia and Latin America (including the Caribbean), and has highlighted five main themes that emerge from the 74 papers reviewed: transnational families, gendered use and effects, information practices, digital inequalities and digital humanitarianism. The use of digital tech pervades all aspects of human life, and migrant experiences thereof represent a particularly interesting sub-set of the literature—the use of mobile technologies by mobile people. Our overwhelming conclusion is that the use of digital technologies generally exacerbates existing inequalities, although the potential still exists for them to be disruptive and to be used to benefit the social, economic, political and cultural experiences of migrant life. Moreover, although the bulk of the literature focuses on perceived positive aspects of digital tech, there is also a much darker side to it that has as yet been insufficiently addressed. The ways through which migrants are increasingly being encouraged or forced into using particular apps, and the rise of digital surveillance of migrants are two topics worthy of much more research and policy influencing. Migrants are often very vulnerable, and it is important that they should all have the benefit of learning how to use digital tech safely, wisely and securely.

Acknowledgements This work has been undertaken as part of the Migration for Development and Equality (MIDEQ) Hub. Funded by the UKRI Global Challenges Research Fund (GCRF) (Grant Reference: ES/S007415/1), MIDEQ unpacks the complex and multi-dimensional relationships between migration and inequality in the context of the Global South. More at www.mideq.org.

Notes

1. Our working papers containing rich empirical evidence from the research are freely available at https://ict4d.org.uk/publications/working-papers/.
2. For a full listing of references, see https://ict4d.org.uk/technology-inequality-and-migration/litrev/.
3. Very similarly named departments were treated as the same. Thus, Communication Studies was considered the same as Communication, but different from Communication and New Media.
4. Dominated by 21 researchers in Singapore, 18 in the USA, 10 in the UK and 8 in South Africa.

5. This chapter also draws from 1,335 responses to our online surveys in Nepal, Malaysia, Ghana, South Africa, Haiti and Brazil, online interviews conducted with Nepalese migrants in Malaysia and returnee migrants and family members in Nepal, online interviews conducted with migrants and returnees in Ghana and in-person interviews and focus groups conducted with migrants in South Africa. See our collection of papers at https://ict4d.org.uk/publications/working-papers/ for detailed results from our online surveys.
6. Both Farbenblum et al. (2018) and Kikkawa et al. (2021) provide reviews of numerous digital applications designed for migrant workers or to facilitate and regulate migrant mobility.

References

Acedera, K. E., & Yeoh, B. S. A. (2018). Facebook, long-distance marriages, and the mediation of intimacies. *International Journal of Communication*, 12, 4123–4142 https://ijoc.org/index.php/ijoc/article/download/9667/2475

Acedera, K. E., & Yeoh, B. S. A. (2019). 'Making time': Long-distance marriages and the temporalities of the transnational family. *Current Sociology*, 67(2), 250–272. https://doi.org/10.1177/0011392118792927

Acedera, K. E., & Yeoh, B. S. A. (2022). The intimate lives of left-behind young adults in the Philippines: Social media, gendered intimacies, and transnational parenting. *Journal of Immigrant and Refugee Studies*, 20(2), 206–219. https://doi.org/10.1080/15562948.2022.2044572

Aricat, R. G. (2015). Is (the study of) mobile phones old wine in a new bottle? A polemic on communication-based acculturation research, research. *Information Technology and People*, 28(4), 806–824. https://doi.org/10.1108/ITP-09-2014-0223

Aricat, R. G., Karnowski, V., & Chib, A. (2015). Mobile phone appropriation and migrant acculturation: A case study of an Indian community in Singapore. *International Journal of Communication*, 9, 2221–2242. https://ijoc.org/index.php/ijoc/article/view/3081

Benitez, J. L. (2012). Salvadoran transnational families: ICT and communication practices in the network society. *Journal of Ethnic and Migration Studies*, 38(9), 1439–1449. https://doi.org/10.1080/1369183X.2012.698214

Canevez, R., Maitland, C., Xu, Y., Hannah, S. A., & Rodrigue, R. (2021). Exploring the relationship between information and communication technology collective behaviors and sense of community: An urban refugee analysis. *Information Technology and People*, 35(2), 536–557. https://doi.org/10.1108/ITP-03-2020-0112

Chib, A., & Nguyen, H. (2018). Essentialist identities as resistance to immobilities: Communicative mobilities of Vietnamese foreign brides in Singapore. *International Journal of Communication, 12*, 4030–4051. https://ijoc.org/index.php/ijoc/article/download/9662/2471

Chib, A., Ang, M. W., Ibasco, G. C., & Nguyen, H. (2021). Mobile media (non-) use as expression of agency. *Mass Communication and Society*. https://doi.org/10.1080/15205436.2021.1970187

Dutta, M. J., & Kaur-Gill, S. (2018). Precarities of migrant work in Singapore: Migration, (im)mobility, and neoliberal governmentality. *International Journal of Communication, 12*, 4066–4084. https://ijoc.org/index.php/ijoc/article/view/9664

Farbenblum, B., Berg, L., & Kintominas, A. (2018). *Transformative technology for migrant workers: Opportunities, challenges and risks*. Open Society Foundations. https://www.migrantjustice.org/transformative-technology

Grant, J. A., Mitchell, M. I., Nyame, F. K., & Yakovleva, N. (2013). Micro-regionalisms, information and communication technologies, and migration in West Africa: A comparative analysis of Ghana's diamond, cocoa and gold sectors. In U. Lorenz-Carl & M. Rempe (Eds.), *Mapping agency: Comparing regionalisms in Africa* (pp. 149–174). Routledge.

Hammersley, M. (2020). Reflections on the methodological approach of systematic reviews. In O. Zawacki-Richter, M. Kerres, S. Bedenlier, M. Bond, & K. Buntins (Eds.), *Systematic reviews in educational research* (pp. 23–29). Springer VS. https://doi.org/10.1007/978-3-658-27602-7_2

Hechanova, M. R. A., Tuliao, A. P., & Hwa, A. P. (2011). If you build it, will they come? Adoption of Online Counselling among Overseas Migrant Workers. *Media Asia, 38*(1), 32–40. https://doi.org/10.1080/01296612.2011.11726889

Hussain, F., & Lee, Y. (2021). Navigating digital borderscapes: A case study from Rohingya refugee settlements in Bangladesh. *Asiascape: Digital Asia, 8*, 190–210. https://brill.com/view/journals/dias/8/3/article-p190_5.xml#d209358195e336

Kikkawa, A., Justo, C. J., & Sirivunnabood, P. (2021). Migtech: How technology is reshaping labour mobility and the landscape of international migration. *Labour migration in Asia*. ADB, OECD and ILO Report. https://www.adb.org/publications/labor-migration-asia-impacts-covid-19-crisis-post-pandemic-future

Lemberg-Pedersen, M., & Haioty, E. (2020). Re-assembling the surveillable refugee body in the era of data-craving. *Citizenship Studies, 24*(5), 607–624. https://doi.org/10.1080/13621025.2020.1784641

Le-Phuong, L., Lams, L., & De Cock, R. (2022). Social media use and migrants' intersectional positioning: a case study of Vietnamese female migrants. *Media and Communication, 10*(2), 192–203. https://doi.org/10.17645/mac.v10i2.5034

Lim, S. S., & Pham, B. (2016). 'If you are a foreigner in a foreign country, you stick together': Technologically mediated communication and acculturation of migrant students. *New Media and Society, 18*(1), 2171–2188. https://doi.org/10.1177/1461444816655698

Madianou, M. (2019). Technocolonialism: Digital innovation and data practices in the humanitarian response to refugee crises. *Social Media and Society, 5*(3), 1–13. https://doi.org/10.1177/2056305119863146

Meyers, C., & Rugunanan, P. (2020). Mobile-mediated mothering from a distance: A case study of Somali mothers in Port Elizabeth, South Africa. *International Journal of Cultural Studies, 23*(5), 656–673. https://doi.org/10.1177/1367877920926645

Molland, S. (2021). Scalability, social media and migrant assistance: Emulation or contestation? *Ethnos*. https://doi.org/10.1080/00141844.2021.1978520

Muswede, T., & Sithole, S. L. (2022). Social media networking as a coping strategy amid the COVID-19 lockdown: The case of migrant women in Limpopo, South Africa. *South African Review of Sociology, 52*(2), 4–19. https://doi.org/10.1080/21528586.2022.2068159

Netto, G., Baillie, L., Georgiou, T., Teng, L. W., Endut, N., Strani, K., & O'Rourke, B. (2022). Resilience, smartphone use and language among urban refugees in the Global South. *Journal of Ethnic and Migration Studies, 48*(3), 542–559. https://doi.org/10.1080/1369183X.2021.1941818

Platt, M., Yeoh, B. S. A., & Lam, T. (2016). Renegotiating migration experiences: Indonesian domestic workers in Singapore and use of information communication technologies. *New Media and Society, 18*(10), 2207–2223. https://doi.org/10.1177/1461444816655614

Porter, G., Hampshire, K., Abane, A., Munthall, A., Robson, E., Tanie, A., Owusu, S., de Lannoy, A., & Bango, A. (2018). Connecting with home, keeping in touch: Physical and virtual mobility across stretched families in sub-Saharan Africa. *Africa, 88*(2), 404–424. https://doi.org/10.1017/S0001972017000973

Raheja, N. (2022). Our sisters and daughters: Pakistani Hindu migrant masculinities and digital claims to Indian citizenship. *Journal of Immigrant and Refugee Studies, 20*(2), 190–205. https://doi.org/10.1080/15562948.2022.2032906

Ritchie, H. A. (2022). An institutional perspective to bridging the divide: The case of Somali women refugees fostering digital inclusion in the volatile context of urban Kenya. *New Media and Society, 24*(2), 345–364. https://doi.org/10.1177/14614448211063186

Rothe, D., Fröhlich, C., & Lopez, J. M. R. (2021). Digital humanitarianism and the visual politics of the refugee camp: (Un)seeing control. *International Political Sociology, 15*(1), 41–62. https://doi.org/10.1093/ips/olaa021

Schoemaker, E., Baslan, D., Pon, B., & Dell, N. (2021). Identity at the margins: Data justice and refugee experiences with digital identity systems in Lebanon, Jordan, and Uganda. *Information Technology for Development, 27*(1), 13–36. https://doi.org/10.1080/02681102.2020.1785826

Thomas, M., & Lim, S. S. (2010). ICT use and female migrant workers in Singapore. In J. E. Katz (Ed.), *Mobile communication: Dimensions of social policy* (pp. 175–190). Routledge.

Vuningoma, S., Lorini, M. R., & Chigona, W. (2021). *How refugees in South Africa use mobile phones for social connectedness*. CandT'21: Proceedings of the 10th

International Conference on Communities and Technologies—Wicked Problems in the Age of Tech, 128–137, https://doi.org/10.1145/3461564.3461569

Van Dijk, J. (2020). *The digital divide*. Polity Press.

Wang, W., & Lim, S. S. (2021). ICTs and transnational householding: The double burden of polymedia connectivity for international 'study mothers'. In M. McAuliffe (Ed.), *Research handbook on international migration and digital technology* (pp. 207–219). Cheltenham: Edward Elgar. https://doi.org/10.4337/9781839100611.00025

Open Access This chapter is licensed under the terms of the Creative Commons Attribution 4.0 International License (http://creativecommons.org/licenses/by/4.0/), which permits use, sharing, adaptation, distribution and reproduction in any medium or format, as long as you give appropriate credit to the original author(s) and the source, provide a link to the Creative Commons license and indicate if changes were made.

The images or other third party material in this chapter are included in the chapter's Creative Commons license, unless indicated otherwise in a credit line to the material. If material is not included in the chapter's Creative Commons license and your intended use is not permitted by statutory regulation or exceeds the permitted use, you will need to obtain permission directly from the copyright holder.

24

Migrant Resource Flows and Development in the Global South

Edward Asiedu, Tebkieta Alexandra Tapsoba, and Stephen Gelb

Introduction

As migrants move from their country of origin to their country of destination, they take with them resources including knowledge and finance. From their country of destination, they send back flows of resources to their families and the wider communities, including finance in the form of remittances and diaspora investment, trade in goods and services, and knowledge such as technology, skills, and business and entrepreneurial capabilities. All these flows directly impact on consumption and investment behaviour, and on employment and economic growth in both origin and destination countries.

Resource flows may have perverse effects on income and wealth inequalities. Although migration may be the result of inequality in a community,

E. Asiedu
Department of Finance, University of Ghana Business School (UGBS), P.O. Box LG78, Legon, Accra, Ghana
e-mail: edasiedu@ug.edu.gh

T. A. Tapsoba
Institut Supérieur Des Sciences de La Population ISSP, Université Joseph Ki-Zerbo, Boulevard Charles de Gaulle, 03 BP 7118, Ouagadougou, Burkina Faso
e-mail: teb_kieta@hotmail.com

S. Gelb (✉)
ODI, 203 Blackfriars Road, London SE1 8NJ, UK
e-mail: srgelb@gmail.com

the effects of migrants' resource flows may lead to further inequalities—related to income, consumption, investment and access to education or health—between the migrants and their families and non-migrants within their community of origin (see also Feyissa, 2022 and Feyissa et al., in this volume), and perhaps also between migrants and natives in the destination country.

The Sustainable Development Goals (SDGs) only mention remittances once, in Goal 10c on the cost of remittances. However, the UN's Global Indicators Framework (UN, 2021) contains a single additional reference which does concern their use in countries of origin. Indicator 17.3.2—the "volume of remittances … as a proportion of total GDP [of recipient countries]"—is linked to sub-goal 17.3 on additional financial resources for developing countries. This sub-goal has a second indicator referring collectively to foreign direct investment (FDI), official development assistance (ODA) and South–South cooperation, so the singling out of remittances accords them greater significance. The Global Compact on Safe, Orderly and Regular Migration does go somewhat further in pointing to the development impact of migrants' resource flows, for example in Objectives 18 and 19.[1]

Research and policy attention on remittances has grown significantly, in part through the work of international organisations like IOM, IFAD, and the KNOMAD network centred at the World Bank, as well as the work of academics (see, for example, de Haas et al., 2020). But there has been much less research and policy focus on resource flows linked to South–South migration, whether remittances or other flows, including diaspora investment, trade and knowledge. This chapter examines the existing literature on all three types of resource flow in the context of South–South migration and considers their potential for development. In the first section, we look at remittances and diaspora investment, before turning to trade in goods and services, looking at both formally recorded and informal trade. In the third section, we look at knowledge flows.

We note that global data on remittances sent and received for about 150 countries is now very usefully provided by the Global Knowledge Partnership on Migration and Development (KNOMAD) at the World Bank,[2] together with estimated bilateral data for countries. But there remain no national or global datasets looking at diaspora investment or bilateral trade flows linked to migrant and diaspora populations, and this is an important policy priority. Moreover, knowledge flows are not measured by a common indicator and as a result they are difficult to measure and compare, whether across countries or even locations, despite having significant impacts (Gelb & Krishnan, 2018).

Financial Flows

South–South Remittances Are Underestimated

Remittances within the Global South suffer from the same underestimation as South–South migration more generally (Ratha & Shaw, 2007). This underestimation is mainly due to the fact that only formal channels are used to estimate them (Amuedo-Dorantes & Pozo, 2004). Transfers sent through informal channels could even be as 50% greater than remittances recorded by the IMF (African Development Bank, 2009; Ahmed et al., 2021; Freund & Spatafora, 2008). Surveys and censuses in developing countries including Living Standards Measurement studies in Burkina Faso and Nigeria provide information about these informal channels, and show that hand-to-hand transfers[3] are sometimes preferred by migrants. Another informal channel is "fax", or "*hawala*" as it is called in many countries, which consists of money changers gathering the funds of multiple people and redistributing them to beneficiaries via a counterpart trader in the origin country (African Development Bank, 2009). Informal channels persist due to high commissions (African Development Bank, 2009). In fact, South–South remittance costs are on average higher than North–South remittance costs and are often excessive. For example, Angola-Namibia transfers cost 22.4% of the total amount and from South Africa–Zambia 18%. In comparison, sending money from Russia to Central Asian countries only cost between 1.3% and 1.7% (World Bank Group/KNOMAD, 2022; World Bank Group, 2019). Of the 30 highest-cost corridors for receiving remittances in 2015, 33% were South–South corridors, all in Africa (World Bank Group, 2016).

This undoubtedly motivated SDG 10.c which targets the reduction of remittance transaction costs below 3% by 2030. It is however important to note that the rise of money transfers by mobile phone operators reduces transfer costs considerably. For example, in WAEMU (West African Economic and Monetary Union) countries sharing the same telephone operators, the costs are derisory. Transferring money between Senegal and another African country sharing the same telephone service sometimes costs a maximum of only 1%.[4] In the case of Kenya, Muguna (2018) shows that between 2010 and 2014, receiving money via a mobile transfer costs an average of 1.93%. By contrast, bank transfers remain high with an average cost of 19%. Generally speaking, money transfers via mobile phones like M-Pesa in Kenya, Orange money, and Moov money in West Africa help remittances to reach remote areas securely and rapidly and also increase the use of formal channels rather than informal (Muguna, 2018).

The World Bank development indicators are usually the source of data used to quantify workers' remittances. They are defined as earnings, either cash or goods, sent to countries of origin by migrants—and are a considerable financial inflow for developing countries. They are recorded by the IMF (International Monetary Fund) and are based on countries' balance of payments.[5] To reflect their significance for developing countries they are often compared to other resource flows. After ranking second above Official Development Aid (ODA) and below Foreign Development Investment (FDI) (Ratha, 2003), remittances now exceed both of these flows in Low and Middle Income Countries (LMICs) (World Bank Group/KNOMAD, 2022). Remittances also have proven themselves resilient during the 2020 recession, even as FDI, for example, decreased by 12% (World Bank Group/KNOMAD, 2022).

When it comes to disaggregating the data by sending countries, one can see that again, South–South financial flows composed of remittances and diaspora finance are not well documented. Organisations like the World Bank are therefore working on the basis of estimates, using migrants' stock in destination countries and GDP per capita. Using the World Bank bilateral remittance matrix and the World Population Review list of Global South countries, we can estimate the importance of South–South remittances. Our calculations show that some countries such as Côte d'Ivoire received in 2021 $348 million in remittances from other countries in the Global South, which represents 68.84% of total remittances received. Remittances from the Global South represented 27.07% for Senegal, 31.43% for Nigeria and 36.72% for Ghana. Despite this important share of South–South remittances, the amounts remain underestimated mainly because they do not include the use of informal remittances channels. Hence, according to Clemens and Mckenzie (2014), aggregate growth in remittances over time may be largely due to measurement improvement rather than to growing numbers of migrants or to rising incomes of migrants. The authors estimate that between 1990 and 2010, measurement improvement accounts for 79% of the rise in remittances.

An Example of South–South Remittance Data

For the Central Bank of West African States, that covers WAEMU countries, transfers in the region are recorded through bank transfers, postal administrations, Money Transfer Companies (MTCs) and foreign banknotes noticed during foreign exchange operations (BCEAO, 2013). Within the WAEMU, postal institutions have the advantage of being spread across the country and being accessible to many. According to Clotteau and Ansón (2011), in sub-Saharan Africa, post offices have a larger geographical coverage, and 80% of them are located in rural areas where also nearly 80% of people live. Transfers received by Burkina Faso's Laposte (post offices) between 2019 and 2020 give insight into South–South remittances, as Laposte represents the main money transfer company in Burkina Faso. Though these inflows only capture a fraction of remittances, the data show that during these two years, transfers rose and the country received more than 57 billion CFA or US$86 million. Money sent from the Global South represented 33.59% of total transfers received during this period, of which Côte d'Ivoire represented 53.9%. The other main sources are the United States and Europe, with 24.87% and 20.17% respectively. Côte d'Ivoire is the main destination country of the majority of Burkinabè migrants (Dabiré et al., 2009), thanks to colonialism, and the economic attraction of the country (see Dabiré & Soumahoro, in this volume). In the case of Kenya, Muguna (2018) shows that South–South remittances represented up to 20% of total remittances, and that the total amounts have been rising. Her work also highlights the fact that remittances sent from the Global South rose faster than those from the Global North between 2012 and 2014, 28% and 18% respectively. The main Global South senders to Kenya are Tanzania, Uganda, South Africa and India.

Remittances Impact on Development: Diaspora Finance

Remittances, which are constantly increasing according to the World Bank, constitute a significant source of income for the families of migrants in the country of origin (Asiedu & Chimbar, 2020). They enable these families to cope with endogenous shocks, but also exogenous ones such as global health crises. Remittances' impact on broader development challenges has been thoroughly discussed in the literature, including their impact on poverty (Acosta et al., 2008), on inequalities (Chauvet & Mesplé-Somps, 2007) on consumption instability (Combes & Ebeke, 2011), on mitigating the effects of natural disasters (Mohapatra et al., 2012) and on their general impact on development (De Paoli & Mendola, 2017). However, their origin is not usually clearly distinguished, so we cannot be certain about whether South–South remittances have distinct effects from North–South remittances. Nevertheless, some examples of South–South studies exist. For example, Tapsoba (2022) focused on the effect of remittances on households' livelihood in the Burkina Faso-Côte d'Ivoire corridor, showing that remittances from Côte d'Ivoire rose during the COVID-19 pandemic and that households that received remittances during this period were less likely to report a negative effect of COVID-19 on their livelihood. In the case of Kenya, Muguna (2018) found that remittances from Kenyan diaspora living in developing countries have had a positive effect on Kenya's GDP and overall development (Muguna, 2018).

Beyond direct remittances, diasporas[6] and migrants direct capital flows and investments towards origin countries (Kugler et al., 2018). In fact, they can support the development of capital markets in their origin countries by enabling the country to diversify investors, introduce new financial products and provide a reliable source of funding, for example, using diaspora bonds (World Bank Group, 2019). As in the case of remittances, there is very little specific analysis of South–South initiatives. Countries do however develop initiatives to foster diaspora investment from the Global South. For example, the treaty of friendship and cooperation between Burkina Faso and Côte d'Ivoire is intended to be a platform for exchanges between the two countries, but also a place for the creation of opportunities for diaspora members wanting to invest in their origin country. Some investors try to attract diaspora investment by offering services that facilitate their investment in real estate, regardless of their destination country. Enterprises, therefore, design special packages for diasporas, especially in Côte d'Ivoire, where the majority of Burkinabè migrants reside (Lefaso.net, 2022).

Mapping 254 diaspora development initiatives in the world, Gelb et al. (2021) found that the two main recipient regions are Africa with 97 initiatives, followed by Asia with 69. But none of these were targeting South–South migration. Some are accompanied by remittances, but overall they concern areas like knowledge sharing, diaspora direct investment in productive activities in origin countries from enterprises connected to diasporas (Rodriguez-Montemayor, 2012), collective remittances for social investments and diaspora bonds and loans (Gelb et al., 2021). For example, the Burkina Faso diaspora in Italy is organised in associations, which contributed to the establishment of development infrastructure in their region of origin, to set up agricultural cooperatives (IOM, 2016). This Italian diaspora invests heavily in the Centre-Est region of Burkina Faso, especially in real estate, education and health (ARBI, 2022). According to the African Development Bank, remittances by better qualified or higher paid migrants from France to the Comoros, Mali, Senegal and Morocco earmarked for real estate investment can account up to 25–60% of all remittances sent (African Development Bank, 2009).

Trade Flows

Bilateral trade flows between the home and host countries may be facilitated by immigrants' ties to their country of origin. Nowadays, it is commonly acknowledged that immigration can increase bilateral commerce through two key mechanisms: immigrant preference effects and transaction cost effects. Because they are more knowledgeable about their native markets, languages, conventions, business practices and laws, immigrants can reduce the costs associated with commercial transactions. When the host and home countries have extremely dissimilar cultures, languages and institutional structures as well as when there are limited sources of information available, this direct trade-stimulating impact is likely to be greatest—that is, when the resulting informal trade barriers are at their highest level (Genç, 2014). The impact of transaction costs is anticipated to extend to both imports and exports. In contrast, immigrant preference effects are anticipated to increase solely imports into the host nation since they come about through the consumption channel because of immigrants' demand for goods from their native countries. It is also likely that the demand for these products rises among the host community as well, perhaps because of the demonstration effect influencing native inhabitants' choices. However, if there are enough immigrants over time for native companies to begin manufacturing those goods, there may also be a countervailing immigrant substitution effect (Genç, 2014).

Global trade patterns have evolved as South–South mobility has increased, shaping, and changing the flow of resources among migrants, including the trading of goods and services. Trade flows are one of the ways that migration affects socioeconomic growth. In the past, there has been limited research on migration, trade flows and development in the Global South, even though studies on trade flows (goods and services) as they are influenced by migration have been explored for the North–North and North–South corridors. According to a study of the literature on the Global South, trade flows among migrants in the form of products frequently outpace trade flows in services between nations (Ehrhart et al., 2014; Müller, 2019). Clothing, shoes, cosmetics, leather, electronic appliances, mobile phones and furniture are examples of manufactured commodities that are transferred between countries of origin and destination supported by migrants. Migration-driven trade flows have an impact on national and personal development in both the country of origin and the country of destination. As a result, improving one's own living situation as well as that of their entire family is related to the necessity to migrate to other nations, which has ramifications for the socioeconomic development of other countries.

Data on South–South trade flows are scarce and, in many cases, even when available, difficult to verify. According to the Chinese customs authorities, trade between China and Africa surged in 2022 to a record US$282 billion (11% year-on-year increase) explained by soaring commodity prices, China's reopening and Beijing's recent push to boost imports from Africa.[7] In terms of the breakdown of the trade data, according to Chinese customs authorities, exports to Africa totalled US$164.49 billion for 2021 (an increase of 11.2% year on year), and imports from Africa to China rose at a similar rate to reach US$117.51 billion in the same period.

In 2020, the largest exporter to China from Africa was South Africa, followed by Angola and the Democratic Republic of Congo. In terms of Chinese exports to Africa, Nigeria remained the largest buyer, followed by South Africa and Egypt.

China's FDI to sub-Saharan Africa has also seen a considerable increase since the 2000s. As shown in Fig. 24.1, Chinese FDI to Africa had increased from close to nothing in 2003 to over US$5 billion by 2008. While Chinese FDI to Africa has been relatively stable since 2009 (just under US$5 billion), US FDI to Africa which was in excess of US$10 billion in 2009 has since declined considerably. The top four (4) sectors in Africa that have received Chinese investments are the energy sector, followed by the transport sector, then metals and real estate.

With regard to other South–South trade, the International Trade Center suggests that there is more than $1 billion in two-way trade potential between Africa and the Caribbean, covering both goods and services. The ITC (2022) contends that the two regions currently ship less than 1% of their exports to each other. African exports to the Caribbean, and Caribbean exports to Africa reached their peak in 2014 but have since declined, and for 2020 were less than 0.1% of each region's total exports. The decline in mutual exports in 2020 is largely attributed to the pandemic.

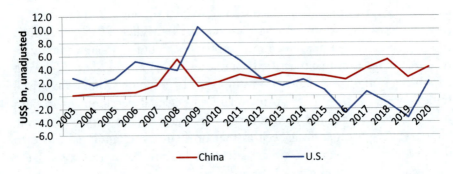

Fig. 24.1 Chinese FDI vs. US FDI to Africa, flow

Within Africa, Northern Africa is observed to be the leading African exporter to the Caribbean (42%), followed by Western Africa (28%), then Southern Africa (23) and then Eastern Africa (7%). Primary minerals and metals account for the bulk of Africa's export to the Caribbean, whereas chemicals are the major items exported to Africa from the Caribbean. Collaborative efforts by ITC and Afreximbank hope to nudge more South–South trade flows between the two regions in the next five years.

Goods Trade Flows

The effects of migration on trade flows are large for nations in the Global South as compared to the Global North or between the Global North and the South, according to studies that have examined trade flows among migrants in countries of origin and destination. For instance, it has been found that migrants in the African region encourage the export of commodities from their place of origin by enhancing information on trading opportunities and product information, as well as by assisting to enforce contracts in a setting with an inadequate institutional framework (Ehrhart et al., 2014). In trade connections between developing nations, it has been found that migrants have a pro-exports influence that is especially significant for African countries (Ehrhart et al., 2014). This result has been attributed to the fact that African nations face particularly high trade hurdles that can be surmounted by migrant networks, including weak legal systems and little to no knowledge of available global commercial opportunities. Around 50% of African migrants remain inside the continent, with North Africa emerging as the top destination (IOM, 2022, 61). These nations host between 1.5 and 2.5 million foreign migrant workers and refugees.[8] Studies examining how immigration affects trade flows in Global South countries include those by Karayil (2007) on India and the Gulf Cooperation Council, Kerby (2018) on Asia and South Africa, Cissé (2013) on Chinese migrants in Senegal and African migrants in China. All these studies have discovered a strong positive impact of the immigrant population on trade flows and the socioeconomic growth of both the country of origin and the country of destination, as well as between immigrants and locals in the country of destination.

Studies in the field of Sino-African migration studies have frequently provided insights into South–South migration related to commercial flows and socioeconomic growth (African migrants in China and Chinese migrants in Africa) (see also Teye et al., in this volume). Although reliable statistics are hard to come by China, Africa's top commercial partner is home to an estimated 500,000 African migrants. Many of them live and operate their own companies in the South of the nation.[9] One of the few studies looking at the relationship between trade and migration in the context of the African trading community in China has been undertaken by Bodomo (2010). His findings show that migration from Africa has a beneficial and large impact on trade, as well as a socioeconomic contribution that helps China move away from the need for migrant communities in the twenty-first century. In particular, the migrant community in China offers employment prospects for Chinese in China. In addition to serving as mentors to the Chinese employees, they also promoted business links between African clients and their Chinese suppliers (Cissé, 2013). In terms of income, studies have shown that Chinese consumer goods in Senegal have given Chinese the chance to support themselves financially, as well as the creation of entrepreneurship opportunities, the creation of social capital in both the country of origin and the country of destination, and the transmission of business relationships and trading skills to other family members and other traders in the country of origin as well as the country of destination (Cissé, 2013).

Goods and Services Trade Flows

South–South migration and the cross-border flow of integrated trade in commodities and services are used in another category of research. According to Gnimassoun (2020), who investigated whether intra-trade and migration are the main sources of income in Africa, the continent's integration has not been sufficiently strong to have a long-term positive, meaningful and robust impact on real per capita income in Africa. Although only through international migration, it does seem to dramatically increase income in the short and medium run. Research by the International Organisation for Migration (IOM) (2022) shows that the movement of goods and services suggests that contributions are typically localised in the host areas where they operate rather than being always direct to the national treasury per se. According to IOM (2022), immigrant-owned enterprises contribute to the economic and social well-being of the communities where they are based in Johannesburg. They close the employment gap in these impoverished areas by not only employing themselves as business owners but also South Africans and other immigrants.

Informal Trade Flows

In the context of informal trade in the developing world, people also cross borders to sell little quantities of items as street vendors, for instance. These people are not precisely categorised as migrants. The economic crises of the 1980s in Latin America led to an increase in the proportion of migrant workers who are self-employed as well as those who work in services and commerce. For example, a significant Dominican Republic border town twice a week grants Haitian traders access to markets without immigration scrutiny (Ratha & Shaw, 2017). For a long time, traders from Mozambique and other southern African nations have frequently entered South Africa, typically on visitor visas that do not authorise trading. For a variety of reasons, including trade, Angolans enter Namibia. Although it does not constitute migration in the legal sense, what migrants from northern neighbours call "suitcase trading" has reached significant levels in Turkey (Ratha & Shaw, 2017). Informal trade should be seen as an integral component of a broader movement of goods. Informal sector cross-border trade provides support, income and direct investment in development to a significant number of people in the region. It also forms an integral part of the African regional economy (Peberdy, 2000). According to the literature, there are several reasons why people engage in informal commerce, including self-employment, the need to subsist, and serving as a stopgap for jobless people who, given the chance, would swiftly quit it in favour of paid employment.

A review of the literature shows that long-standing agreements facilitate migration between countries in the Global South along with allowing the free passage of migrants and trade, with little monitoring, which serves as an opportunity for resource flows in the form of trade that is easily transmitted across countries relative to transmissions between the Global South and Global North. These transmissions are improved by using diaspora networks to get around trade restrictions and lower trade-related transaction costs for both the countries of origin and the countries of destination. Therefore, interest in trade among migrants within the Global South has increased in terms of impacts on both the origin and destination countries' socioeconomic development due to its unpredictable influence compared to trade flows among migrants between the global north and the Global South. Genc et al. (2012) show that a 10% increase in the number of immigrants can cause trade to grow by 1.5% on average. Others have also shown that bilateral trade is higher when the size of the inward migration corridor is larger (see Fagiolo & Mastrorillo, 2014). Overall, therefore, it is clear from the evidence that the presence of large diasporas in a country correlates with trade.

Knowledge

We focus in this section on knowledge as an asset or productive resource, that is, a useful or valuable possession able to be used in future income and wealth generation activities and which will enhance development. Of course, knowledge flows also enable other activities such as consumption, or political and social engagement, but these are not the primary concern here. Knowledge is understood to be structured and organised information capable of being transferred, that is, of *flowing*. The section surveys three bodies of literature on international knowledge flows linked with migration and human mobility, arguing that the conception of knowledge is often static, and too narrowly focused on high- and mid-skill technical and managerial activities. Knowledge related to "low" skills is largely ignored, while the Global South is presented primarily as a recipient of knowledge from the Global North, rather than as itself a source and creator of knowledge. There is almost no literature on South–South knowledge flows, and no aggregate data given the absence of a common metric as well as the fact that so much knowledge flow is informal. We would argue that an adequate understanding of these aspects is possible only through critical engagement with the inadequate conceptions of knowledge in the literature.

Migration-linked knowledge flows have been most commonly studied in the context of the "brain drain", the idea that migration of high- and mid-skill people (as conventionally understood) from the Global South to the Global North countries severely decreases the skills pool in sending countries. The notion of the "brain drain" excludes South–South migration virtually by definition. The "brain drain" effect has a long and contested history including many empirical analyses (Grubel & Scott, 1966; Bhagwati & Hamada, 1974, and Baldwin, 1970, are early examples; Kerr, 2008, and Berger, 2022 provide recent overviews). Policies to stem the flow of migrants through quotas on out-migration or in-migration have not worked well (Clemens & Sandefur, 2014). But the literature identifies a range of other "brain *re*-distribution" processes, linked to migrations of different durations and frequencies, which might offset a "brain drain" (Agrawal et al., 2011; Kone & Özden, 2017; Lowell & Findlay, 2001; Wickramasekara, 2002; Williams & Baláž, 2008a). These include:

- "Brain gain"—expanded mid-level skills training provision in sending countries to increase retention numbers, as in the Global Skills Partnerships mentioned in the Global Compact on Migration, Objective 19e (Clemens, 2014)

- "Brain circulation"—permanent or temporary return migration
- "Brain banks"—diaspora networks facilitating access to knowledge from both diasporas and natives in destination countries
- "Brain exchanges"—temporary work-related movement of skilled people
- "Brain training"—movement for short-term training.

Research has also indicated that migration may increase individuals' incentive to invest in training, resulting in "brain overflow" (skilled unemployment) in origin countries, while South-to-North migration of skilled people can produce "brain waste", in other words migrant underemployment (relative to their skills) in destination countries (Williams & Baláž, 2008a).

Policy debate on "brain distribution" focuses largely on the movement of people with high- and medium skills and on their technical or managerial knowledge. The higher earnings of these migrants are justified by the higher productivity and "scarcity value" of their knowledge. Knowledge is implicitly understood as a "substance" transferable through formal instruction and direct interaction, with acquisition by recipients assured through skills certification. Little attention is paid to "low-skill" people and their knowledge—the oft-used phrase "knowledge workers" is revealing—or non-certifiable transfer processes (Williams & Baláž, 2008a, 2008b), although these are likely more common in South–South flows.

As with financial flows, knowledge flows back to origin countries may be significantly enhanced if an organised diaspora participates in structured "brain distribution" mechanisms. A recently compiled global database of 254 diaspora investment schemes identified 143 (56%) which were either directly knowledge-focused or involved company equity investments which usually involve both financial and knowledge flows (Gelb et al., 2021). Significantly, in *none* of these schemes was the knowledge-sending country located in the Global South. There is plenty of evidence of how diasporas and diaspora organisations have contributed, through knowledge as well as finance, to economic development (not simply growth narrowly defined) in origin countries (Brinkerhoff, 2016; Kuznetsov, 2006; Newland & Tanaka, 2010; Plaza & Ratha, 2011; Saxenian, 2005), but this literature entirely ignores the potential of diasporas located in the Global South. For example, Plaza and Ratha's (2011) important volume on African diasporas and development has only one chapter (by Crush, 2011) on diasporas within Africa, which does not mention knowledge flows. There is also a large body of work on Indian diasporas in the Global South (see several chapters in Hegde & Sahoo, 2018, for example), but work on their contribution to development largely ignores the Global South (see Naujoks, 2018; Kapur, 2001, 2010).

On the other hand, the growing body of material on South–South migration, largely focuses on China (Giese & Marfaing, 2019; Lampert & Mohan, 2019; Mohan et al., 2014; Min Zhou, 2017) and India (Hegde & Sahoo, 2018) does not explicitly examine knowledge flows associated with Global South diasporas, even when concerned with economic development.

Knowledge flows linked to company equity ownership are the focus of the second body of literature of interest, on foreign direct investment (FDI). There is a presumption that foreign corporations transfer technology and skills (that is, knowledge) from home to the host economy. Knowledge is diffused both inside the company via employee training, and to local businesses including suppliers, competitors and new businesses established by former employees (Dunning & Lundan, 2008). The focus is again on high- and medium-skill technical and managerial knowledge, with knowledge conceptualised as a transferable, accumulable "substance" or object. But this literature does recognise the centrality of the *tacit* or uncodifiable dimension of knowledge (as defined by Polanyi), meaning that transfer depends significantly on interpersonal interactions, and therefore on the movement (usually temporary) of employees, especially managers and high-skill employees.

Until recently almost all FDI into the Global South came from the Global North, so the Global South was seen exclusively as a recipient rather than the source of FDI-linked knowledge flows. But as noted above, South–South FDI has increased rapidly in the past two decades, most prominently out of China. It can be argued that South–South investment (and its associated human mobility) facilitates more knowledge transfer than North–South, since the "technology gap" between home and host economy is smaller since the technology or knowledge (including machinery but also organisational structures and practices) is already adapted to "southern" operating environment features such as deficient infrastructure and widespread informality of firms and markets and regulation (Gelb, 2005; UNCTAD, 2006).Case studies of China-Africa FDI show that there is significant knowledge flow from China to Africa (Bräutigam, 2009; Calabrese & Tang, 2022; Oya & Schaefer, 2019) while Gelb (2014) looks at two-way flows between South Africa and China and India. Outward FDI from the Global South has also increased to the Global North, often explicitly intended to enable the South investor to learn—acquire technology and operational knowledge. Though this reverses the direction of flow, which is now from host to home economy, the knowledge flow remains North-to-South.

The third body of literature is the growing interest in migration-linked entrepreneurship, both "entrepreneur FDI" (EFDI) in migrants' destination countries (Granovetter, 1995; Portes et al., 2002; Portes & Yiu, 2013;

Portes & Martinez, 2020) and "entrepreneur diaspora direct investment" (EDDI) undertaken by returnees to origin countries (Elo & Riddle, 2016; Newland & Tanaka, 2010). Entrepreneurs carry knowledge with them as they move between countries. And because they are migrants, both EFDI and EDDI businesses have a competitive advantage: the entrepreneur's "in-betweenness" links them to networks in *both* diaspora and origin countries, providing sources of knowledge, market information, and even finance inaccessible to their competitors (Brinkerhoff, 2016; Mayer et al., 2015). Both businesses and networks are often family-based and often informal, and linked business operations may span several countries. There are many South–South examples, such as the Chinese diaspora in the rest of Asia (Yeung, 2004), Indian and Chinese diasporas in Africa (Dubey, 2016; Gadzala, 2011; Giese & Marfaing, 2019), Africans in China (Bodomo, 2010; Mathews, 2019) and Africans elsewhere in Africa (Simba & Ojong, 2018; Zack & Estifanos, 2018). But knowledge flows are barely examined explicitly.

The migrant entrepreneur literature points towards recognition that *all* migrants are "knowledgeable", even if "low"- or "unskilled" as conventionally defined. This in turn strongly encourages a shift of conceptual focus from skills to competences, or ability and experience derived from lifelong formal and informal learning (Williams & Baláž, 2008a, 34). Both the FDI and the migrant entrepreneur literatures underline that the Global South is not simply a recipient but a significant source of migration- or mobility-linked knowledge flows. And both literatures also point clearly to the centrality of the movement of people in facilitating knowledge flows: migrants are often boundary spanners and knowledge brokers linking networks or groups of people or organisations across borders (Williams & Baláž, 2008a, 77). In these roles, migrants are knowledge *transformers*, translating—both interpreting and converting to another language—and contextualising the knowledge being transferred, so often in effect creating new knowledge.

This approach also emphasises the tacit aspect of knowledge, elaborating that "tacit" does not mean unstructured or unsystematic knowledge, but also that mobility and human interaction is necessary but not always sufficient to transfer (tacit) knowledge, which might be context-specific, within an organisation or another set of social relations. A shift is needed, from conceptualising knowledge as a "substance" or object stored or passed unchanged between people, to recognising that knowledge is transformed, created or recreated, through its transfer. There are almost no studies using this approach to examine migration-linked knowledge flows, and those that do, focus on South–North knowledge flows. Iskander and Lowe (2011) unpack the interaction between tacit and explicit (codified) knowledge to provide a granular analysis of how Mexican construction workers applied their competencies acquired at home to adapt American technologies and practices—and teach American colleagues—when working on US projects, while still conforming to US regulatory standards. Shan (2020) builds on this by showing how immigrants from both the Global South and the Global North have contributed to transforming practices in the engineering workplaces in Canada.

To conclude this section, then, our understanding of the place of knowledge flows in South–South migration is at a very early stage, and this in turn restricts the potential of such flows to contribute to greater equality and more inclusive development in both origin and destination countries. Progress requires the abandonment of outdated but perhaps entrenched assumptions and mindsets, about what knowledge is, who has the knowledge, how knowledge flows between people and places and what happens to it as it flows.

Conclusion

This brief overview of South–South resource flows, looking at finance, goods trade and knowledge resources, leads to three main concluding points, which we have emphasised throughout the chapter.

The first is that despite the significance of South–South migration as a share of global migration, the literature examining these migration-linked flows has barely begun to address their South–South component, focusing overwhelmingly on North–South flows which might have greater aggregate value (at least in terms of formal market values), but ignores the flows involving the majority of the migrant and diaspora population from the Global South.

The second point is related to the first. An important factor in many South–South resource flows is their informality, in part reflecting the extent to which economic activity and markets in most Global South countries are informal. This includes of course financial and goods flows, but consideration of knowledge flows underlines that all economic activities are to some extent informal, as the transfer of tacit knowledge is inherently informal. A major policy aim for most governments is "formalisation" of informal activities, but it is not always acknowledged that this may have costs as well as benefits, for the origin country's governments and populations as well as for migrants. Macroeconomic impact is enhanced by a shift of remittances (and diaspora finance) from informal to formal, resulting in money inflows being recorded in the official balance of payments and entering the banking system. But low-income migrants will continue to use informal remittance agents until the user cost of formal channels is reduced—which digital finance is now making possible, but these are still less than 3% of global remittances and less than 1% in sub-Saharan Africa (GSMA, 2022)—and until more governments adapt cross-border finance regulation to take account of migrants and diasporas. Goods trade flows may be reduced if informal distribution channels are disrupted or blocked, affecting not only migrants operating retail and wholesale enterprises along the chain but also restricting access for domestic consumers and producers in importing countries and producers in exporting countries.

Thirdly, as the literature cited shows, there is not enough focus on the broad development impact of South–South flows, in particular whether their impacts differ from North–South flows, and if so, how—in degree or in kind, or both. This is important, as while these resource flows broadly have positive impact, they may nonetheless be unequalising, within migrant communities or between migrants and native population in host countries, or between migrant-linked and non-migrant-linked households or businesses within origin countries. Optimising the development impact or resource flows, including addressing such inequalities, requires policy plans and implementation, and in the case of migrant-linked resource flows, this involves action by governments not only in origin countries, but often also those in destination countries. More data and analysis of resource flow impact would help to indicate what governments in the Global South could be doing in relation to mobilising resources from their own migrants and diasporas in other South countries, while also facilitating outward resource flows from migrants from other origin countries resident in their countries, where again the focus is entirely on diasporas in the North.

Acknowledgements This work has been undertaken as part of the Migration for Development and Equality (MIDEQ) Hub. Funded by the UKRI Global Challenges Research Fund (GCRF) (Grant Reference: ES/S007415/1), MIDEQ unpacks the complex and multi-dimensional relationships between migration and inequality in the context of the Global South. More at www.mideq.org.

Notes

1. In the GCM, Objective 18 is "Invest in skills development and facilitate mutual recognition of skills, qualifications and competences" and Objective

1. 19 is "Create conditions for migrants and diasporas to fully contribute to sustainable development in all countries". See UN (2018).
2. See www.knomad.org.
3. Migrants entrust money intended for their parents to a relative going back for visits in the country of origin.
4. Orange.sn.
5. They are the result of three components' summation: (a) current transfers (or workers remittances) which are all transfers directly affecting the level of disposable income (IMF, 2022), (b) compensation of employees which are salaries, wages and other income resulting from border or seasonal workers and non-resident workers, (c) migrant transfers (Ratha, 2003).
6. Diasporas include migrants and the descendants of migrants over more than one generation, that is, all people living (on a temporary or permanent basis) outside the country of their birth or ancestry (Gelb et al., 2021).
7. https://www.scmp.com/news/china/diplomacy/article/3207403/china-africa-trade-hits-record-us282-billion-boost-beijing-and-soaring-commodity-prices?module=perpetual_scroll_0&pgtype=article&campaign=3207403.
8. https://reliefweb.int/report/world/african-migration-trends-watch-2021.
9. https://www.migrationpolicy.org/article/migration-trade-china-africa-traders-face-precarity.

References

Acosta, P., Calderon, C., Fajnzylber, P., & Lopez, H. (2008). What is the impact of international remittances on poverty and inequality in Latin America? *World Development, 36*(1), 89–114.

African Development Bank. (2009). *The Bank's Approach to African Migrant Remittances. The Migration and Development Initiative.*

Agrawal, A., Kapur, D., McHale, J., & Oettl, A. (2011). Brain drain or brain bank? The impact of skilled emigration on poor-country innovation. *Journal of Urban Economics, 69*(1), 43–55.

Ahmed, J., Mughal, M., & Martínez-Zarzoso, I. (2021). Sending money home: Transaction cost and remittances to developing countries. *The World Economy, 44*(8), 2433–2459.

Amuedo-Dorantes, C., & Pozo, S. (2004). Workers' Remittances and the Real Exchange Rate: A Paradox of Gifts. *World Development, 32*(8), 1407–1417. https://doi.org/10.1016/j.worlddev.2004.02.004

ARBI. (2022). *Beguedo en Italie—Projets.* https://www.associazionearbi.it/fr/projets

Asiedu, E., & Chimbar, N. (2020). Impact of remittances on male and female labor force participation patterns in Africa: Quasi-experimental evidence from Ghana. *Review of Development Economics, 24*(3), 1009–1026.

Baldwin, G. B. (1970). Brain drain or overflow? *Foreign Affairs, 48*(2), 358–372.
BCEAO. (2013). *Synthèse des résultats des enquêtes ur les envois de fonds des travailleurs migrants dans les pays de l'UEOMOA*. Direction Générale des Etudes Economiques et de la Monnaie Direction de la Recherche et de la Statistique Service de la Balance des Paiements.
Berger S. (2022). *Brain drain, brain gain and its net effect KNOMAD paper 46 November* (World Bank, Washington DC). https://www.knomad.org/sites/default/files/2022-11/knomad_paper_46_brain_drain_brain_gain_and_its_net_effect_sandra_berger_november_2022.pdf
Bhagwati, J., & Hamada, K. (1974). The brain drain, international integration of markets for professionals and unemployment: A theoretical analysis. *Journal of Development Economics, 1*(1), 19–42.
Bodomo, A. (2010). The African trading community in Guangzhou: An emerging bridge for Africa-China relations. *The China Quarterly, 203*, 693–707.
Bräutigam, D. (2009). *The Dragon's gift: The real story of China in Africa*. Oxford University Press.
Brinkerhoff, J. M. (2016). *Institutional reform and diaspora Entrepreneurs: The in-between advantage*. Oxford University Press.
Calabrese, L., & Tang, X. (2022). Economic transformation in Africa: What is the role of Chinese firms? *Journal of International Development, 35*(1), 43–64.
Chauvet, L., & Mesplé-Somps*, S. (2007). Impact des financements internationaux sur les inégalités des pays en développement. *Revue économique, 58*(3), 735–744.
Clemens, M. (2014). *Global skills partnerships: A proposal for technical training in a mobile world*. CGD Policy Paper 40. Centre for Global Development.
Clemens, M. A., & McKenzie, D. J. (2014). *Why don't remittances appear to affect growth?* Center for Global Development working paper, 366.
Clemens, M., & Sandefur, J. (2014). Let the people go: The problem with strict migration limits. *Foreign Affairs, 93*, 152.
Clotteau, N., & Ansón, J. (2011). *Role of post offices in remittances and financial inclusion*. The World Bank Group documents.
Cissé, D. (2013). South-South migration and Sino-African small traders: A comparative study of Chinese in Senegal and Africans in China. *African Review of Economics and Finance, 5*(1), 17–28.
Combes, J. L., & Ebeke, C. (2011). Remittances and household consumption instability in developing countries. *World Development, 39*(7), 1076–1089.
Crush, J. (2011). Diasporas of the South: Situating the African diaspora in Africa. In S. Plaza & D. Ratha (Eds.), *(2011) Diaspora for development in Africa* (pp. 55–77). World Bank.
Dabiré, B. H., Kone, H., & Lougue, S. (2009). *Recensement général de la population et de l'habitation de 2006. Analyse des résultats définitifs. Thème 8 : Migrations*. Ministère de l'économie et des finances.
de Haas, H., Castles, S., & Mark Miller, J. (2020). *The age of migration: International population movements in the modern world* (6th edn.). Macmillan.

De Paoli, A., & Mendola, M. (2017). International migration and child labour in developing countries. *The World Economy, 40*(4), 678–702.

Dubey, A. K. (2016). The Indian diaspora as a heritage resource in Indo–African relations. In A. Kumar Dubey & A. Biswas (Eds.), *India and Africa's partnership: A vision for a new future* (pp. 115–136). Springer-Verlag, New Delhi and Heidelberg.

Dunning, J. H., & Lundan, S. M. (2008). *Multinational enterprises and the global economy* (2nd ed.). Cheltenham.

Ehrhart, H., Le Goff, M., Rocher, E., & Singh, R. J. (2014). Does Migration Foster Exports? Evidence from Africa. In *Policy Research Working Papers*. The World Bank. https://doi.org/10.1596/1813-9450-6739

Elo, M., & Riddle, L. (2016). *Diaspora business*. Brill, Leiden. Available at: https://doi.org/10.1163/9781848884038_003

Fagiolo, G., & Mastrorillo, M. (2014). Does human migration affect international trade? A Complex-Network Perspective. *PLoS One, 9*(5), e97331.

Feyissa, D. (2022). Beyond economics: The role of social-political factors in Hadiya Migration to South Africa. *Zanj: The Journal of Critical Global South Studies, 5*(1/2), 35–58.

Freund, C. L., & Spatafora, N. (2008). *Remittances: Costs, determinants, and informality*. World Bank Policy Research Working Paper 3704, World Bank: Washington.

Gadzala, A. W. (2011). Chinese and Indian entrepreneurs in the East African economies. In E. Mawdsley & G. McCann (Eds.), *India in Africa: Changing geographies of power* (pp. 88–107). Pambazuka Press.

Gelb, S., (2005). South-South investment: The case of Africa in Africa. In J. J. Teunissen & A. Akkerman (Eds.), *Africa in the World Economy: National, regional and international challenges*. The Hague.

Gelb, S. (2014). *FDI links between South Africa and the BRICs: A firm-level overview*. Working Paper, World Trade Institute, University of Bern; and Mandela Institute, University of Witwatersrand Johannesburg. https://doi.org/10.2139/ssrn.2614350

Gelb, S., Kalantaryan, S., McMahon, S., & Perez-Fernandez, M. (2021). *Diaspora finance for development: From remittances to investment*. Publications Office of the European Union.

Gelb, S., & Krishnan, A. (2018). *Technology, migration and the 2030 Agenda for Sustainable Development*. ODI: London for Swiss Development Corporation. https://www.odi.org/publications/11192-technology-migration-and-2030-agenda-sustainable-development

Genç, M. (2014). The impact of migration on trade. *IZA World of Labor*.

Genc, M., Gheasi, M., Nijkamp, P., & Poot, J. (2012). The impact of immigration on international trade: A meta-analysis. In *Migration impact assessment* (pp. 301–337). Edward Elgar Publishing.

Giese, K. (2019). Business partners and employers: Chinese traders as facilitators of grassroots social innovation in West Africa. In K. Giese & L. Marfaing (Eds.),

Chinese and African entrepreneurs: Social impacts of interpersonal encounters (124–146). Brill, Leiden and Boston.

Gnimassoun, B. (2020). Regional integration: Do intra-African trade and migration improve income in Africa? *International Regional Science Review, 43*(6), 587–631.

Granovetter, M. (1995). The economic sociology of firms and entrepreneurs. In A. Portes (Ed.), *The economic sociology of immigration: Essays on networks, ethnicity, and entrepreneurship*. Russell Sage Foundation, New York.

Grubel, H. B., & Scott, A. D. (1966). The international flow of human capital. *American Economic Review, 56*(1/2), 268–274.

GSM Association. (2022). *State of the industry report on mobile money 2022*. GSMA.

Hegde, R. S., & Sahoo, A. K. (Eds.). (2018). *Routledge Handbook of the Indian diaspora*. Routledge.

IMF. (2022). *Balance of payments manual*, 191.

IOM. (2016). *Etude sur la diaspora Burkinabe au Burkina Faso, en Côte d'Ivoire, en Italie et en France*. https://publications.iom.int/system/files/pdf/etude_sur_la_diaspora_burkinabe_fr.pdf

IOM. (2022). *World migration report 2020*, Geneva.

Iskander, N., & Lowe, N. (2011). *The transformers: Immigration and tacit knowledge development*. NYU Wagner Research Paper, 2011–01.

Kapur, D. (2001). Diasporas and technology transfer. *Journal of Human Development, 2*(2), 265–286.

Kapur, D. (2010). *Diaspora, development, and democracy: The domestic impact of international migration from India*. Princeton University Press.

Karayil, S. B. (2007). Does migration matter in trade? A study of India's exports to the GCC countries. *South Asia Economic Journal, 8*(1), 1–20.

Kerby, E. (2018). Bamboo shoots: Asian migration, trade and business networks in South Africa. *Studies in Economics and Econometrics, 42*(2), 103–137.

Kerr, W. R. (2008). Ethnic scientific communities and international technology diffusion. *The Review of Economics and Statistics, 90*(3), 518–537.

Kone, Z. L., & Özden, Ç. (2017). Brain drain, gain and circulation. In K. A. Reinert (Ed.), *Handbook of globalisation and development* (pp. 349–370). Edward Elgar Publishing.

Kugler, M., Levintal, O., & Rapoport, H. (2018). Migration and cross-border financial flows. *The World Bank Economic Review, 32*(1), 148–162.

Kuznetsov, Y. (Ed.) (2006). *Diaspora networks and the international migration of skills: How countries can draw on their talent abroad*. World Bank Publications.

Lampert, B., & Mohan, G. (2019). A transformative presence? Chinese migrants as agents of change in Ghana and Nigeria. In K. Giese & L. Marfaing (Eds.), *Chinese and African Entrepreneurs* (pp. 147–169). Brill.

Lefaso.net. (2022). *Habitat : CGE IMMOBILIER à la conquête du marché ivoirien*. https://www.consulat-burkinaespagne.org/51465_fr/Habitat-:-CGE-IMMOBILIER-%C3%A0-la-conqu%C3%AAte-du-march%C3%A9-ivoirien/

Lowell, B. L., & Findlay, A. (2001). *Migration of highly skilled persons from developing countries: Impact and policy responses*. International migration papers no. 44, International Labour Organisation, pp.1–34.

Mathews, G. (2019). African cultural brokers in South China. In K. Giese & L. Marfaing (Eds.), Chinese and African Entrepreneurs: Social impacts of interpersonal encounters (pp. 64–83). Brill.

Mayer, S. D., Harima, A., & Freiling, J. (2015). Network benefits for Ghanaian diaspora and returnee entrepreneurs. *Entrepreneurial Business and Economics Review, 3*(3), 95.

Mohapatra, S., Joseph, G., & Ratha, D. (2012). Remittances and natural disasters: Ex-post response and contribution to ex-ante preparedness. *Environment, Development and Sustainability, 14*, 365–387.

Mohan, G., Lampert, B., Tan-Mullins, M., & Chang, D. (2014). *Chinese Migrants and Africa's Development: New Imperialists or Agents of Change?* Zed Books.

Müller, J., (2019). Transient trade and the distribution of infrastructural knowledge: Bolivians in China. *Transitions: Journal of Transient Migration, 3*(1), 15–29.

Muguna, A. C. W. (2018). *South-South migration: The impact of diaspora remittance on national development of Kenya*. Doctoral dissertation, United States International University-Africa.

Naujoks, D. (2018). Paradigms, policies, and patterns of Indian diaspora investments. In R. S. Hegde & A. K. Sahoo (Eds.), *Routledge Handbook of the Indian Diaspora*. Routledge.

Nepal—Malaysia. (s. d.). MIDEQ—Migration for diversity and equality. Consulté 26 décembre 2022, à l'adresse https://www.mideq.org

Newland, K., & Tanaka, H. (2010). *Mobilizing diaspora entrepreneurship for development*. Migration Policy Institute.

Oya, C., & Schaefer, F. (2019). *Chinese firms and employment dynamics in Africa: A comparative analysis*. IDCEA Synthesis Report, SOAS, University of London.

Plaza, S., & Ratha, D. (2011). *Diaspora for development in Africa*. World Bank Publications.

Peberdy, S. (2000). Mobile entrepreneurship: Informal sector cross-border trade and street trade in South Africa. *Development Southern Africa, 17*(2), 201–219.

Portes, A., Guarnizo, L. E., & Haller, W. J. (2002). Transnational entrepreneurs: An alternative form of immigrant economic adaptation. *American Sociological Review*, 278–298.

Portes, A., & Yiu, J. (2013). Entrepreneurship, transnationalism, and development. *Migration Studies, 1*(1), 75–95.

Portes, A., & Martinez, B. P. (2020). They are not all the same: Immigrant enterprises, transnationalism, and development. *Journal of Ethnic and Migration Studies, 46*(10), 1991–2007.

Ratha, D. (2003). Workers' remittances: An important and stable source of external development finance. In World Bank, *Global development finance: Striving for stability in development Finance*. Washington DC. Available at SSRN: https://ssrn.com/abstract=3201568

Ratha, D., & Shaw, W. (2007). *South-South migration and remittances.* World Bank Working Paper 102, World Bank: Washington DC.

Ratha, D., & Shaw, W. S. (2017). *Causes of South-South migration and its socioeconomic effects.* Migration Policy Institute.

Rodriguez-Montemayor, E. (2012). *Diaspora direct investment policy: Options for development.* Policy Brief IDB-PB-183, Inter-American Development Bank, Washington DC. Accessed on 23 Sep 2022 https://publications.iadb.org/publications/english/document/Diaspora-Direct-Investment-Policy-Options-for-Development.pdf

Saxenian, A. (2005). From brain drain to brain circulation: Transnational communities and regional upgrading in India and China. *Studies in Comparative International Development, 40,* 35–61.

Shan, H. (2020). Knowledge 'transfer' as sociocultural and sociomaterial practice. Immigrants Expanding Engineering Practices in Canada. *European Journal for Research on the Education and Learning of Adults, 11*(3), 383–397.

Simba, A., & Ojong, N. (2018). Diaspora networks: A social capital source for entrepreneurship in low-income and emerging economies in Africa. In D. Hack-Polay & J. Siwale (Eds.), *African diaspora direct investment: Establishing the economic and socio-cultural rationale* (pp. 113–143). Palgrave Macmillan.

Tapsoba, T. A. (2022). Remittances and households' livelihood in the context of Covid-19: Evidence from Burkina Faso. *Journal of International Development, 34*(4), 737–753.

United Nations. (2018). *Global compact for safe, orderly and regular migration.* Resolution A/RES/73/195, UN General Assembly, New York, 19 December.

United Nations. (2021). *Global indicators framework, resolution A/RES/71/313.* United Nations.

UNCTAD. (2006). World investment report: FDI from Developing and Transition Economies: Implications for Development, Geneva and NY.

Wickramasekara, P. (2002). *Policy responses to skilled migration: Retention, return and circulation.* International Labour Organization.

Williams, A., & Balaz, M. (2008a). *International migration and knowledge.* Routledge.

Williams, A. M., & Baláž, V. (2008b). International return mobility, learning and knowledge transfer: A case study of Slovak doctors. *Social Science and Medicine, 67*(11), 1924–1933.

World Bank. (2016). *Migration and development. A role for the World Bank Group.* World Bank, Washington DC. https://documents1.worldbank.org/curated/en/690381472677671445/pdf/108105-BR-PUBLIC-SecM2016-0242-2.pdf or https://www.knomad.org/publication/migration-and-development-role-world-bank-group

World Bank Group. (2019). *Leveraging economic migration for development. A briefing for the World Bank board.* World Bank, Washington DC. Accessed on 12 Sep 2022. https://www.knomad.org/sites/default/files/2019-08/World%20Bank%20Board%20Briefing%20Paper-LEVERAGING%20ECONOMIC%20MIGRATION%20FOR%20DEVELOPMENT_0.pdf

World Bank Group/KNOMAD. (2022). *A war in a pandemic. Implications of the Ukraine crisis and COVID-19 on global governance of migration and remittance flows. Migration and Development Brief 36*. World Bank: Washington DC.

World Bank. (2022). *Remittance prices worldwide: Making markets more transparent*. World Bank, Washington DC. Accessible at https://remittanceprices.worldbank.org/

Yeung, H. W. C. (2004). *Chinese capitalism in a Global Era: Towards a hybrid capitalism*. Routledge.

Zack, T., & Estifanos, Y. S. (2018). Somewhere else: Social connection and dislocation of Ethiopian migrants in Johannesburg. *African and Black Diaspora: An International Journal, 16*(2), 149–165. https://doi.org/10.1080/17528631.2015.1083179

Zhou, M. (Ed.) (2017). *Contemporary Chinese Diasporas*. Springer.

Open Access This chapter is licensed under the terms of the Creative Commons Attribution 4.0 International License (http://creativecommons.org/licenses/by/4.0/), which permits use, sharing, adaptation, distribution and reproduction in any medium or format, as long as you give appropriate credit to the original author(s) and the source, provide a link to the Creative Commons license and indicate if changes were made.

The images or other third party material in this chapter are included in the chapter's Creative Commons license, unless indicated otherwise in a credit line to the material. If material is not included in the chapter's Creative Commons license and your intended use is not permitted by statutory regulation or exceeds the permitted use, you will need to obtain permission directly from the copyright holder.

25

South–South Migration and Children's Education: Expanded Challenges and Increased Opportunities

Henrietta Nyamnjoh, Mackenzie Seaman, and Meron Zeleke

Introduction

Children are affected by South–South migration[1] in different ways. Some children migrate themselves while other children do not move but live in households or communities impacted by migration. Such diverse ways to participate in migration—moving or remaining—have different impacts which vary depending on the child, their household, and their community, as well. These differences in turn generate inequalities between children, which may leave some more, less, or differently able to benefit from migration.

This chapter draws on research conducted in Ethiopia and South Africa as part of the work package on childhood inequalities which is part of the

---

[1] We understand migration to encompass the entire spectrum from forced through voluntary migration.

H. Nyamnjoh (✉)
Department of Sociology, University of Cape Town Rondebosch, Cape Town, South Africa
e-mail: henrietta.nyamnjoh@uct.ac.za

M. Seaman
Samuel Hall, Olenguruone Road, Lavington, Kenya
e-mail: mackenzie.seaman@samuelhall.org

M. Zeleke
Addis Ababa University Center for Human Rights, Addis Ababam, Ethiopia

© The Author(s) 2024
H. Crawley and J. K. Teye (eds.), *The Palgrave Handbook of South–South Migration and Inequality*, https://doi.org/10.1007/978-3-031-39814-8_25

Migration for Development and Equality (MIDEQ) Hub.[2] The research examined the needs and experiences of Ethiopian children, including both those who stay back and those in South Africa, and how migration affects childhood inequalities, with a focus on education. The research thus aimed to address a knowledge gap on South–South migration as in such migration contexts, children's experiences have been researched less extensively than in the Global North (Bartlett, 2011).

While existing evidence demonstrates that education affects South–South child migration—such as regarding who migrates (Boyden, 2013)—this chapter focuses specifically on the reverse relationship: how migration affects children in unequal ways in regard to education. Importantly, these inequalities in education have spill-over effects in other areas, which continue over time, and ultimately result in varying degrees of inclusion or exclusion for children in the societies in which they live. Reflecting this, the chapter examines how migration and education interact in complex ways to produce inequalities and impact the social mobility of the children and their households via two case studies on migration: children who stay back in Ethiopia, and the children of Ethiopian migrants in South Africa.

Note on Terminology

This article chooses to use the term "children who stay back" instead of the more common "left-behind children" or "children left behind." Albeit imperfect, rejecting the term "left-behind children" restores some agency to these children, as this term does not necessarily preclude them from the migration decision-making process as "left behind" does. Specifically using the "left behind" terminology removes the agency from children (Mondain & Diagne, 2013) who can participate in the decision to migrate with their parents and who can also influence their parents' migration decision-making (Lam & Yeoh, 2019a). Indeed, even when children are not involved in the decision

---

[2] The Migration for Development and Equality (MIDEQ) Hub unpacks the complex and multidimensional relationships between migration and inequality in the context of the Global South. MIDEQ aims to transform the understanding of the relationship between migration, inequality, and development by decentring the production of knowledge about migration and its consequences away from the Global North towards the Global South. MIDEQ mobilises resources for partners in the Global South to define their own research questions and generate their own knowledge, producing robust, comparative, widely accessible evidence on South–South migration, inequality, and development; and engaging national and regional partners on key policy issues. More at www.mideq.org

of remaining or migrating, they remain agents[3] shaping their own lives and do not remain in stasis (Lam & Yeoh, 2019b)—as the left behind terminology indicates. Children exhibit this agency in varying degrees and in various ways according to the specific context in which they live (Deng et al., 2022). For example, in a systematic review of children's agency in migration contexts, children who stayed back were identified to have expressed agency in four distinct ways: (1) in terms of care provision, (2) how they cope with the absence of their caregivers, (3) initiating communication with their parents, and (4) disclosure or withholding of information (Deng et al., 2022).

Further problematising the term, the lack of agency with which the term "left behind" confers on children, and which in turn impacts how migration actors perceive and treat this group of children, is deeply interconnected with Global North notions of childhood that conceptualise such children as having been deserted. This complicates the term's applicability in South–South migration contexts; The ideal childhood from the Global North undergirding this term often fails to find resonance in Global South contexts where children are embedded in wider households rather than nuclear families (Guo, 2022). As Guo writes:

> Quite often researchers and public media use the category "left-behind children" to describe children whose parents have migrated while overlooking that this presumably universal category reflects an ontological view about an ideal childhood from the Global North… [where] parental migration means that they are "deserted." (Guo, 2022)

For the reasons described above, we choose not to not use the term "left-behind children" in this chapter whilst being cognisant of not wanting to replicate binaries between Global South and North.

Methods

The data presented in this chapter comes from two qualitative studies conducted in Ethiopia and South Africa. The studies focused on understanding the nexus between migration and inequality among children. The qualitative studies focused on how inequalities in education develop in childhood in migration contexts. The two studies took a corridor approach,

---

[3] Agents are "individuals as actors with the ability to make sense of their environment, initiate change, and make choices" (Kuczynski, 2002, 9).

examining migration from Ethiopia to South Africa—a common South–South migration movement in the region (Crawley, 2023; Estifanos and Zack, 2019).

In Ethiopia, the research took place in the Hadiya zone, one of the administrative zones in Southern Nations, Nationalities and Peoples Regional State in Ethiopia, and is a hot spot for migration to South Africa (Kefale & Gebresenbet, 2022). Relevant data was collected through semi-structured interviews (SSIs), key informant interviews (KIIs), focus group discussions (FGDs), and field observations. SSIs were conducted with 25 children at different locations in the Hadiya zone and in the capital, Addis Ababa. Three FGDs were also held with 15 children from migrant households in Bonosha town and the zonal capital, Hosana.

In South Africa, data was collected in the Western and Eastern Cape—provinces with vibrant Ethiopian communities and which had comparatively lower COVID-19 infection rates at the time of data collection. This chapter specifically draws on 12 SSIs with Ethiopian children from primary school to university levels, two FGDs with secondary school Ethiopian children, and two additional FGDs with the mothers of these children from these areas.

Review of the Evidence: Children's Education in Migration Contexts

Much of the literature on inequalities in children's education in migration contexts has focused on the Global North, and further, has examined educational inequalities through the lens of integration barriers (see Bohon et al., 2005; Koehler & Schneider, 2019; McIntyre & Hall, 2020; Mestheneos & Ioannidi, 2002) and how such barriers produce inequalities between non-migrant children and child migrants.[4] Common barriers identified in systematic reviews on child migrants' education trajectories in the Global North include: language barriers; a lack of knowledge of the local school system by parents; disadvantaged socioeconomic background of parents; discriminatory individual, policy, and legal treatment; and economic constraints, among others. There have been additional efforts to take an intersectional approach to such educational inequalities, examining how children's education is affected not just by migration, but by other factors such as gender (see Qin, 2006; Ray, 2022) and intergenerational dynamics (see Wallace et al., 2022).

---

[4] This paper uses the term child migrants to describe children who migrate or children who are descended from migrants themselves.

Educational inequalities among children effected by migration,[5] and between such children and those not effected by migration, are deeply connected with migration's influence on social mobility. This is because of education's potentially positive impact on upward social mobility. Given integration barriers for children affected by migration in the Global North can produce severe educational inequalities among children, the potential of education to promote children and their households' upward social mobility can be consequently constricted in migration contexts. Indeed, research has examined education's specific role in social mobility in the context of child migration, such as how migration constricts education's ability to facilitate upward social mobility (see Papademetriou & Terrazas, 2009) and how migration for children's educational purposes is driven by a desire for upward social mobility (see Browne, 2017). The negative impacts of education barriers on children's upward social mobility can expand to familial outcomes, as well (Wallace et al., 2022). The childhood inequalities in education seen in migration contexts thus have both short-term and long-term consequences on the upward social mobility of entire networks—potentially constraining individuals', households', and communities' ability to reap the full benefits of migration.

Given that much of the focus has been on education of child migrants in the Global North, there are two significant gaps within the research. First, existing research has often failed to examine the impact that migration has on the larger educational inequalities of all children affected by migration, namely those who do not reside in the Global North, like children who stay back. This centring of the research in the Global North has thus the additional consequence that children who are affected by South–South migration, as well as those who remain in the Global South while household members migrate to the Global North, are often ignored. Secondly, the focus of the research in the Global North means that much of the studies have focused on an "us" versus "them" approach to childhood inequalities in migration contexts. The research has thus far focused predominantly on how migration, education, and childhood intersect to develop inequalities between child migrants and non-migrant children in Global North communities of destination (see Borgna, 2015; Entorf & Tatsi, 2009; Hillmert, 2013). Thus, while there exists a relatively robust understanding of how migration generates inequalities between migrant communities and non-migrant communities in the Global North, there is very little understanding of how South–South migration generates educational inequalities transnationally among children

---

[5] Children who are affected by migration refers to both child migrants and those who stay back.

of the same communities within the Global South, such as between children who migrate and children who stay back (Bartlett, 2011), and the implications this has on social mobility.

With the current academic discussion on social mobility and migration calling for an incorporation of transnational, as well as intergenerational perspectives to childhood and migration, space, as well as time are thus emerging as critical lens of analyses for understanding inequalities in migration contexts and their impact on social mobility. Indeed, such analyses better reflect how those effected by migration in the Global South achieve and view their own social mobility, as well. For example, Zeleke (2019) found that even in those circumstances when migrants might have experienced a downward social mobility in communities of destination, these migrants' outlook towards upward social mobility is framed in reference to the result that their migration bears for those who stay back—i.e. transnationally and intergenerationally. This chapter thus aims to expand the evidence base on migration, children's education, and inequalities in the Global South while also assuming a transnational and intergenerational analytical frame which better reflects South–South migration realities.

Examining Childhood, Education, and Inequalities in South–South Migration Contexts

The existing evidence indicates that for many families in the Global South, migration is seen as a way of improving the standard of living of the migrants, as well as the families that stay and contributing to upward social mobility (Nyamnjoh, 2020). Importantly, migration is an opportunity for parents to give their (future) children better education and by extension improved opportunities for sustainable livelihoods such as through remittances or through children migrating alongside them. Providing children improved educational opportunities can represent a compensation for the lack or shortfall of education in parents' own lives, whose educational aspirations at times were halted to pursue migration (see Crivello, 2010; Schewel & Fransen, 2018). Parents thus at times envision education in migration contexts as a way to foster intergenerational upward social mobility—in both communities of destination and origin insofar that education is considered to make the children "become somebody in life" (Crivello, 2010, 402). In South–South migration, education of children thus dovetails intergenerational dependencies transnationally and the roles that children play in mitigating family poverty. Despite these intentions, much like in the Global North, children who migrate are seen to be largely disadvantaged when it comes to educational outcomes compared to non-migrant children in countries of destination (Caarls et al., 2021).

Within this limited evidence base, there have been additional efforts in the South–South child migration literature to take an intersectional approach and connect the educational experiences of child migrants to systemic disadvantage or advantage. A 2016 Human Rights Report which examined Syrian refugee children's access to education in Lebanon indicates that age may be an important factor in inequality production in education among child migrants. The report found that children aged 15 or older faced significant challenges when enrolling in secondary school which did not exist or were less impactful for younger children, such as the lack of availability of Arabic-language education (HRW, 2016). The report identified that this is partially due to the higher requirements of secondary school, as well as the increased social pressure on older children to work. Such educational experiences in South–South migration contexts may produce educational inequalities among children within the same migrant household, as well as between age groups of displaced communities, impacting migration's ability to facilitate upward social mobility. Studies on North–South migration have similarly documented the importance of age in determining educational trajectories (Corak, 2012; Lemmermann & Riphahn, 2018).

Other studies on South–South migration have also indicated how child migrants' experiences in education can diverge to generate larger inequalities—again restricting the ability of education to promote upward social mobility. For example, one study on migration from Haiti to the Dominican Republic found that race played an important role in child migrants' experiences in education—with those children with darker skin colours more targeted for bullying (Bartlett, 2011). Another report on out-of-school migrants in Ghana found that migration did little to mitigate gender norms from children's countries of origin which discouraged girls' school enrolment (Kyereko, 2020). Migration thus not only refracted the gendered inequalities existing among children, but continued to produce them in countries of destination. These nuances emphasise that education's impact on social mobility in migration contexts is mitigated by additional social categories, such as gender, age, and race.

However, in contrast to the literature on the Global North, which extensively focuses on child migrants—namely children who migrate or are descendants of migrants—there have been efforts in the literature on South–South migration to examine how migration produces childhood inequalities transnationally by examining the educational experiences of those who stay back (see Robles & Oropesa, 2011). Specifically, there is an ongoing academic debate on the impact of parental migration on the well-being of such children. Hanson and Woodruff (2003) argue that the migration of a parent positively impacts the schooling of children who stay back and improves their academic performance, which other studies support (see Boyden, 2013; Cebotari et al., 2017; Crivello, 2010). Studies with these arguments approach migration as a household strategy for improving the household's economic standing (Semyonov & Gorodzeisky, 2008; Stark & Bloom, 1985) and focus on remittances as a way to facilitate educational opportunities and attainment among children who stay back (Caarls et al., 2021). Other studies nevertheless highlight how parental migration might negatively affect children's educational motivation such as via remittances reducing children's interest in education because of heightened desires and aspirations to migrate (see Kandel & Kao, 2001; Carling, 2001, 2002). Additionally, emerging evidence suggests that the gender of the parent or caregiver who migrates impacts children's education differently. For example, a study by Dunusinghe (2021) found that educational performance of children in Sri Lanka whose mothers had migrated was lower than those whose fathers had migrated. Conversely, Sun et al. (2020) found that in Mexico, the educational aspirations of girls who stay back are more negatively influenced by their mother's migrating than those for boys.

Thus, like child migrants in South–South migration contexts, the literature on children who stay back in the Global South has at times benefitted from a nuanced approach. A review of the evidence on education, migration, and displacement by UNESCO (2019) identified that gender impacts children who stay back in unique ways—contributing to childhood inequalities and thus migration's ability to facilitate upward social mobility. The report found that in South Africa, migrant families may not benefit from an exemption from school fees, which can negatively impact girls more (UNESCO, 2019). Further, the same review found that in Cambodia, girls who stayed back were significantly more likely to drop out of school than boys who stayed back—as well as more likely to drop out compared to children overall from non-migrant households. This may be associated with an increased care burden girls suffer after a care provider has migrated, a finding evidenced in this review, as well (UNESCO, 2019). Such inequalities spurred on by migration can exacerbate the educational inequalities facing girls in the Global South more generally, expanding the gap between girls' and boys' educational opportunities as well as between girls not impacted by migration and those who stay back. Critically, unable to reap the full benefits of education, girls who stay back may thus find their upward social mobility constrained.

Reflecting the bias in the literature in the Global North, the evidence on children who stay back in the Global South, while incorporating an intergenerational perspective, often compares these children belonging to migrant households to those children belonging to non-migrant households (see Caarls et al., 2021; for a notable exception see Zuccotti et al., 2017). Thus, while the more limited literature in the Global South on educational experiences among children in migration contexts examines educational inequalities more holistically by looking at children affected by migration—rather than just child migrants—it fails to provide a compelling intergenerational *and* transnational understanding of how childhood inequalities are generated depending on how children participate in migration.

A nuanced transnational and intergenerational examination of childhood inequalities in migration contexts, and its impact on social mobility, is thus required to better understand how migration impacts children and their entire ecosystem differently depending on their role in migration process. Importantly, such examinations better reflect the realities of migration where migrants often situate themselves not just in relation to the host communities, but also to those in places of origin (Zuccotti et al., 2017) and to their larger family networks (Eresso, 2019).

Educational Inequalities Among Children Who Stay Back

This section presents the lived experiences of children coming from migrant households in Ethiopia and who stay back. It expands on how migration shapes and impacts children's access to education and educational trajectories of children born in migrant households and how the produced inequalities impact social mobility.

Remittance affects children's access to education in migrant households in Ethiopia. The data from Ethiopia shows that migration via remittances simultaneously leads to a devaluing and valuing of education. In terms of valuing education, KIIs conducted with school principals and teachers in Bonosha town and Hosanna in the Hadiya zone described how the parents who migrate actively invest in the education of their children who stay back in Ethiopia through remittances. During one FGD conducted with school principal and teachers at Hosanna town, a participant expressed the comparative advantage of students coming from migrant households and how such transnational investments produced educational inequalities:

> If one thinks of getting a quality education in Ethiopia, it is clear that one would go for private schools. Hadiya is not an exception in this regard…The ones who can afford the high prices are mostly the diaspora…It is rare to find a migrant in the diaspora sending their children to public schools as that is considered a failure.

Data collected from the private schools in Hosanna and Bonosha towns demonstrate how migrant parents tend to prefer private schools, representing a clear monetary investment in their children's education. Indeed, there is a boom of private schools in the area catering to the high demand from migrant households for such schools.

In response to such investments over time, KIIs recount that following the mass migration of Hadiya migrants to South Africa in the aftermath of the 1990s, there has been a growing inequality regarding children's access to education—children from migrant households more often attend private schools in the zonal capital Hosanna and the district town Bonosha. Unlike the public schools, these private schools offer additional extra-curricular activities, skills training, and have relatively well-equipped libraries and resource centres. Further, returnees and migrants are investors and owners of such private schools in the zone. With its roots in transnational and intergenerational remittance flows, children who stay back thus benefit from the produced inequalities, reaping greater educational opportunities and thus opportunities for upward social mobility.

Importantly, the heightened value of education, particularly private education by migrant parents from Hadiya or return migrants—indicated by their investment in their children's education—is seen as a compensatory investment. While Global North perspectives on such children being deserted (Guo, 2022) would indicate such acts are a way to compensate for parents' absence, the data indicates that parents in Ethiopia rather see remittances as a way to compensate for their own lack of educational attainment intergenerationally. A returnee parent from South Africa who owns an international hotel in Addis Ababa and sends his children to one of the most expensive international schools in Ethiopia voiced this reasoning for investing in his children's education:

> It is not only about the money that I brought from South Africa which I used to invest in the hospitality business I am running. It is also about being able to send five of my children to an international school…I dropped out of school in 11th grade to generate some income so that I could migrate to South Africa. Now that I have invested in my children's education, I feel compensated.

Children born in South Africa or born to a parent owning South African citizenship provide such children of migrant households special access to international schools in Ethiopia.

In addition to getting access to better education at private schools, remittances allow children from migrant households to get additional educational support through paid tutoring and having access to educational support materials. During FGDs with children coming from non-migrant households, the participants of the FGDs emphasised how such differential access to additional educational support sets the boundaries for their own educational achievements:

> One of the key things that sets us [children from non-migrant households] apart is the differential access we both have to different educational support such as paid tutoring. Our parents can hardly afford the essential school goods such as notebooks and stationery let alone paying for a tutor. Most of the kids coming from migrant households have private tutors.

Thus, migration not only impacts on the educational quality children receive, but also access to educational support. Importantly, the data indicate that this inequality is produced by migrant parents and is visible to children themselves—producing a recognised and known inequality among children in Ethiopia.

However, migration also at times led to a devaluing of education specifically by children who stay back. In the data, some children, often whose fathers had migrated, devalued education more than children belonging to non-migrant families. Examining children's educational aspirations via their life dreams indicates how the perceived success stemming from migration to South Africa discredited previous avenues for social mobility, such as education. Among rural communities of high migration in the Hadiya zone, there was, in particular, a growing disinterest in education among the younger generation in favour of migration. A key informant described this phenomenon:

> In my time [in the 1990s], it was education which was sought... [When I passed the national exam], families and neighbours brought to my family 20 coffee pots... Years after, I was no longer the socially attractive person. Less intelligent people who made it to South Africa became the new hero. People now mock me: "What do you have to show for your education?" They would say "Your father has lived in a mud house with a thorn fence before and after university, but look at migrant families who live in fancy houses!"

Indeed, despite benefitting from increased educational opportunities provided by remittances, for most children who stay back, migration was the dream. For most children who stay back, migration was viewed as a more viable livelihood pursuit than pursuing education. Hence, in contrast to investing in their own education, children viewed investing in migration as wiser and more attractive in terms of "value for money." This favouring of migration over education is situated within the broader crisis in the education system—there is a growing belief that one cannot change their life through education and employment within Ethiopia.

Further, data collected from community members, law enforcement, school principals, teachers and students highlight that children coming from migrant households have major issues with discipline. While referring to the difference between the non-migrant and migrant families, the teachers and principals emphasised the lack of discipline of students from migrant households and the challenge of managing such students. A principal of a private school in Bonosha described this challenge:

> They often do not attend school properly, their performance is poor, they view education as valueless. On the contrary, children from the civil servant families or other poor households see education as the way out of poverty, and because of continuous follow-up they get from their parents they perform better in class.

Biniyam,[6] a 14-year-old informant whose parents are in Durban, shared the challenges he was facing due to the strong societal bias and stereotype towards children coming from migrant households:

> I do not get where all these biases towards us come from! Our teachers and the local society consider us to be undisciplined and as if we are all disinterested in education. There is a prejudice that we all want to end up in South Africa, where our parents are. We are not treated well by our teachers and the school community.

Preferring migration over education—despite remittances at times providing greater educational opportunities—thus may flow from both children's own perception that migration is the better investment, but also from a discouraging school environment.

In Ethiopia, migrant parents produce greater opportunities for their children's education via remittances and through foreign documentation. This

---

[6] All names are pseudonyms.

produces an inequality of opportunity, whereby children who stay back benefit from greater access to higher quality education and educational support. Importantly, such investment by parents is seen as a compensatory act for migrant parents' at times own lack of education opportunities and attainment. However, this contrasts with children's own educational experience and desires in the Hadiya zone. The data indicates that these children at times devalue education—having seen the benefits of migration. Further, the absence of these parents produces perceived challenges for educational achievement regarding discipline, and a discouraging school environment. This threatens to produce an inequality in educational attainment—rather than opportunity—between children who stay back and children of non-migrant households.

Children of Those who Left and Educational Inequalities

This section turns to the experiences of second-generation children born of Ethiopian migrants in South Africa and the first-generation—those that joined families through family reunion. It examines how lack of documentation keeps children in a permanent state of uncertainty, and thus inequality. In terms of education, lack of documentation forecloses education as the tool which can facilitate upward social mobility.

Like children who stay back in Ethiopia, in South Africa, Ethiopian parents viewed their children's education as a way to achieve upward social mobility. Such parents believe their children's expanded educational opportunities in South Africa will open up the opportunities for their children to have a better life away from their own "tuck shop mentality"[7], as well as that these children will eventually be the ones to lift them out of poverty (Boyden, 2013; Crivello, 2010). Additionally, parents at times saw their children's education as facilitating "better" migration, such as to Canada. Migrant parents' desire for better educational opportunities and attainment for the next generation should be contextualised against their own lack, where migrant parents' aspiration to migrate had often outweighed that of education (Kuschminder & Siegel, 2014; Kuschminder et al., 2012; Mains, 2012).

Despite the intentions of Ethiopian migrant parents in South Africa, education for their children has been incomplete—not adequately providing access to the labour market and greater educational opportunities. Indeed,

---

[7] Almost all Ethiopians in South Africa operate a grocery corner store in the townships popularly referred to as tuck shops.

despite the improved quality of education that Ethiopian children have received in South Africa, such access has yet to have a substantial and meaningful impact on their lives. This clearly deviates from the intended goals of education unlocking their potential and facilitating upward social mobility across generations. As a result, migration produces pronounced inequalities among children in South Africa, as well as between Ethiopian children in South Africa and those in Ethiopia.

It is predominantly a lack of documentation and the failure to move Ethiopian children from refugee status to either a permanent or temporary resident permit holder that produces their marginal and unequal position in education and keeps them in permanent temporality (Tize, 2021). Keeping Ethiopian children permanently on short-term extended refugee status limits their access to education, as well as ability of education to produce further opportunities that could contribute to their well-being and productivity. For example, even with qualifications obtained, the lack of documentation becomes the grounds to deny such adult children access to employment. This causes anxiety and keeps the families stuck in the stagnant realities of their insecure status (see Tize, 2021).

Maya, a 16-year-old girl, highlights the challenges of having a refugee document and the difficulty of navigating the system to procure documentation that will give her access to study:

> My father took me to Pretoria [from Cape Town] to get a document from Home Affairs. It was a document asked for by my school. And it wasn't a great experience, you can feel a great amount of tension and you can feel that you are unwelcome.

Such documentation challenges are further exemplified by Grace. Grace has studied from primary to tertiary education and is currently a third-year chartered accounting student. In order to complete her degree, she has to enrol for an internship that will assist her to write three articles as part of the requirements to obtain her undergraduate degree. She narrates her ordeals and how the lack of document prohibits her mobility from one stage to the other at the university:

> It was so difficult applying for university. Because I don't have a passport, I am on a refugee's permit.... So it's very difficult to apply to a lot of places…And then I have to apply for an internship and to write an article and for that article as well, everywhere I try to apply, everyone is telling me that I need to have a permanent residency.

Without completing the internship Grace will not graduate and cannot enrol for the honour's programme. It is important to note that Grace arrived in South Africa at the age of 8 in 2009, and as an adult she is still struggling with the issue of documentation. The psychological toll was clear during the interview. Grace's demeanour during the interview immediately changed when she began narrating her ordeals at school. It was evident that she was emotionally drained by this process. The restrictions of refugee status keep Ethiopian students in a constant state of uncertainty, as Grace concludes:

> But now they got back to me and I have one [refugee status] until 2025 I think…But even with that, I can't continue into the next phase of my life. I can't apply for the internship that I need.

Second-generation children born of Ethiopian parents and first-generation children who joined their parents for family reunion like Grace are confronted with ongoing documentation issues even as they enter adulthood. Such educational stagnation potentially constrains opportunities throughout their lives and contributes to further inequalities, such as in the labour market.

Grace and Maya's stories were emblematic of the data. For example, since completing her Matric (high school leaving certificate) in 2020, another 21-year-old girl, Helen, had not yet received her result given her lack of documentation and was consequently unable to enrol in university. Others interviewed were also unable to complete their studies in a timely manner because they were kicked out of the system until the right documentation was provided. This is the situation for 25-year-old Faith; Faith's registration was voided, and she lost a year because not even her asylum documentation was accepted by the school as it was considered to be forged document, of which it was not. Although Faith had finally graduated from university, lack of documentation made it difficult to apply for further studies, as well. Such structural barriers engendered by migration policies limit migrants' ability to contribute to intergenerational upward social mobility via education, as well as produce and expand educational inequalities among children.

Discussion

The experiences of the parents and children presented above produce a complex web of inequalities transnationally (i.e. between children in Ethiopia and first and second-generation children born of Ethiopian migrants in South

Africa and those who came for family reunion respectively) and nationally (among children in South Africa and among children in Ethiopia), with such inequalities being perceived differently across generations. Examining the educational experiences and aspirations of children affected by migration in Ethiopia and South Africa demonstrates that migration is producing childhood inequalities in education transnationally, but its impact intergenerationally is less clear.

In the data, educational inequalities were apparent when comparing children's educational aspirations across the two contexts. For example, the eagerness of first-generation Ethiopian students in South Africa to graduate contrasts with children who stayed back in the Hadiya zone. Children of Ethiopian migrants in South Africa acknowledged the growing value of education to "become somebody" (Crivello, 2010, p. 402), implicitly and explicitly acknowledging the positive impact that education can have on their future livelihoods and that education is an "agency of socialisation" through which, in addition to learning knowledge and skills, children are taught particular norms and attitudes (Boyden, 2013; Schewel & Fransen, 2018, p. 556). In contrast, partly given the crisis in the Ethiopian education system, as well as the physical manifestation of the benefits of migration, children in Hadiya at times rather aspired to migrate than achieve educational success. For these Ethiopian children, the notion that a higher formal qualification is always associated with a reduced unemployment risk (Eggert et al., 2010) is an illusion. Thus, depending on how children participated in migration process—i.e. remained in Ethiopia, reunited with parents in South Africa or born into migration households in South Africa—Ethiopian children valued education differently. However, this devaluation or valuation of education was rooted in both groups' desire for, and perception of what generated, upward social mobility. Those in South Africa aspired to achieve educational success because they perceived it allowed them to achieve upward social mobility—something their parents similarly reflected. In contrast, those in Ethiopia at times devalued education because they did not view it as a way to achieve upward social mobility—for them migration was rather the vehicle—which, conversely, contrasted with their parents' own perceptions. In the data, inequalities in educational attainment, insofar that it is influenced by children's aspirations, thus flowed partially from children's different experience with, and thus perception of, migration and its benefits.

Not only were aspirations, and by extension attainment, impacted by migration, but educational opportunities were additionally unequal between the two groups. For example, those children who stayed back in the Hadiya zone benefited from increased educational opportunities which transnational and intergenerational remittances facilitated. Children who stay back appeared to have better access to education and educational support structures than Ethiopian children of non-migrant households, children who united with family in South Africa, first-generation children born to Ethiopian migrants in South Africa, and their parents. Thus, if they desired, children who stay back could reap the benefits of such greater opportunities and attain a higher level and quality of education. In contrast, that Ethiopian migrant children in South Africa remain on refugee status produced a stymied access to education in comparison to those children who stayed back in Ethiopia. These children in South Africa were unable to securely access education. Despite valuing schooling more consistently, in the South African context such restrictions made the opportunities for an improved standard of living and thus upward social mobility via education unlikely. In the data, migration thus produced clear inequalities in terms of education access, and by consequence also attainment, which privileged children who stayed back over those who were born to Ethiopian parents in South Africa.

As indicated, the educational inequalities and upward social mobility of children were contextualised not just across the transnational community, but intergenerationally within the family, as well. For example, data from both Ethiopia and South Africa demonstrates the esteem that parents place on education, as in both contexts children's education was seen as a way for parents to compensate for their own lack of educational attainment and the elevation of the children as the hope and future to improve the families' livelihood. In this way, parents saw migration as facilitating upward social mobility intergenerationally by allowing for greater quality of educational opportunities—regardless of whether children held similar beliefs. Many in the data viewed migration as a way to provide greater opportunities to the next generation—which at times succeeded and thus produced inequalities between Ethiopian migrant and non-migrant households.

Further, in Ethiopia and South Africa, upward social mobility was measured in similar ways vis-à-vis the ability to speak English. Speaking English thus served as a key demarcation of inequalities. In South Africa, despite the challenges posed by access to documentation, parents still appreciated the standard of education that their children received with their children's ability to speak English better than their counterparts in Ethiopia attesting to a perceived better education. Likewise, one of the key variables used to measure the positive impact of migration on educational attainment of children at the place of origin, Ethiopia, is the access children who stay back have in learning English at an earlier age. In public schools in Ethiopia English language is taught as a single subject starting from Grade 1 where all other subjects are taught in local languages. Private schools often offer additional English lessons starting from preschool at kindergartens through extra-curricular activities such as reading clubs. Thus, across the two contexts, parents saw children as achieving upward social mobility intergenerationally via education, with migration opening up such educational avenues.

However, nuancing the intergenerational social mobility is the lived experiences of the children themselves where the perceptions of the inequalities varied. For example, speaking English was a point of pride for respondents in South Africa—and perhaps a way to compensate for migration-produced educational inequalities between children in Ethiopia and Ethiopian migrant children in South Africa. Thus, despite suffering from more restricted education access, particularly after primary education, which is compulsory for all children in South Africa, the children in South Africa themselves experienced this inequality less overtly and instead used their English language ability as a way to position themselves as better than those who stayed back in Ethiopia. Children, similar to parents, thus often viewed their educational experience as better because of migration. While these perceptions at times contradicted the documented experiences of such children—particularly in South Africa, it is important to recognise that for these children migration was a source of opportunity, rather than inequality. Such a finding emphasises the importance of grounding inequalities in the perceptions of children themselves.

Conclusion

The two case studies presented above demonstrate that migration produces inequalities which have intergenerational roots and impacts, and which also vary across space—depending on the reference frame used for discussing the educational inequalities. The inequalities also influence what is seen as facilitating upward social mobility over time, as well as migration's ability to contribute to the upward social mobility of children affected by migration and their larger networks.

That migration produces inequalities in generationally and geographic-specific ways highlights the need to incorporate for incorporating such time and space analyses to future examinations on children, migration, and inequalities. The corridor approach taken in these case studies specifically allows for such analyses by contextualising the experiences of children impacted by migration transnationally. Such a fluid approach to migrant communities is more reflective of the experiences of children affected by migration and their wider network which perceives inequalities and social mobility within communities and across generations.

Acknowledgements The authors would like to thank Nassim Majidi for her input and expert guidance in the development of this chapter. This work has been undertaken as part of the Migration for Development and Equality (MIDEQ) Hub. Funded by the UKRI Global Challenges Research Fund (GCRF) (Grant Reference: ES/S007415/1), MIDEQ unpacks the complex and multi-dimensional relationships between migration and inequality in the context of the Global South. More at www.mideq.org

References

Bartlett, L. (2011). South-south migration and education: the case of people of Haitian descent born in the Dominican Republic. *Compare: A Journal of Comparative and International Education, 42*, 1–22. https://doi.org/10.1080/03057925.2011.633738

Bohon, S. A., Macpherson, H., & Atiles, J. H. (2005). Educational barriers for new latinos in Georgia. *Journal of Latinos and Education, 4*, 43–58. https://doi.org/10.1207/s1532771xjle0401_4

Borgna, C., (2015). *Migration, education, and inequality. Which European educational systems provide fair opportunities to learn?* (WZB Report).

Boyden, J. (2013). 'We're not going to suffer like this in the mud': educational aspirations, social mobility and independent child migration among populations living in poverty. *Compare: A Journal of Comparative and International Education, 43*, 580–600. https://doi.org/10.1080/03057925.2013.821317

Browne, E. (2017). Evidence on education as a driver for migration. Knolwledge, evidence and learning for Development. https://opendocs.ids.ac.uk/opendocs/bitstream/handle/20.500.12413/13050/K4D_HDR_%20Migration%20and%20Education.pdf?sequence=1&isAllowed=y. Accessed 17 March 2023.

Caarls, K., Cebotari, V., Karamperidou, D., Conto, M.C.A., Zapata, J., & Zhou, R.Y., (2021). *Lifting barriers to education: Improving education outcomes for migrant and refugee children in latin America and the Caribbean.* UNICEF Office of Research – Innocenti, Florence.

Carling, J. (2001). *Aspiration and ability in international migration: Cape Verdean experiences of mobility and immobility.* University of Oslo, Centre for Development and the Environment.

Carling, J. (2002). Migration in the age of involuntary immobility: Theoretical reflections and Cape Verdean experiences. *Journal of Ethnic and Migration Studies, 28*, 5–42.

Cebotari, V., Mazzucato, V., & Siegel, M. (2017). Gendered perceptions of migration among ghanaian children in transnational care. *Child Indicators Research, 10*, 971–993. https://doi.org/10.1007/s12187-016-9407-x

Corak, M., (2012). Age at immigration and the education outcomes of children. In A. S. Masten, K. Liebkind, & D. J. Hernandez (Eds.), *Realizing the potential of immigrant youth, the Jacobs foundation series on adolescence* (pp. 90–114). Cambridge University Press. https://doi.org/10.1017/CBO9781139094696.006

Crawley, H., Seaman, M., Ghimire, A., Rbihat, R., Sangli, G., & Zeleke, M. (2023). *From left behind to staying back: Changing how we think about children in migrant households*. (Discussion Paper) (pp. 1–24). United Nations University.

Crivello, G. (2010). 'Becoming somebody': Youth transitions through education and migration in Peru. *Journal of Youth Studies, 14*, 395–411.

Deng, Z., Xing, J., Katz, I., & Li, B. (2022). Children's behavioral agency within families in the context of migration: A systematic review. *Adolescent Research Review, 7*, 1–61. https://doi.org/10.1007/s40894-021-00175-0

Dunusinghe, P. (2021). Impact of parental migration on children's educational performance: Evidence from Sri Lanka. *Journal of Economics and Development Studies, 9*, 35–49.

Eggert, W., Krieger, T., & Meier, V. (2010). Education, unemployment and migration. *Journal of Public Economics, 94*, 354–362. https://doi.org/10.1016/j.jpubeco.2010.01.005

Entorf, H., & Tatsi, E. (2009). Migrants at school: Educational inequality and social interaction in the UK and Germany (IZA Discussion Paper No. 4175). Rochester, NY.

Eresso, M.Z., (2019). Social inequality and social mobility: the construed diversity of Ethiopian female labor migrants in Djibouti. *African Human Mobility Review, 5*, 1749–1773. https://doi.org/10.14426/ahmr.v5i3.890

Estifanos, Y. S., & Zack, T. (2019). *Follow the money: Tactics, dependencies and shifting relations in migration financing on the Ethiopia—South Africa migration corridor* (Working Paper 63). University of Witwatersrand and the University of Sussex.

"Growing Up Without an Education:" Barriers to Education for Syrian Refugee Children in Lebanon. (2016). Human Rights Watch.

Guo, K. (2022). *Reframing 'left-behind' children: Normative understandings, local practices and socio-economic hierarchies | Reimagining childhood studies*. https://reimaginingchildhoodstudies.com/reframing_left_behind_children/

Hanson, G., & Woodruff, C. (2003). *Emigration and educational attainment in Mexico* (UCSD Working Paper). University of California at San Diego.

Hillmert, S. (2013). Links between immigration and social inequality in education: A comparison among five European countries. *Research in Social Stratification and Mobility, 32*, 7–23. https://doi.org/10.1016/j.rssm.2013.02.002

Kandel, W., & Kao, G. (2001). The impact of temporary labor migration on Mexican children's educational aspirations and performance. *The International Migration Review, 35*, 1205–1231.

Kefale, A., & Gebresenbet, F. (2022). *Youth on the move: Views from below on Ethiopian international migration.* Oxford University Press.

Koehler, C., & Schneider, J. (2019). Young refugees in education: The particular challenges of school systems in Europe. *Comparative Migration Studies, 7*, 28. https://doi.org/10.1186/s40878-019-0129-3

Kuschminder, K., & Siegel, M. (2014). *Migration & development: A world in motion Ethiopia country report.* Maastricht University.

Kuschminder, K., Siegel, M., & Andersson, L. (2012). Profiling Ethiopian migration: A comparison of characteristics of Ethiopian migrants to Africa, the Middle East and the North. In C. U. Rodrigues (Ed.), *Crossing African borders: Migration and mobility.* Center of African Studies (CEA), ISCTE-IUL, University Institute of Lisbon.

Kuczynski, L. (Ed.). (2002). Beyond bidirectionality: Bilateral conceptual frameworks for understanding dynamics in parent–child relations. In *Handbook of dynamics in parent-child relations* (pp. 3–24). SAGE Publications.

Kyereko, D. O. (2020). Education for all: The case of out-of-school migrants in Ghana. In M. L. McLean (Ed.), *West African youth challenges and opportunity pathways, gender and cultural studies in Africa and the diaspora* (pp. 27–52). Springer International Publishing. https://doi.org/10.1007/978-3-030-21092-2_2

Lam, T., & Yeoh, B. S. A. (2019a). Parental migration and disruptions in everyday life: Reactions of left-behind children in Southeast Asia. *Journal of Ethnic and Migration Studies, 45*, 3085–3104. https://doi.org/10.1080/1369183X.2018.1547022

Lam, T., & Yeoh, B. S. A. (2019b). Under one roof? Left-behind children's perspectives in negotiating relationships with absent and return-migrant parents. *Population, Space and Place, 25*, 1–10. https://doi.org/10.1002/psp.2151

Lemmermann, D., & Riphahn, R. T. (2018). The causal effect of age at migration on youth educational attainment. *Economics of Education Review, 63*, 78–99. https://doi.org/10.1016/j.econedurev.2017.11.001

Mains, D., (2012). *Hope is cut: Youth, unemployment, and the future in urban Ethiopia.* Temple University Press.

McIntyre, J., & Hall, C. (2020). Barriers to the inclusion of refugee and asylum-seeking children in schools in England. *Educational Review, 72*, 583–600. https://doi.org/10.1080/00131911.2018.1544115

Mestheneos, E., & Ioannidi, E. (2002). Obstacles to refugee integration in the European Union member states. *Journal of Refugee Studies, 15*, 304–320.

Mondain, N., & Diagne, A. (2013). Discerning the reality of 'those left behind' in contemporary migration processes in Sub-Saharan Africa: Some theoretical reflections in the light of data from Senegal. *Journal of Intercultural Studies, 34*, 503–516. https://doi.org/10.1080/07256868.2013.827831

Nyamnjoh, H. M. (2020). Entrepreneurialism and innovation among Cameroonian street vendors in Cape Town. *African Identities, 18*, 295–312. https://doi.org/10.1080/14725843.2020.1777085

Papademetriou, D., & Terrazas, A. (2009). *Immigrants and the current economic crisis: Researche evidence, policy challenges and implications*. Migration Policy Institute.

Qin, D. (2006). The role of gender in immigrant children's educational adaptation. *Current Issues in Comparative Education, 9*, 8–19.

Ray, R. (2022). School as a hostile institution: How black and immigrant girls of color experience the classroom. *Gender & Society, 36*, 88–111. https://doi.org/10.1177/08912432211057916

Robles, V. F., & Oropesa, R. S. (2011). International migration and the education of children: Evidence from Lima. *Peru. Population Research and Policy Review, 30*, 591–618. https://doi.org/10.1007/s11113-011-9202-9

Schewel, K., & Fransen, S. (2018). Formal education and migration aspirations in Ethiopia. *Population and Development Review, 44*, 555–587. https://doi.org/10.1111/padr.12159

Semyonov, M., & Gorodzeisky, A. (2008). Labor migration, remittances and economic well-being of households in the Philippines. *Population Research and Policy Review, 27*, 619–637.

Stark, O., & Bloom, D. E. (1985). The new economics of labor migration. *The American Economic Review, 75*, 173–178.

Sun, F., Liu, Z., & Schiller, K. S. (2020). Parental migration and children's educational aspirations: China and Mexico in a comparative perspective. *Chinese Sociological Review, 52*, 462–486. https://doi.org/10.1080/21620555.2020.1779052

The intersections between education, migration and displacement are not gender-neutral. (2019). *Global Education Monitoring Report*. UNESCO.

Tize, C. (2021). Living in permanent temporariness: The multigenerational ordeal of living under Germany's toleration status. *Journal of Refugee Studies, 34*, 3024–3043. https://doi.org/10.1093/jrs/fez119

Wallace, M., Wilson, B., & Darlington-Pollock, F. (2022). Social inequalities experienced by children of immigrants across multiple domains of life: A case study of the Windrush in England and Wales. *Comparative Migration Studies, 10*, 1–21. https://doi.org/10.1186/s40878-022-00293-1

Zeleke, M. (2019). Too many winds to consider; which way and when to sail!: Ethiopian female transit migrants in Djibouti and the dynamics of their decision-making. *African and Black Diaspora: AN International Journal, 12*(1), 49–63.

Zuccotti, C. V., Ganzeboom, H. B. G., & Guveli, A. (2017). Has migration been beneficial for migrants and their children. *International Migration Review, 51*, 97–126.

Open Access This chapter is licensed under the terms of the Creative Commons Attribution 4.0 International License (http://creativecommons.org/licenses/by/4.0/), which permits use, sharing, adaptation, distribution and reproduction in any medium or format, as long as you give appropriate credit to the original author(s) and the source, provide a link to the Creative Commons license and indicate if changes were made.

The images or other third party material in this chapter are included in the chapter's Creative Commons license, unless indicated otherwise in a credit line to the material. If material is not included in the chapter's Creative Commons license and your intended use is not permitted by statutory regulation or exceeds the permitted use, you will need to obtain permission directly from the copyright holder.

26

Mapping the Linkages Between Food Security, Inequality, Migration, and Development in the Global South

Jonathan Crush and Sujata Ramachandran

Introduction

In 2018, Louise Arbour, former UN Special Representative for Migration and lead architect of the Global Compact for Migration, articulated the relationship between migration and development in highly optimistic and celebratory terms (Arbour, 2018). Her comments focused on the voluntary forms of migration and their related development consequences. International migration was characterised by Arbour as an "overwhelmingly positive" process for migrants as well as their sending and receiving communities, a "potent motor for development", and an "instrument of prosperity, not as a failure of development". She went on to emphasise that migration and development can be mutually supportive processes, operating as a "virtuous circle" that involves beneficial activities, practices, and processes which lead to equally progressive results.

This untempered enthusiasm for migrants as agents of development exemplifies the contemporary framework of "migration and development" that

---

J. Crush (✉) · S. Ramachandran
Balsillie School of International Affairs, Waterloo, ON, Canada
e-mail: jcrush@balsillieschool.ca

S. Ramachandran
e-mail: sramachandran@balsillieschool.ca

J. Crush
University of the Western Cape, Cape Town, South Africa

© The Author(s) 2024
H. Crawley and J. K. Teye (eds.), *The Palgrave Handbook of South–South Migration and Inequality*, https://doi.org/10.1007/978-3-031-39814-8_26

emphasizes the beneficial development-based outcomes of migration for both sending and receiving countries (Faist & Fauser, 2011). The "migration and development nexus" has received much attention from international organisations and national governments. It includes some consideration of the various forms of development as drivers of migration, the linkages between globalisation and migration, and the potential for connecting these two aspects in policy design and execution. Yet, as Crawley et al. (2022) have recently argued, the complex set of structural inequalities that affect migration at local, national, and regional scales and shape its consequences for migrants, their sending communities, and others, have not received adequate critical attention. As Crawley (2018) suggests, the "developmental potential of migration is neither straightforward nor inevitable".

Just as the relationship between inequality, migration, and development remains under addressed, the linkages between food security, migration, and development have been similarly neglected (Anns, 2020; Carney & Krause, 2020; Crush, 2012, 2013; Orjuela-Grimm et al., 2022). Crush (2012, 2013) has previously noted that the key theme of food security has been largely overlooked in the discourse on migration and development, as well as in migration studies. For example, in their discussion on famine-led migration, Sadliwala and de Waal (2018) have underscored the cursory reference to food insecurity in the Global Migration Compact to draw attention to the disregarded connections between acute food crises and population mobility. These omissions are highly problematic since food is essential for survival and food security constitutes a core measure of human security and human wellbeing. As a starting point, Crush (2013) identifies two distinctive dimensions to the linkages between migration, development, and food security: first, the various ways in which migrants take care of their food needs, and second, the ways in which they utilise their wages in the destination country. In addition, Crush and Caesar (2017) propose a research and policy focus on two additional linkages: the relationship between remittances and the food security of both senders and recipients, and the reasons for variability in migrant food security in relation to South-South migration. Carney and Krause (2020) further suggest that a focus is needed on the food security of "migrants on the move". All these aspects can be concretely connected with the configurations of inequality in the origin and destination areas and the spaces in-between.

This chapter provides a corrective in several ways. First, we address their relevance to the ongoing discussion on migration and development within academic and policy circles. We broaden this dialogue beyond regular population flows to and from countries in the Global South to include involuntary and irregular forms of migration. Third, we treat food security and inequality as central themes to capture the multidimensional linkages between migration and development in the context of diverse forms of cross-border and international migratory flows in the Global South. Drawing on a newer body of studies that focus on food security and South-South migration, we highlight the various interactions between migration, food security, and inequality in the Global South.

Inequality, Migration, and Food Security

UNDESA (2015) outlines two key dimensions of inequality: inequality of opportunity and inequality of outcomes. Inequality of opportunity occurs in terms of unequal access to services such as education, health, or employment. Inequality of outcomes occurs when individuals have uneven living standards related to disparities in wealth/incomes, health, education, and food security. Inequalities associated with migration are also often intersectional and multidimensional and tied to structural inequalities within and between countries in the Global South and North (UNU, 2022). Migration processes are a highly visible reflection of global inequalities in terms of wages, labour market conditions, opportunities available to individuals and groups, and general living standards (Crawley, 2018). Migration as a process and migrants as social actors are embedded in "elementary mechanisms" and landscapes of inequality in both origin and destination areas with opportunity and outcomes stretched over space (Safi, 2020). Furthermore, migration can trigger new inequalities and intensify existing asymmetries in both the sending and receiving areas (see also Crawley and Yete this volume).

Safi (2020) identifies three intersecting channels through which migration interacts with inequality dynamics: economic, legal, and ethno-racial. Economically, as a key feature of the capitalist system, international migration nourishes stratified and segmented exploitative labour regimes in terms of types of work available, wages, and other benefits. Labour migrants fall (and often fail) predominantly in poorly remunerated, less stable, and less attractive employment towards the bottom end of the labour market. Legal processes of categorisation through a variety of migrant statuses (temporary workers, irregular migrants, students, accompanying spouses, asylum-seekers, refugees, seasonal migrants), and border control procedures affecting modes of entry, bring differential rewards and benefits. As non-citizens, most migrant groups receive fewer rights and protections. As the final aspect of social stratification, other cross-cutting divisions, especially gender, nationality, ethnicity, and race, exert a decisive influence over access to occupations and positions in the labour market. The ethno-racial categorisation of migrants and related biases exert a strong impact on the economic, social, and political rights of migrants and on uneven access to resources.

Although discussed primarily for South-North migration, the concept of "migrant precarity" and "hyper-precarity" has been used to emphasise their "lifeworlds that are inflected with uncertainty and instability" (Lewis et al., 2015, 581). This condition of precariousness can typify the migrants' working and living conditions, which have a strong impact on their own food insecurity, those of their households in these receiving settings, and their dependents in the sending areas. Similarly, "migrant marginality" highlights the disadvantages and vulnerabilities faced by various categories of migrants and this marginalisation is seen as a predecessor to entrenched inequalities (Netshikulwe et al., 2022). Food insecurity is thus a stark outcome of migrant precarity (Ramachandran et al., 2023). Equally importantly, it is a crucial indicator of the existing social and economic inequalities with which individuals and groups are associated.

As Klassen and Murphy (2020,1) have noted, "access to food is an important marker of how well a society distributes its wealth, reflecting the state of political accountability, economic redistribution, and the society's commitment to uphold the right to food". Shaped by the four dimensions of food availability, food access, food utilisation, and food stability, food security occurs when individuals, households, and groups have physical and economic access to safe and nutritious foods that fulfil their dietary requirements and food preferences for active, healthy lives. Food security and insecurity are inextricably intertwined with poverty and inequality. If migration is a symbol and expression of inequality within and across countries globally, including those in the Global South, then food security is a key measure and expression of these asymmetries.

Food Security, Migration Aspirations, and Actions

An emerging body of work has confirmed that food insecurity tied to escalating inequalities and asymmetries within and across countries and regions can fundamentally influence migration aspirations, intentions, and behaviours. At the macro-scale, Smith and Wesselbaum (2022) find a significant positive correlation between food insecurity at origin and out-migration, and a positive correlation between out-migration and within-country inequality in food insecurity. At the regional scale, Sadiddin et al. (2019) show that in sub-Saharan Africa, food insecurity raises the probability of individual desire to migrate to another country and this aspiration increases with worsening food insecurity. At the household level, personal and/or external shocks, such as job losses, declines in household income, food price hikes, and inflation, inevitably exacerbate the food insecurity of individuals and families and drive out-migration. A recent longitudinal study in southwest Ethiopia, for example, documents an increased migration propensity among young male and female members in households that had suffered severe food insecurity or farm loss shocks (Lindstrom et al., 2022).

Migration-related aspirations are generally higher among individuals and households that face regular deficits in sufficient quantities of nutritious food. Migration is a common livelihood and risk diversification strategy for marginal households facing food insecurity due to economic shocks (Smith & Floro, 2020). Poverty and food insecurity have been identified as key inter-linked determinants of internal migration in the Global South (Choitani, 2017). However, their relationship with international migration is not uncomplicated due to the higher barriers and risks associated with such movements. The nuances of these linkages, and the role of food security and insecurity in migration dynamics, are less understood, and the absence of in-depth research hampers an adequate understanding of the connections. Clearly, the poorest facing severe food insecurity may not be able to migrate despite strong aspirations to do so because of weak access to formal channels of migration. When they do move, it may be across shorter distances to neighbouring countries and using risky informal channels. Short- and long-term migration from rural communities in the South can also exacerbate gender-based inequalities. In Nepal, for example, improved food security from migrant remittances has occurred but at the expense of intensified gender inequality (Kim et al., 2019). While male Nepali migrants face tough working conditions in India, the women left behind have to assume complete responsibility for farming, as well as housework and child care.

Exogenous factors and other developments that deepen existing disparities between individuals, households, and groups have cascading detrimental effects on food insecurity and can lead to increased migratory flows to other countries. A combination of income inequality, poverty, social insecurity, violence, and dire effects of climate-related events have significantly increased food insecurity and, in turn, generated "knock-on effects" including migration from El Salvador, Guatemala, and Honduras (IOM and WFP,

2022; WFP, 2017b). Carney (2015) draws attention to what she calls an "unending hunger" caused by deepened structural inequalities in Mexico with international migration as a common coping strategy. As one outcome of existing and/or intensifying local inequality in migrant-sending areas, food insecurity can thus operate as a powerful "push factor" for migration in most areas of the Global South. Smith and Floro (2020) study the linkages between food insecurity, gender, and migration desires and behaviour in low- and middle-income countries. They argue that migration intentions increase monotonically, and migration preparations decrease with the severity of food insecurity. Women are less likely to have migration intentions and preparations due to gender-based inequalities.

The COVID-19 pandemic has brought into sharp relief the robust connections between food security, inequality, and mobility, with short-term and long-term implications for migratory dynamics, migrants in destination settings, and their sending communities. The pandemic triggered an unprecedented and multidimensional crisis of inequality, including gender-based inequities, intensified extreme poverty, and heightened food insecurity (Crush & Si, 2020). COVID-19 has exacerbated pre-existing imbalances in the labour market and unravelled recent efforts to lower economic disparities on a global scale (Narayan et al., 2022). Global travel bans, lockdowns, and other public health measures to limit contagion have produced disproportionate negative effects on the socioeconomic and health well-being of migrants. Income losses, limited access to relief measures, greater exposure due to their work and living conditions, increased remittance responsibilities, and rising anti-migrant tendencies have exerted new pressures, leading to a significant deterioration of migrant food security (Crush et al., 2021). Although its full effects are still unfolding, some new studies have suggested that migration surges will be long-term global effects of the pandemic and related structural changes (Smith & Wesselbaum, 2020). Longitudinal surveys with Guatemalan farmers recorded a recent three-fold increase in emigration intentions (Ceballos et al., 2022). Despite some improvements in incomes, food security, and dietary diversity, over half of the households were borrowing to cope and had not yet fully recovered from pandemic-related shocks.

Crises, Food Insecurity, and Survival Migration

The linkages between South-South migration, inequality, and food security are particularly transparent with respect to involuntary forms of migration (Chikanda et al., 2020). The *Global Report on Food Crises* notes that in 2017, some 15.3 million persons were displaced by six of the world's worst conflict-related food crises: in Syria, Yemen, Iraq, South Sudan, Northeast Nigeria, and Somalia (FSIN, 2018). In conflict situations, many individuals experience what Carney (2019) has described as "food-specific violence". Access to food resources and food availability can be weaponised and used to control certain groups, greatly deepening power asymmetries between individuals and communities. The destruction of food sources and rural infrastructure, coalescing with large-scale population movements and other events such as natural disasters, can forge pervasive chronic food insecurity (Martin-Shields & Stojetz, 2018). Widespread inequality can persist in crisis-affected settings even after violent conflicts end (Bircan et al., 2010). Access to food resources and food availability can influence the dynamics of violent conflicts. Food insecurity grievances, especially in areas with weaker food supplies, can escalate into violent social and political struggles (Koren & Bagozzi, 2016). Economic hardship and severe forms of food insecurity were major contributory factors to the flight of Syrian refugees to Jordan and Lebanon, although the act of migration only worsened their food insecurity (WFP, 2017a).

Although violent conflict has long been seen as one of the main drivers of enforced "survival migration" (Betts, 2013), recognition of the nexus between conflict, food insecurity, and survival migration is more recent. The 2017 *Global Report on Food Crises*, for example, identifies conflict and the widespread instability it causes as key determinants of acute food insecurity (FSIN, 2017). Food insecurity is also an important contributing factor in the occurrence and severity of the armed conflicts and generalised violence that result in large-scale cross-border migrations in the Global South (WFP, 2017a). Violent conflict severely disrupts and damages regular social and economic processes tied to food systems, such as crop production, the operation of markets and trade, and the circulation of food and other commodities. Vulnerable households lose access to a wide range of resources necessary for survival, and migration becomes necessary to escape and survive (FAO, 2016). Conflict and crisis generate acute and chronic food insecurity and operate as the main determinant of large-scale displacement (WFP and FAO, 2022). Thus, violent conflict, forced migration, and food insecurity often feed into and intensify each other (FAO and IFPRI, 2017).

Food insecurity is also a ubiquitous feature of prolonged economic crisis. Global economic crises and recessionary periods exacerbate deeply embedded socioeconomic hierarchies and produce food security shocks, especially for marginal households with meagre financial resources. Political mismanagement, financial collapse, and hyperinflation contributed to sharp economic contraction, very high unemployment levels, accompanied by widespread deterioration in food access, surges in food costs, and a large-scale exodus to neighbouring countries. Carril-Caccia et al. (2022) estimate that severe food crises affect the directionality of migration, which is increasingly heading to other countries in the Global South. Venezuela and Zimbabwe are good examples in different regions of the Global South. Massive shortages of basic food commodities tied to the country's economic crisis were the final precipitants of out-migration for many Venezuelan migrants to other countries in Latin America (Pico et al., 2021). As one participant explained: "The main reason I left Venezuela was that I couldn't get groceries like milk to feed my granddaughter, and when that happened, I couldn't stand it anymore" (Pico et al., 2021, 6).

Economic and political crises are commonly accompanied by negative changes to labour markets, and low-wage, less skilled workers are likely to be the first to face retrenchment an important driver of the migrant exodus to neighbouring countries. However, survival migration does not automatically mean the restoration of food security. As one Zimbabwean migrant in South Africa noted: "the people in Zimbabwe will be expecting us to feed them and not vice-versa. But we are struggling here" (Crush & Tawodzera, 2016). Persistent difficulties in securing regular income along with the urgent and unrelenting need to support relatives in Zimbabwe contributed to high levels of food insecurity and poor dietary diversity among Zimbabwean migrants in South African cities (Crush & Tawodzera, 2017).

Nawrotzski et al. (2014) also found significant differences in the long-term food insecurity of migrants and refugees in northeastern South Africa during the 2008 global food crisis. Former Mozambican refugees experienced the greatest declines in food and livelihood security. Migrant households fell behind non-migrant households in food security by 2010. Inflation, rising food prices, and recent developments, such as the war in Ukraine, have magnified pandemic-related shocks and stressors to forge a "global food crisis" (FAO, 2023). The latest *State of Food Security and Nutrition in the World* report identifies a sharp spike in moderate and severe food insecurity in 2020, followed by significant surges in severe food insecurity a year later (FAO et al.,

2022). Food insecurity is a "consistent condition" for Afghan refugee families in Pakistan (Khakpour et al., 2019) and for refugees in camps and urban spaces worldwide.

Remittances and Food Security

Migrant remittances have become an increasingly significant part of the resources of left-behind households, with important implications for their expenditure and consumption patterns (Ebadi et al., 2020). Studies focused on migrant-sending areas have shown that households receiving international remittances are more likely to be food secure than those who do not (Moniruzzaman, 2022; Regmi & Paudel, 2017). Other work has shown that remittances expand household food expenditures in sub-Saharan Africa and improve the long-term food security of recipients (Ajefu & Ogebe, 2020). The intensity of the impact on the food security of recipient households is also correlated with national income (Sulemana et al., 2022). Lower income countries with larger cohorts experiencing poverty and poor living standards experienced the strongest positive effects on their food security. Another study found that the level of food supply tends to be higher in developing countries with high remittance flows (Subramaniam et al., 2022).

Analysing a World Bank living standards dataset for Nigeria, Obi et al. (2020) conclude that remittances are a "veritable instrument" to meet short-term and long-term food security for households during food crises. These effects were most pronounced for female-headed households, who are at greater risk of food insecurity. Another assessment found a significant correlation between remittance receipts and food security in all regions of the Global South (Ebadi et al., 2020). Households not receiving remittances were much more likely to be severely food insecure in sub-Saharan Africa as well as Southeast, South, and East Asia. In some countries, such as Liberia, Yemen, Haiti, and Nepal, the non-receipt of remittances was significantly associated with moderate and severe food insecurity. Households in the lowest income quantiles were also the least likely to receive remittances.

Informal food transfers are an important part of remittance landscapes with consequences for the welfare and food security of both sending and receiving households (Crush & Caesar, 2017). One-third of migrant-sending households in one survey of five Southern African countries had received food remittances (Frayne & Crush, 2018). Transnational food transfers improve food supply between sending households. While food remittances may not always enhance dietary diversity, they can ease the harsh burden of absolute hunger and enhance food accessibility. Remittance receipts also function as informal support mechanisms in contexts of weak or absent social welfare systems and improve the general well-being of recipient households. While remittances bring various benefits to recipients, the pressure to constantly remit can worsen migrant vulnerabilities in destination areas (Ramachandran & Crush, 2021). Due to this responsibility, migrants remain tied to mechanisms and structures of inequality and food insecurity in both origin and destination areas (Ramachandran et al., 2023).

Migrants, Food Environments, and Informality

Migrants play an increasingly important role in local and national food systems and supply chains in origin and destination countries. Cross-border migration can support local food production systems in the sending areas. For example, migration from Nicaragua to other Central American countries has sustained small-scale agricultural systems and food production in that country (Carte et al., 2019). Left-behind household members engage in small-scale agricultural practices by producing and remaining on the land in a difficult social, political, and economic environment. Migration has therefore eased rural poverty for farming households and stemmed deagrarianisation. In Southeast Asia, there is evidence that some forms of labour migration have transformed agrarian livelihoods without leading to the complete or absolute exit from agricultural production (Kelley et al., 2020).

Migrants can be key employees and actors in food production, distribution, and retailing in destination countries. This is well-documented in the Global North. However, less work is currently available in relation to South-South migration. The labour-intensive, low-skilled, and often poorly remunerated agricultural sector, including fisheries, livestock, forestry, and other agriculture-related activities, is the largest employer of migrant workers in Algeria, Botswana, Cabe Verde, Liberia, Namibia, Niger, and Nigeria (AU, 2017). Nicaraguan farmworkers face long working hours, physically demanding manual labour, repeated exposure to pesticides, and are often denied their legitimate rights in Costa Rica (Poirier et al., 2022). A new ILO (2021) study shows that female and Myanmarese migrants receive much lower wages and temporary contracts in Thailand's agricultural sector. Migrants from Zimbabwe and Lesotho play a vital role as cheap and exploitable labour on large commercial fruit and vegetable farms in South Africa (Bolt, 2015; Kudejira, 2019).

Migrants are under-recognised participants in local food environments in the urban areas of destination countries. Food environments include the spatial distribution of food outlets such as formal and informal retail food shops, markets, restaurants and are shaped by socioeconomic relationships and structural inequalities (Vonthron et al., 2020). These foodscapes are composite arrangements of formal and informal sector activities in which migrants, especially women, actively participate. Migrants feed cities working as street vendors and small- and medium-scale traders engaged in food retail operations. For example, migrants work in the Malaysian food service sector, with Rohingya refugees active but largely invisible in wholesale fresh markets and other groups placed in restaurants and outdoor food stalls (Muniandy, 2020).

A survey of informal food vendors in Cape Town, South Africa, found that more than half had migrated from other African countries (Tawodzera, 2019). Migrant vendors and traders sell a wide range of reasonably priced cooked and uncooked food products, including fruits and vegetables, on the streets and at transport hubs in poor neighbourhoods not well served by formal grocery stores and supermarkets. They also operate *spazas* (informal grocery shops) and adopt practices such as low markup, credit purchases for regular customers, and bulk-breaking and selling food in miniscule quantities (such as a single bread slice). Nevertheless, migrant food vendors operate in an extremely hostile environment, face rampant xenophobia, with repeated attempts by authorities and citizens to curtail their activities. Migrant street food vendors and spaza operators have faced recurring bouts of xenophobic violence, including physical attacks, looting of stock, and arson in South Africa (Crush & Ramachandran, 2015). Frontline migrant food workers have been targets of racial prejudice and xenophobia in other countries as well (Muniandy, 2020).

Migrant Destinations, Inequality, and Food Insecurity

The social and economic inequalities experienced by migrants in destination countries are another important component of the linkages between inequality, migration, and food security. Although not all migrants experience food insecurity at their destination, it is a core aspect of migrant marginality and precarity in the Global South (Ramachandran et al., 2023). The multiple layering of inequalities that migrants are exposed to can rapidly forge pathways to extreme or hyper-precarity with cascading effects on food insecurity. These inequalities in opportunity and outcomes include exclusion from formal labour markets and/or incorporation in the most menial and dangerous jobs, decent work deficits, erratic work opportunities, inadequate incomes, substandard housing, weak social protection, and discriminatory treatment by the state. Demands for bribes from police, difficulties in renewing legal residence permits, and arrest and deportation without due process all compound vulnerability to food insecurity. For example, Carney and Krause (2020) show that food insecurity and stress were greatly exacerbated for young irregular Haitian male migrants in the Dominican Republic during periods of intensified immigration policing. Migrants transiting through Mexico are forced to rely on migrant shelters, and beg, or offer their services in exchange for food (Deschak et al., 2022). Poverty, racialised violence, stigma, and food insecurity often operate as a vicious cycle in the lives of migrants with precarious migration status (Carney & Krause, 2020).

Gendered biases and gender-based inequities intersect with other forms of discrimination to produce unique hardships for female migrants and differential experiences by gender identity. Most female asylum-seekers and refugees in Durban, South Africa, are forced to skip meals and consume less than their other family members (Napier et al., 2018). Although placed in households with abundant food, Indonesian domestic workers in Singapore often go hungry, are given smaller food portions and less desirable food, and rely on spoilt food or leftovers from their employers' plates (Mohamed, 2017). Food is used as a deliberate tactic to reinforce their low position and weak rights.

Conclusion

Our chapter argues that greater research attention needs to be paid to the intersections between migration, inequality, and food security. As a stark outcome of socioeconomic asymmetries within and across countries and regions, food insecurity is a core challenge of equitable and sustainable development. In this mapping exercise, we position food security and inequality as core components of an emerging research agenda on South-South migratory flows and mobilities. Drawing on recent case study evidence from across the Global South, we identify five distinctive dimensions to the dynamic linkages between food security, inequality, and migration. First, we showed how food security and inequality of opportunity and outcomes interact to influence migration motivations and actions. Second, by providing a discussion of various forms of crisis scenarios and conflict dynamics, we analysed how and under what circumstances food insecurity becomes the main driver and final trigger of forced displacement. Third, we assessed the role of food and cash remittances in addressing the food insecurity of households in sending areas and destination countries. Fourth, we discussed the role of migration and migrants in the food systems and food environments where they often labour under difficult, unequal, and hostile conditions. Finally, we connect migrant precarities with the food security status of various categories of migrants in transit and in destinations. By mapping the ways in which these linkages act upon South-South migration, we aim to temper the celebratory narratives of the migration-development nexus.

References

Arbour, L. (2018, February 5). Migration and development: A virtuous cycle. *Great Insights Magazine*. https://ecdpm.org/work/focus-on-migration-moving-backward-moving-forward-volume-7-issue-1-winter-2018/migration-and-development-a-virtuous-circle

African Union. (2017). *Report on labour migration statistics in Africa*. African Union.

Ajefu, J., & Ogebe, J. (2020). The effects of international remittances on expenditure patterns of the left-behind households in Sub-Saharan Africa. *Review of Development Economics, 25*(1), 405–429.

Anns, L. (2020, July 17). Migrants' rights are key to development: Interview with Heaven Crawley. *Caritas Europe*. https://www.caritas.eu/interview-with-prof-heaven-crawley/

Betts, A. (2013). *Survival migration: Failed governance and the crisis of displacement*. Cornell University Press.

Bircan, C., Brück, T., & Vothknecht, M. (2010). *Violent conflict and inequality* (DIW Berlin Discussion Paper No. 1013). DIW/German Institute for Economic Growth.

Bolt, M. (2015). *Zimbabwe's migrants and South Africa's border farms*. International African Institute and Cambridge University Press.

Carril-Caccia, F., Paniagua, J., & Suarez-Varela, M. (2022). *Forced migration and food crisis* (SUERF Policy Brief No. 440). SUERF The European Money and Finance Program.

Carney, M. (2015). *The unending hunger: Tracing women and food insecurity across borders*. University of California Press.

Carney, M. (2019, February 24). Food insecurity is a legitimate basis for seeking asylum. *The Hill*. https://thehill.com/opinion/immigration/431332-food-insecurity-is-a-legitimate-basis-for-seeking-asylum/

Carney, M. A., & Krause, K. C. (2020). Immigration/migration and healthy publics: The threat of food insecurity. *Palgrave Communication, 6*, 93. https://doi.org/10.1057/s41599-020-0461-0

Carte, L., Radel, C., & Schmook, B. (2019). Subsistence migration: Smallholder food security and the maintenance of agriculture through mobility in Nicaragua. *Geographical Journal, 185*(2), 180–193.

Ceballos, F., Hernandez, M., & Paz, C. (2022). *COVID-19 and extreme weather: Food security and migration attitudes in rural Guatemala* (IFPRI Discussion Paper No. 02126). IFPRI.

Chikanda, A., Crush, J., & Tawodzera, G. (2020). Urban food security and South-South migration to cities of the Global South". In J. Crush, B. Frayne, & G. Haysom (Eds.), *Handbook on Urban Food Security in the Global South* (pp. 261–281). Edward Elgar.

Choitani, C. (2017). Understanding the linkages between migration and household security in India. *Geographical Research, 55*(2), 192–205.

Crawley, H. (2018, October 30). Why understanding the relationship between migration and inequality may be the key to Africa's development. *Development Matters*. https://oecd-development-matters.org/2018/10/30/why-understanding-the-relationship-between-migration-and-inequality-may-be-the-key-to-africas-development/

Crawley, H., Garba, F., & Nyamnjoh, F. (2022). Editorial introduction: Migration and (in)equality in the Global South. *Zanj: The Journal of Critical Global South Studies, 5*(1/2),1–13.

Crush, J. (2012). *Migration, development and urban food security* (Urban Food Security Series No. 9). African Food Security Network.

Crush, J. (2013). Linking food security, migration and development. *International Migration, 51*(5), 61–75.

Crush, J., & Caesar, M. (2017). Food remittances and food security: A review. *Migration and Development, 7*(2), 180–200.

Crush, J., & Ramachandran, S. (2015). Doing business with xenophobia. In J. Crush, A. Chikanda, & C. Skinner (Eds.), *Waterloo: Southern African migration programme* (pp. 25–59). International Migration Research Centre and Balsillie School of International Affairs.

Crush, J., & Si, Z. (2020). COVID-19 containment and food security in the global South. *Journal of Agriculture, Food Systems, and Community Development, 9*(4), 149–151.

Crush, J., & Tawodzera, G. (2016). *The food insecurities of Zimbabwean migrants in urban South Africa* (Urban Food Security Series No. 23). African Food Security Network.

Crush, J., & Tawodzera, G. (2017). South-South migration and urban food security: Zimbabwean migrants in South African cities. *International Migration, 55*(4), 88–102.

Crush, J., Thomaz, D., & Ramachandran, S. (2021). *South-South migration, food insecurity and the Covid-19 pandemic* (MiFOOD Working Paper No. 1), Waterloo.

Deschak, C., Infante, C., Mundo-Rosas, V., Orjuela-Grimm, M., & Aragon-Gama, A. (2022). Food insecurity and coping strategies in international migrants in transit in Mexico. *Journal of Migration and Health, 5*, 100099. https://doi.org/10.1016/j.jmh.2022.100099

Ebadi, N., Ahmadi, D., & Melgar-Quinonez, H. (2020). Domestic and international remittances and food security in Sub-Saharan Africa. *Remittances Review, 5*(1), 37–54.

Faist, T., & Fauser, M. (2011). The migration-development nexus: Towards a transnational perspective. In T. Faist, M. Fauser, & P. Kivisto (Eds.), *The migration-development nexus: A transnational perspective* (pp. 1–26). Springer.

FAO. (2016). *Migration and protracted crises: Addressing the root causes and building resilient agricultural livelihoods.* Food Agriculture Organisation of the United Nations.

FAO. (2023). *The global food crisis: Impact on the Asia Pacific region.* Food Agriculture Organisation of the United Nations.

FAO, Ifad, UNICEF, WFP, & WHO. (2022). *The state of food security and nutrition in the world 2022: Repurposing food and agricultural policies to make healthy diets more available.* Food and Agricultural Organisation of the United Nations.

FAO & IFPRI. (2017). *Conflict, migration and food security: The role of agriculture and rural development.* FAO-IFPRI Joint Brief. https://www.fao.org/3/i7896e/i7896e.pdf

Food Security Information Network. FSIN. (2017). *Global report on food crises 2017.* https://documents.wfp.org/stellent/groups/public/documents/ena/wfp291271.pdf?_ga=2.150479606.1566941052.1677852249-2060118426.1677852249

Frayne, B., & Crush, J. (2018). Food supply and rural-urban links in Southern African cities. In B. Frayne, J. Crush, & C. Mccordic (Eds.), *Food and Nutrition Security in Southern African Cities* (pp. 34–47). Routledge.

International Organisation for Migration and World Food Programme. (2022). *Understanding the adverse drivers and implications of migration from El Salvador, Guatemala and Honduras.* https://www.wfp.org/publications/wfp-and-iom-understanding-adverse-drivers-and-implications-migration-el-salvador

ILO. (2021). *Working and employment conditions in the agriculture sector in Thailand: A Survey of migrants working on Thai sugarcane, rubber, oil palm and maize farms.*

Kelley, L., Peluso, N., Carlson, K., & Afiff, S. (2020). Circular labour migration and land-livelihood dynamics in Southeast Asia's concession landscapes. *Journal of Labour Studies, 73*, 21–33.

Khakpour, M., Iqbal, R., Ghulam-Hussain, N., Engler-Stringer, R., Koc, M., Garcea, J., Farag, M., Henry, C., & Vatanparast, H. (2019). Facilitators and barriers toward food security of Afghan refugees residing in Karachi, Pakistan. *Ecology of Food and Nutrition, 58*(4), 317–334.

Kim, J. J., Stites, E., Webb, P., Constas, M., & Maxwell, D. (2019). The effects of male out-migration on household food security in rural Nepal. *Food Security, 11*, 719–732.

Klassen, S., & Murphy, S. (2020). Equity as both a means and an end: Lessons for resilient food systems from COVID-19. *World Development, 136*, 105104. https://doi.org/10.1016/j.worlddev.2020.105104

Koren, O., & Bagozzi, B. (2016). From global to local, food insecurity is associated with contemporary armed conflicts. *Food Security, 8*, 999–1010.

Kudejira, D. (2019). *Movement of Zimbabwean immigrants into, within and out of farm labour market in Limpopo province of South Africa*. Unpublished MPhil Thesis, University of Western Cape.

Lewis, H., Dwyer, P., Hodkinson, S., & Waite, L. (2015). Hyper-precarious lives: Migrants, work and forced labour in the Global North. *Progress in Human Geography, 39*(5), 580–600.

Lindstrom, D., Randell, & H., Belachew, T. (2022). The migration response to food insecurity and household shocks in southwestern Ethiopia, 2005–2008. *International Migration Review*, 0(0). https://doi.org/10.1177/01979183221139115

Martin-Shields, C., & Stojetz, W. (2018). *Food security and conflict: Empirical challenges and future opportunities for research and policymaking on food security and conflict* (FAO Agricultural Development Economic Working Paper No. 18–04). FAO.

Mohamed, C. (2017). *Indonesian domestic workers and the lack of food security in Singapore* (Migration and Mobilities Paper No. MMP 2017–01). Centre for Asia-Pacific Initiatives, University of Victoria.

Moniruzzaman, M. (2022). The impact of remittances on household food security: Evidence from a survey in Bangladesh. *Migration and Development, 11*(3), 352–371.

Muniandy, P. (2020). From the pasar to mamak stall: Refugees and migrants as surplus ghost labor in Malaysia's food service industry. *Journal of Ethnic and Migration Studies, 46*(11), 2293–2308. https://doi.org/10.1080/1369183X.2018.1529557

Napier, C., Oldewage-Theron, W., & Makhaye, B. (2018). Predictors of food insecurity and coping strategies of women asylum seekers and refugees in Durban South Africa. *Agriculture and Food Security, 7*, 67. https://doi.org/10.1186/s40066-018-0220-2

Narayan, A., Cojocaru, A., Agrawal, S., Bundervoet, T., Davalos, M., Garcia, N., Lakner, C., Mahler, D., Talledo, V., Ten, A., & Yonzan, N. (2022). *COVID-19 and Economic Inequality: Short-Term Impacts with Long-Term Consequences* (Policy Research Working Paper 9902). World Bank.

Nawrotzki, R. J., Robson, K., Gutilla, M. J., Hunter, L. M., Twine, W., & Norlund, P. (2014). Exploring the impact of the 2008 global food crisis on food security among vulnerable households in rural South Africa. *Food Security, 6*, 283–297. https://doi.org/10.1007/s12571-014-0336-6

Netshikulwe, A., Nyamnjoh, F., & Garba, F. (2022). Pushed to the margins: Ethiopian migrants in South Africa. *Zanj: The Journal of Critical Global South Studies, 5*(1/2), 76–92.

Obi, C., Bartolini, F., & D'Haese, M. (2020). International migration, remittance and food security during food crises: The case study of Nigeria. *Food Security, 12*, 207–220.

Orjuela-Grimm, M., Deschak, C., Aragon-Gama, C., Bhatt Carreño, S., Hoyos, L., Mundo, V., Bojorquez, I., Carpio, K., Quero, Y., Xicotencatl, A., & Infante, C. (2022). Migrants on the move and food (in)security: A call for research. *Journal of Immigrant and Minority Health., 24*(5), 118–1327. https://doi.org/10.1007/s10903-021-01276-7

Poirier, M., Barraza, D., Caxaj, C., Martínez, A., Hard, J., & Montoya, F. (2022). Informality, social citizenship, and wellbeing among migrant workers in Costa Rica in the context of COVID-19. *International Journal of Environmental Research and Public Health, 19*(10), 6224. https://doi.org/10.3390/ijerph19106224

Pico, R., Matamoros, S., & Bernal, J. (2021). Food and nutrition insecurity in Venezuelan migrant families in Bogota Columbia. *Frontiers in Sustainable Food Systems, 5*, 634817. https://doi.org/10.3389/fsufs.2021.634817

Ramachandran, S., Crush, J., Tawodzera, G., & Opiyo Onyango. E. (2023). Pandemic food precarity, crisis living and translocality: Zimbabwean migrant households in South Africa during Covid-19. In M. McAuliffe, & C. Bauloz (Eds.), *Research handbook on migration, gender and Covid-19*. Edward Elgar.

Ramachandran, S., and Crush, J. (2021). *Between burden and benefit. Migrant remittances, social protection and sustainable development* (SAMP Migration Policy Series No. 83). Waterloo: SAMP, IMRC and BSIA.

Regmi, M., & Paudel, K. P. (2017). Food security in a remittance-based economy. *Food Security, 9*, 831–848. https://doi.org/10.1007/s12571-017-0705-z

Sadiddin, A., Cattaneo, A., Cirillo, M., & Miller, M. (2019). Food insecurity as a determinant of international migration: Evidence from Sub-Saharan Africa. *Food Security, 11*, 515–530. https://doi.org/10.1007/s12571-019-00927-w

Sadliwala, B., & de Waal, A. (2018, November 15). The emerging crisis: Is famine returning as a major driver of migration? *Migration Information Source*. https://www.migrationpolicy.org/article/emerging-crisis-famine-returning-major-driver-migration

Safi, M. (2020). *Migration and inequality*. Polity Press.

Smith, M., & Floro, M. (2020). Food insecurity, gender and international migration in low- and middle-income countries. *Food Policy, 91*, 101837. https://doi.org/10.1016/j.foodpol.2020.101837

Smith, M., & Wesselbaum, D. (2020). COVID-19, food insecurity, and migration. *The Journal of Nutrition, 150*(11), 2855–2858.

Subramaniam, Y., Masron, T., & Azman, N. (2022). Remittances and food security. *Journal of Economic Studies, 49*(4), 699–715.

Sulemana, I., Anarfo, E., & Doabil, L. (2022). Migrant remittances and food security in sub-Saharan Africa: The role of income classifications. *International Migration Review* 0(0). https://doi.org/10.1177/01979183221107925

Tawodzera, G. (2019). The nature and operations of informal food vendors in Cape Town. *Urban Forum, 30,* 443–459.

UNDESA. (2015, October 21). *Concept of inequality* (UN/DESA Development Issues Brief No. 1). https://www.un.org/en/development/desa/policy/wess/wess_dev_issues/dsp_policy_01.pdf

UNU (2022, January 1). Why we need to centre equality in the implementation of the Global Compact on Migration. *ReliefWeb.* https://reliefweb.int/report/world/why-we-need-centre-equality-implementation-global-compact-migration

Vonthron, S., Perrin, C., & Soulard, C. (2020). Foodscape: A scoping review and a research agenda for food security-related studies. *PLoS ONE, 15*(5), e0233218. https://doi.org/10.1371/journal.pone.0233218

World Food Programme. (2017a). *At the root of exodus: Food security, conflict and international migration.* World Food Programme.

World Food Programme. (2017b). *Food security and emigration: Why people flee and the impact on family members left behind in El Salvador, Guatemala and Honduras.* WFP.

World Food Programme and Food and Agricultural Organisation of the United Nations. (2022). *Hunger hotspots: FAO-WFP early warnings on acute food insecurity. June to September 2022 Outlook.* Rome: World Food Programme, and Food and Agricultural Organisation of the United Nations.

Open Access This chapter is licensed under the terms of the Creative Commons Attribution 4.0 International License (http://creativecommons.org/licenses/by/4.0/), which permits use, sharing, adaptation, distribution and reproduction in any medium or format, as long as you give appropriate credit to the original author(s) and the source, provide a link to the Creative Commons license and indicate if changes were made.

The images or other third party material in this chapter are included in the chapter's Creative Commons license, unless indicated otherwise in a credit line to the material. If material is not included in the chapter's Creative Commons license and your intended use is not permitted by statutory regulation or exceeds the permitted use, you will need to obtain permission directly from the copyright holder.

Part IV

Responses to South–South Migration

27

The Governance of South–South Migration: Same or Different?

Francesco Carella

Introduction: Defining "the South" in South–South Migration

The Global South is a contested concept, whose definition is relatively vague (see also Crawley and Teye, Fiddian-Qasmiyeh, this volume). The expression has partially replaced terms that used to be commonplace, such as the Third World, and developing or underdeveloped countries, which implied both a supposed hierarchy among countries and value judgements (Mawdsley, 2012, 267). In social science literature, some academics have tried to define Global South in purely geographic terms (Bakewell et al., 2009, 2), although it is clear that even for them, the North and the South would not be neatly divided by the equatorial line (Anderson, 2014, 783). Others have defined Global South in economic terms, based on development indexes: either the Gross Domestic Product (GDP) index—widely used by governments and several international institutions, including the World Bank—or the Human Development Index, compiled by UNDP (Bakewell et al., 2009, 2). In this definition, countries in the higher echelons of the rankings (high-income or upper-middle income) are considered Global North, and countries in the lower echelons (low-income and lower-middle income) are classified as Global South. This seems to be a pragmatic and clear-cut solution to the complex issue of definition.

F. Carella (✉)
International Labour Organization (ILO), Lima, Peru
e-mail: carella@ilo.org

© The Author(s) 2024
H. Crawley and J. K. Teye (eds.), *The Palgrave Handbook of South–South Migration and Inequality*, https://doi.org/10.1007/978-3-031-39814-8_27

When discussing South–South migration in this article, however, I will use a more critical and nuanced definition of Global South, one that has become more prominent in the recent humanities and social science literature, and which incorporates anthropological, cultural and historical considerations—including links to the experience of "enslavement, mapping, claiming, conquest and colonisation" (Ndlovu-Gatsheni & Tafira, 2018, 127). In reality, this definition makes the boundary between North and South comparatively blurrier, to the extent that the term Global South becomes "productively ambiguous" (Anderson, 2014, 783). Mignolo compellingly explains that the expression "is not a geographic location; rather it is a metaphor that indicates regions of the world at the receiving end of globalization and suffering its consequences" (Mignolo, 2011, 184). As the North–South distinction transcends equatorial divisions and development indexes, it can be useful to think of it as a distinction between "periphery"—or the many Souths of the world—and the "metropole", as the centre of power (Connell, 2007, 213).[1]

Grasping the complexities inherent in defining the Global South is crucial to research and policy analysis on migration, since southern countries are nowadays origin, transit, destination and return countries for migrants and refugees. Furthermore, evidence suggests that in most continents, South–South migration is greater than South-North migration, and that the growth of the former has outpaced that of the latter (IOM, 2022, 1).

In this chapter, I first try to discern some specificities of South–South migration, before highlighting the limitations of the previous characterisation and nuancing it to take account of the complexity of human mobility in a context characterised by inequalities at the global level, as well as between southern countries and within them. Using examples from labour migration, forced displacement and mixed flows in the Global South, I then consider the implications of these characteristics of migration between the countries of the Global South for policy and programmatic responses—particularly those that can contribute to an effective governance of migration and the protection of the rights of migrants and refugees in the South. Throughout the chapter, I use a broad definition of migration, encompassing the breadth of human mobility. Wherever relevant, I refer specifically to labour migration, forced displacement or mixed flows.

---

[1] From this perspective, one may conceivably find pockets of South in urban and rural areas of North America or Western Europe which have suffered from long-standing political and infrastructural neglect.

What is Different? Discerning Specificities in South–South Migration

According to the International Organisation for Migration (IOM), 37% of international migration occurs along South–South corridors, and only 35% from South to North (IOM, 2022, 1). Forced displacement too occurs mostly within the Global South (Fiddian-Qasmiyeh, 2019, 239): it is a myth that northern countries bear the burden of refugee influxes. So what, if anything, distinguishes these growing South–South migration flows?

To start with, different dynamics can be observed in how migrants reach their countries of destination: the prevalence of porous borders that permit border crossings by land, without transiting through a formal checkpoint, results in comparatively more prevalent irregular migration status. Migrants in irregular status are particularly vulnerable to rights violations and less likely to report abuse out of fear that any involvement with authorities may result in their arrest, detention and deportation.

Specific dynamics can also be observed in the integration of migrants in their host countries. A great deal of the literature on the Global North has focused on the sociological and cultural aspects of integration, contrasting national models such as France's assimilationism and the UK's multiculturalism, and more recently giving way to interculturalism (Rodríguez-García, 2010, 260; Zapata-Barrero, 2015, viii) or the superdiversity of many global cities (Vertovec, 2007, 1028). On the other hand, in southern countries, one of the most pressing concerns seems to be economic, or at least socioeconomic, integration. This may be due to a variety of reasons, including the possible cultural and/or linguistic proximity between the countries of origin and destination; a shared history and skills compatibility (Khan & Hossain, 2017, 17). However, the characteristics of southern economies—and specifically their labour markets—play a role too.

Understanding labour markets is crucial to understanding human mobility because labour migration represents the large majority of international migration flows. According to the International Labour Organisation (ILO)'s latest available estimates on migrant workers, in 2019 there were 169 million migrant workers world-wide, constituting approximately 4.9% of the global workforce, and over 62% of the estimated 272 international migrants (ILO, 2021a, 11). Additionally, out of those who leave their countries for reasons unrelated to work—including refugees and other forcibly displaced people—the overwhelming majority still end up looking for employment or other forms of livelihood in their destination country, thereby turning into workers, who have an impact on labour markets.

Most labour markets in the Global South are characterised by high degrees of informality (Hammer & Ness, 2021, 2; ILO, 2018, 13): the informality rates among the general population reach 88% in India, 70% in Peru and 96% in Senegal (ILOSTAT, 2022). Large informal economies are both enticing and perilous for migrant workers. The attraction lies in the job opportunities for those with no access to a regular status, as well as those who, even in a regular situation, find no better livelihood option than to take up informal employment under conditions that most national workers are unwilling to accept. The peril arises out of the gaps in occupational safety and health, social protection and working conditions associated with informal employment (ILO, 2017, 69), which is largely out of the reach of labour inspection and affords workers little or no transparency about their rights. These protection gaps became particularly evident during the COVID-19 pandemic, when migrants in the South were among the first to lose their jobs, but usually the last to access testing and treatment (African Union, 2020, 6), as well as any social protection measures (Carella et al., 2021, 13).

Irregular status and labour informality are different issues, which are intertwined in a mutually reinforcing relationship. Informality may contribute to irregularity insofar as vast informal economies attract those migrant workers who find no legal channels to migrate; and conversely, irregular status leads to further informality as migrants in an irregular situation have no access to formal jobs.

Even when they obtain a work visa and a formal job, many migrants in the Global South do not fully enjoy their right to work and rights at work. The recruitment process (both transnational and in-country) is insidious and can result in abuses and violations, from the charging of fees and related costs (which should be borne by the employer) to human trafficking and forced labour in the most extreme cases. Indeed, the forced labour prevalence among adult migrant workers is over three times that of national workers (ILO et al., 2022, 36). At their workplace, migrants' occupational safety and health are not always guaranteed, especially in the "3D jobs"—the *Ds* standing for dirty, dangerous and/or difficult (Koser, 2010, 306). Their working environments (private homes, crop fields, construction sites, sweatshops, meatpacking plants, fishing boats, etc.) and living conditions are such that many migrant workers have extremely limited access to justice and remedies if they suffer abuses or rights violations (Hamada, 2017, 157).

Temporariness is another feature of much South–South migration in regions such as Asia (Khan & Hossain, 2017, 16). Short-term, temporary and seasonal labour migration are linked to the economic activities that most migrant workers engage in: occupations that have traditionally been categorised as *low-skilled* and *medium-skilled*, but should more accurately be referred to as *low-wage*. This trend contrasts sharply with the global race for talent that can be observed in South-North labour migration, whereby northern destination countries select the best and brightest professionals from the Global South, opening legal migration channels for them, and often leaving the countries of origin to deal with the consequences of brain drain (Raghuram, 2009, 27). The temporary nature of migration also means that integration prospects are curtailed, as there is no path to permanent residency or nationality acquisition in the host country (ILO, 2022, 36).

Not So Different, After All? Global Inequalities and Diversity Within South–South Migration

Push–pull theories and functionalist migration models with all their limitations (De Haas, 2014, 4) posit that migration occurs as a result of economic and demographic inequalities between countries: those in the Global North tend to attract migrants due to higher development vis-à-vis those in the South. The latter, often experiencing pressures on their labour markets as they cannot offer gainful work opportunities to all jobseekers, are relieved to let their nationals seek opportunities elsewhere.

Contemporary South–South migration can also be considered a by-product of the distinct impacts of globalisation on different parts of the Global South. Some have defined Asia as a South–South migration hub (Hossain et al., 2017, 1), with Asia's newly industrialised economies having become countries of destination requiring more and less skilled labour; and countries of origin such as Nepal, Sri Lanka and the Philippines eager to provide it. Africa, the Arab States and Latin America and the Caribbean also experience, to different degrees, increasing rates of intra-regional human mobility in the forms of labour migration, forced displacement and mixed flows.

While trying to outline some common features that distinguish South–South migration from South-North migration can be useful, it is also crucial to acknowledge that the exercise is a broad-brush characterisation. There is as much diversity and complexity in South–South migration as there is in humanity. Thus, for each trend outlined in the previous section, it is possible to also identify a counterexample to remind us that trends are not mathematical rules.

While northern countries do handpick high-skilled migrant workers for high-pay occupations, many of them also host migrant workers in low-pay sectors; some of these are in informal jobs, and some may be on their territory irregularly. Even under conditions of regularity and formality, some forms of mobility towards northern countries present important challenges to the protection of migrant workers, as they do in the South: many regulated temporary labour migration schemes have roots that can be traced back to colonial indentured labour (ILO, 2022, 1).

By the same token, the diversity of South–South migration also encompasses high-skilled professionals. One clear illustration among many is Venezuelan mixed-flow migration to Latin American and Caribbean countries: in several destination countries, the level of tertiary education attainment among the Venezuelan migrant population is higher than in the host population (ILO & UNDP, 2021, 24). According to one study, approximately 20,000 Venezuelan medical doctors were living in Argentina, Brazil, Chile, Colombia, Mexico and Peru in 2020 (ILO, 2021b, 20). However, in contrast to most medical and healthcare workers migrating to the Global North (such as Indian doctors or Filipino nurses in the UK), most Venezuelans did not reach their countries of destination in Latin America on a work visa. In fact, many of them had to work in sectors unrelated to their training and qualifications upon arrival. In 2020, 40% of the surveyed healthcare professionals who were exercising their profession had been permitted to do so only as a result of the COVID-19 pandemic, which caused a surge in need for medics and paramedics, and led governments to loosen administrative requirements for the recognition of foreign qualifications. Furthermore, although they were employed in high-skilled occupations, most of them were not paid accordingly (ILO, 2021b, 46).

Another illustration of the diversity within South–South migration is that highly regulated labour migration, based on visas and transnational recruitment, can coexist in the Global South alongside the previously described vast informal economies and widespread irregular migration. The migration of South and South-East Asian workers to the Gulf Cooperation Council (GCC) countries and to destinations such as Hong Kong and Singapore are examples of highly regulated South–South migration corridors, where the level of logistics, formality and bureaucracy involved is reminiscent of South–North labour migration as experienced, for instance, by Jamaican agricultural workers going to Canada or Indian engineers migrating to the USA.

One final consideration, which applies to both South–South migration and other migration flows, but with arguably greater impact on the former, is linked to the multi-level governance of migration and the role of local authorities. Although the right to leave any country, including one's own (emigration) and to return to one's own country are universal human rights, entering another country is not a right (Higgins, 2009, 444). The determination of immigration policy, defined as the conditions for non-nationals to enter and reside in the State's territory, is a highly centralised prerogative of each state, considered to touch the very core of state sovereignty. Subnational and local authorities generally have no or little say in it. Nonetheless, cities, regions and other local authorities do play a pivotal role in designing and implementing crucial aspects of migration policy: first and foremost, those related to the reception and integration of migrants and refugees.

The role of cities in the governance of migration has been progressively acknowledged internationally through a number of initiatives: among them, the Mayoral Forum on Human Mobility, Migration and Development; the Mayors Migration Council and the UN Joint Migration and Development Initiative. Local policies for migrant integration have been widely documented (Zapata-Barrero et al., 2017, 241). While local authorities contribute to the governance of migration everywhere, the difference they can make in certain southern settings is critical, due to the higher prevalence of both labour informality and irregular status among migrants. In contexts where migrants can cross borders and reach their destination without producing formal documentation, it is particularly beneficial for a local authority to foster access to livelihoods and self-sufficiency regardless of migration status, thereby limiting the fiscal burden on public finances. These pay-offs at the local level may determine a *de facto* right to work for migrants at that level, even when it does not exist *de jure* at the national level (Betts & Sterck, 2022, 525).

Policy and Programmatic Responses to South–South Migration

The complexity of South–South migration, intertwined with inequalities between and within countries—in both the North and the South—has wide-ranging policy and programmatic implications. Since the governance of migration occurs at several levels—local, national, regional and international—the remainder of this chapter sheds light on some policy and programmatic implications by looking at the interplay between these dimensions.

The SDGs and Development Policy

Starting with the global level, the 2030 Sustainable Development Agenda, adopted by the international community in 2015, plays a role in shaping policy and programmatic responses to South–South migration. The 17 Sustainable Development Goals (SDGs) to be achieved by 2030 are universal: they apply to all countries, not only developing ones, so they should be equally relevant to the Global North and the Global South. This is a major shift from the previous paradigm (the Millennium Development Goals, or MDGs), in which the responsibility for progress towards the achievement of the goals was placed on developing countries, in a top-down approach that set double standards of dubious effectiveness in terms of developmental impact in a globalised world.

Another important distinction from the previous development framework is that migration features expressly in the SDGs, while it had been absent from the MDGs. Crucially, an explicit reference to migration is made in Goal 8: "Promote sustained, inclusive and sustainable economic growth, full and productive employment and decent work for all". Specifically, SDG Target 8.8 sets out to "Protect labour rights and promote safe and secure working environments for all workers, including migrant workers, in particular women migrants, and those in precarious employment". This is a crucial issue since most international migration is labour migration: over 62% of the estimated 272 international migrants (ILO, 2021a, 11). A substantial proportion of this international labour migration occurs within the Global South—approximately half of it, if we consider the Arab states, including the GCC countries, to be part of the Global South (ILO, 2021a, 32)—where the incidence of irregular migration status and labour informality tends to be higher, and dangerous forms of work with little protection are more widespread.

Another Sustainable Development Goal that specifically refers to migration is SDG 10: "Reduce inequality within and among countries". In particular, Target 10.7 aims to "facilitate orderly, safe, and responsible migration and mobility of people, including through implementation of planned and well-managed migration policies". It is worth zooming into one of the indicators established to measure the achievement of this target, namely indicator 10.7.1 on "Recruitment cost borne by employee as a proportion of monthly income earned in country of destination" (ILO, 2020, 3). Measuring how much it costs for a migrant worker to obtain employment in another country matters because labour intermediation—the process by which a jobseeker is matched with a job opportunity—should come at no cost to the worker or job seeker, regardless of whether it is carried out by a public employment service or a private recruitment agency.[2]

To understand how exorbitant recruitment costs can be for migrants along South–South migration corridors, it is worth considering that a Pakistani worker seeking employment in Saudi Arabia can be charged the equivalent of 10.6 months' country of destination earnings in recruitment fees and related costs; while a Bangladeshi worker migrating to Kuwait can be charged the equivalent of nine months' earnings.[3] The effect of these charges can be devastating. Many migrant workers need to take out loans and become heavily indebted before starting their jobs overseas. Once they have arrived at destination, they start working knowing that, for several months, their income will have to go towards repaying debt. Those who end up victims of abuse or violations of their rights at work will be less likely to report their employer, look for an alternative one, or seek justice and redress, since the burden of debt will make them want to keep their source of income at all costs, and regardless of the conditions to be withstood. In this context, the achievement of migration-related SDG targets, such as 8.8, can clearly make a big difference in the lives of migrant workers in the Global South.

Protection of Migrants' Rights

Globally and nationally, certain legal instruments set standards to protect the rights of migrants, refugees and other people on the move in the Global South. Many southern countries have ratified the 1951 Geneva Refugee Convention and/or its 1967 Protocol as well as at least one of the three international, legally binding treaties for the protection of migrant workers: ILO C97 Migration for Employment (Revised) Convention (1949), ILO C143 Migrant Workers (Supplementary Provisions) Convention (1975) and the International Convention on the Protection of the Rights of All Migrant Workers and Members of Their Families (1990). Most have also endorsed the non-binding UN Global Compact for Safe, Orderly and Regular Migration

---

[2] The requirement that no worker should pay for a job, and its corollary that no recruiter should charge fees to workers, is enshrined in the ILO Principles and Guidelines on Fair Recruitment and also appears in the Dhaka Principles for Migration with Dignity (the "Dhaka Principles"), developed by the Institute for Human Rights & Business (IHRB) and endorsed in 2012 by the Confederation of International Recruitment Agencies (now the World Employment Confederation—WEC) and the International Trade Union Confederation (ITUC). For further information, see https://www.ilo.org/global/topics/fair-recruitment/WCMS_536755.

[3] For further details on these, as well as additional examples, please see the KNOMAD-ILO Migration and Recruitment Costs Surveys at https://www.knomad.org/data/recruitment-costs (accessed on 10 September 2022).

(2018). Beyond instruments that are specific to human mobility, a broader framework for the protection of migrant workers' (including refugees') rights can be found in human rights instruments. Because of migrants' and refugees' high participation in labour markets, International Labour Standards (ILS) can be particularly useful.

At the bilateral level, bilateral labour agreements (BLAs) can be negotiated between countries of origin and destination. These are complementary to international standards; they should draw and be based on the latter but have the advantage of being adapted to a specific bilateral context. Practical Guidance on Bilateral Labour Migration Agreements was published in 2022 by the UN Migration Network.[4] A model agreement is annexed to ILO R86 Migration for Employment Recommendation (Revised). As well as having a clear focus on rights, agreements should ideally include provisions on access to, and portability of, social security for migrant workers; if they do not, separate bilateral or multilateral social security agreements are also useful programmatic responses. For South–South migration flows—at least those of the formal kind—BLAs constitute practical and useful governance tools. For example, they make a difference in the lives of Panamanian migrant workers from the indigenous people Ngäbe Buglé, who every year, during coffee harvest season, engage in temporary agricultural work in Costa Rica; or migrant workers from Nicaragua who cross into northern Costa Rica to work in the pineapple fields.

South–South Cooperation on Migration

South–South cooperation has been shaped to a great extent by emerging economies such as the BRICS (Brazil, India, China and South Africa) and it can take a variety of forms. While a plethora of literature exists on South–South cooperation in the broad field of development studies, less attention has been given to South–South cooperation in the specific fields of migration and displacement (Fiddian-Qasmiyeh, 2019, 240). This cooperation has nevertheless occurred in a variety of forms.

One example of migration-related South–South cooperation is the project on the protection of the rights of migrant workers in Latin America and the Caribbean funded by Brazil's Development Cooperation agency from 2015 to 2017. The project was implemented by the ILO, which provided technical assistance as well as programmatic support, and the participating

---

[4] The Guidance on Bilateral Labour Migration Agreements can be downloaded at: https://www.ilo.org/global/topics/labour-migration/publications/WCMS_837529/lang--en/index.htm.

countries were Argentina, Brazil, Costa Rica, Chile, Mexico and Trinidad and Tobago. Government representatives and other stakeholders from these countries participated in dialogue and exchange on their respective experiences, and contributed to the development of a series of studies and guidance tools based on lessons learned and targeted to their specific needs.[5] The fact that some of these tools are still being used today indicates that South–South cooperation can be a useful programmatic instrument for the governance of South–South migration: participating countries felt that the lessons learned on how to foster the socioeconomic integration of migrants and refugees in a context of high informality and high prevalence of irregular status resonated with their own experience, making the guidance particularly valuable.

Of course, the risk of co-opting by the more powerful party exists in any South–South cooperation exercise. In this case, the more powerful party (and potential co-opter) was Brazil, which was not only a participant, but also the donor of the project. Countries in the Global North have used development cooperation as a form of soft power for a long time, leading some to refer to development aid provided by the North as a new form of colonialism (Ziai, 2015, 33). Does it make a difference that, in this case, the development initiative was funded and led by a southern country, and its implementation supported by a United Nations entity?

This is a complex and controversial question. However, in this South–South cooperation project, Brazil imposed only administrative and financial constraints—which were handled by ILO as implementing agency—while the policy and programmatic priorities were set jointly by participating countries, which shared ownership over the South–South cooperation exercise. Regarding the ILO, it is a member of the UN system, with virtually universal membership (member states are from both the North and the South), which in this case was acting with southern funding. It could therefore be argued that this exercise was a true example of South–South cooperation that fostered dialogue on policy and programmatic responses to migration between the countries of the Global South.

Regional Consultative Processes

Regional Consultative Processes (RCPs) have flourished world-wide since the 1990s as mechanisms to improve the governance of migration through regional-level dialogue among countries. The first RCP was established in the

---

[5] A summary of the project and the guidance tools are available online at: https://www.ilo.org/brasilia/programas-projetos/WCMS_365740/lang--pt/index.htm.

Global North (the Budapest Process, est. 1991), and the two that followed involved both northern and southern countries: 1996 saw the establishment of the Inter-governmental Asia–Pacific Consultations on Refugees, Displaced Persons and Migrants and the Regional Conference on Migration (RCM) in Central and North America (Hansen, 2010, 61, 69, 73). The former included Australia, New Zealand, New Caledonia (a French territory), as well as China and several other southern countries throughout Asia and the Pacific. The latter has Canada and the United States among its member countries, as well as Mexico, all Central American countries and the Dominican Republic; with this membership, the RCM covers both South–South and South-North migration.

Several factors affect whether an RCP can be considered an example of South–South cooperation on migration governance. First, of course, the participation of northern countries in the RCP. Second, the possibility that the de facto leadership in setting the RCP's agenda may be exerted not by any member state but by the RCP technical secretariat, which is usually held by an international organisation (Hansen, 2010, 38). In these cases, considerations around co-opting would apply, similar to those addressed in the previous subsection.

An example of South–South cooperation in regional-level response to South–South migration is the Ministerial Consultation on Overseas Employment and Contractual Labour for Countries of Origin in Asia—now known as Colombo Process—established in 2003 at the initiative of the Sri Lankan Government. Sri Lanka, as a country of origin of migrant workers, was interested in exchanging information and improving coordination with other migrant-sending countries in the region, with a view to improving its negotiating position vis-à-vis destination countries and strengthening the protection of its nationals abroad. The Colombo Process currently has twelve member states: Afghanistan, Bangladesh, Cambodia, China, India, Indonesia, Nepal, Pakistan, the Philippines, Sri Lanka, Thailand and Viet Nam.

Interestingly, the countries that received migrant workers from the Colombo Process member states quickly became interested in the initiative and requested to attend Colombo Process meetings as observers. Some were invited to do so for the first time in 2005. At this meeting, the Colombo Process member states formally decided to engage in dialogue with countries of destination, both in Asia and in Europe. This decision crystallised in the 2008 Abu Dhabi Dialogue, which saw Malaysia, Singapore, the GCC countries and Yemen (as receiving countries) meet with the Colombo Process member states (sending countries). Both groups have continued to meet, retaining the "Abu Dhabi Dialogue" denomination, and held their sixth ministerial meeting in late 2021.[6]

The Colombo Process can be considered an at least partially successful example of South–South cooperation in the governance of South–South migration. In contrast to other RCPs, it was not piloted by countries in the Global North or by international organisations. Nevertheless, its activity has been intermittent, as evidenced by the absence of ministerial meetings between 2011 and 2016 (these are supposed to be held every two years, per Colombo Process Operating Modalities) (IOM, 2011, 5). These shortcomings could be attributed to leadership gaps from southern countries, but possibly also to a determination not to let northern parties or international organisations take the lead.

The Abu Dhabi Dialogue could arguably be considered another example of South–South cooperation in the governance of South–South migration. In line with the arguments advanced in the first section of this chapter, some may not agree that all its member states are southern states, since the GCC countries are high-income economies. However others—myself included—would argue that they are part of the Global South due to a variety of reasons (Ferabolli, 2021, 16), including, but not limited to, their development models, and a shared history with other southern countries, involving colonialism, empire and subordination.

Even so, inequalities within the Global South can be such that the power relations arising between countries of origin and countries of destination of migrant workers lead to co-opting dynamics that are quite similar to those experienced in the North. One illustration may be found in the agenda items at Abu Dhabi Dialogue meetings: recruitment and skills—priorities for the countries of destination—feature prominently, but protection issues (including abuse and exploitation of migrant workers, the consequences of the *kafala* system, etc.) not as much. Indeed, one could plausibly argue that the countries of destination's request to attend meetings of the Colombo Process as observers, and the subsequent creation of the Abu Dhabi dialogue, were *metropolitan* attempts at co-opting a *peripherical* initiative for the governance of South–South migration.

---

[6] For further information on the Colombo Process, see https://www.colomboprocess.org/about-the-colombo-process/background and on the Abu Dhabi Dialogue, see http://abudhabidialogue.org.ae/timeline (accessed on 09 October 2022). For details on the January 2008 meeting, see 24/01/2008 press release 'Abu Dhabi Dialogue on Contractual Labour for Cooperation between Countries of Origin and Destination in Asia' https://www.ilo.org/global/topics/forced-labour/news/WCMS_090660/lang--en/index.htm.

Regional Integration Mechanisms

RCPs do not "operate in a vacuum" (Hansen, 2010, 13). Regional economic communities (RECs) and regional integration mechanisms often provide the institutional framework to implement recommendations issued by the RCP. In certain regions, the local RECs are themselves drivers of migration policies that innovate and go beyond international standards—especially when a free movement regime is a component of the regional integration. In the Global North, one good example is the European Union, where intra-regional migration or mobility is virtually unrestricted, not just for the purpose of employment, but based on the principle of EU citizenship.

In the Global South, some regional blocs have also introduced free movement regimes. In the case of South America's MERCOSUR, the regime is quite extensive, insofar as it applies to any national of a member or associate state, who can enter the territory of another such state and request a residence permit valid for up to two years—subject to minimum administrative requirements in addition to proof of nationality—for any purpose, not just employment. In the Caribbean, CARICOM—self-described as "the oldest surviving integration movement in the developing world"[7]—has provisions for the free movement of workers and job seekers. In Africa, the ECOWAS Protocol on Free Movement, Right of Residence and Establishment has successfully accomplished visa-free travel within the region and has made some progress towards residence and establishment (Garba & Yeboah, 2022, 24).

In forced displacement contexts, some regions in the Global South have pioneered the development of regional protection frameworks, such as the 1969 Refugee Convention of the Organisation of African Unity, now African Union and the 1984 Cartagena Declaration in Latin America. Although these frameworks have enjoyed varying degrees of success in their implementation over time and across their respective regions (Hammoud-Gallego & Freier, 2022, 455, 469), southern countries have also demonstrated creativity in developing alternative, ad-hoc responses to mixed flows, as many Latin American countries have done with regularisation programmes for Venezuelans (R4V, 2022, 19).

---

[7] See the CARICOM website: https://caricom.org/our-community/who-we-are/#:~:text=CARICOM%20is%20the%20oldest%20surviving,%2C%20in%20culture%2C%20in%20security.

Southern Cities and the Local Governance of Migration

Finally, at the local level, some southern cities have been at the forefront of policy and programmatic responses to South–South migration. Most have done so by applying the principle of non-discrimination to their offer of public services (mainstreaming migration as a variable into their programmes) while also creating some services specifically targeting migrants and refugees. São Paulo, the largest city in Brazil, created in 2013 a Migrant Policies Coordination Unit (CPMig by its Portuguese acronym) within the Municipal Secretariat for Human Rights and Citizenship. Its role is to oversee the implementation of the Municipal Policy for the Immigrant Population, which has been followed as an example by several other municipalities, in Brazil and beyond (Sampaio & Baraldi, 2019, 27). One key principle on which the policy rests is the acknowledgement of migrants' contribution to the enrichment of the city. The Coordination Unit manages a Migrants' Reference and Assistance Centre (staffed by migrant workers) and promotes, among others, access to decent work, to justice, to the banking system and regularisation for migrants.

In Mexico City, the local Labour Secretariat has mainstreamed human mobility as a key variable in most of its programmes for labour inclusion and social protection, with the objective of making them accessible to all its citizens, including Mexican migrants (returnees, internally displaced and domestic migrants) as well as refugees and migrants arriving from abroad (STyFE & ILO, 2018, 28).

As shown in this section, the set of southern responses to South–South migration encompasses a plethora of diverse policy and programmatic orientations that are not only innovative, but also as sophisticated as those devised and implemented in the North.

Conclusion

So, is South–South migration so different that the policy and programmatic responses required by it differ from those adopted in South-North migration? The answer will probably depend on whether the respondent is from the North or the South.

It is often unclear whether a certain policy or programmatic response is truly southern or has been co-opted by a non-southern actor to such an extent that the latter sets the agenda. In the case of the Colombo Process, at least at the time of the Process's establishment and at several other points in its history, the objectives, priorities and tone were set by southern countries, and the resulting policy and programmatic focus was a truly *southern* response to South–South migration; as such, fundamental southern concerns such as the protection of migrant workers' rights featured prominently.

In a fully southern policy and programmatic orientation, not only the Colombo Process but also the Abu Dhabi Dialogue would have a clear focus on rights, and prioritise issues such as decent work, access to justice, minimum standards for bilateral labour agreements, etc. However, realpolitik and the different economic clouts of sending and receiving countries (*periphery* and *metropole* respectively) mean that policy and programmatic agendas can be easily co-opted, either by decisively northern actors (European and North American countries), or by arguably southern players (e.g. Asian destination countries, such as the GCC states), or even by hybrid stakeholders (international organisations).

Since each South–South migration corridor is unique, it is wise not to promote a one-size-fits-all approach when looking for effective policy and programmatic approaches to migration governance. However, based on past and current experiences, certain practices are worth recommending, since their application entails minimum risk and can improve outcomes for migrants and southern countries.

At the *national level*, framing migration as a human rights issue rather than a security problem, and presenting it as such, helps host communities see what they have in common with migrants as opposed to what sets them apart. This helps protect migrants. Ensuring coherence among policies that directly affect migrants as well as host communities (immigration policy, employment policy, education and training policy) is crucial to facilitating the integration of migrants in the Global South and maximising their contributions to the host economies, thereby also alleviating the fiscal burden on the host state (OECD & ILO, 2018, 33). At the same time, when devising key national policies, such as social protection, health, education, it is paramount to consider a country's complex migration profile (i.e. incoming migration, outgoing migration or nationals abroad, transit migration, return migration), both at present and in future scenarios, since a country's migration profile can change suddenly. Finally, ensuring coordination between different levels of migration governance—the national level, which usually sets immigration and other overarching laws, and the *local level*, where integration happens—maximises the impact of public spending on the policies and programmes devised for migrants and host communities alike.

At the *regional level*, coordinating with neighbouring countries can be an effective way of ensuring migrants' protection and context-specific policy responses to South–South migration. This is particularly important between countries and within regions with substantial migration flows. This coordination can materialise in different modalities: multilaterally, within the contexts of RECs and/or RCPs on migration; or bilaterally, through the negotiation and implementation of bilateral agreements. Bilateral labour agreements are often the best tailor-made policy and programmatic response to South–South labour migration flows. For the BLAs to work effectively, it is crucial that they are developed ensuring inter-institutional coordination (ministries of foreign affairs, labour, interior—all need to have a say) and in broad consultation with other key stakeholders, including employers' organisations, trade unions and relevant civil society actors.

At the *global level*, striving for the achievement of the SDGs, especially targets 8.8 on the protection of labour rights of all workers, including migrant workers, and 10.7 on orderly, safe and responsible migration and mobility, is a sound first step towards ensuring adequate policy responses to South–South migration. The ratification and application of International Labour Standards and other relevant human rights instruments also help ensure sound governance and rights protection, including where the migration-specific treaties have not been ratified.

Policy coordination and coherence at different levels of governance are crucial in South–South migration and other forms of migration alike. However, the challenging contexts that characterise many southern destination countries (vast informal economies, lack of social and labour protection, etc.) and the particular vulnerability of many migrants along South–South migration corridors (higher prevalence of irregular status, obstacles in access to justice, no long-term prospects, etc.) make bespoke programmatic and policy responses to South–South migration particularly urgent.

The inequalities and diversity between the countries of the Global South render each southern context is unique. Yet the wealth of existing, successful southern responses to South–South migration suggests that it pays to examine what has worked elsewhere and consider how it can be adapted. In the foreseeable future, South–South migration will continue to require innovative responses, and to constitute a migration governance laboratory that both the South and the North will observe and learn from.

This article expresses the views of the author and does not reflect the official views of the ILO.

Acknowledgements The author wishes to express his gratitude to Dr Piyasiri Wickramasekara for providing insightful reflections on the Colombo Process, the Abu Dhabi Dialogue and South–South migration more broadly, during an informal conversation held while this chapter was being drafted.

References

African Union. (2020). *Protecting migrant workers in the informal economy – Inclusion of migrant workers in COVID-19 responses*. AU, Addis Ababa. https://au.int/en/documents/20201223/protecting-migrant-workers-informal-economy-inclusion-mw-covid-19-responses

Anderson, W. (2014). Racial conceptions in the Global South. *Race and Ethnicity, the History of Science Society, 105*(4), 782–792. https://doi.org/10.1086/679425

Bakewell, O., de Haas, H., Castles, S., Vezzoli, S., & Jónsson, G. (2009). South–South migration and human development: Reflections on African Experiences. UNDP Human Development Reports Research Paper 2009/07. UNDP.

Betts, A., & Sterck, O. (2022). Why do states give refugees the right to work? *Oxford Review of Economic Policy, 38*(3), 514–530. https://doi.org/10.1093/oxrep/grac017

Carella, F., Frean, S., & Velasco, J. (2021). Migración laboral, movilidad en el mundo del trabajo ante la pandemia de la COVID-19 en América Latina y el Caribe – Nota Técnica. Lima: OIT. https://www.ilo.org/wcmsp5/groups/public/---americas/---ro-lima/documents/publication/wcms_778606.pdf

Connell, R. (2007). *Southern theory: The global dynamics of knowledge in social science*. Polity.

De Haas, H. (2014). Migration theory – Quo Vadis? *University of Oxford International Migration Institute Working Papers*, Paper 100, November 2014. University of Oxford. https://heindehaas.files.wordpress.com/2015/05/de-haas-2014-imi-wp100-migration-theory-quo-vadis.pdf

Ferabolli, S. (2021). Space making in the Global South: Lessons from the GCC-Mercosur Agreement. *Contexto Internacional, 43*(1), 9–30.

Fiddian-Qasmiyeh, E. (2019). Southern-led responses to displacement: Modes of South–South cooperation? In *Routledge Handbook of South–South Relations* (1st ed., pp. 239–255). Routledge. https://doi.org/10.4324/9781315624495-18

Garba, F., Yeboah, T. (2022). Free movement and regional integration in the ECOWAS sub-region. In J. K. Teye (Ed.), *Migration in West Africa*. IMISCOE Research Series. Springer. https://doi.org/10.1007/978-3-030-97322-3_2

Hamada, Y., (2017). South to South migration in Asia. Opportunities, challenges and policy implications for the Sustainable Development Goals of the 2030 agenda for sustainable development. In P. Short, M. Hossain, & M. A. Khan (Eds.), *South–South Migration. Emerging Patterns, Opportunities and Risks*. Routledge.

Hammer, A., & Ness, I. (2021). Informal and precarious work: Insights from the Global South. *Journal of Labor and Society, 24*, 1–15.

Hammoud-Gallego, O., & Freier, L. (2022). Symbolic refugee protection: Explaining Latin America's liberal refugee laws. *American Political Science Review*, 1–20. https://doi.org/10.1017/S000305542200082X

Hansen, R. (2010). An assessment of principal regional consultative processes on migration. *IOM Migration Research Series*. IOM. https://publications.iom.int/system/files/pdf/mrs_38.pdf

Higgins, R. (2009). The Right in International Law of an Individual to Enter, Stay in and Leave a Country. In *Themes and Theories* (Oxford, 2009; online edn, Oxford Academic, 22 Mar. 2012). https://doi.org/10.1093/acprof:oso/9780198262350.003.0030

Hossain, M., Khan, M. A., & Short, P. (2017). An overview of South–South migration. Opportunities, risks and policies. In P. Short, M. Hossain, & M. A. Khan (Eds.), *South–South Migration. Emerging Patterns, Opportunities and Risks*. Routledge, New York.

ILO. (2017). Labour migration in Latin America and the Caribbean. Diagnosis, Strategy and ILO's work in the Region. ILO, Lima. https://www.ilo.org/wcmsp5/groups/public/---americas/---ro-lima/documents/publication/wcms_548185.pdf

ILO. (2018). *Women and men in the informal economy: A statistical picture*. Third edition. ILO, Geneva. https://www.ilo.org/global/publications/books/WCMS_626831/lang--en/index.htm

ILO. (2020). *Global study on recruitment fees and related costs*. ILO, Geneva. https://www.ilo.org/global/topics/labour-migration/publications/WCMS_761729/lang--en/index.htm

ILO. (2021a). *ILO Global Estimates on International Migrant Workers – Results and Methodology*, 3rd edn, International Labour Office, Geneva. https://www.ilo.org/wcmsp5/groups/public/@dgreports/@dcomm/@publ/documents/publication/wcms_808935.pdf

ILO. (2021b). El aporte de las personas refugiadas y migrantes venezolanas frente a la pandemia de la COVID-19 en los servicios esenciales de salud: Argentina, Brasil, Colombia, Chile, México y Perú. ILO, Lima. https://www.ilo.org/wcmsp5/groups/public/---americas/---ro-lima/documents/publication/wcms_794074.pdf

ILO. (2022). *Temporary Labour Migration: Unpacking Complexities*. International Labour Office, Geneva. https://www.ilo.org/global/topics/labour-migration/publications/WCMS_858541/lang--en/index.htm

ILO STAT. *Statistics on the Informal Economy*, https://ilostat.ilo.org/topics/informality/. Accessed on 23 Oct 2022.

ILO, & UNDP. (2021). *Migration from Venezuela: Opportunities for Latin America and the Caribbean*. ILO and UNDP, Geneva. https://www.ilo.org/americas/publicaciones/WCMS_775183/lang--en/index.htm

ILO, Walk Free, & IOM. (2022). *Global Estimates of Modern Slavery: Forced Labour and Forced Marriage*. International Labour Office, Geneva. https://www.ilo.org/global/topics/forced-labour/publications/WCMS_854733/lang--en/index.htm

IOM. (2011). Colombo Process's operating modalities https://www.iom.int/sites/g/files/tmzbdl486/files/jahia/webdav/shared/shared/mainsite/microsites/rcps/colombo/Colombo-Process-Operating-Modalities-2011.pdf

IOM. (2022). *IOM and South–South and Triangular Cooperation* (Factsheet). https://migration4development.org/sites/default/files/2022-09/SSC_IOM_factsheet_EXTERNAL_JULY%202022.pdf

Khan, M. A., & Hossain M. I. (2017). The emerging phenomenon of post-globalized, South–South migration. In search of a theoretical framework. In P. Short, M. Hossain, M. A. Khan (Eds.), *South–South migration. Emerging patterns, opportunities and risks*. Routledge.

Koser, K. (2010). Introduction: international migration and global governance. *Global Governance, 16*(3), 301–315. http://www.jstor.org/stable/29764947

Mawdsley, E. (2012). The changing geographies of foreign aid and development cooperation: Contributions from gift theory. *Transactions of the Institute of British Geographers, 37*(2), 256–272.

Mignolo, W. D. (2011). The Global South and world dis/order. *Journal of Anthropological Research, 67*(2), 165–188.

Ndlovu-Gatsheni, S. J., & Tafira, K. (2018). The invention of the global South and the politics of South–South solidarity. In E. Fiddian-Qasmiyeh & P. Daley (Eds.), *Routledge Handbook of South–South Relations* (pp. 127–140). Routledge.

OECD, & ILO. (2018). *How immigrants contribute to developing countries' economies*. ILO, Geneva/OECD Publishing. https://doi.org/10.1787/9789264288737-en

Raghuram, P. (2009). Caring about "brain drain" migration in a postcolonial world. *Geoforum, 40*(1), 25–33. https://doi.org/10.1016/j.geoforum.2008.03.005

Rodríguez-García, D. (2010). Beyond assimilation and multiculturalism: A critical review of the debate on managing diversity. *Journal of International Migration and Integration, 11*(3), 251–271. https://doi.org/10.1007/s12134-010-0140-x

R4V. (2022). *Programas de regularización y facilidades administrativas para las personas refugiadas y migrantes de Venezuela, Panama*. https://www.r4v.info/sites/default/files/2022-06/PDA55369_1%20-%20R4V-Junio7%20v4.pdf

Sampaio, C., & Baraldi, C. (2019). *Políticas migratórias em nível local. Análise sobre a institucionalização da política municipal para a população imigrante de São Paulo*. Santiago de Chile: CEPAL. https://repositorio.cepal.org/bitstream/handle/11362/44491/4/S1900310_pt.pdf

STyFE, & OIT. (2018). *Programas sociales para población migrante en la Ciudad de México: Identificación de buenas prácticas y recomendaciones en materia de inserción laboral*. STyFE. https://www.trabajo.cdmx.gob.mx/storage/app/uploads/public/5bc/619/621/5bc6196218328636139953.pdf

Vertovec, S. (2007). Super-diversity and its implications. *Ethnic and Racial Studies, 30*(6), 1024–1054. https://doi.org/10.1080/01419870701599465

Zapata-Barrero, R. (Ed.). (2015). *Interculturalism in cities: Concept, policy and implementation*. Edward-Elgar Publishing.

Zapata-Barrero, R., Caponio, T., & Scholten, P. (2017). Theorizing the 'local turn' in a multi-level governance framework of analysis: A case study in immigrant policies. *International Review of Administrative Sciences, 83*(2), 241–246. https://doi.org/10.1177/0020852316688426

Ziai, A. (2015). *Development discourse and global history: From colonialism to the sustainable development goals*. Routledge.

Open Access This chapter is licensed under the terms of the Creative Commons Attribution 4.0 International License (http://creativecommons.org/licenses/by/4.0/), which permits use, sharing, adaptation, distribution and reproduction in any medium or format, as long as you give appropriate credit to the original author(s) and the source, provide a link to the Creative Commons license and indicate if changes were made.

The images or other third party material in this chapter are included in the chapter's Creative Commons license, unless indicated otherwise in a credit line to the material. If material is not included in the chapter's Creative Commons license and your intended use is not permitted by statutory regulation or exceeds the permitted use, you will need to obtain permission directly from the copyright holder.

28

Policies towards Migration in Africa

Joseph Kofi Teye and Linda Oucho

Introduction

Although human mobility has, historically, been an integral part of life in Africa, the region has become the focus of recent policy discussions on migration governance (Knoll & de Weijer, 2016). This is partly due to the fact that Africa experiences massive labour mobility (Olsen, 2011) and worsening forced displacement situations (Teye, 2022a; UNHCR, 2020). Many of the African sub-regions are experiencing "mixed migration", which entails "cross-border movements of people, including refugees fleeing persecution and conflict, victims of trafficking, and people seeking better lives and opportunities" (Mixed Migration Centre, 2021, 2). While media narratives tend to portray an exodus from Africa to the Global North, especially Europe, most African migrants actually migrate intra-regionally (Awumbila et al., 2018; Setrana and Yeoh, this volume; Teye, 2022a). The proportion of African migrants that are living within their own sub-regions is as follows: Middle Africa (79%), Western Africa (72%), Eastern Africa (71%), Southern Africa (52%), and Northern Africa (13%) (UNCTAD, 2018).

J. K. Teye
Centre for Migration Studies (CMS), University of Ghana, Accra, Ghana
e-mail: jteye@ug.edu.gh

L. Oucho (✉)
African Migration and Development Policy Centre (AMADPOC), Westlands, Nairobi, Kenya
e-mail: linda.oucho@amadpoc.org

African migrants represent less than 15% of the total migrant population in all other regions except for Africa, and only 27% of migrants from the continent live in Europe (Mo Ibrahim Foundation and Africa Europe Foundation, 2020). However, migration within the continent has been increasing in recent years (African Centre for Strategic Studies, 2020). This reflects in part growing inequalities, climate change, trade, and demographic imbalances but also a rise in demand for labour in key economic sectors, such as mining and construction, fishing, agriculture as well as services such as retail trade, health care, domestic work, restaurants, and hotel (Hlatshwayo, 2019; ILO, 2022). Outside Africa, Europe is the most popular destination of migrants from Africa. An increasing number of African labour migrants are also recently moving to the Gulf States (Deshingkar et al., 2019; Jamie & Tsega, 2018; Mlambo & Zubane, 2021).

In recognition that an effective labour migration governance system is critical to harnessing the benefits of migration and addressing its challenges, such as abuse of migrants rights, human trafficking, and limited access to social justice (ILO, 2022; Teye, 2022a), the African Union (AU) Commission and its Member States and Regional Economic Communities (RECs) have adopted a number of global and Africa-wide migration governance frameworks to address the challenges of migration. Many of the regional economic communities have also adopted various frameworks to govern migration.

Despite their promising nature, there are gaps in the implementation of these policy frameworks which are poorly understood. Drawing on a review of academic literature, policy documents, and reports of previous studies, this chapter examines the achievements, gaps, and challenges associated with continental, regional, and national level migration policy frameworks in Africa. The chapter argues that despite the progress in designing a number of migration frameworks which have contributed to some modest gains in better migration governance, several challenges continue to exist including a lack of reliable migration data, weak capacity, resource constraints, and lack of commitment on the part of policy makers. These challenges have affected the effective implementation of these frameworks.

The chapter is organised as follows. The first section presents conceptual issues on gaps between stated and actual policy. This is followed by an analysis of continental level migration frameworks, sub-regional migration frameworks, and national migration policies. The next section focuses on challenges inhibiting effective implementation of the continental, regional, and national migration policy frameworks. The chapter concludes with some reflections and recommendations to further improve migration governance in Africa.

Conceptualising Gaps in the Implementation of Migration Policy Frameworks

In explaining why migration policies may not be effectively implemented, we rely on the concept of "stated and actual policy" which is based on insights from the policy science literature (Aucoin, 1971; Grainger & Konteh, 2007). Actual migration policy reflects the true intentions of the governments towards migration issues (Teye et al., 2019). The actual policy may differ from stated migration policy which is published in official documents, as migration policies or frameworks.

The "stated and actual policy" theoretical perspective posits that, since governments cannot satisfy all interest groups, there are times when a government may formulate or sign a policy that it does not intend to implement. This strategy creates policy ambiguities as stated policy remains "symbolic statements" (Smith, 1985, 135) that are never fully implemented. According to Grainger and Konteh (2007, 46–47), there are three scenarios when stated policy may differ from actual policy. Firstly, a government may find it difficult to state its actual policy on an issue that does not support the interest of powerful interest groups. Secondly, actual policy may differ from stated policy when there are changes in government priorities compared with those at the time of the development of the stated policy. Thirdly, actual policy may deviate from stated policy when the government is not fully committed to an international agreement but it has signed it to satisfy its development partners.

Drawing on insights from this theoretical perspective, this chapter argues that some governments of African countries are not committed to the implementation of some of the regional level free movement protocols. These governments have signed such agreements in order to satisfy powerful partners. Our conceptualisation resonates with the assertion of Czaika and de Haas (2013) that despite signing a number of regional level free movement protocols, governments are actually in favour of discouraging immigration of unskilled migrants. We also assume that apart from lack of commitment, institutional weaknesses and resource constraints may also contribute to poor implementation of migration policies (Teye et al., 2019).

Africa Migration Governance Frameworks

This section focuses on migration governance frameworks at the continental level of Africa, focusing on three key migration policy frameworks, namely AU migration policy framework, the Joint Labour Migration Programme, and the AU free movement of person (FMP) protocol.

African Union Migration Policy Framework

Several policy frameworks have been developed and adopted by the AU to govern and manage both voluntary and forced migration in Africa. At the core of these policies is the vision of African economic integration which is clearly articulated in the Treaty Establishing the African Economic Community (Abuja Treaty) of 1994. The Treaty commits Member States—either bilateral, regional group, or individual—to take, "the necessary measures in order to achieve progressively the free movement of persons, and to ensure the enjoyment of the right of residence and the right of establishment by their nationals within [the African Economic] Community" (AU, 1994). According to Article 43 of the Abuja Treaty:

> Member States agree to adopt, individually at bilateral or regional levels, the necessary measures to gradually achieve free movement of persons and to ensure their nations' enjoyment of the right of residence and establishment within the Community.

This Treaty has been ratified by at least 48 AU Member States (Achiume & Landau, 2015). The AU's approach to governing migration in Africa is outlined in the Migration Policy Framework (MPFA) which was first adopted in 2006 by the Executive Council of the AU. The framework was subsequently revised in 2018 to reflect prevailing migration dynamics on the continent and address the challenges associated with migration on the continent. It articulates AU's firm position that a well-managed migration has the potential to promote socio-economic development of Africa (Abebe, 2017; AU, 2018a). The MPFA covers nine key migration thematic issues: border management, labour migration, migration data management, human rights of migrants, forced displacement, irregular migration, inter-state cooperation and partnership, migration and development, and internal migration (AU, 2018a). It further articulates other social dimensions of migration, including gender, migration and health, conflict, and environment, among others.

The relevance of the MPFA cannot be over-emphasised. First, while the MPFA seems overly ambitious, it highlights the need to position humanitarian standards of migration within global human rights law. For instance, the MPFA enjoins Member States and RECs to develop policies to promote and protect the human rights of migrants, including developing guidelines to curb xenophobia and discrimination (Achiume & Landau, 2015, 3). Furthermore, the Migration Policy Framework underscores the need for conflict prevention and resolution (AU, 2018a; IOM, 2022).

Despite these achievements, there are some weaknesses of the MPFA. Achiume and Landau (2015) have identified several potential limits of the MPFA, categorised as political, institutional, and conceptual. The political limits emanate from the framework's own recognition of the potential political resistance of Member States to guarantee migrants' access to employment, services, market, and territories. Existing research has documented how migrants face multiple restrictions in terms of accessing markets, employment, and other services (Teye, 2022a; Yeboah et al., 2021). A major reason for these restrictions is the fact that while African governments have signed the framework (i.e. stated policy) they are concerned about preserving some sectors of employment for their own citizens (see Teye et al., 2019).

Moreover, conceptually, the framework speaks of tension between migrants and national security but encourages Member States to develop strategies to strike a balance in line with international conventions, norms, and standards. However, the already dire security situation in some parts of the continent with reported cases of xenophobia and human rights abuses of migrants suggest that the AU will need to do more to reinforce Member States commitment to promote the welfare of migrants (Achiume & Landau, 2015).

On the institutional front, there is no institutional mechanism embedded in the MPFA to monitor or track AU Member States compliance with the tenets and provisions of the framework. Indeed, the MPFA itself is non-binding and no Member State can be held accountable for failing to implement the framework.

Joint Labour Migration Programme

To further strengthen labour migration governance in Africa, the AU adopted the Joint Labour Migration Programme in 2015, with the overarching goal of recognising migration as one transformative tool for socio-economic development of Africa. The programme is supported by several development partners, including the International Organisation for Migration (IOM), the

International Labour Organisation (ILO), and the United Nations Economic Commission for Africa (UNECA). The programme was envisaged as a fundamental regional strategic framework to harness the developmental benefits of Migration, and to promote the protection of migrant workers' rights in aspects such as fair recruitment practices, social security portability, and portability of skills (AU, 2022; ILO, 2015). Accordingly, the JLMP aims to improve effective labour migration governance not only in Africa but also migration to the Middle East. It provides support towards the realisation of African Union's Agenda 2063 first 10-year Implementation Plan (2013–2023), and the UN Sustainable Development Goals (SDGs). Furthermore, the JLMP is fundamental to realising the provisions of the Global Compact for Migration as well as the Migration Policy Framework for Africa (MPFA) and its 2018–2030 Plan of Action (ILO, 2015). The JLMP has, since 2018, been implemented through several initiatives including Capacity Development in Migration Statistics (CDM) and Priority Implementation Actions of the AU-ILO-IOM-ECA Joint Programme on Labour Migration Governance for Development and Integration in Africa (JLMP Priority) both of which are funded by the Swedish International Development (SIDA) (ILO, 2022).

The JLMP has contributed to labour migration governance in Africa. The programme has been instrumental in developing two key draft policy documents, including the migrant welfare programme for Africa and the AU Declaration on the Protection and Promotion of the Rights of Migrant Workers. An assessment review carried out by the JLMP Steering Committee found some additional achievements worth highlighting. Firstly, the programme has established an effective management structure, and further provided technical and operational support to AUC and three RECs (SADC, ECOWAS, and EAC) in terms of their labour migration portfolios. The assessment also found that the JLMP facilitated the establishment of an AU Labour Migration Advisory Committee (LMAC) (ILO, 2022). Other best practices and achievements include supporting the development of and rolling out of regional instruments on social security portability for migrant workers and the launching of the first and second editions of the Migration Statistics Report (2019) as well as piloting of new mechanisms to collect administrative data in conjunction with the Economic Community of Central African States (ECCAS). Moreover, in 2020, the JLMP organised several capacity training workshops. Employers' organisations as well as workers' organisations have also benefited from capacity building workshops on labour migration governance. Again, by working with the African Regional Labour Administration Centre, JLMP has developed and implemented training modules on labour migration policy coherence, and further trained around 50 persons from some 15 Member States on procedures to strengthening consular and labour attaché services in line with global labour standards. Through the JLMP, the AU-Labour Migration and Advisory Committee has been operationalised. Despite these achievements, the JLMP has not been able to significantly address issues of trafficking in persons and forced labour (Teye et al., 2022).

African Union Free Movement of Persons Protocol

Following a shift in focus from liberation to economic integration in the early 1990s, Africa's economic integration has been a very prominent agenda of the AU. In January 2018, during a summit in Addis Ababa at which the AU decided to establish African Continental Free Trade Area (AfCFTA) to promote free flow of goods and services, Member States adopted a Free Movement Protocol (FMP) to promote free movement on the continent (AU, 2018b; Hirsch, 2021). The FMP protocol, which is a flagship programme of the Agenda 2063 of the AU, aims to harness the benefits associated with interconnectedness, labour migration, integration, and broader trade in line with the SDGs. The long-term goal is to ensure that Africa becomes a borderless community where there is free movement of goods, capital, services, and persons with substantial rise in trade and investments and further improve the bargaining position of Africa in international trade. Embedded in the protocol are several mobility and labour migration related provisions, including: progressive realisation of the free movement of persons, rights of residence and right of establishment (Article 5), Free movement of students and researchers (Article 13), Free movement of workers (Article 14), permit and passes (Article 15), Mutual recognition of Qualifications (Article 18), Social Security Portability Benefits (Article 19), Remittances (Article 23), Procedures for the Movement of specific groups (Article 24), Cooperation between Member States (Article 25), as well as coordination and harmonisation (Article 26) (AU, 2018b).

The protocol is envisaged to be implemented through a three phased approach. Phase one covers right of entry of community citizens to other AU Member States for a period of up to 90 days without a visa. This requires Member States to eliminate visa requirements for community citizens aiming to enter a member country. It places responsibility on AU Member States to enhance their systems for managing migration, for example, the quality and veracity of civic registration systems. Phase two focuses on granting the right of residence to community citizens (i.e. AU migrants and their families) from other nation states. While the roadmap guiding the implementation of the protocol indicates that phase two would commence from 2023, Article 5 of the protocol provides an avenue for speedy implementation of the protocol.

Phase three focuses on right of establishments. This guarantees Member State nationals the opportunity to engage in economic activities as self-employed or seek employment in trade, business, or profession in other Member States. The road map suggests that this phase would only be implemented following a review of progress of phase one and two by AUC. In line with the fears raised by some stakeholders during the negotiations, the Protocol recognises the potential danger that "arrival and settlement of migrants in a given host country will exacerbate inequalities or will constitute challenges to peace and security' and it notes the need to 'ensure that effective measures are put in place to prevent (such) situations" (AU, 2018b; Hirsch, 2021, 18).

The Free Movement Protocol has modestly contributed to removing barriers to entry through the adoption and implementation of free visa regimes (visa on arrival, visa-free travel). The 2020 Africa Visa Openness Report highlights a notable achievement around facilitation of free movement of persons across the continent by some Member States (AU, 2021). The report found that more than half (54%) of Africa is now open to receive migrants without any visas requirements, a rise by 9% from the previous figure in 2016. The implication is that less than half of Africans (46%) require visas to travel to other 46% of African territories. Moreover, nearly a third of Africans can secure visas on arrival to 28% of other African countries, and a further 26% do not require a visa to move to 26% of other African countries. Nevertheless, only three countries on the continent provide visa-free opportunity for all African Countries: the Gambia, Benin, and Seychelles. While visa openness is rated overall as positive, the COVID-19 pandemic and its associated restrictions have impacted on gains regarding human mobility. This highlights the need for the development of visa-free regimes that transcend economic shocks (AU, 2021).

Despite these achievements, there remains low enthusiasm on the part of many Member States in implementing the Protocol. As of 2021, 32 countries were reported to have signed the AU Free Movement of Persons Protocol. While a minimum of 15 countries are required to complete and submit their ratification instruments, only 4 countries, namely Mali, Sao Tome and Principe, Niger, and Rwanda have ratified the FMP. The lack of commitment to ratify the FMP can be explained in terms of "stated and actual" policies. While governments of African countries report that they support the protocol, many of them are concerned that signing the Protocol will lead to an influx of low skilled migrants to their countries. Indeed nearly half of the SADC countries and all North African states are yet to sign the FMP. The issue of giving up sovereign protection in relation to the mass movement of people has been raised as a fundamental concern which has reduced the commitment of member countries to sign and ratify the protocol (Hirsch, 2021). As shown below by a high state official in Ghana, governments of some countries are concerned that FMP would facilitate massive migration of low skilled persons to their territories:

> We have signed it as we are part of the AU and want to be part of these agreements. However, for the ratification, we are still weighing the options carefully. There are concerns that if we ratify this protocol, millions of migrants from other countries will come and take over jobs here. (Interview with a state official in Ghana, 2022).

The above statement indicates that while some countries have signed such protocols so as to demonstrate their commitment to AU agreements, their migration policies are still restrictive and based on fears that the protocol will economically affect their nationals, in terms of competition.

Regional Migration Governance Frameworks

Regional frameworks are used as a blueprint to develop and strengthen migration governance within and among Member States. The Abuja Treaty (1991) established eight Regional Economic Communities (RECs) in Africa which aimed to strengthen regional integration among Member States by removing trade, migration, and commerce barriers, among others. At present, some countries are members of two or three RECs which pushes the countries to find ways of dealing with overlapping commitments in other RECs. Meeting the obligations of each REC, while balancing needs and expectations is a challenge for these states.

Various RECs are at different stages of developing and implementing their regional migration frameworks.

The Economic Community for West African States (ECOWAS) was the first to set the pace by developing the Protocol on Free Movement of Persons, Residence and Establishment (1979). The Protocol was expected to be implemented in three phases. Phase one focused on establishing the "right of entry" by abolishing visas between 1980 and 1985. Phase two was expected to focus on "right of residence" between 1985 and 1990, followed by Phase three which focused on "right of establishment" between 1990 and 1995. The ECOWAS protocol is supported by various supplementary protocols.

Phase one has been fully implemented: all fifteen ECOWAS countries allow nationals of Member states to visa-free entry for up to 90 days. However, free entry is sometimes affected by harassment of travellers at the border by immigration officials who demand unofficial payments, as highlighted below by an ECOWAS migrant interviewed in Ghana as part of the MADE West Africa study:

> If we rely on what is in the ECOWAS protocol, we are supposed to freely
>   move to any country of ECOWAS as long as we have ID or passport. However,
>   at every checking point, especially at the immigration, we have to pay…I have
>   fought with them once but I later decided to just pay and forget about the
>   ECOWAS and this free movement protocol (.B.A., Beninois migrant in Ghana, cited by Teye et al., 2019, 1566).

While the harassment at the borders is often attributed to poor salaries and the desire of border officials to raise income through unofficial payments (Awumbila et al., 2014; Yeboah et al., 2021), some border officials interviewed, during the MADE West African study, attributed harassment to lack of travel documents by some migrants, as highlighted below by an immigration officer who was interviewed as part of the MADE West Africa project in Sierra Leone:

> People blame us [immigration officers] for the delays at the borders. They accuse us of harassing migrants. I will not say that all our officers behave very well. But there are times that travellers pay bribes because they don't have passports. Some travellers sometimes appear without any travel documents. When we ask them to show their passports, they will say they don't need passport because of free movement protocol. But we need the passports to establish their nationalities. In such cases, they are refused entry and some may offer bribes to our officers (Interview with an immigration officer, Sierra Leone, 23rd September 2017).

The statement above clearly shows how a lack of travel documents affects the implementation of the free movement Protocol. It also highlights migrants' misunderstanding of the requirement for free entry. The implementation of the Protocol is also affected by EU border management bilateral agreements with Niger, which "force" Niger to restrict movement of Africans across some of its governable spaces.

Apart from the challenges associated with the free entry (Phase 1), phases 2 (right of residence), and phase 3 (right of establishment) have not been effectively implemented, largely due to lack of contradictions between national policies and the protocol. The contradictions are due to the desire of some governments to reserve some sectors for their citizens. In Ghana, Nigeria, and Sierra Leone, for instance, there are restrictions which prevent non-nationals from working in the public sector, except under special government arrangements. Immigrants also face challenges obtaining business operation permits. The Ghana Investment Promotion Centre Act, 2013 (ACT 865), for instance, requires wholly foreign-owned businesses and trading companies to have foreign equity of $500,000USD, and $1,000,000 US respectively before being allowed to register a business. Given that Ghanaians do not require any capital to register their businesses, the ACT contradicts the ECOWAS protocol, which requires citizens of ECOWAS countries to be treated the same way as nationals of their host countries. Moreover, the Act precludes foreign nationals from operating certain businesses including, for example, supply of retail sachet water, production of exercise books, operation of taxis, retail of finished pharmacy products, operation of taxis, and petty trading (Teye et al., 2019; Yeboah et al., 2020). The investment laws reflect the true intentions (actual policy) of the government while the protocol can be seen as what Smith (1985) terms a "symbolic document" that will not be fully implemented. Similar findings were made in Sierra Leone where some officials think ECOWAS immigrants are taking over jobs, as highlighted below:

> Although we have ratified the ECOWAS protocol, we can't sit down for immigrants to take over all the jobs in our country... Migrants are also involved in human trafficking, robberies and other serious crimes (Interview with Immigration officer, Sierra Leone, 25 September 2017)

The above statement also shows that some officials continue to blame migrants for crimes and that also accounts for anti-migrant sentiments.

Aside from the free movement Protocol, ECOWAS has adopted a number of migration related policies. The ECOWAS Common Approach on Migration (2008) is a non-binding framework which seeks to assist Member States to identify priority areas on migration they can focus on and strengthen migration management within the region. The ECOWAS General Convention on Social Security aims to strengthen access to social security for migrants as well as provide guidance on measures that should be in place at Member State level to ensure portability of contributions at the end of employment of a migrant worker within the region. ECOWAS is developing a regional migration policy framework. The implementation of these frameworks is also affected by lack of commitment on the part of governments and weak resource capacity.

The Common Market for Eastern and Southern Africa (COMESA)'s focus has been on creating a conducive environment where trade between Member States can take place efficiently. The Protocol on the Gradual Relaxation and Eventual Elimination of Visa Requirements (1984) was meant to remove barriers to free movement among Member States. Later, the Protocol on Free Movement of Persons, Labour Services, the Right of Establishment and Residence (1998) was developed to provide guidelines to Member States on how they can ensue free movement of persons by removing visa barriers (Part II), promoting free movement of labour (Part III) and free movement of services (Part IV). The ratification process has been very slow as only Burundi, Kenya, Rwanda, and Zimbabwe have signed and ratified the Protocol on free movement, while other members such as Seychelles and Mauritius have put in place visa waivers and Zambia issued a visa waiver for nationals on official business. Recently, COMESA has revamped discussion on how to implement the protocol starting with the gazetting of Guidelines for the Movement of Goods and Services across the COMESA Region in 2020 that addressed overlapping commitments between members of the EAC and SADC.

The **East African Community (EAC)** does not have a specific framework on migration, but the Protocol on the East African Community Common Market (2010), popularly known as the Common Market Protocol (CMP), provides guidance on free movement of people and workers between Partner States, namely Kenya, Uganda, United Republic of Tanzania, Rwanda, Burundi, South Sudan, and the Democratic Republic of Congo. Part D of the EAC-CMP focuses on free movement of persons and labour that also includes mutual recognition of qualifications from EAC citizens. Part E outlines the approach to right of establishment and residence. The EAC has also developed its Regional Strategic Framework for e-Immigration (2014) focused on digitising the immigration systems in EAC Partner States to make them more efficient. Partner States have agreed to harmonise their national legal instruments that remove barriers to movement. However, the process has been slow as countries are grappling with the idea of maintaining their sovereignty. Partner states had agreed that they would move together towards regional integration however, Kenya, Rwanda, and Uganda have used the Northern Corridor to remove barriers related to trade and free movement of people. This will be complemented by the EAC e-Immigration Policy (draft) currently being developed to provide further guidance on how to manage the e-immigration system regionally.

The EAC One Stop Border Posts Act (2016) aimed to ease the process for cross border migration recognising that there are cross border traders that conduct businesses across borders. The EAC Gender Policy (2018) includes migration as a priority area recognising that although men dominate migration within the region, women are also on the move. At present, the EAC is developing the regional labour migration policy that would address labour migration within the region and for its citizens in other locations. It is also developing the EAC Council Directive on the Coordination of Social Security Benefits to help partner states to harmonise their social security laws to provide access to facilitate portability of contributions. Finally, the EAC is also developing the EAC Refugee Management Policy to provide a regional approach to forced displacement within the region.

The **Southern African Development Community (SADC)** Protocol on the Facilitation of Movement of Persons (2005) covers all forms of migration from regular and irregular migration between Member States (i.e. Democratic Republic of Congo, United Republic of Tanzania, Angola, Namibia, Zambia, Botswana, Zimbabwe, Mozambique, Eswatini, South Africa, Lesotho, Malawi, Comoros, Madagascar, Mauritius, and Seychelles). Ratification has been very low to the present date as the main hosting Member States such as South African, Botswana, and Namibia are hesitant, fearing that it will lead to a spike of immigrants from neighbouring states (Maunganidze, 2021). South Africa prefers bilateral and small multilateral arrangements on labour migration agreements.

The SADC uses Labour Migration Action Plans (L-MAPs) as a guide for Member States to put measures in place to strengthen labour migration within the region. They run over a course of five years with the first L-MAPs initiated between 2013 and 2015 that led to the development of the Labour Migration Policy Framework (2014). The SADC is currently developing its Regional Migration Policy Framework that would guide Member States to take steps towards developing national migration policies.

The **Intergovernmental Authority on Development (IGAD)** was the first REC to develop a Regional Migration Policy Framework (2012), guided by the AUC's Migration Policy Framework (2006). The framework reflects the region's migration needs at the time, though this focus has recently shifted to climate-induced displacement. Civil and political unrest, as well as the negative impact of climate change, have all been linked to forced displacement in the region. The framework also considers the importance of labour migration which tends to be irregular in nature. The IGAD Migration Action Plan (2015–2020) is the implementation tool of the IGAD-RMPF guiding the REC and Member States to address gaps within their migration instruments through research and dialogue between Member States and government ministries and departments at national level. Recently, the IGAD developed and endorsed its Protocol on Transhumance (2020) targeted at pastoral and nomadic populations that move between Member States. The IGAD has developed instruments to guide discussions and activities related to migration in the region. This includes the Declaration on Labour, Employment and Labour Migration in the IGAD region (2022) which advocates for the speedy ratification of ILO conventions extending rights to migrants and their families. In 2021 it also finalised and endorsed the Protocol for Free Movement in the IGAD region that would facilitate free movement of labour and people as well as ensure there is right of residence and establishment between and among Member States. At present, the IGAD is in the process of encouraging its Member States to sign and ratify as it will require at least four ratifications to make the protocol active. IGAD in partnership with the ILO have produced the IGAD Guidelines on Rights Based Bilateral Labour Agreements (BLAs) to help Member States to develop BLAs with countries in the Gulf using a rights-based approach IGAD (2022).

The **Economic Community of Central African States (ECCAS)** Member States (consisting of Angola, Burundi, Cameroon, Central African Republic, Chat, Congo, Democratic Republic of the Congo, Equatorial Guinea, Gabon, Rwanda, and Sao Tome and Principe) developed the Protocol on Freedom of Movement and Rights of Establishment of Nationals of Members States (1983) in the same year the REC was established. Article 2 focuses on the removal of barriers for free movement of persons while Article 40 promotes free movement and right of establishment of its citizens across the REC. Efforts to implement the Protocol have been hampered by the political, economic, and environmental instability within the region (Adeola, 2019) which has dominated discourses over the years. Peace and security are essential for free movement to be possible to reduce any possible tensions that may arise.

The **Treaty Establishing the Community of Sahel-Saharan States CEN-SAD (1998)** that brought together Member States (Benin, Burkina Faso, Central African Republic, Chad, the Comoros, Cote d'Ivoire, Djibouti, Egypt, Eritrea, The Gambia, Ghana, Guinea Bissau, Libya, Mali, Mauritius, Morocco, Niger, Nigeria, Senegal, Sierra Leone, Somalia, Sudan, Togo, and Tunisia) within the Sahel and Sub-Saharan Africa to agree principles for the free movement of persons, capital, and right of residence. A regional framework was drafted on Free Movement (Abebe, 2017), however, the framework was never successfully adopted. Free movement between Member States has been attributed to members of ECOWAS which has already taken measures to remove barriers to mobility (Wood, 2019). Selective Visa Dispensations are extended only to diplomatic passport holders and special envoys to ease their mobility in the 29 Member States (Adeola, 2019). Finally, the **Arab Maghreb Union (AMU),** established in 1989, has had a long history of facilitating economic and political integration among its Member States (i.e. Algeria, Libya, Mauritania, Morocco, and Tunisia) that could lead to free movement of people, goods, and services. At present, Tunisia allows for free movement of UMA citizens as land borders between Morocco and Algeria have been closed since 1994.

The material presented in this section clearly shows that the implementation record of regional frameworks has been poor. Indeed, only ECOWAS has been able to implement a regional free entry regime. One major reason for the poor implementation of free movement regimes is the fact that, in most cases, countries sign these free movement protocols but are not committed to their implementation due to fears that they would lead to influx of migrants from poor countries which will result in competition with nationals (Teye et al., 2019). As a result, the protocols remain symbolic documents while actual policies entail restriction on the entry and residence of low skilled migrants.

National Policies on Migration

Until recently, many African countries did not have national migration policies, and national legislative instruments were instead used to govern immigration. While cross border labour mobility was encouraged in the colonial era due to demand for labour for mines and plantations in coastal countries, "anti-migrant" narratives which suggested that immigrants were a threat to economic development led to the development of restrictive immigration policies in some countries during the early post-independence era (Teye, 2022a). In West Africa, for instance, there were several mass expulsions of nationals of West African countries. At the same time, actual policies in the early post-independence era sought to portray highly skilled emigrants as unpatriotic citizens, because of brain drain which was affecting the health and education sectors of many African countries (Teye, 2022b).

Within the last decade, a number of African countries have been developing their national policies on migration, many of which seek to harness the benefits of migration for socio-economic development (Teye, 2022b). National migration policies often cover a wide range of migration issues from internal migration, regular and irregular migration to forced displacement, while considering cross cutting issues such as climate change, development, and health. The instruments adopt a whole-of-government and whole-of-society approach on migration by providing guidance to ministries, departments, and agencies on the key areas of focus for the country. These policies tend to be aligned with the international, continental, regional instruments. National migration policies have been guided by the AUC Migration Policy Framework for Africa (MPFA) which was endorsed by Member States in 2006. Over a 10-year period since the MPFA was in place, only Nigeria (2014), Mali (2014), Ghana (2016), had finalised their national migration policies targeted at national migration policy or a labour migration policy. The MPFA was revised in 2018 to reflect the limitations identified at regional and national level and a concerted effort was put in place by the AUC to popularise the framework to Member States and RECs. Since the revisions of the MPFA, several countries, including Malawi, Sierra Leone, Zambia, and Zimbabwe have started to develop their own national migration policies guided by the MPFA (2018) where the GCM and GCR principles have been mainstreamed. The policies reflect the migration priorities of the countries, however, they all tend to provide guidelines for harnessing migrant remittances for socio-economic development. For instance, the Nigerian national migration policy states that:

> Strategies should be developed to encourage Nigerians in the diaspora to invest remittances in social infrastructure, human capital and other economic activities. There is a need to promote the transfer of remittances through efficient formal channels at low transfer cost" (Federal Republic of Nigeria, 2015, 26).

Other countries have developed sectoral migration policies focused on labour migration, refugees, internally displaced persons, and diaspora policies which are targeted towards the interests of the government. These sectoral policies are meant to be guided by the national migration policies providing additional strategic direction adopted by the specific ministries mandated to handle the migrant categories. For instance, Ghana, Sierra Leone, and Zimbabwe have drafted labour migration policies which focus only on international labour migration including migration governance, the protection of migrants and harnessing migration for development. In most countries, efforts to leverage skills transfer and remittances for development are discussed as a key component of national labour migration policies. The Sierra Leonean labour migration policy, for example, captures financial and skills transfer clearly in the statement below:

The State shall provide a sound macro-economic environment to facilitate the efficient flow of remittances....the State shall work with financial institutions to reduce the cost of sending remittances to Sierra Leone. The State shall also adopt programmes to enhance the knowledge of migrant workers and their families regarding the management of remittances" (Government of Sierra Leone, 2018, 33)

Some countries (e.g. Ghana, Malawi; Lesotho, Madagascar, Zambia, and Zimbabwe) have developed diaspora engagement policies that tend to focus on how to effectively engage the diaspora in national development by creating pathways that are more focused on financial remittances for development. Diaspora engagement policies also tend to discuss skills transfers, as shown in the Malawi diaspora policy which states that the government should:

Create safe and trusted communication and knowledge sharing platforms through the development and maintenance of ICT infrastructure and virtual networks;....and develop and strengthen existing initiatives to retain, attract, encourage and support permanent or temporary return migrations of high-level expertise" (Republic of Malawi, 2017, 10).

Some countries have also developed national migration strategies (e.g. Burkina Faso) or embed migration within a population policy as is the case with Mali (ECOWAS, 2015) to ensure that migration issues are factored within existing policies. In most cases, these policies are developed based on technical and financial support by international development partners, including IOM, ILO, ICMPD, and European Union.

Despite these achievements some countries still do not have migration policies. Migration policy implementation has also been poor. In some cases, the governments are not committed to implementing certain aspects of the policy. Despite this limitation, there are regional and continental discussions that bring the Member States together to explore ways of strengthening migration governance such as the training workshop on migration governance. In addition, about 35 African countries have used the IOM's Migration Governance Indicator Framework (MiGOF) tool to assist them to identify their national and local migration governance in terms of the laws and policies related to migration ensuring they align with the international conventions, continental and regional frameworks (IOM, 2019). The production of Migration Governance Indicator reports at national and local levels gives a bird's eye view of the key areas that need to be strengthened but also highlights best practices that can provide guidance to other Member

States who are in the process of strengthening their migration governance structures.

Challenges Associated with Implementation of Migration Policies and Frameworks

This chapter has shown that while the adoption of migration governance frameworks has brought migration issues to the limelight of Africa's development, certain constraints impede the implementation of the migration policies across the continent. As demonstrated already, the first challenge relates to lack of political will to implement regional free movement frameworks. The second challenge relates to weak coordination among the different actors responsible for implementation of migration activities. It is worth remarking that enhancing migration governance means strengthening coordination role of diverse stakeholders at the regional, sub-regional, and national levels. While regional cooperation at RECs is improving, more efforts are needed to strengthen mechanisms for more and better information sharing and policy coherence (Le Coz & Pietropolli, 2020). Effective coordination and cooperation between existing institutions and actors within and across regional and national borders remains an important ingredient in efforts to promote better management of migration in Africa. However, SADC, ECOWAS and EAC and other RECs are faced with coordination and cooperation issues with respect to addressing the needs of migrants.

Another challenge stems from a lack of adequate human resource capacity and funds. Studies from various sub-regional communities in Africa (e.g. ECOWAS, SADC) have shown that state institutions responsible for migration governance lack human, technical, and financial resources for effective implementation of migration policies (Teye et al., 2022). Better management of migration will require provision of needed resources, systems, skills, and capacity strengthening for responsible institutions and stakeholders on wide range of issues from migration data, and strategies to addressing the vulnerabilities faced by migrants (Le Coz and Pietropolli, 2020).

Finally, there is a lack of interest and political will on the part of various governments to prioritise migration as critical development issue (Teye et al., 2022). Many countries are unwilling to commit resources or invest in their migration policies over other sectoral policies and this represents a major challenge to implementing existing policies and frameworks. There is therefore a need to secure the commitment of African governments that they will themselves support, invest, and prioritise and invest in migration policies in their national development planning once external funding or support ceases.

Conclusion

This chapter has analysed migration governance from the African perspective. The chapter has shown that a number of migration frameworks have been adopted at the continental level and some modest gains have been made in terms of their implementation. These include the AU MPFA, the Joint Labour Migration Programme, and the recent AU free movement protocol with the goal of better promoting migration governance and addressing the vulnerabilities faced by migrants on the continent. RECs have also developed various protocols which are aimed at promoting safe, orderly, and regular migration. Consistent with the concept of "stated and actual policies" (Aucoin, 1971; Grainger & Konteh, 2007), the chapter shows that while many African governments have signed regional and sub-regional free movement protocols their actual policies still largely focus on restricting an influx of low skilled immigrants. A number of governments have developed national migration related policies aimed at harnessing the benefits of migration for development. Apart from efforts to leverage remittances for development, the implementation of national level migration policies has been poor due to lack of adequate human resources and funds to effectively coordinate the roles and activities of various stakeholders within the migration governance landscape of Africa (Le Coz and Pietropolli, 2020). Improving migration governance in Africa requires the commitment of governments to invest in migration related activities, capacity training of relevant actors, and better coordination of efforts at all levels of government to ensure better information sharing and investment to address the needs of labour migrants on the continent.

References

Abebe, T. T. (2017). *Migration policy frameworks in Africa*. Institute for Security Studies.

Achiume, E. T., & Landau, L. (2015). *The African Union migration and regional integration framework. Policy and Practice Brief*. African Center for the Constructive Resolution of Disputes ACCORD.

Adeola, R. (2019). The African Union Protocol on Free Movement of Persons in Africa: Development, provisions and implementation challenges. *African Human Rights Yearbook*, 260–275.

Africa Centre for Strategic Studies. (2021). *African Migration Trends to Watch in 2022* https://africacenter.org/spotlight/african-migration-trends-to-watch-in-2022/AU (2002) Treaty Establishing the African Economic Community, Article 43. African Union. https://au.int/sites/default/files/treaties/37636-treaty-0016_-_treaty_establishing_the_african_economic_community_e.pdf

AU. (1994). *Treaty establishing the African economic community*. African Union.

AU. (2018a). *The revised migration policy framework for Africa and plan of action (2018–2027)* Draft. Addis Ababa, Ethiopia. https://au.int/sites/default/files/newsevents/workingdocuments/32718-wd-english_revised_au_migration_policy_framework_for_africa.pdf

AU. (2018b). *Protocol to the Treaty Establishing the African Economic Community Relating to Free Movement of Persons, Right of Residence and Right of Establishment*. https://au.int/en/treaties/protocol-treaty-establishing-african-economic-community-relating-free-movement-persons

AU. (2021). Report on the Implementation of Free Movement Of Persons In Africa 2020–2021 Specialised Technical Committee (STC) On Migration, Refugees and Displaced Persons.

AU. (2022). *Joint Labour Migration Programme*. https://au.int/en/jlmp

Aucoin, P. (Ed). (1971). *The structures of policy making in Canada*. Macmillan.

Awumbila, M., Benneh, Y., Teye, J. K., & Atiim, G. (2014). *Across artificial borders: An assessment of labour migration in the ECOWAS region*. ACP Observatory on Migration.

Awumbila, M., Teye, J., and Nikoi, E. (2018). *Assessment of the implementation of the ECOWAS free movement protocol in Ghana and Sierra Leone*. MADE Network.

Czaika, M., & de Haas, H. (2013). The effectiveness of immigration policies. *Population and Development Review*, *39*(3), 487–508.

Deshingkar, P., Awumbila, M., & Teye, J. K. (2019). Victims of trafficking and modern slavery or agents of change? Migrants, brokers, and the state in Ghana and Myanmar. *Journal of the British Academy*, *7*(s1), 77–106.

ECOWAS. (2015). *A survey on migration policies in West Africa*. ICMPD and IOM.

Government of Sierra Leone. (2018). *Sierra Leone labour migration policy*. Ministry of Labour and Social Security.

Grainger, A., & Konteh, W. (2007). Autonomy, ambiguity and symbolism in African politics: The development of forest policy in Sierra Leone. *Land Use Policy*, *24*, 42–62.

Hirsch, A. (2021). The African Union's FREE movement of persons protocol: Why has it faltered and how can its objectives be achieved? *South African Journal of International Affairs*, *28*(4), 497–517. https://doi.org/10.1080/10220461.2021.2007788

Hlatshwayo, M. (2019). Precarious work and precarious resistance: A case study of Zimbabwean migrant women workers in Johannesburg, South Africa. *Diaspora Studies, 12*(2), 160–178.

IGAD. (2022). *IGAD Regional Guidelines on Rights Based Bilateral Labour Agreements (BLAs)*. IGAD.

ILO. (2015). The Joint labour migration program for Africa, 2015. http://www.ilo.org/addisababa/mediacentre/pr/WCMS_402369/lang--en/index.htm

ILO. (2022). *Labour Migration in Africa*. https://www.ilo.org/africa/areas-of-work/labour-migration/lang--en/index.htm

IOM. (2019). *Migration governance indicators: A global perspective*. IOM.

IOM. (2022). IOM and AU Sign New 3-Year Agreement to Strengthen Migration Policies and Frameworks in Africa. https://reliefweb.int/report/world/iom-and-au-sign-new-3-year-agreement-strengthen-migration-policies-and-frameworks

Jamie, F. O. M., & Tsega, A. H. (2018). Ethiopian female labor migration to the Gulf states: The case of Kuwait. In *Ethiopians in an Age of Migration* (pp. 90–103). Routledge.

Knoll, A., & de Weijer, F. (2016). Understanding African and European perspectives on migration – Towards a better partnership for regional migration governance? *Discussion paper no 203*. Maastricht: European Centre for Development Policy Management. https://ecdpm.org/publications/understanding-african-european-perspectives-migration

Le Coz, C., & Pietropoll, A. (2020). Africa Deepens its Approach to Migration Governance, But Are Policies Translating to Action? https://www.migrationpolicy.org/article/africa-deepens-approach-migration-governance

Maunganidze, O. A. (2021). *Migration policy in South Africa: Lessons from Africa's migration magnet for European policymakers*. German Council on Foreign Relations, Vol. 18, September 2021: p.17. https://dgap.org/sites/default/files/article_pdfs/Report-SouthAfrica_18_2021_EN.pdf

Mixed Migration Centre West Africa. (2021). *Quarterly mixed migration update*. https://mixedmigration.org/wp-content/uploads/2021/04/qmmu-q1-2021-wa.pdf

Mlambo, V. H., & Zubane, S. (2021). No rights, No Freedom: The Kafala system and the plight of African migrants in the Middle East. *ADRRI Journal of Arts and Social Sciences, 18*(6), 1–16.

Mo Ibrahim Foundation and Africa-Europe Foundation. (2020). Africa and Europe Facts and Figures on African Migrations. https://mo.ibrahim.foundation/sites/default/files/2022-02/aef_summit_african-migrations.pdf

Olsen, A. S. W. (2011). Reconsidering West African migration. *Danish Insitute for International Studies (DIIS) Working Paper 21*.

Republic of Malawi. (2017). *Malawi diaspora engagement policy*. Ministry of Foreign Affairs and International Cooperation.

Smith, T. B. (1985). Evaluating development policies and programmes in the third world. *Public Administration and Development, 5*(2), 129–144.

Teye, J. K. (2022a). Migration in West Africa: An Introduction. In J. K. Teye (Ed.), *Migration in West Africa* (pp. 3–17). Springer.

Teye, J. K. (2022b). Critical migration policy narratives from West Africa. *Special issue article: International migration*.

Teye, J. K., Awumbila, M., & Nikoi, E. (2019). Ambiguity and symbolism in the implementation of the ECOWAS free movement protocol: Evidence from Ghana and Sierra Leone. *African Human Mobility Review, 5*(2), 1556–1582.

Teye, J. K., Setrana, M., Yeboah, T., & Teye-Kwadwo, E. (2022). *Regional baseline assessment on forced labour, unfair and unethical recruitment practices in the Southern Africa and IOC Region*. A report submitted to the IOM.

UNCTAD. (2018). *Economic development in Africa: Report 2018—migration for structural transformation*. United Nations.

UNHCR. (2020). *Sahel crisis: Responding to the urgent needs of refugees, internally displaced, returnees and others of concern*. UNHCR.

Wood, T. (2019). The role of free movement of persons agreements in addressing disaster displacement: A study of Africa. *Platform on Disasters Displacement: Follow up to the Nansen Initiative*. https://disasterdisplacement.org/wp-content/uploads/2019/06/52846_PDD_FreeMovement_web-single_compressed.pdf

Yeboah, T., Kandilige, L., Bisong, A., & Muhammed, F. G. (2020). The ECOWAS free movement protocol and diversity of experiences of different categories of migrants: A qualitative study. *International Migration, 59*(2).

Yeboah, T., Kandilige, L., Bisong, A., Garba, F., & Teye, J. K. (2021). The ECOWAS free movement protocol and diversity of experiences of different categories of migrants: A qualitative study. *International Migration, 59*(3), 228–244.

Open Access This chapter is licensed under the terms of the Creative Commons Attribution 4.0 International License (http://creativecommons.org/licenses/by/4.0/), which permits use, sharing, adaptation, distribution and reproduction in any medium or format, as long as you give appropriate credit to the original author(s) and the source, provide a link to the Creative Commons license and indicate if changes were made.

The images or other third party material in this chapter are included in the chapter's Creative Commons license, unless indicated otherwise in a credit line to the material. If material is not included in the chapter's Creative Commons license and your intended use is not permitted by statutory regulation or exceeds the permitted use, you will need to obtain permission directly from the copyright holder.

29

Migration Governance in South America: Change and Continuity in Times of "Crisis"

Marcia Vera Espinoza

Introduction

South America's recent history has been marked by distinctive mobility patterns that position the countries of the region as ones of emigration, transit and destination, and in some cases, all of them at once (Jubilut et al., 2021). From the displacement caused by the military dictatorships of the 1970s as well as the mobility flows following re-democratisation in the late 1980s, South America has been mostly considered a region of emigration (Acosta, 2018; Martínez Pizarro & Orrego Rivera, 2016). However, since the second half of the twentieth century, and particularly, since the early 2000s, the region has been also marked by the intensification of intra-regional mobility and the diversification of the countries of origin and destination of extra-regional immigration (Freier et al., this volume; Stefoni, 2018). Since 2014, South America's intra-regional mobility has been shaped by the massive displacement of Venezuelans, who then started to leave the country due of its political and economic downturn (Gandini et al., 2019). With more than 7 million Venezuelans refugees and migrants across the world as of 2022, out of which more than 5.5 million are hosted by countries in South America (R4V, 2022), this is the largest exodus in the region's recent history and one of the largest of the world (UNHCR, 2022).

M. Vera Espinoza (✉)
Institute for Global Health and Development, Queen Margaret University, Edinburgh EH21 6UU, UK
e-mail: MVeraEspinoza@qmu.ac.uk

© The Author(s) 2024
H. Crawley and J. K. Teye (eds.), *The Palgrave Handbook of South–South Migration and Inequality*, https://doi.org/10.1007/978-3-031-39814-8_29

Venezuelan displacement has not only been characterised as a "humanitarian crisis" due to both the conditions that prompt that mobility and the vulnerability of the people on the move, but also perceived as a "migration crisis" that has imposed socio-economic challenges in reception countries, and as a political issue to deal by the countries of the region (Gandini et al., 2019). By December 2022, South American countries were destination to almost 80% of the total number of Venezuelans living outside their county (R4V, 2022). Colombia has the largest Venezuelan population with 2.48 million, followed by Peru with 1.49 million, Ecuador with more than 502,000 Venezuelans, and Chile with more than 444,000. Brazil is the fifth destination country with 388,000 Venezuelans, followed by Argentina, hosting 171,000 Venezuelan migrants (R4V, 2022). The platform of inter-agency Coordination for Venezuelan Migrants and Refugees (R4V)[1] specifies that many governments of the region do not account for Venezuelans without a regular status, which means that the total number of Venezuelans is likely to be higher.

This mobility has not only increased the number of foreign populations in key destination countries such as Argentina, Brazil, and Chile (IOM, 2021), it has also transformed some countries from being transit and sending countries, to destinations of Venezuelan displacement, such as Peru (Palla et al., 2022) and Colombia (López, 2022). Despite the political salience of this displacement and the sheer numbers of people on the move, this is not the only mobility dynamic taking place in the Latin American's sub-region. South America is also experiencing the arrival from people from Central America (Cantor, 2014), and the ongoing mobility of Haitians (Marcelin & Cela, this volume; Yates, 2021) and Cubans (Zapata et al., 2023), among other intra-regional and extra-regional flows. These flows are driven by structural inequalities and labour opportunities, among other complex reasons.

These diverse patterns of mobility, alongside internal economic, social and political changes, as well as international challenges, have shaped the regional and national migration governance that characterised South America during the last two decades (Acosta et al., 2019; Gandini et al., 2019; Jubilut et al., 2021). Since the early 2000s there has been a growing body of literature that discusses the development of a regional framework of human mobility in South America, characterised to be as one of the most developed after the EU mobility regime (Brumat, 2020; Geddes et al., 2019), and shaped by a liberal discourse in terms of migrants' rights (Cantor et al., 2015; Geddes & Vera Espinoza, 2018). However, this same literature recognises that beyond the rhetoric, the liberal approach has not uniformly been reflected in national-level migration laws (Finn et al., 2019) while showing several gaps in implementation (Acosta & Freier, 2015), illustrating the tensions between human rights and security concerns (Domenech, 2013). The same can be said about the regional approach to refugee protection, which has been characterised as "progressive" and promoted under a principle of "solidarity" but criticised by lack of implementation and with gaps in the protection provisions (de Menezes, 2016; Feddersen et al., 2023; Vera Espinoza, 2018; Vera Espinoza, 2021).

The discursive consensus in the regional approach to human mobility and refugee protection, based on the non-criminalisation of irregular migration, human rights rhetoric and multilateral efforts to coordinate policies (Margheritis & Pedroza, 2022), has been discussed as a somehow distinctive regional approach to migration governance in South America (Geddes & Vera Espinoza, 2018; Geddes et al., 2019). However, the regional approach has been put to the test by the Venezuelan displacement and the convergence of multiple crises—including the COVID-19 pandemic, socio-economic crisis and local political unrests, among others (see Gandini et al., 2022; Margheritis, 2022). The regional response to migration and displacement in the last five years has been more fragmented (Brumat, 2022; Margheritis & Pedroza, 2022), with the countries of the region adopting a series of ad hoc measures mostly aimed at temporary protection (Acosta et al., 2019; Gandini et al., 2019) and with a mixed use of already existing mechanisms such as the MERCOSUR residence agreement (Brumat, 2021)[2] or the limited use of the expanded refugee definition provided by the Cartagena Declaration of 1984 (Blouin et al., 2020).[3]

Within this fragmented scenario, I argue that South America shows processes and practices of both change and continuity in its regional approach to migration governance which respond to a mobility framed and driven by multiple "crises" (Gandini et al., 2022; Margheritis, 2022; Vera Espinoza et al., 2021). Some of the changes, however, have reinforced the most restrictive aspects of the "continuities" we see across the region.

Drawing on the review of recent literature, as well as from insights from two research projects conducted between 2017 and 2022,[4] this chapter explores how migration governance in the region has changed, and with what consequences, considering recent migration dynamics, particularly the Venezuelan displacement, and the convergence of multiple "crises". The chapter argues that in a context of multiple "crises", South American migration governance is characterised by a fragmented and reactive approach which shows some continuities (such as the permanence of a regional progressive framework and the continued presence of a securitised approach) and change (which includes the increased militarisation of border controls and the weakening of the asylum regime, among others). Taken together, the chapter shows that South America's patchwork migration governance evidences the fragmentation of regional responses, which in practice translate in more control, the criminalisation of migration, increased irregularity and less protection for people on the move.

The chapter develops this argument by first exploring key ideas associated to regional migration governance and notions of crisis. The text then provides evidence on the continuities we can see across many countries of the region as well as the governance changes that have emerged in the context of multiple "crises". The chapter then discusses how can we make sense of these continuities and changes in context of fragmented and reactive regional migration governance.

Regional Migration Governance in Times of "Crisis"

There is a growing body of literature exploring regional migration governance in South America. A large part of this scholarship has tried to understand the extent to which a "liberal tide" took shape in the region, focusing on the contradictions of developing a progressive regional discourse during the post-dictatorship period and early 2000s, which coexisted with restrictive policies (Ceriani, 2018; Acosta & Freier, 2015; Cantor et al., 2015). Other contributions have also shed light on the potential impact of regional consultations processes (Finn et al., 2019; Ramírez & Alfaro, 2010) as well as the development and influences on mobility mechanisms such as the MERCOSUR residence agreement (Brumat, 2022). There is also scholarship that explores the growing (and continuing) securitisation trends on migration governance (Brumat & Vera Espinoza, 2023; Brumat et al., 2018; Herrera & Berg, 2019), particularly those that started to take shape during the COVID-19 pandemic (Domenech, 2020; Freier & Vera Espinoza, 2021; Vera Espinoza et al., 2021; Zapata et al., 2023). While the region continues to be underrepresented within global academic debates, these contributions—through publications in English, Spanish and Portuguese—have developed relevant knowledge about the specific characteristics of regional migration governance in South America, its role within wider Latin American and global trends, and how it seats within South-South migration debates.

Migration governance has been widely understood as the "norms, rules, principles and decision-making procedures that regulate the behaviour of

States (and other transnational actors)" (Betts, 2011, 4). These are based on a range of formal and informal institutions and processes that operate at different levels. Besides this multi-level understanding (see also Lavenex & Piper, 2019), migration governance has also been understood as epiphenomenal, related to "a much wider set of economic, political, social, demographic and environmental conditions" (Geddes et al., 2019, 8) that determine "change", which governing organisations try to make sense of in order to navigate and coordinate its effects. Governance systems are not just passive or reactive (Geddes et al., 2019, 9), they can also shape mobility. A focus on the sense making process of migration governance has also been developed in Latin America. In the early 2000s, Mármora (2002, 390) described migration governance as "the adjustment between the characteristics, causes and effects of migration, the expectations and social demands about it, and the real possibilities of the States to respond to it".

This "adjustment" between causes, expectations and the possibilities of responding to it, have been mostly articulated around notions of "crisis" and the extent to which states are able to manage the "misgovernance" of migration. Latin American scholars have been critical to the development of notions of governance, by shedding light into the discourses and practices that have been both constructed and facilitated through it, the actors that have imposed these ideas and the impacts they may have in "managing" mobility (see Domenech, 2018; Ramírez & Alfaro, 2010). Domenech (2018) pays particular attention to how discourses of "crisis" are formed around issues such as the increase of irregular migration and the business of trafficking and smuggling, enabling a justification that demands bilateral and multilateral action, therefore promoting specific ideas around regional governance.

The formation of governance discourses is not exclusive to South America and the regional level. For instance, we have seen how the notion of "safe, orderly and regular" migration has been spread globally, first through the adoption of the Sustainable Development Goals (Target 10.7, 2015) and then through the Global Compact on Migration (2018). In the case of South America, Domenech (2018) also puts attention to the actors—such as the International Organization for Migration (IOM).—that through their work with governments contribute to disseminate these ideas. We also see this transfer and development of knowledge in relation to refugee protection, such as the use of the principle of "solidarity" (de Menezes, 2016; Vera Espinoza, 2018) and the search for what it used to be "durable solutions" which has now transitioned to just "solutions" (Vera Espinoza, forthcoming). In a recent text, I explore how the grammar of durable solutions in Latin America has changed over the last 20 years, both in line with the events in the region as well as with changes at the international level, and the changing role of the UNHCR in the governance of forced migration (Vera Espinoza, forthcoming).

The point to emphasise here is that processes of migration governance—at the national, regional or international level—are not merely responses to mobility or situations of "crisis", rather the context itself is discursively constructed around issues that justify governance. For instance, we have recently seen how a process of a categorisation has also mobilised specific actions by States. For example, UNHCR created the category "Venezuelans displaced abroad", which was first introduced in its 2019 Global Trends Report. While the report acknowledges that the group is entitled to international protection, it does not necessarily recognise them as refugees (Freier, 2022). This ambiguity in the category has been instrumental for many South American States that have decided not to use the expanded refugee definition of the Cartagena Declaration, even when is included in their legislations (as is the case of Chile and Uruguay) (see Zapata et al., 2023). So far, only Brazil in the South American context (and Mexico when looking at the wider Latin American region), have recently applied the Cartagena refugee definition to specific national groups, including Venezuelans (Blouin et al., 2020).

The creation of these understandings of governance can also be explored through Geddes (2021) notion of repertoires of migration governance, through which the author invites us to focus not only on the outcomes of governance, such as law and policies, but also on "what actors do and what they think they should be doing". These repertoires comprise narratives, that are social, affective, performative and ongoing. Through the operation and effects of these repertoires they "have powerful effects on migrants and their lived experiences" (Geddes, 2021, 3).

In line with the processes and impacts of governance, it is relevant to briefly unpack the notions of "crisis" that have been developed in South America and how they have informed the development of regional migration governance. Gandini et al. (2022, 17) explain that in the Latin American context, the migration-crisis nexus has been understood both in a preventive and reactive manner, but also as a "strategic decisions in light of an exceptional situation". We identified then that there are two coexisting frameworks: one that shows migration as result of a specific context due to social, political, economic and environmental issues (as in the context that prompted the Venezuelan displacement); and a second that shows crisis as a context, in which the migration processes are those that create contexts of "crisis". The latter process relates to the framing use for example in the so called "European Refugee

Crisis", terminology that emerged in 2015 as a result of the Syrian displacement, particularly in relation to the arrivals at the shores of Europe, and the associated categories related to the "crisis" (see Crawley & Skleparis, 2018). We have seen similar framing in relation to increased mobility patterns in South America. Crisis, then, it is more linked to a political categorisation rather than an empirical one (Rojas & Winton, 2019).

Migration as result of a context of crisis and migration as crisis can also coexist at the same time. Margheritis (2022, 4) suggests that in the South American context we can qualify the Venezuelan displacement as a "nested" crisis, defined as "one occurring within, and closely intertwined with, other crises—as in a Russian doll set. The key point is that such crisis is embedded in a larger context characterized by diverse, interrelated critical conditions/junctures".

The notion of "crisis"—either as context "for" or "of", multiple or nested, crisis—has become, in South America and elsewhere, a framework to justify the implementation of both humanitarian discourses and restrictive State practices (Herrera & Berg, 2019). As we have explained elsewhere (Vera Espinoza et al., 2021) ideas of crisis and exceptionality tend to identify migrants as "humanitarian subjects" and not as subjects of rights, which justify emergency responses that tend to be short term and ad hoc, as we see in the context of South America response to the Venezuelan displacement (see also Gandini et al., 2022). We have also seen an increased criminalisation of migrants and their mobility, and the spectacularisation of control as the main response (Varela-Huerta, 2021). The framing of crisis then becomes a bordering process in itself, shaping governance practices and measures of control—both outside and inside the States' territories (Vera Espinoza, 2022).

The next sections explore patterns of continuity and change in regional migration governance in South America, and how and in which ways these simultaneous processes that control who move, for how long and under what conditions, also shapes how people move. With a focus on processes, actors and outcomes, the sections that come reflect on how notions of "crisis" have shaped the logics and practice of governance in the region.

Continuity: The Coexistence of a Progressive Framework and Security Actors

It has been widely established that South America's migration governance is non-linear, with waves of restrictive and more open migration policies happening one after the other, or—in many cases—simultaneously

(Domenech, 2007; Geddes & Vera Espinoza, 2018). Until the end of the twentieth century, migration policy in South American countries was marked by a vision of national security and a selective approach that created *wanted* and *unwanted* migrants (Acosta, 2018; Herrera & Cabezas, 2019). From the late 1990s and throughout the early 2000s, most South American countries who inherited restrictive immigration legislations from the dictatorships in the 1970s and 1980s, adopted progressive national policies and discourses that emphasised the importance of migrants' human rights and the need to de-criminalise migration (Brumat, 2020). Freier and Rodriguez (2021) state that since 1993, sixteen Latin American countries have reformed their immigration laws. At least nine of them are South American countries.[5]

During this period, we also see a progressive regional framework taking place, which is consistent with the prominence of migration as part of the social agenda in regional integration processes (Margheritis, 2012). For instance, multilateral organisations such as the Southern Common Market (Mercosur) and the Andean Community (CAN) created mechanisms that facilitated a mobility and residence regime for intra-regional migrants (Brumat & Vera Espinoza, 2023). These initiatives were also discursively aided by the non-binding declarations of the South American Conference on Migration (SACM) (Finn et al., 2019). Some of the regional discourses and mechanisms developed through these multilateral organisations remain in place, showing signs of regional continuity. However, the implementation of these measures and the emergence of new regional initiatives show a more complex panorama.[6]

A similar progressive, although complex, regime is in place for international protection of forced migrants in the region. This is characterised by the coexistence of systems across international (the 1951 Convention Relating to the Status of Refugees, its 1967 protocol and the 2018 Global Compact on Refugees), regional (the 1984 Cartagena Declaration on Refugees and the regime derived from its review process; The Inter-American Human Rights System) and national levels (national legislation and complementary protection measures) (Jubilut et al., 2021). Most countries in the region have signed the Cartagena Declaration (1984) and thirteen countries have included the Cartagena refugee expanded definition in their domestic legislation.[7] Although, in South America, only Brazil has used this definition on specific nationalities, such as Venezuelans.

This regional migration norms for protection and residence that emerged from the political discourses in the late 1990s and early 2000s, have been associated to a resurgence of regionalism (Cantor et al., 2015; Geddes et al., 2019), the low number of immigration at that time (Acosta et al., 2019), the social agenda of left-wing governments in power then (Margheritis, 2012) and even to the shared experiences of exile and migration that many actors within governance systems had (Geddes & Vera Espinoza, 2018). According to Brumat and Freier (2021), this progressive turn in migration policies was also "consciously designed" in opposition to the restrictive policies and approaches that were being developed in the USA and Europe.

While this progressive regional framework remains, there are several issues on how countries use or not use these instruments and mechanisms, particularly in times of "crisis". Still, its continuity cannot be understated either. Some of the processes, structures and actors set up as a direct or indirect result of this regional approach, have been relevant to uphold processes or create minimal standards despite political and shifting migration discourses in the region. For instance, Brumat and Geddes (2023) have shown that despite the threats of the far-right government of Jair Bolsonaro in Brazil (2019–2022), the country granted refugee status recognition to thousands of Venezuelans. The authors show that the recognition of Venezuelans as refugees was grounded, among other reasons, in "a pocket of efficiency within the Brazilian state that was associated with the work of CONARE [the Brazilian National Committee for Refugees] served as a basis for the inclusion of CSOs and influence from international actors, particularly UNHCR" (13). The presence of these structures and the influence of the UN Agency would remain as legacies of the progressive reforms associated with the "liberal tide".

One of the key characteristics of this regional approach is the constant calls for migrant regularisation (Acosta & Harris, 2022; Castro, 2021). While in some cases the discourse has met the practice, as it shown by policies in Argentina, Brazil, Colombia and Uruguay towards Venezuelans, the fragmented approach discussed in the next section shows some contradictory policies. Moreover, this regional approach towards migrant regularisation, consistent with the human rights focus of the regional integration project of the 2000s, has been recognised as an approach of "control with human face" (Domenech, 2013), that is policies with a progressive rhetoric, but with mechanisms that may be conducive to control and securitisation (see Brumat & Vera Espinoza, 2023; Finn & Umpierrez de Reguero, 2020).

While the current regional approach is much more rooted in notions of "safe, orderly, and regular migration" and it is characterised by fragmented responses as I show below, there are still calls for regional governance. For instance, the Chilean president, Gabriel Boric, said in 2023 as part of the Community of Latin American and Caribbean States (CELAC) meeting: "One of the biggest challenges we have today is the migration crisis. We cannot respond to it individually, we have to address it together, regionally" (ADN, 2023).

Another continuity that we have seen in the region is the role of "securitist actors" within national migration bureaucracies. In a recent article, we discuss the re-emergence of these securitist actors within countries such as Argentina, Brazil and Chile, to explain migration policy change between 2015 and 2019 (Brumat & Vera Espinoza, 2023). These securitist actors, which mostly consist of bureaucrats within Ministries of Interior, Security and Defence as well as other groups with historical roots in influencing restrictive policy-making (Acosta, 2018), have promoted and/or endorsed national policy proposals aimed at detaining and deporting irregular immigrants, revoque the liberalisation of policy and encouraging migrant selectivity. These actors and their ideas also played a role in Chile's and Brazil's decisions to not sign and to leave, respectively, the 2018 Global Compact on Migration,[8] despite their active participation in the negotiations that led to the non-binding agreement.

The coexistence of progressive regional frameworks and national securitist actors, and their continuity over time, allows to understand some of the tensions, but also the changes in migration governance in the region.

Changes: The Temporalities and Materialities of Control

The confluence of specific crisis, such as the high numbers Venezuelan displaced across the region, then the health, social and economic crises associated with the COVID-19 pandemic, and high political and social polarisation, have provided a perfect mix to justify some of the changes we have observed on regional migration governance in South America. Here, I briefly explore three: the patchwork governance approach (Acosta et al., 2019; Margheritis & Pedroza, 2022); the militarisation of borders (Zapata et al., 2022) and the "weakening" of asylum (Zapata et al., 2023).

Around 2015 is when we start to witness increased political salience of migration in some countries of the region. At the time, the mobility of Haitians and Central Americans and the increased displacement of Venezuelans were starting to make the headlines. It is in 2017/18 when countries such as Chile, Colombia and Peru start to adopt some ad hoc legal instruments in relation to the Venezuelan displacement, while other countries such as Argentina, Brazil and Uruguay early opted to use existing norms such as the Mercosur Residence agreement to include Venezuelans, despite that the country was suspended from the bloc in 2016 (Acosta et al., 2019). Other countries such as Bolivia established a process of migrant regularisation since 2018.

Special attention should be given to the countries adopting ad hoc measures. I use the cases of Colombia and Chile to illustrate the differences among some of these approaches. Colombia, the main receptor country of Venezuelan population with more than 2.5 million people (UNHCR and IOM, 2022), opted to implement a special residence permit (PEP as per the Spanish acronym) in 2017. This permit gave Venezuelans right to residence and to work for a period of two years, a policy that was consistent with the regularisation approach that had characterised the region. However, in 2020 it was estimated that 56% of Venezuelans in Colombia were in an irregular situation as many of them did not accomplish the PEP requirements (Gobierno de Colombia, 2021). In March 2021, Colombia signed Decree No. 216 that created the Temporary Protection Statute for Migrants Venezuelans (ETPV as per the Spanish acronym). This temporary protection mechanism allowed Venezuelan migrants in Colombia at the time of January 31, 2021, to regularise their status and to stay in the country for ten years (Castro, 2021; López, 2022). While these 10 years regularisation time frame has been celebrated by the international community, the temporality imposed to residence raises questions about the lack of use of other already existing mechanisms for international protection (such as the expanded refugee definition of the Cartagena Declaration), which could lead to permanent residency. The implementation of the temporary protection mechanism also included the creation of a Single Registry of Migrants, which according to the Government of Colombia, has the objective of "collecting and updating your biographical and biometric information", which would be used for the formulation and design of policies as well as for identify the applicants for Temporary Protection Permit (Gobierno de Colombia, 2021, p. 8). There are concerns, however, about the use Colombia may give to this biometric information and who they will share it with. More recently, in 2023, Colombia signed an agreement with Panama and the United States to tackle migration through the jungle region that separates Colombia and Panama known as the Darien Gap, further externalising the control of mobility in the wider region.

Another case that is relevant to explore is the one of Chile. In 2018, the then right-wing Chilean government announced a wide migration reform that included a new migration law and the creation of different six visas and a regularisation process, as part of a series of measures to "clean up the house" (Freier & Vera Espinoza, 2021). Alongside the modifications to the bill, which was finally enacted in 2021 (Doña Reveco, 2022), the government of Sebastian Piñera issued two executive decrees to change visa procedures for Venezuelan and Haitian migrants. One of these decrees created the Visa of Democratic Responsibility for Venezuelans. This consular visa could be issued in any Chilean consulate abroad subject to specific requirements such as a passport (or ID national card) and proof of non-criminal record. With time, the requirements to access this visa increased and the visa started to work as a family reunification procedure (Vera Espinoza, 2022). The consular visa, that was promoted in the media as a special visa to help Venezuelans flee Maduro's regime, represents a de facto barrier to legal entry for targeted nationalities. We have seen the same barriers in other countries, such as Ecuador and Peru (Freier & Luzes, 2021; Palla et al., 2022). Before the imposition of the visa, Venezuelans could enter the country without requesting a visa. The government also reinforced the practice of mass deportations, as a key feature of a communication campaign that criminalises migration, reproducing ideas about "good" and "bad" migrants (Brumat & Vera Espinoza, 2023, Vera Espinoza, 2022). This rhetoric was particularly strong during the pandemic, when the government made media statements that associated the increase of COVID-19 cases with the arrival of irregular migrants, fulling the racism and xenophobia in Chile but also present across the region (Freier & Vera Espinoza, 2021). The campaign to criminalise migration has continued in the government of Gabriel Boric, and in early 2023 senators announced the proposal of a bill—with support across the political spectrum—calling to implement measures to allow police stop and search procedures and the preventive detention of undocumented migrants.

South American countries have used a "patchwork approach" to migration management, particularly in response to the Venezuelan displacement, with the adoption of a myriad of measures, instead of using the legal mechanisms already present in their legislations and regional frameworks. Many of these recent measures impose a particular temporality to rights of residency and pushes migrants, refugees and displaced population to navigate confusing and ever-changing laws and requirements (Vera Espinoza et al., 2021; Zapata et al., 2023). The fragmented approach to migration governance (Margheritis & Pedroza, 2022) that we see across the region is undoubtedly reactive to both external and internal dynamics and pressures (Brumat & Vera Espinoza, 2023). While some analysts consider this approach as "pragmatic" and to certain extent open (Gandini & Salee, 2023), is worth noticing that the fragmentation can become a governance tool in itself, as not only develops a confusing system aimed at deterrence, but also delegitimise the existing frameworks and norms.

These normative deterrence measures are also accompanied by other material and symbolic bordering practices, such as the militarisation of the borders that we have seen across the region. Some of these practices were taking place or being designed before the pandemic (as in the case of Uruguay), but in countries such as Brazil, Chile and Peru, among others, was the health crisis and the closure of borders in March 2020 that also led to border militarisation (Domenech, 2020; Palla et al., 2022; Zapata et al., 2023). The Chilean case is illustrative here to explain the knocking effect of these measures. The imposition of new consular visas in 2018 and the closure of borders in 2020 justified under the epidemiological measures to control the pandemic, contributed to a massive increase of migration through unauthorised entry points, with people enduring very dangerous journeys (Vera Espinoza, 2022). The response of the government came through the *Colchane Plan*, by which the militarisation of the border was consolidated. Decree 265 allowed the Armed Forced to contribute and assist the police with the migration control (Stefoni et al., 2021). As in Chile, many countries have allowed the militarisation of borders beyond the initial epidemiological reasons that justify them in the first place. As we have analysed elsewhere, the crisis of the pandemic allowed the normalisation of the exceptionality imposed during the pandemic (Gandini et al., 2022). The framework of "multiple crises" has then facilitated the emergence of new spaces of control and the articulation of actors that either respond or contribute to these exceptional measures.

Finally, but intrinsically linked to the discussion above, we have seen a growing discretionality on the targeting and the limited implementation of existing national laws and regional agreements on refugee protection across the region and the increase of complementary pathways rather than using existing frameworks (Jubilut et al., 2021). In a recent publication (Zapata et al., 2023), we analyse the cases of Brazil, Chile, Mexico and Uruguay to evidence that the emergence of Covid-related measures have further restricted access to refugee protection. In countries such as Brazil, Chile and Mexico the pandemic was used as an excuse to roll out a series of legal and administrative measures that curtail access to asylum, including rejection at the border, deportations and, in some cases, detention. These came to exacerbate other practices we have seen even before the pandemic, such as barriers to access asylum procedures and in some cases pre-admissibility interviews not contemplated in the law. From our analysis, Uruguay seems to be the exception, as the country implemented exceptional measures aimed at migrant and refugee regularisation (Zapata et al., 2023). However, these measures also include a specific temporality that is not conducive to long-term inclusion. Drawing from Mountz (2020) and de Lucas (2016), we argue in the paper that Latin America, and specially the Southern region, is witnessing "an accelerated weakening of refugee protection" which can result in the "*undermining, abandonment and/or replacement* of the region's widely praised refugee governance" [emphasis in original] (Zapata et al., 2023, 15). The ad hoc measures, the militarisation of borders and the weakening of asylum show how that grammar of refugee protection and the articulations of migration governance are changing in the region (Jubilut et al., 2021; Vera Espinoza, forthcoming).

Conclusion

This chapter has explored the changes in migration governance in South America in the last decade, and how it has been framed and justified through the lens of crisis. The analysis shows evidence of both continuity and change within the management of migration. The chapter argues that South America has been developing a patchwork approach to migration governance, characterised by fragmented and reactive measures, with practices and measures that evidence both continuity and change. While this could be justified by the fact that the massive displacement of Venezuelans put to test the norms and structures already present in the countries of the region (measures taken under the pragmatic approach, as it has been called) it is also relevant to recognise how fragmentation itself becomes a tool of governance.

The patchwork governance approach, justified and enacted in a context of multiple crises, tends to normalise the limited use of existing frameworks and inject extra complexity to a system that is increasingly aimed at deterrence of migrant, refugee and displaced population in the region. Some of the regional structures and principles remain as a strategic backdrop that is not fully used, but instead showcased as a progressive framework, when at the national-level short term temporary practices and increasing entry requirements close safe pathways and increase irregularity. At the local level, the expansion and spectacularisation (Varela-Huerta, 2021) of control measures are used to appease very polarised societies. On the ground, many of these practices contribute to further differentiations between *them* and *us*, making more difficult for migrants and refugees to navigate hyper-complex bureaucracies and limiting their access to rights and social protection (Vera Espinoza et al., 2021).

It is undeniable that the large increase of migration flows in South America is imposing new challenges to governments and host societies in the region. At the same time, the patchwork governance increases irregularity, criminalises migration and fuels racism. A real pragmatic approach would be to seriously assess what the increased mobility control has accomplished in the region, what impacts has on migrant population (with particular attention to gender dynamics, children and adolescents), and what is the assessment of the norms and frameworks already in place. Mobility will continue to be a constant feature of South American societies. The challenge is then how to move from a lens of crisis as the main feature of governance, to one that encourages human security and social cohesion.

Notes

1. The Inter-Agency Coordination Platform for Refugees and Migrants from Venezuelans (R4V), jointly coordinated by the UNHCR and IOM, is made up by over 200 organisations (including UN Agencies, civil society, faith-based organisations and NGOs, among others) that as their website specifies: "coordinate their efforts under Venezuela's Refugee and Migrant Response Plan (RMRP) in 17 countries in Latin America and the Caribbean" (R4V, 2023).
2. The Southern Common Market (MERCOSUR for its Spanish initials) Residence Agreement was signed in 2002 and came into force in 2009. The Residence agreement allows citizens of the trade bloc to obtain a temporary residence in another member state, and therefore to have access to the same rights and liberties than the ones of the nationals in the country of reception. Nine countries, both as full and associate members of the bloc, are part of the agreement (Argentina, Brazil, Paraguay, Uruguay, Chile, Bolivia, Peru, Colombia and Ecuador. Excluding Venezuela that was suspended from the bloc).
3. The Cartagena Declaration of 1984 broadened the definition of refugee to include "persons who have fled their countries because their lives, safety or freedom have been threatened by generalised violence, foreign aggression, internal conflicts, massive violation of human rights or other circumstances that have seriously disturbed public" order (Declaración de Cartagena, 1984), which are to be used in addition to the causes contained in the 1951 Geneva Convention and its 1967 Protocol.
4. These projects include: i. Prospects for International Migration Governance (MIGPROSP, Project no. 340430, https://migrationpolicycentre.eu/migprosp/), Advanced Investigator Grant awarded to Professor Andrew Geddes from the European Research Council, in which I was a researcher; ii. Research conducted with the Group CAMINAR—Comparative Analysis on International Migration and Displacement in the Americas (www.caminaramericas.org).
5. Argentina (Act 25,871-2004); Venezuela (Act 32,944-2004); Uruguay (Act 18,250-2008); Bolivia (Act 370-2013); Colombia (Decree 834-2013); Brazil (Act 13,445-2017); Ecuador (Human Mobility Law of 2017); Peru (Legal Decree 1,350, 2017); Chile (Law 21,325-2021).

6. Some of the regional initiatives/norms that have been promoted in the last few years include, among others: i. The establishment of the Quito Process in 2018, a regional forum that gathered 13 countries, supported by IOM and UNHCR, aimed to respond to the Venezuelan displacement; ii. The approval of the Andean Migratory Statute by the Andean Community (CAN for its acronym in Spanish) in 2021, which regulates the community right of movement within the economic bloc and grants temporary residence to citizens of these countries; iii. Los Angeles Declaration on Migration and Protection as part of the Ninth Summit of the Americas in 2022 (see Castro, 2021; Brumat, 2022).
7. These include Argentina, Bolivia, Brazil, Chile, Colombia, Ecuador, Paraguay, Peru and Uruguay in South America.
8. In January 2023, the government of president Lula da Silva announced Brazil's return to the Global Compact on Migration, four years after former president Jair Bolsonaro withdrew from the accord.

References

Acosta, D. (2018). *The national versus the foreigner in South America. 200 years of migration and citizenship law.* Cambridge University Press.

Acosta, D., & Freier, L. F. (2015). Turning the immigration policy paradox upside down? Populist liberalism and discursive gaps in South America. *International Migration Review, 49*(3), 659–696.

Acosta, D., Harris, J. (2022). *Regímenes de Política Migratoria en América Latina y el Caribe Inmigración, libre movilidad regional, refugio y nacionalidad.* Banco Interamericano de Desarrollo.

Acosta, D., Blouin, C., & Freier, L. F. (2019). *La emigración venezolana: respuestas latinoamericanas. 3 (2a época). Documento de Trabajo.* Fundación Carolina.

ADN. (2023). *Celac 2023: Presidente Gabriel Boric aboga por una "respuesta en conjunto" para solucionar la crisis migratoria en la región. ADN Radio.* Tuesday 24 January 2023.

Betts, A. (Ed.). (2011). *Global migration governance.* Oxford University Press.

Blouin, C., Berganza, I., & Freier, L. F. (2020). The spirit of Cartagena? Applying the extended refugee definition to Venezuelans in Latin America. *Forced Migration Review, 63,* 64–66.

Brumat, L. (2020). Four generations of regional policies for the (free) movement of persons in South America (1977–2016). In G. Rayp, I. Ruyssen, & K. Marchand (Eds.), *Regional integration and migration governance in the global south* (pp. 153–176). Springer International Publishing.

Brumat, L. (2021). The residence agreement of MERCOSUR as an alternative form of protection: The challenges of a milestone in regional migration governance. In

L. L. Jubilut, M. Vera Espinoza, & G. Mezzanotti (Eds.), *Latin America and refugee protection: Regimes, logics and challenges* (pp. 237–255). Berghahn Books.

Brumat, L. (2022). América Latina y la agenda de movilidad humana (2021–2022). In Sanahuja, J. Antonio & P. Stefanoni (Eds.), *América Latina: transiciones ¿hacia dónde? Informe Anual 2022–2023* (pp. 79–90). Fundación Carolina. ISBN: 978-84-09-46409-8.

Brumat, L., & Freier, L. F. (2021). Unpacking the unintended consequences of European migration governance: The case of South American migration policy liberalisation, *Journal of Ethnic and Migration Studies, 49*(12), 3060–3084.

Brumat, L., & Geddes, A. (2023). Refugee recognition in Brazil under Bolsonaro: The domestic impact of international norms and standards. *Third World Quarterly*. https://www.tandfonline.com/. https://doi.org/10.1080/01436597.2022.2153664

Brumat, L., & Vera Espinoza, M. (2023). Actors, ideas, and international influence: Understanding migration policy change in South America. *International Migration Review.*

Brumat, L., Acosta, D., & Vera Espinoza, M. (2018). Gobernanza migratoria en América del Sur: ¿hacia una nueva oleada restrictiva? In L. Bizzozero Revelez & W. Fernández Luzuriaga (Eds.), *Anuario de Política Internacional y Política Exterior 2017- 2018* (pp. 205–211). Ediciones Cruz del Sur. ISSN: 2393-6924.

Cantor, D. J. (2014). The new wave: Forced displacement caused by organized crime in Central America and Mexico. *Refugee Survey Quarterly, 33*(3), 34–68.

Cantor, D. L., Freier, F., & Gauci, J.-P. (Eds.). (2015). *A liberal tide: Towards a paradigm shift in Latin American migration and asylum policy-making*. Institute of Latin American Studies.

Castro, A. (2021, November). Displaced Venezuelans in Latin America: A test of regional solidarity? *Notes de L'Ifri, Ifri.*

Ceriani, P. (2018). Migration policies and human rights in Latin America. Progressive practices, old challenges, worrying setbacks and new threats. *Global Campus Policy Brief*. https://repository.gchumanrights.org/items/c8951d47-2f67-492e-b345-8dfe8f1e7880

Crawley, H., & Skleparis, D. (2018). Refugees, migrants, neither, both: Categorical fetishism and the politics of bounding in Europe's "migration crisis." *Journal of Ethnic and Migration Studies, 44*(1), 48–64.

De Lucas, J. (2016). Sobre el proceso de vaciamiento del derecho de asilo por parte de los Estados de la UE. *Ars Iuris Salmanticensis*, AIS: revista Europea e Iberoamericana de Pensamiento y Análisis de Derecho, Ciencia Política y Criminología, *4*(1), 21–27.

de Menezes, F. L. (2016). Utopia or reality: Regional cooperation in Latin America to enhance the protection of refugees. *Refugee Survey Quarterly, 35*(4), 122–141.

Declaración de Cartagena. (1984). Declaración de Cartagena. Cartagena: Coloquio Sobre la Protección Internacional de los Refugiados en América Central, Problemas Jurídicos y Humanitarios. https://www.acnur.org/5b076ef14.pdf

Domenech, E. (2013). Las migraciones son como el agua: Hacia la instauración de políticas de 'control con rostro humano'. La gobernabilidad migratoria en la Argentina. *Polis. Revista Latinoamericana, 12*(35), 119–142.

Domenech, E. (2007). La agenda política sobre migraciones en América del sur: El caso de la Argentina. *Revue Européenne des Migrations Internationales, 23*(1), 71–94

Domenech, E. (2018). Gobernabilidad migratoria: producción y circulación de una categoría de intervención política. *Revista Temas de Antropología y Migración, 10*, 110–125. ISSN: 1853-354.

Domenech, E. (2020). *Pandemia y control de fronteras en el espacio sudamericano. Boletín (Trans)Fronteriza Año 1—Número #3 "(In)movilidades en las Américas y COVID-19" November 2020.* Clacso.

Doña Reveco, C. (2022, May 18). *Chile's Welcoming Approach to Immigrants Cools as Numbers Rise.* Migration Policy Institute. https://www.migrationpolicy.org/article/chile-immigrants-rising-numbers

Feddersen, M., Morales, A., Ramaciotti, J. P., & Vera Espinoza, M. (2023). *Ley de Refugio en Chile. Nudos críticos, desafíos urgentes y alternativas hacia el futuro.* Centro de Políticas Migratorias. https://www.politicasmigratorias.org/publicaciones

Finn, V., Doña-Reveco, C., & Feddersen, M. (2019). Migration governance in South America: Regional approaches versus national laws. In A. Geddes, M. Vera Espinoza, L. Hadj-Abdou, & L. Brumat (Eds.), *The dynamics of regional migration governance* (pp. 15–35). Edward Elgar Publishing.

Finn, V., & Umpierrez de Reguero, S. (2020). Inclusive Language for exclusive policies: Restrictive migration governance in Chile, 2018. *Latin Amermican Policy, 11*(1), 42–61.

Freier, F. (2022). *The power of categorization: Reflections on UNHCR's category of 'Venezuelans displaced abroad'.* Measuring migration conference 2022 proceedings. pp. 51–54.

Freier, F., & Vera, E. M. (2021). COVID-19 and immigrants' increased exclusion: The politics of immigrant integration in Chile and Peru. *Frontiers in Human Dynamics, 3*, 606871.

Freier, L. F., & Luzes, M. (2021). How humanitarian are humanitarian visas? An analysis of theory and practice in South America. In in L. L. Jubilut, M. Vera Espinoza, & G. Mezzanotti (Eds.), *Latin America and Refugee Protection: regimes, logics and challenges* (pp. 276–293). Berghahn Books.

Freier, L. F., & Rodríguez, F. (2021). Trends in latin American domestic refugee Law. In L. L. Jubilut, M. Vera Espinoza, & G. Mezzanotti (Eds.), *Latin America and refugee protection: Regimes, logics and challenges.* (pp. 256–275). Berghahn Books.

Gandini, L., & Salee, A. (2023). *Betting on legality: Latin American and Caribbean responses to the Venezuelan displacement crisis.* Migration Policy Institute. https://www.migrationpolicy.org/research/latin-american-caribbean-venezuelan-crisis

Gandini, L., Prieto Rosas, V., Lozano-Ascencio, F. (2019). El éxodo venezolano: migración en contextos de crisis y respuestas de los países latinoamericanos. In L. Gandini, F. Lozano-Ascencio & V. Prieto Rosas (Coords.), *Crisis y migración de población venezolana. Entre la desprotección y la seguridad jurídica en Latinoamérica* (pp. 9–32). UNAM.

Gandini, L., Vera Espinoza, M., & Zapata, G. P. (2022). Movilidades y 'crisis' en América Latina: brechas en las políticas de inclusión social antes y durante la pandemia. In G. P. Zapata, M. Vera Espinoza & L. Gandini (Eds.), *Movilidades y Covid-19 en América Latina: inclusiones y exclusiones en tiempos de "crisis"* (pp. 15–36). UNAM.

Geddes, A. (2021). *Governing migration beyond the state*. Oxford University Press.

Geddes A., & Vera Espinoza, M. (2018). Framing understandings of international migration: How governance actors make sense of migration in Europe and South America. In A. Margheritis (Ed.), *Shaping migration between Europe and Latin America. New approaches and challenges* (pp. 27–50). ILAS publications.

Geddes, A., Vera Espinoza, M., Hadj-Abdou, L., & Brumat, L. (Eds.). (2019). *The dynamics of regional migration governance*. Edward Elgar Publishing.

Gobierno de Colombia. (2021). Abecé del estatuto temporal de protección para migrantes venezolanos. Ministerio de Relaciones Exteriores. https://www.cancilleria.gov.co/sites/default/files/FOTOS2020/ok._esp-_abc_estatuto_al_migrante_venezolano-_05mar-2021.pdf

Herrera, G., & Berg, U. (2019), 'Migration crises' and humanitarianism in Latin America: The case of Ecuador. In N. Sorensen & S. Plambech (Eds.), *Global perspectives on humanitarianism*. Danish Institute for International Studies.

Herrera, G., & Cabezas, G. (2019). Ecuador: de la recepción a la disuasión. Políticas frente a la población venezolana y experiencia migratoria 2015–2018. In L. Gandini, F. Lozano-Ascencio & V. Prieto Rosas (Eds.), *Crisis y migración de población venezolana. Entre la desprotección y la seguridad jurídica en Latinoamérica* (pp. 125–156). UNAM.

IOM. (2021). *Migration data in South America. Migration data portal*. October 2021 update. https://www.migrationdataportal.org/regional-data-overview/migration-data-south-america#recent-trends

Jubilut, L. L., Vera Espinoza, M., & Mezzanotti, G. (Eds.). (2021). *Latin America and refugee protection: Regimes, logics and challenges*. Berghahn Books.

Lavenex, S., & Piper, N. (2019). Regional migration governnce: Perspectives 'from above' and 'from below'. In A. Geddes, M. Vera Espinoza, L. Hadj-Abdou, & L. Brumat (Eds.), *The dynamics of regional migration governance* (pp. 15–35). Edward Elgar Publishing.

López, S. (2022). Población venezolana en Colombia durante la pandemia: exclusión latente. In G. P. Zapata, M. Vera Espinoza, & L. Gandini (Eds.), *Movilidades y covid-19 en América Latina: Inclusiones y exclusiones en tiempos de "crisis"* (pp. 111–129). UNAM.

Margheritis, A. (2012). Piecemeal regional integration in the post-neoliberal era: Negotiating migration policies within Mercosur. *Review of International Political Economy, 20*(3), 541–575.

Margheritis, A. (2022). Migration governance evolution amidst a nested crisis: The case of South America. *International Migration*. https://onlinelibrary.wiley.com/doi/abs/. https://doi.org/10.1111/imig.13109

Margheritis, A., & Pedroza, L. (2022). *Is there a "Latin American" approach to migration governance? Análisis Carolina 16-2022, September*. Fundación Carolina.

Mármora, L. (2002). *Las políticas de migraciones internacionales*. Paidós/OIM.

Martínez Pizarro, J., & Orrego Rivera, J. (2016). Nuevas tendencias y dinámics migratorias en América Latina y el Caribe. CEPAL Población y Desarrollo ISSN 1680-8991. https://www.cepal.org/es/publicaciones/39994-nuevas-tendencias-dinamicas-migratorias-america-latina-caribe

Mountz, A. (2020). *The death of asylum: Hidden geographies of the enforcement archipielago*. University of Minnesota Press.

Palla, I., Zamora Gómez, C., & Blouin, C. (2022). Entre (des) protección social y ayuda humanitaria: El control de las y los migrantes durante la COVID-19 en Perú. In G. P. Zapata, M. Vera Espinoza, & L. Gandini (Eds.), *Movilidades y covid-19 en América Latina: inclusiones y exclusiones en tiempos de "crisis"* (pp. 155–174). UNAM.

Ramírez, J., & Alfaro, Y. (2010). Espacios multilaterales de diálogo migratorio: El proceso Puebla y la Conferencia Sudamericana de Migración. *Andina Migrante., 9*, 2–10.

Rojas, M. L. Y., & Winton, A. (2019). Precarious mobility in Central America and southern Mexico: Crises and the struggle to survive. In C. Menjívar, M. Ruiz, & E. I. Ness (Eds.), *The oxford handbook of migration Crises* (pp. 245–260). Oxford University Press.

R4V. (2022, December). *Venezuelan refugees and migrants in the region. Latin America and the Caribbean*. R4V inter-agency coordination platform for refugees and migrants from Venezuela.

R4V. (2023). Inter-agency coordination platform for refugees and migrants from Venezuela. UNHCR and IOM.

Stefoni, C. (2018). *Panorama de la migración internacional en América del Sur*. CEPAL Población y Desarrollo ISSN 1680-9009. https://www.cepal.org/es/publicaciones/43584-panorama-la-migracion-internacional-america-sur

Stefoni, C., Cabieses, B., & Blukacz, A. (2021). Migraciones y COVID-19: Cuando el discurso securitista amenaza el derecho a la salud. *Simbiótica, 8*(2), 38–66.

UNHCR. (2022). *UNHCR Venezuela situation fact sheet June 2022*. https://reliefweb.int/report/venezuela-bolivarian-republic/unhcr-venezuela-situation-fact-sheet-june-2022

Varela-Huerta, A. (2021). *De bestias, caravanas y jaulas. Espectáculo de frontera, luchas migrantes y porno-miseria*. Nexos. https://migracion.nexos.com.mx/author/amarela-varela-huerta/

Vera Espinoza, G., & Mezzanotti (Eds.) (2021). *Latin America and refugee protection: Regimes, logics and challenges*. (pp. 256–275). Berghahn Books.

Vera Espinoza, M. (2018). The limits and opportunities of regional solidarity: Exploring refugee resettlement in Brazil and Chile. *Global Policy, 9*(1), 85–94.

Vera Espinoza, M. (2021). The mixed legacy of the Mexico declaration and plan of action: Solidarity and refugee protection in Latin America. In L. L. Jubilut, M. Vera Espinoza & G. Mezzanotti (Eds.), *Latin America and refugee protection: Regimes, logics and challenges* (pp. 77–95). Berghahn Books.

Vera Espinoza, M. (2022). Gobernanza excluyente vs. resistencia inclusiva: el manejo de las migraciones durante la pandemia en Chile. In G. P. Zapata, M. Vera Espinoza, & L. Gandini (Eds.), *Movilidades y covid-19 en América Latina: inclusiones y exclusiones en tiempos de "crisis"* (pp. 87–109). UNAM.

Vera Espinoza, M., Prieto Rosas, V., Zapata, G. P., Gandini, L., Fernández de la Reguera, A., Herrera, G., López Villamil, S., Zamora Gómez, C., Blouin, C., Montiel, C., Cabezas Gálvez, G., & Palla, I. (2021). Towards a typology of social protection for migrants and refugees in Latin America during the COVID-19 pandemic. *Comparative Migration Studies, 9*, 52.

Vera Espinoza, M. (2023). The shifting grammar of durable solutions in Latin America. In K. Jacobsen & N. Majidi (Eds.), *Handbook in forced migration*. Edward Elgar Publishing.

Yates, C. (2021). *Haitian migration through the Americas: A decade in the making*. Migration policy institute. https://www.migrationpolicy.org/article/haitian-migration-through-americas

Zapata, G. P., Vera Espinoza, M., & Gandini, L. (Eds.), *Movilidades y Covid-19 en América Latina: inclusiones y exclusiones en tiempos de "crisis"*. UNAM.

Zapata, G. P., Gandini, L., Vera Espinoza, M., & Prieto, R. (2023, in press). Weakening practices amidst progressive laws: Refugee governance in Latin America during COVID-19. *Journal of Immigrant and Refugee Studies*.

Open Access This chapter is licensed under the terms of the Creative Commons Attribution 4.0 International License (http://creativecommons.org/licenses/by/4.0/), which permits use, sharing, adaptation, distribution and reproduction in any medium or format, as long as you give appropriate credit to the original author(s) and the source, provide a link to the Creative Commons license and indicate if changes were made.

The images or other third party material in this chapter are included in the chapter's Creative Commons license, unless indicated otherwise in a credit line to the material. If material is not included in the chapter's Creative Commons license and your intended use is not permitted by statutory regulation or exceeds the permitted use, you will need to obtain permission directly from the copyright holder.

30

Perú and Migration from Venezuela: From Early Adjustment to Policy Misalignment

Jacqueline Mazza and Nicolás Forero Villarreal

Introduction

Beginning in 2015, the world began witnessing the surreal unravelling of one of South America's strongest economies. The outflow of Venezuelans seeking refuge from both political repression and economic collapse grew exponentially. Within seven years Venezuelans fleeing their country would top 7.18 million (RV4, January 2023), putting Venezuela in league with the world's two other modern mass migration crises, Syria and Ukraine. The Venezuelan economy shrunk to one-quarter of its former size and over 75% of the remaining population is now living in extreme poverty (ENCOVI, 2021). The Inter-American Commission on Human Rights and the Organisation of American States (OAS) designated Venezuela as a country of "forced displacement" (2018). The economic-political-social "implosion" of Venezuela has created the largest mass migration crisis in Latin American and Caribbean history (Alvarez et al., 2022; Mauricia, 2019). Venezuelans have moved overwhelmingly to South American countries, which received more than 80% of all Venezuelan refugees and migrants (RV4, January 2023, Selee et al.,

J. Mazza (✉)
Johns Hopkins University-SAIS-Europe, Via Benjamino Andreatta 3 (Formerly Via Belmeloro 11), Bologna, Italy
e-mail: jmazza1@jhu.edu

N. F. Villarreal
Universidad de los Andes, Bogotá, Colombia
e-mail: n.forero703@uniandes.edu.co

2019). Colombia, which shares multiple borders with Venezuela, has received the largest number of migrants—2.5 million by January 2023 (RV4, January 2023). But Perú is the number two destination country, even though it has no direct borders with Venezuela. Perú has received the second largest number of Venezuelans every year since April 2018, many walking 4,500 kilometres through neighbouring Colombia (Rossiasco, 2019). By the end of 2022, more than 1.5 million Venezuelans were resident in Perú, comprising 4% of Perú's national population and highly concentrated in the capital city of Lima and local port of Callao (RV4, January 2023).

This chapter addresses the principal question *how* and then *how well* did Perú adapt to the mass migration of Venezuelan migrants? To answer *how*, the chapter constructs a historical chronology of three phases: (I) 2015–2018; (II) 2018–early 2020; and, (III) 2020 to present (2023) and details the principal national migration policy steps taken together with the changing size and nature of the inflows of Venezuelan migrations. The three phases correspond to different Peruvian presidencies, and as the chapter will detail, each phase varied dramatically on a spectrum of receptivity and restrictiveness to Venezuelan migrants.

To answer both *how* and *how well*, the chapter draws on the principal regional literature, including economic studies and surveys, and utilises migration data of the United Nations to track the flows of migrants in and out of Perú both before and during the Venezuelan migration crisis. To specifically analyse *how well*, the chapter cites and analyses evidence on a range of impacts: bureaucratic and administrative, impacts on the Peruvian economy, labour market, and social conditions as well as impacts on the Venezuelan migrants themselves. In 2018, a unique multilateral level of aid coordination and management was created by the United Nations in response to the Venezuelan crisis, known as the Regional Interagency Coordination Platform (R4V). To further answer *how well*, the chapter explores Perú's national policies in the context of R4V's multilateral migration coordination and support that was only drawn on to a limited extent.

The first section introduces Perú's long, multi-cultural history with migration and places Venezuela's current crisis within the literature of forced displacement. The second section lays out in three phases how Perú national migration management moved from early accommodation in Phase I under Umberto Humala and Pedro Pablo Kuczynski to restrictive migration policies in Phase 2 under Martin Vizcarra to a COVID-19-dominated Phase 3 of even further restrictions that began under Martin Vizcarra and continued with the Presidencies of Pedro Castillo and Dina Botuarte. This section also describes the formation of RV4 and what became Perú's limited reliance on this resource. The chapter concludes by evaluating Perú's migration management as maladapted to the dimensions and nature of the Venezuelan forced migration crisis, creating clear contrasts with approaches undertaken by its South American neighbours, in particular, Colombia and Argentina.

Overall, the Venezuelan migration crisis has given rise to a substantial body of regional (Latin American and Caribbean) literature drawn on in this chapter. There is, however, comparatively less academic literature analysing Perú in a South-South context with regions outside of Latin America (Levaggi & Freier, 2022); this chapter thus contributes by placing Perú's challenges as part of the Global South. Even further, academic literature is only beginning to look at Venezuela as part of a more modern phenomenon of "mass" migration crises that link Syria, Ukraine, and Venezuela (Mazza & Caballero, 2022). As this chapter will argue, "mass" migration crises have a greater set of demands on countries of the Global South for which traditional national case-by-case migration management policies such as those pursued by Perú are particularly poorly suited.

Perú's Migration History

Perú's origins as the seat of the Inca Empire and indigenous culture in the Americas were fundamentally reshaped in the early colonial period by the influx of Europeans, African slaves, and Asian immigrants. From independence in 1824 to the abolition of slavery in 1854, Perú's early history was redrawn by more than a century of immigrants coming from the East and West. The draw of Perú's vast natural resources as well as commodity booms in guano and rubber attracted labourers and merchants from Spain, China, Italy, Japan as well as other countries shaping an early history of multi-ethnic migration. Today the impact of this early immigration made Perú into one of the most culturally and ethnically diverse nations in South America (Takenaka et al., 2010).

But beginning in the 1960s, Perú's economic and political troubles reversed the migration trend to outmigration. By the 1990s, Peruvians were fleeing hyperinflation, the terrorism toll of Sendero Luminoso, and frequent political crises. Peruvians migrated particularly to the United States, Spain, Japan, and Italy, and to the stronger regional economies of Chile and Argentina. As shown in Fig. 30.1, for more than 50 years from 1960 through 2014, Perú had become a country of net outmigration. As Fig. 30.1 demonstrates this large volume of emigration drove net emigration rates to nearly—8% of the population by 2008. The global financial crisis of 2008–9 and the return of (principally) commodity-based growth in Perú was able to slow substantially the net outflows of Peruvians after this low point. Spain, in particular, provided incentives for South Americans to return home given economic troubles in Spain.

Just prior to the Venezuelan crisis, Perú had reached a net migration rate of 0 (Fig. 30.1), but 2014 would be the last year that emigrants and immigrants netted to zero.

From the arrival of the first significant numbers of Venezuelans in 2015, Venezuelans fleeing political and economic chaos under Maduro became the principal factor transforming Perú into a net receiving nation in the modern era, with a high 3% net migration rate in 2018 when Venezuelan migrants had topped 700,000.

As shown in Fig. 30.2, Venezuelan migration to Perú escalated sharply beginning in 2017, displaying a spurt characteristic of "forced" rather than voluntary migration. The crisis unfolded in a surreal fashion: mismanagement of the oil industry and the economy, brutal repression of the opposition, then massive economic contraction, inflation spiralling to one million per cent, food shortages, widespread hunger and malnutrition, violence, criminal gangs, with the government and military the seat of drug running, and other crimes.

Fig. 30.1 Perú: Net migration rates, 1960–2022

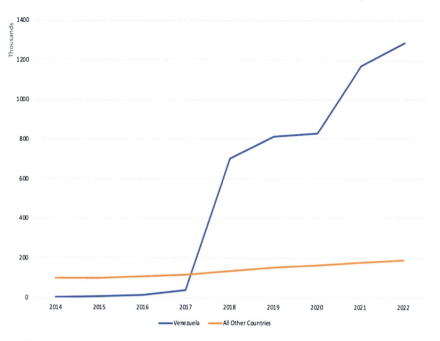

Fig. 30.2 Venezuelan migrants to Perú vs. all other migrants, 2014–2022

Most internal and international migration is broadly considered to fall into the category of voluntary migrants, typically moving in search of economic opportunities, for family reunification, and/or for education (Castles et al., 2005). In contrast, involuntary or forced migration is more applicable to the current Venezuelan crisis. Reed, Ludwig, and Braslow (Reed et al., 2016) define forced migration "as coerced or involuntary movement from one's home". Involuntary migration is understood within the United Nations system as coming from four broad types of which Venezuela constitutes the first type:

- Conflict-induced displaced migrants;
- Environmental- or disaster-induced displacement;
- Human trafficking;
- Development-induced displacement such as the construction of dams (Reed et al., 2016).

According to Stankovic, Ecke, and Wirtz, forced migration refers to the "forcibly induced migration of people, for example, when migrants are forced to flee to escape conflict or persecution or become trafficked" (Stankovic et al., 2021). By 2018, the Interamerican Commission on Human Rights

(IACHR) and the Organisation of American States had issued Resolution 2/18 clearly placing Venezuela in the category of forced migration, due to the "massive" violations of human rights, violence, and insecurity (IACHR and OAS, February 2018). The IACHR stated that not only the massive violations of human rights but also the internal economic and health crisis that Venezuela has been facing as a result of the shortage of food and medicines were factors for which, hundreds of thousands of Venezuelans were *forced to migrate* to other countries in the region as a survival strategy (IACHR and OAS, February 2018).

Three Phases of Venezuelan Migration

The first "wave" of Venezuelan migrants was visible in the capital city of Lima in large numbers by 2015. These waves multiplied yearly with the exception of 2020 when the COVID-19 pandemic led to border closures for nearly a year. By 2022, the number of Venezuelan migrants in Perú reached nearly 1.3 million (87% of all immigrants) dwarfing all other migrants who numbered only 200,000 (Fig. 30.2).

The scale and the profile of these migrants-their age, gender, education, and whether they migrated with family members or alone-would change markedly in just seven years. Forced migration from Venezuela coincided and was shaped by the country's political turmoil and ongoing administrative instability (Paredes & Encinas, 2020). Since 2015, Perú's executive branch of government has been ruled by six different presidents. In 2020 alone, Perú had three different heads of State. The last six presidents of Perú have been either investigated or convicted for corruption-related charges.

The objective and content of Perú's migration policy can be most accurately described in three historical phases that followed the ups and downs of Peruvian politics: Phase 1 (2015–late 2018), Phase 2 (late 2018–March 2020), and Phase 3—COVID-19 (March 2020–2023+).

Phase I: 2015–18: Relative Openness to Relatively Fewer Numbers

Perú had substantially modernised its legal framework for migrants and refugees well before the start of the Venezuelan crisis. In 2002, Perú renewed its law regarding refugees, endorsing the Cartagena Declaration's definition of refugee status, which defines refugees as persons who have fled their countries or origin if their lives, safety, or freedom has been threatened by generalised violence, foreign aggression, internal conflicts, massive violations of human rights, or other circumstances that have seriously disturbed public order (Law n.º 27.891, 2002, art. 3). The definition of refugee under the Cartagena Declaration expands on the 1951 Refugee Convention, which had predominantly relied on persecution as the key element to determine refugee status (Cartagena Declaration, 1984). By 2015, Perú had already signed and ratified major international conventions related to the protection of migrants. Many experts believed the country remained faithful to Latin America's exceptionalism regarding political asylum (Blouin, 2021).

In 2015, under the government of Ollanta Humala, Perú adopted a National Migration Policy which guaranteed a relative openness to immigrants, reforming the State's migration infrastructure, and increasing frontier controls among its measures (Decree n.º 1236, 2015) This landmark decree coincided with the first wave of highly skilled and educated Venezuelan migrants arriving in Perú. Perú's 2015 National Migration Policy, however, was never truly implemented confronting both legislative and administrative obstacles. During the last year of the Humala presidency corruption-related scandals overwhelmed the capacity of the government to promote implementation of many policies, including the National Migration Policy (Quiñón et al., 2016).

The election of Pedro Pablo Kuczynski to the presidency in 2016 marked the start of Perú's more open-door policy to Venezuelan migrants, in line with a dramatic change in the country's foreign policy in opposition to the Maduro regime in Venezuela (Vidarte, 2018). In contrast to the Humala administration's ambiguity and neutrality towards the Venezuelan government, Kuczynski was adamant in denouncing human rights conditions in Venezuela and he started a regional movement to oppose the Maduro regime (Freier & Parent, 2018). The Kuczynski government created the Lima Group in 2017 to bring together regional pressure on the Maduro government. He also expelled the Venezuelan ambassador from Perú (Arcarazo Acosta et al., 2019).

Most importantly, six months after arriving to the presidency Kuczynski enacted the decree providing the Temporary Permanence Permit (hereinafter "PTP"). The PTP granted Venezuelans two years of stay and could serve as a pathway to achieve legal residence. The measure provided for the permanence of Venezuelan migrants, allowing them access to health, education most importantly employment (Supreme Decree N. 002, 2017). This first version had very flexible requirements covering Venezuelans whether they entered regularly or irregularly. The PTP was widely regarded as an accommodating move in support of migrant inclusion in Perú (Blouin & Freier, 2019, Wolfe, 2021). The PTP granted Venezuelans two years of stay and was to serve as a pathway to achieve legal residence. The PTP was renewed four times during Kuczynski's presidency. During this period, the Kuczynski administration, in particular, framed Perú's policy as one honouring how Venezuelans welcomed Peruvians during Perú's political crises of the 70 s and 80 s (Gestión, 2018).[1]

Even though Perú had its own economic troubles post-2015, economic studies indicate that immigrant labour has been well accommodated in the economy largely given the underlying positive economic conditions in Perú in the first years of the Venezuelan migrant crisis. Vera and Jimenez find in the specific case of Venezuelans in Perú that there was no negative impact on wages for native Peruvians. They find that the pre-2019 labour market absorbed migrant labour quite well but that was done principally by expanding jobs in the informal sector. So, although the net employment effect in Perú was positive, the growth was nearly all in informal employment (Boruchowicz et al., 2021). Perú's early national policy approach of creating a new migration instrument, the PTP, was not granted under the framework of international protection based on refugee status or asylum. Instead, it was a broader instrument intended to favour social integration and economic development of Venezuelans in Perú. In this early stage (2015–18), Perú's early openness to Venezuelan migrants was considered the"most accommodating" of all the South American receiving nations (Blouin, 2021; Selee et al., 2019; Wolfe, 2021). Perú's regional leadership towards Venezuela ended abruptly with the tumultuous fall and resignation of President Kuczynski amid a corruption-related scandal. The subsequent two phases of Peruvian migration policy would lead to substantial backtracking from its lauded initial policy.

Phase II: Late 2018–March 2020: Greater Legal Restrictions, Numbers, and Exclusion

Martin Vizcarra replaced Kuczynski as president of Perú in March 2018. From the beginning of his presidency Vizcarra signalled he would be undoing Perú's accommodating policy towards Venezuelan migrants, in particular making work authorisation more difficult to qualify for through a series of changes to the PTP. Gone from public discourse was the idea that better economic and social integration of Venezuelans would be good for Perú. In August 2018, the government introduced Decree 007 which moved up the deadline to request the PTP from 30 June 2019 to 31 December 2018

(Republic of Perú, 2018). That decree also provided that the PTP could only be requested if the entry to Peruvian territory was made before 31 October 2018. Later in October 2018, the government enacted a resolution requiring the submission of a valid passport as a requirement to access the PTP (Resolution N. 00000270), knowing full well that the Maduro government was collapsing bureaucratically and no longer issuing passport renewals.[2]

The increasing restrictions did not have the impact on reducing migratory flows that the Vizcarra government intended. Venezuelan migration to Perú surged past the half million mark to 700,000 by the end of 2018 (Fig. 30.2) driven by the external factors of forced migration. The Vizcarra government added to the bureaucratic burdens on the Peruvian government by failing to provide additional resources or infrastructure to process migrants under its more complicated requirements. President Vizcarra stated publicly in an interview with CNN in 2018 that Perú had reached its limits and capacity to host Venezuelan migrants, ignoring its own role in enacting requirements without resources to carry them out (CNN, 2018).

In 2019, the Vizcarra administration launched the ironically-named "Operation Safe Migration", going even further in restricting legal immigration and setting difficult-to-meet requirements to enter Peru legally. This policy had two principal measures. First, it created a specialised police force in charge of deporting all Venezuelan migrants that committed crimes. It also required all Venezuelan migrants wishing to enter Perú to apply for a Humanitarian Visa (Republic of Perú, 2019). The humanitarian visa required Venezuelans to present a valid passport and a certificate of criminal records that had to be duly notarised and apostilled before leaving Venezuela. There were only two Peruvian consulates in Venezuela that could process humanitarian visas, alongside three more in Colombia (Bogotá, Leticia, and Medellín) and five consulates in Ecuador (Guayaquil, Quito, Cuenca, Machala, and Loja).

The onerous requirement to possess a valid passport and go through additional procedures and qualifications for a humanitarian visa led to a surge in Venezuelan migrants asking for refugee status and asylum as the only alternatives to legally enter Perú (Camino & López Montreuil, 2020). Overnight, asylum and refugee claims skyrocketed and again the Vizcarra government was both unprepared, making no provision to handle increased claims. Venezuelans who went through the lengthy process in Perú found that the vast majority of claims were denied, even though Venezuelans fit refugee and asylum requirements under international norms. A report of the Peruvian

Ministry of Foreign Affairs showed Perú received 158,311 refugee applications from Venezuelans in 2019, 548 were denied and 497 were approved, which represents just 0.3% in acceptance rate (Morales Tovar, 2019).

The enormous increase in refugee/asylum requests put a spotlight on how fragile and unprepared Perú's refugee/asylum infrastructure was. Weak implementation infrastructure is a noted common feature in Latin America despite the existence of robust legal mechanisms (Gandini et al., 2020). In the case of Perú, the asylum process was set up to take just 60 days (Camino & Montreuill, 2020).

Seeing that Ecuador had become the largest point of entry to Perú, the Vizcarra government tried to patch that hole by adding a new pre-screening application at the border through Ecuador (Camino & López Montreuil, 2020). Peruvian border authorities could now refuse entry to asylum seekers while their central office staff reviewed the request for asylum/refugee status. Perú's actions were viewed by many international NGOs and human rights advocates as being contrary to not only the Refugee Convention of 1951 (which prohibits the return or rejection at the border of asylum seekers), but also the Cartagena Declaration whose spirit had been at least embraced by Peruvian law (Amnesty International, 2020).

By early 2020, even before the COVID-19 health crisis hit, the Vizcarra government increased public attacks on Venezuelan migrants, claiming the need for greater security and border control. He promoted a hardline policy to deport Venezuelan migrants that had committed crimes, even the most minor ones. Venezuelan migrants were easy targets of the now poorly performing economy, and the negative stereotyping of Venezuelan migrants would be further accelerated once the COVID-19 crisis hit.

Phase III: March 2020–2023: Dual Health and Migration Crises with Deteriorating Conditions for Migrants

On the 15th of March 2020, the Peruvian government declared a strict State of Emergency lockdown with rising cases of COVID-19 (Republic of Perú, 2020b). Under the State of Emergency, a mandatory quarantine was enacted, and all travel was suspended by the closure of land, air, and water borders to both foreigners and Peruvian nationals. Venezuelan migration flows did dramatically decrease. What is not known is how many migrants came across porous land borders evading border control during the early COVID period. Vizcarra steered an early strict lockdown of COVID-19, but it was not able to prevent the later soaring deaths on an overwhelmed, fragile hospital system, and now collapsing economy.

Under lockdown, Venezuelan migrants who had lost the legal right to work under Phase II were now principally working in the informal sector, suddenly cut off from any way to earn a daily living as open markets were not operating. While international organisations tried to step in and help, migrants were not eligible to receive nationwide emergency cash transfers enacted by the government (Republic of Perú., 2020a) as they were in most countries of South America except for greater limitations in Chile. The national identity document (DNI) was used to qualify as a beneficiary of the cash assistance programme. Individuals with a DNI number could receive the allotted 320 soles (about $115) a month but few qualified (Mazza & Forero Villareal, 2020).

To access the national health system, the SIS (*Seguro de Salud Integral*), migrants were required to have legal status (at least temporary residence) or a Foreign Identification Card (*Carta de Extranjera*), except for those under five. Migrants could buy into the SIS system, but few of them could afford this. In theory, access to emergency medical assistance for those with COVID-19 was provided under an extraordinary national government measure. Nevertheless, many health providers continued to request the national identity document (DNI) or simply refused services to Venezuelans (Levaggi & Freier, 2022; Mazza & Forero Villareal, 2020).

Housing conditions for Venezuelan migrants also deteriorated greatly during the pandemic, as many were in precarious housing, without a rental contract and were thus not often protected from eviction (Mazza & Forero Villareal, 2020). Statistics indicate that in both 2018 and 2019 at least 94% of Venezuelan migrants in Perú were living in rented, many daily-rate housing (INEI, 2018). The Peruvian Ombudsperson reported in 2020 that due to the pandemic at least 39% of Venezuelans in Perú were at risk of losing their housing (República del Perú, Defensoría del Pueblo, 2020). The Peruvian government remained silent and inactive regarding evictions of Venezuelans which placed more Venezuelans on the streets during lockdowns.

In October of 2020, the government introduced the Temporary Permit Carnet (CPT) which allowed Venezuelan migrants to remain legally in Peruvian territory for one year during the health crisis. According to the Decree of 2020, the CTP must be renewed annually, and it allows Venezuelans access to health, education, and labour services. The CTP, however, had provisions discouraging its use. Venezuelans had to register and pay a fee, including an additional penalty fee for those that have overstayed their visas in Perú before the pandemic period. Despite appearing to be a similar measure to the PTP of the Kuczynski administration, the additional penalty fee was regarded by many as a particular burden to an already vulnerable population and penalised migrants who were not able to qualify for legal residence under Perú's difficult to comply with requirements (e.g. valid Venezuelan passport).

President Vizcarra played into the growing xenophobia against Venezuelans portraying migrants as criminals and carriers of COVID-19 (Aron & Castillo, 2020; Freier & Perez, 2021). Echoing the voices of Perú's leadership, the pandemic led to an increase in xenophobia against Venezuelan migrants (Freier et al., 2021; Winter, 2020). Several congressmen introduced limits on the rights of Venezuelan migrants. In 2020, a draft law was presented in the Peruvian Congress for Perú to reject and withdraw its support from the UN Migration Compact of 2018 (de la Vega et al., 2021). The increased xenophobia had little to do with evidence, a 2021 survey, for example, found that the largest immigrant areas of Lima and Callao had lower levels of non-violent crime than non-immigrant dominated areas (Boruchowicz et al., 2021).

In November of 2020, the dramatic death toll from the pandemic and continued internal political turmoil led to President Vizcarra's ousting by vote of Congress. Rather than abate, political turmoil now focused on how a succession would proceed. The incumbent president of Congress remained the interim president until elections were held in 2021. During this time, the Peruvian government did begin vaccinations, including of some Venezuelan migrants and the more systematic application of the CTP.

The 2021 elections pitted an extreme left and an extreme right candidate both of whom espoused xenophobic views of Venezuelan migrants. The winning candidate of the left, Pedro Castillo, publicly tied Venezuelan migrants to COVID-19, insecurity, and crime. When Castillo took office in July 2021, he made the situation of Venezuelan migrants even more precarious by restoring diplomatic relations with Venezuela and signalling a friendlier, less critical policy towards Maduro. The Castillo government did extend the CTP in 2022 to last two years, but this was more a bureaucratic measure rather than an attempt to improve conditions for Venezuelan migrants.

Economic and health recovery was undermined amidst growing political paralysis, and Venezuelan migrants were portrayed as part of the problem. After months of continuous changes in his cabinet and several failed impeachment votes, Castillo announced the closure of Congress in December 2021. Castillo's announcement, however, rallied most members of Congress to finally vote in favour of his impeachment accompanied by his dramatic removal from power and imprisonment on charges of conspiracy and rebellion.

The Congress named the former Vice-President, Dina Boluarte to replace Castillo. Boularte's interim government has not been recognised by several key actors in the region, including Colombia and Mexico. Domestic turmoil in Perú only worsened with tens of thousands of Peruvians protesting against the new government and its legitimacy. Boluarte's tough response to protests has been widely condemned by international organisations, national and international human rights NGOs (UN News, 2023). Domestic turmoil has overwhelmed national policy and economic recovery, migration policy being but a subset of these.

The Boluarte government introduced a National Development and Social Inclusion Policy (PNDIS) 2030 with the goal of reducing poverty to 15% in seven years. This Plan, although it recognises migration as a key issue, did not introduce any specific measure to support the inclusion of migrants (La Republica, 2023). Perú's restrictive migration policies (with some adjustments made to the COVID-19 crisis with the CTP) even if faithfully carried out would have required resources, attention to good management, and the ability to seek help from international authorities or its own small NGO community; none of these steps were undertaken.

Migration Management: How Well Did It Work?

The mass migration of millions of Venezuelans to South America represents a historic challenge for all South American receiving nations. In recognition of the extraordinary crisis presented by forced migration from Venezuela, the United Nations created a unique platform in 2018, the Regional Interagency Coordination Platform (R4V). R4V became the principal source of both regional data and information on the crisis unfolding in the region and helped guide, coordinate aid, and identify needs for international assistance in the key receiving nations (see below). Migratory management after 2018 thus became a combination of national government policies and programmes and a combination of international, national, and coordinated assistance to support Venezuelan migrants in destination countries.

Perú's national migration policies, as documented above, changed dramatically from an accommodating migration policy in Phase I to restrictive and often counterproductive policies in Phases II and III, intended to discourage inflows by enacting difficult-to-meet legal entry criteria and bureaucratic delays. In Phase III, the restrictive policies interacted with the onset of COVID-19 policies and deepening national political crises, the combination of which led to deteriorating living conditions for barely-surviving Venezuelan migrants and a near breakdown of migration management by bureaucratic inaction.

This section explores in more detail the component parts of "how well" Perú's migration management went in Phases II and III as more and poorer Venezuelans were forced out of their country. It reviews key studies, surveys, and analyses regarding Perú's bureaucratic and administrative management approach, particularly in terms of discouragement of migrant flows, bureaucratic demands on its public sector, migration policy outcomes, and impacts on Venezuelan migrants themselves. It also reviews Perú's limited use of both international assistance and international coordination under RV4 which further undermined Perú's ability to cope with mass migration.

Administrative Burdens and Policy Dysfunction

As the size of the Venezuelan migrant population exceeded all expectations by 2017–18, new bureaucratic and hard-to-meet eligibility requirements were put in place by President Vizcarra as described under Phase II. These heavy requirements were put in place with neither additional resources nor staff nor streamlined procedures. Many analysts argue this may have been intentional, a policy designed not to work as a way to discourage Venezuelans from entering the country in the first place.

There is no evidence that the increased "bureaucratic burdens approach" discouraged Venezuelans from entering Perú. Ecuador and Chile also enacted migration restrictions at the same time, so Venezuelans could not be expected to be easily diverted to a neighbouring country based on news of particular country's legal work requirements. The factors of forced migration, compelling Venezuelans to leave—political repression, hunger, collapse of health, and other basic institutions—were not responsive to a set of restrictive policies that would more appropriate for voluntary migration.

The principal impacts of Peru's difficult to comply with administrative policy were instead on i) a massive increase in the number (and percentage) of Venezuelans crossing over non-official land borders and ii) increases in those "illegally" working and residing in Perú. Irregularity increased from just 10% of all Venezuelans before late 2018 to over 50% afterwards (Chaves-González et al., 2021).

Despite increased restrictions on legal migration, Perú quickly became the number two destination country for Venezuelan migrants after Colombia. Venezuelans were particularly drawn into informal work in the cities of Lima and Callao as part of a growing diaspora of Venezuelans around Lima. Perú advanced ahead of Chile as number two beginning in April 2018 and every year thereafter, even though the biggest restrictions on migration began in December 2018 (RV4, 2022).

By enacting bureaucratic burdens to legal residence and cancelling the PTP work permit of President Kuzinski, Perú created another bureaucratic burden for itself—a "flood" of new political asylum claims they were unprepared to process. Asylum claims (for which Venezuelans qualified under international definitions) became the only viable option to those without valid passports. As with its other migration policy changes, the Vizcarra administration did not provide additional resources or capacity to handle the increased political asylum claims.

Despite Perú's refugee law which states a decision on political asylum should be granted within 60 days of presentation of the request (Republic of Perú, 2002), by 2019, less than 1% of asylum claims were processed and Venezuelans were waiting up to two years for their claims to be considered (Guerrero et al., 2020). On humanitarian visas, Venezuelan applicants have waited up to 4 years to get a response to their humanitarian visa application, a response that was typically negative (Morales, 2019). As of January 2022, Perú's Special Commission for Refugees reported that of the 615,771 applicants for refugee status; of which the vast majority were Venezuelans, only 4125 Venezuelan citizens have been recognised with refugee status (Defensoría del Pueblo, 2022). Perú's Ombudpersons's Office found that immigration and police authorities were simply not advancing the processing of refugee applications, despite the national legislative requirements (Defensoria del Pueblo, 2022).

Limited Reliance on International Coordination (RV4)

With the rapid expansion of Venezuelan migration into a regional crisis, the United Nations Secretary-General called for the IOM and UNHCR to co-lead and coordinate multilateral assistance to the key receiving nations.[3] In April 2018, the R4V regional response platform was created and headquartered in Colombia. The RV4 regional coordination mechanism links the key relevant United Nations agencies and international donors, and provides up-to-date assessments of migrant needs, numbers, and profiles of migrants. In addition, R4V became a multilevel management platform that also incorporated domestic and local organisations involved in the protection of migrants creating a novel hybrid system between international, national, and non-governmental organisations.

Each receiving nation in the Latin American and Caribbean region creates a "chapter" affiliated with RV4, and that national RV4 chapter can have very different relations and reliance on the help of RV4. The chapters are made up of distinct organisations of the UN, non-governmental organisations working throughout Latin America to support Venezuelan migrants, the Catholic Church, and other organisations. State entities from the local, regional, and national level are often invited to assist at the meetings of the RV4.

The organisations that are members of the Regional Interagency Coordination Platform for Perú are active in poverty alleviation in Perú (CARE, Save the Children, *Ayuda en Acción*, World Vision). Levaggi and Freier noted that Perú had a smaller, less active NGO community pushing for greater inclusion of Venezuelan migrants which undermined both advocacy for national policy and for greater use of international resources (Levaggi & Freier, 2022).

Perú has not actively sought high levels of financing nor has finance tracked well the dramatic increase of needs as Venezuelan migrants topped over 1 million from 2019 onwards. While all countries face levels of underfunding relative to RV4's estimated needs, Perú's financing deficits are considered particularly severe. In 2022, only 17% ($52.7 million) of the estimated $304 million needed has been granted via the Regional Interagency Coordination Platform. (RV4, November 2022; Fig. 30.3).

Perú's lower levels of financing have been attributed in large part to its own foreign policy positions. Levaggi and Freier argue that Perú has shunned the level of international support that Colombia embraced in the Venezuelan crisis (Levaggi & Freier, 2022). They point out this trend can be traced back to the presidency of Alan Garcia who rejected large-scale international aid as a symbol that Perú had advanced beyond its third world country status.

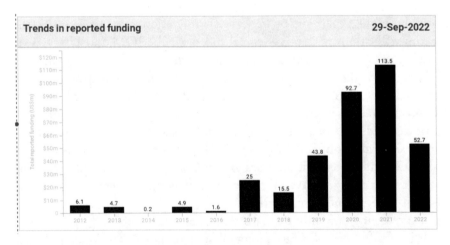

Fig. 30.3 International funding received by Perú for the Venezuelan migrant crisis

Additionally, RV4's platform was introduced by the time Kuczynski's government had already ended. At this point for Perú, the Vizcarra government's less open approach to migration reflected a low priority to seek funding provided through RV4. With limited national state capacity itself, Perú further constrained the effectiveness of even its more restrictive policies by not drawing sufficiently on international resources and its own non-governmental community. Local governments such as the city of Lima, already strapped by the COVID-19 crisis, were left to sort out responsibilities more rationally allocated to national governments.

Deteriorating Economic and Social Impacts on Migrants Despite Labour Market Effects

In contrast to the negative rhetoric of Phases II and III, a range of scholarly works and economic analysis found that Perú largely accommodated migrant labour and that it contributed to the countries' growth, particularly best during Phase I. The Peruvian Central Bank assessed in 2019 that migrants had contributed. 3% to GDP growth and had a net positive impact on the country's fiscal balance. The study determined these impacts were positive despite the country's 2015 slowdown (IMF, 2020). The World Bank calculated a net positive economic contribution both to the economy and the Treasury of $365 million by 2019 (Rossiasco Uscategui, 2019). The study posited three pathways through which these results might have come: (i) from the increase in local demand for services (e.g. food, clothing, restaurants to serve migrants); (ii) from the "freeing" up Peruvian women to seek higher wage work as Venezuelans occupied a greater percentage of the lower wage informal work; and, (iii) from potentially higher productivity in the informal sector as higher skilled Venezuelans were likely more productive in these informal jobs (Boruchowicz et al., 2021). Morales and Pierola of the Interamerican Development Bank found that the economic effects on Perú were positive but generally low, except for significant effects on low-income Peruvian women, perhaps again from greater sales and being able to move up in earnings (Morales & Pierola, 2020).

The combination of the particular deleterious effects of COVID-19 on migrants and less widely available services for migrants as discussed in Phase III led to a dramatic increase in precarious daily life for migrants. Of the 1.3 million Venezuelans in Perú in January 2022, UNHCR (United Nations Commission on Refugees) estimated that 810,000 of them (over 60%) were in conditions of extreme vulnerability and require greater support in food, health, shelter, and daily living (UNHCR, January 2022). The existing high informality-over 70%-combined with low legalisation rates of migrants resulting from Phase II and III policies—led to an extraordinary rate of over 90% of Venezuelan migrants ending up working in the informal sector or self-employed before COVID-19 hit; informality that only increased as a result of the pandemic (Mazza & Forero Villareal, 2020). Multiple studies have linked the lack of legal status for migrants in Perú to their high presence in low-skilled informal work and limited benefits, leading to poorer socio-economic conditions overall (CIUP, 2020; Koechlin et al., 2019).

The high vulnerability and informality of Venezuelans led to significant labour exploitation according to Blouin and Freier (Blouin & Freier, 2019). Migrants faced different types of discrimination with different impacts by gender (Boruchowicz et al., 2021). For example, a World Bank study found particularly discrimination in public transit against female migrants and in public places against all migrants, with males having a higher rate of discrimination than females (Boruchowicz et al., 2021).

The children of Venezuelan migrants faced increasing problems to access education even though it was in theory guaranteed to them under Peruvian law. Key problems cited identified were the lack of space in schools to include migrant children, delays in getting certification of their grades from Venezuela or taking a placement exam, and poor information given to migrant parents regarding the eligibility of their children (Blouin, 2019). A Save the Children survey in late 2021 found nearly one-quarter of Venezuelan migrant children in Lima and la Libertad ido not go to school (OCHA, 2021).

Misaligned Migration Policy and Its Alternatives

To conclude, it is important to remember that Perú was dealt an extremely difficult, and unpredictable hand with the mass influx of forced migrants from Venezuela. There simply is no precedent in South America for the size of such flows and then a health crisis the scale of the COVID pandemic.

After successfully accommodating the first, and comparatively smaller wave of migrants under Phase 1, Perú switched to restrictive strategies, promoted by its political leadership yet without the national capacity nor resources to carry out even what it said were its policies. Perú's more restrictive approach was "poorly adaptive" (Aron & Castillo, 2020) both to forced migration flows as well as to creating more workable social services delivery particularly in the time of a health crisis. The road not taken would have fostered better economic integration of migrant talents, expand and strengthen its institutions, relying more heavily on an expanded non-governmental sector and international community and taking more care not to create highly discriminatory treatment of such a large group of migrants. Levaggi and Freier explain how Perú's policy choices turned counterproductive: "The country's new immigration law [late 2018] lacks institutional consolidation and there is no strong civil society to act as a counterweight to restrictive policy developments" (Levaggi & Freier, 2022, 311).

Accommodating migrants on a mass scale was not in Perú's modern historical experience as it had been for neighbouring Argentina, although Perú did have a post-colonial experience to draw on. Argentina was able to do a better job at integrating Venezuelans, albeit at smaller numbers (Levaggi and Freier, 2022). Argentina had learned the lessons of how legal status, institutional capacity, and labour market and social integration of migrants can contribute to national well-being. Perú's approach was the opposite. It restricted legal status with virtually no impact on diminishing flows, merely increasing the precariousness of Venezuelans living in Perú and reducing more positive impacts on the economy. Levaggi and Freier note that Argentina was better able to integrate Venezuelan refugees for three reasons: smaller numbers and higher socio-economic characteristics of Venezuelans, a progressive legislative framework, and the prominent role of civil society actors in pushing for more inclusive public policies (Levaggi & Freier, 2022).

Perú's policy became more misaligned to better socio-economic performance as migration levels rose. A more productive use of resources would be to invest in more universal migration management and better integration of migrants in the local economy. A less burdensome administrative alternative would have been to grant migration status based on group or country-based criteria rather than individual, case-by-case proceedings. Other South American countries used more group-based criteria with greater administrative ease; Brazil determined a priori that all Venezuelans were designated refugees. Colombia, the country with the greatest number of Venezuelans by far, took the bold step of granting all Colombian Temporary Protective Status (TPS) (Freier et al., 2021). The group-based designation enabled Colombia to register over 900,000 Venezuelans for 10-year TPS work and residency status just by mid-2022 (*Migración* Colombia, 2022).

De Haas has written about the importance of states in shaping favourable conditions for a positive developmental role for migration (De Haas, 2010). While the education levels of Venezuelan migrants decreased overtime in Perú, the overall high level of education represented a "brain bonus" to Perú that was not taken advantage of. Adequate state capacity to advance development via migration includes fiscal resources, administrative capacity, technical knowledge, legal and political capacity, and territorial control (Cingolani,

2013). The World Bank and others argue that what most helps determine positive economic impact are the conditions in destination countries and Perú was in a favourable moment in the early phase of Venezuelan migration with a complementary migration policy (Boruchowicz et al., 2021). This World Bank study argued that Perú's high informality rate, typically considered a liability, gave the country greater flexibility to deal with the shock of migrant influxes.

Perú remains something of an outlier in South America, undertaking a comparatively limited range of state actions to integrate or accommodate the escalating migrant population. Cynthia Aronson of the Wilson Center noted that Colombia and Ecuador are proceeding with integration policies at a much faster pace than Perú (Arnson, 2019). Perú does provide international experience in the contrasting lessons between its Phase I and its Phases II–III policies, two periods that contrasted both in "how" and "how well" it responded to forced migration from Venezuela. Today, Peru remains a contrast between what could have been a greater contributory role to economic growth and humanitarian outreach rather than a policy approach more associated with a mass of marginalised informal workers, maligned by Perú's political leadership. Learning how to advance national development while adapting to large migration flows is becoming ever relevant to the Global South as they face the out-of-size role human migration now plays in the twenty-first century.

Acknowledgements The authors would like to thank Guillermo Caballero Ferreira for his superb research assistance.

Notes

1. See also "Entrevista al presidente de la República Pedro Pablo Kuczynski," 2018, *TV Perú*, 5 de marzo.
2. This last restriction was challenged in court as discriminatory and violating the rights of Venezuelan migrants to access international protection. The Peruvian courts ultimately upheld the legality of the resolution (Costa Checa, 2021).
3. R4V stands for the Inter-Agency Coordination Platform for Refugees and Migrants from Venezuela https://rv4.info.

References

Acosta, D. A., Blouin, C. A., & Freier, L. F. (2019). *La emigración venezolana: respuestas latinoamericanas. Documentos de trabajo*. Fundación Carolina: Segunda época, 3, 1.

Alvarez, J., Arena, M., Brousseau, A., Faruqee, H., Corugedo, E. W. F., Guajardo, J., Peraza, G., & Yepez, J. (2022). Regional spillovers from the Venezuelan crisis: Migration flows and their impact on Latin America and the Caribbean. *Departmental Papers, 2022* (019).

Amnesty International. (2020). *Seeking refuge: Perú turns its back on those fleeing Venezuela*. Amnesty International. https://www.amnesty.org/es/documents/amr46/1675/2020/es/

Arnson, C. (2019). Moving hemisphere: Shifting migration trends in the Americas [Audio podcast]. *Wilson Center*. https://www.wilsoncenter.org/audio/moving-hemisphere-shifting-migration-trends-americas

Aron Said, V., & Castillo Jara, S. (2020). Reacting to change within change: Adaptive leadership and the Peruvian response to Venezuelan immigration. *International Migration, 60*(1), 57–76.

Blouin, C. (2021). Migration policy towards Venezuelan migrants in Perú: Complexities and contradictions. *Colombia Internacional, 106*, 141–164.

Blouin, C., & Freier, L. F. (2019). Población venezolana en Lima: entre la regularización y la precariedad. *Crisis y migración de la población venezolana. Entre la desprotección y la seguridad jurídica en Latinoamérica*, 157–184.

Boruchowicz, C., Martinelli, C., & Parker, S. W. (2021, May 17). Economic consequences of mass migration: The Venezuelan exodus in Perú. *Social Science Research Network (SSRN)*. https://doi.org/10.2139/ssrn.3847897

Camino, P., & López Montreuil, U. (2020). Asylum under pressure in Perú: The impact of the Venezuelan crisis and COVID-19. *Forced Migration Review, 65*, 53–56.

Castles, S., Miller, M. J., & Ammendola, G. (2005). *The age of migration: International population movements in the modern world*. The Guilford Press.

Castro Padrón, M. (2020). *Niños, niñas y adolescentes cenezolanos en Colombia: hacia una estrategia de permanencia educativa y convivencia escolar*. Equilibrium CenDE.

Chaves-González, D., Amaral, J., & Mora, M. J. (2021). Socioeconomic integration of Venezuelan migrants and refugees: The Cases of Brazil, Chile, Colombia, Ecuador, and Perú. *International Migration, 59*(3), 1–17.

Cingolani, L. (2013). The state of state capacity: A review of concepts, evidence and measures. *MERIT Working Papers* 2013-053. United Nations University—Maastricht Economic and Social Research Institute on Innovation and Technology (MERIT).

CIUP (Centro de Investigación de la Universidad del Pacífico). (2020). *Cuarta propuesta de política pública. Hacia intervenciones para migrantes y comunidades de acogida*. Available at https://www.migrationportal.org/es/resource/propuesta-politica-publica-4-migracion-venezolana-salud-mental-intervenciones-migrantes-comunidades-acogida/

CNN. (2018). *Entrevista al presidente del Perú Martin Vizcarra*. Available at https://www.youtube.com/watch?v=GlO2hifGPcA

Colloquium on the International Protection of Refugees in Central America, Mexico and Panamá. (1984). *Cartagena declaration on refugees*. Available at https://www.refworld.org/docid/3ae6b36ec.html

Costa Checa, M. (2021). *De la apertura a la restricción: Los cambios en la política migratoria del Perú respecto a los migrantes venezolanos entre el 2016 y el 2019*. Pontifica Universidad Católica del Perú.

De Haas, H. (2010). Migration and development: A theoretical perspective. *International Migration Review, 44*(1), 227–264.

De la Vega, M. J. B., Perez, D. E., & Vargas, V. R. (2021). Venezuelan population in Perú in times of COVID-19: Fighting against adversity to achieve social inclusion. *Precedente*, 9–42.

Defensoría del Pueblo. (2022, June 20). *Defensoría del Pueblo: Estado debe reforzar sistema de refugio y garantizar derechos de quienes buscan protección internacional. Defensoría del Pueblo.* https://www.defensoria.gob.pe/defensoria-del-pueblo-estado-debe-reforzar-sistema-de-refugio-y-garantizar-derechos-de-quienes-buscan-proteccion-internacional/

El Camino a Cero. (2022, January 18). *Continua entrega asiva de política por protección temporal a migrantes venezolanos*.

ENCOVI. (2021). *Encuesta nacional de condiciones de vida, Caracas, Venezuela*. Universidad Catolica Andres Bello, 7th edn.

Entrevista al presidente de la república Pedro Pablo Kuczynski. (2018, March 5). *TV Perú*. Available at https://www.youtube.com/watch?v=A4NiiTGqAY0

Freier, L. F. (2022, February 15). Colombia went big on migration. Will others follow? *Americas Quarterly*. Available at https://www.americasquarterly.org/article/colombia-went-big-on-migration-will-others-follow/

Freier, L. F., & Parent, N. (2018, July 18). A South American migration crisis: Venezuelan outflows test neighbours' hospitality. *Migration Information Source*. Available at https://www.migrationpolicy.org/article/south-american-migration-crisis-venezuelan-outflows-test-neighbours-hospitality

Freier, L. F., & Pérez, L. M. (2021). Nationality-based criminalization of south-south migration: The experience of Venezuelan forced migrants in Perú. *European Journal on Criminal Policy and Research, 27*(1), 113–133.

Freier, L. F., Bird, M., Brauckmeyer, G., Kvietok, A., Licheri, D., Román, E. L., & Ponce, L. (2021). *Diagnóstico de la cobertura mediática de la situación de personas refugiadas y migrantes*. Universidad del Pacifico and UNHCR ACNUR.

Gandini, L., Prieto Rosas, V., & Lozano-Ascencio, F. (2020). Nuevas movilidades en América Latina: La migración venezolana en contextos de crisis y las respuestas en la región. *Cuadernos Geográficos, 59*(3), 103–121.

Gestión. (2018). *Pedro Pablo Kuczynski a Venezolanos: "Vengan al Perú y les pagaremos los sueldos de ley."*, Lima. Available at https://gestion.pe/peru/politica/ppk-venezolanos-vengan-Perú-les-pagaremos-sueldos-ley-228593-noticia/

Groeger, A., León-Ciliotta, G., & Stillman, S. (2022). *Immigration, labour markets and discrimination (English), policy research working paper, no. WPS 9982*. World Bank Group.

Guerrero Ble, M., Leghtas, I., & Graham, J. (2020). *From displacement to development: How Peru can transform Venezuelan displacement into shared growth*. Center for Global Development.

Infobae. (2022, June 21). *Perú, el segundo país a nivel mundial con mayor número de refugiados y migrantes venezolanos*. Infobae. https://www.infobae.com/america/peru/2022/06/21/peru-el-segundo-pais-a-nivel-mundial-con-mayor-numero-de-refugiados-y-migrantes-venezolanos/

Instituto Nacional de Estadistica e Informatica (INEI). (2018). *Encuesta dirigida a la población venezolana que reside en el país*. ENVOPE.

Inter-American Commission on Human Rights and The Organisation of American States. (2018). *Resolution 2/18, forced migration of Venezuelans*. IACHR AND OAS [online]. Available at https://www.oas.org/en/iachr/decisions/pdf/Resolution-2-18-en.pdf

International Monetary Fund. (2020, January 13). *Perú: 2019 Article IV consultations-press release*. Staff report: Staff statement and statement by the executive director of Perú.

Koechlin, J., Solórzano, X., Larco, G., & Fernández-Maldonado, E. (2019). *Impacto de la inmigración venezolana en el mercado laboral de tres ciudades: Lima, Arequipa y Piura*. Organización Internacional para las Migraciones (OIM), Lima, Perú: Editorial Solvima Graf. SAC. Available at https://peru.iom.int/sites/default/files/Documentos/IMPACTOINM2019OIM.pdf

La República. (2023, February 17). ONU recomienda al Perú ayudar a migrantes venezolanos a salir de la pobreza. *La República*. https://larepublica.pe/economia/2023/02/17/onu-recomienda-al-peru-ayudar-a-migrantes-venezolanos-a-salir-de-la-pobreza-pndis-1555874

Levaggi, A. G., & Feline Freier, L. (2022). *'Immigrants' contribution to development in the Global South: Comparing policy responses to Venezuelan immigration in Perú and Argentina*. International Development Policy| Revue internationale de politique de développement, 14.

Martin, S. (2019, May 14). *Effective practices in managing mass migration*. Georgetown University. Mimeo.

Mauricia, J. (2019). Venezuelan economic crisis: Crossing Latin American and Caribbean borders. *Migration and Development, 8*(3), 437–447.

Mazza, J., & Caballero Ferreira, G. (2022). Learning from crises: Perspectives from Europe's Ukrainian and South America's Venezuelan migration crises. *SAIS Journal of Global Affairs, 25*(1), Spring.

Mazza, J., & Forero Villareal, N. (2020, December). Venezuelan migrants under COVID-19: Managing South America's pandemic amidst a migration crisis. Latin America working paper. *Wilson Center for International Scholars*.

Migración Colombia. (2022). *Cifras sobre el estatuto temporal de protección*. Ministerio de Relaciones Exteriores. https://www.cancilleria.gov.co/estatuto-temporal-proteccion-migrantes-venezolanos

Ministerio de Desarrollo e Inclusión Social in Perú. (2022). *Plan Nacional para la reducción de la anemia en el Perú al 2030*. Retrieved from https://cdn.www.gob.pe/uploads/document/file/4090334/PNDIS%20al%202030.pdf.pdf

Morales Tovar, M. (2019). Solicitar refugio en Perú: un trámite que toma hasta 4 años. Proyecto Migración Venezuela. *Revista Semana*. https://migravenezuela.com/web/articulo/refugiados-y-migrantes-venezolanos-en-peru/1627

Morales, F., & Pierola, M. D. (2020). Venezuelan migration in Perú: Short-term adjustments in the labour market. *IDB Working Paper Series*, no. IDB-WP-1146.

OCHA. (2021). *Perú 2022*. Financial tracking service. https://fts.unocha.org/countries/175/donors/2022?order=total_funding&sort=desc

Paredes, M., & Encinas, D. (2020). Perú 2019: Crisis política y salida institucional. *Revista De Ciencia Política (santiago), 40*(2), 483–510.

Quiñón, A., Rodríguez, A., & Alva, J. (2016). Presidentes en problemas: Aprobación presidencial de Alan García (2005–2011) y Ollanta Humala (2011–2016). *Politai, 7*(13), 93–119.

R4V Inter-Agency Coordination Platform for Refugees and Migrants from Venezuela. (2022, November). *Perú RMRP*.

R4V Inter-Agency Coordination Platform for Refugees and Migrants from Venezuela. (2023, January). *Venezuelan refugees and migrants in the region*.

Reed, H. E., Ludwig, B., & Braslow, L. (2016). Forced migration. *International handbook of migration and population distribution*, 605–625.

Republic of Perú. (2002). *Law on refugees*, Law N. 27.891, viewed 26 February 2023. https://docs.peru.justia.com/federales/leyes/27891-dec-20-2002.pdf

Republic of Perú. (2015). *Legislative decree n.º 1236 on migrants adopted September 2015*. Available at https://ihl-databases.icrc.org/en/national-practice/legislative-decree-no-1236-migrations-2015

Republic of Perú. (2017). *Supreme Decree approving the guidelines for the granting of temporary residence permits for foreign mothers or fathers of Peruvian children who are minors and children of legal age with permanent disabilities*. Law N. 002-2017. Available at https://www.acnur.org/fileadmin/Documentos/BDL/2017/11018.pdf

Republic of Perú. (2018). *Supreme Decree modifying the guidelines for the granting of the temporary permanence permit for people of Venezuelan nationality*. N.

007-2018. Available at https://busquedas.elperuano.pe/normaslegales/modifican-lineamientos-para-el-otorgamiento-del-permiso-temp-decreto-supremo-n-007-2018-in-1682426-2/#:~:text=Los%20presentes%20lineamientos%20tienen%20por,31%20de%20octubre%20de%202018.%E2%80%9D

Republic of Perú, Migration Superintendency. (2018). *Resolution providing that the presentation of a valid passport must be required from persons of Venezuelan nationality for the purposes of migratory control of entry into the national territory*. N. 00000270-2018. Available at https://cdn.www.gob.pe/uploads/document/file/1499248/RS_270_2018_Migraciones.pdf?v=1645457122

Republic of Perú. (2019, July). Operation safe migration. *Revista Migraciones*. Available at https://cdn.www.gob.pe/uploads/document/file/1273955/RevistaMigraciones_Julio_2019.pdf

Republic of Perú. (2020a). *Emergency Decree approving extraordinary measures to reduce the negative impact on the economy of households affected by the mandatory social isolation and immobilization measures at the national level*. N. 052-2020. Available at https://busquedas.elperuano.pe/normaslegales/decreto-de-urgencia-que-establece-medidas-extraordinarias-pa-decreto-de-urgencia-n-052-2020-1866033-1/

Republic of Perú. (2020b). *Supreme Decree declaring a State of National Emergency due to the serious circumstances that affect the life of the nation as a result of the COVID-19 outbreak*. N. 044-2020. Available at https://cdn.www.gob.pe/uploads/document/file/566448/DS044-PCM_1864948-2.pdf?v=1584330685

República del Perú, Defensoría del Pueblo. (2020, May 16). *Desalojos sin orden judicial son ilegales*. Available at https://www.defensoria.gob.pe/defensoria-del-pueblo-desalojos-sin-orden-judicial-son-ilegales/

Rossiasco Uscategui, P. A. (2019). *Una Oportunidad para Todos: Los Migrantes y Refugiados Venezolanos y el Desarrollo del Perú* (Vol. 2) [online]. World Bank Group. Available at http://documents.worldbank.org/curated/en/107621574372585665/Una-Oportunidad-para-Todos-Los-Migrantes-y-Refugiados-Venezolanos-y-el-Desarrollo-del-Perú

Selee, A., Bolter, J., Muñoz-Pogossian, B., & Hazán, M. (2019). *Creativity amid crisis: Legal pathways for Venezuelan migrants in Latin America*. Migration Policy Institute.

Stankovic, S., Ecke, J., & Wirtz, E. (2021). Forced migration. In *Oxford Research Encyclopedia of Anthropology*.

Takenaka, A., Paerregaard, K., & Berg, U. (2010). Peruvian migration in a global context. *Latin American Perspectives, 37*(5), 3–11.

UN News. (2023, January 30). *La ONU solicita un aumento en la ayuda humanitaria para Venezuela*. Retrieved from https://news.un.org/es/story/2023/01/1517817

UNHCR. (2022, January). *Fact sheet Perú*. Available at https://www.acnur.org/es-mx/623023114.pdf

Vidarte, O. (2018). La política exterior en tiempos de Kuczynski. *Perú Hoy, 33*, 109–124.

Winter, B. (2020, April). The backlash to Venezuelan migration is here. *Americas Quarterly* [online]. Available at https://www.americasquarterly.org/article/the-backlash-to-venezuelan-migration-is-here/

Wolfe, G. (2021). Where are Venezuelan migrants and refugees going? An analysis of legal and social contexts in receiving countries. *Center for Migration Studies*, 4.

Open Access This chapter is licensed under the terms of the Creative Commons Attribution 4.0 International License (http://creativecommons.org/licenses/by/4.0/), which permits use, sharing, adaptation, distribution and reproduction in any medium or format, as long as you give appropriate credit to the original author(s) and the source, provide a link to the Creative Commons license and indicate if changes were made.

The images or other third party material in this chapter are included in the chapter's Creative Commons license, unless indicated otherwise in a credit line to the material. If material is not included in the chapter's Creative Commons license and your intended use is not permitted by statutory regulation or exceeds the permitted use, you will need to obtain permission directly from the copyright holder.

31

The "ASEAN Way" in Migration Governance

Rey P. Asis and Carlos L. Maningat

Introduction: Migration in the ASEAN Region

Southeast Asia is no stranger to large movements of people, as it was home to transnational labour migration mainly due to empire-wide sourcing of labour during the late nineteenth century and then the emigration of Chinese and Indian migrants up until the mid-twentieth century (Kaur, 2007, 2008). International migrant stock for Association of Southeast Asian Nation (ASEAN)[1] was recorded at 23.6 million in 2020, 13.44% higher than in 2015, and accounts for 8.4% of the 281 million total migrant stock (UN DESA, 2020). During the first year of the COVID-19 pandemic, overseas deployment sharply dropped in several ASEAN member-states, notably for the Philippines (−78%), Thailand (−64%) and Indonesia (−59%) (ABDI, 2022).

Various studies have pointed out that the uneven economic development and wage differentials across the region, aside from generally porous borders,

---

R. P. Asis
Asia Pacific Mission for Migrants, G/F, No. 2 Jordan Road, Kowloon, Hong Kong SAR
e-mail: reyasis@gmail.com

C. L. Maningat (✉)
Ecumenical Institute for Labor Education and Research, Inc, Quezon City, Philippines
e-mail: jo.maningat@gmail.com

contribute to increasing levels of migrant mobility among ASEAN countries (see Kaur, 2007; Kikkawa & Suan, 2019; Basir, 2019). Two principal migration corridors have been documented: the archipelagic ASEAN corridor and the Mekong sub-regional corridor. In the first, Malaysia, Singapore and Brunei are the major destination countries, importing workers largely from Indonesia and the Philippines. In the second, Thailand is the main destination for migrant workers from countries through which the Mekong River flows, specifically, Burma, Cambodia, Lao PDR and Vietnam (Kaur, 2007).

It is acknowledged that the vast majority of migrants, roughly nine out of every ten, searching for work within ASEAN are low-skilled or semi-skilled (Orbeta, 2013). Despite this, regional frameworks such as the ASEAN Economic Community (AEC) Blueprint only cover the flow of professionals and skilled manpower, and do not cover the much larger flow of unskilled and semi-skilled workers. As noted by Geiger (2015, 190), the governments in the region tend to be less welcoming towards low-skilled migrant workers, "who are subject to various restrictive policies pertaining to such activities as switching jobs, bringing families with them, or pursuing permanent settlement in the host country." Skeldon (2009, 13) wrote that Asian economies "operate essentially exclusive immigration policies" which are different from those in Australia, Canada or the United States of America, while Lavenex and Piper (2022) use the ASEAN case as an example of a model wherein cooperation from "above" is least formalised, contrary to the top-down regional migration governance of the European Union and, to a certain extent, the African Union.

Migration patterns, particularly irregular migration, have led to most governments in the region endeavouring to exert tighter control over cross-border movements through national policies and bilateral agreements and by linking their security interests to the wider Asia Pacific region in the ASEAN Regional Forum (Kaur, 2007). Part of the irregular migration flows in the region is the movement of refugees: in Northern ASEAN countries where refugees from Vietnam, Cambodia, Burma and Laos settled in Thailand, and in Sabah, Malaysia where Filipinos fleeing the conflict in Mindanao in the 1970s sought refuge (see Battistela, 2002). Human trafficking remains a pressing concern, with more than 85% of victims trafficked within the Southeast Asia region with Malaysia and Thailand as leading destination countries (Luong, 2020).

The share of female migrants originating from Southeast Asia is close to 50%, which is higher than the global average (see also Bastia and Piper, this volume). Yamanaka and Piper (2005, 1) note that the traditional unequal gender ideology and hierarchy in the region "mediates between state migration policy and global labour demands, thus producing employment opportunities and constraints that are segregated by sex." Elias (2020) points out the lack of state support for social reproductive labour as among the reasons for the dependence of well-off households in the ASEAN region on live-in domestic workers who are mostly women. Female migrants in the region are highly vulnerable to widespread abusive practices, and generally work in the informal service economies of their destination countries often under unprotected and undocumented status. But there were some inroads for female migrant workers into the formal economy, mainly in the manufacturing where they could be paid lower wages compared to male workers, for instance in Singapore, Malaysia and Thailand (Kaur, 2007).

The "ASEAN Way" in Migration Governance: Disengagement, Decentralisation

Based on available literature seeking to decode the ASEAN approach in migration governance, two fundamental features can be identified. Firstly, there is disengagement from international commitments on migration and human rights, and secondly, decentralisation of recruitment in the migrant labour market. Such an approach places migrant workers, most especially those who are undocumented and in a very vulnerable and precarious situation, while at the same time creating a space for contestations from "below," i.e. from civil society groups which seek to fill in the gaps or challenge the policy framework on migration.

Disengagement, Non-interference

While regional frameworks and numerous bilateral agreements on migration are already in place, Southeast Asian countries have, for a long time, exhibited a disengaged stance as far as entering into and enforcing legal instruments on migration and human rights are concerned. This attitude is reflected in the very limited ratification or concurrence with international instruments. For instance, Indonesia and the Philippines are the only two ASEAN countries which ratified the 1990 United Nations Migrant Workers Convention. As for the UN Protocol to Prevent, Suppress and Punish Trafficking in Persons, Especially Women and Children, there are a limited number of countries that are signatories: Indonesia, Vietnam, Singapore and Thailand who signed most recently.

Notably, the 1967 ASEAN founding document did not touch on labour mobility, and it was only in 1995 that limited provisions on labour mobility were tackled under the 1995 Framework Agreement on Services (AFAS) (Lavenex & Piper, 2022). In 1966, the Principles of Bangkok on the Status and Treatment of Refugees were adopted, with a final version only affirmed in 2011 which are merely declaratory and non-binding and are merely aimed at inspiring member-states to enact national legislation (Moretti, 2016). In 2012, ASEAN ministers signed the Agreement on Movement of Natural Persons which is largely linked to investment and business flows to facilitate the temporary movement of highly skilled professionals. These provisions affect only a very small fraction of the total migrant flows as informal migration movements constitute more than half of the migrants flows in the region. Moreover, implementation has been poor (Jurje & Lavenex, 2018).

This reluctance on the part of Southeast Asian countries to enter into or enforce international, regional and multilateral instruments, frameworks and commitments on migration and human rights is rooted in the general ASEAN principle of non-interference. Corthay (2015) explains that one reason for this approach is the racial and cultural diversity among ASEAN countries, combined with the weak state structures and a lack of stable regime legitimacy: hence the policy of non-interference is intended to prevent the aggravation of conflicts. Acharya (2017) describes this preference for an explicitly non-legalistic, voluntarist mode of governance as the "ASEAN Way."

Representing a departure from the absence of monitoring mechanisms in ASEAN (Nikomborirak et al., 2013), Member States adopted in 2007 the Declaration on Protection and Promotion of the Rights of Migrant Workers, which, ten years later, was revamped into the 2017 ASEAN Consensus on The Protection and Promotion of The Rights of Migrant Workers. But Piper and Iredale (2003) have noted that the Consensus only applies to legally resident migrant workers, and that it is much more limited than the 1990 UN Migrant Workers Convention. Again, the large irregular migration flows that exist in the region are left out in the discussion. Bal and Gerard (2017) provide a context on the negotiations for the document which resulted in an impasse, as Indonesia became the lone voice in asserting a binding declaration for migrant workers' rights. Labour-recipient countries such as Thailand, Singapore and Malaysia registered their opposition to a legally binding instrument as migration is generally seen as a livelihood and a development strategy, a position which was later supported by the Philippines, albeit surprisingly.

In 2012, all Member States signed the ASEAN Human Rights Declaration, another non-binding agreement, which contains more protective language than other major multilateral rights treaties as it notes that migrant workers' rights "are an inalienable, integral and indivisible part of human rights and fundamental freedoms."[2] In 2015, the ASEAN Convention Against Trafficking in Persons, Especially Women and Children (ACTIP) was adopted, although it only came into force in March 2017 after the Philippines became the sixth ASEAN Member State to ratify. The Convention exemplifies a criminalisation approach to trafficking, including mandating higher penalties for aggravating circumstances as well as specific penalties for participation in an "organized criminal group," laundering "proceeds of crime" and corruption (Ramji-Nogales, 2017).

ASEAN Member States have also crafted Mutual Recognition Agreements (MRAs) as another instrument for skilled labour mobility in line with the liberalisation of trade in services. While framework agreements have been completed in specific areas such as engineering services, nursing services and architecture, permission to work is still subject to domestic laws and regulations which remain to be highly restrictive in many ASEAN countries (Huelser & Heal, 2014). Thus, MRAs constitute an additional but weak and non-binding layer of institutional migration governance which only affirms the generally disengaged stance of ASEAN countries. In place of formal arrangements, countries in the region also engage in regional consultative processes (RCPs) for working out regional-level responses to issues related to migration. Examples of these include the Colombo Process, the Abu Dhabi Dialogue, the Bali Process and the Global Forum on Migration and Development (Geiger, 2015).

Since regional migration flows are not governed by binding regional mechanisms and frameworks, host and origin governments ensure the signing of bilateral agreements and memoranda of understanding (MOU) on the movement of migrant labour. Kikkawa and Suan (2019) note that Thailand has a separate MOU with the governments of Cambodia, the Lao PDR and Myanmar, while Malaysia has MOUs with countries such as Indonesia. While numerous bilateral arrangements exist in the ASEAN region, these agreements generally leave out the core issue of migrant rights protection and are primarily focused on the procedures for regulating the flow of workers (Skeldon, 2009).

Decentralised Recruitment

Alongside the generally weak and voluntary modes of regional migration governance in the ASEAN region, relations between and among private recruitment agencies, brokers, traffickers and employers have drastically flourished over the years. Goh et al. (2017) call this the "middle space" of migration that transcends statism, while Lindquist et al. (2012) refers to the "black box" of institutions, networks and people that move migrants from one point to another. Shrestha and Yeoh (2018) offered a nuanced take on the practices of brokerage and the making of migration infrastructures in Asia, moving away from the purely negative conceptions of migration brokerage under the mainstream crisis-centric narrative by taking into account shifting relations, complex historical temporalities and international labour and global migratory regimes.

It is important to note that there exists a paradox in the making of the middle space in migration or migration infrastructures particularly in Southeast Asian countries. Peck and Tickell (2002) note that such deregulation of markets has been matched by renewed state intervention while Xiang (2008, 175) frames the contradiction as the "upward concentration of capital and downward outsourcing of labour and the tension between the dispersion/fragmentation of labour management and the centralization of migration control."

On one hand, several states in the ASEAN region have taken steps to institutionalise mechanisms for the licensing of the growing number of private recruitment agencies, although the requirements involved vary per country. In Indonesia, the number of licensed recruitment companies grew from less than 50 in 1995 to around 500 recruitment companies in 2007, sending nearly 700,000 workers abroad annually (Xiang & Lindquist, 2014). On the other hand, informal brokers fill in the gaps and facilitate irregular migration flows as exemplified by *tekongs* (former migrants) in Malaysia and *calo* (labour brokers) in Indonesia who have established a network of contacts in destination countries (Battistela, 2022; Testaverde et al., 2017) (Table 31.1).

Table 31.1 Licensing requirements for recruitment agencies in ASEAN's main sending countries

Licensing requirement	PHL	IDN	VNM	KHM	LAO	MMR
Minimum capital	X	X	X	O	X	O
Security deposit	X	X	X	X	X	O
Orientation	X	O	O	O	O	O
Employer accreditation/job order review	X	X	X	O	O	O
Representative abroad	O	O	X	X	O	O

Note X = the licensing requirement is present; O = the licensing requirement is not present; ASEAN = Association of Southeast Asian Nations; IDN = Indonesia; KHM = Cambodia; LAO = Lao PDR; MMR = Myanmar; PHL = Phillipines; VNM = Vietnam
Source Testaverda et al. (2017)

As pointed out by Lindquist et al. (2012), the relationship between licensed recruitment agencies and informal brokers constitutes a continuum rather than a dichotomy, with one functioning alongside the other. Profit-making recruiters for instance are accused of manufacturing irregularity by bypassing state regulations, imposing onerous debts on migrants that lead to debt bondage, deceiving migrants about the terms of employment and inflicting emotional or physical violence on migrants (Goh et al., 2017). Interestingly, Molland (2022) demonstrates that increased efforts to legalise migration channels did not lead to a decline or alteration of brokering services and dubious transactions, using the case of the commercial sex industry along the Thai-Lao border. In fact, it is suggested that transparent and deceptive recruitment co-exist and are characterised by asymmetrical relationships and patronage, and that "trafficking is taking place in the very same contexts that are deemed 'safe' by anti-trafficking programs" (Molland, 2022, 117). Young Lao sex workers are playing the role of "dilettante-brokers" as they recruit from their informal social networks upon their return. Others have also shown that increased regulation of migration flows can lead to increased vulnerability, as migration brokers, migrants and employers seek ways to circumvent what are perceived as onerous or unfair restrictions (see Yamanaka & Piper, 2006).

Testaverde et al. (2017) note that several ASEAN countries have used self-enforcement and public ranking of recruitment agencies as a tactic to improve the recruitment process—which is itself a form of labour market deregulation. This approach is underscored in no less than the 2018 UN Global Compact for Safe, Orderly and Regular Migration, which seeks to "enhance the "availability and flexibility of pathways for regular migration," and to "facilitate fair and ethical recruitment and safeguard conditions that ensure decent work" as among its key objectives.[3] Under the devolved setting, employment agents and recruiters on whom the placement of migrant domestic workers produce paperwork, bear risks and responsibilities and administer a "debt-financed migration regime" as particularly illustrated in Singapore (Goh et al., 2017). Recruiters and employment agents exercise functions in regulating worker mobilities—from control of entry, recruitment, health checks, placement, labour market segmentation, financing, training and repatriation, among others. As businesses, they also respond to forces of supply and demand, matching the needs of families for domestic services such as upkeep of the household, preparation of meals and care for children and elderly dependents (see Chee, 2020).

Aside from bearing the risks and regulatory functions, recruitment agencies and brokers consciously shape the image of the ideal migrant. Labour export-oriented educational institutions in the Philippines, for instance, are complicit in reinforcing existing hierarchies, steering away students from academic pursuits and redirecting them to acquire technical skills and service work to fit the global labour demand in the service sector (Shrestha & Yeoh, 2018, citing Ortiga, 2018). In the realm of recruitment of domestic workers, recruitment agencies play a key part in creating the "ideal maid" and, in the process, construct women as submissive, docile non-citizen workers (Elias & Louth, 2016). In Elias' (2020) discussion of the "labour brokerage" model, the labour-sending state accommodates the demands of the host state, ensuring outsourced regulatory functions of workers to guarantee a "quality product" in return for more favourable terms and conditions of work for its citizens.

Migration Policies in Labour-Sending and Labour-Receiving ASEAN Countries

Labour-Sending Countries

From the viewpoint of labour-sending ASEAN countries such as the Philippines and Indonesia, migrant labour has become an important means of addressing poverty and generating foreign exchange through remittances while providing an escape valve for unemployment pressures (Bal & Gerard, 2017). The state's regulatory mechanisms are geared towards the facilitation of employment abroad, licensing of private recruitment agencies and pre-departure trainings. As succinctly put by Elias (2020), this labour brokerage model is about "states being able to continue to send low-cost workers abroad but without significantly challenging the exploitative terms on which this takes place" (p. 32).

The following section discusses the salient features of migration governance in Indonesia, the Philippines and Vietnam as key ASEAN labour-sending countries.

Indonesia

In Indonesia, the national government has moved from a lax approach to a more state-managed system through regulation of recruitment agencies and streamlining of recruitment processes. In 2004, it passed Law No. 39/2004 or the National Law on the Placement and Protection of Indonesian

Overseas Workers, which primarily centralised the placement and protection of migrant workers to the national government. At the same time, it devolved pre-departure activities such as training, completion of documentation requirements and enrolment in insurance programmes to private recruitment agencies. In 2006, the National Authority for the Placement and Protection of Indonesian Overseas Workers (commonly known as BNP2TKI was established for the licensing of private recruitment agencies upon the issuance of Presidential Regulation No. 81/2006. Bal and Palmer (2020, 4) note that Indonesia's labour ministry officials are in a "symbiotic relationship" with labour recruiters in order to promote the export of Indonesian labour overseas, using "overseas labour migration, and remittances earned, to offset their inability to generate meaningful employment and social protection for vast proportions of their citizens at home."

In the years that followed, Indonesia's move towards the decentralisation of migration governance to local government units contributed to the lack of coordination and clarity regarding jurisdiction and responsibility at the local level. This confusion and regulatory maze made more migrants resort to unlicensed agents to exploit loopholes and commit illegal practices (Ford & Lyons, 2013).

Philippines

Ahead of its ASEAN neighbours, the Philippines has passed major laws on migrants workers' rights and has been often cited in existing literature as model for migration governance infrastructure, although gaps in implementation remain. As early as 1974, the country had already embedded provisions on overseas contract workers in the Labour Code. Provisions on overseas contract workers in the 1974 Labour Code was "seen at that time as a stop-gap measure to help arrest challenges in the economy, like the dollar shortfall and unemployment" (Dalupang, 2017).

In 1995, the country passed the Republic Act 8042, otherwise known as the Migrant Workers and Overseas Filipinos Act, which has detailed provisions and penalties for illegal recruitment. This legislation was amended in 2009 through Republic Act 10022 to introduce the following key provisions: (1) recruitment and manning agencies are required to shoulder the insurance coverage of each migrant worker deployed; (2) forging of Bilateral Labour Agreements (BLAs) with receiving country is encouraged; the BLA will specify the rights and obligations of the countries regarding grievances and settling of claims and (3) state officials who facilitate the deployment of overseas Filipino workers (OFWs) to countries that do not guarantee or follow international labour standards face dismissal from public service or disqualification from government appointments for five years (Orbeta & Abrigo, 2013). In December 2021, the country signed into law the Republic Act 11641 which created the Department of Migrant Workers. The Filipino migrants' alliance Migrante International (2022) has pointed out that the creation of the new department only further institutionalised the existing labour export thrust of the national government.

Private deployment agencies sit at the centre of the deployment management system in the Philippines, as they facilitate the biggest proportion of migrant workers. Except for government-to-government arrangements and a few name-hires (or those workers who have found employment without assistance from the government or from private recruitment agencies), deployment can only be undertaken through private recruitment agencies (Orbeta, 2013). Deployment is regulated through agency fees and employment standards, and through monitoring and redress.

The Philippine Overseas Employment Administration (POEA), which was established in 1982 and is currently under the newly created Department of Migrant Workers, reserves the privilege of recruiting and placing workers for overseas employment positions primarily through the licensing of private recruitment agencies and manning agencies. However, it does not prescribe a strict minimum wage for OFWs except for household service workers/domestic workers (Orbeta & Abrigo, 2013).

Vietnam

Labour export in Vietnam was originally encouraged under the Doi Moi policy (open door policy) through the principles of market socialism and multilateralism. It was carried out through centrally managed labour exchange and technical support programmes with European socialist countries and a number of African countries in the 1970s and 1980s. In the aftermath of the USSR's collapse, the country expanded its foreign relations in 1991 and began to commercialise labour export services by empowering the Ministry of Labour, War Invalids and Social Affairs (MOLISA) to manage the flow of the international labour population (Nguyen, 2014). During the same period, the government issued Decree 370 which established the mechanism for the licensing of recruitment agencies for deployment of workers abroad. Initially, labour export services were monopolised by state-owned enterprises or certain mass organisations, until it was expanded to include domestic private firms (Ishizuka, 2013).

In 2006, Vietnam's national assembly passed the Law on Vietnamese Guest Workers under Contract which stipulates the rights and obligations of enterprises sending workers abroad under contracts. The law sets requirements and conditions for the licensing of recruitment enterprises, and outlines the responsibility of enterprises in case the worker dies or suffers from occupational accidents or abuse, among others (Nguyen, 2021). However, the legal framework only refers to protection of migrant workers under contract, and does not stipulate interventions for undocumented migrant workers.

Labour-Receiving Countries

Among ASEAN countries, Singapore and Malaysia stand out as net labour-receiving countries and have varied approaches in their governance frameworks for migrant labour. As described by Malaysia is "somewhat more generous" as it provides some forms of social security to migrant workers compared to Singapore which has no social security coverage at all to temporary migrant workers. Various authors have also pointed out that Singapore's immigration strategy is aligned with its national development strategy unlike in Malaysia (see Kaur, 2007; Orbeta et al., 2013). In terms of similarity in approach to migrant workers, both countries employ low-skilled migrant workers in specific sectors such as construction, manufacturing, service sectors and as household workers, on a transient basis (Bal & Gerard, 2017).

Singapore

Singapore's foreign labour policy is two-pronged, consisting of unrestricted inflow of foreign talents and professionals and managed inflow of foreign low-skilled labour through the use of work permits, worker levies and other criteria (Orbeta et al., 2013). Augmentation of the national labour force with migrant labour is explicitly stated as a key element in the country's economic plans and policies (Kaur, 2007).

The Employment Agencies Act, which was passed in 1958, governs the rules on the recruitment and placement of migrant domestic workers by employment agencies. The law was amended in 2011 to introduce stricter regulations on employment agencies, including the need to put up a security deposit for large employment agencies and publication of an employment agency's performance indicators on the Ministry of Manpower's website (Goh et al., 2017). Meanwhile, employment entry requirements are contained in the Employment of Foreign Workers Act signed in 1990 and which features a two-tier framework for admission of migrants. The first component is the Employment Pass for professionals and skilled migrants, and the other one is the Work Permit for less-skilled foreign workers. While skilled workers are entitled to subsidised healthcare, education and housing, migrant workers in the work permit category are excluded from social protection coverage and their employers are required to post a security bond (Kaur, 2007).

Malaysia

While Malaysia is both a sending and receiving country, it is considered a net receiver due to its dependence on contract migrant workers (Orbeta et al., 2013). It is also confronted with the challenge of large numbers of irregular migrant workers within its borders, owing to the fact that it had no mechanism for the legal recruitment and employment of low-skilled workers up until 1992 (Orbeta, 2013). As noted by Hickey et al. (2013), Malaysia's framing of migration and the influx of irregular migrant workers in particular as a national security problem has led to many cases of abuse and maltreatment, and has been the subject of growing criticisms domestically and by the international community.

Regulatory legislation and governance of foreign workforce distinguishes migrants as "pegawai dagang" or expatriates, and *pekerja asing* or foreign contract workers. There are correspondingly two types of employment-related work permits or work visas, namely an employment or work pass (Pas Penggajian) for expatriates, and a work permit or contract worker pass (Pas Lawatan Kerja Sementara) or visit pass for the temporary (contract) employment of less-skilled workers, including domestic workers (Kaur, 2008).

The Role of Civil Society in Migration Governance

Country-level frameworks in migration governance, which for the most part focus on regulating the licensing of recruitment agencies for labour-sending countries and that which regulate the inflow of low-skilled migrant labour for labour-receiving countries, have left wide gaps for civil society organisations (CSOs) to intervene. Interventions and engagements by civil society groups and migrants' organisations take the form of advocacy work for improved migration governance frameworks at the international, regional and national levels, stronger regulation of recruitment agencies, provision of support services to migrants suffering from poor treatment and other rights violations and organising of migrant workers and support groups.

As a whole, Asia has been home to vibrant civil society space engaged in migrant rights activism (Lavenex & Piper, 2022), with Southeast Asian migrant CSOs and transnational social movements playing a notable part in calling out abuses of migrant workers. As noted by, ASEAN non-state actors, CSOs and transnational social movements in the region can invoke international law and use it "to name and shame actors who mistreat migrants." At the regional level, the Solidarity for Asian People's Advocacy (SAPA) Task Force on ASEAN and Migrant Workers, which was formed in April 2006, united various civil society groups in lobbying the ASEAN Declaration on the Protection and Promotion of the Rights of Migrant Workers (ACMW). Bal and Gerard (2017) noted that the task force was linked to focal points with domestic CSOs, which include TWC2 (Transient Workers Count Too, Singapore), Tenaganita (Malaysia), Federations of Trade Unions, Burma (Thailand), and with regional networks as well such as CARAM-Asia (Co-ordination of Action Research on AIDS and Mobility). There are also sub-regional trade union councils which work with migrant networks to call for the suspension of trade benefits contained in regional trade policies which are detrimental to workers' rights, while "network of networks" work to concretise protection of migrant workers and their families (Lavenex & Piper, 2022). Gerard (2014) notes however that civil society engagements in ASEAN-established channels have limitations, as CSOs are required to go through affiliation and with the continued lack of institutionalised political participation.

Outside formal and established channels for CSO advocacy, migrant workers are organising themselves to seek changes in the migration policies both in the host country and their country of origin. Exercising their agency, Southeast Asian migrants have been very active in a broad range of advocacy work for rights protection and in challenging unjust policies. For advocacy organisations, the Philippines has served as a model given the depth and breadth of migrant rights advocacy efforts (Chavez & Piper, 2015). This stems from the long history of vibrant social movements and migrant worker activism in the country (Piper & Rother, 2021). Transnational Filipino migrants' alliance Migrante International has actively opposed and criticised the Philippines' systematic brokering of migrant workers while assisting distressed overseas Filipino workers and their families.

Piper (2010) lists the expressions of migrants' rights claims in various campaigns and contexts, from the "right to be paid" campaign by Tenaganita in Malaysia, to one-day off and opposition to impending wage cuts by Southeast Asian migrants in Hong Kong, the regulation of recruitment agencies in the origin countries and campaigning for the rights of migrants' families in the Philippines. In the case of Indonesia, the preoccupation of immigration officials with enforcement issues in regulating borders has left gaps on providing legal services and other assistance to migrants, which are being filled by churches, trade unions and NGOs, functioning as components of the state migration management model (Ford & Lyons, 2013).

Regional advocacy networks have taken on the crusade for fair and ethical recruitment of migrants by private enterprises which is reflective of the emphasis in the agenda of international organisations such as the International Labour Organisation (ILO) and the International Organisation for Migration (IOM). More recently, these international organisations have advocated licensing, regulating and incentivising ethical recruitment in the industry (Gordon, 2015; Jones, 2015; Tayah, 2016). For instance, the IOM is promoting the International Recruitment Integrity System (IRIS), which focuses on developing an accreditation framework for recruitment, while the ILO has a multi-stakeholder Fair Recruitment Initiative. More concretely, the UN Global Compact for Safe, Orderly and Regular Migration lists among its objectives the facilitation of fair and ethical recruitment to ensure decent work.

Elias (2020) sees a dilemma in advocating both for migrant workers' rights and for more ethical standards in the recruitment of migrant workers, noting that the "search for practical solutions to migration governance that uphold the labour brokerage model perpetuates a dehumanising model of migration in which the migrant worker is seen largely as product" (p. 24). The Open Working Group on Labour Migration and Recruitment has also acknowledged the limits of such model, as solutions to recruitment enable the private enterprises' profit motive and the state's desperation to deploy workers abroad.[4]

Conclusion

Unlike the European Union (EU) which has been characterised as a regional migration regime, ASEAN demonstrates a disengaged and decentralised framework for migration governance wherein a host of actors—from country-level policymakers and regulators to private sector recruitment agencies and civil society groups fill in the gaps. While the ASEAN adopts the human rights framework in its declarations and multilateral engagements related to migration, it does little in following up on the commitments of its member-states in line with its time-honoured principle of non-interference. Such stance has left a huge space for contestations and engagements from below, although formal channels for CSO engagement remain limited and selective. Civil society groups and transnational networks have for the longest time engaged ASEAN member-states in established platforms, although the results have only manifested in the language of declarations while decisive ASEAN action on the refugee crisis, sex trafficking and issues related to labour conditions of migrant workers in the region have yet to materialise.

At the national level, the labour brokerage model stands out as the common feature across the Southeast Asian region, with regulatory mechanisms treating migrants as labour for export-import. Labour-sending countries merely facilitate the deployment of overseas workers mainly through licensing of recruitment agencies and bilateral agreements while labour-receiving countries tap migrant workers for both professional and low-skilled jobs, albeit with different sets of discriminatory migration policies. Quite interestingly, informal brokers ("tekong," "calo" and fixers) exist alongside formal labour brokerage channels as workers try to circumvent migration policies and regulations all in the name of seeking better opportunities abroad. Intrinsic in the labour brokerage model is the outsourcing of risks and responsibilities by state instrumentalities to private recruitment agencies, informal brokers and loose social networks, and here lies the problem as far as accountability over abuses is concerned.

Southeast Asian migrant workers, who are the primary stakeholders in the complex migration governance ecosystem, are asserting their voice in various spaces to influence policymaking and to pressure governments to act on their demands. However, their meaningful participation in established ASEAN platforms and channels have yet to be institutionalised. There is a need to reflect on the current migrant rights advocacy in the region, with the aim of leveraging engagements to truly empower migrant workers and raise their capacities to organise and lobby for significant reforms.

Notes

1. The Association of Southeast Asian Nations, or ASEAN, is the regional organisation of 10 member-states in Southeast Asia, namely Brunei, Cambodia, Indonesia, Laos, Malaysia, Myanmar, the Philippines, Singapore, Thailand and Vietnam. It was established on 8 August 1967 in Bangkok, Thailand with the signing of the ASEAN Declaration.

2. ASEAN Human Rights Declaration, https://asean.org/asean-human-rights-declaration/.
3. UN Global Compact for Safe, Orderly and Regular Migration, https://refugeesmigrants.un.org/sites/default/files/180711_final_draft_0.pdf.
4. Policy brief on ethical recruitment, written based on contributions of the Open Working Group on Labour Migration and Recruitment, http://mfasia.org/migrantforumasia/wp-content/uploads/2017/01/5-Policy-Brief-Support-for-Ethical-Recruitment.pdf.

References

Acharya, A. (2017). The Myth of ASEAN Centrality, *Contemporary Southeast Asia: A Journal of International and Strategic Affairs 39* (2), 273–279.

Asian Development Bank Institute. (2022). *Labor migration in Asia: COVID-19 impacts, challenges, and policy responses.* https://www.adb.org/sites/default/files/publication/797536/labor-migration-asia.pdf

Bal, C. S., & Gerard, K. (2017). ASEAN's governance of migrant worker rights. *Third World Quarterly, 39*(4), 799–819.

Bal, C. S., & Palmer, W. (2020). Indonesia and circular labour migration: Governance, remittances and multi-directional flows. *Asian and Pacific Migration Journal, 29*(1), 3–11.

Basir, S. M. (2019). Irregular migrations in Southeast Asia: challenges for protection and migration policy. *Indonesian Journal of International Law, 17*, 145.

Battistella, G. (2002). Unauthorized migrants as global workers in the ASEAN region. *Japanese Journal of Southeast Asian Studies, 40*(3), 350–371.

Caballero-Anthony, M., & Menju, T. (Eds.). (2015). *Asia on the move: Regional migration and the role of civil society.* Brookings Institution Press.

Chee, L. (2020). "Supermaids": Hyper-resilient subjects in neoliberal migration governance. *International Political Sociology, 14*(4), 366–381.

Chia, J., & Kenny, S. (2012). The children of Mae La: reflections on regional refugee cooperation. *Melbourne Journal of International Law, 13*(2), 838–858.

Corthay, E. (2015). The ASEAN doctrine of non-interference in light of the fundamental principle of non-intervention. *APLPJ, 17,* 1.

Dalupang, Denison Rey A. (2017). *Should Marcos get the credit for the OFW boom? Manpower and one man's power.* Philstar.com. https://newslab.philstar.com/31-years-of-amnesia/ofws

Elias, J. (2020). Governing domestic worker migration in Southeast Asia: Public-private partnerships, regulatory grey zones and the household. In S. Breslin & H. Nesadurai (Eds.), *Non-state actors and transnational governance in Southeast Asia* (pp. 92–114). Routledge.

Elias, J., & Louth, J. (2016). Producing migrant domestic work: Exploring the everyday political economy of Malaysia's 'maid shortage.' *Globalizations, 13*(6), 830–845.

Ford, M., & Lyons, L. (2013). Outsourcing border security: NGO involvement in the monitoring, processing and assistance of Indonesian nationals returning illegally by sea. *Contemporary Southeast Asia*, 215–234.

Francisco, V., & Rodriguez, R. M. (2014). Countertopographies of migrant women: Transnational families, space, and labor as solidarity. *WorkingUSA, 17*(3), 357–372.

Geiger, A.Y. (2015). Regional Frameworks for Managing Migration and the Role of Civil Society Organisations, in Caballero-Anthony, M. and Menju, T. (Eds) Asia on the Move: *Regional Migration and the Role of Civil Society*, Tokyo: Japan Center for International Exchange, pp.183-201.

Gerard, K. (2014). ASEAN and civil society activities in 'created spaces': The limits of liberty. *The Pacific Review, 27*(2), 265–287.

Goh, C., Wee, K., & Yeoh, B. S. (2017). Migration governance and the migration industry in Asia: Moving domestic workers from Indonesia to Singapore. *International relations of the Asia-Pacific, 17*(3), 401–433.

Gonzalez, J. L. (1998). *Philippine labour migration: Critical dimensions of public policy*. Institute of Southeast Asian Studies.

Gordon, J. (2015). *Global labour recruitment in a supply chain context*. International Labour Organisation Fundamentals Working Paper (2015).

Hickey, M., Narendra, P., & Rainwater, K. (2013). A review of internal and regional migration policy in Southeast Asia. *Migrating Out of Poverty Working Paper*, 8.

Huelser, S., & Heal, A. (2014). Moving freely?: Labour mobility in ASEAN. *ARTNeT Policy Brief* No. 40.

Ishizuka, F. (2013). *International labor migration in Vietnam and the impact of receiving countries' policies*. Inst. of Developing Economies, Japan External Trade Organisation.

Jones, K. (2015). *Recruitment monitoring and migrant welfare assistance: what works?* International Organisation for Migration (IOM).

Jurje, F., & Lavenex, S. (2018). Mobility norms in free trade agreements: Migration governance in Asia between regional integration and free trade. *European Journal of East Asian Studies, 17*(1), 83–117.

Kaur, A. (2007). International labour migration in Southeast Asia: Governance of migration and women domestic workers. *Intersections: Gender, History and Culture in the Asian Context, 15*, 2007.

Kaur, A. (2008). International migration and governance in Malaysia: Policy and performance. *UNEAC Asia Papers, 22*, 4–18.

Kikkawa, A., & Suan, E. B. (2019). Trends and patterns in intra-ASEAN migration. In E. Gentile (Ed.), *Skilled labour mobility and migration* (pp. 1–24). Edward Elgar Publishing.

Lavenex, S., & Piper, N. (2022). Regions and global migration governance: Perspectives 'from above', 'from below' and 'from beyond.' *Journal of Ethnic and Migration Studies, 48*(12), 2837–2854.

Leigh, M. (2007). The contested basis of nationhood: Key issues when analysing labour flows in Southeast Asia. *International Journal on Multicultural Societies (IJMS), 9*(2), 174–184.

Lindquist, J., Xiang, B., & Yeoh, B. S. (2012). Opening the black box of migration: Brokers, the organisation of transnational mobility and the changing political economy in Asia. *Pacific Affairs, 85*(1), 7–19.

Luong, H. T. (2020). Transnational crime and its trends in South-East Asia: A detailed narrative in Vietnam. *International Journal for Crime, Justice and Social Democracy, 9*(2), 88.

Migrante International. (2022). *DMW's 5 months expose Marcos' labor export thrust*. https://migranteinternational.org/dmws-5-months-expose-marcos-labor-export-thrust/

Molland, S. (2022). *Safe migration and the politics of brokered safety in Southeast Asia*. Taylor and Francis.

Moretti, S. (2016). Addressing the Complexity of Regional Migration Regimes through a Mixed Migration Approach. Paper Presented at the *Asylum & Migration Symposium Organised at the University of Geneva, Geneva, Switzerland,* 10-11 October 2016, Available at SSRN: https://ssrn.com/abstract=2960596

Nikomborirak, D., Jitdumrong, S., Basu Das, S., Menon, J., & Severino, R. C. (2013). ASEAN trade in services. In S. Basu et al. (Eds.), *The ASEAN economic community: A work in progress* (pp. 95–140). ADB and Institute of Southeast Asian Studies.

Nguyen, C. H. (2014). Development and brain drain: A review of Vietnamese labour export and skilled migration. *Migration and Development, 3*(2), 181–202.

Nguyen, T. H. Y. (2021). Challenges in ensuring the rights of Vietnamese migrant workers in the globalization context–The two sides of the development process. In *Asian Yearbook of International Law, 25* (2019), 154–184. Brill Nijhoff.

Nurdin, M. R., Sathian, M. R., & Hussin, H. (2020). Forced migration governance in Southeast Asian countries: 'Same but different'? *Otoritas: Jurnal Ilmu Pemerintahan, 10*(1), 58–78.

Orbeta Jr., A. (2013). Enhancing labour mobility in ASEAN: Focus on lower-skilled workers (No. 2013-17). *PIDS Discussion Paper Series.*

Orbeta, A., Jr., & Abrigo, M. R. M. (2013). Managing international labour migration: The Philippine experience. *Philippine Journal of Development, XXXVIII* (1/2), 58–83.

Orbeta Jr., A., & Gonzales, K. G. (2013). Managing international labour migration in ASEAN: Themes from a six-country study (No. 2013-26). *PIDS Discussion Paper Series.*

Peck, J., & Tickell, A. (2002). Neoliberalizing Space. Antipode 34, 380 - 404. https://doi.org/10.1111/1467-8330.00247.

Pedroza, L., Palop-García, P., & Chang, S. Y. (2022, January). Migration policies in Singapore 2017-2019. *IMISEM Case Report*. German Institute for Global and Area Studies(GIGA). https://doi.org/10.57671/imisem-22027

Piper, N. (2010). All quiet on the Eastern front? Temporary contract migration in Asia revisited from a development perspective. *Policy and Society, 29*(4), 399–411.

Piper, N. (2015). The reluctant leader: The Philippine journey from labour export to championing a rights-based approach to overseas employment. In E. Berman & M. S. Haque (Eds.), *Asian leadership in policy and governance. Public policy and governance* (pp. 305–344). Emerald Group Pub Ltd.

Piper, N., & Iredale, R. (2003). "Identification of the obstacles to the signing and ratification of the UN convention on the protection of the rights of all migrant workers 1990—*The Asia Journal of Ethnic and Migration Studies Pacific Perspective.*" prepared for UNESCO, APMRN working paper no. 14. University of Wollongong.

Piper, N., & Rother, S. (2021). Governing regional migration from the 'bottom-up': A nodal approach to the role of transnational activist networks in Asia. *Journal of Ethnic and Migration Studies*, 1–18.

Piper, N., & Yamanaka, K. (2006). *Feminised migration in East and Southeast Asia: policies, actions and empowerment*. UNRISD Occassional Paper 11 https://repositorio.unal.edu.co/bitstream/handle/unal/75181/9290850647.2005.pdf?sequence=1&isAllowed=y NB

Ramji-Nogales, J. (2017). Under the canopy: Migration governance in Southeast Asia. UCLA. *Journal of International Foreign Affairs, 21*, 10.

Rother, S., & Piper, N. (2015). Alternative regionalism from below: Democratizing ASEAN's migration governance. *International Migration, 53*(1), 36–49.

San Juan Jr., E. (2009). Overseas Filipino workers: The making of an Asian-Pacific diaspora. *The Global South, 3*(2), 99–129.

Shrestha, T., & Yeoh, B. S. (2018). Introduction: Practices of brokerage and the making of migration infrastructures in Asia. *Pacific Affairs, 91*(4), 663–672.

Skeldon, R. (2009). *Managing Irregular Migration as a Negative Factor in the Development of Eastern Asia*, ILO Asian Regional Programme on Governance of Labour Migration Working Paper No.18 https://www.ilo.org/wcmsp5/groups/public/---asia/---ro-bangkok/documents/publication/wcms_105108.pdf

Tayah, M. J. (2016). *Decent work for migrant domestic workers: Moving the agenda forward*. ILO.

Testaverde, M., Moroz, H., Hollweg, C. H., & Schmillen, A. (2017). Migrating to opportunity: Overcoming barriers to labor mobility in Southeast Asia. World Bank Publications.

United Nations Department of Economic and Social Affairs—UN DESA. (2020). *International migrant stock*. Data set accessed at https://www.un.org/development/desa/pd/content/international-migrant-stock

Xiang, B. (2008). Transplanting labor in East Asia. *Senri Ethnological Reports, 77*, 175–186.

Xiang, B., & Lindquist, J. (2014). Migration Infrastructure. *International Migration Review*, 48(1_suppl), 122–148. https://doi.org/10.1111/imre.12141

Yamanaka, K. and Piper, N. (2005). Feminized migration in East and Southeast Asia: Policies, actions and empowerment (No. 11). *UNRISD Occasional Paper*. https://repositorio.unal.edu.co/bitstream/handle/unal/75181/9290850647.2005.pdf?sequence=1&isAllowed=y

Open Access This chapter is licensed under the terms of the Creative Commons Attribution 4.0 International License (http://creativecommons.org/licenses/by/4.0/), which permits use, sharing, adaptation, distribution and reproduction in any medium or format, as long as you give appropriate credit to the original author(s) and the source, provide a link to the Creative Commons license and indicate if changes were made.

The images or other third party material in this chapter are included in the chapter's Creative Commons license, unless indicated otherwise in a credit line to the material. If material is not included in the chapter's Creative Commons license and your intended use is not permitted by statutory regulation or exceeds the permitted use, you will need to obtain permission directly from the copyright holder.

32

Unfair and Unjust: Temporary Labour Migration Programmes in and from Asia and the Pacific as Barriers to Migrant Justice

Pia Oberoi and Kate Sheill

Introduction

Access to justice in the context of migration is often centred on the formal or practical access of migrants to systems of justice, both in the country of destination as well as their origin countries (in the context of portability of benefits or remedies, for instance) including access to informal institutions, such as customary frameworks, and quasi-judicial alternative dispute mechanisms. The United Nations (UN) Special Rapporteur on the human rights of migrants has asserted that "[e]ffective access to justice means that everyone, without discrimination, has the right to access the system provided for conflict resolution and the restoration of rights" (UN, 2018a, para. 7). He elaborates further that the key elements that make up effective access to justice include the right to legal aid and representation, the right to information and an interpreter, the right to consular assistance, the competent authority to which access is provided, as well as remedies and redress.

From numerous studies and the testimony of migrant workers employed on temporary labour migration programmes (TLMPs), we know that many are consistently excluded by policy or practice from access to justice and remedies for human rights abuses whether in the workplace or outside (UN,

---

P. Oberoi (✉)
UN Secretariat Building, Rajadamnoen Nok Avenue, Bangkok 10200, Thailand
e-mail: poberoi@ohchr.org

K. Sheill
Independent Human Rights Consultant, Bangkok, Thailand

© The Author(s) 2024
H. Crawley and J. K. Teye (eds.), *The Palgrave Handbook of South–South Migration and Inequality*, https://doi.org/10.1007/978-3-031-39814-8_32

2022b). A range of barriers function to keep justice out of reach for migrant workers on such programmes, who face multiple obstacles in navigating non-judicial, often employer-led, dispute resolution and mediation mechanisms or accessing legal services and the judicial system. These include their lack of knowledge of the local law, the precarity of their status in the country, prohibition of or restrictions on their right to freedom of association, language and cultural barriers and the requirements of a foreign jurisdiction.

While we concur that enhancing remedy for migrant workers is an important facet of a rights-based approach to labour migration, we argue in this chapter that it is not enough. Improving access to justice for migrants on TLMPs or ensuring that the programmes themselves are "lawful" (in terms of their compliance with domestic legal standards), is not sufficient in itself to ensure that these pathways promote human rights and dignity in their design, scope and implementation. Nor would it prevent in the first place the human rights abuses often reported on the schemes. In this inquiry, we seek to go further in our understanding of the concept of justice within the context of TLMPs, including but going beyond the principle of "access to justice" and building on concepts of social justice and fairness.

Social justice as a societal organising principle can be understood in many ways as centring fairness in relations between individuals within society. It builds on an understanding of justice itself as a manifestation of fairness, and imports concepts of equity and non-discrimination, enabling people to live lives of dignity. The concept of fairness is equally rooted in the UN Sustainable Development Agenda's focus on reducing inequalities within and between countries, aiming to ensure equal opportunity and reduce inequalities of outcome (UN, 2015). The UN has observed the persistence of inequalities based on characteristics such as income, race, class and opportunity, stating "We cannot achieve sustainable development and make the planet better for all if people are excluded from the chance for a better life" (UN, n.d.).

It is therefore through the lens of fairness as understood above that we come to explore the human rights (including access to justice) parameters of TLMPs. Do they reduce inequalities and promote equal opportunities? Do they respect, protect and fulfil the rights of the human beings involved? Are they fair?

In its 2014 report on *Fair Migration*, the International Labour Organization (ILO) called for the construction of an "agenda for fair migration" based on respect for the rights of migrant workers and one which offers them meaningful opportunities for decent work as well as the guarantee of a fair sharing of the prosperity which migration helps to create. The ILO notes that this call is indeed premised on its social justice mandate and the related imperative to "inject a social dimension into globalization" (International Labour Office, 2014, para. 18).

There has long been recognition in the academy as well as in the policy-making context that TLMPs come with a high risk of abuse to migrant workers and their families (see, for example, Ruhs, 2003; Shamir, 2017; Strauss & McGrath, 2017). In its recent report entitled *We wanted workers, but human beings came': Human rights and temporary labour migration programmes in and from Asia and the Pacific*, the UN Human Rights Office has called for a human rights-based assessment of TLMPs which examines migrants' full lived experience of temporary labour migration—at and away from the workplace—as well as the consequences of these programmes for their families and communities (UN Office of the High Commissioner for Human Rights, 2022).

Temporary Labour Migrations in and from Asia and the Pacific

Labour migration dominates policy discussion on mobility in Asia and the Pacific. Within this, TLMPs,[1] fixed-term agreements which delineate organised schemes for contract labour, are often the only option for regular migration for low-wage workers in and from the region.[2] Though TLMPs also operate across different wage levels and labour sectors, the focus in this analysis is on migration to low-wage work because those migrants typically have fewer options for justice and remedy along these pathways. For Asia Pacific migrants, most labour migration is to destinations either within the region or in the Middle East. Major destinations for these migrations are the ASEAN destination countries of Malaysia, Singapore and Thailand and also East Asia including the Republic of Korea and Taiwan; migrants from South Asia in particular also migrate to the countries of the Gulf Cooperation Council (GCC) as well as Lebanon and Jordan; and Pacific Island State migrants go to Australia and New Zealand.

As well as offering time-bound contracts, TLMPs—particularly for low-wage workers—typically contain a range of restrictive terms and conditions, including that migrants must return to their states of origin on completion of the contract, that their visas tie them to one employer and that they are not permitted to change work sectors or specific employers, they are prohibited from seeking citizenship or entering other permanent or long-term residence pathways, they are often prevented from accessing public services and they are not entitled to bring family members with them or to reunify with family once in the country of employment (Costa & Martin, 2018). Governed often by vaguely worded and non-legally binding agreements[3] that may explicitly deny, restrict or omit any reference to human rights, especially outside of labour rights and the workplace, TLMPs have generated human rights concerns even where they are highly regulated and monitored (New Zealand Human Rights Commission, 2022).

The role that employers play—or that States require employers to play—in the governance of TLMPs is outsized. On the one hand, such a system enables unprincipled employers to abuse migrant workers with impunity. In particular, the threat or fear of deportation, in the context of debt burdens, consequent inability to recoup the investment already made and the sociocultural impacts of "failed migration", has a chilling effect on complaint and can force compliance in abusive working and living conditions (Costa & Martin, 2018; Reilly, 2011). On the other hand, the system enables States to delegate to employers nearly all responsibility for the well-being of migrant workers on TLMPs. From the provision of housing, sanitation, healthcare and other services to making travel arrangements and handling immigration procedures, employers—or the agents to whom they subcontract these responsibilities—loom large in migrants' lives. Coupled with their temporary—often precarious—immigration status and other related barriers, the power differential that this dynamic creates can locate the migrant worker in a position of subservience and supplication vis-à-vis their employer—far removed from the equality of an employer–employee relationship demanded by human rights and decent work standards.[4] While much focus has recently been placed on the misconduct of private recruitment agents and sub-agents, in view of the proliferation of intermediaries in temporary labour migration and while recruitment reform must be part of the solution, it is not in itself a solution to the inequalities that are built into TLMPs including in the context of enforced and coercive temporariness (ILO, 2015). That TLMPs either explicitly forbid or implicitly prevent migrant workers from enjoying their right to freedom of association, through forming or joining trade unions or knowing about and participating in other forms of association, serves to exacerbate this inequality, lack of voice and powerlessness.

While these human rights deficits are stark, TLMPs also demand our attention because they are widely *promoted* by a wide range of actors as the optimal governance model for safe, orderly and regular labour migration (Abu Dhabi Dialogue, n.d.; UN General Assembly, 2018 para. 21(d)). The schemes promise a quadruple win, focusing on the potential economic benefits of TLMPs—for the origin and destination States, the employing industries and businesses, as well as for the migrants (Castles & Ozkul, 2014; Underhill-Sem et. al., 2019; Wickramasekara, 2011).[5] The Global Forum on Migration and Development (GFMD), a State-led forum established in 2007 for multilateral dialogue on migration, has long focused on temporary labour migration primarily from an economic development perspective. Through such forums, migration and development have been interconnected in the international policy space (Geiger & Pécoud, 2013; Hao'uli, 2013), where the focus has been on migration as a driver of economic development in countries of origin and destination, with an emphasis on economic remittances (Delgado Wise et al., 2013). Discussion of TLMPs is also centred in similarly informal and non-binding regional consultative processes devoted to migration governance along the Asia-Middle East corridors such as the Abu Dhabi Dialogue and the Colombo Process. As State-centric spaces, they have promoted TLMPs as the default governance model of labour migration along these corridors, often ignoring or downplaying the programmes' risks while exaggerating their benefits (Global Unions, 2010). The GFMD and similar spaces have also been criticised for lacking transparency and accountability in what has been described as a "politically-sheltered format" (Crépeau & Atak, 2016, 133).

TLMPs as Barriers to Justice

How can low-wage migrants on TLMPs access justice and effective remedy when through their design and implementation the programmes themselves constitute barriers to justice? Most obviously they are a barrier to economic justice, serving an economic model that subordinates large segments of the world's population and requires and produces inequalities by providing a low-cost flexible workforce without the economic, social or cultural demands made by integration (Triandafyllidou, 2022). They are a barrier to climate justice, for example in States' lack of mitigation efforts adequate to prevent the adverse effects of the climate crisis that drive some of these migrations and in the elevation of temporary labour migration as a preferred adaptive response to climate change with little regard to the conditions and impacts of these migrations. Moreover, TLMPs exacerbate injustice by creating a narrative that recasts unequal and racialised migration practices as development wins while ignoring the structural injustices that create and increase situations of vulnerability (UN Office of the High Commissioner for Human Rights & Global Migration Group, 2018) that drive and complicate temporary migrations.

The denial of the human rights of low-wage migrant workers on TLMPs is a means and a result of dehumanising them, which in turn enables other rights abuses including through preventing access to justice. Such dehumanisation is reflected in the narratives that commodify migrant workers as units of labour rather than fully human individuals—the use of language such as "sending" and "receiving" countries and statistical terminology of migrant "stocks" denies migrant agency and even personhood, minimising migrants and their work as low-skilled or unskilled. This resonates with populist usage of water metaphors ("waves", "flows", "floods") or other pejorative and dehumanising terminology such as "swarms", "hordes" or "invasion".

TLMPs are a Barrier to Development Justice

The framing of migration as a development issue in the international governance of the migration, such as through the GFMD, has served as a justification for TMLPs, with a focus on maximising the strictly economic benefits for development in both countries of origin and destination, the former through the transfer of financial remittances and the latter through migrants' low-wage labour in certain sectors. Some Asia Pacific countries of destination such as New Zealand and South Korea explicitly list development of the country of origin as an objective of their TLMPs (Cho et al., 2018; Wickramasekara, 2015). Similarly, where TLMPs are promoted as means to foster climate resilience in the Global South, again arguing in favour of economic remittances, this time as an adaptation strategy and again shifting the adaptation burden from the main carbon-emitting States to the Global South and even to migrants themselves (Draper, 2022; Gonzalez, 2020).

For countries of origin, instead of meeting their responsibility to invest in human rights inclusive economies (United Nations, 1990, 2008), TLMPs enable reliance on a model of privatisation and individual reliance. With remittances constituting an important macroeconomic income stream for countries of origin, often equal to or in excess of foreign direct investment (Barne & Pirlea, 2019), migrants' own governments may be structurally dependent on their migration (UN, 2022a).[6] Their reluctance to challenge unequal or even abusive conditions faced by their citizens—on grounds of the economic benefits of TLMPs—can lead to a "race to the bottom" as countries of origin compete with each other for the prized MOU or bilateral agreement, dissuading their citizens from raising complaints about conditions and outcomes of TLMPs.

However, there is at best mixed evidence that financial remittances generate equitable development outcomes for individuals, communities and countries of origin (Withers, 2019). TLMPs thus represent an archetype of a limited approach to development, considerably at odds with the more expansive commitment in the 2030 sustainable development agenda to "leaving no one behind" (UN System Chief Executives Board for Coordination, 2017).

For migrant workers and their families, TLMPs' claimed economic benefit can be—and often is—undermined by a range of factors from non- or underpayment of wages and benefits, lack of social protection of portability of accrued benefits and the exploitative recruitment costs and associated debt that many migrants carry. Similarly, the promised TLMP benefit of skills transfer is often undercut by there being little training or investment offered, the absence of processes to recognise skills, qualifications and competences that have been gained, or the reality that the experience gained abroad may not be relevant for the domestic labour market on return (Castles & Ozkul, 2014). Further, related costs to society such as the consequences of long-term family separation are rarely counted within the cost–benefit analysis of temporary labour migrations. Even within the economic development equation for countries of employment, it is often the case that the labour needs TLMPs are ostensibly responding to (including the structural deficits or crises that give rise to these needs) may be ongoing or permanent and not well served by the cyclical disruptions to the workforce (International Labour Organization, 2021).

TLMPs are a Barrier to Racial Justice

The historical legacy of TLMPs as rooted in racialised and unequal forms of mobility pervades their contemporary nature: as the ILO has noted "[c]ontemporary temporary labour migration schemes have their roots in colonial indentured labour and can be traced back to the end of the nineteenth century, when the idea first appeared of 'creating an immigrant who could be made to leave.' Since then, countries have experimented with multiple forms of temporary labour migration that have varied over time and within regions" (ILO, 2022, para. 5). These forces continue to demarcate who is entitled to occupy a social and physical space, that is, to move or to stay. In this way, TLMPs are based on and reproduce racial and other hierarchies that exemplify the management, instrumentalisation and exclusion of the undesirable Other (Bradley & de Noronha, 2022; Carstensen, 2021). In countries such as Qatar, for instance, the denial of space to racialised migrants is made physical reality through laws and policies which require single, male Asian and African migrant workers to reside in remote or segregated areas (UN, 2020).

Such barriers to physical presence replicate those faced by racialised migrants in a global sense; citizens from the South and Southeast Asian countries of origin for example are among those who face the most barriers to travel generally, with more destination countries requiring they secure a visa prior to travel (see, Henley & Partners, 2022). As such it is unsurprising that discriminations are entrenched through these programmes, including along nationality, class and caste lines. Any intersectional analysis of TLMPs must acknowledge the structural condition of many low-wage migrant workers on these programmes who are seeking to escape conditions of poverty and inequality (UN, 2022a), highlighting their disproportionate disadvantages and lack of bargaining power on the basis of their socioeconomic status. The structural conditions of TLMPs also embed racist and class-based societal associations between certain types of work and specific nationalities (UN, 2020). Class-based inequality is built into TLMPs particularly in those contexts where different standards are offered for workers framed as "high-skilled" in contrast to those for low-wage workers where, for example, the former are entitled to bring their families with them and to access social security benefits or pathways to permanent residence, while the latter are not (Dauvergne & Marsden, 2014; Triandafyllidou, 2022).

TLMPs are a Barrier to Gender Justice

TLMPs reinscribe gendered ideas about labour, operating mostly in highly gendered labour sectors for low-wage migrants and offering more opportunities for men who constitute the vast majority of migrant workers on TLMPs in and from Asia and the Pacific particularly in sectors such as construction in the GCC countries, fisheries in East and Southeast Asia and seasonal work to Australia and New Zealand (IOM, 2021). Bilateral agreements for these schemes often centre men's migrations, for example, they usually do not include provision for sexual and reproductive health, an omission that discriminates against women in particular but is in keeping with the reduction of people to workers that would cast pregnancy as a hindrance to economic productivity. In some destination States where Asia Pacific women do migrate under these programmes, they are restricted to women-dominated sectors such as domestic work.

On the other hand, the assumption of maleness that dominates TLMPs itself subscribes to a retrograde stereotype that does not understand men migrant workers as fathers and partners engaged with child development and care or with family life broadly, or indeed as individuals needing protections in the course of their migration such as health rights (including for mental health) (see for a related discussion, Arsenijević et al., 2018).

When TLMPs do consider the family lives of migrant workers it is generally to mandate family separation, both in terms of prohibiting the migration of workers' family members and imposing strict limits on forming families in the countries of destination. One example is Singapore where the government exercises a high degree of policing of migrant workers' intimate life and sexual and reproductive rights. The Employment of Foreign Manpower (Work Passes) Regulations (2012)[7] prohibit marriage to a Singapore citizen or permanent resident without express government permission and involvement in any "immoral or undesirable activities, including breaking up families in Singapore" (Section 8). There are also prohibitions on migrants getting pregnant or delivering a child while in the country and women migrant workers are required to take mandatory pregnancy tests, a form of gender-based discrimination, prior to arrival in Singapore and at regular intervals during their stay (Ministry of Manpower, (n.d.). Given that most migrant workers undertake TLMPs at a time in their life when they would be expecting—or expected—to start families, this inability to make or sustain family life is particularly iniquitous.

Where migrants have made families in their countries of origin, enforced family separations have resulted in a range of harms ranging from abuse suffered by spouses who are left behind to breakdown of the parent–child relationship. Rasika Jayasuriya (2021) observes in this context that TLMPs undermine the child–parent relationship through structural features that create unnecessarily protracted periods of parental absence in children's lives.[8] In another context, research in the Pacific has observed that the absence of men on seasonal labour migration places a greater burden of work on the women who have been left behind and tends to confine them to traditional gender roles—within the sphere of their house and family—thereby limiting the possibility of them being able to seek and sustain paid employment (Chattier, 2019). Any allowances for family life on TLMPs within South–South corridors are limited to close family members within a nuclear family structure and within patriarchal, heteronormative values and structures. Even in those few instances where family members are permitted to join the migrant worker, there may be a lack of housing suitable for families of migrant workers, and they may also face practical and legal barriers to access education, health or other necessary social services.

Temporariness

Temporariness is central to the privileging of TLMPs in contemporary migration governance. It allows policymakers to treat each migration as singular, time-limited event and, crucially, to normalise the imposition of various restrictions on the human rights of migrants undertaking TLMPs on the basis that their stay in the country of employment is fleeting (Dauvergne & Marsden, 2014). States justify these rights restrictions as acceptable because migrants are only temporarily present in the jurisdiction and some advocates argue they are a necessary trade-off for access to the State and its labour market (Ruhs, 2013). Countries of origin and destination view such restrictions, particularly those preventing low-wage migrant workers enjoying a wider economic and social life and denying their right to family life, as necessary to ensure that migrant workers make minimal demands on the destination State and return to their countries of origin at the end of their contract. In this way, TLMPs provide the required low-cost flexible workforce within a context of securitised migration control (Horvath, 2014). Further, by ensuring that migrants will not stay on longer than their short-term contracts, much less formally integrate into the societies in which they live, States claim that TLMPs enable a response to populist hostility towards migrants and migration. The essential unfairness of such utilitarian arguments is revealed not only in the questionable assumption that human rights—universal, inalienable rights—can be forfeited in the first place but is rendered more stark when we appreciate that in far too many instances of TLMPs the financial cost–benefit analysis does not actually land in favour of low-wage migrant workers. Many themselves directly assume steep costs to recruiters, brokers or other intermediaries, they are forced to accept high deductions, unpaid overtime, irregular or non-payment of wages, in addition to which they indirectly—by virtue of the fact that States do not incur costs for healthcare, housing or other rights—relieve the financial burden on these countries.

In a challenge to the notion of "temporariness", along many of these corridors migrants often take on repeated TLMPs in the same or another destination State, such that although each TLMP lasts between a season and a few years, the migrant may spend a decade or more on these "temporary" schemes and for some, will spend effectively their whole (working) life on TLMPs. Extended or repeated stay does not ameliorate the risks of the programmes' temporariness: longer but still temporary stays may increase situations of vulnerability as migrant workers have more invested in the country of destination including community ties and the employment relationship and therefore have more to lose (Reilly, 2011).

However long they stay on TLMPs, in most cases the temporary labour migration pathway is completely untethered from options for longer-term or permanent stay.[9] Although many workers on these programmes will migrate with no intention of staying long-term or permanently in the country of destination, the removal of this option renders TLMPs potentially abusive if or when circumstances change (if a changing climate and environmental degradation means that return to their homes is no longer possible for instance) or migrants' intentions evolve (if they form a relationship and/or have children in the country of employment for instance) (Merla & Smit, 2020).

TLMPs formalise, enforce and celebrate temporariness, operating in practice to impede migrants' agency in deciding the length of stay and time of return, constricting their decision-making and plans about their wider lives, including family life. That they do not permit migrants to have histories, families or aspirations and deny them full personhood, renders these programmes fundamentally unjust and unfair, "anchored in a fundamental subordination" (Dauvergne & Marsden, 2014, 237).

Indisputably, human rights standards are clear that every person remains a rights-holder when they cross an international border and become migrants. Human rights—fundamental albeit minimal standards to which we are all entitled without discrimination—attach to migrants as people and they are unchanging: they are not bestowed by countries of origin or citizenship, nor do they need to be renegotiated as people move across borders.[10] The temporariness of a migrants' presence in the country or the delegation of duty of care or immigration functions to companies or private citizens do not therefore absolve States of their responsibility to respect, protect and fulfil the human rights of all persons under their jurisdiction including in the design and practice of TLMPs.

Yet, as is often the case, the devil lies in the detail. One challenge for advocates seeking policy change on temporary labour migration is the wide latitude in respect of migration governance ostensibly afforded to—and often loudly claimed by—States under the shroud of "sovereign prerogative". International human rights law permits limited differential—but not discriminatory—treatment on the basis of migration status. The question we must ask is whether, when and how are legal exclusions to human rights standards permissible in the case of migrants who are in a regular but temporary immigration status?[11] While the UN Committee on Economic, Social and Cultural Rights has guided that *all* migrants within a State's jurisdiction are entitled equally to the right to health (UN, 2017), for example, and the near-universally ratified UN Convention on the Rights of the Child (1989) provides that it is in children's best interests to have their relationship with their parents and family life protected, these broad principles require further operational guidance—and then of course effective implementation—in order to be rendered meaningful to the lives of people embarking on TLMPs. For example, where does responsibility and accountability lie for the health rights of Bangladeshi construction workers in Malaysia who are dependent on sub-agents to grant them access only to sub-standard private medical clinics in a context where they are not entitled to sick leave (Uddin et al., 2020)? What are the duties of States of origin and of destination to protect the parent–child relationship in the context of prolonged family separation through TLMPs (Jayasuriya, 2021)? Whereas some international human rights mechanisms have issued broad-based guidance related to migrant workers (UN, 2013), further specific and targeted advice in respect of the parameters of legal inclusions and exclusions in TLMPs and the scope and content of the rights of migrants on these programmes is urgently needed as is normative guidance at regional and national levels. In their consideration of issues relating to the rights of migrant workers, these expert bodies could explicitly analyse temporariness and issue guidance to ensure that it is not being used to justify discriminatory treatment.

Conclusion

> Viewing people on the move as an economic issue has led to a series of policies and practices that too often treat them as silent commodities to be exploited in the national labour market. ... They are, in effect, incorporated into the economy on terms not dissimilar to other inputs in the production process; their capacity to exercise their labour power is no more than a commodity. (UN, 2018b, para. 27)

TLMPs are extractive in nature, creating a situation where migrants are permitted only as labour, not as fully human. As currently conceived and managed, TLMPs derive from, thrive on and heighten the global inequalities that "create migration but constrict mobility" (Walia, 2022). They are prime examples of what Virginia Mantouvalou has termed "state-mediated structures of injustice" (2022, 711), legislating inequality and precarity. Seen from a human rights perspective, the programmes are fundamentally unjust, often designed to reduce people to commodities.[12]

The reality is that for many migrant workers, TLMPs result in precarious and discriminatory conditions leading to immediate and long-term negative human rights consequences for migrants and their families, including in terms of access to civil, political, economic, social and cultural rights, including the right to family life, access to services and ability to access remedy for violations of their rights. This results in an unacceptably high human cost for migrants and their families, while the negative consequences of these programmes extend beyond temporary migrant workers to also worsen conditions more broadly in these industries and harm wider social discourse, as well as undermining the value of these programmes to countries of origin. Inhabiting a situation of "permanent temporariness", many migrants are neither able to establish meaningful lives in their countries of employment nor in their home countries.

Migrant workers embark on TLMPs often knowing that the conditions they will face will not be optimal (see for a discussion on unfree labour, Strauss & Fudge, 2013; LeBaron & Phillips, 2019). It is also a fact that many—and particularly those migrants who experience the worst deprivations on TLMPs—are compelled to leave countries of origin in response to deep structural inequalities and exclusions (Lester, 2010). Yet, it is important too to respect that in undertaking these programmes, migrants are exercising their agency with experience or understanding of the realities of the poor living and working conditions offered to them, what Mai (2016) has described as "bounded exploitation". That migrant workers are willing or have little option but to tolerate poor standards, or that countries of destination promise similar or better conditions than those in their origin countries, does not vindicate either the conditions offered by TLMPs or the lack of dedicated attention to the systemic failures in these programmes (Reilly, 2011).

TLMPs are often incompatible with States' existing human rights commitments and deny the human rights goals that States have agreed for the full inclusion and social cohesion of migrants including through the objective of "minimizing disparities" agreed in the Global Compact for Migration (UN General Assembly, 2018, paras. 13 and 32). Reform is urgently needed. The UN Human Rights Office has called on States to devise and implement human rights-based labour migration pathways that function as effective alternatives to TLMPs and the human rights deficits that are at their heart (UN Office of the High Commissioner for Human Rights, 2022). These alternatives may indeed in part resemble those aspects of TLMPs that are prized both by policy makers and migrants, enabling flexibility and responsiveness, for example. But systemic policy reform of labour migration needs above all to centre the migrant and their family in the design and implementation of the programmes to ensure that migrant workers, even on a temporary stay, enjoy equal human rights and are fully included under national laws and policies.

In seeking to understand the normative parameters of contemporary TLMPs, the overall context of fairness (and unfairness) in which these programmes are situated becomes paramount. Critical inequities in the global economic and financial architecture as well as neoliberal economies that present structural barriers to equality, social justice and sustainability lie at the heart of these migrations. The temporariness of legal status that is embedded in TLMPs then magnifies these systemic vulnerabilities faced by low-wage migrant workers in these countries and along these corridors. Rather than allowing those who are compelled to take to these pathways to become collateral damage within an agenda narrowly focused on economic growth at the expense of equity, we are called to reimagine and realise a world where migration is undertaken in dignity and justice leading to equitable, rights-based and fair outcomes for migrants and their families.

Notes

1. There is no internationally agreed legal definition of TLMPs and there are several terms in use to describe these programmes and the workers on them including: circular migrations, seasonal work, guest worker programmes, Technical Intern Training Program and others.
2. Such schemes are found in most, if not all, destination countries, not only those in the Global South.
3. Governments in Asia have become increasingly interested in TLMPs with IOM reporting that while only four agreements were signed by these governments between 1990 and 1999, 38 were signed between 2000 and 2009, and 18 more between 2010 and 2014 (IOM, 2021).
4. ILO Employment Relationship Recommendation, 2006 (No. 198). The ILO has observed that "[i]t is through the employment relationship, however defined, that reciprocal rights and obligations are created between the employee and the employer" (ILO, 2006, para. 5).
5. Also often described as a triple win, subsuming the industry benefits within the destination State.
6. Following his 2021 visit to Nepal, the UN Special Rapporteur on extreme poverty and human rights voiced concern about the government's reliance on outward migration as a solution to unemployment arguing that it was

7. hindering the country's development, terming it "a symptom of structural problems that the Government must address" (UN, 2022a, para. 16).
7. See, Part VI, Sections 6–8.
8. Jayasuriya further notes that TLMPs force parents into a position where they must fracture their physical relationships with their children in order to provide materially for them.
9. There will be some cases in destination countries for Asia Pacific migrants where they are able to transition to a protection status having proved human rights harm or criminal acts against them, such as trafficking in persons or domestic violence, though barriers of access to justice render this option illusory for many low-wage migrants and in most cases this status too is temporary.
10. For more on this see, UN Office of the High Commissioner for Human Rights and Global Migration Group (2018).
11. In comparison to the "rights versus numbers" trade-off argument, we argue that these parameters arise not from the politics of TLMPs but from an inquiry into the permissible limitations on human rights through the lens of the principles of universality, interdependence and indivisibility and in the context of standards of necessity, proportionality and non-discrimination.
12. The International Labour Organization, the specialised agency of the United Nations dedicated to promoting decent work, is founded on the principle that labour is not a commodity (ILO, 1944, see Part I, para. (a)).

References

Abu Dhabi Dialogue. (n.d.). About Abu Dhabi dialogue: What is temporary labour migration? http://abudhabidialogue.org.ae/about-abu-dhabi-dialogue. Accessed 23 January 2023.

Arsenijević, J., Burtscher, D., Ponthieu, A., Severy, N., Contenta, A., Moissaing, S., Argenziano, S., Zamatto, F., Zachariah, R., Ali, E., & Venables, E. (2018). 'I feel like I am less than other people': Health-related vulnerabilities of male migrants travelling alone on their journey to Europe. *Social Science & Medicine, 209*, 86–94. https://doi.org/10.1016/j.socscimed.2018.05.038

Barne, B., & Pirlea, F. (2019, July 2). Money sent home by workers now largest source of external financing in low- and middle-income countries (excluding China). *Data Blog* (World Bank). https://blogs.worldbank.org/opendata/money-sent-home-workers-now-largest-source-external-financing-low-and-middle-income. Accessed 9 March 2022.

Bradley, G. M., & de Noronha, L. (2022). *Against borders: The case for abolition*. Verso.

Carstensen, A. L. (2021). Unfree labour, migration and racism: Towards an analytical framework. *Global Labour Journal, 12*(1). https://doi.org/10.15173/glj.v12i1.4159

Castles, S., & Ozkul, D. (2014). Circular migration: Triple win, or a new label for temporary migration? In G. Battistella (Ed.), *Global and Asian perspectives on international migration* (pp. 27–49). Springer.

Chattier, P. (2019). Beyond development impact: Gender and care in the Pacific Seasonal Worker Programme. *Gender & Development, 27*(1), 49–65.

Cho, Y., Denisova, A., Yi, S., & Khadka, U. (2018). *Bilateral arrangement of temporary labor migration: Lessons from Korea's employment permit system.* World Bank.

Costa, D., & Martin, P. (2018, August 1). *Temporary labor migration programs: Governance, migrant worker rights, and recommendations for the U.N. Global Compact for Migration.* Economic Policy Institute.

Crépeau, F., & Atak, I. (2016). Global migration governance: Avoiding commitments on human rights, yet tracing a course for cooperation. *Netherlands Quarterly of Human Rights, 34*(2), 113–146.

Dauvergne, C., & Marsden, S. (2014). The ideology of temporary labour migration in the post-global era. *Citizenship Studies, 18*(2), 224–242. https://doi.org/10.1080/13621025.2014.886441

Delgado Wise, R., Márquez Covarrubias, H., & Puentes, R. (2013). Reframing the debate on migration, development and human rights. *Population, Space and Place, 19*(4), 430–443. https://doi.org/10.1002/psp.1783

Draper, J. (2022). Labor migration and climate change adaptation. *American Political Science Review, 116*(3), 1012–1024. https://doi.org/10.1017/S0003055421001313

Employment of Foreign Manpower (Work Passes) Regulations. (2012). Fourth schedule, part VI. https://sso.agc.gov.sg/SL/EFMA1990-S569-2012. Accessed 21 July 2021.

Geiger, M., & Pécoud, A. (2013). Migration, development and the "migration and development nexus." *Population, Space and Place, 19*(4), 369–374. https://doi.org/10.1002/psp.1778

Global Unions. (2010). Global Unions' statement to the global forum on migration and development, Puerto Vallarta, 8 and 9 November 2010.

Gonzalez, C. G. (2020). Climate change, race, and migration. *Journal of Law and Political Economy, 1*(1). https://doi.org/10.5070/LP61146501

Hao'uli, E. (2013). Triple wins or trojan horse? Examining the recognised seasonal employer scheme under a TWAIL lens. *New Zealand Yearbook of International Law,* (11), 183–220.

Henley & Partners. (2022). The Henley passport index: Compare my passport. https://www.henleyglobal.com/passport-index/compare. Accessed 4 February 2023.

Horvath, K. (2014). Securitisation, economisation and the political constitution of temporary migration: The making of the Austrian seasonal workers scheme. *Migration Letters, 11*(2), 154–170.

International Labour Office. (2006). *The employment relationship: International labour conference, 95th session, 2006*. Report V(1). International Labour Office.

International Labour Office. (2014). *Fair migration: Setting an ILO agenda*. Report of the Director-General. Report I(B). International Labour Conference, 103rd Session, ILC.103/DG/IB.

International Labour Organization. (1944). *Declaration concerning the aims and purposes of the International Labour Organisation* (Declaration of Philadelphia).

International Labour Organization. (2015, August 19). *Regulating labour recruitment to prevent human trafficking and foster fair migration: Models, challenges and opportunities*.

International Labour Organization. (2021). *Temporary labour migration: The business community experience*.

International Labour Organization. (2022, October 13). *Temporary labour migration, governing body 346th session, Geneva, October–November 2022*. GB.346/POL/1.

International Organization for Migration (IOM). (2021). *Spotlight on labour migration in Asia*. IOM.

Jayasuriya, R. (2021). *Children, human rights and temporary labour migration: Protecting the child-parent relationship*. Routledge.

LeBaron, G., & Phillips, N. (2019). States and the political economy of unfree labour. *New Political Economy, 24*(1), 1–21. https://doi.org/10.1080/13563467.2017.1420642

Lester, E. (2010). Socioeconomic rights, human security and survival migrants: Whose rights? Whose security? In A. Edwards & C. Ferstman (Eds.), *Human security and non-citizens: Law, policy and international affairs* (pp.314–356). Cambridge University Press.

Mai, N. (2016). 'Too much suffering': Understanding the interplay between migration, bounded exploitation and trafficking through Nigerian sex workers' experiences. *Sociological Research Online, 21*(4). https://doi.org/10.5153/sro.415

Mantouvalou, V. (2022). The UK seasonal worker visa. *European Law Open, 1*(3), 711–719. https://doi.org/10.1017/elo.2022.39

Merla, L., & Smit, S. (2020). Enforced temporariness and skilled migrants' family plans: Examining the friction between institutional, biographical and daily timescales. *Journal of Ethnic and Migration Studies*. https://doi.org/10.1080/1369183X.2020.1857228

Ministry of Manpower. (n.d.). Six-monthly medical examination (6ME) for female migrant workers. https://www.mom.gov.sg/passes-and-permits/work-permit-for-foreign-worker/sector-specific-rules/six-monthly-medical-examination. Accessed 19 October 2021.

New Zealand Human Rights Commission. (2022). *The RSE scheme in Aotearoa New Zealand: A human rights review*. Human Rights Commission.

Reilly, A. (2011). The ethics of seasonal labour migration. *Griffith Law Review, 20*(1), 128–152.

Ruhs, M. (2003). *Temporary foreign worker programmes: Policies, adverse consequences, and the need to make them work*. Social Protection Sector, International Migration Programme, International Labour Office.

Ruhs, M. (2013). *The price of rights: Regulating international labor migration*. Princeton University Press.

Shamir, H. (2017). The Paradox of 'Legality': Temporary migrant worker programs and vulnerability to trafficking. In P. Kotiswaran (Ed.), *Revisiting the law and governance of trafficking, forced labor and modern slavery* (pp. 471–502). Cambridge University Press.

Strauss, K., & Fudge, J. (2013). Temporary work, agencies and unfree labour: Insecurity in the new world of work. In K. Strauss & J. Fudge (Eds.), *Temporary work, agencies and unfree labour* (pp. 1–25). Routledge.

Strauss, K., & McGrath, S. (2017). Temporary migration, precarious employment and unfree labour relations: Exploring the 'continuum of exploitation' in Canada's temporary foreign worker program. *Geoforum, 78*, 199–208.

Triandafyllidou, A. (2022). Temporary migration: Category of analysis or category of practice? *Journal of Ethnic and Migration Studies, 48*(16), 3847–3859. https://doi.org/10.1080/1369183X.2022.2028350

Uddin, M. S., Masud, M. M., & Hye, Q. M. A. (2020). Barriers to health-care access: A case study of Bangladeshi temporary migrant workers in Kuala Lumpur, Malaysia. *Humanities and Social Sciences Letters, 8*(2), 215–223. https://doi.org/10.18488/journal.73.2020.82.215.223

UN General Assembly. (2015). *Transforming our world: The 2030 agenda for sustainable development*. UN Doc. A/RES/70/1.

UN General Assembly. (2018). *Global compact for safe, orderly and regular migration (GCM)*. Adopted 19 December 2018. UN Doc. A/RES/73/195.

UN Office of the High Commissioner for Human Rights and Global Migration Group. (2018). *Principles and guidelines, supported by practical guidance, on the human rights protection of migrants in vulnerable situations*.

UN Office of the High Commissioner for Human Rights. (2022). *'We wanted workers, but human beings came': Human rights and temporary labour migration programmes in and from Asia and the Pacific*. UN OHCHR.

UN System Chief Executives Board for Coordination. (2017). *Leaving no one behind: Equality and non-discrimination at the heart of sustainable development: A shared United Nations System framework for action*. UN, Chief Executives Board.

UN. (1990). *Committee on economic, social and cultural rights, general comment no. 3: The nature of states parties' obligations, in UN doc. E/1991/23*.

UN. (2008, February 4). *Committee on economic, social and cultural rights, general comment no. 19: The right to social security (art. 9)*. UN Doc. E/C.12/GC/19.

UN. (2013, August 28). *Committee on the protection of the rights of all migrant workers and members of their families: General comment no. 2 on the rights of migrant workers in an irregular situation and members of their families.* UN Doc. CMW/C/GC/2.

UN. (2017, February 24). *Duties of states towards refugees and migrants under the international covenant on economic, social and cultural rights: Statement by the Committee on economic, social and cultural rights.* UN Doc. E/C.12/2017/1.

UN. (2018a, September 25). *Report of the Special Rapporteur on the human rights of migrants: Access to justice for migrant persons.* UN Doc. A/73/178/Rev.1.

UN. (2018b, January 16). *Report of the Special Rapporteur on the situation of human rights defenders.* UN Doc. A/HRC/37/51.

UN. (2020, April 27). *Report of the Special Rapporteur on contemporary forms of racism, racial discrimination, xenophobia and related intolerance, visit to Qatar.* UN Doc. A/HRC/44/57/Add.1.

UN. (2022a, May 13). *Report of the Special Rapporteur on extreme poverty and human rights on his visit to Nepal.* UN Doc. A/HRC/50/38/Add.2.

UN. (2022b, April 25). *Report of the Special Rapporteur on trafficking in persons, especially women and children: Trafficking in persons in the development sector: Human rights due diligence and sustainable development, A/HRC/50/33.*

UN. (n.d.). *Reduced inequalities: Why it matters.* https://www.un.org/sustainabledevelopment/wp-content/uploads/2018/01/10_Why-It-Matters-2020.pdf. Accessed 25 February 2023.

Underhill-Sem, Y., Marsters, E., Bedford, R., Naidu, V., Friesen, W. (2019). *Are there only winners?—Labour mobility for sustainable development in the Pacific.* New Zealand Institute for Pacific Research. https://apo.org.au/sites/default/files/resource-files/2019-05/apo-nid244881.pdf. Accessed 4 September 2022.

Walia, H. (2022). *Why climate justice must go beyond borders.* Open Democracy, 20 January 2022. https://www.opendemocracy.net/en/oureconomy/climate-justice-migrant-labour-harsha-walia/. Accessed 28 January 2022.

Wickramasekara, P. (2011). *Circular migration: A triple win or a dead end? Global union research network.* International Labour Office.

Wickramasekara, P. (2015). *Bilateral agreements and memoranda of understanding on migration of low skilled workers: A review.* ILO.

Withers, M. (2019). *Sri Lanka's remittance economy: A multiscalar analysis of migration underdevelopment.* Routledge.

Open Access This chapter is licensed under the terms of the Creative Commons Attribution 4.0 International License (http://creativecommons.org/licenses/by/4.0/), which permits use, sharing, adaptation, distribution and reproduction in any medium or format, as long as you give appropriate credit to the original author(s) and the source, provide a link to the Creative Commons license and indicate if changes were made.

The images or other third party material in this chapter are included in the chapter's Creative Commons license, unless indicated otherwise in a credit line to the material. If material is not included in the chapter's Creative Commons license and your intended use is not permitted by statutory regulation or exceeds the permitted use, you will need to obtain permission directly from the copyright holder.

33

Migrant Political Mobilisation and Solidarity Building in the Global South

Mariama Awumbila, Faisal Garba, Akosua K. Darkwah, and Mariama Zaami

Introduction

This chapter examines how migrants from the Global South who move within the region organise themselves, the forms of solidarity that they extend to each other, and how these relate to broader working-class formations. It interrogates the dynamics of migrant organising, both formal and informal, and alliances, visible and not-so-visible, formed by migrants in the Global South. This is particularly important given the fact that South-South migration forms about 36% of total migrant stock (UN DESA, 2019) and that South-South migration is increasingly becoming a significant factor in the economic and social development of many developing countries. While xenophobia and othering are regular features of migrant-local interactions in the migration literature (Darkwah, 2019; Desai, 2008; Dodson, 2010), the extent to which its opposite, solidarity, occurs as a result of the workplace and

---

M. Awumbila (✉) · M. Zaami
Department of Geography and Resource Development, University of Ghana, Legon, Ghana
e-mail: mawumbila@ug.edu.gh

F. Garba
Department of Sociology, University of Cape Town, Cape Town, South Africa
e-mail: faisal.garbamuhammed@uct.ac.za

A. K. Darkwah
Department of Sociology, University of Ghana, Legon, Ghana

© The Author(s) 2024
H. Crawley and J. K. Teye (eds.), *The Palgrave Handbook of South–South Migration and Inequality*, https://doi.org/10.1007/978-3-031-39814-8_33

community activism of migrants has received scant attention in the literature, hence our focus. How migrants organise themselves and how they relate to locals of similar social standing is important for a nuanced understanding of migrant experiences especially in the Global South where the majority of human mobility takes place (Dakas, 2018).

A desk study on migrant solidarity and political mobilisation undertaken as part of research for the Migration for Development and Equality (MIDEQ) Hub in 2021,[1] identified three main levels (micro, meso, and macro) at which migrants mobilise to respond to their circumstances or conditions. At the micro-level, migrants organise largely around individual working conditions and terms of employment, while at the macro-level, the set of issues that migrants organise around takes a more structural approach where the focus is often on shifting society-wide structures of oppression and discrimination. However, as Pande (2012) notes, migrants also engage in mobilising and resistive activities that are neither micro nor macro and that may rather be labelled as meso-level resistance. We argue that meso-level organising and the solidarity networks formed by migrants in the Global South may provide them with the space to build solidarity in their own ways, and to fight their exploitation and oppression. This is because it provides them with the space to draw on the labour power of the group as a leverage against workplace abuses and unfavourable social conditions. Migrant meso-level organising therefore mirrors social movement unionism in that the issues of production, social reproduction, and social participation coalesce.

This chapter therefore focuses on how migrants within the Global South organise at the meso-level to defend and access their rights and the solidarity that they build among themselves as migrants and with social movements, working-class organisations, and other civil society actors. Although we focus on migrant mobilisation and solidarity building at the meso-level, we also draw attention to the linkages between the meso and the macro/micro-levels and examine how the different levels of organising reinforce each other and the many ways in which they relate with one another. Given the problems inherent in conceptualising a complex, multi-dimensional, and normative concept of transnational solidarity, we adopt a nuanced analysis of mobilisation and transnational solidarity practices for a better understanding of the complexities of the political action of both migrants and citizens.

Conceptualising Political Mobilisation and Solidarity Building

As with all other measurable theoretical constructs, there are multiple ways of defining and conceptualising mobilisation. A good starting point for any conceptualisation of political mobilisation is the work by Deutsch (1961), which has largely been accepted as the standard framework for research on mobilisation (Cameron, 1974). Deutsch (1961) defines social mobilisation as a process in which "old social, economic, and psychological commitments are eroded or broken and people become available for new patterns of socialization and behavior" (Deutsch, 1961, 493). Deutsch suggests that this uprooting and erosion occurs, with urbanisation, commercialisation, and industrialisation. He views these changes as the necessary prior conditions for political mobilisation, which involves the induction of the socially uprooted into stable, new patterns of behaviour and commitment (Deutsch, 1961).

This conception of political mobilisation has several drawbacks, however, as highlighted by a number of authors (Cameron, 1974). Cameron (1974) notes that these problems are not unique to Deutsch, but that indeed, they are evident in the work of virtually all who use the concept. Cameron (1974) categorises these problems into three: firstly, the failure to explain the process of mobilisation, that is, the process by which the socially available are inducted into new patterns of behaviour; secondly, the tendency to assume that mobilisation is one of the most significant features of the larger process of change termed "modernization"; and thirdly, the view that political mobilisation is socially determined and the dependent variable in a process of social change. (Cameron, 1974).

Critiquing Deutsch's (1961) conceptualisation further, Huntington (1996) argues that a major failure of all process analysis (as in Deutsch's definition), is a lack of linkage between the social and political aspects of the changes being described. That is, "the relation between the 'macro' socio- economic changes and 'macro' political changes which have to be mediated through 'micro' changes in the attitudes, values, and behavior of the individuals" (Huntington, 1996, 310). He argues further that most theories of change do not specify the manner in which "macro" change affects an individual's behaviour and therefore most conceptions of mobilisation retain the passivity implicit in Deutsch's definition (Huntington, 1996).

From the perspective of political communication, mobilisation is defined as "the process by which a passive collection of individuals in a society is transformed into an active group in the pursuit of common goals" (Kalyango & Adu-Kumi, 2013, 8). Kalyango and Adu-Kumi (2013) further highlight how with globalisation and the introduction of new technologies, mobilisation processes have become more sophisticated. They argue that in today's globalised world of online media discussion groups, virtual social media platforms and other virtual participatory electronic devices have become the new tools for national or global mobilisation. In Africa particularly, the massive acquisition of social media tools and the adoption of new media technologies has provided opportunities for political as well as social mobilisation (Fair et al., 2009). For example, in 2008 the Committee for Joint Action (CJA) in Ghana was able to mobilise thousands of sympathisers to organise a demonstration to press for the reduction of fuel prices in 2008 (Kalyango & Adu-Kumi, 2013). The use of social media for purposes of political mobilisation is of course not unique to Ghana. Scholars have noted similar practices among the Rohingya (Ansar & Khaled, 2023), Nigerians (Nwoye & Okafor, 2014), and perhaps most well-known of all, among the participants in what became known as the Arab Spring (Comunello & Anzera, 2012; Khamis & Vaughn, 2014).

The above discussion indicates that conceptualisations of mobilisation until recent times were mainly in the area of political and electoral mobilisation (Rokkan, 1966). Linking this to migrants' mobilisation, studies indicate that migrants political mobilisation often revolves around obtaining more political, social, and economic rights in receiving states, and is determined by both transnational and domestic forces (Ostergaard-Nielsen, 2003; Wright & Bloemraad, 2012). Sending countries may assist their citizens in improving their status abroad and migrants' incorporation trajectories and receiving countries' integration policies both co-determine immigrants' desire to participate politically, and their capabilities. However, such a view risks overlooking important complexities, since migrants may also desire to participate politically when they experience social exclusion. Migrants may then organise around race and ethnicity, display solidarity through daily interactions and activities, and strategically mobilise relations with the majority society in order to protect group interests (Portes & Rumbaut, 2001).

Although the concept of solidarity has a long history in the social sciences and more recently in migration and refugee studies, there is no consistent definition of or approach to this concept in the literature. Rather, various types of solidarity with different philosophical underpinnings co-exist. A common starting point for a conceptualisation of solidarity is the recognition that solidarity means different things to different actors, takes on different shapes in different contexts, and is invoked to explain and define a wide range of practices, discourses, positionings, and social relations (Birey et al., 2019). The concept of solidarity is thus complex, multi-dimensional, and normative.

Lahusen et al. (2021) define solidarity as a disposition and practice of help or support towards others but solidarity transcends unilateral concepts such as care, empathy, or altruism (Passy, 2001), even though it shares some of the same features. Solidarity is thus often linked to reciprocal expectations and practices between people expressing sameness, togetherness, and inclusiveness. However, solidarity could also be restricted to national communities, thus excluding outsiders (for instance, migrants), but often, solidarity implies a wider community of equals, thus eliminating the distinction between insiders and outsiders. In all cases, solidarity presupposes a conception of shared rights, responsibilities, and obligations (Lahusen et al., 2021).

Lahusen et al. (2021) further argue that solidarity particularly at the grassroots level, involves both civic and political components. With regard to the civic component of solidarity, these solidarity groups usually follow a philanthropic or humanitarian mission, aiming to meet the needs of fellow citizens and/or non-nationals. This approach to solidarity tends to focus on compassion, altruism, and care (Schroeder et al., 1995; Skitka & Tetlock, 1993; van Oorschot, 2000). Correspondingly, action activities usually focus on the provision of help and support, primarily in terms of services and goods. The political component of solidarity tends to highlight the advocacy element of collective actions with a focus on denouncing injustice, discrimination, and oppression suffered by specific groups or communities, because they speak out on behalf of their rights and engage in activities geared to improving their situation (Scholz, 2008). These groups might also be engaged in the delivery of services and goods, as well, (i.e. in civic solidarity) but the advocacy element is a more dominant part of their mission and activism, given that they rally publicly in order to pressure governments, political and economic elites, and other stakeholders to step up remedial actions. Action repertoires for political solidarity therefore make use of advocacy activities such as public awareness campaigns, consumer boycotts, lobbying activities, and various forms of political protests (della Porta & Caiani, 2009).

Other writers draw out the complex and at times contradictory microdynamics, tensions, and conflicts expressed in the everyday work of migrant activists, support groups, and solidarity actions. These studies question, for example, the view that solidarity is only possible between people with shared identities and a common history. They also raise questions about power hierarchies that generate gendered, racialised, class positionalities entangled with politics of place and history within migrants' solidarity movements (Ünsal, 2015). This highlights the need for any studies of migrant solidarity to draw out the complexities and nuances of solidarity struggles that involve differently positioned actors.

From the above analysis, we conclude that the plethora of meanings given to the concept of solidarity which generally follow different philosophical traditions, has led to the difficulties in defining and generally differentiating the concept from other core concepts of the social sciences. The use of the concept is therefore often complex, multi-dimensional, and normative. Reflecting this, and in line with other authors (Bauder & Juffs, 2020), we do not advocate for developing a single definition or application of the concept of solidarity, but rather, highlight the different types of solidarity occurring in the Global South, showing the variability and often contradictory uses of the concept.

The discussion in this chapter also highlights the need for migration scholars and researchers to adopt a more nuanced analysis of mobilisation and transnational solidarity practices for a better understanding of the complexities of the political action of both migrants and citizens. This will entail a conceptualisation of political mobilisation and solidarity building that captures the interaction and possible mutual influence between the micro, meso, and macro levels and at different levels in each society.

Migrant Organising at the Micro, Meso, and Macro Levels: An Overview

Migrants respond to their circumstances in various ways, including through mobilising one another and allies. Migrants often combine informal protection measures with their version of (semi) formal organising in/as part of working-class struggles. The literature on resistance to forms of subjugation and the different ways in which migrants respond can broadly be classified into three types; the private, the public, and what Pande (2012) refers to as the meso-level of collective activity. Private level activities (or the micro-level) are "individual and symbolic" forms of resistance that migrants engage in, while the public forms of resistance (macro-level organising) are "overt and organised" forms of resistance engaged in either by migrants alone or with the support of citizens (Pande, 2012, 382). In describing the resistive activities of domestic workers in Lebanon, Pande (2012) suggests that they engage in meso-level resistance, forms of resistance that are "neither private nor public."

Beginning with the private level or micro-level organising, the literature abounds with examples. Migrants and migrant workers respond to the oppressions they face through a range of identity-based loosely formed associations based on ethnic, national, or religious affiliation. These include those among undocumented Myanmar migrants in Thailand (Campbell,

2016), Ghanaian migrants in China (Obeng, 2019), Nigerian migrants in Ghana (Bosiakoh, 2011), Caribbean and Mexican migrants in rural Canada (Preibisch, 2004), and Senegalese migrants in Argentina (Freier & Zubrzycki, 2021). These associations are simply directed at building a sense of community to help migrants better cope with their circumstances and to enable them to survive in their host countries. Often, they organise social and religious events to enable them bond with each other (Pande, 2020). Bosiakoh's (2011) study of Nigerian immigrants in Ghana, for example, highlights how migrant associations support new arrivals to settle down, including providing temporary housing if needed, directing them to locations with affordable rent, providing financial assistance to cover medical bills and generally encouraging them through the struggles and challenges that come with being a refugee or a migrant worker. Similarly, Chereni (2018) documents how Zimbabwean migrants in South Africa draw on informal social support systems to survive the stresses of living in South Africa. These support systems can be created in church, at work, or among friends. While these informal forms of social protection are not necessarily substitutes for formal forms of protection, they nonetheless help migrants navigate the harsh social reality of life as migrants.

An important dimension of micro-level organising is the use of information communication technologies (ICTs) in mobilisation and defensive struggles against abuses and the protection of livelihoods (see also Harinandrath etal., this volume). These include the LGBTQI+ migrant community in Brazil (Theodoro & Cogo, 2019), and community organising among Chin refugees in Malaysia (McConnachie, 2019). Theodoro and Cogo (2019), for example, document how the LGBTQI+ migrant community in Sao Paolo drew on the social networking site, Facebook, to make visible their otherwise invisible status as members of a double minority group—migrant and non-heterosexual.

Unlike micro-level organising, macro-level organising among migrants is overtly political in nature, designed to change the circumstances under which they live and work as migrants, with the focus on shifting society-wide structures of oppression and discrimination such as documentation and right to work, among others. The nature of the protests ranges widely but regardless of the mode of protest they employ, the basis is to call for change for the better. Even when these macro-level organising efforts do not result in concrete changes in favour of the migrants, it does have symbolic value. For example, marches to protest about specific situations make visible an otherwise invisible population. Other forms of organising at the macro-level are not simply for the symbolic value, but result in real, structural change. Cooke (2007), for example, documents the successful efforts of rural migrant workers in China who finally began in 2004 to vote with their feet, abandoning their jobs to protest the poor conditions of work that they had endured for several years. Employers who relied heavily on rural workers suddenly found it difficult to recruit them (Cooke, 2007, 560). Only then did a range of actors—the central government, local government, employment agencies, legal centre, and "*tongxiang hui*" (association of workers from the same region/village)—begin a much more concerted effort to address the issue at hand (Cooke, 2007; Froissart, 2005). These actions therefore tend to highlight the political component of solidarity.

Besides access to work and improved conditions of work, another major concern of migrants, particularly for migrants in the Global South, is access to basic services such as water and electricity. Alvarado (2020) describes the ways in which Nicaraguan migrants in Costa Rica do not necessarily engage in contestation with the state. Rather, they create their own avenues for gaining access to public services such as tapping water and electricity lines and then request local officials to legitimise that which they have accessed already. Scholars who focus on migrants in urban informal spaces thus highlight the fact that encounters with the state do not always have to be in the form of protests. Alvarado (2020) identifies informal interactions, moral claims, and face to face encounters with local state officials as equally effective strategies to provide migrants with services.

With regard to meso-level organising, while unionisation is a formal mechanism for channelling migrant grievances, in many countries in the Global South, migrants, especially those considered to be doing menial jobs—jobs characterised by the 3Ds, dangerous, dirty, and difficult—are denied the right to unionise. Yet, as Pande (2012) has documented for migrant domestic workers in Lebanon, that has not prevented them from organising to improve their circumstances as workers in precarious circumstances. She documents the meso-level resistance they engage in which ranges from strategic dyads restricted to balconies, smaller collectives of live-in workers that operate outside of ethnic churches to the much larger collectives operating in rented apartments that comprise illegal freelancers and runaways (Pande, 2012, 382). This form of resistance, neither private nor public, serves as the beginnings of what could become powerful acts of resistance against the domination they face. Similarly, Genc (2017) explains how migrants formed solidarity networks to address the precarity they faced in detention camps in Kumkapi, Istanbul. Over a hundred migrants protested over several issues, including the bureaucratic nature of the legal assistance and administrative supervision measures. These solidarity events eventually led to the formation of a Migrant Solidarity Network (MSN) in February 2010 (Genc, 2017).

Although there is a dearth of literature on migrant organising in sub-Saharan Africa at the meso-level, recent research indicates that migrants are using migration brokers to exercise and extend their agency and to cope with oppression and gain some improvements in working conditions (Awumbila et al., 2019; Deshingkar et al., 2019; Wee et al., 2019). In examining the inner workings of the migration industry and the roles of brokers, Deshingkar et al. (2019) note the role of the state and employers in positioning migrants from Ghana and Myanmar in exploitative work in Libya, the Middle East, Singapore, and Thailand, highlighting the ways in which migrants use brokerage to exercise agency by taking advantage of irregular migration routes and informal employment. Awumbila et al's (2017a, 2017b, 2019) research in Ghana indicates that brokers are integral to migrants being able to exercise agency by transcending local power inequalities, by accessing more remunerative work, and by switching jobs at the destination point. Although the transformative effects of migrant agency on structures of inequality and the potential for brokerage to offer opportunities for resistance against unequal power relations at destination have been questioned, they remain important parts of migrants' risk management strategies and efforts to minimise exploitation through meso-level actors.

Migrant Political Mobilisation Through Trade Unions

Across the globe, perhaps the most public form of meso-level organising to improve conditions of work for all workers is the trade union. Trade unions can give protection to all workers regardless of immigration status. The power of trade unions to change the working conditions and circumstances of workers is perhaps best illustrated in the work of the All-China Federation of Trade Unions (ACFTU). Through their efforts, the central government took a major step in 2003 to address the needs of migrant workers by finally classifying rural migrant workers in urban areas as members of the working class. Accepting rural migrant workers as part of the membership of the union was a significant step because the ACFTU was the only union recognised by the central government (Cooke, 2007). The legitimising impact of this act was very significant because it allowed for migrant workers to engage in collective action for better working conditions (Froissart, 2005). However, the success of their efforts was thwarted by the delay tactics employed by firms in recognising trade unions in their workplaces. Cooke (2007, 574) recounts the words of one trade union worker as follows:

... They [employers] don't say no to us each time we go to see them about setting up a trade union. They are always very friendly and sound very sincere. They will say, "Yes, it is a very good idea [to set up a trade union in the company], we will think about it", "we are thinking about it", "we are making preparation to set one up", or "we are setting it up ..." Five years later, they are still in the early stage of preparation to set one up.

Foreign owned companies were particularly notorious in this regard. In one such company, it took trade union workers 12 years to finally get a union in place. In addition to the fact that it took a long time to set up unions in various workplaces, trade unions also seem to have very little impact on the ground. They are not able to significantly improve wage levels or social insurance (Cooke, 2007). Trade unions seemed to serve as the mouthpiece of management, not workers with there being clear cases where it was obvious that trade unions had colluded with the management of enterprises, sometimes receiving bribes for such collusion. The general opinion migrants had of trade unions was thus not very positive. Froissart (2005, 37) notes:

Migrants were scathing about the union: "No point to seek trade unions' help. They take your money and run", "Trade unions serve the capital, not the people", "Trade unions are full of conmen, and they never settle conflicts" were wide spread statements.

This is due perhaps to the fact that the ACFTU had not translated its interest in incorporating rural migrant workers into its ranks with a policy document outlining union operations and regulations (Cooke, 2007). It may also point to the weakness in general of trade unions in a state like China and point to the importance of the central government in passing and implementing regulations that protect workers (Froissart, 2005, 33).

Although Chinese urban workers were willing to incorporate rural migrants into their unions, this is not always the case especially when migrants originate from outside a nation state. Often in such circumstances, workers with legal protection are uncomfortable with the idea of including migrants in their unions because of the fear that migrants, given their insecure legal status, will simply serve to drive down wages and conditions of work in general (Munck & Hyland, 2014). In South Africa for example, this tension between migrant and indigenous workers is evident in spite of the conciliatory language of major South African trade unions. At a policy level, the Congress of South African Trade Unions (COSATU), South Africa's largest trade union federation, has firmly supported the rights of migrants to decent work. In a communique on the Immigration Act of 2002, COSATU submitted as follows:

[A] preoccupation with undocumented migration [which] results in a failure to provide a coherent immigration policy and in certain respects the avoidance of issues … [such a preoccupation would] further engender paranoia, which will then make it difficult to have a rational and humane approach to undocumented migration (Gordon & Maharaj, 2014, 131).

At a grassroots level, however, it is clear that citizens are not in favour of such an approach. Gordon and Maharaj (2014) document the logic provided by native members of the private security trade union for their reluctance to include undocumented migrant workers in the union. Rather than see these migrant workers as comrades, these workers, who live themselves on the economic margins given the precarious conditions (Standing, 2011) under which they work, see the undocumented foreign workers as competitors and are thus reluctant to partner with them to improve working conditions for both groups.

Other countries on the African continent have been slow to incorporate migrants into unions, but nonetheless have done so after years of effort on the part of migrant associations to ensure the regularisation of their migrant status. This is evident in Morocco where in the early part of the twenty-first century, two sub-Saharan African migrant associations were set up. These include the Council of sub-Saharan Migrants in Morocco established in 2005 and the Collective of sub-Saharan Migrants in Morocco set up in 2010. These political associations, although not legally recognised, advocate for the legalisation of sub-Saharan Africans initially enroute to Europe who choose to stay in Morocco instead (Üstübici, 2016, 310). The purpose of these associations is succinctly described by a member of one such organisation in the following words:

There are many sub-Saharans living in Takadoum, it is the hottest neighborhood in Rabat. This [the neighbourhood violence] motivated us, sub-Saharans to come together to create an association, ALECMA. This is to denounce different problems we encounter in the country, then to defend our rights because as migrants, our rights need to be respected. This is why we regrouped under an association. We started this fight to be recognised (Üstübici, 2016, 311).

Another continued, "We are mobilising people to rise for their rights …. You have the right of workers, right to papers, right to access health, right to liberty. You should not stay in your corner. You need to claim your rights" (Üstübici, 2016, 311).

In 2012, the advocacy efforts of these political associations were eventually heard by the unions when Morocco's Democratic Organisation of Workers set up its first branch that included migrants. This new branch advocates for the regularisation of migrants within Morroco (Üstübici, 2016) and has support from transnational groups. One such transnational organisation offering crucial support to the work of the Democratic Organisation of Workers was the Association of Maghrebian Workers in France. Members of this association were particularly supportive of the efforts of migrant associations in Morocco because as migrants themselves, they were in a similar position as the migrants in Morocco. As the national coordinator of this association explained: "We do not comprehend claiming regularisation for hundreds of thousands of Moroccans abroad while Morocco will not even do it for a few thousand sub-Saharan immigrants" (Üstübici, 2016, 316). In 2013,[2] the state finally responded to the calls for regularisation of migrants with a revised migration policy, one that adopts a human rights rather than security approach to migrants. Concrete steps emanating from that policy include the creation of a Ministry concerned with migrant affairs, the Ministry in Charge of Moroccans Living Abroad and Migration Affairs (Üstübici, 2016).

In Ghana, trade unions have been slow to incorporate migrants into their unions, however, with the increased arrival of migrants, particularly from the West African sub region in response to conflicts and crises in neighbouring countries, and a rise in some migration streams such as migration for domestic work in the Middle East and Gulf Countries, the Ghana Trades Union Congress (GTUC) has had to address issues of migrants. In Ghana, migrant workers, face some of the most serious decent work deficits. Migrant workers are largely employed in the informal economy, in particular in hard-to-reach sectors, such as on cocoa farms, oil farms in rural areas, in quarries, on fishing vessels, or in private households as domestic workers or as commercial workers, thus making it difficult for unionisation.

Despite the importance of the informal economy in the Global South, employing about 83% of total labour force in Africa (ILO, 2021), and employing a large number of migrant workers as shown above, little attention has been focused on collective organising among people in the informal economy. Indeed, their collective organising is often ignored and in some cases, they are seen outright as lacking collective mobilisation capabilities. Rather than engaging in collective demand-making, it is argued that informal actors act in a quiet and "atomized " fashion to address their immediate needs (Lindell, 2010). In trying to rectify this, trade unions are increasingly attempting to reach out to informal and casual workers, many of whom are migrants, seeking to organise the "unorganized". Lindell (2010) argues that such an approach may be dangerous as it implies that people in the informal economy are passive targets awaiting the "rescuing hand of trade unions." He further argues that people in the informal economy should be seen as *actors*, capable of various initiatives, including organising themselves, despite the many obstacles they often face (Lindell, 2010).

More recently, the significance of trade unions engaging more closely with *all* kinds of workers irrespective of *where* they work, including the informal economy, has gained international acceptance. (Trade unions therefore figure as key actors in the International Labour Organizations (ILO) campaign for creating decent work in the informal economy. The GTUC, for example, has subscribed to a decent work agenda that focuses on decent work for everyone regardless of location (GTUC, 2016). The Ghana TUC is also a member of the Trades Union Migration Network (ATUMNET), a network that addresses fair recruitment in relation to labour migration and has as recently as 2022 launched a national Migrant Recruitment Advisor (MRA), an internet hub that seeks to raise awareness of the rights of migrant workers, including informal sector workers and protect migrant workers from abusive employment practices (GTUC, 2022).

Informal sector workers comprising many internal migrants have also mobilised around their work associations in Ghana. These include the formation of workers' groups such as the Union of Informal Workers' Association (UNIWA), the Domestic Workers Union, the Ghana Youth Porters Association, and informal hawkers and vendors associations. These groups or associations have helped in giving voice, space, and protection to migrant workers, particularly internal migrants. For instance, the first trade union for workers in the informal sector, namely UNIWA, is set up to address and promote the interest of workers in the informal economy, a large percentage of whom are internal migrants. Despite this, immigrants particularly from the West African region are seen as threats to the livelihoods of Ghanaians as seen by recent tensions between the Ghana Union of Traders (GUTA) and the Nigerian Association of Traders (NAT).

In Tunisia, to address migrant workers' challenges with recruitment agencies, the Tunisian General Labour Union (UGTT) has set up a regional network where they are the point of contact when migrants arrive in Tunisia. This has helped to increase access to reliable information and to provide them with legal information on their rights and also providing them a directory of organisations that could help address the needs of migrants (ILO, 2021).

This evidence suggests that rather than seeing immigrants as a potential threat to conditions of work for citizens, adopting policies to ease the legalisation status of immigrants ensures that their bargaining power will improve ultimately securing the bargaining power of citizens as well. Citizens' interests as workers are ultimately best served when they align their interest in better working conditions with migrant workers' interests in routes to citizenship and thus access to secure jobs with decent working conditions.

Migrants Workers, Non-migrant Workers: Solidarity and Contradiction

Other scholarly discussions on solidarity focus less on its origins and much more on the process by which solidarity is displayed or enacted. Solidarity between migrants and citizens, on one hand, or among different groups of migrants, on the other hand, is founded on shared political beliefs among these two groups. Brysk and Wehrenfenning (2010) explain that it is quite common to see solidarity among oppressed ethnic groups because the dominant group sets a threshold of their availability for normative appeals. Once the minority group, now rooted in the dominant group's society, has access to education and the media which provides them a sense of the dominant group's threshold for such appeals, they can then conceptualise their own experiences and appeal for better conditions. To ensure that the dominant group sympathises with the suppressed minority group, Brysk and Wehrenfenning (2010) explain that articulating and establishing the history of the group's persecution is important. Their argument draws on the experience of US Jews whom they argue were particularly successful at drawing on narratives of slavery, religious discrimination, and genocide to highlight their suppression and oppression.

Another set of literature emphasises the fact that solidarity movements that incorporate migrants and citizens are a positive step away from the overly humanitarian or philanthropic approach that has characterised the relationship between migrants and citizens as discussed under the conceptual issues section. When citizens are described as humanitarians giving charity, it places migrants in a passive category as victims, lacking agency to mitigate their own circumstances. The solidarity literature moves the discussion away from a focus on charity from citizens towards migrants, to a recognition of a transaction between peers. As Tazzioli (2018, 6) explains, "acting in solidarity entails supporting migrant struggles ... more than it does acting in order to save or bring help to them." As described above, there are many ways in which this can be done. In Morocco, for example, Moroccan CSOs use their legal status to secure permission from the state to organise public protests at which sub-Saharan migrant associations can make their requests (Üstübici, 2016).

Another critique of the humanitarian approach centres less on the powerlessness it evokes of migrants but also on the ways in which it simply maintains the status quo without seeking to subvert it in any crucial manner. While humanitarianism can be described as a form of resistance, its effectiveness is increasingly being questioned in recent times with many scholars arguing that humanitarianism simply alleviates pain and suffering without dealing directly with the root causes of the suffering. Or as Cantat (2018) puts it, humanitarianism simply stabilises the dominant social order, it does not subvert it. In discussing humanitarianism, however, Zamponi (2017, 97) has developed the concept of direct social actions which he defines as "actions that do not primarily focus upon claiming something from the state or other power-holders but that instead focus upon directly transforming some specific aspects of society by means of the action itself." Unlike protest where the disenfranchised make claims on the state or employers, direct social action focuses on providing support of various forms to the disenfranchised such as food supplies, translation services, legal aid, free accommodation, and so on. Zamponi (2017) cautions us against reading protest as a higher form of politics than direct social action. He argues that direct social action is not simply humanitarian aid as often conceptualised in the literature but political action as well. One of his interviewees, a Lampendusa based activist echoes a similar sentiment in the words, "when we describe what we do, we always say that giving them tea, for us, is a political act" (Zamponi, 2017, 108).

In the current discourse on the matter, it is clear that solidarity movements that seek real substantive change are preferred to the humanitarian movements of the past that alleviated the suffering of migrants without necessarily changing their circumstances. Solidarity movements are also preferred because they incorporate migrants and do not distance them from the activity that is designed to improve their circumstances.

Conclusion

Although the literature is skewed towards migrant organising in the Global North, this chapter addresses an important gap and contributes to our understanding of how migrants in the Global South organise themselves. The chapter highlights the fact that at the meso-level, migrant organising in the Global South is varied, changing, and intersects with questions of livelihoods. Migrants' self-organisation in small, intermediate, and umbrella bodies enables them to cope and attempt to shift immediate questions of livelihood, discrimination, and their structural underpinnings in the form of exclusionary state policy and xenophobia.

The success of these efforts varies. While in some countries, such as Morocco, migrant self-organsing has received the support of Moroccans living abroad leading to the eventual creation of a Ministry in Charge of Moroccans Living Abroad and Migration Affairs, other countries on the African continent have done a dismal job of incorporating the needs and concerns of migrant workers into that of citizens. While the largest South African trade union, COSATU ostensibly speaks to the interests of migrant workers, on the ground, average South Africans are antagonistic towards migrants seeing them more as a threat than as fellow workers subject to similar exploitation by capitalists. The discussion has also highlighted the more recent attempts by trade unions in African countries to engage more closely with all categories of workers irrespective of *where* they work. It is the hope that these engagements will centre on migrants, many of whom are in the informal economy, not as passive targets, but as actors capable of collective mobilisation. Successful or not, each effort on the part of migrants to have their needs met is important in its own right because it legitimises migrants and serves as a reminder that they are not victims but have agency.

Indeed, increasingly, humanitarian activists recognise the need to move away from conceptualising the migrants to whom they offer support as victims but rather as agents in their own right with whom they can build solidarity movements. A focus on meso-level organising in the Global South thus orients us to the possibilities for agency on the part of migrants both in terms of self-organising but also in terms of building community with citizens in the new nation states in which they find themselves.

Acknowledgements This work has been undertaken as part of the Migration for Development and Equality (MIDEQ) Hub. Funded by the UKRI Global Challenges Research Fund (GCRF) (Grant Reference: ES/S007415/1), MIDEQ unpacks the complex and multi-dimensional relationships between migration and inequality in the context of the Global South. More at www.mideq.org

Notes

1. The Migration for Development and Equality (MIDEQ) Hub unpacks the complex and multi-dimensional relationships between migration and inequality in the context of the Global South. More at www.mideq.org
2. Morocco is not alone in its late interest in the status of migrants within their borders. Mexico passed its first migration law in 2011 (Basok & Rojas Wiesner, 2017).

References

Alvarado, N. A. (2020). Migrant politics in the urban Global South: The political work of Nicaraguan migrants to acquire urban rights in Costa Rica. *Geopolitics, 27*(4), 1180–1204. https://doi.org/10.1080/14650045.2020.1777399

Ansar, A., & Khaled, A. F. M. (2023). In search of a Rohingya digital diaspora: Virtual togetherness, collective identities and political mobilisation. *Humanities and Social Sciences Communications, 10*(1), 1–13.

Awumbila, M., Deshingkar, P., Kandilige, L., Teye, J. K., & Setrana, M. (2019). Please, thank you and sorry–brokering migration and constructing identities for domestic work in Ghana. *Journal of Ethnic and Migration Studies, 45*(14), 2655–2671. https://doi.org/10.1080/1369183X.2018.1528097

Awumbila, M., Teye, J. K., & Yaro, J. A. (2017a). Of silent maids, skilled gardeners and careful madams: Gendered dynamics and strategies of migrant domestic workers in Accra, Ghana. *GeoJournal, 82*, 957–970. https://doi.org/10.1007/s10708-016-9711-5

Awumbila, M., Teye, J. K., & Yaro, J. A. (2017b). Social networks, migration trajectories and livelihood strategies of migrant domestic and construction workers in Accra, Ghana. *Journal of Asian and African Studies, 52*(7), 982–996. https://doi.org/10.1177/0021909616634743

Basok, T., & Rojas Wiesner, M. L. (2017). Winning a battle, losing the war: Migrant rights advocacy and its "influence" on the Mexican state. *Canadian Journal of Latin American and Caribbean Studies, 42*(1), 17–35. https://doi.org/10.1080/08263663.2017.1281941

Bauder, H., & Juffs, L. (2020). 'Solidarity' in the migration and refugee literature: Analysis of a concept. *Journal of Ethnic and Migration Studies, 46*(1), 46–65. https://doi.org/10.1080/1369183X.2019.1627862

Birey, T., Cantat, C., Maczynska, E., et al. (2019). *Challenging the political across borders. Migrants' and solidarity struggles*. Central European University.

Bosiakoh, T. A. (2011). The role of migrant associations in adjustment, integration and social development: The case of Nigerian migrant associations in Accra, Ghana. *Ghana Journal of Development Studies, 8*(2), 64–83. https://doi.org/10.4314/gjds.v8i2.5

Brysk, A., & Wehrenfennig, D. (2010). 'My brother's keeper'? Inter-ethnic solidarity and human rights. *Studies in Ethnicity and Nationalism, 10*(1), 1–18. https://doi.org/10.1111/j.1754-9469.2010.01067.x

Cameron, D. R. (1974). Toward a theory of political mobilization. *The Journal of Politics, 36*(1), 138–171.

Campbell, S. (2016). Everyday recomposition: Precarity and socialization in Thailand's migrant workforce. *American Ethnologist, 43*(2), 258–269. https://doi.org/10.1111/amet.12303

Cantat, C. (2018). The politics of refugee solidarity in Greece: Bordered identities and political mobilization. *CPS/MigSol Working Paper, 1*. https://core.ac.uk/download/pdf/151739941.pdf

Chereni, A. (2018). Risk, vulnerability and Zimbabwean migrants' post-arrival adaptation in Johannesburg: Reflections on relational aspects of informal social protection. *Journal of Social Development in Africa, 33*(1), 53–80.

Comunello, F., & Anzera, G. (2012). Will the revolution be tweeted? A conceptual framework for understanding the social media and the Arab Spring. *Islam and Christian-Muslim Relations, 23*(4), 453–470.

Cooke, F. L. (2007). Migrant labour and trade union's response and strategy in China. *Indian Journal of Industrial Relation, 42*(4), 558–588.

Dakas, S. (2018). *The future of human mobility: Four things to keep in mind when debating migration and displacement*. UNDP.

Darkwah, A. K. (2019). Fluid mobilities? Experiencing and responding to othering in a borderless world. *Contemporary Journal of African Studies, 6*(2), 51–69.

della Porta, D., & Caiani, M. (2009). *Social movements and Europeanization*. Oxford University Press.

Desai, A. (2008). Xenophobia and the place of the refugee in the rainbow nation of human rights. *African Sociological Review, 12*(2), 49–68.

Deshingkar, P., Awumbila, M., & Teye, J. K. (2019). Victims of trafficking and modern slavery or agents of change? Migrants, brokers, and the state in Ghana and Myanmar. *Journal of the British Academy, 7*(s1), 77–106. https://doi.org/10.5871/jba/007s1.077

Deutsch, K. W. (1961). Social mobilization and political development. *American Political Science Review, 55*(3), 493–514.

Dodson, B. (2010). Experience locating xenophobia: Debate, discourse, and everyday in Cape Town, South Africa. *Africa Today, 56*(3), 2–22.

Fair, J. E., Tully, M., Ekdale, B., & Asante, R. K. (2009). Crafting lifestyles in urban Africa: Young Ghanaians in the world of online friendship. *Africa Today, 55*(4), 28–49. https://doi.org/10.2979/aft.2009.55.4.28

Freier, L. F., & Zubrzycki, B. (2021). How do immigrant legalization programs play out in informal labor markets? The case of Senegalese street hawkers in Argentina. *Migration Studies, 9*(3), 1292–1321. https://doi.org/10.1093/migration/mnz044

Froissart, C. (2005). The rise of social movements among migrant workers: Uncertain strivings for autonomy. *China Perspective, 61*, 30–40. https://doi.org/10.4000/chinaperspectives.526

Genç, F. (2017). Migration as a site of political struggle. An evaluation of the Istanbul migrant solidarity network movements. *Journal for Critical Migration and Border Regime Studies, 3*(2), 117–132.

Ghana Trade Union Congress (GTUC). (2012–2016). *Policies*. https://ghanatuc.com/wp-content/uploads/2020/03/TUC-POLICIES-2012-2016.pdf

Ghana Trade Union Congress (GTUC). (2022). Launches migrant recruitment advisory platform. *Graphic Online*. https://www.graphic.com.gh/news/general-news/tuc-launches-migrant-recruitment-advisory-platform.html

Gordon, S., & Maharaj, B. (2014). Representing foreign workers in the private security industry: A South African perspective on trade union engagement. *The Journal of Modern African Studies, 52*(1), 123–149.

Huntington, S. (1996). *The clash of clash of civilizations and the remaking of the world order*. Touchstone.

International Labour Migration (ILO). (2021). *Trade unions manual to promote migrant workers' rights and foster fair labour migration governance in Africa*. https://www.ilo.org/wcmsp5/groups/public/---africa/---ro-abidjan/---sro-cairo/documents/publication/wcms_853297.pdf

Kalyango, Y., Jr., & Adu-Kumi, B. (2013). Impact of social media on political mobilization in East and West Africa. *Global Media Journal, 12*, 1–20.

Khamis, S., & Vaughn, K. (2014). Cyberactivism and citizen mobilization in the streets of Cairo. In F. Miraftab & N. Kudva (Eds.), *Cities of the global south reader* (pp. 300–303). Routledge.

Lahusen, C., Zschache, U., & Kousis, M. (2021). *Transnational solidarity in times of crises: Citizen organisations and collective learning in Europe*. Springer Nature.

Lindell, I. (2010). Introduction: The changing politics of informality–collective organizing, alliances and scales of engagement. In I. Lindell (Ed.), *Africa's informal workers collective agency, alliances and trans-national organizing in urban Africa* (pp. 1–30). Zed Books.

McConnachie, K. (2019). Securitization and community-based protection among Chin refugees in Kuala Lumpur. *Social and Legal Studies, 28*(2), 158–178. https://doi.org/10.1177/0964663918755891

Munck, R., & Hyland, M. (2014). Migration, regional integration and social transformation: A North-South comparative approach. *Global Social Policy, 14*(1), 32–50. https://doi.org/10.1177/1468018113504773

Nwoye, K. O., & Okafor, G. O. (2014). New media and political mobilization in Africa: The Nigerian experience. *American Journal of Social Sciences, 2*(2), 36–42.

Obeng, M. K. M. (2019). Journey to the East: A study of Ghanaian migrants in Guangzhou, China. *Canadian Journal of African Studies/Revue Canadienne Des Études Africaines, 53*(1), 67–87. https://doi.org/10.1080/00083968.2018.1536557

Ostergaard-Nielsen, E. (2003). *Transnational politics: The case of Turks and Kurds in Germany*. Routledge.

Pande, A. (2012). From "balcony talk" and "practical prayers" to illegal collectives: Migrant domestic workers and meso-level resistances in Lebanon. *Gender and society, 26*(3), 382–405. https://doi.org/10.1177/0891243212439247

Pande, A. (2020). Body, space and migrant ties: Migrant Domestic Workers And Embodied Resistances in Lebanon. In M. Baas (Ed.), *The Asian migrant's body: Emotion, gender and sexuality*. Amsterdam University Press.

Passy, F. (2001). Political altruism and the solidarity movement: An introduction. In M. Giugni & F. Passy (Eds.), *Political altruism? Solidarity movements in international perspective* (pp. 3–26). Rowman and Littlefield.

Portes, A., & Rumbaut, R. G. (2001). The forging of a new America: Lessons for theory and policy. In R. G. Rumbaut & A. Portes (Eds.), *Ethnicities: Children of immigrants in America* (pp. 301–317). University of California Press.

Preibisch, K. L. (2004). Migrant agricultural workers and processes of social inclusion in rural Canada: Encuentros and desencuentros. *Canadian Journal of Latin American and Caribbean Studies, 29*(57–58), 203–239. https://doi.org/10.1080/08263663.2004.10816857

Rokkan, S. (1966). Electoral mobilisation, party competition and national integration. In J. Lapalombara & M. Weiner (Eds.), *Political parties and political development* (pp. 261–265). Princeton University Press.

Scholz, S. J. (2008). *Political solidarity.* Penn State University Press.

Schroeder, D. A., Penner, L. A., Dovidio, J. F., & Piliavin, J. A. (1995). *The psychology of helping and altruism: Problems and puzzles.* McGraw-Hill.

Skitka, L. J., & Tetlock, P. E. (1993). Providing public assistance: Cognitive and motivational processes underlying liberal and conservative policy preferences. *Journal of Personality and Social Psychology, 65*(6), 1205–1223. https://doi.org/10.1037/0022-3514.65.6.1205

Standing, G. (2011). *The Precariat: The new dangerous class.* Bloomsbury.

Tazzioli, M. (2018). Crimes of solidarity: Migration and containment through rescue. *Radical Philosophy, 201,* 4–10.

Theodoro, H. G., & Cogo, D. (2019). LGBTQI+ immigrants and refugees in the city of São Paulo: Uses of ICTs in a South-South mobility context. *Revue française des sciences de l'information et de la communication,* (17). https://doi.org/10.4000/rfsic.7053

UN DESA. (2019). *International migrant stock: The 2019 revision. (Unite Nations database, POP/DB/MIG/Stock/Rev.2019).* UNDESA.

Ünsal, N. (2015). Challenging 'refugees' and 'supporters'. Intersectional power structures in the refugee movement in Berlin. *Movements. Journal für kritische Migrations-und Grenzregimeforschung, 1*(2), 1–18.

Üstübici, A. (2016). Political activism between journey and settlement: Irregular migrant mobilisation in Morocco. *Geopolitics, 21*(2), 303–324. https://doi.org/10.1080/14650045.2015.1104302

van Oorschot, W. (2000). Who should get what, and why? On deservingness criteria and the conditionality of solidarity among the public. *Policy and Politics, 28*(1), 33–48. https://doi.org/10.1332/0305573002500811

Wee, K., Goh, C., & Yeoh, B. S. (2019). Chutes-and-ladders: The migration industry, conditionality, and the production of precarity among migrant domestic workers in Singapore. *Journal of Ethnic and Migration Studies, 45*(14), 2672–2688. https://doi.org/10.1080/1369183X.2018.1528099

Wright, M., & Bloemraad, I. (2012). Is there a trade-off between multiculturalism and socio-political integration? Policy regimes and immigrant incorporation in comparative perspective. *Perspectives on Politics, 10*(1), 77–95.

Zamponi, L. (2017). Practices of solidarity: Direct social action, politicisation and refugee solidarity activism in Italy. *Mondi Migranti, 3*, 97–117. https://doi.org/10.3280/MM2017-003005

Open Access This chapter is licensed under the terms of the Creative Commons Attribution 4.0 International License (http://creativecommons.org/licenses/by/4.0/), which permits use, sharing, adaptation, distribution and reproduction in any medium or format, as long as you give appropriate credit to the original author(s) and the source, provide a link to the Creative Commons license and indicate if changes were made.

The images or other third party material in this chapter are included in the chapter's Creative Commons license, unless indicated otherwise in a credit line to the material. If material is not included in the chapter's Creative Commons license and your intended use is not permitted by statutory regulation or exceeds the permitted use, you will need to obtain permission directly from the copyright holder.

Index

A

Access to justice 19, 590, 602, 603, 699, 700, 704
Advocacy 128, 288, 396, 405, 491, 506, 511, 512, 668, 690–693, 723, 730
Africa 2, 3, 9, 11–13, 17, 18, 26, 27, 29, 34–37, 39, 50, 55, 56, 58, 60, 106, 107, 109, 110, 112–114, 120, 127, 136, 139, 157, 169, 170, 172, 175, 178, 184–186, 188, 189, 191–193, 195, 196, 205, 223, 319, 320, 326, 335, 345, 350, 355, 356, 499, 500, 513, 521, 524, 526–528, 531–533, 591, 600, 609, 610, 612–618, 626, 627, 730
Agriculture 15, 163, 169, 189, 218, 227, 234, 240, 274, 298, 320, 321, 327, 336, 576, 610
Art 12, 65, 110, 128, 132, 133, 135, 136, 141, 142, 144, 204, 659
Asia 2, 6, 12, 17, 19, 58, 139, 172, 178, 186, 309, 345, 396, 397, 406, 477, 479, 481, 483, 484, 488, 499, 500, 513, 524, 527, 533, 590, 591, 598, 684, 691, 701, 706
Aspirations 15, 17, 86, 170, 187, 205, 286, 296, 300–303, 335, 344–347, 360, 374–376, 381, 382, 438, 439, 445, 456, 460, 461, 464–466, 468, 470, 505, 548, 550, 553, 558, 570, 571, 709
Asylum 108, 129, 153, 156, 169, 176, 177, 247, 253, 344, 347, 349–352, 355, 356, 358–360, 491, 569, 578, 634, 640, 643, 644, 659–662, 667. *See also* Refugees

B

Bordering 63, 130, 224, 252, 296, 314, 446, 482, 483, 485, 637, 643
Borders 3, 10, 16, 63, 76, 126, 127, 129–132, 142, 143, 153, 156,

190, 206, 213, 216, 226, 260, 312, 378, 384, 395, 396, 406, 442, 444–446, 456, 478, 479, 482, 483, 491, 529, 533, 589, 593, 618, 621, 623, 626, 640, 643, 644, 654, 662, 666, 679, 690, 692, 709

Brazil 2, 6, 15, 25, 26, 31, 34, 251, 253, 261, 262, 274–277, 279, 282, 283, 286, 289, 343, 344, 346, 348–350, 353, 354, 356–358, 360, 413–415, 417–428, 500, 592, 597, 601, 632, 636, 638–640, 643, 671, 725

Burkina Faso 2, 13, 126, 129, 189, 223–227, 229–237, 240, 242, 372, 375, 380–383, 386, 387, 395, 521, 523, 524, 622, 625

C

Camp 12, 39, 76, 77, 118, 467

Capacity, capability 10, 59, 64, 89, 108, 138, 139, 175, 178, 201, 204, 211, 214, 218, 232, 233, 248, 260, 279, 302, 307, 359, 378, 385, 461, 465, 610, 614, 620, 626, 627, 659, 661, 667, 669–671, 710

Care 117, 239–241, 335, 394, 396, 400–403, 407, 460, 503, 508, 545, 550, 571, 610, 685, 706, 709, 723

Categories 8, 85–88, 91, 93–95, 108, 142, 154, 155, 195, 238, 259, 263, 322, 377, 446, 463, 549, 570, 579, 624, 637, 734

Childhood 125, 224, 231, 240, 241, 543–545, 547–551, 558

Children 13, 17, 26, 28, 29, 77, 113, 131, 188, 211, 212, 216, 231, 235, 238–241, 301, 333, 335, 401, 402, 407, 419, 425, 502–504, 507, 510, 512, 543–560, 645, 670, 685, 707, 709, 710

China 50, 158, 159, 162, 165, 167–169, 172, 178, 319, 321–323, 325, 326, 328, 334–337, 344, 376, 377, 442, 510, 526–528, 532, 533, 598, 655, 725, 728

Circulation 14, 138, 272, 280, 394, 531, 573

Civil society 19, 248, 256, 306, 311, 315, 357, 405, 406, 491, 603, 671, 681, 690–693, 720

Civil war 11, 27, 37, 38

Class 14, 19, 40, 53, 88, 89, 114, 204, 280, 302, 314, 333, 337, 396, 397, 401, 405, 416, 421, 461, 463, 468, 487, 503, 506, 554, 700, 706, 723, 727

Climate, climate change 16, 175, 176, 188, 189, 302, 435–446, 621, 624, 703, 704, 709

Climate mobilities 436, 437, 439, 441, 442, 446

Colonialism 7, 13, 40, 60, 88, 108, 112–115, 117, 120, 196, 416, 417, 487, 523, 597, 599

Coloniality 51, 52, 56, 62, 88, 89, 97, 109, 110, 120, 133, 417

Conflict 3, 4, 12, 33, 35–39, 126, 154, 169, 170, 185, 187, 191, 218, 219, 238, 345, 379, 380, 383, 444, 461, 483, 485, 573, 578, 609, 612, 613, 657, 659, 680, 682, 699, 723, 730

Corridor(s) 10, 12, 158, 169, 178, 202, 212, 224, 236, 296, 314, 372, 375–377, 381, 383, 384, 386, 387, 405, 431, 509, 521, 525, 529, 560, 602, 603, 680, 707, 712

Côte d'Ivoire 13, 38, 170, 223–227, 229, 231–234, 236, 239, 242, 375, 380, 383, 522–524
COVID-19 7, 18, 188, 261, 297, 298, 303, 307, 310, 312, 336, 506, 523, 572, 592, 616, 634, 642, 662, 664, 665, 669, 679
Culture 36, 57, 107, 113, 114, 120, 127, 128, 132, 137, 144, 190, 191, 205, 218, 282, 304, 305, 335, 417, 420, 441, 464, 504, 505, 510, 511, 655

D

Data 15, 52, 92, 107, 110, 116, 154–156, 169, 175, 178, 186, 193, 202, 224, 232, 233, 248, 262, 263, 272, 276, 277, 279, 281, 289, 309, 320, 321, 326, 349, 360, 414, 421, 423, 424, 428, 508, 509, 520, 522, 535, 546, 551, 553, 555, 559, 612, 614, 665
Decision-making 5, 16, 193, 206, 208, 210, 282, 286, 374, 376, 436, 455, 456, 458, 459, 462, 463, 465, 467–470, 544, 709
Decolonial 11, 52–54, 59, 61, 62, 64, 87, 88, 93, 96–98, 105, 109, 132, 142, 481, 487
Development 4, 6, 8, 10, 16–18, 36, 38, 54, 85, 89, 90, 96, 116, 128, 154, 163, 167, 184, 185, 196, 197, 206, 232, 258, 274, 331, 335, 345, 347, 375, 383, 394, 397, 398, 403, 404, 406, 440, 441, 470, 481, 487, 506, 520, 523–525, 529, 531, 535, 544, 567–569, 588, 591, 594, 597, 600, 611, 613, 614, 616, 621, 623–626, 634–636, 671, 700, 703–705

Diaspora 17, 196, 259, 283, 445, 520, 522, 524, 531, 533, 535, 536, 552, 624, 625, 666
Digital technologies 16, 17, 500, 502–506, 509–511, 513
Discrimination 40, 50, 118, 265, 302, 303, 315, 346–348, 354, 357, 398, 405, 417, 421, 424, 428, 463, 465, 466, 469, 470, 488, 489, 511, 578, 613, 670, 699, 706, 707, 720, 723, 725, 732, 734
Displacement 5, 11, 37–39, 47, 53, 127, 129, 155, 175, 176, 187, 188, 248, 253, 349, 438, 440, 441, 550, 573, 588, 591, 596, 600, 612, 621, 623, 631–633, 637, 640, 644, 646, 653, 657
Documentation 3, 7, 172, 249, 263, 280, 325, 378, 481, 486, 555–557, 559, 687, 725

E

Economics 2, 4, 6, 8, 13, 28, 33, 36, 58, 88, 111, 112, 115, 118, 120, 129, 154, 155, 165, 170, 178, 183–185, 189, 190, 192, 195, 207, 224, 228, 234, 247, 249, 250, 258, 264, 273, 275, 283, 301, 311, 315, 322, 323, 328, 330, 332, 335, 337, 347, 359, 374–376, 378, 380, 382, 384, 385, 394, 397, 400, 414, 417, 421, 428–431, 456–460, 465, 468, 469, 480, 487, 491, 503, 519, 523, 529, 532, 546, 570, 572–574, 576, 587, 591, 602, 610, 612, 615, 623, 636, 646, 653, 655, 656, 660, 669, 672, 689, 702–705, 708, 712, 719, 723, 729
Education 17, 90, 169, 170, 193, 196, 205, 212, 236, 237, 239,

241, 248–251, 258, 259, 261, 264, 279, 300, 301, 305, 327, 335, 357, 373, 376, 380, 388, 419, 420, 457, 461, 520, 544–556, 558–560, 569, 592, 602, 623, 657–659, 670, 671, 690, 707, 732

Employment 15, 33, 167, 192, 193, 196, 230, 235–238, 250, 274, 278, 279, 285–287, 298, 302, 314, 320, 325, 331, 357, 376, 387, 397, 399, 460, 461, 480, 484, 486, 489, 490, 505, 519, 528, 554, 556, 569, 590, 594, 595, 598, 600, 613, 619, 659, 660, 685, 687–690, 705, 707, 709, 711, 720, 726, 731

Environment 130, 185, 189, 203, 305, 322, 377, 436, 440, 441, 443, 466, 482, 490, 505, 506, 532, 545, 577, 579, 590, 594, 612, 620, 625

Epistemic injustice 11, 83, 84, 89, 90, 92–94, 98

Epistemic oppression 83, 84, 89, 91, 93, 94

Equality 14, 37, 258, 259, 418, 427, 430, 534, 702, 712

Ethics 11, 83, 105, 106, 109–113, 115–118, 120

Ethiopia 17, 162, 202, 205–208, 213, 217, 381, 384, 386, 545, 546, 551, 552, 557–560

Ethnographic network tracing 272

Ethnography 53, 110, 120

Eurocentrism 11, 47, 48, 52–54, 60, 84, 91, 94–96, 98

Europe 8, 9, 25, 28, 29, 40, 48, 49, 53, 60, 87, 92, 107, 109, 159, 162, 164, 170, 185, 186, 210, 252, 344, 345, 347, 350, 376, 395, 396, 446, 459, 460, 479, 482, 523, 588, 609, 610, 637, 729

F

Family 5, 7, 10, 19, 39, 40, 133, 170, 190, 193, 209–211, 215, 216, 230, 233–235, 238, 242, 276, 278–285, 301, 312, 325, 335, 336, 378, 380, 381, 396, 399–403, 423, 458, 460, 464, 466, 483, 486–488, 502, 503, 505, 509–512, 514, 523, 525, 548, 550, 553–555, 557, 559, 571, 578, 615, 642, 658, 680, 692, 702, 705–708, 710–712

Family migration 373, 381

Feminisation of migration 394, 395, 402

Feminism 54, 61

Fieldwork 11, 92, 105, 107, 110, 114, 116, 119, 120, 238, 296, 336, 383, 388

Food security 16, 218, 332, 568–575, 577, 578

Forced labour 164, 225–227, 306, 307, 310, 590, 615

G

Gender 13, 15, 16, 89, 154, 157, 162, 237, 250, 262, 324, 337, 394, 396, 398, 404–406, 417, 421, 423, 431, 437, 458, 460, 461, 466, 468, 469, 503, 507, 512, 546, 550, 571, 578, 645, 670, 707

Gendered migration 393, 394, 397, 406

Geopolitics 11, 48, 51, 61, 95–97

Ghana 9, 14, 28, 30, 35, 38, 39, 189, 197, 226, 227, 320–323, 325–329, 331, 333, 335–337, 346, 349, 376, 385–387, 479, 514, 549, 617, 619, 625, 727, 730, 731

Global South 1, 2, 5–13, 15, 17–19, 27, 49, 51, 53, 59, 87, 92, 95,

96, 98, 109, 126, 127, 130, 141–143, 153–155, 157, 158, 161, 177, 178, 183, 184, 197, 203, 219, 224, 275, 288, 295, 321, 377–379, 394, 405, 407, 435, 436, 439, 445, 446, 457, 461, 467, 469, 478, 482, 483, 486, 500, 521–524, 527, 529–532, 534, 544, 547, 548, 551, 568, 569, 571, 574, 575, 578, 587–589, 591, 592, 594, 595, 599, 602, 655, 704, 712, 719, 724, 726, 733, 734

Governance 4, 18, 19, 39, 86, 89, 90, 114, 143, 178, 214, 273, 396, 404, 442, 588, 593, 597–599, 602, 603, 610, 612, 614, 617, 624–627, 632–637, 639, 640, 642, 644, 680, 681, 683, 686, 687, 690, 693, 702–704, 709

H

Haiti 14, 31, 35, 248, 254, 271–273, 276, 277, 279–281, 283–286, 288, 349, 357, 421, 425, 426, 428, 514, 549, 575

Health 196, 232, 237–240, 249, 258, 259, 263, 336, 338, 380, 467, 523, 524, 569, 572, 590, 602, 624, 640, 643, 662–664, 669, 670, 707, 710, 729

History 2, 6, 10, 29, 35, 37, 53, 62, 113, 127, 136, 271, 300, 357, 382, 394, 436, 530, 589, 599, 602, 631, 653, 655, 691, 723, 732

I

Inclusion 13, 61, 247–250, 258, 259, 261, 264, 383, 456, 544, 601, 643, 665, 668, 711. *See also* Integration

Indigenous peoples 33, 37, 250, 355, 415, 430, 596

Inequality 6–8, 10–18, 20, 34, 38, 52, 54, 57, 84, 96, 108, 118, 154, 184, 204, 210, 219, 224, 230–232, 234–242, 249–251, 262–264, 271, 275, 296, 303, 305, 315, 321, 322, 333, 336–338, 371, 372, 374–377, 379, 380, 382–388, 396, 407, 413, 414, 417, 419, 424, 427, 429, 435, 445, 456–465, 467–470, 478, 479, 482, 486, 487, 489, 491, 505, 507, 508, 512, 513, 519, 523, 535, 543–547, 549–553, 555, 557–560, 568–572, 577, 578, 591, 594, 610, 700, 702, 710, 727, 734

Informality 18, 169, 250, 264, 378, 383, 384, 430, 532, 534, 590, 594, 597, 670, 672

Information 91, 117, 119, 202–204, 212, 214, 216, 277, 281, 282, 286, 304, 309, 325, 326, 374, 375, 421, 429, 431, 456, 480, 490, 505, 506, 510, 513, 521, 525, 527, 533, 595, 598, 599, 627, 641, 670, 699, 731

Integration 13, 17, 87, 107, 137, 172, 176, 177, 184, 185, 189, 241, 256, 264, 285, 347, 348, 354, 357, 360, 443, 508, 528, 546, 589, 591, 593, 600, 602, 612, 615, 617, 623, 638, 639, 660, 670–672, 722. *See also* Inclusion

Intermediaries 4, 16, 212, 280, 281, 283, 284, 288, 295, 296, 300, 325, 376, 378, 398, 477–492, 702, 708. *See also* Smugglers; Traffickers

746 Index

Inter-regional migration 14, 407
Intersectionality 437, 445
Intra-regional migration 2, 13, 159, 172, 186, 196, 600

J

Journey, journeys 3, 7, 15, 26, 29, 30, 52, 63, 131, 137, 139, 143, 203, 206–209, 211, 212, 215, 219, 282, 284, 287, 343, 344, 346, 347, 375, 383, 400, 406, 445, 455, 456, 464, 466, 478, 479, 485, 486, 491, 500, 510, 643
Justice 18, 19, 98, 111, 119, 131, 309, 418, 422, 429, 447, 457, 508, 509, 595, 601, 610, 700, 703, 706, 712, 713

K

Kinship 4, 11, 105, 106, 326, 437, 460, 478
Knowledge production 9, 11, 48, 51, 54, 61, 85, 86, 90, 94, 95, 97, 98, 428

L

Labour migration 19, 33, 165, 274, 300, 309, 375, 397, 404, 480, 481, 488, 576, 588, 589, 591, 592, 594, 596, 603, 610, 612–615, 621, 624, 679, 692, 700–703, 705, 707, 709, 712, 731
Latin America 27, 58, 172, 175, 178, 248–250, 260, 272, 274, 276, 277, 279, 286–288, 344, 346–350, 354–356, 360, 395, 500, 513, 529, 574, 591, 592, 600, 635, 644, 645, 655, 662, 668. *See also* South America

Liberia 11, 27, 32, 37–39, 576

M

Malaysia 6, 14, 33, 50, 165, 167, 295–299, 301, 303, 305–310, 312, 314, 315, 407, 511, 514, 598, 680, 681, 683, 689, 690, 692, 701, 725
Media 14, 130, 132, 155, 175, 185, 205, 282, 286, 300, 311, 313, 328, 343, 344, 358, 385, 402, 445, 464, 491, 503, 505, 506, 510, 511, 513, 545, 642, 722, 732
Middle East 6, 12, 58, 127, 139, 158, 159, 161, 162, 165, 170, 178, 405, 730
Migration research 10, 11, 48, 53, 83–90, 92, 93, 95, 98, 105, 394, 407
Migration studies 13, 15, 47–49, 52–55, 85, 86, 88, 89, 91, 97, 98, 105, 106, 108, 109, 112, 120, 202, 204, 205, 344, 371, 480, 527, 568
Mobilisation 19, 239, 447, 506, 512, 720–722, 724, 730, 734

N

Nepal 3, 6, 295–297, 301, 302, 304, 305, 309, 310, 313, 314, 464, 483
Network tracing 275, 276
Non-governmental organisations (NGO) 117, 241, 309, 325, 481, 490, 662, 665, 667, 668, 692

P

Pacific 19, 58, 164, 436, 440, 441, 445, 447, 598, 701, 706, 707, 713

Index   747

Participatory 53, 109, 110, 405, 722
Path dependency 14, 271, 272, 275, 285, 286, 288
Perú 18, 654–656, 658–672
Poetry 12, 65, 134, 137, 144
Policy 6–8, 10, 18, 19, 34, 48–50, 58, 86, 87, 93, 95, 96, 109, 130, 178, 184, 186, 196, 227, 248, 259, 264, 271, 274, 275, 285, 288, 295, 309, 315, 346, 347, 354, 356, 358–360, 377, 383, 394, 396–398, 403, 404, 427, 429, 441, 443–445, 460, 461, 467, 469, 470, 478, 482, 483, 487, 520, 530, 534, 568, 588, 593, 594, 597, 600–603, 610–612, 616, 619, 621, 623–627, 634, 637–641, 654, 659, 660, 662, 665, 666, 668, 670–672, 680, 688, 689, 691, 693, 694, 701, 703, 710, 712, 728, 730, 731, 734
Population 8, 25, 29, 35, 37, 38, 128, 154–157, 161, 168, 175–177, 184, 186, 190, 192, 225, 227, 247–254, 259, 262–265, 271, 273, 275, 279, 296, 297, 344, 351, 355, 358, 359, 386, 395, 414, 415, 417, 420, 421, 425, 428–431, 441, 457, 520, 527, 534, 568, 573, 592, 610, 632, 642, 645, 654, 666, 672, 703, 725
Postcolonial 50, 52–54, 59, 109, 114, 375, 442, 443, 445–447
Poverty 3, 15, 20, 35, 37, 94, 115, 184, 185, 192, 230, 232–234, 236, 238, 242, 250, 345, 348, 371–375, 379, 380, 383, 386–388, 395, 456, 468, 482, 486, 487, 523, 555, 570, 571, 576, 665, 686, 706, 712
Power 5, 11, 38, 47, 52, 58, 90, 105, 106, 109, 110, 112, 117–120, 128, 133, 135, 137, 139, 140, 203, 204, 228, 260, 319, 323, 354, 387, 404, 416, 417, 420, 421, 427, 429, 430, 442, 482, 491, 502–504, 508, 511, 573, 588, 597, 599, 664, 702, 710, 723, 727, 731
Precarity 8, 15, 128, 398, 406, 407, 570, 579, 700, 710, 726

R

Race 6, 15, 40, 53, 54, 61, 66, 88, 258, 348, 396, 416–419, 421, 427, 437, 445, 463, 469, 549, 570, 591, 700, 722
Racism 15, 40, 59, 284, 348, 354, 357, 360, 414, 416–421, 424–429, 469, 644
Recruitment 19, 227, 228, 296, 302, 309, 310, 326, 423, 479, 484, 491, 510, 590, 592, 595, 599, 614, 681, 684–690, 692–694, 702, 705, 731
Refugees 4, 8, 12, 39, 64, 75–77, 85, 108, 109, 118, 127, 130, 131, 139, 153, 156, 167, 176, 177, 249, 258–261, 264, 265, 274, 288, 310, 347, 349, 350, 352, 356–358, 379, 405, 441, 446, 504, 506–509, 549, 556, 559, 574, 577, 589, 596, 601, 609, 624, 633, 636, 638, 642–644, 658, 659, 662, 667, 680, 725. *See also* Asylum
Religion 5, 113, 127, 258, 420, 464, 469
Remittances 4, 8, 14, 17, 163, 165, 196, 206, 214, 229, 232, 242, 286, 302, 335, 338, 371, 374, 379–382, 387, 397, 403, 404, 458, 459, 486, 490, 502, 519–524, 535, 536, 548,

748 Index

550–552, 554, 559, 568, 572, 575, 576, 579, 624, 625, 687
Representation 27, 85, 88, 106, 108, 112, 113, 115, 120, 210, 348, 385, 405, 418, 426, 699
Research 4, 7, 8, 11, 12, 15, 36, 48–51, 53–55, 60, 83, 85–88, 90–95, 97, 98, 105, 106, 109–111, 114, 116, 117, 119, 128, 168, 176, 184, 186, 212, 215, 217, 233, 235, 262, 276, 320, 325, 336, 360, 394, 402, 407, 423, 435, 437, 438, 446, 462, 464, 470, 478, 488, 492, 499, 501, 509, 511, 512, 525, 544, 546, 547, 568, 578, 588, 622, 707, 720, 727
Resistance 58, 128, 136, 137, 143, 420, 430, 439–441, 487, 491, 504, 508, 613, 720, 724, 726, 727
Resource flows 17, 519, 520, 522, 534, 535
Rights 7, 12, 14, 17, 19, 37, 134, 172, 204, 205, 235–237, 248, 251, 256, 258, 259, 261, 263, 272, 275, 285, 288, 357, 358, 378, 388, 399, 404, 405, 421, 457, 489, 549, 569, 576, 588, 594, 596, 602, 603, 613, 614, 622, 633, 644, 645, 658, 662, 665, 672, 682, 683, 689, 691–693, 699, 700, 702, 704, 709–711, 713, 723, 729–731

S

Sexuality 40, 66, 89, 463, 466, 504
Slavery 11, 27, 33–37, 40, 185, 311, 348, 418, 430, 655, 732
Smugglers 130, 212, 280, 359, 376, 478, 485. *See also* Intermediaries; Traffickers

Smuggling 130, 155, 259, 274, 307, 378, 635
Social networks 5, 202, 203, 210, 213, 230, 242, 276, 277, 279, 281, 283, 288, 300, 321, 325, 326, 334, 376, 388, 438, 444, 459, 465, 481, 486, 505, 511, 685, 693
Social reproduction 394, 407, 720
Solidarity 19, 116, 205, 288, 487, 490, 507, 719, 720, 722–724, 726, 732, 733
South Africa 6, 189, 190, 201–203, 205–212, 214, 216–218, 376, 378, 381, 384, 386, 394, 407, 513, 514, 523, 532, 543, 546, 552, 553, 555, 557, 558, 560, 574, 577, 725, 728
South America 14, 17, 18, 131, 139, 159, 168, 172, 247, 249, 252, 258, 263, 264, 402, 631–633, 635, 637, 644, 646, 655, 663, 665, 670. *See also* Latin America
South-South migration 51, 58, 568, 569, 576, 579, 588, 589, 591–595, 597–599, 601–603, 634, 719
Survey data 262
Sustainable Development Goals (SDGs) 6, 271, 405, 482, 520, 594, 603, 614, 615, 635

T

Temporariness 18, 590, 702, 708–712
Temporary migration 394, 398, 399, 403, 406, 703
Time, temporality 3, 5, 36, 76, 78, 86, 97, 116, 126, 129, 139, 142, 157, 170, 192, 194, 202, 214, 218, 229, 252, 253, 274, 286, 296, 308, 314, 333, 396,

Index

399, 401, 420, 438, 444, 502, 506, 522, 548, 556, 598, 611, 641–643, 669, 684, 687, 705, 728

Trade 2, 4, 7, 17, 25–29, 34–37, 39, 40, 169, 188, 190, 206, 237, 238, 240, 320, 321, 323, 326, 327, 330, 338, 385, 445, 519, 520, 525–527, 529, 535, 573, 610, 615, 616, 620, 645, 691

Trade unions 19, 306, 405, 603, 691, 692, 702, 727, 728, 730, 731, 734

Traffickers 130, 212, 307, 308, 485, 684. *See also* Intermediaries; Smuggling

Transit migration 95, 287, 602

Transnational borders 482

Transnational families 396, 399, 502, 513

Transnational solidarity 18, 720, 724

V

Venezuela 31, 248, 252, 253, 256, 260, 349, 357, 407, 574, 645, 653–655, 657–661, 664, 665, 670, 672

Violence 7, 26, 35, 38, 62, 64, 127, 132, 134–138, 141, 167, 215, 217, 256, 259, 271, 280, 286, 301, 345, 356, 359, 360, 386, 417, 421, 485, 504, 573, 577, 578, 645, 656, 658, 685, 713, 729

Vulnerability 4, 7, 13, 14, 108, 118, 127, 130, 132, 175, 217, 236, 240, 250, 271, 272, 275, 280, 285, 288, 305–307, 348, 360, 380, 382, 384, 385, 430, 435, 506, 570, 576, 578, 626, 627, 632, 669, 670, 703, 708

W

Wages 6, 165, 185, 195, 229, 250, 262, 302, 305–307, 322, 323, 333, 355, 399, 406, 456, 463, 489, 536, 568, 569, 576, 660, 669, 679, 688, 701, 705, 728

Wellbeing 7, 19, 20, 115, 116, 205, 218, 261, 262, 264, 273, 310, 315, 348, 399, 402, 403, 407, 488, 502, 509, 512, 528, 550, 556, 568, 572, 576, 671, 702

West Africa 11, 25–29, 35, 37, 39, 116, 185, 193, 195, 223, 343, 443, 477, 521, 618, 623

Women 2, 26, 36, 38, 54, 63, 65, 157, 162, 188, 190, 193, 196, 224, 230, 231, 238, 250, 251, 262, 278, 282, 283, 286, 298, 301–303, 309, 330, 337, 393–397, 399–407, 415, 417, 422, 431, 439, 460, 464, 466, 468, 470, 487, 488, 504–506, 571, 577, 594, 621, 669, 681, 686, 706, 707

X

Xenophobia 55, 242, 260, 265, 357, 358, 386, 577, 613, 664, 719, 734

Printed in the United States
by Baker & Taylor Publisher Services